The Philosophy of Love and Sex

An Anthology

by

Carol Hay

Clancy Martin

OXFORD
UNIVERSITY PRESS

Oxford University Press is a department of the University of Oxford.
It furthers the University's objective of excellence in research, scholarship,
and education by publishing worldwide. Oxford is a registered trade mark
of Oxford University Press in the UK and in certain other countries.

Published in the United States of America by Oxford University Press
198 Madison Avenue, New York, NY 10016, United States of America.

For titles covered by Section 112 of the US Higher Education Opportunity
Act, please visit www.oup.com/us/he for the latest information about
pricing and alternate formats.

Library of Congress Cataloging-in-Publication Data

Library of Congress Control Number: 2023014203
ISBN: 978-0-19-064475-8

9 8 7 6 5 4 3 2 1
Printed by Marquis, Canada

We'd like to thank our editors Jeff Marshall, Jessica McLaughlin, and Robert Miller, who first proposed this book; Alice MacLachlan, Susanne Sreedhar, and Helga Varden for helpful discussions about which readings to include; Reetika Kalita and Paul Goldberg, who helped with the manuscript; and most especially Nico, Amie, and our children.

TABLE OF CONTENTS

ACKNOWLEDGMENTS

GLORIA ANZALDÚA, "La Conciencia de la Mestiza: Towards a New Consciousness" from *Borderlands/La Frontera: The New Mestiza*, pp. 77–81, 83–85. © 1987, Aunt Lute Books. All rights reserved.

SAINT AUGUSTINE, *The Confessions of Saint Augustine*. Urbana, Illinois: Project Gutenberg, 2002.

SANDRA BARTKY, "Feminine Masochism and the Politics of Personal Transformation." Copyright (1990) From Femininity and Domination: Studies in the Phenomenology of Oppression. Reproduced by permission of Taylor and Francis Group, LLC, a division of Informa PLC.

JENNIFER BARTLETT, "Longing for the Male Gaze" from *The New York Times* in 2016 https://www.nytimes.com/2016/09/21/opinion/longing-for-the-male-gaze.html. © The New York Times.

NANCY BAUER, "Pornutopia," from *n + 1*, Issue 5, Winter 2007, pp. 65–73. © 2007. Reprinted with permission.

VERA BERGELSON, "The Meaning of Consent." Ohio State Journal of Criminal Law, Vol. 12, No. 1 (2014), 171–180. Reprinted with permission.

TALIA MAE BETTCHER, When Selves Have Sex: What the Phenomenology of Trans Sexuality Can Teach About Sexual Orientation, *Journal of Homosexuality*, 61:5, 605–620, 2014. Reprinted by permission of the publisher (Taylor & Francis Ltd, http://www.tandfonline.com).

ELIZABETH BRAKE, "Minimal Marriage: What Political Liberalism Implies for Marriage Law." Ethics 2010 120:2, 302–337. © 2010. Reprinted by permission of University of Chicago Press Journals.

JUDITH BUTLER, "Doing Justice to Someone: Sex Reassignment and Allegories of Transsexuality," *in GLQ: A Journal of Lesbian and Gay Studies*, Volume 7, no. 4, pp. 621–636. Copyright 2001, Duke University Press. All rights reserved. Republished by permission of the copyright holder, Duke University Press.

ANN J. CAHILL, reprinted from Rethinking Rape. Copyright © 2001 by Cornell University. Used by permission of the publisher, Cornell University Press.

CLAUDIA CARD, "Against Marriage and Motherhood." Hypatia, 11(3), 1–23. © 1996. Reprinted by permission of Cambridge University Press.

MANDY LEN CATRON, "To Fall in Love With Anyone, Do This" from *The New York Times*, 2015. © The New York Times.

GRETA CHRISTINA, "Are We Having Sex Now, or What?" from *The Erotic Impulse* edited by David Steinberg, copyright © 1992 by David Steinberg. Used by permission of Tarcher, an imprint of Penguin Publishing Group, a division of Penguin Random House LLC. All rights reserved.

JAMES CONLON, "Why Lovers Can't Be Friends" from Adrianne Leigh McEvoy (ed.), *Sex, Love, and Friendship: Studies of the Society for the Philosophy of Sex and Love*, 1993–2003, pp. 2–7.

JOHN CORVINO, "Man on Man, Man on Dog, or Whatever the Case May Be" from *What's Wrong With Homosexuality*, pp. 125–137. Copyright © 2013, Oxford University Press. All rights reserved.

KIMBERLÉ CRENSHAW, "Beyond Racism and Misogyny: Black Feminism and 2 Live Crew" by

Kimberlé Crenshaw. Copyright © 1991 by Kimberlé Crenshaw. Originally published by Boston Review, 1991. Reprinted with the permission of the author; all rights reserved.

IVAN COYOTE, "Fear and Loathing in Public Bathrooms, or How I Learned to Hold My Pee" from *Gender Failure* by Ivan E. Coyote and Rae Spoon, © 2014, Arsenal Pulp Press. Reprinted with permission. All rights reserved.

ELIZABETH EMENS, "Monogamy's Law: Compulsory Monogamy and Polyamorous Existence" from N.Y.U. *Review of Law & Social Change*, Volume 29, Issue 2. © 2004. Reprinted with permission.

JANE ENGLISH, "What Do Grown Children Owe Their Parents?" *Having Children*, Oxford University Press, 1979, pp. 148–154. Copyright © 1979, Oxford University Press. All rights reserved.

MICHEL FOUCAULT, The History of Sexuality: Volume I: An Introduction, translated by Robert Hurley, translation copyright © 1978 by Penguin Random House LLC. Used by permission of Pantheon Books, an imprint of the Knopf Doubleday Publishing Group, a division of Penguin Random House LLC. All rights reserved. The History of Sexuality by Michel Foucault. Originally published in French as La Volonté du Savoir. Copyright © 1976 by Editions Gallimard. Reprinted by permission of Georges Borchardt, Inc., for Editions Gallimard.

ALAN GOLDMAN (1977). "Plain Sex." *Philosophy & Public Affairs*, 6(3), 267–287. © 1977. Reprinted by permission of John Wiley & Sons Inc.

EMMA GOLDMAN, "Love and Marriage" from *Anarchism and Other Essays*. Urbana, Illinois: Project Gutenberg, 2000.

ELIZABETH GROSZ, "Refiguring Lesbian Desire," pp. 70–81 from The Lesbian Postmodern, by Laura Doan. Copyright © 1994. Columbia University Press. Reprinted with permission of Columbia University Press.

CAROL HAY, The Obligation to Resist Oppression. Journal of Social Philosophy, 42: 21–45. © 2011. Reprinted by permission of John Wiley & Sons Inc.

bell hooks, "Reflections on Race and Sex." Copyright (2014) From Yearning: Race, Gender, and Cultural Politics by bell hooks. Reproduced by permission of Taylor and Francis Group, LLC, a division of Informa PLC.

CATHERINE MACKINNON, "Pornography, Civil Rights, and Speech." Harvard Civil Rights-Civil Liberties Law Review, 1985, pp. 3–11, 13–23, 27, 44, 51–68. © 1985. Reprinted with permission.

BONNIE MANN, "Creepers, Flirts, Heroes and Allies: Four Theses on Men and Sexual Harassment" from *The American Philosophical Association's Newsletter on Feminism and Philosophy*, pp. 24–30. © 2012.

CLANCY MARTIN, Excerpt from "Marriage" from Love and Lies: An Essay on Truthfulness, Deceit, and the Growth and Care of Erotic Love by Clancy Martin. Copyright © 2015 by Clancy Martin. Reprinted by permission of Farrar, Straus and Giroux. All rights reserved.

SIMON MAY, "Love as Perfect Friendship: Aristotle" from *Love: A History*. Copyright © 2011, Yale University Press. Reprinted with the permission of Yale University Press. All rights reserved.

THOMAS MERTON, Excerpt from "Love and Need: Is Love a Package or a Message?" from LOVE AND LIVING by Thomas Merton. Copyright © 1979 by The Merton Legacy Trust. Reprinted by permission of Farrar, Straus and Giroux. All rights reserved.

CHARLES MILLS, "Do Black Men Have A Moral Duty To Marry Black Women?" *Journal of Social Philosophy*, 25: 131–153. © 1994. Reprinted by permission of John Wiley & Sons Inc.

EDITH GWENDOLYN NALLY, "Case for Platonic Love." Edith Gwendolyn Nally, University of Missouri-Kansas City. All rights reserved.

ROBERT NOZICK, from *The Examined Life: Philosophical Meditations*. Copyright © 1989 by Robert Nozick. Reprinted with the permission of Simon & Schuster, Inc. All rights reserved. *The Examined Life* by Robert Nozick. Copyright © 1989 by Robert Nozick. (Simon & Schuster, 1989).

Reprinted by permission of Georges Borchardt, Inc., on behalf of the author.

MARTHA NUSSBAUM, "Whether From Reason or Prejudice": Taking Money for Bodily Services. *The Journal of Legal Studies*, 1998 27:S2, 693–723. © 1998. Reprinted by permission of University of Chicago Press Journals.

EVANGELIA PAPADAKI, Reprinted by permission of Springer Nature. "Sexual Objectification: From Kant to Contemporary Feminism." *Contemporary Political Theory* 6, 330–348 (2007). © 2007

JORDAN PASCOE, "Kant and Kinky Sex" from "What Philosophy Can Tell You about Your Lover," Sharon M. Kaye, pp. 25–35. © 2012. Open Court Publishing Company, a subdivision of Cricket Media. Reprinted with permission. All rights reserved.

CAROL PATEMAN, "Feminism and the Marriage Contract" from The Sexual Contract, 1988 pp. 154–197, 168–169, 183–187. Reprinted by permission of Stanford University Press.

PLATO, *Symposium*, trans. Paul Woodruff and Alexander Nehamas, (Hackett 1989). Reprinted by permission of Hackett Publishing Company, Inc. All rights reserved.

POPE FRANCIS, "Amoris Laetitia" ("The Joy of Love") 2016, Passages 9–13 and 71–75. © Libreria Editrice Vaticana.

RAJA ROSENHAGEN, "Iris Murdoch: Love as Just Attention." Raja Rosenhagen, Ashoka University. All rights reserved.

DEBORAH SATZ, "Markets in Women's Sexual Labor," *Ethics* 1995 106:1, 63–85. © 1995. Reprinted by permission of University of Chicago Press Journals.

MARY-LYNDON SHANLEY, "II. Marital Slavery and Friendship: John Stuart Mill's The Subjection of Women," *Political Theory*. 1981; 9(2):229–247. © 1981. Reprinted by Permission of SAGE Publications, Ltd.

IRVING SINGER, "Appraisal and Bestowal" from *The Nature of Love*, Volume 1, pp. 3–20, © 2009 Irving Singer, by permission of The MIT Press.

STENDHAL, "Love as Crystallization." On Love. Urbana, Illinois: Project Gutenberg, 2016.

GLORIA STEINEM, "Erotica and Pornography: A Clear and Present Difference" from *Ms. Magazine*. © 1978. Reprinted with permission.

LORI WATSON, "Why Sex Work Isn't Work" from *Logos: A Journal of Modern Society & Culture*, vol. 13, nos. 2–3, pp. 1–4. © 2014. Reprinted with permission.

ROBIN WEST, "The Harms of Consensual Sex" from American Philosophical Association newsletter, pp. 177–181. © 1995.

CHARLOTTE WITT, "A Critique of the Bionormative Concept of the Family" from *Family-Making*, 2014 pp. 2–12, 18–19. Copyright © 2014, Oxford University Press. All rights reserved.

In her prizewinning 2011 short story "William Wei," the contemporary American writer Amie Barrodale tells a tale about romance gone wrong. It's a narrative many of us have lived. Two people meet, at first remotely and then in person, they have a connection, they share secrets, they have sex, they even develop a fascinating intimacy, and yet, for some reason neither can explain, it doesn't work out. The narrator nevertheless concludes: "I think I can safely say it changed my life."

Why did these two find each other in the first place? Maybe they were just lonely, and though many of us prize our alone time, none of us likes loneliness. What were they expecting from the relationship? The great Buddhist teacher Dzongsar Khyentse Rinpoche says that we should treat romantic love like a motel: you check in for a while, hopefully you have a nice time while you're there, and then you check out again. It doesn't last forever—after all, nothing does. But we tend to want more than that. We want to find our soulmate, the one person in the entire world we are fated to meet and with whom our entire selves can merge. This ideal of all-consuming and salvatory romantic love dominates cultural narratives about what we should hold out hope for. June Jordan captures it in "Poem Number Two on Bell's Theorem, or The New Physicality of Long Distance Love": "There is no chance we will fall apart/There is no chance/There are no parts." We want long-term romantic relationships; maybe we want marriage; perhaps we hope for a partner who will be with us until the day one of us dies (probably most of us, in this scenario, prefer to be the one who goes first, and not to be the grieving one left behind). We want that one special person we imagine will be with us through all of life's ups and downs. "For better or for worse, for richer or for poorer, in sickness and in health."

But so many marriages wind up in divorce, and that is almost always a bitter destructive process—is marriage really what we want? Perhaps a very long partnership is ideal, and yet marriage as an institution is presently growing in popularity in the United States and many other countries. And of course for those who were denied the right to be married in this country, such as queer couples until quite recently, the freedom to marry is reasonably seen as an important right. Nevertheless, it's hard to forget the old joke about marriage: "It's a great institution, if you want to live in an institution." And when we look at the history of marriage, we see that it has all too often been a means of exerting social and legal power—specifically, power exerted by men over women and children, maintained chiefly for the purpose of allowing men to assure the paternity of their offspring in the days before modern DNA testing made this possible without exercising total control over who women had sex with. The emergence of divorce as a legal right is correctly seen as a tremendously liberating event in the history of feminism, and many queer people are suspicious of viewing heterosexual marriage as a way of life worth emulating. Still, many continue to see marriage—or at least some form of long-term partnership—as the moral heart of the family, and also to see the family as the place where we first learn to be good people and learn what it means to love. Certainly most of us do first learn what we know about how to love within the context of a family, whatever that family may look like. But the concept of a family can be a fluid one, and many are coming to realize that we need not stay bound by traditional patriarchal conceptions.

Maybe the young lovers in Barrodale's story just wanted to have sex—or maybe that's what one of them wanted, while the other wanted something more. Is there anything wrong with that? Most of us will agree that pleasure is a good in itself, so long as it doesn't involve the harm of another—why shouldn't two people just have sex for the fun of it? But of course it can often get more complicated than that, as we all know, because so often with sex we begin the process of intimacy: we share something of ourselves with another that we don't generally share with the world at large. For us human beings, sex and love so often blend into one another. Many of us have desperately probably hoped to hear from the lips of a lover, "I love you," or equally as desperately feared to say it first. And yet there is a paradox at the heart of intimacy and sex, identified by Esther Perel: "When people become fused—when two become one—connection can no longer happen. There is no one to connect with." The separateness that erotic love has us try so desperately to overcome is, paradoxically, a precondition for the possibility of desire. Also of course most of us will have sex with many different people in our lives, and few if any of those intimate encounters will result in love affairs. So it's interesting to think about how sex and love really work together, and why sex is given so much importance in our ideas about romantic love.

What about this whole idea of romantic or erotic love? Should we be a bit suspicious of it? After all, for centuries it was depicted as a very particular kind of relationship between a man and a woman. And that style of relationship is only one of an enormous variety of erotic opportunities presented to human beings, which expand further once we challenge the ideas that heterosexuality is the only possible sexual orientation, and that woman and man are the only possible gender identities. Many thinkers argue that we should completely reconceptualize the notion of romantic or erotic love, and admit that the old way of considering it has been too narrow and repressive or even violent. Polyamory and other forms of ethical nonmonogamy are now gaining popularity and acceptance in many quarters. In the long-overdue #MeToo era the question of whether it is even possible to have liberating rather than repressive and coercive forms of *eros* is an urgent one. None of us actively want to harm or manipulate each other—or at least, such people seem rare—and yet it happens all the time, maybe particularly in the context of sexual relationships. We need to have open and honest conversations about the morality of sex, but those discussions are difficult. In our culture as in many others, so much about our erotic lives has been carefully hidden from view.

There are many kinds of love other than romantic or erotic love: the love between children and parents; the love between any caregiver and the cared for; the love between siblings; the love of God or other forms of devotional love; the love between friends. Do these different kinds of love have anything important in common? Should they all be called "love," or should they have different names? In many cultures, there are lots of different words for love—when it comes to love, the English language, which is so rich, nuanced, and complex in most instances, is a bit simpleminded. And why is love so important to us? Most of us would happily give our lives for the ones we love, but can we say why this is the case? (Then there's the unforgettable line by the great Lauryn Hill: "You say you'll die for me/why won't you live for me?") Many feminists argue that the concepts of love and care are at the very heart of the actual day-to-day morality most of us live by, but how much have we really tried to think through what we mean when we say we love someone? And when we feel unloved—which we all do, sometimes—what does that mean to us?

In this book, we can only scratch the surface of these profound questions. What we have tried to do—and what the people included in these pages here also do—is to illuminate some of the questions posed by love and sex. That is, we are trying to start a more honest, open, and healthy conversation about love and sex. We hope you will learn a lot about how complicated love and sex are, as you read the work here—and how much fun it is to think about this subject (or subjects). We think that there is almost nothing more important for our culture to be talking about today.

PART

I

Philosophy of Love

Introduction

You've known this person for years. You've been best friends, then not so much, then friends again. One time you kissed at a party but pretended it never happened the next day. Then unexpectedly you decided to go on a "real date." One thing led to another, and now you're madly in love. You plan to spend the rest of your lives together. You know each other completely: every secret, every intimate thought, no matter how terrifying or embarrassing. Sometimes you think you know this person better than you know yourself.

You've just met this person. Your parents announce: "This is your future spouse. You two will be married." But you don't even know this person! How are you ever to come to

love a stranger? Plus you're not even sure you believe in marriage. . . .

You've been dating the same person since high school. You promised each other that even though you're going to be long-distance, you'd "stay true." But now you're in college, and there are so many new people to meet, so many romantic possibilities, and you yourself seem to be changing. Suddenly you wonder if you ever really were in love, or it was just a young game you were playing. What if you still don't even know what love is?

You've never been in love, and you don't know what it is. Yes, you love your parents. Yes, you love your sisters and brothers. Sure, you love your friends. But the kind of love they make movies and write songs about? You're starting to wonder if the whole thing isn't just some giant made-up nonsense, like Santa Claus. Then, BAM! The French call it *coup de foudre*, literally "being struck by the lightning bolt," what we in English call "love at first sight." You see that person, and you're *gone*.

You've been in love so many times, had a thousand crushes, but that love has never been returned. You worry that you're addicted to love. You're convinced that your whole life will be a series of unrequited loves. You have so much love to give, and yet no one seems to want it. When will you find someone to love you back?

We could go on and on with such scenarios, which are familiar to us all, if only from movies and television shows. And these are just examples of romantic love, or what is also often called erotic love. You love your family, you love your dog, you love to exercise, you even love your school, and your side job. You have friends who love God, and other friends who say they love the planet. And when people say, as they so often do, that the meaning of life is to be found in love—"All you need is love," as The Beatles insisted—it sounds somewhat plausible to you. But you also quickly want to add: What kind of love? How do all of these different kinds of love relate to each other, if they do? And maybe there's much more to life than love? Maybe we've been exaggerating its importance, because our culture has an obsession with love?

In these articles the authors tend to share one fundamental assumption: Whatever love is, it's important. It is at the core of what it is to be a human being in the way that few other things are. Many of our authors think that to learn to love, and to love well, is indeed the most important aspect of human experience. But their accounts of what love is are many and various, and often differ in crucial ways. Some think that to love is to experience the truth of another; others, that deception and self-deception are always at work in ordinary human love. Some think that love leads us up to God or the realm of the Gods; others, that love is a very earthly thing, that binds us to the earth and reveals us to ourselves as both natural and sacred. Some argue that love is to be discovered; others, that love is to be created; others, that it's a little of both.

The good news is, whether you know it or not, you're already an expert at love. By the time you've come to this class and this book, you've done so much loving, and thought about love so frequently and deeply (an interesting question: Can you remember a day when you didn't think about love, at least fleetingly?), that you already have a great variety of opinions about love. But like most of our opinions, you may not have taken the time to sort through them. What these readings are designed to do is to help you to think, write, and argue more carefully about this, perhaps the most mysterious and compelling of all human experiences—not to change your way of thinking about what you already know concerning love but, hopefully, to open your mind to the vast array of ways of considering its multifarious nature.

Love and Need: Is Love a Package or a Message?

BY THOMAS MERTON

Thomas Merton (1915–1968) was an American Trappist monk, social activist, and scholar of comparative religion. In this prescient essay, Merton argues that instead of taking existential responsibility for who and how we love, we allow our increasingly consumerist culture to commodify love. In so doing, we sacrifice the possibility of a sublime opportunity for self-knowledge and growth in favor of a superficial exchange of sexual and emotional services with equally needy and shallow partners.

We speak of "falling in love," as though love were something like water that collects in pools, lakes, rivers, and oceans. You can "fall into" it or walk around it. You can sail on it or swim in it, or you can just look at it from a safe distance. This expression seems to be peculiar to the English language. French, for instance, does not speak of "*tomber en amour*" but does mention "falling amorous." The Italian and Spanish say one "enamors oneself." Latins do not regard love as a passive accident. Our English expression "to fall in love" suggests an unforeseen mishap that may or may not be fatal. You are at a party: you have had more drinks than you need. You decide to walk around the garden a little. You don't notice the swimming pool . . . all at once you have to swim! Fortunately, they fish you out, and you are wet but none the worse for wear. Love is like that. If you don't look where you are going, you are liable to land in it: the experience will normally be slightly ridiculous. Your friends will all find it funny, and if they happen to be around at the time, they will do their best to steer you away from the water and into a nice comfortable chair where you can go to sleep.

Sometimes, of course, the pool is empty. Then you don't get wet, you just crack your skull or break your arm.

To speak of "falling into" something is to shift responsibility from your own will to a cosmic force like gravitation. You "fall" when you are carried off by a power beyond your control. Once you start you can't stop. You're gone. You don't know where you may land.

The expression to "fall in love" reflects a peculiar attitude toward love and toward life itself—a mixture of fear, awe, fascination, and confusion. It implies suspicion, doubt, hesitation, in the presence of something unavoidable—yet not fully reliable. For love takes you out of yourself. You lose control. You "fall." You get hurt. It upsets the ordinary routine of life. You become emotional, imaginative, vulnerable, foolish. You are no longer content to eat and sleep, make money and have fun. You now have to let yourself be carried away with this force that is stronger than reason and more imperious even than business!

Obviously, if you are a cool and self-possessed character, you will take care never to *fall*. You will accept the unavoidable power of love as a necessity that can be controlled and turned to good account. You will confine it to the narrow category of "fun" and so you will not let it get out of hand. You will have fun by making others fall without falling yourself.

But the question of love is one that cannot be evaded. Whether or not you claim to be interested in it, from the moment you are alive you are bound to be concerned with love, because love is not just something that happens to you: *it is a certain special way of being alive.*

Love is, in fact, an intensification of life, a completeness, a fullness, a wholeness of life. We do not live merely in order to vegetate through our days until we die. Nor do we live merely in order to take part in the routines of work and amusement that go on around us. We are not just machines that have to be cared for and driven carefully until they run down. In other words, life is not a straight horizontal line between two points, birth and death. Life curves upward to a peak of intensity, a high point of value and meaning, at which all its latent creative possibilities go into action and the person transcends himself or herself in encounter, response, and communion with another. It is for this that we came into the world—this communion and self-transcendence. We do not become fully human until we give ourselves to each other in love. And this must not be confined only to sexual fulfillment: it embraces everything in the human person—the capacity for self-giving, for sharing, for creativity, for mutual care, for spiritual concern.

Love is our true destiny. We do not find the meaning of life by ourselves alone—we find it with another. We do not discover the secret of our lives merely by study and calculation in our own isolated meditations. The meaning of our life is a secret that has to be revealed to us in love, *by the one we love.* And if this love is unreal, the secret will not be found, the meaning will never reveal itself, the message will never be decoded. At best, we will receive a scrambled and partial message, one that will deceive and confuse us. We will never be fully real until we let ourselves fall in love—either with another human person or with God.

Hence, our attitude toward life is also going to be in one way or another an attitude toward love. Our conception of ourselves is bound to be profoundly affected by our conception—and our experience—of love. And our love, or our lack of it, our willingness to risk it or our determination to avoid it, will in the end be an expression of ourselves: of who we think we are, of what we want to be, of what we think we are here for.

We consciously or unconsciously tailor our notions of love according to the patterns that we are exposed to day after day in advertising, in movies, on TV, and in our reading. One of these prevailing ready-made attitudes toward life and love needs to be discussed here. It is one that is seldom consciously spelled out. It is just "in the air," something that one is exposed to without thinking about it. This idea of love is a corollary of the thinking that holds our marketing society together. It is what one might call a package concept of love.

Love is regarded as a deal. The deal presupposes that we all have needs which have to be fulfilled by means of exchange. In order to make a deal you have to appear in the market with a worthwhile product, or if the product is worthless, you can get by if you dress it up in a good-looking package. We unconsciously think of ourselves as objects for sale on the market. We want to be wanted. We want to attract customers. We want to look like the kind of product that makes money. Hence, we waste a great deal of time modeling ourselves on the images presented to us by an affluent marketing society.

In doing this we come to consider ourselves and others not as *persons* but as *products*—as "goods," or in other words, as packages. We appraise one another commercially. We size each other up and make deals with a view to our own profit. We do not give ourselves in love, we make a deal that will enhance our own product, and therefore no deal is final. Our eye is already on the next deal—and this next deal need not necessarily be with the same customer. Life is more interesting when you make a lot of deals with a lot of new customers.

This view, which equates lovemaking with salesmanship and love with a glamorous package, is based on the idea of love as a mechanism of instinctive needs. We are biological machines endowed with certain urges that require fulfillment. If we are smart, we can exploit and manipulate these urges in ourselves and in others. We can turn them to our own advantage. We can cash in on them, using them to satisfy and enrich our own ego by profitable deals with other egos. If the partner is not too smart, a little cheating won't hurt, especially if it makes everything more profitable and more satisfactory for me!

If this process of making deals and satisfying needs begins to speed up, life becomes an exciting gambling game. We meet more and more others with the same needs. We are all spilled out helter-skelter onto a roulette wheel hoping to land on a propitious number. This happens over and over again. "Falling in love" is a droll piece of luck that occurs when you end up with another person whose need more or less fits in with yours. You are somehow able to fulfill each other, to complete each other. You have won the sweepstake. Of course, the prize is good only for a couple of years. You have to get back in the game. But occasionally you win. Others are not so lucky. They never meet anyone with just the right kind of need to go with their need. They never find anyone with the right combination of qualities, gimmicks, and weaknesses. They never seem to buy the right package. They never land on the right number. They fall into the pool and the pool is empty.

This concept of love assumes that the machinery of buying and selling of needs and fulfillment is what makes everything run. It regards life as a market and love as a variation on free enterprise. You buy and you sell, and to get somewhere in love is to make a good deal with whatever you happen to have available. In business, buyer and seller get together in the market with their needs and their products. And they swap. The swapping is simplified by the use of a happy-making convenience called money. So too in love. The love relationship is a deal that is arrived at for the satisfaction of mutual needs. If it is successful it pays off, not necessarily in money, but in gratification, peace of mind, fulfillment. Yet since the idea of happiness is with us inseparable from the idea of prosperity, we must face the fact that a love that is not crowned with every material and social benefit seems to us to be rather suspect. Is it really *blessed*? Was it really a *deal*?

The trouble with this commercialized idea of love is that it diverts your attention more and more from the essentials to the accessories of love. You are no longer able to really love the other person, for you become obsessed with the effectiveness of your own package, your own product, your own market value.

At the same time, the transaction itself assumes an exaggerated importance. For many people what matters is the delightful and fleeting moment in which the deal is closed. They give little thought to what the deal itself represents. That is perhaps why so many marriages do not last, and why so many people have to remarry. They cannot feel real if they just make one contract and leave it at that!

From the moment one approaches it in terms of "need" and "fulfillment," love has to be a deal. And what is worse, since we are constantly subjected to the saturation bombing of our senses and imagination with suggestions of impossibly ideal fulfillments, we cannot help revising our estimate of the deal we have made. We cannot help going back on it and making a "better" deal with someone else who is more satisfying.

The situation then is this: we go into love with a sense of immense need, with a naïve demand for perfect fulfillment. After all, this is what we are daily and hourly told to expect. The effect of overstimulation by advertising and other media keeps us at the highest possible pitch of dissatisfaction with the second-rate fulfillment we are actually getting and with the deal we have made. It exacerbates our need. With many people, sexual cravings are kept in a state of high irritation, not by authentic passion, but by the need to prove themselves attractive and successful lovers. They seek security in the repeated assurance that they are still marketable, still a worthwhile product. The long word for all this is narcissism. It has disastrous affects, for it leads people to manipulate each other for selfish ends.

When you habitually function like this, you may seem to be living a very "full" and happy life. You may seem to have everything. You go everywhere, you are in the middle of everything, have lots of friends, "love" and are "loved." You seem in fact to be "perfectly adjusted" sexually and otherwise with your partner(s). Yet underneath there may be a devouring sense that you have nevertheless been cheated, and that the life you are living is not the real thing at all. That is the tragedy of those who are able to measure up to an advertising image which is presented to them on all sides as ideal. Yet they know by experience that there is nothing to it. The whole thing is hollow. They are perhaps in some ways worse off than those who cannot quite make the grade and who therefore always think that perhaps there is a complete fulfillment which they can yet attain. These at least still have hope!

The truth is, however, that this whole concept of life and of love is self-defeating. To consider love merely as a matter of need and fulfillment, as something which works itself out in a cool deal, is to miss the whole point of love, and of life itself.

The basic error is to regard love merely as a need, an appetite, a craving, a hunger which calls for satisfaction. Psychologically, this concept reflects an immature and regressive attitude toward life and toward other people.

To begin with, it is negative. Love is a lack, an emptiness, a nothingness. But it is an emptiness that can be exploited. Others can be drafted into the labor of satisfying this need—provided we cry loud enough and long enough, and in the most effective way. Advertising begins in the cradle! Very often it stays there—and so does love along with it. Psychologists have had some pretty rough things to say about the immaturity and narcissism of love in our marketing society, in which it is reduced to a purely egotistical need that cries out for immediate satisfaction or manipulates others more or less cleverly in order to get what it wants. But the plain truth is this: love is not a matter of getting what you want. Quite the contrary. The insistence on always having what you want, on always being satisfied, on always being fulfilled, makes love impossible. To love you have to climb out of the cradle, where everything is "getting," and grow up to the maturity of giving, without concern for getting anything special in return. Love is not a deal, it is a sacrifice. It is not marketing, it is a form of worship.

When people are truly in love, they experience far more than just a mutual need for each other's company and consolation. In their relation with each other they become different people: They are more than their everyday selves, more alive, more understanding, more enduring, and seemingly more endowed. They are made over into new beings. They are transformed by the power of their love.

Love is the revelation of our deepest personal meaning, value, and identity. But this revelation remains impossible as long as we are the prisoner of our own egoism. I cannot find myself in myself, but only in another. My true meaning and worth are shown to me not in my estimate of myself, but in the eyes of the one who loves me; and that one must love me as I am, with my faults and limitations, revealing to me the truth that these faults and limitations cannot destroy my worth in *their* eyes; and that I am therefore valuable as a person, in spite of my shortcomings, in spite of the imperfections of my exterior "package." The package is totally unimportant. What matters is this infinitely precious message which I can discover only in my love for another person. And this message, this secret, is not fully revealed to me unless at the same time I am able to see and understand the mysterious and unique worth of the one I love.

What are we going to do about it? Well, for one thing, we can be aware of these immature and inadequate ideas. We do not have to let ourselves be dominated by them. We are free to think in better terms. Of course, we cannot do this all by ourselves. We need the help of articulate voices, themselves taught and inspired by love. This is the mission of the poet, the artist, the prophet. Unfortunately, the confusion of our world has made the message of our poets obscure and our prophets seem to be altogether silent—unless they are devoting their talents to the praise of toothpaste.

Meanwhile, as our media become more sophisticated and more subtle, there is no reason why they should not also create for us a better and saner climate of thought—and present us with a less fallacious fantasy world of symbolic fulfillments.

There is no reason except, of course, that it is easier to make money by exploiting human weakness!

DISCUSSION QUESTIONS

1. Why is Merton suspicious of the expression "to fall in love"? Explain how this suspicion is informed by a sense that it is important that we take existential responsibility for our lives.

2. What is "the package concept of love"? Explain why this commercialized understanding of love might be alluring, but is always ultimately unfulfilling. Explain how it is designed to prey on our weakness and immaturity.

3. How have Merton's criticisms of the commercialization of love become even more trenchant since 1979 when this essay was originally published? Discuss how technological advances such as the invention of the internet and social media exacerbate the problems he describes.

4. Describe Merton's positive conception of love—what he thinks love can truly be, and what it can teach us about ourselves.

Symposium (selections)

BY PLATO

Plato (424/423–348/347 BCE) was an Ancient Greek philosopher who founded the Platonist school of thought and the Academy, one of the first institutions of higher learning in the world. These selections focus on four of the speeches found in his dialogue, the Symposium:

(i) Aristophanes's familiar story of love as a search for a soulmate, understood literally as your other half from whom you were separated by angry gods;

(ii) Phaedrus's explanation of the ancient Athenian institution of paiderastia as the means by which young boys learned the civic virtues required for citizenship;

(iii) Diotima's description of love as "giving birth in beauty"—as the means by which mortal human beings can strive for immortality (either through procreation or through fame and respect); and

(iv) Alcibiades's flirtation with and rejection by Socrates, which casts Socrates's ultimate death for "corrupting the youth" in new light.

For we all know that Love is inseparable from Aphrodite, and if there were only one Aphrodite there would be only one Love; but as there are two goddesses there must be two Loves. And am I not right in asserting that there are two goddesses? The elder one, having no mother, who is called the heavenly Aphrodite—she is the daughter of Uranus; the younger, who is the daughter of Zeus and Dione—her we call common; and the Love who is her fellow-worker is rightly named common, as the other Love is called heavenly. All the gods ought to have praise given to them, but not without distinction of their natures; and therefore I must try to distinguish the characters of the two Loves. Now actions vary according to the manner of their performance. Take, for example, that which we are now doing, drinking, singing, and talking—these actions are not in themselves either good or evil, but they turn out in this or that way according to the mode of performing them; and when well done they are good, and when wrongly done they are evil; and in like manner not every kind of loving nor every Love is noble and worthy of praise, but only that which inspires men to love nobly. The Love who is the offspring of the common Aphrodite is essentially common, and has no discrimination, being such as moves the meaner sort of men. They are apt to love women as well as youths, and the body rather than the soul—the most foolish beings they can find are the objects of this love which desires only to gain an end, but never thinks of accomplishing the end nobly, and therefore does good and evil quite indiscriminately. The goddess who is the mother of this love is far younger than the other, and she was born of the union of the male and female, and partakes of both. But the offspring of the heavenly Aphrodite is derived from a mother in whose birth the female has no part,—she is from the male only; this is that love which is of youths, and the goddess being older, there is nothing of wantonness in her. Those who are inspired by this love turn to the male, and delight in him who is the more valiant and intelligent nature; anyone may recognize the pure enthusiasts in the very character of their attachments. For they love not boys, but intelligent beings whose reason is beginning to be developed, much about the time at which their beards begin to grow. And starting from such a choice, they are ready, I apprehend, to be faithful to their companions, and pass their whole life with them, not to take them in their inexperience, and deceive them, and make fools of them, and then run away to others of them.

For, observe that open loves are held to be more honourable than secret ones, and that the love of the noblest and highest, even if their persons are less beautiful than others, is especially honourable. Consider, too, how great is the encouragement which all the world gives to the lover, not treating him as though he were doing something dishonourable; but if he succeeds he is praised, and if he fails he is blamed. And in the pursuit of his love the custom of mankind allows him to do many strange things, which philosophy would bitterly censure if they were done from any other interest or motive, such as the desire for money or office or some other kind of power. He may pray, and entreat, and supplicate, and vow upon oath, and lie on a mat at the door, and endure a slavery worse than that of any slave—in any other case friends and enemies would be equally ready to prevent him, but now there is no friend who will be ashamed of him and admonish him, and no enemy will charge him with meanness or flattery; the actions of a lover have a grace which ennobles them; and custom has decided that they are open to no reproach, because they have a noble purpose: and, what is strangest of all, he only may swear and forswear himself (so men say), and the gods will forgive his transgression, for there is no such thing as a lover's oath. Such is the entire liberty which gods and men have allowed the lover, according to the custom which prevails in our part of the world—from this point of view a man might fairly argue that in Athens to love and to be loved is held to be a most honourable thing. But when parents forbid their sons to talk with their lovers, and

place them under a tutor's care who is instructed to that effect, and their companions and equals cast in their teeth anything of the sort which they may observe, and their elders refuse to silence the reprovers and do not rebuke this mistaken censure,—anyone who reflects on all this will, on the contrary, think that we hold these practices to be most disgraceful. But the truth as I imagine is, that judgement on such practices cannot be absolute; in themselves they are neither honourable nor dishonourable, as was said at the beginning; they are honourable to him who follows them honourably, dishonourable to him who follows them dishonourably. There is dishonour in yielding to the evil, or in an evil manner; but there is honour in yielding to the good, or in an honourable manner. Evil is the vulgar lover who loves the body rather than the soul, inasmuch as he is not even stable, because he loves a thing which is in itself unstable, and therefore when the bloom of youth which he was desiring is over, he takes wing and flies away, dishonouring all his words and promises; whereas the love of the noble disposition is lifelong, for it becomes one with the perdurable. The custom of our country would have both of them proven well and truly, and would have us yield to the one sort of lover and avoid the other; and therefore encourages some to pursue, and others to fly, testing both the lover and beloved in contests and trials, until they show to which of the two classes they respectively belong. And this is the reason why, in the first place, a hasty attachment is held to be dishonourable, because time is the true test of this as of most other things; and secondly there is dishonour in being overcome by the love of money or political power, whether one is frightened into surrender by much hardship or, living in enjoyment of the advantages they offer, is unable to rise above their seductions. For none of these things are of a permanent or lasting nature; not to mention that no generous friendship ever sprang from them. There remains, then, only one road of honourable attachment which our custom allows the beloved to follow; for it is our rule that as any menial service which the lover does to him is not to be accounted flattery or a reproach to himself, so the beloved has one way only of voluntary service which is not open to reproach, and this is service directed to virtue.

For you know it is our custom that anyone who does service to another under the idea that he will be improved by him either in wisdom, or in some other particular of virtue—such a voluntary service, I say, is not to be regarded as a dishonour, and is not open to the charge of flattery. And these two customs, one the love of youth, and the other the practice of philosophy and virtue in general, ought to meet in one, and then the beloved may honourably indulge the lover. For when the lover and beloved come together, having each of them an inner law, the lover thinking that he is right in doing any service which he can to his gracious love, and the other that he is right in showing any kindness which he can to him who is making him wise and good; the one capable of communicating understanding and virtue, the other seeking to acquire them with a view to education and wisdom; when the two laws of love are fulfilled and meet in one—then, and then only, may the beloved yield with honour to the lover. Nor when love is of this disinterested sort is there any disgrace in being deceived, but in every other case there is equal disgrace in being or not being deceived. For he who is gracious to his lover under the impression that he is rich, and is disappointed of all gain because he turns out to be poor, is disgraced all the same: for he has done his best to show that he would give himself up to anyone's "uses base" for the sake of money; but this is not honourable. And on the same principle he who gives himself to a lover because he is a good man and in the hope that he will be improved by his company, shows himself to be virtuous, even though the object of his affection turn out to be a villain, and to have no virtue; and though he is deceived he has committed a noble error. For he has proved that for his part he will do anything for anybody with a view to virtue and improvement, than which there can be nothing nobler. Thus noble in every case is the acceptance of another, if it be for the sake of virtue. This is that love which comes from the heavenly goddess, and is heavenly, and of great price to individuals and cities, making the lover and the beloved alike

eager in the work of their own improvement. But all other loves are the offspring of the other, who is the common goddess. To you, Phaedrus, I offer this my contribution in praise of love, which is as good as I could make, extempore.

Aristophanes professed to open another vein of discourse; he had a mind to praise Love in another way, unlike that of either Pausanias or Eryximachus. Mankind, he said, judging by their neglect of him, have never, as I think, at all understood the power of Love. For if they had understood him they would surely have built noble temples and altars, and offered solemn sacrifices in his honour; but this is not done, and most certainly ought to be done: since of all the gods he is the best friend of men, the helper and the healer of the ills which are the great impediment to the happiness of the race. I will try to describe his power to you, and you shall teach the rest of the world what I am teaching you. In the first place, let me treat of the nature of man and what has happened to it. The original human nature was not like the present, but different. The sexes were not two as they are now, but originally three in number; there was man, woman, and the union of the two, of which the name survives but nothing else. Once it was a distinct kind, with a bodily shape and a name of its own, constituted by the union of the male and the female: but now only the word "androgynous" is preserved, and that as a term of reproach. In the second place, the primeval man was round, his back and sides forming a circle; and he had four hands and the same number of feet, one head with two faces, looking opposite ways, set on a round neck and precisely alike; also four ears, two privy members, and the remainder to correspond. He could walk upright as men now do, backwards or forwards as he pleased, and he could also roll over and over at a great pace, turning on his four hands and four feet, eight in all, like tumblers going over and over with their legs in the air; this was when he wanted to run fast. Now the sexes were three, and such as I have described them; because the sun, moon, and earth are three; and the man was originally the child of the sun, the woman of the earth, and the man-woman of the moon, which is made up of sun and earth, and they were all round and moved round and round because they resembled their parents. Terrible was their might and strength, and the thoughts of their hearts were great, and they made an attack upon the gods; of them is told the tale of Otys and Ephialtes who, as Homer says, attempted to scale heaven, and would have laid hands upon the gods. Doubt reigned in the celestial councils. Should they kill them and annihilate the race with thunderbolts, as they had done the giants, then there would be an end of the sacrifices and worship which men offered to them; but, on the other hand, the gods could not suffer their insolence to be unrestrained. At last, after a good deal of reflection, Zeus discovered a way. He said: "Methinks I have a plan which will enfeeble their strength and so extinguish their turbulence; men shall continue to exist, but I will cut them in two and then they will be diminished in strength and increased in numbers; this will have the advantage of making them more profitable to us. They shall walk upright on two legs, and if they continue insolent and will not be quiet, I will split them again and they shall hop about on a single leg." He spoke and cut men in two, like a sorb-apple which is halved for pickling, or as you might divide an egg with a hair; and as he cut them one after another, he bade Apollo give the face and the half of the neck a turn in order that man might contemplate the section of himself: he would thus learn a lesson of humility. Apollo was also bidden to heal their wounds and compose their forms. So he gave a turn to the face and pulled the skin from the sides all over that which in our language is called the belly, like the purses which draw tight, and he made one mouth at the centre, which he fastened in a knot (the same which is called the navel); he also moulded the breast and took out most of the wrinkles, much as a shoemaker might smooth leather upon a last; he left a few, however, in the region of the belly and navel, as a memorial of the primeval state. After the division the two parts of man, each desiring his other half, came together, and throwing their arms about one another, entwined in mutual embraces, longing to grow into one, they began to die from hunger and self-neglect, because they did not like to do anything apart; and when one of the halves

died and the other survived, the survivor sought another mate, man or woman as we call them,—being the sections of entire men or women,—and clung to that. Thus they were being destroyed, when Zeus in pity invented a new plan: he turned the parts of generation round to the front, for this had not been always their position, and they sowed the seed no longer as hitherto like grasshoppers in the ground, but in one another; and after the transposition the male generated in the female in order that by the mutual embraces of man and woman they might breed, and the race might continue; or if man came to man they might be satisfied, and rest, and go their ways to the business of life. So ancient is the desire of one another which is implanted in us, reuniting our original nature, seeking to make one of two, and to heal the state of man. Each of us when separated, having one side only, like a flat fish, is but the tally-half of a man, and he is always looking for his other half. Men who are a section of that double nature which was once called androgynous are lovers of women; adulterers are generally of this breed, and also adulterous women who lust after men. The women who are a section of the woman do not care for men, but have female attachments; the female companions are of this sort. But they who are a section of the male follow the male, and while they are young, being slices of the original man, they have affection for men and embrace them, and these are the best of boys and youths, because they have the most manly nature. Some indeed assert that they are shameless, but this is not true; for they do not act thus from any want of shame, but because they are valiant and manly, and have a manly countenance, and they embrace that which is like them. And these when they grow up become our statesmen, and these only, which is a great proof of the truth of what I am saying. When they reach manhood they are lovers of youth, and are not naturally inclined to marry or beget children,—if at all, they do so only in obedience to custom; but they are satisfied if they may be allowed to live with one another unwedded; and such a nature is prone to love and ready to return love, always embracing that which is akin to him. And when one of them meets with his other half, the actual half of himself, whether he be a lover of youth or a lover of another sort, the pair are lost in an amazement of love and friendship and intimacy, and one will not be out of the other's sight, as I may say, even for a moment: these are the people who pass their whole lives together, and yet they could not explain what they desire of one another. For the intense yearning which each of them has towards the other does not appear to be the desire of lover's intercourse, but of something else which the soul of either evidently desires and cannot tell, and of which she has only a dark and doubtful presentiment.

***

And as you have set forth his nature with such stately eloquence, may I ask you further, Whether Love is by his nature the love of something or of nothing? And here I must explain myself: I do not want you to say that Love *is* the love of a father or the love of a mother—that would be ridiculous; but to answer as you would, if I asked, Is a father a father of something? to which you would find no difficulty in replying, of a son or daughter: and the answer would be right.

Very true, said Agathon.

And you would say the same of a mother?

He assented.

Yet let me ask you one more question in order to illustrate my meaning: Is not a brother to be regarded essentially as a brother of something?

Certainly, he replied.

That is, of a brother or sister?

Yes, he said.

And now, said Socrates, I will ask about Love:— Is Love of something or of nothing?

Of something, surely, he replied.

Keep in mind what this is, and tell me what I want to know—whether Love desires that of which love is.

Yes, surely.

And does he possess, or does he not possess, that which he loves and desires?

Probably not, I should say.

Nay, replied Socrates, I would have you consider whether "necessarily" is not rather the word. The

inference that he who desires something is lacking in that thing, and that he who does not desire a thing is not in lack of it, is in my judgement, Agathon, absolutely and necessarily true. What do you think?

I agree with you, said Agathon.

Very good. Would he who is great, desire to be great, or he who is strong, desire to be strong?

That would be inconsistent with our previous admissions.

True. For he who has those qualities cannot be lacking in them?

Very true.

Suppose that a man being strong desired to be strong, or being swift desired to be swift, or being healthy desired to be healthy,—since in that case he might be thought to desire something which he already has or is, I refer to the point in order that we may not be led astray—you will see on reflection that the possessors of these qualities must have their respective advantages at the time, whether they choose or not; and who can desire that which he has? Therefore, when a person says, I am well and wish to be well, or I am rich and wish to be rich, and I desire to have exactly what I have—to him we shall reply: "You, my friend, having wealth and health and strength, want to have the continuance of them; for at this moment, whether you choose or no, you have them. And when you say, I desire that which I have and nothing else, is not your meaning that you want to have in the future what you have at present?" He must agree with us—must he not?

He must, replied Agathon.

Then, said Socrates, he desires that what he has at present may be preserved to him in the future, which is equivalent to saying that he desires something which is non-existent to him, and which as yet he has not got?

Very true, he said.

Then he and everyone who desires, desires that which he has not already, and which is future and not present, and which he has not, and is not, and which he lacks;—these are the sort of things which love and desire seek?

Very true, he said.

Then now, said Socrates, let us recapitulate the argument. First, is not love of something, and of something too which is wanting to a man?

Yes, he replied.

Remember further what you said in your speech, or if you like I will remind you: you said that the love of the beautiful set in order the empire of the gods, for that of deformed things there is no love—did you not say something of that kind?

Yes, said Agathon.

Yes, my friend, and the remark was a just one. And if this is true, love is the love of beauty and not of deformity?

He assented.

And the admission has been already made that love is of something which one lacks and has not?

True, he said.

Then Love lacks and has not beauty?

Certainly, he replied.

And would you call that beautiful which lacks beauty and does not possess it in any way?

Certainly not.

Then would you still say that Love is beautiful?

Agathon replied: I fear that I said what I did without understanding.

Indeed, you made a very good speech, Agathon, replied Socrates; but there is yet one small question which I would fain ask:—Is not the good also the beautiful?

Yes.

Then in lacking the beautiful, love lacks also the good?

I cannot refute you, Socrates, said Agathon:— Be it as you say.

Say rather, beloved Agathon, that you cannot refute the truth; for Socrates is easily refuted.

And now, taking my leave of you, I will rehearse a tale of love which I heard from Diotima of Mantinea,[1] a woman wise in this and many other kinds of knowledge, who in the days of old, when the Athenians offered sacrifice before the coming of the plague, delayed the disease ten years. She was my instructress in the art of love, and I shall try to repeat to you what she said to me, beginning with the propositions on which Agathon and I are agreed; I will do the best I can do without any help.[2] As you, Agathon, suggested,[3] it is proper to speak first of the being and nature of Love, and then of his works. (I think it will be easiest for me if in recounting my conversation with the wise woman I follow its actual course of question and answer.) First I said to her in nearly the same words which he used to me, that Love was a mighty god, and likewise fair; and she proved to me, as I proved to him, that by my own showing Love was neither fair nor good. "What do you mean, Diotima," I said, "is Love then evil and foul?" "Hush," she cried; "must that be foul which is not fair?" "Certainly," I said. "And is that which is not wise, ignorant? do you not see that there is a mean between wisdom and ignorance?" "And what may that be?" I said. "Right opinion," she replied; "which, as you know, being incapable of giving a reason, is not knowledge (for how can knowledge be devoid of reason?) nor again ignorance (for neither can ignorance attain the truth), but is clearly something which is a mean between ignorance and wisdom." "Quite true," I replied. "Do not then insist," she said, "that what is not fair is of necessity foul, or what is not good evil; or infer that because Love is not fair and good he is therefore foul and evil; for he is in a mean between them." "Well," I said, "Love is surely admitted by all to be a great god." "By those who know or by those who do not know?" "By all." "And how, Socrates," she said with a smile, "can Love be acknowledged to be a great god by those who say that he is not a god at all?" "And who are they?" I said. "You and I are two of them," she replied. "How can that be?" I said. "It is quite intelligible," she replied; "for you yourself would acknowledge that the gods are happy and fair—of course you would—would you dare to say that any god was not?" "Certainly not," I replied. "And you mean by the happy, those who are the possessors of things good and things fair?" "Yes." "And you admitted that Love, because he was in want, desires those good and fair things of which he is in want?" "Yes, I did." "But how can he be a god who has no portion in what is good and fair?" "Impossible." "Then you see that you also deny the divinity of Love."

"What then is Love?" I asked; "Is he mortal?" "No." "What then?" "As in the former instance, he is neither mortal nor immortal, but in a mean between the two." "What is he, Diotima?" "He is a great spirit ($\delta\alpha\acute{\iota}\mu\omega\nu$), and like all spirits he is intermediate between the divine and the mortal." "And what," I said, "is his power?" "He interprets between gods and men, conveying and taking across to the gods the prayers and sacrifices of men, and to men the commands of the gods and the benefits they return; he is the mediator who spans the chasm which divides them, and therefore by him the universe is bound together, and through him the arts of the prophet and the priest, their sacrifices and mysteries and charms, and all prophecy and incantation, find their way. For God mingles not with man; but through Love all the intercourse and converse of gods with men, whether they be awake or asleep, is carried on. The wisdom which understands this is spiritual; all other wisdom, such as that of arts and handicrafts, is mean and vulgar. Now these spirits or intermediate powers are many and diverse, and one of them is Love." "And who," I said, "was his father, and who his mother?" "The tale," she said, "will take time; nevertheless I will tell you. On the day when Aphrodite was born there was a feast of all the gods, among them the god Poros or Plenty, who is the son of Metis or Sagacity. When the feast was over, Penia or Poverty, as the manner is on such occasions, came about the doors to beg. Now Plenty, who was the worse for nectar (there was no wine in those days), went into the garden of Zeus and fell into a heavy sleep; and Poverty considering that for her there was no plenty, plotted to have a child by him, and accordingly she lay down at his side and conceived Love, who partly because he is naturally a lover of the beautiful, and because Aphrodite is herself beautiful, and also because he was begotten during her birthday feast, is her follower and attendant. And as his parentage is, so also are his fortunes. In the first place he is always poor, and anything but tender and fair, as the many imagine him; and he is rough and squalid, and has no shoes, nor a house to dwell in; on the bare earth exposed he lies under the open heaven, in the streets, or at the doors of houses, taking his rest; and like his mother he is always in distress. Like his father too, whom he also partly resembles, he is always plotting against the fair and good; he is bold, enterprising, strong, a mighty hunter, always weaving some intrigue or other, keen in the pursuit of wisdom, fertile in resources; a philosopher at all times, terrible as an enchanter, sorcerer,

sophist. He is by nature neither mortal nor immortal, but alive and flourishing at one moment when he is in plenty, and dead at another moment in the same day, and again alive by reason of his father's nature. But that which is always flowing in is always flowing out and so he is never in want and never in wealth.

"Then," she said, "the simple truth is, that men love the good." "Yes," I said. "To which must be added that they love the possession of the good?" "Yes, that must be added." "And not only the possession, but the everlasting possession of the good?" "That must be added too." "Then love," she said, "may be described generally as the love of the everlasting possession of the good?" "That is most true."

"Then if this be always the nature of love, can you tell me further," she went on, "what is the manner of the pursuit? what are they doing who show all this eagerness and heat which is called love? and what is the object which they have in view? Answer me." "Nay, Diotima," I replied, "if I knew, I should not be wondering at your wisdom, neither should I come to learn from you about this very matter." "Well," she said, "I will teach you:—The object which they have in view is birth in beauty, whether of body or soul." "I do not understand you," I said; "the oracle requires an explanation." "I will make my meaning clearer," she replied. "I mean to say, that all men are bringing to the birth in their bodies and in their souls. There is a certain age at which human nature is desirous of procreation—procreation which must be in beauty and not in deformity. The union of man and woman is a procreation; it is a divine thing, for conception and generation are an immortal principle in the mortal creature, and in the inharmonious they can never be. But the deformed is inharmonious with all divinity, and the beautiful harmonious. Beauty, then, is the destiny or goddess of parturition who presides at birth, and therefore, when approaching beauty, the procreating power is propitious, and expansive, and benign, and bears and produces fruit: at the sight of ugliness she frowns and contracts and has a sense of pain, and turns away, and shrivels up, and not without a pang refrains from procreation.

And this is the reason why, when the hour of procreation comes, and the teeming nature is full, there is such a flutter and ecstasy about beauty whose approach is the alleviation of the bitter pain of travail. For love, Socrates, is not, as you imagine, the love of the beautiful only." "What then?" "The love of generation and of birth in beauty." "Yes," I said. "Yes, indeed," she replied. "But why of generation? Because to the mortal creature, generation is a sort of eternity and immortality, and it, as has been already admitted, love is of the everlasting possession of the good, all men will necessarily desire immortality together with good: whence it must follow that love is of immortality."

I was astonished at her words, and said: "Is this really true, O most Wise Diotima?" And she answered with all the authority of an accomplished sophist: "Of that, Socrates, you may be assured;— think only of the ambition of men, and you will wonder at the senselessness of their ways, unless you consider how they are stirred by the passionate love of fame. They are ready to run all risks, even greater than they would have run for their children, and to pour out money and undergo any sort of toil, and even to die, 'if so they leave an everlasting name.' Do you imagine that Alcestis would have died to save Admetus, or Achilles to avenge Patroclus, or your own Codrus in order to preserve the kingdom for his sons, if they had not imagined that the memory of their virtues, which still survives among us, would be immortal? Nay," she said, "I am persuaded that all men do all things, and the better they are the more they do them, in hope of the glorious fame of immortal virtue; for they desire the immortal.

"Those who are pregnant in the body only, betake themselves to women and beget children— this is the character of their love; their offspring, as they hope, will preserve their memory and give them the blessedness and immortality which they desire for all future time. But souls which are pregnant—for there certainly are men who are more creative in their souls than in their bodies, creative of that which is proper for the soul to conceive and bring forth: and if you ask me what are these conceptions, I answer, wisdom, and virtue in general—among such souls are all creative poets

and all artists who are deserving of the name inventor. But the greatest and fairest sort of wisdom by far is that which is concerned with the ordering of states and families, and which is called temperance and justice. And he who in youth has the seed of these implanted in his soul, when he grows up and comes to maturity desires to beget and generate. He wanders about seeking beauty that he may get offspring—for from deformity he will beget nothing—and naturally embraces the beautiful rather than the deformed body; above all, when he finds a fair and noble and well-nurtured soul, he embraces the two in one person, and to such a one he is full of speech about virtue and the nature and pursuits of a good man, and he tries to educate him. At the touch and in the society of the beautiful which is ever present to his memory, even when absent, he brings forth that which he had conceived long before, and in company with him tends that which he brings forth; and they are married by a far nearer tie and have a closer friendship than those who beget mortal children, for the children who are their common offspring are fairer and more immortal.

"These are the lesser mysteries of love, into which even you, Socrates, may enter; to the greater and more hidden ones which are the crown of these, and to which, if you pursue them in a right spirit, they will lead, I know not whether you will be able to attain. But I will do my utmost to inform you, and do you follow if you can. For he who would proceed aright in this matter should begin in youth to seek the company of corporeal beauty; and first, if he be guided by his instructor aright, to love one beautiful body only—out of that he should create fair thoughts; and soon he will of himself perceive that the beauty of one body is akin to the beauty of another; and then if beauty of form in general is his pursuit, how foolish would he be not to recognize that the beauty in every body is one and the same! And when he perceives this he will abate his violent love of the one, which he will despise and deem a small thing, and will become a steadfast lover of all beautiful bodies. In the next stage he will consider that the beauty of the soul is more precious than the beauty of the outward form; so that if a virtuous soul have but a little comeliness, he will be content to love and tend him, and will search out and bring to the birth thoughts which may improve the young, until he is compelled next to contemplate and see the beauty in institutions and laws, and to understand that the beauty of them all is of one family, and that personal beauty is a trifle; and after institutions his guide will lead him on to the sciences, in order that, beholding the wide region already occupied by beauty, he may cease to be like a servant in love with one beauty only, that of a particular youth or man or institution, himself a slave mean and narrow-minded; but drawing towards and contemplating the vast sea of beauty, he will create many fair and noble thoughts and discourses in boundless love of wisdom, until on that shore he grows and waxes strong, and at last the vision is revealed to him of a single science, which is the science of beauty everywhere. To this I will proceed; please to give me your very best attention:

"He who has been instructed thus far in the things of love, and who has learned to see the beautiful in due order and succession, when he comes toward the end will suddenly perceive a nature of wondrous beauty (and this, Socrates, is the final cause of all our former toils)—a nature which in the first place is everlasting, knowing not birth or death, growth or decay; secondly, not fair in one point of view and foul in another, or at one time or in one relation or at one place fair, at another time or in another relation or at another place foul, as if fair to some and foul to others, or in the likeness of a face or hands or any other part of the bodily frame, or in any form of speech or knowledge, or existing in any individual being, as for example, in a living creature, whether in heaven, or in earth, or anywhere else; but beauty absolute, separate, simple, and everlasting, which is imparted to the ever growing and perishing beauties of all other beautiful things, without itself suffering diminution, or increase, or any change. He who, ascending from these earthly things under the influence of true love, begins to perceive that beauty, is not far from the end. And the true order of going, or being led by another, to the things of love, is to begin from the beauties of earth and mount upwards for the sake of that other beauty, using

these as steps only, and from one going on to two, and from two to all fair bodily forms, and from fair bodily forms to fair practices, and from fair practices to fair sciences, until from fair sciences he arrives at the science of which I have spoken, the science which has no other object than absolute beauty, and at last knows that which is beautiful by itself alone. This, my dear Socrates," said the stranger of Mantinea, "is that life above all others which man should live, in the contemplation of beauty absolute; a beauty which if you once beheld, you would see not to be after the measure of gold, and garments, and fair boys and youths, whose presence now entrances you; and you and many a one would be content to live seeing them only and conversing with them without meat or drink, if that were possible—you only want to look at them and to be with them. But what if a man had eyes to see the true beauty—the divine beauty, I mean, pure and clear and unalloyed, not infected with the pollutions of the flesh and all the colours and vanities of mortal life—thither looking, and holding converse with the true beauty simple and divine? Remember how in that communion only, beholding beauty with that by which it can be beheld, he will be enabled to bring forth, not images of beauty, but realities (for he has hold not of an image but of a reality), and bringing forth and nourishing true virtue will properly become the friend of God and be immortal, if mortal man may. Would that be an ignoble life?"

When Socrates had done speaking, the company applauded, and Aristophanes was beginning to say something in answer to the allusion which Socrates had made to his own speech,[4] when suddenly there was a great knocking at the door of the house, as of revellers, and the sound of a flute-girl was heard. Agathon told the attendants to go and see who were the intruders, "If they are friends of ours," he said, "invite them in, but if not, say that the drinking is over." A little while afterwards they heard the voice of Alcibiades resounding in the court; he was in a great state of intoxication, and kept roaring and shouting "Where is Agathon? Lead me to Agathon," and at length, supported by the flute-girl and some of his attendants, he found his way to them. "Hail, friends," he said, appearing at the door crowned with a massive garland of ivy and violets, his head flowing with ribands. "Will you have a very drunken man as a companion of your revels? Or shall I crown Agathon, which was my intention in coming, and go away? For I was unable to come yesterday, and therefore I am here today, carrying on my head these ribands, that taking them from my own head, I may crown the head of this fairest and wisest of men, as I may be allowed to call him. Will you laugh at me because I am drunk? Yet I know very well that I am speaking the truth, although you may laugh. Come now, I have stated my term:[5] am I to come in or not? Yes or no, will you drink with me?"

The company were vociferous in begging that he would take his place among them, and Agathon specially invited him. Thereupon he was led in by the people who were with him; and as he was being led, intending to crown Agathon, he took the ribands from his own head and held them in front of his eyes; he was thus prevented from seeing Socrates, who made way for him, and Alcibiades took the vacant place between Agathon and Socrates, and in taking the place he embraced Agathon and crowned him. Take off his sandals, said Agathon, and let him make a third on the same couch.

By all means; but who makes the third partner in our revels? said Alcibiades, turning round and starting up as he caught sight of Socrates. Good heavens, he said, what is this? Why, it is Socrates! Here you are, always laying an ambush for me, and always, as your way is, pouncing out upon me at all sorts of unsuspected places: and now, what have you to say for yourself, and why are you lying here, where I perceive that you have contrived to find a place, not by a joker or lover of jokes like Aristophanes, but by the fairest of the company?

Socrates turned to Agathon and said: I must ask you to protect me, Agathon; for my passion for this man has grown quite a serious matter to me. Since I became his admirer I have never been allowed to speak to any other beauty, or so much as to look at them. If I do, he goes wild with envy and jealousy, and not only abuses me but can hardly keep his hands off me, and at this moment he may do me some harm, Please to see to, this, and either

reconcile me to him, or, if he attempts violence, protect me, as I am in bodily fear of his mad and passionate attempts.

There can never be reconciliation between you and me, said Alcibiades; but for what you have just said, I will chastise you some other time. At the moment, Agathon, I must beg you to give me some of the ribands that I may crown his head, his marvellous head—I would not have him complain of me for crowning you, and neglecting him, who in his eloquence is the conqueror of all mankind; and this not only once, as you were the day before yesterday, but always. Whereupon, taking some of the ribands he crowned Socrates, and again reclined.

Then he said: You seem, my friends, to be sober, which is a thing not to be endured; you must drink—for that was the agreement under which I was admitted—and I elect myself master of the feast until you have drunk an adequate amount. Let us have a large goblet, Agathon, if there is one; or rather, he said, addressing the attendant, bring me that wine-cooler. The wine-cooler which had caught his eye was a vessel holding more than two quarts—this he filled and emptied, and bade the attendant fill it again for Socrates. Observe, my friends, said Alcibiades, that this ingenious trick of mine will have no effect on Socrates, for he can drink any quantity of wine and not be at all nearer being drunk. Socrates drank the cup which the attendant filled for him.

I will begin at once, said Alcibiades, and if I say anything which is not true, you may interrupt me if you will, and say "that is a lie," though my intention is to speak the truth. But you must not wonder if I speak anyhow as things come into my mind; for the fluent and orderly enumeration of all your singularities is not a task which is easy to a man in my condition.

And now, my boys, I shall praise Socrates in a figure which will appear to him to be a caricature, and yet I speak, not to make fun of him, but only for the truth's sake. I say, that he is exactly like the busts of Silenus, which are set up in the statuaries' shops, holding pipes or flutes in their mouths; and they are made to open in the middle, and have images of gods inside them. I say also that he is like Marsyas the satyr. You yourself will not deny,

Socrates, that your face is like that of a satyr. Aye, and there is a resemblance in other points too. For example, you are a bully, as I can prove by witnesses, if you will not confess. And are you not a flute-player? That you are, and a performer far more wonderful than Marsyas. He indeed with instruments used to charm the souls of men by the power of his breath, and the players of his music do so still: for the melodies of Olympus[6] are derived from Marsyas who taught them, and these, whether they are played by a great master or by a miserable flute-girl, have a power which no others have; they alone possess the soul and reveal the wants of those who have need of gods and mysteries, because they are divine. But you produce the same effect with your words only, and do not require the flute: that is the difference between you and him. When we hear any other speaker, even a very good one, he produces absolutely no effect upon us, or not much, whereas the mere fragments of you and your words, even at second hand, and however imperfectly repeated, amaze and possess the souls of every man, woman, and child who comes within hearing of them. And if I were not afraid that you would think me hopelessly drunk, I would have sworn as well as spoken to the influence which they have always had and still have over me. For my heart leaps within me more than that of any Corybantian reveller, and my eyes rain tears when I hear them. And I observe that very many others are affected in the same manner. I have heard Pericles and other great orators, and I thought that they spoke well, but I never had any similar feeling; my soul was not shaken by them, nor was I angry at the thought of my own slavish state. But this Marsyas has often brought me to such a pass, that I have felt as if I could not endure the life which I am leading (this, Socrates, you will admit); and at this very moment I am conscious that if I did not shut my ears against him, and fly as from the voice of the siren, I could not hold out against him, and my fate would be like that of others,—he would pin me down, and I should grow old sitting at his feet. For he makes me confess that I ought not to live as I do, neglecting the many wants of my own soul and busying myself with the concerns of the Athenians; therefore I

hold my ears and tear myself away from him. And he is the only person who ever made me ashamed, which you might think not to be in my nature, and there is no one else who does the same. For I know that I cannot answer him or say that I ought not to do as he bids, but when I leave his presence the love of popularity gets the better of me. And therefore I steal away and fly from him, and when I see him I am ashamed of what I have confessed to him. Many a time have I wished that he were dead, and yet I know that I should be much more sorry than glad if he were to die: so that I am at my wit's end what to do about the fellow.

And this is what I and many others have suffered from the flute-playing of this satyr. Yet hear me once more while I show you how exact the image is, and how marvellous his power. For be assured of this, none of you know him; but I will reveal him to you, since, having begun, I must go on. See you how fond he is of the fair? He is always with them and is always being smitten by them, and then again he knows nothing and ignorant of all things—such is the appearance which he puts on. Is he not like a Silenus in this? To be sure he is: his outer mask is the carved head of the Silenus; but, O my companions in drink, when he is opened, what temperance there is residing within! Know you that beauty and wealth and all the other blessings which in popular opinion bring felicity, are of no account with him, and are utterly despised by him: he regards not at all the persons who are gifted with them, nor us ourselves—this is fact; but he spends all his life in teasing mankind, and hiding his true intent. When, however, I opened him, and looked within at his serious purpose, I saw in him divine and golden images of such fascinating beauty that I was ready to do in a moment whatever Socrates commanded: they may have escaped the observation of others, but I saw them. Now I fancied that he was seriously enamoured of my beauty, and I thought it a marvellous piece of luck; I had the means of persuading him to tell me everything that he knew, for I had a wonderful opinion of the attractions of my youth. In the prosecution of this design, when I next went to him, I sent away the attendant who usually accompanied me (I will confess the whole truth, and beg you to listen; and if I speak falsely, do you, Socrates, expose the falsehood). Well, he and I were alone together, and I thought that when there was nobody with us, I should hear him speak the language which lovers use to their loves when they are by themselves, and I was delighted. Nothing of the sort; he conversed as usual, and spent the day with me and then went away. Afterwards I challenged him to the palaestra; and he wrestled and closed with me several times when there was no one present: I fancied that I might succeed in this manner. Not a bit; I made no way with him. Lastly, as I had failed hitherto, I thought that I must take stronger measures and attack him boldly, and, as I had begun, not give him up, but see how matters stood between him and me. So I invited him to sup with me, just as if he were a fair youth, and I a designing lover. He was not easily persuaded to come; he did, however, after a while accept the invitation, and when he came the first time, he wanted to go away at once as soon as supper was over, and I had not the face to detain him. The second time, still in pursuance of my design, after we had supped, I went on conversing far into the night, and when he wanted to go away, I pretended that the hour was late and compelled him to remain. So he lay down on the couch next to me, on which he had reclined at supper, and there was no one but ourselves sleeping in the apartment. All this may be told without shame to anyone, but what follows I could hardly tell you if I were sober; yet as the proverb says, *In vino veritas*, whether there are also the mouths of children or not;[7] and therefore I may speak. Nor should I be justified in concealing a resplendent action of Socrates when I have set out to praise him. Moreover I have felt the serpent's sting; and he who has suffered, as they say, is willing to tell only his fellow sufferers as they alone will be likely to understand him, and will not be extreme in judging of the sayings or doings which have been wrung from his agony. For I have been bitten by a worse than a viper's tooth; I have known in my soul, or in my heart, or however else it ought to be described, that worst of pangs, more violent in ingenuous youth than any serpent's tooth, the pang of philosophy, which will make a man say or do anything. And you whom I see around me,

Phaedrus and Agathon and Eryximachus and Pausanias and Aristodemus and Aristophanes, all of you, and I need not say Socrates himself, and multitudes of others, have had experience of the same dionysiac madness and passion of philosophy. Therefore listen and excuse my doings then and my sayings now. But let the attendants and other profane and unmannered persons close tightly the doors of their ears.

When the lamp was put out and the servants had gone away, I thought that I must be plain with him and have no more ambiguity. So I gave him a shake, and I said: "Socrates, are you asleep?" "No," he said. "Do you know what I am thinking?" "What is it?" he said. "I think," I replied, "that of all the lovers whom I have ever had you are the only one who is worthy of me, and you appear to be too modest to speak. Now I feel that I should be a fool to refuse you this or any other favour, and therefore I come to lay at your feet all that I have and all that my friends have, in the hope that you will assist me in the way of virtue, which I desire above all things, and in which I believe that you can help me better than anyone else. And I should certainly have more reason to be ashamed of what wise men would say if I were to refuse my favour to such as you, than of what the world, who are mostly fools, would say of me if I granted it." To these words he replied in the ironical manner which is so characteristic of him:—"Alcibiades, my friend, you have indeed an elevated aim if what you say is true, and if there really is in me any power by which you may become better; truly you must see in me some rare beauty of a kind infinitely higher than the comeliness which I see in you. And therefore, if you mean to share with me and to exchange beauty for beauty, you will have greatly the advantage of me; you will gain true beauty in return for appearance— like Diomede, gold in exchange for brass. But look again, sweet friend, and see whether you are not deceived in me. The mind begins to grow critical when the bodily eye fails, and you are still a long way from that point." Hearing this, I said: "I have told you my own thoughts, saying exactly what I mean; and now it is for you to consider what you think best for you and me." "That is good," he said; "at some other time then we will consider and act as seems best about this and about other matters." After this interchange, I imagined that he was wounded by my shafts, and so without waiting to hear more I got up, and throwing my coat about him crept under his threadbare cloak, as the time of year was winter, and there I lay during the whole night having this truly superhuman wonder in my arms. This again, Socrates, will not be denied by you. And yet, notwithstanding all, he was so superior to my solicitations, so contemptuous and derisive and disdainful of my beauty—which really, as I fancied, had some attractions—hear, O judges; for judges you shall be of the haughty virtue of Socrates—nothing more happened, but in the morning when I awoke (let all the gods and goddesses be my witnesses) I arose as from the couch of a father or an elder brother.

This, friends, is my praise Socrates. I have added my blame of him for his ill treatment of me; and he has ill treated not only me, but Charmides the son of Glaucon, and Euthydemus the son of Diodes, and many others in the same way—beginning as their lover, the deceiver has ended by making them pay their addresses to him. Wherefore I say to you, Agathon, "Be not deceived by him; learn from me and take warning, and do not be a fool and learn by experience, as the proverb says."

When Alcibiades had finished, there was a laugh at his outspokenness; for he seemed to be still in love with Socrates. You are sober, Alcibiades, said Socrates, or you would never have gone so far about to hide the purpose of your satyr's praises, for all this long story is only an ingenious circumlocution, of which the point comes in by the way at the end; you want to get up a quarrel between me and Agathon, and your notion is that I ought to love you and nobody else, and that you and you only ought to love Agathon. But the plot of this Satyric or Silenic drama has been detected, and you must not allow him, Agathon, to score a success, and set us at variance.

I believe you are right, said Agathon; so I infer from the way in which he has placed himself between you and me with the intention of dividing us; but he shall gain nothing by that move, for I will go and lie on the couch next to you.

Yes, yes, replied Socrates, by all means come here and lie on the couch below me.

Alas, said Alcibiades, how the fellow goes on persecuting me; is determined to get the better of me at every turn. I do beseech you, at least allow Agathon to lie between us.

Certainly not, said Socrates; as you praised me, and I in turn ought to praise my neighbour on the right, he will be out of order in praising me again when he ought rather to be praised by me, and I must entreat you to consent to this, and not be jealous, for I have a great desire to praise the youth.

Hurrah! cried Agathon, I cannot possibly stay here, Alcibiades; I must move instantly, that I may be praised by Socrates.

The usual way, said Alcibiades; where Socrates is, no one else has any chance with beauty; and now how readily has he invented a specious reason for attracting Agathon to himself.

Agathon arose in order that he might take his place on the couch by Socrates, when suddenly a large band of revellers entered, and spoiled the order of the banquet. Someone who was going out having left the door open, they had found their way in, and made themselves at home; great confusion ensued, and everyone was compelled to drink large quantities of wine. Aristodemus said that Eryximachus, Phaedrus, and others went away—he himself fell asleep, and as the nights were long took a good rest: he was awakened towards daybreak by a crowing of cocks, and when he awoke, the others were either asleep, or had gone away; there remained only Socrates, Aristophanes, and Agathon, who were drinking out of a large goblet which they passed round, and Socrates was discoursing to them. Aristodemus was only half awake, and he did not hear the beginning of the discourse; the chief thing which he remembered was Socrates compelling the other two to acknowledge that the genius of comedy was the same with that of tragedy, and that the true artist in tragedy was an artist in comedy also. To this they were constrained to assent, being drowsy, and not quite following the argument. And first of all Aristophanes dropped off, then, when the day was already dawning, Agathon. Socrates, having laid them to sleep, rose to depart; Aristodemus, as his manner was, following him. At the Lyceum he took a bath, and passed the day as usual. In the evening he retired to rest at his own home.

DISCUSSION QUESTIONS

1. While there are many similarities between ancient Athenian views of love and sex and our own, there are also some stark differences. The biggest difference is the practice of *paiderastia*—a relationship between boys and men whose primary purpose was seen as educational rather than sexual. By associating with someone who was already a man, a boy learned *arête*—civic virtue or excellence. Discuss who plays this educational role in our contemporary society, and why we now condemn those who would sexualize or romanticize this relationship.

2. Explain how when Socrates chastises Alcibiades for wanting to "exchange bronze for gold" he is tacitly criticizing the social institution of *paiderastia*. Your answer should include a discussion of what the social purpose of *paiderastia* was supposed to be, as well as a discussion of why Socrates was ultimately put to death by the people of Athens.

3. Explain how Plato's conception of love as "giving birth in beauty" makes love "what morals have in place of immortality." Your answer should focus on a discussion of the difference between being pregnant in body and pregnant in soul.

NOTES

1. Cf. *Alcibiades I.*
2. Cf. *Gorg.* 505 c.
3. *Supra*, 195 a.
4. p. 205 e.
5. *Supra*, 212 e: "Will you have a very drunken man? &c."
6. Cf. Arist. *Pol.* viii. 5, § 16.
7. In allusion to the two proverbs, *olvos καί παεδες ἀληθεῖς*, and *olvos καί ἀλήθεια*.

Love as Crystallization

BY STENDHAL

> Stendhal—the pen name of Marie-Henri Beyle (1783–1842), a nineteenth-century French writer—offers a classic, hugely influential account of the imaginative transformation of the beloved in the development of romantic or erotic love. This brief excerpt includes both the first and second stages of his "love as crystallization" process of the imagination.

Chapter I Of Love

My aim is to comprehend that passion, of which every sincere development has a character of beauty. There are four kinds of love.

1. Passion-love—that of the Portuguese nun (1), of Héloïse for Abelard, of Captain de Vésel, of Sergeant de Cento.
2. Gallant love—that which ruled in Paris towards 1760, to be found in the memoirs and novels of the period, in Crébillon, Lauzun, Duclos, Marmontel, Chamfort, Mme. d'Épinay, etc. etc.

'Tis a picture in which everything, to the very shadows, should be rose-colour, in which may enter nothing disagreeable under any pretext whatsoever, at the cost of a lapse of etiquette, of good taste, of refinement, etc. A man of breeding foresees all the ways of acting, that he is likely to adopt or meet with in the different phases of this love. True love is often less refined; for that in which there is no passion and nothing unforeseen, has always a store of ready wit: the latter is a cold and pretty miniature, the former a picture by the Carracci. Passion-love carries us away in defiance of all our interests, gallant love manages always to respect them. True, if we take from this poor love its vanity, there is very little left: once stripped, it is like a tottering convalescent, scarcely able to drag himself along.

3. Physical love. Out hunting—a fresh, pretty country girl crosses your path and escapes into the wood. Everyone knows the love founded on this kind of pleasure: and all begin that way at sixteen, however parched and unhappy the character.
4. Vanity-love. The vast majority of men, especially in France, desire and have a fashionable woman, in the same way as a man gets a fine horse, as something which the luxury of a young man demands. Their vanity more or less flattered, more or less piqued, gives birth to transports of feelings. Sometimes there is also physical love, but by no means always: often there is not so much as physical pleasure. A duchess is never more than thirty for a bourgeois, said the Duchesse de Chaulnes, and those admitted to the Court of that just man, king Lewis of Holland, recall with amusement a pretty woman from the Hague, who could not help finding any man charming who was Duke or Prince. But true to the principle of monarchy, as soon as a Prince arrived at Court, the Duke was dismissed: she was, as it were, the decoration of the diplomatic body.

The happiest case of this uninspiring relationship is that in which to physical pleasure is added habit. In that case store of memories makes it resemble love a little; there is the pique of self-esteem and sadness on being left; then, romance forces upon us its ideas and we believe that we are in love and melancholy, for vanity aspires to credit itself with a great passion. This, at least, is certain that, whatever kind of love be the source of pleasure, as soon as the soul is stirred, the pleasure is keen and its memory alluring, and in this passion, contrary to most of the others, the memory of our losses seems always to exceed the bounds of what we can hope for in the future.

Sometimes, in vanity-love habit or despair of finding better produces a kind of friendship, of all kinds the least pleasant: it prides itself on its security, etc.[1]

Physical pleasure, being of our nature, is known to everybody, but it takes no more than a subordinate position in the eyes of tender and passionate souls. If they raise a laugh in the *salons*, if often they are made unhappy in the intrigues of society, in return the pleasure which they feel must remain always inaccessible to those hearts, whose beat only vanity and gold can quicken.

A few virtuous and sensitive women have scarcely a conception of physical pleasures: they have so rarely risked them, if one may use the expression, and even then the transports of passion-love caused bodily pleasure almost to be forgotten.

There are men victims and instruments of diabolical pride, of a pride in the style of Alfieri. Those people who, perhaps, are cruel because, like Nero, judging all men after the pattern of their own heart, they are always a-tremble—such people, I say, can attain physical pleasure only in so far as it is accompanied by the greatest possible exercise of pride, in so far, that is to say, as they practise cruelties on the companion of their pleasures. Hence the horrors of *Justine* (2). At any rate such men have no sense of security.

To conclude, instead of distinguishing four different forms of love, we can easily admit eight or ten shades of difference. Perhaps mankind has as many ways of feeling as of seeing; but these differences of nomenclature alter in no degree the judgments which follow. Subject to the same laws, all forms of love, which can be seen here below, have their birth, life and death or ascend to immortality.[2]

Chapter II Of the Birth of Love

This is what takes place in the soul:—

1. Admiration.
2. A voice within says: "What pleasure to kiss, to be kissed."
3. Hope (3).

We study her perfections: this is the moment at which a woman should yield to realise the greatest possible physical pleasure. In the case even of the most reserved women, their eyes redden at the moment when hope is conceived: the passion is so strong, the pleasure so keen, that it betrays itself by striking signs.

4. Love is born.

To love—that is to have pleasure in seeing, touching, feeling, through all the senses and as near as possible, an object to be loved and that loves us.

5. The first crystallization begins.

The lover delights in decking with a thousand perfections the woman of whose love he is sure: he dwells on all the details of his happiness with a satisfaction that is boundless. He is simply magnifying a superb bounty just fallen to him from heaven,—he has no knowledge of it but the assurance of its possession.

Leave the mind of a lover to its natural movements for twenty-four hours, and this is what you will find.

At the salt mines of Salzburg a branch stripped of its leaves by winter is thrown into the abandoned depths of the mine; taken out two or three months later it is covered with brilliant crystals; the smallest twigs, those no stouter than the leg of a sparrow, are arrayed with an infinity of sparkling, dazzling diamonds; it is impossible to recognise the original branch.

I call crystallization the operation of the mind which, from everything which is presented to it, draws the conclusion that there are new perfections in the object of its love.

A traveller speaks of the freshness of the orange groves at Genoa, on the sea coast, during the scorching days of summer.—What pleasure to enjoy that freshness with her!

One of your friends breaks his arm in the hunting-field.—How sweet to be nursed by a woman you love! To be always with her, to see every moment her love for you, would make pain almost a blessing: and starting from the broken arm of your friend, you conclude with the absolute conviction of the angelic goodness of your mistress. In a word, it is enough to think of a perfection in order to see it in that which you love.

This phenomenon, which I venture to call crystallization, is the product of human nature, which commands us to enjoy and sends warm blood rushing to our brain; it springs from the conviction that the pleasures of love increase with the perfections of its object, and from the idea: "She is mine." The savage has no time to go beyond the first step. He is delighted, but his mental activity is employed in following the flying deer in the forest, and with the flesh with which he must as soon as possible repair his forces, or fall beneath the axe of his enemy.

At the other pole of civilisation, I have no doubt that a sensitive woman may come to the point of feeling no physical pleasure but with the man she loves.[3] It is the opposite with the savage. But among civilised peoples, woman has leisure at her disposal, while the savage is so pressed with necessary occupations that he is forced to treat his female as a beast of burden. If the females of many animals are more fortunate, it is because the subsistence of the males is more assured.

But let us leave the backwoods again for Paris. A man of passion sees all perfections in that which he loves. And yet his attention may still be distracted; for the soul has its surfeit of all that is uniform, even of perfect bliss.[4]

This is what happens to distract his attention:—

6. Birth of Doubt.

After ten or twelve glances, or some other series of actions, which can last as well several days as one moment, hopes are first given and later confirmed. The lover, recovered from his first surprise and, accustomed to his happiness or guided by theory, which, always based on the most frequent cases, must only take light women into account—the

lover, I say, demands more positive proofs and wishes to press his good fortune.

He is parried with indifference,[5] coldness, even anger, if he show too much assurance—in France a shade of irony, which seems to say: "You are not quite as far as you think."

A woman behaves in this way, either because she wakes up from a moment of intoxication, and obeys the word of modesty, which she trembles to have infringed, or simply through prudence or coquetry.

The lover comes to doubt of the happiness, to which he looked forward: he scans more narrowly the reasons that he fancied he had for hope.

He would like to fall back upon the other pleasures of life, and finds them annihilated. He is seized with the fear of a terrible disaster, and at the same time with a profound preoccupation.

7. Second crystallization.

Here begins the second crystallization, which forms diamonds out of the proofs of the idea—"She loves me."

The night which follows the birth of doubts, every quarter of an hour, after a moment of fearful unhappiness, the lover says to himself—"Yes, she loves me"—and crystallization has its turn, discovering new charms. Then doubt with haggard eye grapples him and brings him to a standstill, blank. His heart forgets to beat—"But does she love me?" he says to himself. Between these alternatives, agonising and rapturous, the poor lover feels in his very soul: "She would give me pleasures, which she alone can give me and no one else."

It is the palpability of this truth, this path on the extreme edge of a terrible abyss and within touch, on the other hand, of perfect happiness, which gives so great a superiority to the second crystallization over the first.

The lover wanders from moment to moment between these three ideas:—

1. She has every perfection.
2. She loves me.
3. What means of obtaining the greatest proof of her love?

The most agonising moment of love, still young, is when it sees the false reasoning it has made, and must destroy a whole span of crystallization.

Doubt is the natural outcome of crystallization.

Chapter VI The Crystals of Salzburg

Crystallization scarcely ceases at all during love. This is its history: so long as all is well between the lover and the loved, there is crystallization by imaginary solution; it is only imagination which makes him sure that such and such perfection exists in the woman he loves. But after intimate intercourse, fears are continually coming to life, to be allayed only by more real solutions. Thus his happiness is only uniform in its source. Each day has a different bloom.

If the loved one yields to the passion, which she shares, and falls into the enormous error of killing fear by the eagerness of her transports,[6] crystallization ceases for an instant; but when love loses some of its eagerness, that is to say some of its fears, it acquires the charm of entire abandon, of confidence without limits: a sense of sweet familiarity comes to take the edge from all the pains of life, and give to fruition another kind of interest.

Are you deserted?—Crystallization begins again; and every glance of admiration, the sight of every happiness which she can give you, and of which you thought no longer, leads up to this agonising reflexion: "That happiness, that charm, I shall meet it no more. It is lost and the fault is mine!" You may look for happiness in sensations of another kind. Your heart refuses to feel them. Imagination depicts for you well enough the physical situation, mounts you well enough on a fast hunter in Devonshire woods.[7] But you feel quite certain that there you would find no pleasure. It is the optical illusion produced by a pistol shot.

Gaming has also its crystallization, provoked by the use of the sum of money to be won.

The hazards of Court life, so regretted by the nobility, under the name of Legitimists, attached themselves so dearly only by the crystallization they provoked. No courtier existed who did not dream of the rapid fortune of a Luynes or a Lauzun, no charming woman who did not see in prospect the duchy of Madame de Polignac. No

rationalist government can give back that crystallization. Nothing is so *anti-imagination* as the government of the United States of America. We have noticed that to their neighbours, the savages, crystallization is almost unknown. The Romans scarcely had an idea of it, and discovered it only for physical love.

Hate has its crystallization: as soon as it is possible to hope for revenge, hate begins again.

If every creed, in which there is absurdity and inconsequence, tends to place at the head of the party the people who are most absurd, that is one more of the effects of crystallization. Even in mathematics (observe the Newtonians in 1740) crystallization goes on in the mind, which cannot keep before it at every moment every part of the demonstration of that which it believes.

In proof, see the destiny of the great German philosophers, whose immortality, proclaimed so often, never manages to last longer than thirty or forty years.

It is the impossibility of fathoming the "why?" of our feelings, which makes the most reasonable man a fanatic in music.

In face of certain contradictions it is not possible to be convinced at will that we are right.

Chapter VII Differences Between the Birth of Love in the Two Sexes

Women attach themselves by the favours they dispense. As nineteen-twentieths of their ordinary dreams are relative to love, after intimate intercourse these day-dreams group themselves round a single object; they have to justify a course so extraordinary, so decisive, so contrary to all the habits of modesty. Men have no such task; and, besides, the imagination of women has time to work in detail upon the sweetness of such moments.

As love casts doubts upon things the best proved, the woman who, before she gave herself, was perfectly sure that her lover was a man above the crowd, no sooner thinks she has nothing left to refuse him, than she is all fears lest he was only trying to put one more woman on his list.

Then, and then only appears the second crystallization, which, being hand in hand with fear, is far the stronger.[8]

Yesterday a queen, to-day she sees herself a slave. This state of soul and mind is encouraged in a woman by the nervous intoxication resulting from pleasures, which are just so much keener as they are more rare. Besides, a woman before her embroidery frame—insipid work which only occupies the hand—is thinking about her lover; while he is galloping with his squadron over the plain, where leading one wrong movement would bring him under arrest.

I should think, therefore, that the second crystallization must be far stronger in the case of women, because theirs are more vivid fears; their vanity and honour are compromised; distraction at least is more difficult.

A woman cannot be guided by the habit of being reasonable, which I, Man, working at things cold and reasonable for six hours every day, contract at my office perforce. Even outside love, women are inclined to abandon themselves to their imagination and habitual high spirits: faults, therefore, in the object of their love ought more rapidly to disappear.

Women prefer emotion to reason—that is plain: in virtue of the futility of our customs, none of the affairs of the family fall on their shoulders, so that reason is of no use to them and they never find it of any practical good.

On the contrary, to them it is always harmful; for the only object of its appearance is to scold them for the pleasures of yesterday, or forbid them others for tomorrow.

Give over to your wife the management of your dealings with the bailiffs of two of your farms—I wager the accounts will be kept better than by you, and then, sorry tyrant, you will have the *right* at least to complain, since to make yourself loved you do not possess the talent. As soon as women enter on general reasonings, they are unconsciously making love. But in matters of detail they take pride in being stricter and more exact than men. Half the small trading is put into the hands of women, who acquit themselves of it better than their husbands. It is a well-known maxim that, if you are speaking business with a woman, you cannot be too serious.

This is because they are at all times and in all places greedy of emotion.—Observe the pleasures of burial rites in Scotland.

Chapter X

In proof of crystallization I shall content myself with recalling the following anecdote. A young woman hears that Edward, her relation, who is to return from the Army, is a youth of great distinction; she is assured that he loves her on her reputation; but he will want probably to see her, before making a proposal and asking her of her parents. She notices a young stranger at church, she hears him called Edward, she thinks of nothing but him—she is in love with him. Eight days later the real Edward arrives; he is not the Edward of church. She turns pale and will be unhappy for ever, if she is forced to marry him.

That is what the poor of understanding call an example of the senselessness of love.

A man of generosity lavishes the most delicate benefits upon a girl in distress. No one could have more virtues, and love was about to be born; but he wears a shabby hat, and she notices that he is awkward in the saddle. The girl confesses with a sigh that she cannot return the warm feelings, which he evidently has for her.

A man pays his attentions to a lady of the greatest respectability. She hears that this gentleman has had physical troubles of a comical nature: she finds him intolerable. And yet she had no intention of giving herself to him, and these secret troubles in no way blighted his understanding or amiability. It is simply that crystallization was made impossible.

In order that a human being may delight in deifying an object to be loved, be it taken from the Ardennes forest or picked up at a Bal de Coulon, that it seems to him perfect is the first necessity—perfect by no means in every relation, but in every relation in which it is seen at the time. Perfect in all respects it will seem only after several days of the second crystallization. The reason is simple—then it is enough to have the idea of a perfection in order to see it in the object of our love.

Beauty is only thus far necessary to the birth of love—ugliness must not form an obstacle.

The lover soon comes to find his mistress beautiful, such as she is, without thinking of ideal beauty.

The features which make up the ideally beautiful would promise, if he could see them, a quantity of happiness, if I may use the expression, which I would express by the number one; whereas the features of his mistress, such as they are, promise him one thousand units of happiness.

Before the birth of love beauty is necessary as advertisement: it predisposes us towards that passion by means of the praises, which we hear given to the object of our future love. Very eager admiration makes the smallest hope decisive.

In gallant-love, and perhaps in passion-love during the first five minutes, a woman, considering a possible lover, gives more weight to the way in which he is seen by other women, than to the way in which she sees him herself.

Hence the success of princes and officers.[9] The pretty women of the Court of old king Lewis XIV were in love with that sovereign.

Great care should be taken not to offer facilities to hope, before it is certain that admiration is there. It might give rise to dullness, which makes love for ever impossible, and which, at any rate, is only to be cured by the sting of wounded pride.

No one feels sympathy for the simpleton, nor for a smile which is always there; hence the necessity in society of a veneer of rakishness—that is, the privileged manner. From too debased a plant we scorn to gather even a smile. In love, our vanity disdains a victory which is too easy; and in all matters man is not given to magnifying the value of an offering.

Chapter XI

Crystallization having once begun, we enjoy with delight each new beauty discovered in that which we love.

But what is beauty? It is the appearance of an aptitude for giving you pleasure.

The pleasures of all individuals are different and often opposed to one another; which explains very well how that, which is beauty for one individual, is ugliness for another. (Conclusive example of Del Rosso and Lisio, 1st January, 1820.)

The right way to discover the nature of beauty is to look for the nature of the pleasures of each individual. Del Rosso, for example, needs a woman who allows a certain boldness of movement, and who by her smiles authorises considerable licence; a woman who at each instant holds physical pleasures before his imagination, and who excites in him the power of pleasing, while giving him at the same time the means of displaying it.

Apparently, by love Del Rosso understands physical love, and Lisio passion-love. Obviously they are not likely to agree about the word beauty.[10]

The beauty then, discovered by you, being the appearance of an aptitude for giving you pleasure, and pleasure being different from pleasure as man from man, the crystallization formed in the head of each individual must bear the colour of that individual's pleasures.

A man's crystallization of his mistress, or her *beauty*, is no other thing than the collection of all the satisfactions of all the desires, which he can have felt successively at her instance.

Chapter XII Further Consideration of Crystallization

Why do we enjoy with delight each new beauty, discovered in that which we love?

It is because each new beauty gives the full and entire satisfaction of a desire. You wish your mistress gentle—she is gentle; and then you wish her proud like Emilie in Corneille, and although these qualities are probably incompatible, instantly she appears with the soul of a Roman. That is the moral reason which makes love the strongest of the passions. In all others, desires must accommodate themselves to cold realities; here it is realities which model themselves spontaneously upon desires. Of all the passions, therefore, it is in love that violent desires find the greatest satisfaction.

There are certain general conditions of happiness, whose influence extends over every fulfilment of particular desires:—

1. She seems to belong to you, for you only can make her happy.
2. She is the judge of your worth. This condition was very important at the gallant and chivalrous Courts of Francis I and Henry II, and at the elegant Court of Lewis XV. Under

a constitutional and rationalist government women lose this range of influence entirely.

3. For a romantic heart—The loftier her soul, the more sublime will be the pleasures that await her in your arms, and the more purified of the dross of all vulgar considerations.

The majority of young Frenchmen are, at eighteen, disciples of Rousseau; for them this condition of happiness is important.

In the midst of operations so apt to mislead our desire of happiness, there is no keeping cool.

For, the moment he is in love, the steadiest man sees no object such as it is. His own advantages he minimises, and magnifies the smallest favours of the loved one. Fears and hopes take at once a tinge of the romantic. (Wayward.) He no longer attributes anything to chance; he loses the perception of probability; in its effect upon his happiness a thing imagined is a thing existent.[11]

A terrible symptom that you are losing your head:—you think of some little thing which is difficult to make out; you see it white, and interpret that in favour of your love; a moment later you notice that actually it is black, and still you find it conclusively favourable to your love.

Then indeed the soul, a prey to mortal uncertainties, feels keenly the need of a friend. But there is no friend for the lover. The Court knew that; and it is the source of the only kind of indiscretion which a woman of delicacy might forgive.

DISCUSSION QUESTIONS

1. Explain Stendhal's "crystallization" metaphor for love. Can you think of examples to support his metaphor?
2. Are there better and worse romantic partners on Stendhal's view? Why or why not?
3. For Stendhal, what happens when relationships fall apart? Are we suddenly seeing our former lovers more accurately? Or is something else going on?

NOTES

1. Well-known dialogue of Pont de Veyle with Madame du Deffant, at the fireside.
2. This book is a free translation of an Italian MS. of M. Lisio Visconti, a young man of the highest distinction, who died recently at Volterra, the place of his birth. The day of his sudden death he gave the translator permission to publish his Essay on Love, if means were found to shape it to a decorous form. Castel Fiorentino, June 10th, 1819.
3. If this peculiarity is not observed in the case of man, the reason is that on his side there is no modesty to be for a moment sacrificed.
4. That is to say, that the same tone of existence can give but one instant of perfect happiness; but with a man of passion, his mood changes ten times a day.
5. The *coup de foudre* (thunderbolt from the blue), as it was called in the novels of the seventeenth century, which disposes of the fate of the hero and his mistress, is a movement of the soul, which for having been abused by a host of scribblers, is experienced none the less in real life. It comes from the impossibility of this defensive manœuvre. The woman who loves finds too much happiness in the sentiment, which she feels, to carry through successful deception: tired of prudence, she neglects all precaution and yields blindly to the passion of loving. Diffidence makes the *coup de foudre* impossible.
6. Diane de Poitiers, in the *Princesse de Clèves*, by Mme. de Lafayette.
7. If you could imagine being happy in that position, crystallization would have deferred to your mistress the exclusive privilege of giving you that happiness.
8. This second crystallization is wanting in light women, who are far away from all these romantic ideas.
9. Those who remarked in the countenance of this young hero a dissolute audacity mixed with extreme haughtiness and indifference to the feelings of others, could not yet deny to his countenance that sort of comeliness, which belongs to an open set of features well formed by nature, modelled by art to the usual rules of courtesy, yet so far frank and honest that they seemed as if they disclaimed to conceal the natural working of the soul. Such an expression is often mistaken for manly frankness, when in truth it arises from the reckless indifference of a libertine disposition, conscious of

superiority of birth and wealth, or of some other adventitious advantage totally unconnected with personal merit.*Ivanhoe*, Chap. VIII

10. *My Beauty*, promise of a character useful to *my* soul, is above the attraction of the senses; that attraction is only one particular kind of attraction (7). 1815.

11. There is a physical cause—a mad impulse, a rush of blood to the brain, a disorder in the nerves and in the cerebral centre. Observe the transitory courage of stags and the spiritual state of a soprano. Physiology, in 1922, will give us a description of the physical side of this phenomenon. I recommend this to the attention of Dr. Edwards (8).

Appraisal and Bestowal

BY IRVING SINGER

Irving Singer (1925–2015) was an American philosopher whose work focused on issues ranging from cinema, love, sexuality, to the philosophy of George Santayana. In Singer's famous and influential account, love is not merely recognizing admirable and desirable qualities in the beloved, but also actively creating those qualities. Both modes of thinking and feeling are constitutive of meaningful loving.

I start with the idea that love is a way of valuing something. It is a positive response *toward* the "object of love"—which is to say, anyone or anything that is loved. In a manner quite special to itself, love affirms the goodness of this object. Some philosophers say that love *searches* for what is valuable in the beloved; others say that love *creates* value in the sense that it makes the beloved objectively valuable in some respect. Both assertions are often true, but sometimes false; and, therefore, neither explains the type of valuing which is love.

But what is it to value or evaluate? Think of what a man does when he sets a price upon a house. He establishes various facts—the size of the building, its physical condition, the cost of repairs, the proximity to schools. He then weights these facts in accordance with their importance to a hypothetical society of likely buyers. Experts in this activity are called appraisers; the activity itself is appraisal or appraising. It seeks to find an objective value that things have in relation to one or another community of human interests. I call this value "objective" because, although it exists only insofar as there are people who want the house, the estimate is open to public verification. As long as they agree about the circumstances—what the house is like and what a relevant group of buyers prefer—all fair-minded appraisers should reach a similar appraisal, regardless of their own feelings about this particular house. In other words, appraising is a branch of empirical science, specifically directed toward the determining of value.

But now imagine that the man setting the price is not an appraiser, but a prospective buyer. The price that he sets need not agree with the appraiser's. For he does more than estimate objective value: he decides what the house is worth to *him*. To the extent that his preferences differ from other people's, the house will have a different value for him. By introducing such considerations, we relate the object to the particular and possibly idiosyncratic interests of a single person, his likings, his needs, his wants, his desires. Ultimately, all objective value depends upon interests of this sort. The community of buyers whose inclinations the appraiser must gauge is itself just a class of individuals. The appraiser merely predicts what each of them would be likely to pay for the house. At the same time, each buyer must be something of an appraiser himself; for he must have at least a rough idea of the price that other buyers will set. Furthermore, each person has to weigh, and so appraise, the relative importance of his own particular interests; and he must estimate whether the house can satisfy them. In principle these judgments are verifiable. They are also liable to mistake: for instance, when a man thinks that certain desires matter more to him than they really do, or when he expects greater benefits from an object than it can provide. Deciding what something is worth to *oneself* we may call an "individual appraisal." It differs from what the appraiser does; it determines a purely individual value, as opposed to any objective value.

Now, with this in mind, I suggest that love creates a new value, one that is not reducible to the individual or objective value that something may also have. This further type of valuing I call bestowal. Individual and objective value depend upon an object's ability to satisfy prior interests—the needs, the desires, the wants, or whatever it is that motivates us toward one object and not another. Bestowed value is different. It is created by the affirmative relationship *itself*, by the very act of responding favorably, giving an object emotional and pervasive importance regardless of its capacity to satisfy interests. Here it makes no sense to speak of verifiability; and though bestowing may often be injurious, unwise, even immoral, it cannot be erroneous in the way that an appraisal might be. For now it is the valuing alone that *makes* the value.

In saying that a woman is beautiful or that a man is handsome, or that a man or woman is good in any other respect, we ascribe objective value. This will always be a function of *some* community of human interests, though we may have difficulty specifying which one. And in all communities people have individual value for one another. We are means to each other's satisfactions, and we constantly evaluate one another on the basis of our individual interests. However subtly, we are always setting prices on other people, and on ourselves. But we also bestow value in the manner of love. We then respond to another as something that cannot be reduced to *any* system of appraisal. The lover takes an interest in the beloved as a *person*, and not merely as a commodity—which she may also be. (The lover may be female, of course, and the beloved may be male; but for the sake of brevity and grammatical simplicity I shall generally retain the old convention of referring to lovers as "he" and beloveds as "she.") He bestows importance upon *her* needs and *her* desires, even when they do not further the satisfaction of his own. Whatever her personality, he gives it a value it would not have apart from his loving attitude. In relation

to the lover, the beloved has become valuable for her own sake.

In the love of persons, then, people bestow value upon one another over and above their individual or objective value. The reciprocity of love occurs when each participant receives bestowed value while also bestowing it upon the other. Reciprocity has always been recognized as a desired outcome of love. Since it need not occur, however, I define the lover as one who bestows value, and the beloved as one who receives it. The lover makes the beloved valuable merely by attaching and committing himself to her. Though she may satisfy his needs, he refuses to use her as just an instrument. To love a woman as a person is to desire her for the sake of values that appraisal might discover, and yet to place one's desire within a context that affirms her importance regardless of these values. Eventually the beloved may no longer matter to us as one who is useful. Treating her as an end, we may think only of how we can be useful to *her*. But still it is we who think and act and make this affirmative response. Only in relation to *our* bestowal does another person enjoy the kind of value that love creates.

Through bestowal lovers have "a life" together. The lover accords the beloved the tribute of expressing *his* feelings by responding to *hers*. If he sends her valuable presents, they will signify that he too appreciates what she esteems; if he makes sacrifices on her behalf, he indicates how greatly her welfare matters to him. It is as if he were announcing that what is real for her is real for him also. Upon the sheer personality of the beloved he bestows a framework of value, emanating from himself but focused on her. Lovers linger over attributes that might well have been ignored. Whether sensuous or polite, passionate or serene, brusque or tender, the lover's response is variably fervent but constantly gratuitous. It dignifies the beloved by treating her as *someone*, with all the emphasis the italics imply. Though independent of our needs, she is also the significant object of our attention. We show ourselves receptive to her peculiarities in the sense that we readily respond to them. Response is itself a kind of affirmation, even when it issues into unpleasant emotions such as anger and jealousy. These need not be antithetical to love; they may even be signs of it. Under many circumstances one cannot respond to another person without the unpleasant emotions, as a parent cannot stay in touch with a wayward child unless he occasionally punishes him. It is when we reject the other person, reducing him to a nothing or expressing our indifference, that love disappears. For then instead of bestowing value, we have withdrawn it.

In general, every emotion or desire contributes to love once it serves as a positive response to an independent being. If a woman is *simply* a means to sexual satisfaction, a man may be said to want her, but not to love her. For his sexual desire to become a part of love, it must function as a way of responding to the character and special properties of this particular woman. Desire wants what it wants for the sake of some private gratification, whereas love demands an interest in that vague complexity we call another person. No wonder lovers sound like metaphysicians, and scientists are more comfortable in the study of desire. For love is an attitude with no clear objective. Through it one human being affirms the significance of another, much as a painter highlights a figure by defining it in a sharpened outline. But the beloved is not a painted figure. She is not static: she is fluid, changing, indefinable—*alive*. The lover is attending to a *person*. And who can say what that is?

In the history of philosophy, bestowal and appraisal have often been confused with one another, perhaps because they are both types of valuation.[1] Love is related to both; they interweave in it. Unless we appraised we could not bestow a value that goes beyond appraisal; and without bestowal there would be no love. We may speak of lovers accepting one another, or even taking each other as is. But this need not mean a blind submission to some unknown being. In love we *attend* to the beloved, in the sense that we respond to what *she* is. For the effort to succeed, it must be accompanied by justifiable appraisals, objective as well as individual. The objective beauty and goodness of his beloved will delight the lover, just as her deficiencies will distress him. In her, as in every other human being, these are important properties.

How is the lover to know what they are without a system of appraisals? Or how to help her realize her potentialities—assuming that is what she wants? Of course, in bestowing value upon this woman, the lover will "accentuate the positive" and undergo a kind of personal involvement that no disinterested spectator would. He will feel an intimate concern about the continuance of good properties in the beloved and the diminishing of bad ones. But none of this would be possible without objective appraisals.

Love would not be love unless appraising were accompanied by the bestowing of value. But where this conjunction exists, *every* appraisal may lead on to a further bestowal. By disclosing an excellence in the beloved, appraisal (whether individual or objective) makes it easier for us to appreciate her. By revealing her faults and imperfections, it increases the importance of acting on her behalf. Love may thus encompass all possible appraisals. Once bestowal has occurred, a man may hardly care that his beloved is not deemed desirable by other men. Given a choice, he may prefer her to women who are sexually more attractive. His love is a way of compensating for and even overcoming negative appraisals. If it were a means of repaying the object for value received, love would turn into gratitude; if it were an attempt to give more than the object has provided, it would become generosity or condescension. These are related attitudes, but love differs from them in bestowing value without calculation. It confers importance no matter *what* the object is worth.

When appraisal occurs alone, our attitude develops in the direction of science, ambition, or morality. To do "the right thing" we need not bestow value upon another person; we need only recognize the truth about his character and act appropriately.

When love intervenes, morality becomes more personal but also more erratic. It is almost impossible to imagine someone bestowing value without caring about the other person's welfare. To that extent, love implies benevolence. And yet the lover does not act benevolently for the sake of doing the right thing. In loving another person, we respect *his* desire to improve himself. If we offer to help, we do so because *he* wants to be better than he is, not because *we* think he ought to be. Love and morality need not diverge, but they often do. For love is not *inherently* moral. There is no guarantee that it will bestow value properly, at the right time, in the right way. Through love we enjoy another person as he is, including his moral condition; yet this enjoyment may itself violate the demands of morality. Ethical attitudes must always be governed by appraisal rather than bestowal. They must consider the individual in his relations to other people, as one among many who have equal claims. Faced with the being of a particular person, morality tells us to pick and choose those attributes that are most desirable. It is like a chef who makes an excellent stew by bringing out one flavor and muffling another. The chef does not care about the ingredients as unique or terminal entities, but only as things that are good to eat. In loving another person, however, we enact a nonmoral *loyalty*—like the mother who stands by her criminal son even though she knows he is guilty. Her loyalty need not be *im*moral; and though she loves her son, she may realize that he must be punished. But what if the value she has bestowed upon her child blinds her to the harm he has done, deters her from handing him over to the police, leads her to encourage him as a criminal? Her love may increase through such devotion, but it will be based on faulty appraisals and will not be a moral love.

Possibly the confusion between appraisal and bestowal results from the way that lovers talk. To love another person is to *treat* him with great regard, to confer a new and personal value upon him. But when lovers describe their beloved, they sometimes sound as if she were perfect just in being herself. In caring about someone, attending to her, affirming the importance of her being what she is, the lover resembles a man who has appraised an object and found it very valuable. Though he is bestowing value, the lover *seems* to be declaring the objective goodness of the beloved. It is *as if* he were predicting the outcome of all possible appraisals and insisting that they would always be favorable.

In being primarily bestowal and only secondarily appraisal, love is never elicited by the object in the sense that desire or approbation is. We desire things or people for the sake of what will satisfy us. We approve of someone for his commendable properties. But these conditions have only a causal tie to love: as when a man loves a woman *because* she is beautiful, or *because* she satisfies his sexual, domestic, and social needs, or *because* she resembles his childhood memory of mother. Such facts indicate the circumstances under which people love one another; they explain why this particular man loves this particular woman; and if the life sciences were sufficiently developed, the facts could help us to predict who among human beings would be likely to love whom. But explaining the occurrence of love is not the same as explicating the concept. The conditions for love are not the same as love itself. In some circumstances the bestowing of value will happen more easily than in others; but *whenever* it happens, it happens as a new creation of value and exceeds all attributes of the object that might be thought to elicit it. Even if a man loves only a woman who is beautiful and looks like his mother, he does not *love* her for these properties in the same sense in which he might *admire* her for being objectively valuable or *desire* her for satisfying his needs.

For what then does a man love a woman? For being the person she is, for being herself? But that is to say that he loves her for nothing at all. Everyone is himself. Having a beloved who is what she is does not reveal the nature of love. Neither does it help us to understand the saint's desire to love all people. They are what they are. Why should they be loved for it? Why not pitied or despised, ignored or simply put to use? Love supplements the human search for value with a capacity for bestowing it gratuitously. To one who has succeeded in cultivating this attitude, *anything* may become an object of love. The saint is a man whose earthly needs and desires are extraordinarily modest; in principle, every human being can satisfy them. That being so, the saint creates a value-system in which all persons fit equally well. This disposition, this freely given response, cannot be elicited from him: it bestows itself and happens to be indiscriminate.

To the man of common sense it is very upsetting that love does not limit itself to some prior value in the object. The idea goes against our purposive ways of thinking. If I wish to drink the best wine, I have reason to prefer French champagne over American. My choice is dictated by an objective goodness in the French champagne. If instead I wish to economize, I act sensibly in choosing a wine I value less highly. We act this way whenever we use purposive means of attaining the good life, which covers a major part of our existence. But love, unlike desire, is not wholly purposive. Within the total structure of a human life it may serve as a lubricant to purposive attitudes, furthering their aims through new interests that promise new satisfactions; but in creating value, bestowing it freely, love introduces an element of risk into the economy. Purposive attitudes are safe, secure, like money in the bank; the loving attitude is speculative and always dangerous. Love is not *practical,* and sometimes borders on madness. We take our life in our hands when we allow love to tamper with our purposive habits. Without love, life might not be worth living; but without purposiveness, there would be no life.

The creativity of love is thus primarily a self-creation. Lovers create within themselves a remarkable capacity for affective response, an ability to use their emotions, their words, their deeds for bestowing as well as appraising value. Each enhances the other's importance through an imaginative play within valuation itself. Indeed, love may be best approached as a subspecies of the imagination. Not only does the lover speak in poetic metaphors, but also he behaves like any artist. Whatever his "realistic" aspirations, no painter can duplicate reality. The scene out there cannot be transferred to a canvas. The painter can only *paint* it: that is, give it a new importance in human life by presenting his way of seeing it through the medium of his art and the techniques of his individual talent. These determine the values of his painting, not the external landscape that may have originally inspired him. The artist may vary the scene to his heart's content, as El Greco did when he rearranged the buildings of Toledo. What matters is his way of seeing as a function of the imagination, not the disposition in space of stones and mortar. Similarly, a lover sees a woman not as others might, but through the creative agency of bestowing value. He need not change her any more than El Greco changed the real Toledo. But he renews her personality by subsuming it within the imaginative system of his own positive responses. Through her he expresses the variety of feelings that belong to love. Artists, even the most abstract, do not create out of nothing: they re-create, create anew. So too, the lover re-creates another person. By deploying his imagination in the art of bestowing value, by caring about the independent being of another person, the lover adds a new dimension to the beloved. In relation to him, within his loving attitude, she becomes the object of an affirmative interest, even an aesthetic object. She is, as we say, "*appreciated*"—made more valuable through the special media and techniques in which love consists.

Treating love as an aspect of the imagination enables us to confront problems I have thus far ignored. For instance, I said it was *as if* the lover were predicting that no appraisal would discover any significant fault. If we now inquire into the meaning of these "as ifs," I can only remind you how they operate in other situations involving the imagination. Think of yourself as a spectator in the theater, watching an engrossing drama. The hero dies, and you begin to weep. Now for whom are you crying? Surely not for the actor: you know that as soon as the curtain falls, he will scramble to his feet and prepare for a great ovation. Is it then the character in the play? But there is no such person. You are fully aware that Hamlet (at least Shakespeare's Hamlet) never existed. How can his death, which is purely fictional, sadden you? Yet it does, more so perhaps than the death of real people you may have known. What happens, I think, is that you respond *as if* the actor were really Hamlet and *as if* Hamlet really existed. The "as if" signifies that although you *know* the actor is only acting and Hamlet only fictitious, your imaginative involvement causes you to express feelings appropriate to real people. At no point are you deluded. The "illusion" of the theater is not an illusion at all. It is an act of imagination—nothing like a mistake of judgment, nothing like the derangement that causes Don Quixote to smash the cruel puppet show in order to save the unfortunate heroine. On entering the theater, you have entered the dramatic situation. You have allowed your imagination to engage itself in one specific channel. With the assistance of the realistic props, the surrounding darkness, the company of other people doing the same imagining, you have invested the actors and the characters they represent with a capacity to affect your feelings as real persons might.

In love the same kind of thing occurs. The as ifs of love are imaginative, not essentially delusional. Of course, the lover *may* be deluded about his beloved. That is the familiar joke about lovers: they live in constant illusion, Cupid is blinded by emotion, etc. That this often happens I do not care to deny. But that this should be the essence of love, that by its very nature love should be illusory, seems to me utterly absurd. Even if people frequently clambered on stage and acted like Don Quixote, we would not say that their behavior revealed what it is to be a theatrical spectator. We would say they did not know how to look at a play. Likewise, it is not in the acting out of illusions that people become lovers. Though lovers do commit errors of judgment and are sometimes carried away by their feelings, love itself is not illusory. Emotional aberrations are adventitious to it, not definitive. As love is not primarily a way of knowing, neither is it a way of making mistakes. Appraisal is a way of knowing, and emotions may always interfere with its proper employment. But love is an imaginative means of bestowing value that would not exist otherwise. To the extent that a man is a lover, rather than a person seeking knowledge or yielding to self-delusion (which he may also be), he accords his beloved the courtesy of being treated affirmatively regardless of what he knows about her. In refusing to let his appraisive knowledge deflect his amorous conduct, he bestows a tribute which can only be understood as an imaginative act.

In a similar fashion the lover's attention fixes upon the sheer presence of the beloved. In that extreme condition sometimes called "falling in love," such attentiveness often approaches self-hypnosis.

Freud was one of the first to recognize the kinship between hypnosis and certain types of love; but his analysis neglects the philosophical import of these occurrences, their linkage to valuation. For me the loving stare of one human being visually glued to another signifies an extraordinary bestowal of value, an imaginative (though possibly excessive) response to the presence of another person. The lover's glance illuminates the beloved. He celebrates her as a living reality to which he attends. As in celebration of any sort, his response contributes something new and expressive. He introduces the woman into the world of his own imagination—as if, through some enchantment, she were indeed his work of art and only he could contemplate her infinite detail. As long as they intensify her presence, the lover will cherish even those features in the beloved that appraisal scorns.

I am sure that the similarity between love and the theater could be pushed much further. Love is the art of enjoying another person, as theater is the art of enjoying dramatic situations. Because it inevitably suggests the possibility of *enjoyment*, love is the most frequent theme in all entertainments based on human relations: it is the only subject that interests everyone. Nevertheless, the analogy between love and the theater can also be misleading. The actor portrays a character; the beloved does not portray anything, though she may symbolize a great deal. The beloved is not an *image* of perfection in the sense in which an actor is an image or representation of Hamlet. The lover uses his imagination to appreciate the beloved as she is, to accept her in herself; but the audience uses the actor as a vehicle for the fiction. That is why an actor can only rarely look his audience in the eye. In so direct a communication his presence crowds out his aesthetic function, and we respond to him as the person he happens to be, not as the character he represents. On the other hand, lovers may well be stereotyped (as they are often photographed or painted) in a joint posture of immediate confrontation, face to face, each searching for the other's personality, each peering into the other's eyes: "Our eyebeams twisted, and did thread / Our eyes, upon one double string."

DISCUSSION QUESTIONS

1. What is "appraisal"? What is "bestowal"? Give concrete examples.
2. Suppose we are in a love relationship not of our choosing (such as familial love). Do we still appraise and bestow? How does that work?
3. When we bestow love upon someone, can we be mistaken in that bestowal? Please give concrete examples.

NOTE

1. Though not of "*evaluation*." That word is usually reserved for appraisal.

To Fall in Love with Anyone, Do This

BY MANDY LEN CATRON

> Canadian writer Mandy Len Catron describes using psychologist Arthur Aron's techniques for an unusual experiment: to see if she and a friend can force themselves to fall in love.

More than 20 years ago, the psychologist Arthur Aron succeeded in making two strangers fall in love in his laboratory. Last summer, I applied his technique in my own life, which is how I found myself standing on a bridge at midnight, staring into a man's eyes for exactly four minutes.

Let me explain. Earlier in the evening, that man had said: "I suspect, given a few commonalities, you could fall in love with anyone. If so, how do you choose someone?"

He was a university acquaintance I occasionally ran into at the climbing gym and had thought, "What if?" I had gotten a glimpse into his days on Instagram. But this was the first time we had hung out one-on-one.

"Actually, psychologists have tried making people fall in love," I said, remembering Dr. Aron's study. "It's fascinating. I've always wanted to try it."

I first read about the study when I was in the midst of a breakup. Each time I thought of leaving, my heart overruled my brain. I felt stuck. So, like a good academic, I turned to science, hoping there was a way to love smarter.

I explained the study to my university acquaintance. A heterosexual man and woman enter the lab through separate doors. They sit face to face and answer a series of increasingly personal questions. Then they stare silently into each other's eyes for four minutes. The most tantalizing detail: Six months later, two participants were married. They invited the entire lab to the ceremony.

"Let's try it," he said.

Let me acknowledge the ways our experiment already fails to line up with the study. First, we were in a bar, not a lab. Second, we weren't strangers. Not only that, but I see now that one neither suggests nor agrees to try an experiment designed to create romantic love if one isn't open to this happening.

I Googled Dr. Aron's questions; there are 36. We spent the next two hours passing my iPhone across the table, alternately posing each question.

They began innocuously: "Would you like to be famous? In what way?" And "When did you last sing to yourself? To someone else?"

But they quickly became probing.

In response to the prompt, "Name three things you and your partner appear to have in common," he looked at me and said, "I think we're both interested in each other."

I grinned and gulped my beer as he listed two more commonalities I then promptly forgot. We exchanged stories about the last time we each cried, and confessed the one thing we'd like to ask a fortuneteller. We explained our relationships with our mothers.

The questions reminded me of the infamous boiling frog experiment in which the frog doesn't feel the water getting hotter until it's too late. With us, because the level of vulnerability increased gradually, I didn't notice we had entered intimate territory until we were already there, a process that can typically take weeks or months.

I liked learning about myself through my answers, but I liked learning things about him even more. The bar, which was empty when we arrived, had filled up by the time we paused for a bathroom break.

I sat alone at our table, aware of my surroundings for the first time in an hour, and wondered if anyone had been listening to our conversation. If they had, I hadn't noticed. And I didn't notice as the crowd thinned and the night got late.

We all have a narrative of ourselves that we offer up to strangers and acquaintances, but Dr. Aron's questions make it impossible to rely on that narrative. Ours was the kind of accelerated intimacy I remembered from summer camp, staying up all night with a new friend, exchanging the details of our short lives. At 13, away from home for the first time, it felt natural to get to know someone quickly. But rarely does adult life present us with such circumstances.

The moments I found most uncomfortable were not when I had to make confessions about myself, but had to venture opinions about my partner. For example: "Alternate sharing something you consider a positive characteristic of your partner, a total of five items" (Question 22), and "Tell your partner what you like about them; be very honest this time saying things you might not say to someone you've just met" (Question 28).

Much of Dr. Aron's research focuses on creating interpersonal closeness. In particular, several studies investigate the ways we incorporate others into our sense of self. It's easy to see how the questions encourage what they call "self-expansion." Saying things like, "I like your voice, your taste in beer, the way all your friends seem to admire you," makes certain positive qualities belonging to one person explicitly valuable to the other.

It's astounding, really, to hear what someone admires in you. I don't know why we don't go around thoughtfully complimenting one another all the time.

Why don't we?

We finished at midnight, taking far longer than the 90 minutes for the original study. Looking around the bar, I felt as if I had just woken up. "That wasn't so bad," I said. "Definitely less uncomfortable

than the staring into each other's eyes part would be."

He hesitated and asked. "Do you think we should do that, too?"

"Here?" I looked around the bar. It seemed too weird, too public.

"We could stand on the bridge," he said, turning toward the window.

The night was warm and I was wide-awake. We walked to the highest point, then turned to face each other. I fumbled with my phone as I set the timer.

"O.K.," I said, inhaling sharply.

"O.K.," he said, smiling.

I've skied steep slopes and hung from a rock face by a short length of rope, but staring into someone's eyes for four silent minutes was one of the more thrilling and terrifying experiences of my life. I spent the first couple of minutes just trying to breathe properly. There was a lot of nervous smiling until, eventually, we settled in.

I know the eyes are the windows to the soul or whatever, but the real crux of the moment was not just that I was really seeing someone, but that I was seeing someone really seeing me. Once I embraced the terror of this realization and gave it time to subside, I arrived somewhere unexpected.

I felt brave, and in a state of wonder. Part of that wonder was at my own vulnerability and part was the weird kind of wonder you get from saying a word over and over until it loses its meaning and becomes what it actually is: an assemblage of sounds.

So it was with the eye, which is not a window to anything but rather a clump of very useful cells. The sentiment associated with the eye fell away and I was struck by its astounding biological reality: the spherical nature of the eyeball, the visible musculature of the iris and the smooth wet glass of the cornea. It was strange and exquisite.

When the timer buzzed, I was surprised—and a little relieved. But I also felt a sense of loss. Already I was beginning to see our evening through the surreal and unreliable lens of retrospect.

Most of us think about love as something that happens to us. We fall. We get crushed.

But what I like about this study is how it assumes that love is an action. It assumes that what matters to my partner matters to me because we have at least three things in common, because we have close relationships with our mothers, and because he let me look at him.

I wondered what would come of our interaction. If nothing else, I thought it would make a good story. But I see now that the story isn't about us; it's about what it means to bother to know someone, which is really a story about what it means to be known.

It's true you can't choose who loves you, although I've spent years hoping otherwise, and you can't create romantic feelings based on convenience alone. Science tells us biology matters; our pheromones and hormones do a lot of work behind the scenes.

But despite all this, I've begun to think love is a more pliable thing than we make it out to be. Arthur Aron's study taught me that it's possible—simple, even—to generate trust and intimacy, the feelings love needs to thrive.

You're probably wondering if he and I fell in love. Well, we did. Although it's hard to credit the study entirely (it may have happened anyway), the study did give us a way into a relationship that feels deliberate. We spent weeks in the intimate space we created that night, waiting to see what it could become.

Love didn't happen to us. We're in love because we each made the choice to be.

DISCUSSION QUESTIONS

1. How do we fall in love, according to Catron? Walk me through the steps.
2. Do you think we can fall in love with anyone? Why or why not?
3. Are we ever just struck by love, like a lightning bolt striking from the sky? How does this fit with Catron's view?

Love's Bond

BY ROBERT NOZICK

Robert Nozick (1938–2002) was an American philosopher best known for his libertarian political philosophy. In this essay, Nozick argues that love involves— even requires—a metamorphosis of the individual into something more than just the individual. Love changes the self, and ideally expands the boundaries of the self.

The general phenomenon of love encompasses romantic love, the love of a parent for a child, love of one's country, and more. What is common to all love is this: Your own well-being is tied up with that of someone (or something) you love. When a bad thing happens to a friend, it happens to her and you feel sad for her; when something good happens, you feel happy for her. When something bad happens to one you love, though, something bad also happens *to you*. (It need not be exactly the same bad thing. And I do not mean that one cannot also love a friend.) If a loved one is hurt or disgraced, you are hurt; if something wonderful happens to her, you feel better off. Not every gratification of a loved one's preference will make you feel better off, though; her well-being, not merely a preference of hers, has to be at stake. (Her well-being as who perceives it, she or you?) When love is not present, changes in other people's well-being do not, in general, change your own. You will be moved when others suffer in a famine and will contribute to help; you may be haunted by their plight, but you need not feel you yourself are worse off.

This extension of your own well-being (or ill-being) is what marks all the different kinds of love: the love of children, the love of parents, the love of one's people, of one's country. Love is not necessarily a matter of caring equally or more about someone else than about yourself. These loves are large, but love in some amount is present when your well-being is affected to whatever extent (but in the same direction) by another's. As the other fares, so (to some extent) do you. The people you love are included inside your boundaries, their well-being is your own.[1]

Being "in love," infatuation, is an intense state that displays familiar features: almost always thinking of the person; wanting constantly to touch and to be together; excitement in the other's presence; losing sleep; expressing one's feelings through poetry, gifts, or still other ways to delight the beloved; gazing deeply into each other's eyes; candlelit dinners; feeling that short separations are long; smiling foolishly when remembering actions and remarks of the other; feeling that the other's minor foibles are delightful; experiencing joy at having found the other and at being found by the other; and (as Tolstoy depicts Levin in *Anna Karenina* as he learns Kitty loves him) finding *everyone* charming and nice, and thinking they all must sense one's happiness. Other concerns and responsibilities become minor background details in the story of the romance, which becomes the predominant foreground event of life. (When major public responsibilities such as commanding Rome's armies or being king of England are put aside, the tales engross.) The vividness of the relationship can carry artistic or myth is proportions— lying together like figures in a painting, jointly living a new tale from Ovid. Familiar, too, is what happens when the love is not equally reciprocated: melancholy, obsessive rumination on what went wrong, fantasies about its being set right, lingering in places to catch a glimpse of the person, making telephone calls to hear the other's voice, finding that all other activities seem flat, occasionally having suicidal thoughts.

However and whenever infatuation begins, if given the opportunity it transforms itself into continuing romantic love or else it disappears. With this continuing romantic love, it feels to the two people that they have united to form and constitute a new entity in the world, what might be called a *we*.[2] You can be in romantic love with someone, however, without actually forming a *we* with her or him—that other person might not be in love with you. Love, romantic love, is *wanting* to form a *we* with that particular person, feeling, or perhaps wanting, that particular person to be the right one for you to form a *we* with, and also wanting the other to feel the same way about you. (It would be kinder if the realization that the other person is not the right one with whom to form a *we* always and immediately terminated the desire to form it.) The desire to form a *we* with that other person is not simply something that goes along with romantic love, something that contingently happens when love does. That desire is intrinsic to the nature of love, I think; it is an important part of what love intends.

In a *we,* the two people are not bound physically like Siamese twins; they can be in distant places, feel differently about things, carry on different occupations. In what sense, then, do these people together constitute a new entity, a *we*? That new entity is created by a new web of relationships between them which makes them no longer so separate. Let me describe some features of this web; I will begin with two that have a somewhat cold and political-science sound.

#1

First, the defining feature we mentioned which applies to love in general: Your own well-being is tied up with that of someone you love romantically. Love, then, among other things, can place you at risk. Bad things that happen to your loved one happen to you. But so too do good things; moreover, someone who loves you helps you with care and comfort to meet vicissitudes—not out of selfishness although her doing so does, in part, help maintain her own well-being too. Thus, love places a floor under your well-being; it provides insurance in the face of fate's blows. (Would economists explain some features of selecting a mate as the rational pooling of risks?)

People who form a *we* pool not only their well-being but also their autonomy. They limit or curtail their own decision-making power and rights; some decisions can no longer be made alone. Which decisions these are will be parceled differently by different couples: where to live, how to live, who friends are and how to see them, whether to have children and how many, where to travel, whether to go to the movies that night and what to see. Each transfers some previous rights to make certain decisions unilaterally into a joint pool; somehow, decisions will be made together about how to be together. If your well-being so closely affects and is affected by another's, it is not surprising that decisions that importantly affect well-being, even in the first instance primarily your own, will no longer be made alone.[3]

#2

The term *couple* used in reference to people who have formed a *we* is not accidental. The two people also view themselves as a new and continuing unit, and they present that face to the world. They want to be perceived publicly as a couple, to express and assert their identity as a couple in public. Hence those homosexual couples unable to do this face a serious impediment.

To be part of a *we* involves having a new identity, an additional one. This does *not* mean that you no longer have any individual identity or that your sole identity is as part of the *we*. However, the individual identity you did have will become altered. To have this new identity is to enter a certain psychological stance; and each party in the *we* has this stance toward the other. Each becomes psychologically part of the other's identity. How can we say more exactly what this means? To say that something is part of your identity when, if that thing changes or is lost, you feel like a different person, seems only to reintroduce the very notion of identity that needs to be explained. Here is something more helpful: To love someone might

#3

be, in part, to devote alertness to their well-being and to your connection with them. (More generally, shall we say that something is part of your identity when you continually make it one of your few areas of special alertness?) There are empirical tests of alertness in the case of your own separate identity—for example, how you hear your name mentioned through the noise of a conversation you were not consciously attending to; how a word that resembles your name "jumps out" from the page. We might find similar tests to check for that alertness involved in loving someone. For example, a person in a *we* often is considerably more worried about the dangers of traveling—air crashes or whatever—when the other is traveling alone than when both travel together or when he himself or she herself is traveling alone; it seems plausible that a person in a *we* is alert, in general, to dangers to the other that would necessitate having to go back to a single individual identity, while these are made especially salient by a significant physical separation. Other criteria for the formation of a joint identity also might be suggested, such as a certain kind of division of labor. A person in a *we* might find himself coming across something interesting to read yet leaving it for the other person, not because he himself would not be interested in it but because the other would be more interested, and one of them reading it is sufficient for it to be registered by the wider identity now shared, the *we*. If the couple breaks up, they then might notice themselves reading all those things directly; the other person no longer can do it *for them*. (The list of criteria for the *we* might continue on to include something we discuss later, not seeking to "trade up" to another partner.) Sometimes the existence of the *we* can be very palpable. Just as a reflective person can walk along the street in friendly internal dialogue with himself, keeping himself company, so can one be with a loved person who is not physically present, thinking what she would say, conversing with her, noticing things as she would, for her, because she is not there to notice, saying things to others that she would say, in her tone of voice, carrying the full *we* along.

If we picture the individual self as a closed figure whose boundaries are continuous and solid, dividing what is inside from what is outside, then we might diagram the *we* as two figures with the boundary line between them erased where they come together. (Is that the traditional heart shape?) The unitive aspects of sexual experience, two persons flowing together and intensely merging, mirror and aid the formation of the *we*. Meaningful work, creative activity, and development can change the shape of the self. Intimate bonds change the boundaries of the self and alter its *topology*—romantic love in one way and friendship (as we shall see) in another.

The individual self can be related to the *we* it identifies with in two different ways. It can see the *we* as a very important *aspect* of itself, or it can see itself as part of the *we*, as contained within it. It may be that men more often take the former view, women the latter. Although both see the *we* as extremely important for the self, most men might draw the circle of themselves containing the circle of the *we* as an aspect *within* it, while most women might draw the circle of themselves within the circle of the *we*. In either case, the *we* need not consume an individual self or leave it without any autonomy.

Each person in a romantic *we* wants to possess the other completely; yet each also needs the other to be an independent and nonsubservient person. Only someone who continues to possess a nonsubservient autonomy can be an apt partner in a joint identity that enlarges and enhances your individual one. And, of course, the other's well-being—something you care about—requires that nonsubservient autonomy too. Yet at the same time there is the desire to possess the other *completely*. This does not have to stem from a desire to dominate the other person, I think. What you need and want is to possess the other as completely as you do your own identity. This is an expression of the fact that you *are* forming a new joint identity with him or her. Or, perhaps, this desire just *is* the desire to form an identity with the other. Unlike Hegel's description of the unstable dialectic between the master and the slave, though, in a romantic *we* the autonomy of the other and complete possession too are reconciled in the formation of a joint and wondrous enlarged identity for both.

The heart of the love relationship is how the lovers view it from the inside, how they feel about their partner and about themselves within it, and the particular ways in which they are good *to* each other. Each person in love delights in the other, and also in giving delight; this often expresses itself in being playful together. In receiving adult love, we are held worthy of being the primary object of the most intense love, something we were not given in the childhood oedipal triangle.[4] Seeing the other happy with us and made happy through our love, we become happier with ourselves.

To be englowed by someone's love, it must be we ourselves who are loved, not a whitewashed version of ourselves, not just a portion. In the complete intimacy of love, a partner knows us as we are, fully. It is no reassurance to be loved by someone ignorant of those traits and features we feel might make us unlovable. Sometimes these are character traits or areas of incompetence, clumsiness, or ignorance; sometimes these are personal bodily features. Complex are the ways parents make children uncomfortable about sites of pleasure or elimination, and these feelings can be soothed or transformed in the closest attentive and loving sexual intimacy. In the full intimacy of love, the full person is known and cleansed and accepted. And healed.

To be made happy with yourself by being loved, it must be you who is loved, not some feature such as your money. People want, as they say, to be loved "for themselves." You are loved for something else when what you are loved for is a peripheral part of your own self-image or identity. However, someone for whom money, or the ability to make it, was central to his identity, or for whom good looks or great kindness or intelligence was, might not be averse to love's being prompted by these characteristics. You can fall in love with someone because of certain characteristics and you can continue to delight in these; but eventually you must love the person himself, and not *for* the characteristics, not, at any rate, for any delimited list of them. But what does this mean, exactly?

We love the person when being together with that person is a salient part of our identity as we think of it: "being with Eve," "being with Adam,"

rather than "being with someone who is (or has) such-and-such. . . ." How does this come about? Characteristics must have played some important role, for otherwise why was not a different person loved just as well? Yet if we continue to be loved "for" the characteristics, then the love seems conditional, something that might change or disappear if the characteristics do. Perhaps we should think of love as like imprinting in ducks, where a duckling will attach itself to the first sizable moving object it sees in a certain time period and follow that as its mother. With people, perhaps characteristics set off the imprint of love, but then the person is loved in a way that is no longer based upon retaining those characteristics. This will be helped if the love is based at first upon a wide range of characteristics; it begins as conditional, contingent upon the loved person's having these desirable characteristics, yet given their range and tenacity, it is not insecure.

However, love between people, unlike imprinting with ducks, is not unalterable. Though no longer dependent upon the particular characteristics that set it off, it *can* be overcome over time by new and sufficiently negative other characteristics. Or perhaps by a new imprinting onto another person. Yet this alteration will not be sought by someone within a *we*. If someone were loved "for" certain desirable or valuable characteristics, on the other hand, then if someone else came along who had those characteristics to a greater extent, or other even more valuable characteristics, it seems you should love this new person more. And in that case, why merely wait for a "better" person to turn up; why not actively seek to "trade up" to someone with a "higher score" along valuable dimensions? (Plato's theory is especially vulnerable to these questions, for there it is the Form of Beauty that is the ultimate and appropriate object of love; any particular person serves merely as a bearer of characteristics that awaken in the lover a love of the Form, and hence any such person should be replaceable by a better awakener.)

A readiness to trade up, looking for someone with "better" characteristics, does not fit with an attitude of love. An illuminating view should explain why not, yet why, nevertheless, the attitude of love is not irrational. One possible and boring explanation is economic in form. Once you have come to know a person well, it would take a large investment of time and energy to reach the comparable point with another person, so there is a barrier to switching. (But couldn't the other person promise a greater return, even taking into account the new costs of investment?) There is uncertainty about a new person; only after long time and experience together, through arguments and crises, can one come to know a person's trustworthiness, reliability, resiliency, and compassion in hardships. Investigating another candidate for coupledom, even an apparently promising one, is likely eventually to reach a negative conclusion and it probably will necessitate curtailing or ending one's current coupled state. So it is unwise to seek to trade up from a reasonably satisfactory situation; the energy you'd expend in search might better be invested in improving your current *we*.

These counsels of economic prudence are not silly—far from it—but they are external. According to them, nothing about the nature of love itself focuses upon the particular individual loved or involves an unwillingness to substitute another; rather, the likelihood of losses from the substitution is what militates against it. We can see why, if the economic analysis were so, we would welcome someone's directing an attitude of love toward us that includes commitment to a particular person, and we can see why we might have to trade the offering or semblance of such an attitude in order to receive it. But why would we want actually to give such a commitment to a particular person, shunning all other partners? What special value is reached through such a love relationship committed to particularism but in no other way? To add that we care about our partners and so do not want to cause them hurt by replacing them is true, yet does not answer the question fully.

Economic analysis might even provide somewhat more understanding. Repeated trading with a fixed partner with special resources might make it rational to develop in yourself specialized assets for trading with that partner (and similarly on the partner's part toward you); and this specialization gives some assurance that you will continue to trade *with that party* (since the invested resources could be worth much less in exchanges with any third party). Moreover, to shape yourself and specialize so as to better fit and trade with that partner, and therefore to do so less well with others, you will want some commitment and guarantee that the party will continue to trade with you, a guarantee that goes beyond the party's own specialization to fit you. Under some conditions it will be economically advantageous for two such trading firms to combine into *one* firm, with all allocations now becoming internal. Here at last we come to something like the notion of a joint identity.

The intention in love is to form a *we* and to identify with it as an extended self, to identify one's fortunes in large part with its fortunes. A willingness to trade up, to destroy the very *we* you largely identify with, would then be a willingness to destroy your self in the form of your own extended self. One could not, therefore, intend to sink into another *we* unless one had ceased to identify with a current one—unless, that is, one had already ceased to love. Even in that case, the intention to form the new *we* would be an intention to *then* no longer be open to trading up. It is intrinsic to the notion of love, and to the *we* formed by it, that there is not that willingness to trade up. One is no more willing to find another partner, even one with a "higher score," than to destroy the personal self one identifies with in order to allow another, possibly better, but discontinuous self to replace it. (This is not to say one is unwilling to improve or transform oneself.) Perhaps here lies one function of infatuation, to pave and smooth the way to uniting in a *we;* it provides enthusiasm to take on over the hurdles of concern for one's own autonomy, and it provides an initiation into *we*-thinking too, by constantly occupying the mind with thoughts of the other and of the two of you together. A more cynical view than mine might see infatuation as the temporary glue that manages to hold people together until they are stuck.

Part of the process by which people soften their boundaries and move into a *we* involves repeated expression of the desire to do so, repeatedly telling each other that they love each other. Their statement often will be tentative, subject to withdrawal if the other does not respond with similar avowals. Holding hands, they walk into the water together, step by step. Their caution may become as great as when two suspicious groups or nations—Israel and the Palestinians might be an example—need to recognize the legitimacy of one another. Neither wants to recognize if the other does not, and it also will not suffice for each to announce that it will recognize if the other one does also. For each then will have announced a conditional recognition, contingent upon the other's unconditional recognition. Since neither one has offered this last, they haven't yet gotten started. Neither will it help if each says it will recognize conditional upon the other's conditional recognition; "I'll recognize you if you'll recognize me if I'll recognize you." For here each has given the other a three-part conditional announcement, one which is contingent upon, and goes into operation only when there exists, a two-part conditional announcement from the other party; so neither one has given the other exactly what will trigger that other's recognition, namely a two-part announcement. So long as they both symmetrically announce conditionals of the same length and complexity, they will not be able to get started. Some asymmetry is needed, then, but it need not be that either one begins by offering unconditional recognition. It would be enough for the first to offer the three-part recognition (which is contingent upon the other's simple two-part conditional recognition), and for the second to offer the two-part conditional recognition. The latter triggers the first to recognize outright and this, in turn, triggers the second to do the same. Between lovers, it never becomes this complicated explicitly. Neither makes the nested announcement "I will love you if you will love me if I will love you," and if either one did, this would not (to put it mildly) facilitate the formation of a *we*. Yet the frequency of their saying to each other, "I love you," and their attention to the other's response, may indicate a nesting that is implicit and very deep, as deep as the repeated triggering necessary to overcome caution and produce the actual and unconditional formation of the *we*.

Even after the *we* is formed, its motion is Aristotelian rather than Newtonian, maintained by frequent impetus. The avowals of love may not stop, and neither may romantic gestures, those especially apt actions, breaking the customary frame, that express and symbolize one's attachment to the *we* or, occurring earlier, the desire to form it.

Granting that a willingness to trade up is incompatible with love and with the formation of a *we* with a particular person, the question becomes one of whether it is rational to love in that particular way. There is the alternative of serious and significant personal ties without a joint identity, after all—friendships and sexual relationships, for instance. An answer could be given by the long and obvious list of the things and actions and emotions especially made possible and facilitated by the *we*. It is not unreasonable to want these, hence not irrational to enter into a *we* including forgoing the option of trading up. Yet it distorts romantic love to view it through the lens of the egoistic question "What's in it for me?" What we want when we are in love is to be with that person. What we want is to be with her or him—not *to be someone who is with her or him*. When we are with the other person, to be sure, we are someone who is with that person, but the object of our desire is not being that kind of someone. We want to make the other person happy, and also, but less so, to be the kind of person who makes her or him happy. It is a question of the emphasis, of how we describe what we want and seek—to use the philosophers' language, a question of the intentional object of our desire.

The way the egoistic question distorts romantic love is by switching the focus of attention from the relation between the lovers to the way each lover in the relation is. I do not mean that the way they are then is unimportant; how good reciprocated romantic love is for us is part of the reason why we desire and value it. But the central fact about love is the relation between the lovers. The central concern of lovers, as lovers, what they dwell upon and nurture, is the other person, and the relation between the two of them, not their own state. Of course, we cannot completely abstract a relation from whatever stands in it. (Contemporary extensional logic treats a relation simply as a set of the ordered pairs of things that—as we would say—stand in the relation.) And in fact, the particularity of a romantic relation does arise from the character of the lovers and then enhances that. Yet what is most salient to each is the other person and what holds between the two of them, not themselves as an endpoint of the relation. There is a difference between wanting to hug someone and using them as an opportunity for yourself to become a hugger.

The desire to have love in one's life, to be part of a *we* someday, is not the same as loving a particular person, wanting to form a *we* with that person in particular. In the choice of a particular partner, reasons can play a significant role, I think. Yet in addition to the merits of the other person and her or his qualities, there also is the question of whether the thought of forming a *we* with that person brings excitement and delight. Does that identity seem a wonderful one for you to have? Will it be *fun*? Here the answer is as complicated and mysterious as your relation to your own separate identity. Neither case is completely governed by reasons, but still we might hope that our choices do meet what reasoned standards there are. (The desire to continue to feel that the other is the right partner in your *we* also helps one surmount the inevitable moments in life together when that feeling itself becomes bruised.) The feeling that there is just "one right person" in the world for you, implausible beforehand—what lucky accident made that one unique person inhabit your century?—becomes true after the *we* is formed. Now your identity is wrapped up in that particular *we* with that particular person, so for the particular *you* you now are, there *is* just one other person who is right.

In the view of a person who loves someone romantically, there couldn't be anyone else who was better as a partner. He might think that person he is in love with could be better somehow—stop leaving toothpaste in the sink or whatever—but any description he could offer of a better mate would be a description of his mate changed, not one of somebody *else*. No one else would do, no matter what her qualities. Perhaps this is due to the particularity of the qualities you come to love, not just a sense of humor but that particular one, not just some

way of looking mock-stern but that one. Plato got the matter reversed, then; as love grows you love not general aspects or traits but more and more particular ones, not intelligence in general but that particular mind, not kindness in general but those particular ways of being kind. In trying to imagine a "better" mate, a person in romantic love will require her or him to have a very particular constellation of very particular traits and—leaving aside various "science fiction" possibilities—no other person *could* have precisely those traits; therefore, any imagined person will be the same mate (perhaps) somewhat changed, not somebody else. (If that same mate actually alters, though, the romantic partner may well come to love and require that new constellation of particulars.) Hence, a person in romantic love *could not* seek to "trade up"—he would have to seek out the very same person. A person not in love might seek someone with certain traits, yet after finding someone, even (remarkably) a person who has the traits sought, if he loves that person she will show those traits in a particularity he did not initially seek but now has come to love—her particular versions of these traits. Since a romantic mate eventually comes to be loved, not for any general dimensions or "score" on such dimensions—that, if anything, gets taken for granted—but for his or her own particular and nonduplicable way of embodying such general traits, a person in love could not make any coherent sense of his "trading up" to *another*.

This does not yet show that a person could not have many such different focused desires, just as she might desire to read this particular book and also that one. I believe that the romantic desire is to form a *we* with that particular person *and* with no other. In the strong sense of the notion of identity involved here, one can no more be part of many *wes* which constitute one's identity than one can simultaneously have many individual identities. (What persons with multiple personality have is not many identities but not quite one.) In a we, the people *share* an identity and do not simply each have identities that are enlarged. The desire to share not only our life but our very identity with another marks our fullest openness. What more central and intimate thing could we share?

The desire to form a *we* with that person and no other includes a desire for that person to form one with you yourself and with no other; and so after sexual desire links with romantic love as a vehicle for its expression, and itself becomes more intense thereby, the mutual desire for sexual monogamy becomes almost inevitable, to mark the intimacy and uniqueness of forming an identity with that one particular person by directing what is the most intense physical intimacy toward her or him alone.

It is instructive here to consider friendship, which too alters and recontours an individual's boundaries, providing a distinct shape and character to the self. The salient feature of friendship is *sharing.* In sharing things—food, happy occasions, football games, a concern with problems, events to celebrate—friends especially want these to be had together; while it might constitute something good when each person has the thing separately, friends want that it be had or done by both (or all) of them *together.* To be sure, a good thing does get magnified for you when it is shared with others, and some things can be more fun when done together—indeed, fun, in part, is just the sharing and taking of delight in something together. Yet in friendship the sharing is not desired simply to enlarge our individual benefits.

The self, we shall see later, can be construed as an appropriative mechanism, one that moves from reflexive awareness of things to *sole* possession of them. The boundaries between selves get constituted by the specialness of this relation of possession and ownership—in the case of psychological items, this generates the philosophical "problem of other minds." Things shared with friends, however, do not stand in a unique and special relationship to any one self as its sole possession; we join with friends in having them and, to that extent at least, our selves and theirs overlap or the boundaries between them are less sharp. The very same things—experiences, activities, conversations, problems, objects of focus or of amusement—are part of us both. We each then are related closely to many things that another person also has an equally close relationship to. We therefore are not separate selves—not so separate anyway. (Should we diagram friendship as two circles that overlap?)

A friendship does not exist *solely* for further purposes, whether a political movement's larger goals, an occupational endeavor, or simply the participant's separate and individual benefits. Of course, there can be many further benefits that flow within friendship and from it, benefits so familiar as not to need listing. Aristotle held one of these to be most central; a friend, he said, is a "second self" who is a means to your own self-awareness. (In his listing of the virtuous characteristics one should seek in a friend, Aristotle takes your parents' view of who your friends should be.) Nevertheless, a relationship is a friendship to the extent that it shares activities for no further purpose than the sharing of them.

People seek to engage in sharing beyond the domain of personal friendship also. One important reason we read newspapers, I think, is not the importance or intrinsic interest of the news; we rarely take action whose direction depends upon what we read there, and if somehow we were shipwrecked for ten years on an isolated island, when we returned we would want a summary of what had happened meanwhile, but we certainly would not choose to peruse the back newspapers of the previous ten years. Rather, we read newspapers because we want to *share* information with our fellows, we want to have a range of information in common with them, a common stock of mental contents. We already share with them a geography and a language, and also a common fate in the face of large-scale events. That we also desire to share the daily flow of information shows how very intense our desire to share is.

Nonromantic friends do not, in general, share an *identity.* In part, this may be because of the crisscrossing web of friendships. The friend of your friend may be your acquaintance, but he or she is not necessarily someone you are close to or would meet with separately. As in the case of multiple bilateral defense treaties among nations, conflicts of action and attachment can occur that make it difficult to delineate any larger entity to which one safely can cede powers and make the bearer of a larger identity. Such considerations also help explain why it is not feasible for a person simultaneously to be part of multiple romantic couples (or of a trio), even were the person to desire this. Friends want to share the things they do *as* a sharing, and they think, correctly, that friendship is valuable partly *because* of its sharing—perhaps specially valuable because, unlike the case of romantic love, this valued sharing occurs *without* any sharing of identity.

We might pause over one mode of sharing that, while it is not done primarily for its own sake, produces a significant sense of solidarity. That is participating with others in joint action directed toward an external goal—perhaps a political cause or reform movement or occupational project or team sport or artistic performance or scientific endeavor—where the participants feel the pleasures of joint and purposeful participation in something really worthwhile. Perhaps there is a special need for this among young adults as they leave the family, and that in part constitutes youth's "idealism." Linked with others toward a larger joint purpose, *joined* with them at the same node of an effectual casual chain, one's life is no longer simply private. In such a way citizens might think of themselves as creating together, and sharing, a memorable civilization.

We can prize romantic love and the formation of a *we*, without denying that there may be extended times, years even, when an adult might best develop alone. It is not plausible, either, to think that every single individual, at some or another time in his life, would be most enhanced as part of a romantically loving *we*—that Buddha, Socrates, Jesus, Beethoven, or Gandhi would have been. This may be, in part, because the energy necessary to sustain and deepen a *we* would have been removed from (thereby lessening) these individuals' activities. But there is more to say. The particular vivid way these individuals defined themselves would not fit easily within a romantic *we*; their special lives would have had to be very different. Of course, a *we* often falls short of its best, so a prudent person might seek (or settle for) other modes of personal relationship and connection. Yet these extraordinary figures remind us that even at its best a *we* constitutes a particular formation of identity that involves forgoing some extraordinary possibilities. (Or is it just that these figures needed equally extraordinary mates?)

Just as the identity of the self continues over an extended period of time, so too is there the desire for the *we* to continue; part of identifying fully with the *we* is intending that it continue. Marriage marks a full identification with that *we*. With this, the *we* enters a new stage, building a sturdier structure, knitting itself together more fully. Being a couple is taken as given though not for granted. No longer focusing upon whether they *do* constitute an enduring *we*, the partners now are free confidently to build together a life with its own focus and directions. The *we* lives their life together. As egg and sperm come together, two biographies have become one. The couple's first child is their union—their earlier history was prenatal.

A *we* is not a new physical entity in the world, whether or not it is a new ontological one. However, it may want to give its web of love relationships a physical incarnation. That is one thing a home is about—an environment that reflects and symbolizes how the couple feel (and what they do) together, the spirit in which they are together; this also, of course, makes it a happy place for them to be. In a different way, and to a much greater extent, children can constitute a physical realization of the parents' love, an incarnation in the world of the valuable extended self the two of them have created. And children might be loved and delighted in, in part as this physical representation of the love between the parents. However, of course and obviously, the children are not merely an adjunct to the parents' love, as either a representation of it or a means of heightening it; they primarily are people to be cared for, delighted in, and loved for themselves.

Intimate bonds change the contours and boundaries of the self, altering its topology: in love, as we have seen, in the sharings of friendship, in the intimacy of sexuality. Alterations in the individual self's boundaries and contours also are a goal of religious quest: expanding the self to include all of being (Indian Vedanta), eliminating the self (Buddhism), or merging with the divine. There also are modes of general love for all of humanity, often religiously enjoined—recall how Dostoyevsky depicts Father Zossima in *The Brothers Karamazov*—that greatly alter the character and contours of the self, now no longer so appropriately referred to as "individual."

It may not be an accident that people rarely do simultaneously combine building a romantic *we* with a spiritual quest. It seems impossible to proceed full strength with more than one major alteration in the self's topology at a time. Nevertheless, it may well be important at times to be engaged in *some* or another mode of change in the boundaries and topology of the self, different ones at different times. Any such change need not be judged solely by how it substantively feeds back into the individual self, though. The new entity that is created or contoured, with its own boundaries and topology, has its own evaluations to make. An individual self justifiably might be proud to be supple enough to enter into these changes and exfoliate them, yet its perspective before the changes does not provide the only relevant standard. It *is* in the interests of an individual sperm or egg cell to unite to form a new organism, yet we do not continue to judge the new life by that gamete's particular interests. In love's bond, we metamorphose.

DISCUSSION QUESTIONS

1. How does love create curtailed autonomy, according to Nozick? What does curtailed autonomy mean?
2. What is "adult love"? Do you think the name is appropriate? Why or why not?
3. Have you experienced the kind of radiance of loving that Nozick describes? Can you say a bit more about that? Why does it matter?

NOTES

1. A somewhat sharper criterion can be formulated of when another's well-being is *directly* part of your own. This occurs when (1) you say and believe your well-being is affected by significant changes in hers; (2) your well-being is affected in the same *direction* as hers, an improvement in her well-being producing an improvement in your own, a decrease, a decrease; (3) you not only judge yourself worse off, but feel some emotion appropriate to that state; (4) you are affected by the change in *her* well-being directly, merely through knowing about it, and not because it symbolically represents to you something else about yourself, a childhood situation or whatever; (5) (and this condition is especially diagnostic) your *mood* changes: you now have different occurrent feelings and changed dispositions to have particular other emotions; and (6) this change in mood is somewhat enduring. Moreover, (7) you have this general tendency or disposition toward a person or object, to be thus affected; you *tend* to be thus affected by changes in that person's well-being.

2. For a discussion of love as the formation of a *we*, see Robert Solomon, *Love* (Garden City, N.Y.: Anchor Books, 1981).

3. This curtailment of unilateral decision-making rights extends even to a decision to end the romantic love relationship. This decision, if any, you would think you could make by yourself. And so you can, but only in certain ways at a certain pace. Another kind of relation might be ended because you feel like it or because you find it no longer satisfactory, but in a love relationship the other party "has a vote." This does not mean a permanent veto; but the other party has a right to have his or her say, to try to repair, to be convinced. After some time, to be sure, one party may insist on ending the relationship even without the other's consent, but what they each have forgone, in love, is the right to act unilaterally and swiftly.

4. Another Greek tale, that of Telemachus at home with Penelope while Odysseus wanders, provides a different picture of the family triangle's character. A father is a needed protector, not just someone to compete with for the mother's love. If the mother is as attractive as the child thinks, in the absence of the father other suitors will present themselves before her. And unlike the father, who will not kill the competitive child or maim him (despite what the psychoanalytic literature depicts as the child's anxieties), these suitors *are* his enemies. Telemachus *needs* his father—to maintain the *safe* triangle—and so he sets out to find him.

The Case for Platonic Love

BY EDITH GWENDOLYN NALLY

Edith Gwendolyn Nally is associate professor of philosophy at the University of Missouri–Kansas City. In this essay, she argues against critics who have found Plato's vision of love in the Symposium disturbingly impersonal. In particular, she argues that, although his view is not a satisfactory account of interpersonal love, this is potentially less of a moral failing than an honest assessment of the nature of human desire. The Symposium suggests that human beings are capable of varieties of desire so vast and of satisfaction so deep that no person, no matter how unique or beloved, could ever be expected to fill such a void. If this is correct, then contemporary thinkers may be wrong to take interpersonal connection as the chief erotic paradigm. Theories of love that focus too narrowly on personal attachment set us up for a great deal of dissatisfaction.

The Challenge

Take a moment to ask yourself what you think love is. What comes to mind? A romantic partner? Couples like Romeo and Juliet, Gertrude and Alice, or Beyoncé and Jay-Z? If so, you're thinking about *romantic* love. This is usually understood as some combination of social, intellectual, or emotional bond, plus sexual desire. Maybe, though, you picture love between family members, friends, or community? These are also social, intellectual, and emotional relationships, but generally exist without sexual desire. Wherever your mind goes, however, chances are you picture some kind of love between people. This is because, for most contemporary readers, love is largely synonymous with *interpersonal* love.

Now, consider whether love plays a role in a good life. If you're still thinking about interpersonal love, you probably think it does. A life without romantic partners, family, friends, or community sounds pretty unappealing. People explain this in different ways. Psychologists, for example, claim that loving relationships fulfill an essential human need.[1] Philosophers sometimes argue that love is necessary for moral understanding.[2] Alfred Lord Tennyson puts it more intuitively: "Tis better to have loved and lost than never to have loved at all."[3] These explanations differ, yet all take interpersonal love to be a vital part of the human experience. A life without loving relationships would be an incomplete one.

Plato thinks about love somewhat differently. One major difference is on display in Diotima's speech in the *Symposium* (which will be our primary focus[4]). Here, the sort of love in question, the sort that Plato thinks brings about the best life (call it "Platonic love" for short[5]), is love for the form of beauty itself (211a–d). Beauty, for Plato, is largely coextensive with what is good or valuable. So, the best kind of love is, roughly, a love for what is good. Even without unpacking the finer points of this view, it's clear that Plato isn't interested in interpersonal love so much as love for an *idea* or *quality*.

Critics have sometimes found this aspect of Plato's vision morally troubling. Gregory Vlastos famously challenges that, because Platonic love is for beauty or goodness, it cannot make sense of genuine interpersonal affection. The problem is that the Platonic lover, when he does form personal attachments, will be in love with certain of his beloved's ideal qualities. But this seems like a moral mistake, since "the individual, in the uniqueness and integrity of his or her individuality, will never be the object of our love."[6] Put simply, loving Platonically seems like a failure to engage with a person as a whole, complicated, and potentially flawed individual.

Some have defended Plato by showing that his archetypal lover cares more for particular individuals than it first appears.[7] This defense is promising, but two facts about Platonic love are nevertheless inescapable. First, the best variety of Platonic love is not interpersonal. It occurs between a lover and a form. Second, what the Platonic lover values in all his pursuits is beauty. For these reasons, the remainder of this chapter explores a different kind of defense. It argues that we should accept Vlastos's critique; Plato doesn't give a satisfying account of interpersonal love. Yet, when properly understood, this oversight is less a moral failing than an honest assessment of the nature of human desire.[8] In particular, once we understand that Plato conceives of love differently than we do—he thinks love includes *all* of our desires for what is good or valuable—it emerges that he thinks we humans are capable of varieties of love (desire) that no person, no matter how unique or beloved, could ever be expected to satisfy.

Extrapersonal *Eros*

Of course, Plato isn't writing about "love" as we know it. His topic is ancient Greek *eros*. This is difficult to translate, at least in part because in English "erotic" almost always denotes something sexual. The ancient Greek term has a broader range. It's breadth is on display in the six speeches in the *Symposium*, where we find two distinct erotic paradigms, both of which were likely common in ancient Greek thought.[9] Three of the speeches address the more familiar (to us) *interpersonal* manifestations of *eros*, while the other three address its less familiar *extrapersonal* dimensions. Extrapersonal *eros*, the speakers argue, can exist between non-persons (i.e., forces of nature) or between a person

and an object of desire (i.e., between a poet and poetry). In the following section, we shall see that recognizing these two paradigms is crucial for understanding Platonic love.

Phaedrus, an Athenian youth, gives the first speech. He thinks *eros* inspires social virtues, like shame and bravery (178d–179b). Alcestis dies for Admetus, Orpheus searches for Eurydice, and Achilles avenges Patroclus because of *eros* (179b–180a). Put simply, Phaedrus explores the social bonds that exist in interpersonal erotic relationships. Pausanias, an older male lover, comes second. He distinguishes between lower and higher varieties of *eros*. The lower variety is entirely sexual (181b–c), while the higher manifests as a psychic bond between lover and beloved (181c–e). What Pausanias highlights, then, are the intellectual aspects of interpersonal *eros*. Aristophanes, the comic dramatist and fourth speaker,[10] considers another dimension of interpersonal *eros*. He tells a story about conjoined lovers, who are cleaved apart by Zeus and must therefore always seek their other halves (189d–192b). Aristophanes imagines Hephaestus offering to weld them together so that they can live as a unified physical and spiritual whole (192d4–e1). They would accept. This tale seems to highlight the familiar sexual-emotional aspects of interpersonal *eros*.

Were we to synthesize these three speeches, we would find a view of *eros* that closely mirrors our ideas about interpersonal love: it manifests as some combination of social (Phaedrus), intellectual (Pausanias), and/or sexual-emotional (Aristophanes) bond between individuals. The remaining speeches, however, enter into far less familiar territory. Eryximachus, Agathon, and Socrates take up extrapersonal *eros*.[11]

Eryximachus, the doctor and third speaker (see n. 10), claims that *eros* causes unions throughout the cosmos (186b2). It balances bodily humors, notes in harmony, and seasons in a year. This is perhaps the most strange (by our lights) vision of *eros* anywhere in the dialogue, since it exists between completely non-personal entities. But this view has recognizable ancient Greek precedents. In the philosophy of Empedocles, for example, Love (*Philotes*) and Strife (*Neikos*) are the forces responsible for the unification and disunification of natural elements.[12] Eryximachus appears, therefore, to be giving a natural scientific account of love. Agathon, the tragedian and host, comes fifth. His account is similar in that he praises *eros* for, among other things, causing productive activities. *Eros* brings about biological procreation (197a2). It also causes poetry, archery, medicine, prophecy, music, bronzework, and governance (196e–197b). Here, *eros* is something like inspiration, what drives a lover to pursue what he loves (e.g., the poet has *eros* for poetry; the governor has *eros* for governing).

Extrapersonal *eros* may seem bizarre at first glance. Does love really occur between natural elements? Notice, however, that in some ways we already admit of extrapersonal erotic pursuits like the ones Agathon mentions. We dub important life projects our "passions" or "loves." We say things like "a poet feels passion for poetry" or that "Shakespeare's greatest love was drama." Of course, this could be mere metaphor; perhaps we don't really mean that Shakespeare had *eros* for drama only that he was intensely devoted to it. But if we're being fair to the Greeks, we should resist assuming that *eros* must be interpersonal. And, once we jettison this assumption, we might wonder why a desire for a pursuit shouldn't be thought of as genuinely *erotic*. What, after all, is the difference between Shakespeare's desire for playwriting and Romeo's desire for Juliet? Their objects are different (one is for artistic expression and the other sexual/emotional fulfillment). But are the desires themselves different in kind? Is longing for a person fundamentally distinct from longing for one's work? Agathon's view invites us to think that they could be of a piece.

Understanding this extrapersonal erotic framework is the first step to properly understanding Plato's view. This is because, if one grants that extrapersonal *eros* exists—if, for example, one grants that we can have erotic desire for projects and goals—then it makes sense to think that *eros* might function in important ways in a good life beyond causing and sustaining interpersonal relationships.

Platonic Love

Socrates' speech comes sixth. He first questions Agathon, before recounting Diotima's view of love and putting it forward as his own. Our examination of Socrates' (Plato's) view begins with three qualifications about *eros*.

First, Socrates claims that *eros* is always for an object that the lover lacks (200a4–5). What it means to love gemstones, for example, is to want gems not currently in one's possession. Of course, people sometimes have *eros* for what they already possess, as when a healthy person desires health (200d4–5). In these cases, the lover has *eros* for the object in the future, as well. *Eros*, if it exists at all, exists as an unsatisfied desire.

Diotima puts forward the second qualification. She thinks there are both interpersonal and extrapersonal varieties of *eros*. People overlook *eros*'s extrapersonal manifestations, because "we divide out a special kind of love, and we refer to it by the word that means the whole—'love'; and for the other kinds of love we use other words" (b5–7).[13] Because we are so focused on one narrow species of *eros*, we miss that it is a wider genus. As Diotima puts it (and we saw at the start of this essay), just about everyone assumes that "lovers are those people who seek their other halves" (205e2). Remember Aristophanes? Diotima thinks that most people conceive of love as his cleaved-apart lovers do. We are so concerned with interpersonal love, specifically with finding sexual and emotional romantic attachments, that we overlook *eros*'s other domains. But if we were to pay attention, we'd realize that *eros* actually drives "every desire for good things or for happiness." (205d3) In fact, *eros* occurs whenever someone desires something that they value. This even includes the love of money, love of sports, and love of wisdom (philosophy) (205d4–7). All are *erotic*, since they are ways of pursuing what one thinks is good. So, *eros* doesn't just manifest in interpersonal relationships; there are as many different kinds of *eros* as there are ideas about what is good or valuable.

The rest of Diotima's speech investigates this wider notion of *eros*. It asks what role *eros*, understood as the unsatisfied desire to possess and reproduce what is good or valuable, plays in a good life (206c–212c).[14] Before looking at Diotima's answer to this question, however, we should add a third, albeit brief, qualification to her definition of *eros*. For Diotima, *eros* isn't just a desire for something good or valuable. It's also about trying to *reproduce* that goodness or value (206e5). This, she thinks, is the human way of dealing with mortality (207a). Because we are mortal, we attempt to make what we really love (value) outlast ourselves.

With this definition of *eros* in hand, let's turn to the central question of Diotima's account: What role does *eros* play in a life well lived? The answer has two phases. The first distinguishes between bodily and psychic *eros* (those "pregnant in body" and "pregnant in soul" [208e3, 209a1]). The bodily group has *eros* for the beauty of another person, so this is what they aim to reproduce, "providing themselves through childbirth with immortality and remembrance and happiness, as they think, for all time to come" (208e4–6). These lovers mate and have kids, creating a flesh and blood duplicate of their beloved. Yet, because of the short-lived nature of physical offspring, it is better, Diotima thinks, to be a psychic lover. Psychic lovers engage in intellectual exchange and procreation. They pass on ideas and values, which are longer lasting and therefore come closer to love's goal of forever preserving what one values.

The second phase divides these psychic lovers into two camps, according to whether they practice the *lower* or *higher* rites of love (cf. 210a1). Hesiod, Homer, Lycurgus, and Solon (209c–e), were all successful in the lower rites. All successfully passed on their worldviews. Homer's *eros* for poetry created a highly influential religio-socio-ethical system that influenced generations to come. Solon's *eros* for lawgiving laid the foundations for the Athenian democracy, one of the longest-lived ideas in history. The higher psychic rites are similar, since the lover also aims to pass on ideas and values to future generations. They do better, however, since what they value is *actually* good/valuable. To understand this, we must wade into the famously complex passage dubbed "the ladder of love."

For our purposes it will suffice to notice that the ladder consists of different "rungs" of erotic development. At each rung, the lover has *eros* for the beauty/value of a different object. The first rung lover has *eros* for a single body (210a8). Think Romeo struck by the appearance of Juliet. At the second rung, however, the lover begins to feel *eros* for the same quality in other bodies (210b1). He realizes that there are, so to speak, other physically beautiful "fish in the sea." The third rung lover progresses to appreciating the beauty of souls (210b5). He comes to have *eros* for beauty that lies within.

The first three rungs are about interpersonal *eros*. The fourth rung takes an extrapersonal turn. The lover becomes infatuated with the beauty of laws and customs (210c4). This makes a certain amount of sense; he will have already spent a good deal of time infatuated with psychic beauty. Since customs and laws are arguably what (in Plato's political works[15]) account for the beauty/goodness of people's souls, the fourth stage lover simply begins to appreciate the extrapersonal causes of his earlier interpersonal desires.

The fifth rung goes deeper in extrapersonal territory: "After customs [the lover] must move on to various kinds of knowledge. The result is that he will see the beauty of knowledge and be looking mainly not at beauty in a single example . . . but the lover is turned to the great sea of beauty." (210d1–6) The fifth-rung lover learns to appreciate beauty across disciplines, i.e. the beauty of a mathematical proof, the beauty of a sonata, or the beauty of an astronomical trajectory.[16] Plus, Diotima adds, he's no longer interested in any single instance of beauty. Instead, he is now a lover of wisdom (a philosopher) (d6) and begins to pursue the beauty of entire systems of thought.

Because the lover accumulates such a vast perspective (210d5), because he now understands the beauty/value of so many varied instantiations, this ultimately results, at the sixth rung, in a vision of the form of beauty itself (211a–d). The lover, "who has beheld beautiful things in the right order and correctly, is coming now to the goal of Loving: all of a sudden he will catch sight of something wonderfully beautiful in its nature" (210e3–211a1).

Now, you're probably wondering what this vision of beauty is actually like. In one sense, Diotima is very clear: the form is constantly and entirely beautiful (211a2–4); it is immaterial (a7–8); and beautiful things participate in it without affecting it (b3–5). But in another sense, her description is somewhat opaque. Do you come away feeling like you understand what the form of beauty is like? Probably not. The ladder of love doesn't offer a complete description of beauty. Instead, it functions as a blueprint for how to love, for how to most productively let *eros* into one's life. This is understandable, since Diotima has been attempting to decipher the role of *eros* in life well lived. The ladder of love suggests that *eros*, properly pursued, not only alights on physically and psychically beautiful persons, but also beautiful customs, laws, theories, and eventually beauty itself. This is ultimately what makes for a good life: "there if anywhere should a person live his life, beholding that Beauty" (211d3).

What's so great about understanding beauty itself? One possibility is that contemplating beauty appears to be the only truly *satisfying* erotic endeavor. Remember that love is always for an object that the lover lacks. The lover feels a void for something good or valuable, something that he wants to exist forever. Diotima thinks that contemplating beauty itself will fill this void to a greater degree than any other pursuit. Other varieties of love, like those that "measure beauty by gold or clothing or beautiful boys and youths" (211d3–4), are focused on particular instances of beauty, not the pure, unmixed, eternal concept itself. As a result, all other erotic pursuits focus on shorter-lived incarnations of beauty, so that even when their objects are acquired, they never really attain love's goal. Gold is spent. Bodies age. Partners, family, and friends die. Great works of art are lost. Even value systems change. The form of beauty is, however, an eternal, unchanging, indestructible ideal. The philosopher alone encounters a beauty that never fades.

Is Platonic Love Morally Deficient?

Let's return to the original challenge. Vlastos alleges that Platonic *eros*, because it is for beauty, cannot account for genuine interpersonal love. It should now be clear that, although this may be correct, Plato is not attempting to account for interpersonal connection. Plato's philosophizing about love has an altogether different focus. He conceives of *eros* as the force which draws us toward whatever is good or valuable, whether it be interpersonal infatuation or extrapersonal pursuits. And, his project is to appraise the different ways that *eros*, thus understood, might manifest in a life. He concludes that one extrapersonal *erotic* pursuit, contemplating beauty itself, is truly satisfying. All other pursuits (love of individuals, money, poetry, etc.) are for objects that are less beautiful/valuable than the eternal, unchanging form of beauty. No matter how deeply and genuinely we love others, then, they simply cannot fill the void human beings feel for beauty.

What we should be asking, then, is whether there is anything morally defective about *this* view. Ask yourself: what would a life without any extrapersonal erotic endeavors be like? Would being a partner, parent, friend, and neighbor be enough for you? Probably not.

Still, it might be objected, Plato doesn't just think that extrapersonal erotic pursuits are important for a meaningful existence but that extrapersonal erotic pursuits are *more important* than interpersonal ones.[17] The ladder of love seems to be ranking manifestations of *eros*, such that the philosopher's desire for ideal beauty is more choiceworthy than a desire for any individual instantiation thereof. And, this objection continues, there is something deeply wrong with caring more for projects than for people. To understand the wrong, we need only to consider famous egoists, like the artist Paul Gaugin who abandoned his wife and children to pursue his painting in Tahiti. Gaugin is by no means a paradigm of love. If Plato's vision supports Gaugin's choice, then it's clearly gone awry.

In response, notice first that this challenge is quite different from the one with which we began. The original objection was that Plato's view makes a mess of interpersonal devotion. We have dealt with this objection already: it is perhaps true that Plato's view doesn't properly account for interpersonal love, but he's pursuing a different project. He is attempting to appraise all the different possible manifestations of *eros*, more broadly understood, in a good life. Disagreeing with Plato's appraisal, thinking he is wrong to value extrapersonal *eros* so highly is an entirely different challenge.

Notice also that this new challenge is weaker than it may first seem. There are at least three reasons. First, it's pretty clear that Plato isn't actually endorsing Gauguin-ism. As was mentioned in the introduction to this essay, scholars have argued that meaningful personal relationships occur throughout the Platonic lover's erotic development.[18] Perhaps the most poignant occurs in the final stage of the ladder, where *eros* for beauty drives the lover not only to contemplate the form of beauty but to perpetuate his understanding, becoming a moral educator to others (212a7–8). Despite how the Platonic lover has been characterized in the literature, then, he is clearly not the type who sets sail for Tahiti.

Second, it's not clear whether the ladder of love is *ranking* erotic endeavors. Perhaps Plato's point is merely that we're so focused on interpersonal connection that we overlook the other, crucially-important, dimension of love. Extrapersonal erotic desires can leave huge voids within the human psyche, which no other person, no matter how special or dear, could ever be expected to fill. In particular, we are capable of loving (desiring) ideas, knowledge, and understanding. Other people can help us pursue these ends, but they cannot replace them.

Third, and finally, even if Plato is ranking extrapersonal endeavors above interpersonal ones, there may be less morally problematic ways of making sense of this. Here's an attempt: Plato is investigating the nature of human desire. What he finds is that deeper forms of satisfaction exist beyond interpersonal attachments. The question is whether he is correct. Could anything be more satisfying than the love we have for one another? Is there anything more gratifying than the love of a partner, child, or friend? This essay won't answer this. It can't. What it can do, however, is suggest that answering "yes" isn't clearly indicative of a moral failure. After all, imagine someone who, despite having genuine and fulfilling relationships, despite really caring for the other people in their life, still desires *more*. Furthermore, suppose that what this person longs for is the immense satisfaction that results from contemplation and understanding. These activities fill the deepest wells within the person's soul, wells that would dry out if others were expected to fill them. Many of us will recognize ourselves, or parts of ourselves, in this description. And, realizing this is not necessarily indicative of a moral infraction or character flaw. Perhaps, after all, those of us who have realized this have simply made an honest assessment of what we need to feel satisfied.

DISCUSSION QUESTIONS

1. What are some examples of extrapersonal *eros* that Diotima gives? Why might we consider these examples to be genuine cases of erotic longing?

2. Why does contemplating the form of beauty satisfy *eros* on Plato's view?

3. This essay claims that even if the *Symposium* ranks extrapersonal love above interpersonal love, this might not be a morally defective view. Why?

NOTES

1. Perhaps the most influential view comes from A. H. Maslow (1943) "A Theory of Human Motivation." *Psychological Review*, 50, 370–396.

2. See, for example, I. Murdoch (1971) *The Sovereignty of Good*. Routledge, 29. See also J. D. Velleman (1999). "Love as a Moral Emotion." *Ethics*, 109, 338–374.

3. A. T. Tennyson (1850). *In memoriam*. London: E. Moxon.

4. *Republic*, *Lysis*, and *Phaedrus* also contain Plato's views on love.

5. This term refers to Plato's expressed views about love (*eros*) in the *Symposium*. It is not to be confused with the colloquial "platonic love" which denotes a friendship lacking sexual feelings.

6. G. Vlastos (1999). "The Individual as Object of Love in Plato." In Gail Fine (ed.), *Plato 2: Ethics, Politics, Religion, and the Soul*. Oxford University Press, 160–161.

7. See, for example, A. W. Price (1989). *Love and Friendship in Plato and Aristotle*. Oxford University Press, 33.

8. F. Sheffield (2012). "The "Symposium" and Platonic Ethics: Plato, Vlastos, and a Misguided Debate." *Phronesis*, 57 (2), 117–141 also thinks Vlastos has misdiagnosed Plato's project. This discussion owes much to her scholarship.

9. See J. Larson (2012) 4 on how *eros* is commonly used in ancient Greek. Plato may be adapting *eros* to his own purposes.

10. Eryximachus and Aristophanes switch places because Aristophanes has a comic case of hiccups (185c4–e7). In fact, Aristophanes' speech, since it focuses on the interpersonal, belongs with the earlier accounts.

11. While there is not space to explore it here, Alcibiades' impromptu speech might be a reflection on these two paradigms. His account is that of someone utterly enmeshed in finding interpersonal eros (Alcibiades) encountering a devotee of extrapersonal *eros* (Socrates).

12. Simplicius, *in Phys.* B35, B36.

13. Although she's discussing the ancient Greek word *eros*, a similar phenomenon happens in English with "love." All translations are A. Nehamas and P. Woodruff (1997). "Symposium." In *Plato's Complete Works*. J. Cooper and D. Hutchinson (Eds.). Indianapolis: Hackett Publishing.

14. See Sheffield (2012) 133 for a similar point.

15. Cf. *Republic* II-III.

16. This reading is heavily indebted to Nussbaum (1986) 180.

17. For this objection, see Sheffield (2012) 132–137.

18. See especially Price (1989).

Iris Murdoch on Love as Just Attention

BY RAJA ROSENHAGEN

> Raja Rosenhagen is associate professor of philosophy at Ashoka University in New Delhi. He specializes in love, the philosophy of science, epistemology, and many other philosophical subjects. In this essay he presents and defends the influential theory of love offered by Iris Murdoch. Iris Murdoch (1919–1999) was an Irish and British novelist and philosopher best known for her novels about good and evil, sexual relationships, morality, and the power of the unconscious. Murdoch argues that love is properly understood as giving someone the appropriate kind of attention, "a just and loving gaze directed upon an individual reality."

How can we make ourselves (morally) better? To Iris Murdoch, philosopher and award-winning novelist, this is among the most important questions moral philosophers should address—a task she sets herself in *The Sovereignty of Good*.[1] Moral agents, Murdoch thinks, should work to acquire an increasingly clear vision—of the Good, other individuals, and of what is good for them.[2] Such work requires *love*, which she characterizes as *just* (and *unselfish*) *attention*.[3] Some philosophers regard love as interfering with morality. To be motivated by love, these philosophers think, conflicts with, e.g., the moral requirement to be impartial.[4] As we will see, for Murdoch—as for Plato and Aristotle before her—love is not foreign to morality, but at its core.[5]

In recent years, philosophical interest in Murdoch's work has increased, various questions about it have been raised. [6] Some concern how her philosophical work relates to her novels, her *fables of unselfing*,[7] in which her protagonists struggle with various facets of love, faith, its loss, and the vagaries and vicissitudes of moral life. Given the novels' strong philosophical overtones, it is tempting to ask whether Murdoch's philosophy shows up in her novels, or how. But one must also square

one's answers with Murdoch's explicit views on how philosophy and art differ in their respective aims, functions, and tools.[8] Other questions are exegetical, but inevitably point to broader philosophical issues. Here is a non-exhaustive list: What does Murdoch's proclaimed moral realism amount to and how are we to understand her proposed proof of the existence of Good?[9] Does Murdoch offer a viable account of moral perception?[10] What is her conception of conceptual change and can it be extended beyond the realm of the moral?[11] What is Murdoch's notion of the self,[12] what the nature of her affinity with Buddhism,[13] and what the role of moral rules and duties in her work; is she a moral particularist?[14] Do demands of love outweigh those of reason?[15] How plausible is Murdoch's hyper-internalist[16] claim that true vision occasions right conduct, and: Must we love everyone? In the following, none of these can be settled. Instead, I will highlight some pertinent aspects of Murdoch's conception of love by contrasting it with a kind of view she opposes and leave it to the reader to follow up on these interesting, yet much thornier issues.

The philosophical camp Murdoch explicitly opposes comprises existentialists, behaviorists and, arguably, Kantians. All of these are said to hold that the locus of moral activity is the will[17] and moral activity its overt movement—its choices.[18] By behaviorist lights, a moving will, to be real, must manifest as publicly observable action. As per the existentialists, in authentically choosing between the publicly available options for action, subjects don't respond to antecedently existing moral facts, but freely generate and embrace their values. All facts relevant to this procedure are taken to be publicly available and accessible. Moral activity, the expression of the agent's freedom, is construed as a moving about between such publicly accessible facts, a leaping of the will in moments of choice between publicly available options, as something entirely public. Inner private episodes have only a shadowy, parasitic existence and derive their meanings, if any, from the public meanings of words we use to describe them, which are, in turn, spelled out in terms of observable behavior. Unless I act, on this view, I haven't really decided, no matter what I tell myself privately; there either is no privileged access to my decision, or it is irrelevant.[19] Further, moral activity is discontinuous. It occurs when an agent, faced with moral choices, thoroughly examines the public facts and freely exercises her will.

We will not ask whose views such characterizations may capture.[20] For our purposes, what matters is that Murdoch rejects them all. A moral subject, she thinks, is more than a moving will; a realistic picture must be more complex and suitably linked to some workable psychological terminology ("motive," "drive," "emotion," "subconscious mechanism," "neurosis," "transference," etc.). Over metaphors of movement she prefers those of vision and imagination. Seeing others clearly—and what one's various actions vis-à-vis them morally amount to—Murdoch insists, is no mean feat. Many morally relevant facts, she thinks, are not easily publicly accessible, nor are they private or subjectively created. They are simply hard to see. But a central moral activity, she insists, *is* private, need not involve or terminate in overt behavior, and happens continuously:[21] the activity of attending to, imagining, and (re-)evaluating others and their actions.

Why should such (re-)evaluations be private? To Murdoch, proponents of the opposing camp model moral concepts too closely on a common understanding of scientific concepts. On it, requirements regarding the mastery of scientific concepts are specifiable in terms of communally determinable and publicly intelligible norms, norms that govern behavioral (including linguistic) patterns that competent concept users must exhibit. But moral concepts (and perhaps scientific ones too), Murdoch holds, work differently.[22] Learning moral concepts does involve mastering conventional, publicly acknowledged rules and publicly observable behavioral patterns. Yet with moral concepts, this is not the end of the story (nor, Murdoch insists, the beginning).[23] Acquiring a better understanding of moral concepts is a "deepening process, at any rate an altering and complicating process," involving a movement of understanding with respect to our moral concepts which is "onward into increasing privacy."[24] One's image of courage at forty differs from that which one had at twenty,[25] she points out and emphasizes that word-utterances and concept uses are historical occasions, whose meanings must be understood in the relevant contexts of use. But such understanding cannot be gleaned from crude public rules. To understand how particular concept applications emerge as results of idiosyncratic trajectories generated through different occasions of use, and changes in such applications, something else must enter the equation: how we attend to others, the quality of our attention, and what we can, accordingly, see. Attention, understanding, evaluations, and changes therein are shaped both by individual, contingent, historical details and by the attending individual's quality of attention. Typically, such evaluations and re-evaluations are thus highly idiosyncratic and are performed privately in the sense that nobody but the subject who engages in them could engage in (let alone readily understand or describe) them.[26]

Arguably, even if partly unconsciously, we constantly evaluatively characterize real and imagined situations and the individuals in them. This ongoing activity, Murdoch thinks, in turn affects which options for acting toward others we see and consider; we differ, for example, in what options we consider vis-à-vis those we evaluate differently, as *cowards*, as *brave, reckless, hesitant,* or as *prudent,* say. Through evaluative activity we build up, continuously and imperceptibly, "structures of value round about us"[27]—the world we can see, within which we move and choose. Our evaluations may predetermine the outcome of our choices before we face them. Yet they may also miss the mark; the structures of value we build up and the images we create of the people we face may become distorted, caricaturesque even. The following passage from Murdoch brings this out nicely:

> The world which we confront is not just a world of "facts" but a world upon which our imagination has, at any given moment, already worked; and although such working may often be "fantasy" and may constitute a barrier to our seeing "what is really there," this is not necessarily so. [. . .] The formulation of beliefs about other people often proceeds and must proceed imaginatively [. . .]. We have to *attend* to people, we may have to have *faith* in them, and here justice and realism may demand the inhibition of certain pictures, the promotion of others. Each of us lives and chooses within a partly private, partly fabricated world [. . .]. To be a human being is to know more than one can prove, to conceive of a reality which goes "beyond the facts" in these familiar and natural ways. This activity is, moreover, usually and often inevitably, an activity of evaluation. We evaluate not only by intentions, decisions, choices [. . .], but also, and largely, by the constant quiet work of attention and imagination.[28]

How, then, does Murdoch's notion of moral activity contrast with that of her opponents? First, moral activity, construed as attending to and (re-)evaluating others, is in an important sense a private activity. Second, it is constant, quiet, and at least partly unconscious. Third, morally relevant facts are *not* readily publicly accessible. Whether we can see what is real and act in ways that truly promote what is good depends on how accurately we evaluate, on whether we attend lovingly and *justly* to those with whom we interact, on whether we do justice to them in how we picture them. Just vision is unselfish, Murdoch insists, and requires that we remove distorting veils created and interposed between us and the world by our private fantasies, by our desires and anxieties concerning how others may serve or obstruct our egocentric goals. Just vision also requires taking into account that the views of others, too, might be clouded. Just like it is difficult for us to see them clearly, it may be difficult for them to see *us* and *our* intentions well, what *we* take to be the best course of action, and *why*. A corollary of this, fourth, is that for Murdoch, freedom is not primarily the freedom to choose.[29] It is the ability to see and respond to what is real and to pursue a vision of what is good that is also informed by an understanding of the good we realistically imagine others as pursuing. This ability is gained by freeing oneself from (selfish) fantasy and if, as Murdoch suggests, true vision occasions right conduct,[30] then mastering it yields good actions almost automatically.[31]

Like the Socrates of the *Symposion*, for whom a properly cultivated *eros* can propel us from appearance to reality, and like Aristotle, for whom complete friendship-love requires that one know one's friend well (as one can only truly benefit those whom one knows), Murdoch ties "love" to "knowledge," "reality," and "truth."[32] Love, she aphorizes, is "knowledge of the individual,"[33] the "extremely difficult realization that something other than oneself is real."[34] It is "the general name of the quality of attachment,"[35] and, if developed, it aids us in determining what is true. Again, developing this ability, Murdoch concedes, is extremely difficult, its full realization a distant ideal.[36] Striving toward it requires fighting what Murdoch thinks is the biggest enemy in moral life—the fat relentless ego[37]—and only few manage to free themselves from fantasy and from the anxious avaricious tentacles of the self. The humble, Murdoch suspects, may most likely become good,[38] not least because just attention involves compassion and humility both. One must be compassionately mindful of what may cloud others' perspectives and humbly accept that they may see more clearly where our own vision is murky.

Acting toward others based on loving attention thus importantly differs from acting that results from merely imagining what one *oneself* would do in their stead. Individuals *differ*, so walking the proverbial mile in their shoes is hard. It takes moral effort, perhaps faith, to see them and to properly understand their actions as directed at the good *they* seek to achieve.[39] When facing an angry person, we will act better toward them if, instead of automatically showing indignation or reciprocating anger, we understand how their rage may blind them, if we consider that, initial appearances notwithstanding, we may not in fact be its main target, and succeed in imagining their pain, needs, motives, and desires realistically. Perhaps we realize how we helped trigger their pain, are humbled, moved by compassion, and learn and grow by looking. We need not, perhaps will not, endorse what good we imagine them as pursuing. Yet if we attend to them lovingly and appreciate what drives their actions and imbues these actions with meaning, our actions will be better attuned to what is truly there, possibly better overall, even vis-à-vis those who morally go astray. Love, for Murdoch, rather than extraneous to morality, is quite the opposite: as it enables realistic vision and good action, it is tied to morality at its heart.

DISCUSSION QUESTIONS

1. According to Murdoch, unselfishly imagining who others are and attending to them justly are moral activities that, if perfected, enable us to engage in actions that are truly responsive to others and serve to do well by them. Suppose we take it, like Murdoch, that the moral progress required for improving our ability to attend justly and imagine realistically is a matter of improving our ability to issue accurate evaluative judgments, a matter of using the right concepts in evaluating the situations we face, perhaps a matter of using our concepts in an increasingly better way. Should we think of this process as the acquisition of a perceptual capacity that is sensitive to antecedently existing moral properties or facts? How else might one understand what "getting things right" would amount to?

2. "True vision occasions right conduct," Murdoch claims. In doing so she suggests that we do the right thing automatically once we recognize it. But is this plausible? Don't we often recognize what is right and still decide to do something else? On Murdoch's account, does true vision make weakness of the will (*akrasia*) impossible? More generally, when Murdoch attacks the opposing conception of the moral self as a moving will, does she go too far and leave too little room for the will in her own conception? How is her position like (or unlike) a conception on which once the right option is truly recognized, all competing considerations are silenced?

3. Suppose one is inclined to agree with Murdoch that true vision occasions right conduct. But why should it only be *true* vision that occasions right conduct? More specifically, why not think that not-so-true vision occasions not-so-right conduct, too? If we pursue this line of thinking, what are the implications for how we should think about moral responsibility and obligation?

4. As indicated in note 22, Murdoch hints at the possibility that the mastery of scientific concepts, too, may be ill-described in terms of the mastery of publicly available rules. The requirements on conceptual mastery and the appurtenant injunction to improve the quality of one's attention that Murdoch thinks enable moral progress, might they apply to non-moral concepts as well? What might implementing an analogous account with respect to scientific observation look like? Would such an account be plausible?

NOTES

1. Cf. Murdoch (1974), 53, 78, 83.
2. "good for S" can mean "what seems good to S" or "what is (in fact) good for S." Both senses are implied here.
3. Murdoch adopts the emphasis on attention from Simone Weil. See Murdoch 1974, 34; Justin Broackes' introduction in Broackes 2012, and Broackes 2019.
4. See Schaubroeck 2018 for a helpful overview.
5. For a discussion of Murdoch in terms of Plato's *eros*, see Hopwood 2018, for a juxtaposition of just attention with Aristotelian *philia*, see Rosenhagen 2019.
6. Various philosophers have cited Murdoch as an influence, e.g., Cora Diamond, John McDowell,

Hilary Putnam, Charles Taylor, Bernard Williams, Susan Wolf (see Setiya 2013), others are Martha Nussbaum and Philippa Foot, who was also one of Murdoch's close friends. Some monographs and anthologies highlighting various aspects of Murdoch's work that have been influential in stimulating debate are Antonaccio & Schweiker 1996; Antonaccio 2000, 2012; Widdows 2005; Rowe 2007; Laverty 2007; Rowe & Horner 2010; Lovibond 2011; Broackes 2012; Forsberg 2013; and, more recently, Browning 2018a, 2018b; and Hämäläinen & Dooley 2019.

7. See Gordon 1995.
8. See Rowe & Horner 2010 for some such attempts. Bryan Magee's interview with Murdoch in Murdoch 1998, the contributions in Dooley 2003, Forsberg 2013, and Browning 2018b (especially chapters 1 & 3) provide a good entry point to Murdoch's thoughts about philosophy and literature.
9. One influential view is developed in Antonaccio 2000, for a critical response see Robjant 2011a.
10. See, e.g., Blum 1991, Clarke 2012, Clifton 2013, Cooper 2019, and Panizza 2019 for discussion.
11. See Forsberg 2013; Rosenhagen 2021.
12. See Antonaccio 2012, ch. 2. A critical assessment of Murdoch's view from a feminist point of view is provided in Lovibond 2011, discussion of the latter in Robjant 2011b and Hämäläinen 2015.
13. A thorough investigation of Murdoch's interest in Buddhism, which she appreciatively mentions in her letters as the greatest religion and as something she has learnt from, has yet to be undertaken. Interested readers might consult Conradi 2004, Robjant 2011a, and the pertinent letters in Horner & Rowe 2015.
14. For a proposal of how moral particularists could benefit from turning to Murdoch, see Millgram 2002.
15. Murdoch suggests this in Murdoch 1974, 102.
16. "hyper-internalist" here refers to a kind of conception according to which seeing what is good intrinsically carries with it a motivation to do it. See Setiya 2013, also Bakhurst 2020 for a productive response.
17. To the Kant of the *Groundwork*, nothing is good without qualification except for a good will (cf. *Kants Schriften*, Akademie Ausgabe, Berlin:

deGruyter, 1902–, Vol. 4, 393). Though she is not a Freudian, Murdoch engages with Freud's work repeatedly (e.g., in Murdoch 1974, 1977, and throughout Murdoch 1992). She praises him for having provided a realistic, complex, and detailed picture of the fallen man and a substantial notion of the self and the various egocentric quasi-mechanical processes it involves that often remain opaque to the subject (cf. Murdoch 1974, 51–54). To the extent that Kant's moral subject can appear as lacking such substance and as being reduced to the will, it strikes her as unrealistic.
18. There is another camp Murdoch opposes that I don't have space to discuss here. It comprises those according to whom the individual is determined and absorbed without remainder by the framework of social relations and determinations it inhabits. For Murdoch, the picture of the individual this view affords is under-complex and thus, again, unrealistic. See Antonaccio 2012, ch. 2, esp. her discussion of the Natural Law view.
19. We sometimes attribute decisions to φ to agents who do not φ, e.g., when we judge that they would have φ-ed had not the world intervened. But even such attributions, Murdoch's opponents might say, rest on publicly observable behavior and one could anyway doubt whether attributions about what someone *would* have done require that in the agent some inner act, one called "deciding," has taken place. See Murdoch 1974, 13ff.
20. See Moran 2012 for a critical discussion of Murdoch's characterization of existentialism.
21. The classic Murdochian example of such an activity appears in *The Idea of Perfection*, the first essay in *The Sovereignty of Good*. In it, M, a mother in law, engages in a reevaluation of her daughter in law, D, upon whom she had previously looked down for, she suspects, possibly selfish reasons. For a recent discussion of this example and its role in *Sovereignty* see Jamieson 2020.
22. Perhaps the meanings scientific concepts are *taken* to have within the scientific community are curled up in the inferences deemed acceptable within the community that they figure in. Such inferences change along with new discoveries and the *real* meanings of scientific concepts may transcend the individual attitudes, even those of the community as a whole. To introduce talk of the *real* meanings

of scientific terms is to introduce into the notion of a scientific concept an ideal limit. It is also to raise some doubt with respect to the idea that the scientific facts lie out there, open to all. While even on such an account what is real is at least potentially open to all observers, the ability to appreciate the facts will in practice depend on the details of how the concepts forming the perceiver's conceptual apparatus are interconnected. Murdoch briefly considers a general position along these lines, but only to put it to one side. (See Murdoch 1974, 11.) For her, just as for us here, the focus lies not on arguing that the idea of publicly available facts is *in general* too crude to be of use in providing an account of perception and proper concept use—scientific or otherwise. Rather, she focuses more narrowly on *moral* perception and *moral* concepts, arguing that no matter what one thinks about scientific concepts, for moral concepts, an account according to which the understanding of moral concepts and the appreciation of moral facts are, at heart, a matter of publicly conforming to certain behavioral regularities is particularly unconvincing.

23. Murdoch 1974, 29.
24. Murdoch 1974, 28f.
25. Murdoch 1974, 28.
26. With respect to particular acts of re-evaluation, Murdoch says that "[i]ts details are the details of *this* personality; and partly for this reason it may well be an activity which can only be performed privately." Murdoch 1974, 23.
27. Murdoch 1974, 37.
28. Cf. Murdoch (1998), 199f.
29. Indeed, referring to the preparatory work of attention, she suggests that "at crucial moments of choice most of the business of choosing is already over." Murdoch 1974, 37.
30. See Murdoch 1974, 66.
31. "Good," Murdoch says, "is the magnetic center towards which love naturally moves." Murdoch 1974, 102. Murdoch's claim that the good—though hard to see and undefinable—works as a magnetic center towards which love naturally strives betrays an important Platonic debt (about which Murdoch is quite explicit). I take it that for her, our understanding of others and their actions is transformed once we acquire an understanding of what they deem good. Likewise, such understanding will enrich and contextualize our own conception of the (common) Good and affect how we respond to others, as we obey to the normative pressures of the reality we can now see (cf. Murdoch 1974, 40ff., for how Murdoch adopts Weil's idea of obedience). The idea that true vision occasions right conduct is part of what Setiya 2013 seeks to capture by the term 'hyper-internalism' (see note 16 above).

32. As I have argued elsewhere (cf. Rosenhagen 2019), parallels between Murdoch and Aristotle abound: note, e.g., that i) *philia* requires time and familiarity (NE 1156b25–32), ii) complete friends love and wish well alike to each other *qua* good (NE 1156b8f.), iii) becoming familiar with others is very hard (NE 1158a11–17), iv) friendship and justice are closely related (NE 1159b25–1160a8), v) friendship asks a man to do what he can, not what is proportional to the merits of the case (for that may be more than he could do) (NE 1163b13–18), and vi) bestowing benefits on others appropriately is laborious (for, as Murdoch would say, it is hard to realize that others are different) (NE 1165a14–1165a36; also: NE 1168a21–27).

33. Murdoch 1974, 28.
34. Murdoch 1959, 51.
35. Murdoch 1974, 103f.
36. Murdoch typically avoids characterizing the ideal moral agent. Here is a rare exception: "The good (better) man is *liberated* from selfish fantasy, can see himself as others see him, imagine the needs of other people, love unselfishly, lucidly envisage and desire what is truly valuable. This is the ideal picture." Murdoch 1992, 331.
37. See Murdoch 1974, 52.
38. See Murdoch, 1974, 103. Presumably, part of her reasoning is that those who are humble are not already full of themselves, which, in turn, makes it easier for them to see (e.g., others) more clearly.
39. See Murdoch 1998, 199.

REFERENCES

Antonaccio, M. & W. Schweiker (eds.) (1996). *Iris Murdoch and the Search for Human Goodness*. University of Chicago Press.

Antonaccio, M. (2000). *Picturing the Human. The Moral Thought of Iris Murdoch*. Oxford University Press.

Antonaccio, M. (2012). *A Philosophy to Live By: Engaging Iris Murdoch*. Oxford University Press.

Aristotle; Barnes, J. (ed.) (1984): *Complete Works of Aristotle, Volume II. The Revised Oxford Translation*. Princeton University Press. [NE: Nicomachean Ethics]

Bakhurst, D. (2020). "Analysis and transcendence in *The Sovereignty of Good*," in: *European Journal of Philosophy*. https://10.1111/ejop.12539

Blum, L. (1991). "Moral perception and particularity," in: *Ethics* 101 (4): 701–725.

Broackes, J. (ed.) (2012). *Iris Murdoch: Philosopher*. Oxford University Press.

Broackes, J. (2019). "Iris Murdoch and Simone Weil." Talk at the Royal Institute of Philosophy, uploaded to YouTube on Jan 28, 2019. URL = https://www.youtube.com/watch?v=LmCRWqkOiqs [last access: 03/15/2021].

Browning, G. (ed.) (2018a). *Murdoch on Truth and Love*. Palgrave Macmillan.

Browning, G. (2018b). *Why Iris Murdoch Matters*. Bloomsbury.

Clarke, B. (2012). "Iris Murdoch and the prospects for critical moral perception," in: Broackes (ed.) (2012), 227–254.

Clifton, W. S. (2013). "Murdochian Moral Perception," in *Journal of Value Inquiry* 47 (2013), 207–220.

Conradi, P. (2004). *Going Buddhist: Panic and Emptiness, The Buddha and Me*. London: Short Books.

Cooper, A. (2019). "Iris Murdoch on Moral Perception," in: *The Heythrop Journal* 2019, 1–13.

Dooley, G. (ed.) (2003). *From a tiny corner in the house of fiction: Conversations with Iris Murdoch*. Columbia: University of South Carolina Press.

Forsberg, N. (2013). *Language Lost and Found. On Iris Murdoch and the Limits of Philosophical Discourse*. Bloomsbury.

Gordon, D. J. (1995). *Iris Murdoch's Fables of Unselfing*. Columbia/London: University of Missouri Press.

Hämäläinen, N. (2015). "Reducing Ourselves to Zero?: Sabina Lovibond, Iris Murdoch, and Feminism," in: Hypatia 30 (4), 743–759.

Hämäläinen, N. & G. Dooley (eds.) (2019). *Reading Iris Murdoch's Metaphysics as a Guide to Morals*. Palgrave Macmillan.

Hopwood, M. (2018). "'The Extremely Difficult Realization That Something Other Than Oneself Is Real': Iris Murdoch on Love and Moral Agency," in: *European Journal of Philosophy* 26 (1): 477–501.

Horner, A. & Rowe, A. (eds.) (2015). *Living on Paper. Letters from Iris Murdoch 1934–1995*. Princeton University Press.

Jamieson, L. (2020). "The Case of M and D in Context: Iris Murdoch, Stanley Cavell and Moral Teaching and Learning," in: *Journal of Philosophy of Education* 54 (2): 425–448.

Laverty, M. (2007). *Iris Murdoch's Ethics: A Consideration of her Romantic Vision*. New York: Continuum.

Lovibond, S. (2011). *Iris Murdoch, Gender and Philosophy*. Routledge.

Millgram, E. (2002). "Murdoch, Practical Reasoning, and Particularism," in: *notizie di POLITEIA* XVIII, 66L 64–87.

Moran, R. (2012). "Iris Murdoch and Existentialism," in Broackes (ed.) (2012), 181–196.

Murdoch, Iris (1959). The Sublime and the Good, in: the *Chicago Review*, Vol. 13 (3) (Autumn 1959).

Murdoch, Iris (1974). *The Sovereignty of Good*. Routledge & Kegan Paul [3rd reprint, first published in 1970].

Murdoch, Iris (1977). *The Fire & the Sun. Why Plato Banished the Artists*. Oxford: Clarendon Press.

Murdoch, Iris (1998). *Existentialists and Mystics: Writings on philosophy and literature*, edited and with a preface by Peter Conradi; foreword by Georg Steiner. New York/London: Allen Lane. The Penguin Press.

Murdoch, Iris (1992). *Metaphysics as a Guide to Morals*. Allen Lane The Penguin Press.

Panizza, S. (2019). "Moral Perception Beyond Supervenience: Iris Murdoch's Radical Perspective," in: *Journal of Value Inquiry* 1 2019, 2: 1–16

Robjant, D. (2011a). "As a Buddhist Christian; The Misappropriation of Iris Murdoch," in: *The Heythrop Journal* 2011, 992–1008.

Robjant, D. (2011b). "Is Iris Murdoch an unconcious misogynist? Some trouble with Sabina Lovibond, the mother in law, and gender," in: *Heythrop Journal* 52 (6): 1021–1031.

Rosenhagen, R. (2019). "Toward Virtue: Moral Progress through Love, Just Attention, and Friendship," in Dalferth, I. U. & T. Kimball (eds.): *Love and Justice:*

Consonance or Dissonance? Claremont Studies in the Philosophy of Religion, Conference 2016. Tübingen: Mohr Siebeck, 217–239.

Rosenhagen, R. (2021). "Murdochian Presentationalism, Autonomy, and the Ideal Lovers' Pledge," in: Fedock, R., M. Kühler, & R. Rosenhagen (eds.) (2021). *Love, Justice, and Autonomy. Philosophical Perspectives.* Routledge, 102–130.

Rowe, A. (2007). *Iris Murdoch: A Reassessment.* Palgrave Macmillan.

Rowe, A. & A. Horner (eds.) (2010). *Iris Murdoch and Morality.* Palgrave Macmillan.

Schaubroeck, K. (2018). "Reasons of Love," in: Martin A. (ed.): *The Routledge Handbook of Love in Philosophy.* New York: Routledge, 288–299.

Setiya, K. (2013). "Murdoch on the Sovereignty of Good," in: *Philosophers' Imprint* 13.

Widdows, H. (2005). *Murdoch's morality.* Aldershot, UK: Ashgate.

Love as Perfect Friendship: Aristotle

BY SIMON MAY

> Simon May is a British philosopher who draws on Aristotle in this essay to provide an account of the importance of friendship for a fully flourishing human life.

Crucially, Aristotle makes friendship, rather than sexual relationships or contemplation of the Good, the supreme form of love. Indeed he so elevates the best sort of friendship-love—what he calls perfect *philia*: wishing and doing well to others for their own sake; intensely identifying with them as if they were "a second self"; seeking deep mutual harmony—that all other forms of relationship, whether to spouses, siblings, children, parents, or sexual partners, are, for him, valuable mainly insofar as they exhibit the features of such *philia*.[1]

The last point is of great importance: *philia* is a form of devotion that is best translated as "friendship-love," but that flourishes not only between what we normally think of as friends, but also in all these other sorts of relationship at their best. And so sexual intimacy, for example, isn't in principle opposed to friendship-love; but since it is motivated merely by the hope of pleasure, Aristotle regards it as no more important to a flourishing life (and possibly less) than, say, a good sense of humour, an adequate income, or handling your drink well.

For him the purest love—love that is based on wishing and doing well to others for their own sake, and not merely on pleasure or gain to oneself—is, in its very essence, ethical. It is possible only between two individuals who are good—and indeed are good in similar ways. What Aristotle means by "good" is much more than simply agreeing on rules like telling the truth, or not stealing, or keeping promises. He means that they share an entire conception of the best way to live life, of the

right ends of life, and of the excellences of character with which our choices and actions must accord.[2] Only friendship-love, he maintains, can fully exemplify this sort of ethical relationship. Erotic associations are driven by desire for pleasure and gain; and though they can be accompanied by friendship-love that seeks the good of the other regardless of pleasure or gain to oneself, or even develop into friendship-love, they are not themselves founded on such love and so are not intrinsically ethical associations.

Philia is inescapably conditional on the excellences of character that we perceive in the other person. Since character is realised in concrete acts and desires over the course of a lived life,[3] we love someone not just for dispositions that we detect in her but for how these dispositions are revealed, over time, in her actual life. Revealed in heroic actions or personal crises or pursuits like thinking, artistic creation and political leadership; and also revealed in ordinary everyday life: in eating, drinking, having sex, party-giving, even telling jokes—all of which can be pursued with varying degrees of excellence or baseness.[4] Hence for Aristotle ideal love "is a thoroughgoing and unconstrained sharing in *all* activities that people judge to be pertinent to their human good living"—all activities, that is, "according to the recognised excellences of character."[5]

But if love is so conditional, then—contrary to another myth about ideal love—it isn't necessarily constant, let alone eternal. We don't go on loving someone regardless of whether they remain the same. Aristotle would disagree with Shakespeare that "Love is not love/ Which alters when it alteration finds."[6] Love will be undermined precisely to the degree that the loved one changes for the worse. Such as through a moral deterioration that isn't reversed. Or through the deterioration of old age, which can "bring about a loss in sensitivity and in enjoyment that can lead to the dissolution or at least the diminution of love."[7] Or through the departure of the loved one. This is how separation and death can, after sufficient time, help us to get over love.[8] (Nor is this far-fetched: some people do after all manage to find new loves when they are deserted or to marry again when a spouse dies.) Anything that seriously undermines trust can also destroy love: suspicion, jealousy, fear, self-protectiveness are all enemies of *philia*.[9]

Friendship-love has a second condition: the goodness of the *lover*. It takes virtue to recognise virtue, to desire it, and to crave unity with another person who possesses it. Only lovers who are themselves virtuous are able, and motivated, to love the good in another. Only they can do what all genuine love must do: bear witness to the other's life and specifically to his quality as an ethical being.

So "perfect" friendship-love, the sort that doesn't simply use the other for pleasure or utility, but wants the best for him for his own sake, is found only between two virtuous people.

Not just any virtuous people, though, but people of *similar* virtue. Like is attracted—and suited—to like. We bind to another through our love of similar ideals, through our possession of similar virtues. "Perfect friendship is the friendship of men who are good, and alike in excellence."[10]

Indeed likeness *is* friendship.[11] Aristotle's claim here is startlingly extreme. In his ideal friendship the likeness of the friends would encompass not only their virtue—and the key choices, desires, motivations, and tastes that it expresses—but also their social status as well as all the pleasures and advantages that they bestow on each other.

This rules quite a few relationships out of the running for friendship. Spouses, for example; or in general men and women. Since female virtue is, he thinks, naturally inferior to male virtue, the best a woman can be never matches the best a man can

be. So perfect *philia* couldn't exist between a man and a woman, no matter how virtuous the woman.[12]

Nor can it exist between parents and their children[13]—for they too are unequal, at least until the children have reached ethical maturity. And certainly not between masters and those who, Aristotle believes, are slaves by nature, rather than merely in subservient positions through bad luck or birth. He adds that although one can be friends with such a person insofar as he is a man, one cannot be friends with the slave in their nature.[14]

Can We Be Friends with Our Lovers?

Aristotle's philosophy suggests a simple answer to this long-running question: friendship-love and erotic love are such different sorts of devotion that they can flourish within the same relationship only if we remember not to expect things from erotic love that don't properly belong to it, and similarly from friendship.

To summarise the features of friendship-love: It is mutual—friendship is reciprocal goodwill—and is seen by both parties as such.[15] It involves wishing the other what is good for his sake.[16] It requires clear mutual recognition of the independence of the two friends: despite thinking of one another as a "second self," they do not expect to "merge" into that indistinguishable union celebrated, as we will see, by much of the erotic-mystical tradition, from early Neoplatonism through Christian unity-mysticism to nineteenth-century Romanticism. Friendship takes time to develop: two lives and their myriad activities must be mutually intertwined for long enough to enable both parties to get to know and love each other's characters well and also to benefit from their joint activities. And it is durable to the extent that good qualities of character—the object of this sort of love—are stable. Whereas these conditions aren't necessary for erotic love, which can be both passionate and genuine without being reciprocated, or making the other's wellbeing a central goal, or scrupulously respecting his separateness, or taking much time to mature, or being particularly durable. Erotic relationships are fragile because they depend on expectations of beauty or sexual pleasure which are either unfulfilled or do not last:

. . . in the friendship of lovers sometimes the lover complains that his excess of love is not met by love in return (though perhaps there is nothing lovable about him), while often the beloved complains that the lover who formerly promised everything now performs nothing. Such incidents happen when the lover loves the beloved for the sake of pleasure while the beloved loves the lover for the sake of utility, and they do not both possess the qualities expected of them . . . ; for each did not love the other person himself but the qualities he had, and these were not enduring; this is why the friendships also are transient. But the love of characters, as has been said, endures because it is self-dependent.[17]

Aristotle is clear: sex is not necessary for the most fulfilling love.[18] So if sex "gets in the way" of friendship-love, say by inducing intense possessiveness of the other at the expense of acting for the sake of his welfare, or an excessive emphasis on physical beauty rather than ethical attractiveness, or on spontaneity rather than constancy, then we can infer that the first of these pairs will always have to yield to the second. At least if we are to aim for "perfect" *philia*, where two people love each other for their own sakes and not merely for pleasure or utility.

But where does that leave relationships that seek both *philia* and Eros—relationships like marriages and other forms of rich intimacy? The conclusion that Aristotle's philosophy suggests—though he doesn't explicitly reach it himself—is that *philia* and Eros, and therefore relationships embracing them both, will always be vulnerable to tensions, where respect for autonomy vies with possessiveness, an emphasis on character and virtue with a fixation on pleasure and physical beauty, the pleasures of reciprocation with the pain of unrequited desire, harmony with turbulence, trust with jealousy. The battles in all love of this sort are not so much between the sexes as between the different forms of love that a particular relationship encompasses.

Self-Love and Self-Knowledge

But, for all Aristotle's talk of *philia* making the other's well-being an end in itself, isn't even "perfect" *philia* extraordinarily self-regarding, given that we love people in this way only if their virtues of character are similar to ours—only if they feel like a "second self" and so are, in a sense, us? Though Aristotle claims that *philia* is the highest form of love, isn't it essentially about loving oneself in another? About a rather self-conscious mutual admiration society?

To which the answer is unashamedly yes. This is not a problem for Aristotle. He sees no necessary conflict between loving another and loving oneself. Nor between altruism and self-interest. Unselfish altruism, where I do something for someone else because his needs or wants are a sufficient reason for helping him, is perfectly consistent with my benefiting from doing these things. It is even consistent with my also having a self-interested reason for doing them.

Indeed, Aristotle goes further: he believes that the highest love essentially involves the desire for *one's own* good. Since the natural and proper aim of life is to fulfil our human potential, our first concern in everything we do, including in loving others, *should* be our own flourishing.[19] Not in the sense that we look for a return from every good thing we do for another person. Rather in the sense that we flourish precisely by loving her for whom she is "in herself." As a "second self" her flourishing is also my own flourishing. And so in caring for her life I care for mine.

What, then, are the blessings that flow to us by loving another? There are two main ones that we can broadly infer from Aristotle's discussion of *philia*.

First among them is self-love. In particular, close friendships deepen one's esteem for oneself,[20] and they dispose one to act in ways that express what is best in one—that are, as we would now say, "true to oneself." For loving others inspires the energy and tenacity to dedicate oneself to one's own flourishing. We are better at sticking with what we care about, at sustaining our motivation, if we share our life with a loved one:[21] "by oneself it is not easy to be continuously active; but with others and towards others it is easier."[22]

This doesn't mean that two friends need to live under the same roof, but it does involve the closest regular association in all the activities that they find necessary to living a good life, from ordinary things like eating, drinking, and giving parties, to thinking, reasoning, law-making, conversing, working, and confronting danger.[23] ("[F]or this is what living together would seem to mean in the case of man, and not, as in the case of cattle, feeding in the same place."[24])

Such continuous association isn't therefore about meeting in order to take a break from life's weightier preoccupations. On the contrary, it involves spending time precisely on those activities that are most central to each other's lives and taking pains to avoid the prolonged separations that, Aristotle insists, endanger the firmness and trust of a friendship.[25]

Plainly, no contemporary man with a job, a mortgage and a family could have time for many friendships of this sort, and it is hard to imagine a wife who would be happy if her husband undertook everything he most cherished only with his friend. But if we jettison Aristotle's assumption that women are inferior to men, ethically as well as in terms of understanding, and therefore incapable of the same quality of friendship-love, it is clear that the ideal arena for this sort of continuous intimacy would be a marriage or other long-term partnership in which all the aspirations and values that make life most worth living for both parties are accommodated.

Aristotle insists that human flourishing needs such long-term intimacy, however it is achieved; and that this is precisely what distinguishes us from wild beasts—as well as from God, who requires no company to be fully himself:

 . . . with us [humans] welfare involves a something beyond us, but the deity is his own well-being.[26]

 . . . he who is unable to live in society, or who has no need because he is sufficient for himself, must be either a beast or a god . . .[27]
This brings us to the second great blessing of loving for Aristotle: self-knowledge.[28] Self-knowledge was much prized by Greek thinkers and mystics—the Delphic Oracle famously charged its votaries to "know thyself"; and Socrates, Plato's teacher, and so Aristotle's intellectual grandfather, went round Athens preaching that "the unexamined life is not worth living." But Aristotle thinks that one sort of self-knowledge is particularly essential to our flourishing: knowing our *motives* for acting in the ways we do. The point is this: our motives aren't arbitrary whims; they embody our inbuilt conceptions of what is good, they express our "core values" (as we would put it nowadays). To understand what sort of life we are leading we need to study not only our actions but also what drives them; we need to know whether we have chosen the right actions out of the right motives.[29] Giving money to a hungry child, for example, has quite a different ethical quality if we accidentally drop a coin into his lap or if our motive is to stop him harassing us with his suffering, than if we give it to him out of genuine empathy and want to help him flourish. Leading a good life isn't about pursuing worthwhile things on autopilot.

And so only by examining our motives can we discover our hidden conceptions of what is good. Only by understanding what values drive us can we be sure that our actions are true to them, and so to who we are.

But why must we love *another* in order to get such self-knowledge? Why can't we obtain it just by looking inwards or by observing ourselves in action?

Because, Aristotle says, it is so hard to know ourselves. Which is, for example, "plain from the way in which we blame others without being aware that we do the same things ourselves."[30] Or in which we claim virtues that we don't have. As Nietzsche was to say over twenty-two centuries later: ". . . we are necessarily strangers to ourselves, we do not comprehend ourselves, we *have* to misunderstand ourselves, for us the law 'Each is furthest from himself' applies to all eternity—we are not 'men of knowledge' with respect to ourselves."[31]

Nietzsche goes much further than Aristotle: he believes that we can never really understand our actions, let alone their motives; they are too complicated, too opaque. If we think we know precisely what we are about, we are almost certainly deluded. Aristotle thinks we *can* gain knowledge of ourselves emotionally, just as we can physically; but we need the aid of mirrors—in this case the mirror of someone who is just like us in his essential nature, a "second self" whom we love; not an enemy (though, one might add, enemies—our choice of them and the behaviour they evoke—can surely give us valuable insight into ourselves):

> [Just as] when we wish to see our own face, we do so by looking into the mirror, in the same way when we wish to know ourselves we can obtain that knowledge by looking at our friend. For the friend is, as we assert, a second self. If, then, it is pleasant to know oneself, and it is not possible to know this without having someone else for a friend, the self-sufficing man will require friendship in order to know himself.[32]

In other words, we learn about ourselves from a loved one not so much because of what he tells us, but rather by observing our own reflections in him. By coming to know him as a "second self," we come to know our own self. By discovering that our intuitions of kinship with him are reliable and well-founded, we discover our own character and why we choose and act as we do.

Aristotle's idea of friends as mirrors hardly exhausts the ways in which intimacy can foster self-knowledge. As important as mirroring is, surely, what we learn from the many unexpected ways in which a close relationship makes us feel secure or frightened, relaxed or uneasy, happy or angry, powerful or weak, sure or unsure of our own values and projects. But Aristotle offers us a crucial insight: that our idea of who we are is formed through intimate, sustained relations with others, based on a sense of deep affinity which has stood the test of time. In other words, individuality is fundamentally relational.

Which brings us back to Aristotle's point that these benefits of love will flow only if lover and beloved are sufficiently virtuous. His idea that love is unjustified—and unjust—if it isn't rooted in appropriate excellences of character might seem distasteful. But it is more profound than meets the eye. It echoes an archaic Greek idea that the cosmos has an essential order—a "just" order—to which everything, whether human or inanimate, must be attuned if it is to flourish. Justice, in the sense of such an attunement, is therefore not simply a matter of respecting rules, like keeping promises or not lying, that we hive off into an area of life called "morality." Instead, justice is acting in accordance with what are taken to be the deepest laws of the universe. Anything that disobeys them does so at its peril. Heraclitus remarks that this includes even the sun: "The sun will not transgress his measures. If he does, the Furies, ministers of Justice, will find him out."[33]

Aristotle is firmly within this tradition when he asserts that everything unfair is unlawful and everything fair is lawful. Greek has a special word for this lawfulness: *dikaios*, meaning "fair," "just," "right" *or* "in accordance with the laws." Love is *dikaios* when it is in accordance with the laws of the other person's nature, when it is strictly justified by his character, when it gives him his due. If love isn't in such accordance it is inauthentic and hollow (as everything is ungenuine when untrue to the laws governing it).

Each of us can therefore only love—and be loved by—very particular people. The bond we feel with such people isn't the result of some mysterious "chemistry," but is based on tangible and observable features of their character and of their conceptions of what is good. Love affirms only those features of the beloved that are virtuous and good, and otherwise is far from "all-accepting." And though we might "fall" in love with inappropriate people—for Aristotle, those who lack virtue, or don't share similar ideals, or fail to wish and do each other well—it won't work. Such an urge will go against the laws of (human) nature: and so, with such people, no lasting intimacy will be possible.

The moral? We are probably much too casual in our choice of lovers; for the wrong choice can knock our life off a flourishing course. Passion and chemistry are no proof of love, let alone of whether a relationship will be good for us. Out of our powerful urge to become similar to those we are attracted to—to heed their advice, to emulate their values and tastes—we pay a real and often disastrous price for associating with the wrong people: those of insufficient virtue, those whose values are too different to our own. We become worse with a worse person, better with a better person; but the secret to durable love is two people who are not only virtuous, but *similarly* virtuous.

DISCUSSION QUESTIONS

1. What are the stages of friendship, for Aristotle? You may use other resources to supplement your answer to this question (try the *Stanford Encyclopedia of Philosophy*, for example).
2. Why might friendship be an even more important and challenging form of love than romantic love?
3. Can lovers be best friends? Why or why not?

NOTES

1. Apart from perfect *philia*, based on the friends' goodness, Aristotle also uses the term *philia* in two other senses, which will not concern us here: to denote relationships based on utility—such as business relationships, where these are cooperative rather than competitive—and to denote those based on pleasure.
2. Character, for Aristotle as for many other Greeks, is a far more significant determinant of a person's life than it tends to be for us today. For them virtues of character—like courage, benevolence, reliability, truthfulness, self-command, wisdom, or generosity—dictate the entire capacity of a person to fulfil his human potential. "Man's character is his fate," says Heraclitus (flourished *c.* 500 BCE), one of the founders of Greek thought. Charles H. Kahn, *The Art and Thought of Heraclitus* (Cambridge, 1979), fragment CXIV (Diels-Kranz fragment 119), p. 81.
3. Price, *Love and Friendship*, p. 108.
4. Nussbaum, *The Fragility of Goodness*, pp. 358–359. Cf. A.W. Price, who, similarly, makes the point that since "the self is primarily realised in its choices," the best love is based on a very broad sharing of the activities by which these choices are manifested. See Price, *Love and Friendship*, p. 107.
5. Nussbaum, *The Fragility of Goodness*, p. 358.

6. Sonnet 116, in William Shakespeare, *The Sonnets and a Lover's Complaint* (London, 1995), p. 134.
7. Nussbaum, *The Fragility of Goodness*, p. 360.
8. " . . . if the absence is of long duration it appears to bring about forgetfulness of the love itself." Quoted in Nussbaum, *The Fragility of Goodness*, p. 360.
9. Nussbaum, *The Fragility of Goodness*, pp. 338–339.
10. *NE*, 1156b7–8, p. 1827.
11. "Now equality and likeness *are* friendship": *NE* 1159b3, p. 1832, my italics.
12. Relationships between husbands and wives belong, for Aristotle, to intrinsically unequal relationships (*NE*, 1158b13–19, p. 1831), and in these the better party should be loved more than he loves and the worse less than he loves (*NE*, 1158b24–8, p. 1831).
13. *NE*, 1158b13–14, p. 1831.
14. "*Qua* slave then, one cannot be friends with him. But *qua* man one can" (*NE*, 1161b4–8, p. 1835). Cf. C.C.W. Taylor, "Politics," in *The Cambridge Companion to Aristotle*, ed. Jonathan Barnes (Cambridge, 1995), pp. 256–257.
15. " . . . goodwill [*eunoia*] when it *is* reciprocal being friendship." *NE*, 1155b33, and 1156a3–5, p. 1826. See John M. Cooper, "Aristotle on Friendship," in *Essays on Aristotle's Ethics*, ed. Amélie Oksenberg Rorty (Berkeley and Los Angeles, 1980), pp. 308–311. My discussion is greatly indebted to Cooper's chapter.
16. *NE*, 1155b31–2, p. 1826.
17. *NE*, 1164a3–13, p. 1839.
18. As Martha Nussbaum, to whom this section is much beholden, puts it: "unlike Plato, he does not appear to believe that intense sexual desire or excitement plays any essential role in the values and benefits of love." Nussbaum, *The Fragility of Goodness*, p. 358.
19. *NE*, 1159a11–12, p. 1832.
20. John M. Cooper suggests that, for Aristotle, "*in* loving and valuing the other person for his own sake one becomes able to love and value oneself" ("Aristotle on Friendship," p. 333).
21. "For there is nothing so characteristic of friends as living together." *NE*, 1157b19–20, p. 1829.
22. *NE*, 1170a4–11, especially 5–6, p. 1849.

23. I owe this interpretation of what Aristotle means by "living together" to Nussbaum, *The Fragility of Goodness*, pp. 358–359.

24. *NE*, 1170b12–13, p. 1850.

25. *NE*, 1156b4–5, p. 1827; 1157b11–12, p. 1829.

26. Aristotle, *Eudemian Ethics*, 1245b18–19, in *The Complete Works of Aristotle*, ed. Jonathan Barnes (Princeton, NJ, 1984), vol. II, p. 1974.

27. Aristotle, *Politics*, 1253a28–9, in *The Complete Works of Aristotle*, ed. Jonathan Barnes (Princeton, NJ, 1984), vol. II, p. 1988.

28. My discussion here is much indebted to Cooper, "Aristotle on Friendship," pp. 320–324.

29. *NE*, 1105a29–33, p. 1746.

30. Aristotle, *Magna Moralia*, 1213a16–17, in *The Complete Works of Aristotle*, ed. Jonathan Barnes (Princeton, NJ, 1984), vol. II, p. 1920.

31. Friedrich Nietzsche, *On the Genealogy of Morals*, in *The Basic Writings of Nietzsche*, trans. W. Kaufmann (New York, 1968), p. 451 (Preface, sect. 1).

32. Aristotle, *Magna Moralia*, 1213a20–6, p. 1920. Cf. *NE*, 1169b28–1170a3, p. 1849, and *Eudemian Ethics*, 1245a35–6, p. 1974: "Therefore, to perceive a friend must be in a way to perceive one's own self and to know a friend is to know one's self." Some scholars doubt that *Magna Moralia* is really by Aristotle, but the passage cited here is typically Aristotelian.

33. In Kahn, *Art and Thought*, fragment XLIV (Diels-Kranz fragment 94), p. 49.

Love & Lies (selections)

BY CLANCY MARTIN

Clancy Martin is a Canadian philosopher, novelist, and essayist. In this selection from his book Love & Lies, Martin contests the traditional view, offered by Plato, bell hooks, and others, that love and truthfulness go hand in hand. He argues that many different kinds of love—parental, in friendship, romantic—include deception and may depend on deception. He also proposes that we may trust our beloved to lie to us, to confirm our self-deceptions.

The Marriage Paradox

If only the brain weren't so nimble, so practiced at partitioning itself! If self-deception were impossible or even rare—rather than, as is the case, the rule—perhaps there would be few affairs, and many fewer failed marriages. How many of us have looked at our spouses and thought, "How I love her," only to notice, fifteen, twenty minutes later, after she's left the room, an attractive woman glancing our way, and wondered, "Now she's interesting. . . ." When you're thinking about that other woman—probably (only?!) to think, how nice that she's attracted to me! But maybe also: who is she? What makes her tick? I wonder what an affair with her would be like?—your love for, need of and commitment to your wife has for that moment or minute flown entirely from your brain. The thought "Now she's interesting . . ." is not a violation of your marriage vow. And the thought itself may not even be under your control. But most adulteries and destroyed marriages begin with precisely that thought. And whether or not you choose to act on the thought is certainly a decision you make.

I remember the night my second marriage ended. For hours that night I had told myself that the woman I was with—a friend was there, too—was not interested in me, and that I was not interested in her. She was drinking; I was not. By the end of the evening, I knew what was going to happen. I knew that it could well end my marriage. I told the woman, once we were in bed: "I'm happily married. I love my wife." She said: "I know." And a month later my marriage was effectively over, and I was already sneaking shots of vodka. I never decided: okay, my marriage is over now. But when I got into that bed that's what I was deciding. And yet the whole time I was telling myself: no, I won't let this happen, this is not what it is.

Remember the paradox of self-deception . . . ? To believe a proposition p and convince oneself that not-p. It ought to be impossible. And yet we do it with such fluency from such a young age. "This is not what it is": that belief is the core of self-deception. "What I know is true is not true." I both knew and did not know that I was ending my marriage that night. But somehow, also, as I was lying to myself, I knew I was lying to myself. I remember thinking: "You've done this before. You can't tell yourself this lie again."

The bad side of self-deception allows us to get ourselves into the kinds of love-destroying situations that I created when I destroyed my first two marriages. But there is also a good side to self-deception. And I think that the benevolent power of self-deception is in fact what makes long-term happy marriages possible—just as I think almost all successful relationships depend upon the benevolent power of self-deception. The crucial difference between bad self-deception, and good self-deception, I think, is *knowing that you're doing it* and *knowing why you're doing it.*

Now this is a bit complicated, because it doesn't sound like self-deception if you understand what it is you're up to. But the process is more complicated than it initially appears. It is rarely the case that we simply "know the true belief" or "accept the false belief": our belief processes are not like on/off switches. We are much more often in the domain of what Sartre called "troubled belief," when truth and falsehood are blended together, and multiple beliefs are combating each other, like waves tossing the boat of the mind on a troubled sea. When I claim that we should acknowledge that we are engaged in self-deception and why we are engaged in self-deception, I mean that we can play these sorts of truth and lie games less dangerously when we recognize that this is the sort of activity we are engaging in. If you refuse to recognize that you are playing the game, you are almost certainly going to lose. If you don't admit to yourself that the sea you are sailing is stormy, you are that much more likely to drown.

Here's an example that might be helpful: a child sees a rainbow and wants to go find it, or sees a cloud from an airplane and wants to play in it. The rainbow and the cloud are no less real for the adult who sees them than they are for the child, but in better understanding the nature of those phenomena the adult will not make the cognitive mistakes that the child might want to make. The naïve lover believes his self-deceptions with the same naïve earnestness that the child believes in the rainbow.

Here's another, cleverer example. It is Shakespeare's *Sonnet 138*, one of the best meditations on love and deception in all of literature:

When my love swears that she is made of truth
I do believe her, though I know she lies,
That she might think me some untutor'd youth,
Unlearned in the world's false subtleties.
Thus vainly thinking that she thinks me young,
Although she knows my days are past the best,
Simply I credit her false speaking tongue:
On both sides thus is simple truth suppress'd.
But wherefore says she not she is unjust?
And wherefore say not I that I am old?

O, love's best habit is in seeming trust,
And age in love loves not to have years told:
Therefore I lie with her and she with me,
And in our faults by lies we flatter'd be.

Let's take the time to analyze this a bit. The first two lines are a delightful double-paradox: lying, the lover swears she is made of truth, and he believes her, though he knows she's lying. But for him to believe her he can't know she's lying: a lie only works when we don't believe it. Here we have self-deception illustrated as deception taking place between the couple. And better still, her lie is that she is made of truth: she lies about the fact that she is lying (she goes on to tell some other lies, too, that he also chooses to believe, knowing they are lies). Even ordinary self-deception—when we lie to ourselves about something—is, as we have seen, usually considered to be paradoxical by philosophers, despite the fact that we do it all the time. But if we are experts at the pretzel-logic that enables us to believe the lies we tell ourselves, how does one believe a lie someone else is telling him, while knowing it's a lie? Here Shakespeare stacks up the paradoxes: next his narrator admits that he lets his lover believe that he believes her lies so that she will think he is young, which is also the lie she is telling him (that he is young), and he uses his acting like he believes her lie to convince himself of the lie she is telling him ("thus vainly thinking that she thinks me young"). This is so subtle, so convoluted, so hilarious, and yet so true to the phenomenology of how love actually works that suddenly we remember why, from just a few lines, Shakespeare was the greatest writer—the greatest thinker?—the English language has ever produced.

It gets better yet: "O, love's best habit is in seeming trust": not in trust, but in *seeming* trust, and not one of love's habits—controversial enough—but love's *best* habit. That is, real trust in love comes in trusting even when we know there may be some grounds for distrust, when we recognize that complete trust is an illusion and should not even be a goal for the best lovers. To truly trust is to seem to trust, to trust with the acceptance of doubt, to be willing to extend the feigning of trust while hoping, even expecting, that the feint will be returned. It is a kind of "seeming trust," but Wallace Stevens got it right when he wrote "let be be finale of seem": sometimes the being is in the finale, the climax, of the seeming. Or, as Nietzsche teaches us, the profundity of the Ancient Greeks was in the fact that, at least prior to Plato, they were content to let appearances be enough, they didn't want truth's veils withdrawn, they understood that "the naked truth" was not what we lovers desire.

Of course, Shakespeare saves the best two lines for last: "Therefore I lie with her and she with me, / And in our faults by lies we flatter'd be."

There is the lovely pun on "lie," Shakespeare characteristically playful, and the introduction of "flattery," the most common and the most harmless form of lie. Flattery is crucial here, because of course we flatter one another all the time—even politeness is merely formalized flattery—but in flattery (as in politeness) we all recognize what is going on, the lie succeeds while being recognized as a lie. Language acts in many different ways, and so do lies: not every lie is of the bald-faced-I'm-trying-to-cruelly-manipulate-you-for-my-own-evil-ends variety, and the lies of love are rarely of this type. When we are falling in love we tell one another and ourselves so many lies—who among us hasn't had the feeling, while falling in love, of "wait, but aren't I making this all up?"—and yet the lies are an essential part of the process. We are faulted by our lies, but our lies recover us from our faults, and the lies, flatteries. We see through all of this, and yet we do it, and the lies work, and we love. The story of Beatrice and Benedick is a kind of illustration of how they come to recognize the necessity of this process, and how it culminates in their marriage. We don't expect that the games Beatrice and Benedick play with one another will end with the wedding—and we'd be sad if they did.

In marriage, I want to argue, this kind of activity of playful, open-eyed deception and self-deception—the willingness to engage in this kind of activity, even the necessity that one learn to engage in this kind of activity—is how love is fostered, nurtured, and maintained. "Couples last longer if they have a tendency to overrate each other compared to the other's self-evaluation," Robert Trivers

tells us. If we tend to glamorize our partners, if we willfully encourage crystals to grow on them in the way that Stendhal describes, we will have stronger marriages. This comes as no surprise: if we take seriously the process by which we fell in love in the first place, it simply makes good sense strategically to encourage an ongoing falling in love.

Adam Phillips puts the same point from the negative perspective, but succinctly: "The point about trust is that it is impossible to establish. It is a risk masquerading as a promise." But we can take blind risks, foolish risks, ill-advised risks; we can also take practiced risks; we can enjoy risk; we can risk because to risk—what we have earlier called, to gamble—is to live. A friend of mine, R. J. Hankinson, a scholar of the ancient skeptic Sextus Empiricus and the ancient physician Galen, once raised the argument that being a skeptic might not be much fun, because it threatens to take the risk out of life. If you aren't willing to be swayed by appearances, so this line goes, what's the fun of it all?

The lama Dzongsar Khyentse Rinpoche teaches that Buddhism doesn't address erotic love—and certainly not marriage—except as a problem. "In relationships, we don't really have a choice. When it comes, it comes. What is important about relationships is not to have expectations. That always ruins the relationships. If you are a couple, your attitude should be that you have checked into a hotel for a few days together. I might never see her again tomorrow. This might be our last goodbye, our last kissing, together. Maybe it will help, it will bring the preciousness of the relationship. When the relationship comes, you should not be afraid." When he married me and my third wife, in a shrine room in a monastery in Bir, in the southern Himalayas, he warned us: "You know, Buddhism doesn't have a marriage ceremony. We don't really believe in marriage. But the best thing you can do is live in the world. I would tell you from the day you when are married, your practice is—let's forget about giving freedom to the sentient beings—start with giving freedom to your husband, and husband to the wife. By freedom what I mean is not craving from your own ego's gratification, and you can start in that way." What he meant, of course, is that we knew—that we should acknowledge—that if life is impermanent (a core Buddhist belief), marriage is that much more so: but here we are, stuck in the world, so, why not risk it? Part of the risk is acknowledging that the other human being, your spouse, is free: there's no telling what she or he might do.

"Now, go run behind a tree or something," he added, after the ceremony was over, and everyone laughed.

Here a little more wisdom from Robert Trivers is helpful. Reflecting with admirable candor on his own marriage, he writes: "I will never forget the sense of vulnerability I felt when I first realized my wife of eighteen months had been catching me in a series of lies without telling me. She was building up a library of my behavior for future use." He doesn't discuss the library he may have been building of her lies. He has the intuition, which I share, that women are more naturally honest than men—and also, perhaps, more naturally inclined towards making inventories and catalogues of truths and falsehoods.

When Trivers had this very personal realization—and it is one of the more charming moments in his refreshingly frank, terrific book on lies and self-deception—he did not abandon his marriage, nor confront his wife about it, nor even, so far as we learn, significantly modify his behavior. What happened is that he realized that she was a more sophisticated lover than he was—that she understood what the narrator of "Sonnet 138" understands, and Trivers, until that moment, did not. The lies he was telling to his wife were not being collected for use *against him*: on the contrary, they were being collected with the anticipation that they might be necessary in order to protect the marriage. His wife recognized his naivete, and was happy to work with it; she would introduce him slowly and gradually, as the *Kama Sutra* instructs wives to do, into the finer points of love, which are a mixture of truth and falsehood.

I remember when my own first wife admitted to me that I had a "tell"—as they say in poker, for recognizing a bluff—that gave away when I was lying. "What is it?" I asked. "I'm not going to tell *you*," she said, laughing, and of course she was right not to. I would have tried to mask it (who knows if I would have been effective, these kinds of tells tend to be subconscious, and are notoriously hard to overcome. My own little brother yawns every time before he tells a lie).

The Violence of Creating the Truth

As I've mentioned more than once, my favorite philosopher on the subject of cultivating truthfulness in the context of intimate love relationships is Adrienne Rich. "An honorable human relationship—that is, one in which two people have the right to use the word 'love'—is a process, delicate, violent, often terrifying to both persons involved, a process of refining the truths they tell each other." The crucial notion here, the phrase on which the plausibility of her entire account depends, is "refining the truths they tell." *Refining the truth*: this is very much like Bonhoeffer's notion of the living truth. It is not an out-and-out lie; but it is a kind of creative approach to the truth that recognizes the frailty of love—and of the human psyche, of what we can bear to hear, especially from someone we love—and embraces the idea that what we are *really saying* is different than the literal words we are speaking. For Rich, to learn to love another human being is to learn how to speak to that person, to develop a language between the two of you, a language that ultimately captures the truth of your love for each other, but need not expose "the naked truth" of what each individual lover may be happening to be feeling or thinking from one moment to the next.

The philosopher Irving Singer is useful here: in appraisal of another, in finding value, we do a kind of truth-estimation (but also—though he only gestures toward this—a kind of projection, a kind of self-deception, a kind of illusion-making), and this a more individual process, a beginning, starting with me, something I do to you; in bestowal of value we are explicitly and necessarily creative, and this is ideally an interactive process. An artist can also interact with her novel, which reveals some of the possible dangers of bestowal, but real bestowal surely takes another human being, and that's where creation is much richer and more demanding, where love becomes really unique among human experiences. My wife can never really love her novel in the way she loves me or her mother or her stepchildren or her friends. But she can love it, she does in fact bestow her love upon it—as I try to bestow my love on my own creative work—and we know the story about the creative act: at the end of the day it has its roots in truth-telling, but that truth-telling takes place almost entirely in fantasy worlds, possible worlds, projections, fictions, dreams. For Rich, then, we might say that love begin in appraisal, and is cultivated through bestowal, and the process of refining the truths we tell one another is a process of creating truths about our love for each other together.

Stanley Cavell argues that we should understand "the ability to perceive distinctions as an intellectual and moral talent essential to the intimacy of marriage." Here he is thinking especially of verbal distinctions (he uses the example of "I missed you" "I missed you too" in Liman's "Mr. and Mrs. Smith"). This is the ability to understand what the partner is *really* saying. To understand the subtext. To become the good reader of another person—which is also to recognize that as you are reading, you are writing—and so is your partner.

Marriage for Grown-Ups

"I'm too romantic for marriage," one of Sandra Cisneros's characters remarks. One might also say: I'm too childish for marriage. The view here—that romance is somehow importantly at odds with marriage—is much like the view of a child who refuses to give up her belief in Santa Claus. Such a person is, in fact, too romantic for love, unless she accepts that to love will mean continual disappointment. To erotically love at all, once we are no longer first lovers, means to accept that romance requires an active participation in the romantic activity: to accept that illusion, disillusionment, and reenchantment are all part of the process, and that, particularly in marriage, both lovers have to commit to that process.

The opposite view—that, as unmarried friends of mine often say, "marriage is an atavism"—is equally naïve. But the activity of marriage isn't going anywhere. Whatever we call it, lifelong monogamous erotic commitment is with us to stay. If we want an "ism" for marriage, we'd more

accurately say: "Marriage is a quixotism." It's a way of looking at erotic love that vigorously defies what superficially seems to be the obvious case: that it's very difficult to stay in love with another human being for years and years. It requires the kind of artistry of a Don Quixote. To enjoy a play or any work of art, Coleridge argued, we must adopt a certain attitude: the suspension of disbelief. What attitudes are the opposites of the suspension of disbelief? What do we express when we refuse to play the game of the artist? Cynicism. Boredom. Disappointment.

To lie to yourself—to be willing to lie to yourself—and, when required, to be willing to lie to the ones you love—might not be, as Adrienne Rich thought, an expression of unutterable loneliness, but on the contrary an assertion of your love. How, when, and why we sort out the right kind of lying from the right kind of truthtelling—and the wrong kind of lying from the wrong kind of truthtelling—is a lifetime's pursuit.

When Aristotle discusses virtue in *Nicomachean Ethics*, he generally argues for what we often call "the golden mean": the virtue of an activity lies between the deficiency and the excess. To be insufficiently brave is to be cowardly; to be excessively so is to be rash. To be insufficiently generous is to be cheap; to be excessively generous is to be a spendthrift. One exception he makes to this rule of moderation is truthtelling: despite his generally good-natured tolerance for most kinds of lying as a relatively harmless vice, he insists that in the activities of truthseeking and truthtelling there is no excess.

But perhaps here Aristotle's vocation as a philosopher and "lover of the truth" led him into an unhelpful inconsistency. I think that he would have done well to stick to his theory. Because in our everyday lives, and especially our love lives, moderation in truthseeking and truthtelling is precisely what is needed. A deficiency in truthtelling—being a bald-faced liar, or always hiding the truth—is clearly a vice; but, and similarly, an excess of truthtelling—always and only trying to confront the ones we love with the naked truth—looks similarly vicious. The territory we are all trying successfully navigate, both in deception and self-deception, is the middle ground, the golden mean, where truthfulness and deception blend together, when communication, trust, love and commitment require sensitivity and nuance.

When I think about my belief that the intimacy I've found and am continuing to develop in my marriage is a good thing, one of the best things in my life, one of my highest pursuits, I think about the joke that Alvy Singer tells at the end of *Annie Hall*, and how he explains it to the audience:

> This guy goes to a psychiatrist and says, "Doc, my brother's crazy; he thinks he's a chicken." And the doctor says, "Well, why don't you turn him in?" The guy says, "I would, but I need the eggs." Well, I guess that's pretty much now how I feel about relationships; y'know, they're totally irrational, and crazy, and absurd. But I guess we keep going through it because most of us need the eggs.

I also think about the discussion at the breakfast table at the end of *Moonstruck*, when Cher's mother, who knows that her husband has been cheating on her, demands that he end the affair. He stands up, strikes the table, and then sits back down again. He's surrounded by his family, and his daughter is about to announce her own, equally crazy marriage. And he speaks these words of despair: "A man understands one day that his life is built on nothing, and that's a bad, crazy day." His wife looks back at him, knowing that he's had an affair, and seeing that it means nothing, really, now that he's agreed to end it, says: "Your life is not built on nothing! Ti amo." And he replies to her: "Ti amo." Yes, the truth is out—but what was at stake is so much more than the simple truth of the fact that he had cheated on her. The point was that they loved each other, and their love was the real, fundamental truth. The "subjective truth." "The living truth," the "refined truth," the "most important truth."

Of course my account of my third marriage and the way it informs how I think about the truth is really just a philosopher stumbling awkwardly around the real story, which is that Amie called one afternoon to do a Tarot card reading on me for a column she wrote for a magazine (the cards said I should work and avoid romance); I google-imaged her and, single at the time, I flirted with her; Facebook led to emails led to texts and then long phone calls. I flew Amie to Kansas City, and one morning, coming upstairs from the basement of my apartment with laundry in my arms, I caught sight of her in the eastern sunlight making coffee in the kitchen, smiling with that half-frown she makes when she's working, her long black hair in her face and on her shoulders; I flew back with her to Seattle, and walking through the jewelry department of Barney's I saw a ring. That afternoon I proposed. That's the truth of it. We met; we fell in love; I asked her to spend the rest of her life with me; she said Yes.

Yes, you might have your heart broken; yes, the whole thing might be an impossible joke, a game with outrageous odds; yes, you might have failed at it twice before and there's no guarantee—just the opposite, really—that the third time's the charm. As we remarked above: life is risky; love, riskier still; marriage might be riskiest of all. But it's worth the risk. To choose to be married is, *contra* Montaigne, a paradoxical expression of one's freedom. When we marry we proclaim: I will love this person, come what may. I willingly, deliberately, actively participate in my erotic commitment. It's an insistence that, whatever the odds are, to have the chance to spend the rest of our lives with person we love most is worth defying the odds.

I know my wife does not always tell me the truth. She knows I do not always tell her the truth. Our intimacy is deeply involved with our ability to try to create some truth together—which always necessarily involves some lying to each other and lying to ourselves. I think we try to tell each other the most important truths. We willingly take the risk of love. We hope to succeed in loving each other. I think our eyes are mostly open. We both know we need the eggs.

And when I am with my wife, I do not feel alone.

DISCUSSION QUESTIONS

1. Why does Martin controversially argue that deception may be valuable or even indispensable for love to exist? Can you think of any examples from your own experience? Is he right or wrong?

2. How does self-deception work in loving relationships, according to Martin?

3. Usually we think that intimacy and the willingness to "bare our souls" or speak hidden truths to someone are interwoven. But Martin seems to think that intimacy may require lying. What do you think? Do you lie to your intimates? Does that create intimacy or detract from it, even destroy it?

Amoris Laetitia ("The Joy of Love")

BY POPE FRANCIS

In this post-synodal apostolic exhortation, Pope Francis, who became the leader of the Catholic Church in 2013, provides astute recommendations on the care and feeding of love. Pope Francis especially emphasizes the importance of the family for our understanding of love.

You and Your Wife

9. Let us cross the threshold of this tranquil home, with its family sitting around the festive table. At the centre we see the father and mother, a couple with their personal story of love. They embody the primordial divine plan clearly spoken of by Christ himself: "Have you not read that he who made them from the beginning made them male and female?" (*Mt* 19:4). We hear an echo of the command found in the Book of Genesis: "Therefore a man shall leave his father and mother and cleave to his wife, and they shall become one flesh (*Gen* 2:24)."

10. The majestic early chapters of Genesis present the human couple in its deepest reality. Those first pages of the Bible make a number of very clear statements. The first, which Jesus paraphrases, says that "God created man in his own image, in the image of God he created them; male and female he created them" (1:27). It is striking that the "image of God" here refers to the couple, "male and female." Does this mean that sex is a property of God himself, or that God has a divine female companion, as some ancient religions held? Naturally, the answer is no. We know how clearly the Bible rejects as idolatrous such beliefs, found among the Canaanites of the Holy Land. God's transcendence is preserved, yet inasmuch as he is also the Creator, the fruitfulness of the human couple is a living and effective "image," a visible sign of his creative act.

11. The couple that loves and begets life is a true, living icon—not an idol like those of stone or gold prohibited by the Decalogue—capable of revealing God the Creator and Saviour. For this reason, fruitful love becomes a symbol of God's inner life (cf. *Gen* 1:28; 9:7; 17:2–5, 16; 28:3; 35:11; 48:3–4). This is why the Genesis account, following the "priestly tradition," is interwoven with various genealogical accounts (cf. 4:17–22, 25–26; 5; 10; 11:10–32; 25:1–4, 12–17, 19–26; 36). The ability of human couples to beget life is the path along which the history of salvation progresses. Seen this way, the couple's fruitful relationship becomes an image for understanding and describing the mystery of God himself, for in the Christian vision of the Trinity, God is contemplated as Father, Son and Spirit of love. The triune God is a communion of love, and the family is its living reflection. Saint John Paul II shed light on this when he said, "Our God in his deepest mystery is not solitude, but a family, for he has within himself fatherhood, sonship and the essence of the family, which is love. That love, in the divine family, is the Holy Spirit."[1] The family is thus not unrelated to God's very being.[2] This Trinitarian dimension finds expression in the theology of Saint Paul, who relates the couple to the "mystery" of the union of Christ and the Church (cf. *Eph* 5:21–33).

12. In speaking of marriage, Jesus refers us to yet another page of Genesis, which, in its second chapter, paints a splendid and detailed portrait of

the couple. First, we see the man, who anxiously seeks "a helper fit for him" (vv. 18, 20), capable of alleviating the solitude which he feels amid the animals and the world around him. The original Hebrew suggests a direct encounter, face to face, eye to eye, in a kind of silent dialogue, for where love is concerned, silence is always more eloquent than words. It is an encounter with a face, a "thou," who reflects God's own love and is man's "best possession, a helper fit for him and a pillar of support," in the words of the biblical sage (*Sir* 36:24). Or again, as the woman of the Song of Solomon will sing in a magnificent profession of love and mutual self-bestowal: "My beloved is mine and I am his . . . I am my beloved's and my beloved is mine" (2:16; 6:3).

13.　This encounter, which relieves man's solitude, gives rise to new birth and to the family. Significantly, Adam, who is also the man of every time and place, together with his wife, starts a new family. Jesus speaks of this by quoting the passage from Genesis: "The man shall be joined to his wife, and the two shall become one" (*Mt* 19:5; cf. *Gen* 2:24). The very word "to be joined" or "to cleave," in the original Hebrew, bespeaks a profound harmony, a closeness both physical and interior, to such an extent that the word is used to describe our union with God: "My soul clings to you" (*Ps* 63:8). The marital union is thus evoked not only in its sexual and corporal dimension, but also in its voluntary self-giving in love. The result of this union is that the two "become one flesh," both physically and in the union of their hearts and lives, and, eventually, in a child, who will share not only genetically but also spiritually in the "flesh" of both parents.

The Sacrament of Matrimony

71.　"Scripture and Tradition give us access to a knowledge of the Trinity, which is revealed with the features of a family. The family is the image of God, who is a communion of persons. At Christ's baptism, the Father's voice was heard, calling Jesus his beloved Son, and in this love we can recognize the Holy Spirit (cf. *Mk* 1:10–11). Jesus, who reconciled all things in himself and redeemed us from sin, not only returned marriage and the family to

their original form, but also raised marriage to the sacramental sign of his love for the Church (cf. *Mt* 19:1–12; *Mk* 10:1–12; *Eph* 5:21–32). In the human family, gathered by Christ, 'the image and likeness' of the Most Holy Trinity (cf. *Gen* 1:26) has been restored, the mystery from which all true love flows. Through the Church, marriage and the family receive the grace of the Holy Spirit from Christ, in order to bear witness to the Gospel of God's love."[3]

72.　The sacrament of marriage is not a social convention, an empty ritual or merely the outward sign of a commitment. The sacrament is a gift given for the sanctification and salvation of the spouses, since "their mutual belonging is a real representation, through the sacramental sign, of the same relationship between Christ and the Church. The married couple are therefore a permanent reminder for the Church of what took place on the cross; they are for one another and for their children witnesses of the salvation in which they share through the sacrament."[4] Marriage is a vocation, inasmuch as it is a response to a specific call to experience conjugal love as an imperfect sign of the love between Christ and the Church. Consequently, the decision to marry and to have a family ought to be the fruit of a process of vocational discernment.

73.　"Mutual self-giving in the sacrament of matrimony is grounded in the grace of baptism, which establishes the foundational covenant of every person with Christ in the Church. In accepting each other, and with Christ's grace, the engaged couple promise each other total self-giving, faithfulness and openness to new life. The couple recognizes these elements as constitutive of marriage, gifts offered to them by God, and take seriously their mutual commitment, in God's name and in the presence of the Church. Faith thus makes it possible for them to assume the goods of marriage as commitments that can be better kept through the help of the grace of the sacrament . . . Consequently, the Church looks to married couples as the heart of the entire family, which, in turn, looks to Jesus."[5] The sacrament is not a "thing" or a "power," for in it Christ himself "now encounters Christian spouses . . . He dwells with them, gives them the strength to take up their crosses and so follow him, to rise again after they have fallen, to forgive one another, to bear one another's burdens."⁶ Christian marriage is a sign of how much Christ loved his Church in the covenant sealed on the cross, yet it also makes that love present in the communion of the spouses. By becoming one flesh, they embody the espousal of our human nature by the Son of God. That is why "in the joys of their love and family life, he gives them here on earth a foretaste of the wedding feast of the Lamb."⁷ Even though the analogy between the human couple of husband and wife, and that of Christ and his Church, is "imperfect,"⁸ it inspires us to beg the Lord to bestow on every married couple an outpouring of his divine love.

74. Sexual union, lovingly experienced and sanctified by the sacrament, is in turn a path of growth in the life of grace for the couple. It is the "nuptial mystery."⁹ The meaning and value of their physical union is expressed in the words of consent, in which they accepted and offered themselves each to the other, in order to share their lives completely. Those words give meaning to the sexual relationship and free it from ambiguity. More generally, the common life of husband and wife, the entire network of relations that they build with their children and the world around them, will be steeped in and strengthened by the grace of the sacrament. For the sacrament of marriage flows from the incarnation and the paschal mystery, whereby God showed the fullness of his love for humanity by becoming one with us. Neither of the spouses will be alone in facing whatever challenges may come their way. Both are called to respond to God's gift with commitment, creativity, perseverance and daily effort. They can always invoke the assistance of the Holy Spirit who consecrated their union, so that his grace may be felt in every new situation that they encounter.

75. In the Church's Latin tradition, the ministers of the sacrament of marriage are the man and the woman who marry;¹⁰ by manifesting their consent and expressing it physically, they receive a great gift. Their consent and their bodily union are the divinely appointed means whereby they become "one flesh." By their baptismal consecration, they were enabled to join in marriage as the Lord's ministers and thus to respond to God's call. Hence, when two non-Christian spouses receive baptism, they need not renew their marriage vows; they need simply not reject them, since by the reception of baptism their union automatically becomes sacramental. Canon Law also recognizes the validity of certain unions celebrated without the presence of an ordained minister.¹¹ The natural order has been so imbued with the redemptive grace of Jesus that "a valid matrimonial contract cannot exist between the baptized without it being by that fact a sacrament."¹² The Church can require that the wedding be celebrated publicly, with the presence of witnesses and other conditions that have varied over the course of time, but this does not detract from the fact that the couple who marry are the ministers of the sacrament. Nor does it affect the centrality of the consent given by the man and the woman, which of itself establishes the sacramental bond. This having been said, there is a need for further reflection on God's action in the marriage rite; this is clearly manifested in the Oriental Churches through the importance of the blessing that the couple receive as a sign of the gift of the Spirit.

DISCUSSION QUESTIONS

1. In what ways does the reading focus on love in the family, and why? Can you think of ways your own understanding of love comes from your family?

2. How do romantic love, familial love, and the love of God relate to each other?

3. We often speak of "unconditional love." But it seems very difficult to love each other unconditionally. How does the reading help us to understand what might be meant by unconditional love?

4. Dostoevsky wrote that "to love someone is to see them as God intended them." Use the reading to explain this idea to a friend.

NOTES

1. *Homily at the Eucharistic Celebration in Puebla de los Ángeles* (28 January 1979), 2: AAS 71 (1979), 184.
2. Cf. *ibid.*

3. *Relatio Finalis* 2015, 38.

4. John Paul II, Apostolic Exhortation *Familiaris Consortio* (22 November 1981), 13: AAS 74 (1982), 94.

5. *Relatio Synodi* 2014, 21.

6. Catechism of the Catholic Church, 1642.

7. *Ibid.*

8. Catechesis (6 May 2015): *L'Osservatore Romano*, 7 May 2015, p. 8.

9. Leo the Great, *Epistula Rustico Narbonensi Episcopo*, Inquis. IV: PL 54, 1205A; cf. Hincmar of Rheims, *Epist.* 22: PL 126, 142.

10. Cf. Pius XII, Encyclical Letter *Mystici Corporis Christi* (29 June 1943): AAS 35 (1943), 202: "*Matrimonio enim quo coniuges sibi invicem sunt ministri gratiae . . .* "

11. Cf. Code of Canon Law, cc. 1116; 1161–1165; Code of Canons of the Eastern Churches, 832; 848–852.

12. *Ibid.*, c. 1055 §2.

Marriage and Love

BY EMMA GOLDMAN

Emma Goldman (1869–1940) was an influential activist and writer who played a pivotal role in the development of anarchist political philosophy. In this essay, Goldman argues on anarchist and feminist grounds that the institution of marriage amounts to nothing more than an "insurance pact"—one whose returns on investment are bad for both men and women, but particularly stifling and demeaning for women.

The popular notion about marriage and love is that they are synonymous, that they spring from the same motives, and cover the same human needs. Like most popular notions this also rests not on actual facts, but on superstition.

Marriage and love have nothing in common; they are as far apart as the poles; are, in fact, antagonistic to each other. No doubt some marriages have been the result of love. Not, however, because love could assert itself only in marriage; much rather is it because few people can completely outgrow a convention. There are today large numbers of men and women to whom marriage is naught but a farce, but who submit to it for the sake of public opinion. At any rate, while it is true that some marriages are based on love, and while it is equally true that in some cases love continues in married life, I maintain that it does so regardless of marriage, and not because of it.

On the other hand, it is utterly false that love results from marriage. On rare occasions one does hear of a miraculous case of a married couple falling in love after marriage, but on close examination it will be found that it is a mere adjustment to the inevitable. Certainly the growing-used to each other is far away from the spontaneity, the intensity, and beauty of love, without which the intimacy of marriage must prove degrading to both the woman and the man.

Marriage is primarily an economic arrangement, an insurance pact. It differs from the ordinary life insurance agreement only in that it is more binding, more exacting. Its returns are insignificantly small compared with the investments. In taking out an insurance policy one pays for it in dollars and cents, always at liberty to discontinue payments. If, however, woman's premium is a husband, she pays for it with her name, her privacy, her self-respect, her very life, "until death doth part." Moreover, the marriage insurance condemns her to life-long dependency, to parasitism, to complete uselessness, individual as well as social. Man, too, pays his toll, but as his sphere is wider, marriage does not limit him as much as woman. He feels his chains more in an economic sense.

Thus Dante's motto over Inferno applies with equal force to marriage. "Ye who enter here leave all hope behind."

That marriage is a failure none but the very stupid will deny. One has but to glance over the statistics of divorce to realize how bitter a failure marriage really is. Nor will the stereotyped Philistine argument that the laxity of divorce laws and the growing looseness of woman account for the fact that: first, every twelfth marriage ends in divorce; second, that since 1870 divorces have increased from 28 to 73 for every hundred thousand population; third, that adultery, since 1867, as ground for divorce, has increased 270.8 per cent; fourth, that desertion increased 369.8 per cent.

Edward Carpenter says that behind every marriage stands the life-long environment of the two sexes; an environment so different from each other that man and woman must remain strangers. Separated by an insurmountable wall of superstition, custom, and habit, marriage has not the potentiality of developing knowledge of, and respect for, each other, without which every union is doomed to failure.

Henrik Ibsen, the hater of all social shams, was probably the first to realize this great truth. Nora leaves her husband, not—as the stupid critic would have it—because she is tired of her responsibilities or feels the need of woman's rights, but because she has come to know that for eight years she had lived with a stranger and borne him children. Can there be anything more humiliating, more degrading than a life-long proximity between two strangers? No need for the woman to know anything of the man, save his income. As to the knowledge of the woman—what is there to know except that she has a pleasing appearance? We have not yet outgrown the theologic myth that woman has no soul, that she is a mere appendix to man, made out of his rib just for the convenience of the gentleman who was so strong that he was afraid of his own shadow.

Perchance the poor quality of the material whence woman comes is responsible for her inferiority. At any rate, woman has no soul—what is there to know about her? Besides, the less soul a woman has the greater her asset as a wife, the more readily will she absorb herself in her husband. It is this slavish acquiescence to man's superiority that has kept the marriage institution seemingly intact for so long a period. Now that woman is coming into her own, now that she is actually growing aware of herself as a being outside of the master's grace, the sacred institution of marriage is gradually being undermined, and no amount of sentimental lamentation can stay it.

From infancy, almost, the average girl is told that marriage is her ultimate goal; therefore her training and education must be directed towards that end. Like the mute beast fattened for slaughter, she is prepared for that. Yet, strange to say, she

is allowed to know much less about her function as wife and mother than the ordinary artisan of his trade. It is indecent and filthy for a respectable girl to know anything of the marital relation. Oh, for the inconsistency of respectability, that needs the marriage vow to turn something which is filthy into the purest and most sacred arrangement that none dare question or criticize. Yet that is exactly the attitude of the average upholder of marriage. The prospective wife and mother is kept in complete ignorance of her only asset in the competitive field—sex. Thus she enters into life-long relations with a man only to find herself shocked, repelled, outraged beyond measure by the most natural and healthy instinct, sex. It is safe to say that a large percentage of the unhappiness, misery, distress, and physical suffering of matrimony is due to the criminal ignorance in sex matters that is being extolled as a great virtue. Nor is it at all an exaggeration when I say that more than one home has been broken up because of this deplorable fact.

If, however, woman is free and big enough to learn the mystery of sex without the sanction of State or Church, she will stand condemned as utterly unfit to become the wife of a "good" man, his goodness consisting of an empty brain and plenty of money. Can there be anything more outrageous than the idea that a healthy, grown woman, full of life and passion, must deny nature's demand, must subdue her most intense craving, undermine her health and break her spirit, must stunt her vision, abstain from the depth and glory of sex experience until a "good" man comes along to take her unto himself as a wife? That is precisely what marriage means. How can such an arrangement end except in failure? This is one, though not the least important, factor of marriage, which differentiates it from love.

Ours is a practical age. The time when Romeo and Juliet risked the wrath of their fathers for love, when Gretchen exposed herself to the gossip of her neighbors for love, is no more. If, on rare occasions, young people allow themselves the luxury of romance, they are taken in care by the elders, drilled and pounded until they become "sensible."

The moral lesson instilled in the girl is not whether the man has aroused her love, but rather is it, "How much?" The important and only God of practical American life: Can the man make a living? can he support a wife? That is the only thing that justifies marriage. Gradually this saturates every thought of the girl; her dreams are not of moonlight and kisses, of laughter and tears; she dreams of shopping tours and bargain counters. This soul poverty and sordidness are the elements inherent in the marriage institution. The State and the Church approve of no other ideal, simply because it is the one that necessitates the State and Church control of men and women.

Doubtless there are people who continue to consider love above dollars and cents. Particularly is this true of that class whom economic necessity has forced to become self-supporting. The tremendous change in woman's position, wrought by that mighty factor, is indeed phenomenal when we reflect that it is but a short time since she has entered the industrial arena. Six million women wage workers; six million women, who have the equal right with men to be exploited, to be robbed, to go on strike; aye, to starve even. Anything more, my lord? Yes, six million wage workers in every walk of life, from the highest brain work to the mines and railroad tracks; yes, even detectives and policemen. Surely the emancipation is complete.

Yet with all that, but a very small number of the vast army of women wage workers look upon work as a permanent issue, in the same light as does man. No matter how decrepit the latter, he has been taught to be independent, self-supporting. Oh, I know that no one is really independent in our economic treadmill; still, the poorest specimen of a man hates to be a parasite; to be known as such, at any rate.

The woman considers her position as worker transitory, to be thrown aside for the first bidder. That is why it is infinitely harder to organize women than men. "Why should I join a union? I am going to get married, to have a home." Has she not been taught from infancy to look upon that as her ultimate calling? She learns soon enough that the home, though not so large a prison as the factory, has more solid doors and bars. It has a keeper so faithful that naught can escape him. The most tragic part, however, is that the home

no longer frees her from wage slavery; it only increases her task.

According to the latest statistics submitted before a Committee "on labor and wages, and congestion of population," ten per cent, of the wage workers in New York City alone are married, yet they must continue to work at the most poorly paid labor in the world. Add to this horrible aspect the drudgery of housework, and what remains of the protection and glory of the home? As a matter of fact, even the middle-class girl in marriage can not speak of her home, since it is the man who creates her sphere. It is not important whether the husband is a brute or a darling. What I wish to prove is that marriage guarantees woman a home only by the grace of her husband. There she moves about in *his* home, year after year, until her aspect of life and human affairs becomes as flat, narrow, and drab as her surroundings. Small wonder if she becomes a nag, petty, quarrelsome, gossipy, unbearable, thus driving the man from the house. She could not go, if she wanted to; there is no place to go. Besides, a short period of married life, of complete surrender of all faculties, absolutely incapacitates the average woman for the outside world. She becomes reckless in appearance, clumsy in her movements, dependent in her decisions, cowardly in her judgment, a weight and a bore, which most men grow to hate and despise. Wonderfully inspiring atmosphere for the bearing of life, is it not?

But the child, how is it to be protected, if not for marriage? After all, is not that the most important consideration? The sham, the hypocrisy of it! Marriage protecting the child, yet thousands of children destitute and homeless. Marriage protecting the child, yet orphan asylums and reformatories overcrowded, the Society for the Prevention of Cruelty to Children keeping busy in rescuing the little victims from "loving" parents, to place them under more loving care, the Gerry Society. Oh, the mockery of it!

Marriage may have the power to bring the horse to water, but has it ever made him drink? The law will place the father under arrest, and put him in convict's clothes; but has that ever stilled the hunger of the child? If the parent has no work, or if he hides his identity, what does marriage do then? It invokes the law to bring the man to "justice," to put him safely behind closed doors; his labor, however, goes not to the child, but to the State. The child receives but a blighted memory of its father's stripes.

As to the protection of the woman,—therein lies the curse of marriage. Not that it really protects her, but the very idea is so revolting, such an outrage and insult on life, so degrading to human dignity, as to forever condemn this parasitic institution.

It is like that other paternal arrangement—capitalism. It robs man of his birthright, stunts his growth, poisons his body, keeps him in ignorance, in poverty, and dependence, and then institutes charities that thrive on the last vestige of man's self-respect.

The institution of marriage makes a parasite of woman, an absolute dependent. It incapacitates her for life's struggle, annihilates her social consciousness, paralyzes her imagination, and then imposes its gracious protection, which is in reality a snare, a travesty on human character.

If motherhood is the highest fulfillment of woman's nature, what other protection does it need, save love and freedom? Marriage but defiles, outrages, and corrupts her fulfillment. Does it not say to woman, Only when you follow me shall you bring forth life? Does it not condemn her to the block, does it not degrade and shame her if she refuses to buy her right to motherhood by selling herself? Does not marriage only sanction motherhood, even though conceived in hatred, in compulsion? Yet, if motherhood be of free choice, of love, of ecstasy, of defiant passion, does it not place a crown of thorns upon an innocent head and carve in letters of blood the hideous epithet, Bastard? Were marriage to contain all the virtues claimed for it, its crimes against motherhood would exclude it forever from the realm of love.

Love, the strongest and deepest element in all life, the harbinger of hope, of joy, of ecstasy; love, the defier of all laws, of all conventions; love, the freest, the most powerful moulder of human destiny; how can such an all-compelling force be synonymous with that poor little State and Church-begotten weed, marriage?

Free love? As if love is anything but free! Man has bought brains, but all the millions in the world have failed to buy love. Man has subdued bodies, but all the power on earth has been unable to subdue love. Man has conquered whole nations, but all his armies could not conquer love. Man has chained and fettered the spirit, but he has been utterly helpless before love. High on a throne, with all the splendor and pomp his gold can command, man is yet poor and desolate, if love passes him by. And if it stays, the poorest hovel is radiant with warmth, with life and color. Thus love has the magic power to make of a beggar a king. Yes, love is free; it can dwell in no other atmosphere. In freedom it gives itself unreservedly, abundantly, completely. All the laws on the statutes, all the courts in the universe, cannot tear it from the soil, once love has taken root. If, however, the soil is sterile, how can marriage make it bear fruit? It is like the last desperate struggle of fleeting life against death.

Love needs no protection; it is its own protection. So long as love begets life no child is deserted, or hungry, or famished for the want of affection. I know this to be true. I know women who became mothers in freedom by the men they loved. Few children in wedlock enjoy the care, the protection, the devotion free motherhood is capable of bestowing.

The defenders of authority dread the advent of a free motherhood, lest it will rob them of their prey. Who would fight wars? Who would create wealth? Who would make the policeman, the jailer, if woman were to refuse the indiscriminate breeding of children? The race, the race! shouts the king, the president, the capitalist, the priest. The race must be preserved, though woman be degraded to a mere machine,—and the marriage institution is our only safety valve against the pernicious sex awakening of woman. But in vain these frantic efforts to maintain a state of bondage. In vain, too, the edicts of the Church, the mad attacks of rulers, in vain even the arm of the law. Woman no longer wants to be a party to the production of a race of sickly, feeble, decrepit, wretched human beings, who have neither the strength nor moral courage to throw off the yoke of poverty and slavery. Instead she desires fewer and better children, begotten and reared in love and through free choice; not by compulsion, as marriage imposes. Our pseudo-moralists have yet to learn the deep sense of responsibility toward the child, that love in freedom has awakened in the breast of woman. Rather would she forego forever the glory of motherhood than bring forth life in an atmosphere that breathes only destruction and death. And if she does become a mother, it is to give to the child the deepest and best her being can yield. To grow with the child is her motto; she knows that in that manner alone can she help build true manhood and womanhood.

In our present pygmy state love is indeed a stranger to most people. Misunderstood and shunned, it rarely takes root; or if it does, it soon withers and dies. Its delicate fiber can not endure the stress and strain of the daily grind. Its soul is too complex to adjust itself to the slimy woof of our social fabric. It weeps and moans and suffers with those who have need of it, yet lack the capacity to rise to love's summit.

Some day, some day men and women will rise, they will reach the mountain peak, they will meet big and strong and free, ready to receive, to partake, and to bask in the golden rays of love. What fancy, what imagination, what poetic genius can foresee even approximately the potentialities of such a force in the life of men and women. If the world is ever to give birth to true companionship and oneness, not marriage, but love will be the parent.

DISCUSSION QUESTIONS

1. Explain how Goldman thinks marriage is like an insurance pact. What are the terms of this arrangement for both women and men, and why does Goldman think both parties get a bad deal?

2. How do gender norms that restrict women's social respectability doom most marriages to failure, according to Goldman?

3. What is the connection between marriage and capitalism, according to Goldman?

4. Discuss whether, and in what ways, our culture's attitudes toward marriage and love have changed since Goldman wrote this essay in 1910. Do you think she would be pleased with these changes?

Marital Slavery and Friendship: John Stuart Mill's *The Subjection of Women*

BY MARY LYNDON SHANLEY

Mary Lyndon Shanley is a feminist legal scholar specializing in issues of the American family and reproductive technologies. Shanley argues here that J. S. Mill's influential book was intended to defend not only the importance of equal opportunity between men and women in the public sphere, but also in the private sphere. Mill, Shanley insists, was arguing for marital friendship.

The Subjection of Women challenged much more than Victorian decorum, however; it was a radical challenge to one of the most fundamental and preciously held assumptions about marriage in the modern era, which is that it was a relationship grounded on the consent of the partners to join their lives. Mill argued to the contrary that the presumed consent of women to marry was not, in any real sense, a free promise, but one socially coerced by the lack of meaningful options. Further, the laws of marriage deprived a woman of many of the normal powers of autonomous adults, from controlling her earnings, to entering contracts, to defending her bodily autonomy by resisting unwanted sexual relations. Indeed, the whole notion of a woman "consenting" to the marriage "offer" of a man implied from the outset a hierarchical relationship. Such a one-way offer did not reflect the relationship which should exist between those who were truly equal, among beings who should be able to create together by free discussion and mutual agreement an association to govern their lives together.

In addition, Mill's view of marriage as slavery suggested a significantly more complicated and skeptical view of what constituted a "free choice" in society than did either his own earlier works or those of his liberal predecessors. Hobbes, for example, regarded men as acting "freely" even when moved by fear for their lives. Locke disagreed, but he in turn talked about the individual's free choice to remain a citizen of his father's country, as if emigration were a readily available option for all. In other of his works Mill himself seemed overly sanguine about the amount of real choice enjoyed, for example, by wage laborers in entering a trade. Yet Mill's analysis of marriage demonstrated the great complexity of establishing that any presumed agreement was the result of free volition, and the fatuousness of presuming that initial consent could create perpetual obligation. By implication, the legitimacy of many other relationships, including supposedly free wage and labor agreements and the political obligation of enfranchised and unenfranchised alike, was thrown into question. *The Subjection of Women* exposed the inherent fragility of traditional conceptualizations of free choice, autonomy, and self-determination so important to liberals, showing that economic and social structures were bound to limit and might coerce any person's choice of companions, employment, or citizenship.

Mill did not despair of the possibility that marriages based on true consent would be possible. He believed that some individuals even in his own day established such associations of reciprocity and mutual support. (He counted his own relationship with Harriet Taylor Mill as an example of a marriage between equals.)[1] But there were systemic impediments to marital equality. To create conditions conducive to a marriage of equals rather than one of master and slave, marriage law itself would have to be altered, women would have to be provided equal educational and employment opportunity, and both men and women would have to become capable of sustaining genuinely equal and reciprocal relationships within marriage. The last of these, in Mill's eyes, posed the greatest challenge.

The Fear of Equality

Establishing legal equality in marriage and equality of opportunity would require, said Mill, that men sacrifice those political, legal, and economic advantages they enjoyed "simply by being born male." Mill therefore supported such measures as women's suffrage, the Married Women's Property Bills, the Divorce Act of 1857, the repeal of the Contagious Diseases Acts, and the opening of higher education and the professions to women. Suffrage, Mill contended, would both develop women's faculties through participation in civic decisions and enable married women to protect themselves from male-imposed injustices such as lack of rights to child custody and to control of their income. Access to education and jobs would give women alternatives to marriage. It would also provide a woman whose marriage turned out badly some means of self-support if separated or divorced. The Divorce Act of 1857, which established England's first civil divorce courts, would enable women and men to escape from intolerable circumstances (although Mill rightly protested the sexual double standard ensconced in the Act).[2] And for those few women with an income of their own, a Married Women's Property Act would recognize their independent personalities and enable them to meet their husbands more nearly as equals.

However, Mill's analysis went further. He insisted that the subjection of women could not be ended by law alone, but only by law and the reformation of education, of opinion, of social inculcation, of habits, and finally of the conduct of family life itself. This was so because the root of much of men's resistance to women's emancipation was not

simply their reluctance to give up their position of material advantage, but many men's fear of living with an equal. It was to retain marriage as "a law of despotism" that men shut all other occupations to women, Mill contended (1: 156). Men who "have a real antipathy to the equal freedom of women" were at bottom afraid "lest [women] should insist that marriage be on equal conditions" (1: 156). One of Mill's startling assertions in *The Subjection of Women* was that "[women's] disabilities [in law] are only clung to in order to maintain their subordination in domestic life: *because the generality of the male sex cannot yet tolerate the idea of living with an equal*" (3: 181; italics added). The public discrimination against women was a manifestation of a disorder rooted in family relationships. The progression of humankind could not take place until the dynamics of the master-slave relationship were eliminated from marriages, and until the family was instead founded on spousal equality.

Mill did not offer any single explanation or account of the origin of men's fear of female equality. Elsewhere, he attributed the general human resistance to equality to the fear of the loss of privilege, and to apprehensions concerning the effect of leveling on political order.[3] But these passages on the fear of spousal equality bring to a twentieth-century mind the psychoanalytic works about human neuroses and the male fear of women caused by the infant boy's relationship to the seemingly all-powerful mother, source of both nurturance and love and of deprivation and punishment.[4] But it is impossible to push Mill's text far in this direction. His account of the fear of equality was not psychoanalytic. He did, however, undertake to depict the consequences of marital inequality both for the individual psyche and for social justice. The rhetorical purpose of *The Subjection of Women* was not only to convice men that their treatment of women in law was unjust, but also that their treatment of women in the home was self-defeating, even self-destructive.

Women were those most obviously affected by the denial of association with men on equal footing. Women's confinement to domestic concerns was a wrongful "forced repression" (1: 148). Mill shared Aristotle's view that participation in civic life was an enriching and ennobling activity, but Mill saw that for a woman, no public-spirited dimension to her life was possible. There was no impetus to consider with others the principles which were to govern their common life, no incentive to conform to principles which defined their mutual activity for the common good, no possibility for the self-development which comes from citizen activity.[5] The cost to women was obvious; they were dull, or petty, or unprincipled (2: 168; 4: 238). The cost to men was less apparent but no less real; in seeking a reflection of themselves in the consciousness of these stunted women, men deceived, deluded, and limited themselves.

Mill was convinced that men were corrupted by their dominance over women. The most corrupting element of male domination of women was that men learned to "worship their own will as such a grand thing that it is actually the law for another rational being" (2: 172). Such self-worship arises at a very tender age, and blots out a boy's natural understanding of himself and his relationship to others.

A boy may be "the most frivolous and empty or the most ignorant and stolid of mankind," but "by the mere fact of being born a male" he is encouraged to think that "he is by right the superior of all and every one of an entire half of the human race: including probably some whose real superiority he had daily or hourly occasion to feel" (4: 218). By contrast, women were taught "to live for others" and "to have no life but in then-affections," and then further to confine their affections to "the men with whom they are connected, or to the children who constitute an additional indefeasible tie between them and a man" (1: 141). The result of this upbringing was that what women would tell men was not, could not be, wholly true; women's sensibilities were systematically warped by their subjection. Thus the reflections were not accurate and men were deprived of self-knowledge.

The picture which emerged was strikingly similar to that which Hegel described in his passages on the relationship between master and slave in *The Phenomenology of Mind*.[6] The lord who sees himself solely as master, wrote Hegel, cannot obtain an independent self-consciousness.

The master thinks he is autonomous, but in fact he relies totally upon his slaves, not only to fulfill his needs and desires, but also for his identity: "Without slaves, he is no master." The master could not acquire the fullest self-consciousness when the "other" in whom he viewed himself was in the reduced human condition of slavery: to be *merely* a master was to fall short of full self-consciousness, and to define himself in terms of the "thing" he owns. So for Mill, men who have propagated the belief that all men are superior to all women have fatally affected the dialectic involved in knowing oneself through the consciousness others have of one. The present relationship between the sexes produced in men that "self-worship" which "all privileged persons, and all privileged classes" have had. That distortion deceives men and other privileged groups as to both their character and their self-worth.[7]

No philosopher prior to Mill had developed such a sustained argument about the corrupting effects on men of their social superiority over and separation from women. Previous philosophers had argued either that the authority of men over women was natural (Aristotle, Grotius), or that while there was no natural dominance of men over women prior to the establishment of families, in any civil society such preeminence was necessary to settle the dispute over who should govern the household (Locke), or the result of women's consent in return for protection (Hobbes), or the consequence of the development of the sentiments of nurturance and love (Rousseau).[8] None had suggested that domestic arrangements might diminish a man's ability to contribute to public debates in the agora or to the rational governing of a democratic republic. Yet Mill was determined to show that the development of the species was held in check by that domestic slavery produced by the fear of equality, by spousal hierarchy, and by a lack of the reciprocity and mutuality of true friendship.

III. The Hope of Friendship

Mill's remedy for the evils generated by the fear of equality was his notion of marital friendship. The topic of the rather visionary fourth chapter of *The*

Subjection of Women was friendship, "the ideal of marriage" (4: 233, 235). That ideal was, according to Mill, "a union of thoughts and inclinations" which created a "foundation of solid friendship" between husband and wife (4: 231, 233).

Mill's praise of marital friendship was almost lyrical, and struck resonances with Aristotle's, Cicero's, and Montaigne's similar exaltations of the pleasures as well as the moral enrichment of this form of human intimacy. Mill wrote:

> When each of two persons, instead of being a nothing, is a something; when they are attached to one another, and are not too much unlike to begin with; the constant partaking of the same things, assisted by their sympathy, draws out the latent capacities of each for being interested in the things . . . by a real enriching of the two natures, each acquiring the tastes and capacities of the other in addition to its own [4: 233].

This expansion of human capacities did not, however, exhaust the benefits of friendship. Most importantly, friendship developed what Montaigne praised as the abolition of selfishness, the capacity to regard another human being as fully as worthy as oneself. Therefore friendship of the highest order could only exist between those equal in excellence.[9] And for precisely this reason, philosophers from Aristotle to Hegel had consistently argued that women could not be men's friends, for women lacked the moral capacity for the highest forms of friendship. Indeed, it was common to distinguish the marital bond from friendship not solely on the basis of sexual and procreative activity, but also because women could not be part of the school of moral virtue which was found in friendship at its best.

Mill therefore made a most significant break with the past in adopting the language of friendship in his discussion of marriage. For Mill, no less than for any of his predecessors, "the true virtue of human beings is the fitness to live together as equals." Such equality required that individuals "[claim] nothing for themselves but what they as freely concede to every one else," that they regard command of any kind as "an exceptional necessity,"

and that they prefer whenever possible "the society of those with whom leading and following can be alternate and reciprocal" (4: 174–175). This picture of reciprocity, of the shifting of leadership according to need, was a remarkable characterization of family life. Virtually all of Mill's liberal contemporaries accepted the notion of the natural and inevitable complimentariness of male and female personalities and roles. Mill, however, as early as 1833 had expressed his belief that "the highest masculine and the highest feminine" characters were without any real distinction.[10] That view of the androgynous personality lent support to Mill's brief for equality within the family.

Mill repeatedly insisted that his society had no general experience of "the marriage relationship as it would exist between equals," and that such marriages would be impossible until men rid themselves of the fear of equality and the will to domination.[11] The liberation of women, in other words, required not just legal reform but a reeducation of the passions. Women were to be regarded as equals not only to fulfill the demand for individual rights and in order that they could survive in the public world of work, but also in order that women and men could form ethical relations of the highest order. Men and women alike had to "learn to cultivate their strongest sympathy with an equal in rights and in cultivation" (4: 236). Mill struggled, not always with total success, to talk about the quality of such association. For example, in *On Liberty*, Mill explicitly rejected von Humbolt's characterization of marriage as a contractual relationship which could be ended by "the declared will of either party to dissolve it." That kind of dissolution was appropriate when the benefits of partnership could be reduced to monetary terms. But marriage involved a person's expectations for the fulfillment of a "plan of life," and created "a new series of moral obligations . . . toward that person, which may possibly be overruled, but cannot be ignored."[12] Mill was convinced that difficult though it might be to shape the law to recognize the moral imperatives of such a relationship, there were ethical communities which transcended and were not reducible to their individual components.

At this juncture, however, the critical force of Mill's essay weakened, and a tension developed between his ideal and his prescriptions for his own society. For all his insight into the dynamics of domestic domination and subordination, the only specific means Mill in fact put forward for the fostering of this society of equals was providing equal opportunity to women in areas outside the family. Indeed, in *On Liberty* he wrote that "nothing more is needed for the complete removal of [the almost despotic power of husbands over wives] than that wives should have the same rights and should receive the same protection of law in the same manner, as all other persons."[13] In the same vein, Mill seemed to suggest that nothing more was needed for women to achieve equality than that "the present duties and protective bounties in favour of men should be recalled" (1: 154). Moreover, Mill did not attack the traditional assumption about men's and women's different responsibilities in an on-going household, although he was usually careful to say that women "chose" their role or that it was the most "expedient" arrangement, not that it was theirs by "nature."

Mill by and large accepted the notion that once they marry, women should be solely responsible for the care of the household and children, men for providing the family income: "When the support of the family depends ... on earnings, the common arrangement, by which the man earns the income and the wife superintends the domestic expenditure, seems to me in general the most suitable division of labour between the two persons" (2: 178). He did not regard it as "a desirable custom, that the wife should contribute by her labour to the income of the family" (2: 179). Mill indicated that women alone would care for any children of the marriage; repeatedly he called it the "care which ... nobody else takes," the one vocation in which there is "nobody to compete with them," and the occupation which "cannot be fulfilled by others" (2: 178; 3: 183; 4: 241).

DISCUSSION QUESTIONS

1. Is male-female equality necessary for marital friendship? Give the argument. Also give examples from your own observation of marriage.

2. How might friendship in marriage contribute to the moral progression of society?

3. What is marital slavery? Does it still exist in our society? In other societies around the world? Discuss.

NOTES

1. On the relationship between John Stuart Mill and Harriety Taylor see F. A. Hayek, *John Stuart Mill and Harriet Taylor: Their correspondence and subsequent marriage* (Chicago: University of Chicago Press, 1951); Michael St. John Packe, *The Life of John Stuart Mill* (New York: Macmilllan, 1954); Alice Rossi, "Sentiment and Intellect" in *Essays on Sex Equality* (Chicago: University of Chicago Press, 1970); and Gertrude Himmelfarb, pp. 187–238.

2. The Matrimonial Causes Act of 1857, as the divorce measure was known, allowed men to divorce their wives for adultery, but women had to establish that their husbands were guilty of either cruelty or desertion in addition to adultery in order to obtain a separation. Mill was reluctant to say what he thought the terms of divorce should be in a rightly ordered society (see note 31), but he was adamant that the double standard was wrong in policy and unjust in principle. Mill also spoke out sharply against that sexual double standard in his testimony before the Commission studying the repeal of the Contagious Diseases Act, an act which allowed for the arrest and forced hospitalization of prostitutes with venereal disease, but made no provision for the arrest of their clients. "The Evidence of John Stuart Mill taken before the Royal Commission of 1870 on the Administration and Operation of the Contagious Diseases Acts of 1866 and 1869" (London, 1871).

3. For a discussion of Mill's views on equality generally, see Dennis Thompson, *John Stuart Mill and Representative Government* (Princeton: Princeton University Press, 1976), pp. 158–173.

4. See, for example, Dorothy Dinnerstein, *The Mermaid and the Minotaur: Sexual Arrangements and Human Malaise* (New York: Harper and Row, 1976); Nancy Chodorow, *The Reproduction of Mothering: Psychoanalysis and the Sociology of Gender* (Berkeley: University of California Press, 1978); and Philip Slater, *The Glory of Hera* (Boston: Beacon Press, 1971) and the references therein.

5. See also Mill's *Considerations on Representative Government* (1861) where he lambasted benevolent despotism because it encouraged "passivity" and "abdication of [one's] own energies" and his praise of Athenian dicastry and ecclesia. *C.W.*, XIX, pp. 399–400, 411. During his speech on the Reform Bill of 1867, Mill argued that giving women the vote would provide "that stimulus to their faculties . . . which the suffrage seldom fails to produce." Hansard v. 189 (May 20, 1867), 824.

6. G. W. F. Hegel, *The Phenomenology of Mind*, trans J. B. Baillie (New York: Harper and Row, 1969). This paragraph is indebted to the excellent study of the *Phenomenology* by Judith N. Shklar, *Freedom and Independence* (Cambridge: Cambridge University Press, 1976), from which the quote is taken, p. 61. Mill's analysis also calls to mind Simone de Beauvoir's discussion of "the Other" and its role in human consciousness: in *The Second Sex*, trans H. M. Parshley (New York: Random House, Vintage Books, 1974), pp. xix ff.

7. Mill argued in addition that men's injustices to women created habits which encouraged them to act unjustly towards others. In *The Subjection of Women* Mill asserted that the habits of domination are acquired in and fostered by the family, which is often, as respects its chief, "a school of wilfulness, overbearingness, unbounded self-indulgence, and a double-dyed and idealized selfishness" (2: 165). Virtue, for Mill, was not simply action taken in accordance with a calculus of pleasure and pain, but was habitual behavior. In *Consideration on Representative Government*, he lamented the effects "fostered by the possession of power" by "a man, or a class of men" who "finding themselves worshipped by others . . . become worshippers of themselves." *C.W.*, XIX, p. 445.

8. For excellent studies of each of these authors views on women (except for Grotius) see Okin. Grotius' views can be found in his *De Juri Belli ac Pacis Libri Tres* [*On the Law of War and Peace.*] (1625), trans. Francis W. Kelsey (Oxford: Clarendon Press, 1925), Bk. II, ch. V, sec. i, p. 231.

9. Montaigne's essay, "Of Friendship" in *The Complete Works of Montaigne*, trans. Donald M. Frame (Stanford: Stanford University Press, 1948), pp. 135–144.

10. Letter to Thomas Carlyle, October 5, 1833, *C.W.*, XII, *Earlier Letters*, p. 184.

11. Letter to John Nichol, August 1869, *C.W.*, XVII, *The Later Letters*, ed. Francis C. Mineka and Dwight N. Lindley (Toronto: University of Toronto Press, 1972), p. 1634.

12. *C.W.*, XVIII, 300. Elsewhere Mill wrote, "My opinion on Divorce is that . . . nothing ought to be rested in, short of entire freedom on both sides to dissolve this like any other partnership." Letter to an unidentified correspondent, November 1855, *C.W.* XIV, *Later Letters*, p. 500. But against this letter was the passage from *On Liberty*, and his letter to Henry Rusden of July 1870 in which he abjured making any final judgements about what a proper divorce law would be "until women have an equal voice in making it." He denied that he advocated that marriage should be dissoluable "at the will of either party," and stated that no well-grounded opinion could be put forward until women first achieved equality under the laws and in married life. *C.W.*, XVII, *Later Letters*, pp. 1750–1751.

13. *C.W.*, XVIII, p. 301.

Why Lovers Can't Be Friends

BY JAMES CONLON

James Conlon is a professor of philosophy at Mount Mary University in Milwaukee. In this essay, Conlon uses Plato's work to argue that romantic or erotic love and friendship are irreconcilable goods. On Conlon's controversial view, to say that your romantic partner is "your best friend" is nonsense—unless it means that the person you are speaking about is no longer genuinely your romantic partner.

That one's spouse is also one's closest friend is a common claim and seems innocent enough. Often it is offered as a gentle boast—for example, by a celebrity introducing a spouse at a formal gathering. Usually, its tone is that of achievement, as if being able to combine lover and friend is the epitome of human intimacy, as desirable as it is rare.

I found myself reacting to such claims with intense hostility. At first, I blamed my reactions on an unhealthy cynicism, perhaps even an unconscious resentment. However, as I explored the nature of my hostility more carefully, especially in conjunction with certain texts of Plato, I realized that it was intellectually grounded. It is not that the union of friend and lover is an ideal more difficult to achieve than facile introductions would have us believe. It is, rather, that the union is impossible; its desirability is founded on a mistaken model of human intimacy. Therefore, the claim to combine lover and friend is not just a harmless exaggeration, but a seriously misguided ideal. To show this, I must first make explicit the theory of human relationships that the claim assumes. Like most theories in Western thought, it has its roots in Plato.

On this theory, each human self is a discrete substance combining essential and unique qualities. All attraction between selves is a desire for union, for sharing these qualities, possessing them, taking part in them in some way. One can hierarchically order the various types of attraction between selves by the essential importance (reality) of the qualities shared. Thus, according to Plato's famous scala amoris in The Symposium, attraction to, and participation in, the beauties of an individual body are ranked lower than attraction to, and participation in, the beauties of an individual soul. Hence, lovers of souls "enjoy a far fuller community with each other . . . and enjoy a far surer friendship" (Plato, 1989, 209c).

Applying this basic approach to concrete contemporary categories of relationship yields the following analysis. Two colleagues in the same profession and institution have a certain closeness; they share each other's expertise, like working on specific projects together, and hope for similar goals. Suppose, as often happens, these colleagues become friends. Now, they no longer meet only on work-related tasks, but go to the movies together, have dinner at each other's houses and participate in activities associated with friendship. What has happened, according to the standard theory, is that the relationship has moved up a notch on the scale. It has become a fuller intimacy because more is shared, both in quantity and essential quality. If these friends subsequently become lovers, this change would be interpreted in the same manner: as an increase in their degree of intimacy.

This cumulative ascent is central to the appeal of Plato's model. For him, the lover who has climbed to the apex of love and "turned to the great sea of beauty" (ibid., 210d) has not really left anything of consequence behind. The beauty of "face or hands or anything else that belongs to the body" (ibid., 211a) is included as part of loving the form of Beauty itself. Nothing of real value is lost. It is not just that the vision of the Sun is superior to other visions, it includes them in itself. There is nothing to be loved in the shadows that is not present in the Sun. Its light subsumes and completes all other experience.

Plato's notion is, of course, carried over into Christianity. Everything said of Plato's vision of the Beautiful could equally be said of Dante Alighieri's vision of God at the climax of the *Divine Comedy*. Vergil and Beatrice are subsumed in God. Nothing would be lost in choosing God over these lesser intimacies.

In summary then, the standard model of intimacy views the differences between friend, lover and colleague as basically differences of degree. Each form of intimacy represents a level of quality sharing which can be placed somewhere along a continuum, with minimal sharing at one end and total sharing at the other.

My criticism of this model centers on the fact that it does not present an accurate account of what happens when relationships change form. Even when the change is positive, it is not simply additive. There is an inevitable deprivation as well.

There is a revealing scene in Robertson Davies' novel of academe, *Rebel Angels*. In it, Simon Darcourt, an Anglican parson and Greek scholar, asks a treasured graduate student, Maria, to marry him. She has already had an affair with another mentor and it is out of its failure that she responds to Simon:

> I love him [the mentor] the way I love you— for the splendid thing that you are, in your own world of splendid things. Like a fool I wanted him in the way you are talking about, and whether it was because I wanted him or he wanted me I don't know and

never shall know, but it was a very great mistake. Because of that stupidity, which didn't amount to a damn as an experience, I think I have put something between us that has almost lost him to me. Do you think I want to do that with you? Are all men such greedy fools that they think love only comes with that special favor? . . . Simon, you called me Sophia: the Divine Wisdom, God's partner and playmate in Creation. . . . [I]f we go to bed it will be Sophia who lies down but it will certainly be Maria—and not the best of her who gets up, and Sophia will be gone forever. And you, Simon dear, would come into bed as my Rebel Angel, but very soon you would be a stoutish Anglican parson, and a Rebel Angel no more. (1981, p. 256)

Simon's proposal clearly comes out of the standard model we have been analyzing. In his mind, it seems only logical to move the teacher/student intimacy to a deeper level by adding romance. Maria, however, has been that route and experienced something the theory did not predict—loss. For her, romantic intimacy did not augment the old; instead, it destroyed it.

But, you will say, this destruction is peculiar to the change from student to lover and not true of relational changes in general. Surely, for example, it does not apply to the change from colleague to friend. There, it is a simple case of addition. Colleagues limit their discussions to professional concerns. If they become friends, they continue to have professional discussions, but include personal and emotional concerns as well. A simple case of addition!

But a closer analysis reveals that it is too simple. Even in this change something is definitely lost. A relationship that was once purely professional (and to read "purely" as "merely" here, begs the question) is so no longer. This is not to claim that the relationship now becomes shady or incompetent, but it does lose the intimacy that pure professionals have between each other and assumes another form.

Suppose, for example, two colleagues on a promotion and tenure committee meet privately to discuss a difficult applicant. They are not friends. Although they deeply admire each other's professional competence, their lives connect only through work. Thus, their conversation is "purely professional," that is, they focus primarily on the matter at hand and are unconcerned about each other's private selves. But make no mistake: there is significant intimacy here. As they dissect the pros and cons of the applicant, their own cherished ideals are an integral, if indirect, part of the discussion. Who they are as scholars, teachers and institutional members is shared with intensity unique to the action-focused work of "unconcerned" professionals.

Obviously, the kind of intimacy that comes with shared professional action could never exist with someone outside the profession—even with the closest of friends. Equally obvious, of course, is that a professional could share with a nonprofessional friend things she never could with a colleague. She might, for example, explore with a friend her own jealousies toward the applicant in a way impossible in professional discussion.

But could friends in the same profession combine both types of sharing? I do not see how. Friends would be continuously conscious of, and concerned about, personal factors extending far beyond the topic at hand. They could not put these on hold while they discussed professional matters. Thus, the joys and powers of purely professional conversation would be lost to them.

But if loss is inescapable whenever relationships change form, then the standard model of human intimacy is fundamentally mistaken. It differentiates relationships according to degree, according to what level they occupy on a continuum. The reality of loss suggests that relationships actually differ not in degree, but in kind. They are not steps on the way toward anything fuller; they are just what they are, modes of relation, each possessing distinct and—sometimes—incompatible strengths and weaknesses.

What does this mean for a model of intimacy? If the standard model has its roots in Plato, perhaps a counter-model would have its roots in Friedrich Nietzsche (arguably the first Western thinker to be truly non-Platonic). Nietzsche's critique of Plato's theory of knowledge, his perspectival alternative to it, provides equally effective possibilities in relation to Plato's theory of love.

On a Nietzschean model, each type of intimacy is a perspective on, creates an interpretation of, the sharing of selves. Since there are only interpretations, with no correct or complete sharing conceivable, the various types of intimacy do not accumulate toward a definitive beatific communion. Each interpretation has its distinctive mode of operation and its own individual value. In contrast to Plato, however, these values are not all commensurable. There exist some real and positive goods that are fundamentally incompatible with others.

An analogy can best illustrate the model I have in mind. Each type of relationship (friend, lover, colleague) is like a literary genre (poem, novel, play). Obviously, differences between genres do not represent steps toward a perfect and complete artistic expression (despite Georg Wilhelm Friedrich Hegel's efforts). Rather, they are just different ways of doing it. Although new ways may be created, they are not progressions toward a perfect way. To describe the poem as "fuller" or "deeper" than the novel, makes no sense. The novel does things a poem could never do; but since the reverse is equally true, efforts to set up a hierarchy between them are clearly misguided. A poem may, in certain contexts and circumstances, be more meaningful than a novel, but this is a practical decision not a metaphysical one. And the practical value of such a decision involves recognizing when genres are incommensurable. Although efforts to explore the limits of any genre are crucial to the creation of new ones, it is precisely a genre's distinctive limits which provide for its meaning. The value of the poem is lost if it tries to be a novel.

So far I have said very little about my title, about the incompatibility of friendship and love. My plan was to lay the groundwork for my thesis on less controversial territory. Now, however, I can state it sharply and with better understanding. Love and friendship are, I believe, two distinct genres of intimacy. Like the poem and the novel, they cannot be combined. Likewise, it is a mistake to rank one as deeper than the other. Each is unique—and each is limited.

Before I argue this, two clarifications are in order. The term "love" is often used indiscriminately to refer to all forms of attraction (one "loves" ice cream, children and god). It should be clear that I am using the term to refer specifically to passionate, romantic love—that characterized by Tristan for Isolde, Anna Karenina for Vronsky, and Swann for Odette. Secondly, it should also be clear that, although passionate love has an inextricable sexual component, it is not synonymous with sexual desire. Although one cannot love romantically without sexual desire, one can certainly desire sexually those one does not love.

What is it, then, about romantic love that makes it incompatible with friendship? In one sense, the answer is so obvious as to seem simplistic. Friends share each other's experience of the world; they see it in similar ways and enjoy it together. Lovers, in contrast, as the rhetoric of romance insists repeatedly, are each other's world. Passion for the beloved is the organizing force of the lover's life, if not in actuality, at least in desire. In love, the world happens only through the other's eyes.

A concrete example will illustrate my point. A man is visiting an art museum in a foreign land. As he marvels at its beauties, he regrets that his friend, who shares his taste in art, was not able to make the trip with him. He anticipates the dinner they have planned for next week and the pleasure his friend will take in the detailed stories of his trip.

If, however, the man is in love, his trip will be quite different. His experience of the museum will seem somehow hollow—like everything else he experiences without the beloved. In love, one does not so much delight in sharing separate experiences, as want every experience, even the most minute, not to be separate. This is the meaning of Catherine's famous "I am Heathcliff" declaration in *Wuthering Heights* (Bronte, p. 51). It is also the source of the jealousy so foreign to friendship and so integral to romance.

C. S. Lewis, in *The Four Loves*, claims that we picture friends side-by-side and lovers face-to-face (Lewis, 1960, p. 98). This insight seems essentially correct to me, and essentially the difference I am trying to describe. Friends are fascinated primarily

by the world (and by each other as objects in it). They delight in exchanging the world with each other. Lovers, on the other hand, are fascinated primarily by each other, and see the world only in each other's eyes. The focus and delight of friends is decidedly different from that of lovers.

In pointing out this difference, I am not claiming to have finally identified the true meaning of love or friendship—or even to have said very much about either. My intent is the minimal one of demonstrating that they are incompatible. Lewis' image is particularly helpful in this. People can stand side-by-side or they can stand face-to-face, but they obviously cannot do both at the same time. Each stand has its own unique delights, but having one logically requires losing the other.

Historically, when differences were emphasized, it was usually to serve a particular hierarchical order. I want to avoid this historical tendency. While insisting that love and friendship are irreconcilably different, I also want to insist on their equality. Though circumstances may make one better than another, this is a practical and not a metaphysical superiority. In themselves they are equal.

The overwhelming tendency of popular culture is to deny this equality and place romantic love above everything else, to view it as the most intimate relationship possible between human beings. The language of romance, with its penchant for totalizing and divine superlatives, feeds this popular hierarchy. But the "made for each other," "everything to me," rhetoric is obviously exaggerated. Romance surely unites people in a way unlike any other, but so does colleagueship. Not enough is said about romance's limits (or colleagueship's strengths). For instance, there is not the level of choice in romance that there is in other relationships. Also, its narrow focus generates an idealized intensity detrimental to the broader context (love's proverbial blindness). Finally, it is notoriously temporary. In short, to proclaim that romance is the most important of life's offerings is simplistic at best, and has often been downright dangerous.

But in detailing the limitations of romance I am not trying, like Michel de Montaigne (1580 [1958]), to invert the popular hierarchy and proclaim friendship as the height of intimacy. If the populace has tended to over-rate passion, intellectuals—from Plato to Shulamith Firestone—have been too prone to vilify it. While it is true that in the constancy of friendship aspects of the self get shared and enacted that would never be possible in the frenzy of passion, there are glories that exist only amidst that madness. This is the truth at the heart of Heloise's famous protestation to the intellectualizing Abelard: "The name of wife may seem more sacred or more binding, but sweeter for me will always be the word mistress, or, if you will permit me, that of concubine or whore" (Abelard and Heloise, 1974, p. 113). Like any genre, passionate romance has values that only it can deliver.

At the outset of this paper, I said that the claim to have united love and friendship was not merely innocent bragging, but a significant and dangerous error. This may have seemed melodramatic at the time, but I want now to reassert and explain it.

The two models of intimacy I have been contrasting reflect profoundly differing views on the meaning of human life and the possibilities inherent in it. Plato's view is marked by a radical and unbounded optimism—which is what made him so useful to Christianity. To him, all genuine goods are compatible; therefore, it is possible to "have them all," possible for the human being to achieve perfect communion with all of reality. For him, the struggle of the moral life involves discerning the narrow path toward this total union and unflinchingly ascending it. When Plato has Socrates reject the passionate advances of Alcibiades, he is absolutely confident that Socrates would find nothing in the arms of Alcibiades that would not also be found in the transcendent arms of Beauty itself. Given the right choices, nothing is really lost; all tears will be wiped from our eyes. In other words, when Plato chooses, he assumes he can have it all—an inviting but dangerous assumption!

The perspectival model of intimacy that I am suggesting is more modest. There is no totalizing genre that subsumes all others in itself, no perfect communion. Since some goods, some forms of intimacy, are incompatible with others, one must choose between them. What gives this choice its poignancy is the realization that having some forms, albeit powerful and splendid, means the death of others powerful and splendid in their own right. On this model, morality is not so much an ascent to totality, but—to use a different metaphor—a kind of quilting in which one struggles to arrange as many compatible goods as one can into a significant and individual unity. But any effective arrangement realizes that choice involves real losses, real goods eternally excluded. The drama of the moral life, its tragic edge, consists in deciding which things to let die. Yes, truth demands that we embrace and reverence and enjoy the goods we choose, but it also demands mourning for the goods our choice excludes. That Socrates chose well that cold night he slept in the arms of Beauty itself, I do not for an instant deny. His quilt works like no other. But his quilt does not include Alcibiades; it never will—and such a terrible loss demands appropriate tears (My thoughts on Alcibiades owe a great deal to Martha Nussbaum, 1986).

DISCUSSION QUESTIONS

1. Why can't lovers be friends? Explain the argument. Do you agree? Give an example from your own experience.
2. What does Conlon mean when he says that the standard or standards for ordinary human intimacy are completely mistaken? Is he right?
3. Explain how Conlon uses Plato's theory of relationships to make his argument. Do you think he correctly captures how relationships develop?

REFERENCES

Abelard and Heloise. (1101–1164 [1974]) *Letters of Abelard and Heloise*. Translated by Betty Radice. New York: Penguin.

Bronte, Emily. (1943) *Wuthering Heights*. New York: Random House.

Davies, Robertson. (1981) *Rebel Angels*. New York: Penguin.

Lewis, C. S. (1960) *The Four Loves*. New York: Harcourt, Brace & World.

de Montaigne, Michel. (1580 [1958]) *Essays*. Translated by J. M. Cohen. New York: Penguin.

Nussbaum, Martha. (1986) *The Fragility of Goodness*. Cambridge: Cambridge University Press.

Plato (c. 360 BCE [1989]) *Symposium*. Translated by Alexander Nehemas and Paul Woodruff. Indianapolis, Ind.: Hackett.

Feminism and the Marriage Contract

BY CAROLE PATEMAN

> Carole Pateman is a feminist and political theorist best known for her radical feminist critique of liberal democracy and the social contract tradition. In this essay, Pateman explains the reforms to marriage law that were achieved by nineteenth-century feminists and argues that despite these successes, marriage remains an institution that unfairly burdens women with (and exempts men from) the responsibility of caring for children.

From at least 1825, when William Thompson published his attack on the "white slave code" of marriage, feminists have persistently criticized marriage on the grounds that it is not a proper contract. In 1860, for example, Elizabeth Cady Stanton stated, in a speech to the American Anti-Slavery Society, that "there is one kind of marriage that has not been tried, and that is a contract made by equal parties to lead an equal life, with equal restraints and privileges on either side."[1] Marriage is called a contract but, feminists have argued, an institution in which one party, the husband, has exercised the power of a slave-owner over his wife and in the 1980s still retains some remnants of that power, is far removed from a contractual relationship. However, not all feminist critics of the marriage contract conclude that marriage should become a purely contractual relationship.

Marriage, according to the entry under "contract" in the *Oxford English Dictionary*, has been seen as a contractual relationship since at least the fourteenth century, and Blackstone states that "our law considers marriage in no other light than as a civil contract."[4] The attraction of contractual marriage for feminists is not hard to see. Feminist criticism takes a "contract" to be an agreement between two equal parties who negotiate until they arrive at terms that are to their mutual advantage. If marriage were a proper contract, women would have to be brought into civil life on exactly the same footing as their husbands.

Feminist writers have stressed the deficiencies of a contract in which the parties cannot set the terms themselves. They have also pointed to the respects in which the marriage contract differs from economic contracts, but, by and large, their criticisms offer little insight into *why* this contract is so curious.

Blackstone explained the singular situation of married women as follows; under coverture, for a man to contract with his wife, "would be only to covenant with himself: and therefore it is, also generally true, that all compacts made between husband and wife, when single, are voided by the intermarriage."[9] Blackstone, like the classic contract theorists, assumes that women both are, and are not, able to enter contracts. If a man and a woman agreed to draw up the terms of their contract when they married, the contract would be void. A married woman lacks a civil existence so she could not have made a contract with her husband. No wonder there are still problems about the contractual character of marriage! To concentrate on the defects of the marriage contract as contract deflects attention from the problems surrounding women's participation in this agreement. In particular, enthusiastic embrace of contractarianism by some contemporary critics presupposes that contract is unproblematic for feminists. The solution to the problem of the marriage contract is presented as completion of the reforms that have eroded coverture; wives can take their place as "individuals," and contract appears once again as the enemy of the old world of status or patriarchy. All the anomalies and contradictions surrounding women and contract, brought to light in the story of the sexual contract, remain repressed.

William Thompson's *Appeal of One Half the Human Race, Women, Against the Pretensions of the Other Half, Men, to Retain them in Political, and Thence in Civil and Domestic, Slavery*, laid the foundation for subsequent feminist criticism of marriage as a contractual relation. The vehemence of his polemic has rarely been equalled, but Thompson places little weight on a proper contract as a solution to the problems of conjugal relations. In this respect, his argument differs not only from much contemporary feminist argument but also from John Stuart Mill's much better known *The Subjection of Women*. According to Thompson, political rights for women and an end to the economic system of individual competition (capitalism) are the crucially important changes that are needed. Only political rights can bring an end to "the *secrecy* of domestic wrongs,"[10] and free relations between the sexes will be possible only within a social order based on "labour by mutual co-operation," or co-operative socialism.

Thompson built model dwellings for his workers on his Cork estate and established mechanics institutes—he argued that women should be admitted to the institutes, to libraries and other educational establishments. He worked out a detailed scheme for co-operative, communal socialism but he died before his plan could be fulfilled. The co-operative or utopian socialists included communal house-work in their blueprints for their new communities and, in the *Appeal*, Thompson emphasizes that provision for children, for instance, would be a communal responsibility. When women contributed to all the work of the community along with men, and could make equal call on communal resources in their own right, the basis of sexual domination would be undermined. When man had "no more wealth than woman, and no more influence over the general property, and his superior strength [is] brought down to its just level of utility, he can procure no sexual gratification but from the voluntary affection of woman."[11]

Once women had secured their civil and political rights and were economically independent in the new world of voluntary co-operation, they would have no reason to be subject to men in return for their subsistence and men would have no means to become women's sexual masters.

The *Appeal* was occasioned by the argument of John Stuart's father, James Mill, that women did not need the vote because their interests were subsumed in the interests of their fathers or their husbands. Unlike his fellow utilitarians then and now, and the economists who incorporate members of the family into one welfare function, Thompson extended his individualism to women. He argued that the interests of each individual member of a family must be counted separately and equally. Individual interests of wives and daughters could not be subsumed under those of the master of the family, nor could his benevolence be assumed to be sufficient to ensure that their interests were protected. Thompson says that close examination must be made of the "so mysteriously operating connexion in marriage," and of the "moral miracle, of the philosophy of utility of the nineteenth century—of reducing two identities into one."[12] The marriage contract was the means through which the "moral miracle" was wrought, but it was anything but a contract.

Women were forced to enter into this supposed contract. Social custom and law deprived women of the opportunity to earn their own living, so that marriage was their only hope of a decent life. The marriage "contract" was just like the contract that the slave-owners in the West Indies imposed on their slaves; marriage was nothing more than the law of the strongest, enforced by men in contempt of the interests of weaker women.

Thompson makes the very important point that no husband can divest himself of the power he obtains through marriage. I have found in discussing this subject that confusion easily arises because we all know of marriages where the husband does not use, and would not dream of using, his remaining powers, and it thus seems that feminist criticism is (today, at least) very wide of the mark. But this is to confuse particular examples of married couples with the *institution* of marriage. Thompson, carefully draws a distinction between the actions of any one husband and the power embodied in the structure of the relation between "husband" and "wife." To become a "husband" is to attain patriarchal right with respect to a "wife." His right is much diminished today from the extensive power he enjoyed in 1825, but even if a man does not avail himself of the law of male sex-right, his position as a husband reflects the institutionalization of that law within marriage. The power is still there even if, in any individual case, it is not used.[14] Thompson adds the further important observation that, even if a husband renounces his power, his wife's freedom is always contingent on his willingness to continue the renunciation.

Some husbands may, as Thompson puts it, allow their wives equal pleasure to their own. However, the wife's enjoyment depends entirely on the benevolence of her husband and what he does, or does not, *permit* her to do. The husband can make the marital home into a prison and cut off "his household slave from all sympathy but with himself, his children, and cats or other household animals." A wife can be excluded from all intellectual and social intercourse and pleasures, and can be prevented from forming her own friendships; "is there a wife who dares to form her own acquaintances amongst women or men, without the permission, direct or indirect, of the husband . . . or to retain them when formed?"[15] If a husband chooses to forego all his legal powers, his wife still has "but the pleasures of the slave, however varied," because her actions are always contingent upon the permission of her husband.[16] Thompson claims that in these matters wives are worse off than the female slaves of the West Indies, and husbands have wider jurisdiction than slave-masters.

In one respect the marriage contract differs from slavery or from the extended employment contract of civil slavery. Slavery originated in and was maintained through physical coercion. In the civil slave contract, like the employment contract, service (labour power) is exchanged for subsistence or wages. Civil slavery cannot be maintained through time unless the worker (slave) is obedient to the commands of the employer; obedience is constitutive of contract. As Thompson emphasizes,

in the marriage contract a wife explicitly agrees to obey her husband. The marriage contract is distinguished by reserving for wives "this gratuitous degradation of swearing to be slaves." Thompson wonders why it is that men do not find the "simple pleasure of commanding to be sufficient, without the gratification of the additional power of taunting the victim with her pretended *voluntary* surrender of the control over her own actions?"[17] The vow of obedience is now no longer always included in the marriage ceremony but nor has it entirely disappeared, and I shall come back to this feature of the marriage contract.

Just as wives' social pleasures depend on the benevolence of their husbands, so, Thompson argues, do their sexual pleasures. In his brief conjectural history of the origins of marriage, Thompson speculates that men's sexual desires led them to set up "isolated breeding establishments, called married life," instead of using women merely as labourers.[18] With the establishment of marriage and the pretence of a contract, men's domination is hidden by the claim that marriage allows equal, consensual sexual enjoyment to both spouses. Husbands, it is held, depend upon the voluntary compliance of their wives for their pleasure. Thompson declares this to be an "insulting falsehood"; a husband is physically strong enough, and is allowed by public opinion and the law, to compel his wife to submit to him, whether she is willing or not. She, however, has no right to enjoyment at all; she can beg, like a child or slave, but even that is difficult for women who are not supposed to have sexual desires. Thompson concludes that "sexual desires increase tenfold the facility of exercising, and of continuing for life, the despotism of men in marriage."[19] Thompson's argument implies that, to bring the audacious falsehood of the marriage contract to an end, not only sweeping political and economic changes are required, but also a radical change in what it means to be a masculine or feminine sexual being; the original contract must be declared null and void.

Four decades later, John Stuart Mill drew much less far-reaching conclusions from his attack on the marriage contract as a contract. In some ways this is rather surprising, since there are some striking parallels between Mill's arguments in *The Subjection of Women* and Thompson's *Appeal*.

John Stuart Mill was one of the rare men who not only supported the feminist movement but attempted to put his sympathies into practice. His criticism of the marriage contract was summed up in a statement that he drew up two months before he and Harriet Taylor were married in 1851. Mill completely rejected the legal powers that he would acquire as a husband—though has rejection had no legal standing—undertaking "a solemn promise never in any case or under any circumstances to use them." He states that he and Harriet Taylor entirely disapproved of existing marriage law, because it "confers upon one of the parties to the contract, legal power and control over the person, property and freedom of action of the other party, independent of her own wishes and will." Mill concluded his declaration by stating that Harriet Taylor "retains in all respects whatever the same absolute freedom of action and freedom of disposal of herself and of all that does or may at any time belong to her, as if no such marriage had taken place; and I absolutely disclaim and repudiate all pretension to have acquired any such rights whatever by virtue of such marriage."[23]

Mill agrees with Thompson on several issues. He argues, for example, that women have no alternative, they are compelled to marry. "Wife" is the only position that their upbringing, lack of education and training, and social and legal pressures realistically leave open to them. Mill also distinguishes between the behaviour of individual husbands and the structure of the institution of marriage. He argues that defenders of existing marriage law rely on the example of husbands who refrain from using their legal powers, yet marriage is designed for every man, not merely a benevolent few, and it allows men who physically ill-treat their wives to do so with virtual impunity. Again, like Thompson, Mill argues that to become a wife is tantamount to becoming a slave, and in some ways is worse; a wife is the "actual bond-servant of her husband: no less so, as far as legal obligation goes, than slaves commonly so called."[24] Mill is much more reticent than Thompson about a wife's sexual subjection, although, as I have already noted, he

drew attention to the right of a husband to compel his wife to grant his "conjugal rights."

Where Mill parts company with Thompson is that he denies that there is any connection between conjugal domination and a wife's position as housewife and economic dependant. Mill calls for reform of marriage law to bring the marriage contract in line with other contracts. Echoing Pufendorf, he notes that "the most frequent case of voluntary association, next to marriage, is partnership in business," but marriage compares very unfavourably with business. No one thinks that one partner in a business must be the absolute ruler; who would enter a business partnership if that were the case? Yet, if power were placed in the hands of one man, the arrangement would be less dangerous than in marriage, since the subordinate partner can always terminate the contract; such a course is not open to a wife (and Mill, who was very cautious in public on the highly charged question of divorce, adds that even if a wife could withdraw from a marriage she should do so only as a last resort). In business, theory and experience both confirm that the appropriate arrangement is for the conditions of partnership to be negotiated in the articles of agreement. Similarly, Mill argues, in marriage, the "natural arrangement" is a division of powers between husband and wife, "each being absolute in the executive branch of their own department, and any change of system and principle requiring the consent of both."

How is the division to be made? Mill suggests, on the one hand, that an arrangement will be made according to the capacities of the partners; they could "pre-appoint it by the marriage contract, as pecuniary arrangements are now often pre-appointed." On the other hand, as feminist critics have recently pointed out, Mill is ultimately inconsistent in his argument. He falls back on the appeals to custom and nature that he had rejected at an earlier stage of his argument in *The Subjection of Women*. Mill, like the classic social contract theorists, assumes that sexual difference necessarily leads to a sexual division of labour, a division that upholds men's patriarchal right. He remarks that, because a husband is usually older than his wife, he will have more authority in decision-making, "at least until they both attain a time of life at which the difference in their years is of no importance." However, he does not say why the husband would be willing to relinquish his power, or how the appropriate time of life is to be recognized. Again, Mill notes that the spouse (and he disingenuously writes, "whichever it is") who provides greater support will have a greater voice, but his own argument ensures that the wife's voice will remain subordinate.[25]

Mill states that when the family is reliant on earnings for support, "the common arrangement, by which the man earns the income and the wife superintends the domestic expenditure, seems to me in general the most suitable division of labour between the two persons." Mill assumes that when women have equal opportunity in education and thus "the *power* of earning," and marriage has been reformed so that husbands are no longer legally sanctioned slave masters, a woman, by virtue of becoming, a wife, will still choose to remain in the home, protected by her husband. He explicitly equates a woman's choosing to marry with a man's choice of a career. When a woman marries and has a household and family to attend to, she will renounce all other occupations "which are not consistent with the requirements of this."[26] Even if marriage became a freely negotiable contract, Mill expected that women would accept that they should render domestic service.

Harriet Taylor was much closer to William Thompson on this issue. In 1851 in *The Enfranchisement of Women*, she responded to the objection that opening all occupations to both sexes on merit would lead to too many competitors and the lowering of wages and salaries. Taylor argued that, at worst, such an enlargement of opportunity for women would mean that a married couple could not then earn more than the man could now earn on his own. The great change would be that the wife "would be raised from the position of a servant to that of a partner." As long as economic life was governed by competition the exclusion of half the competitors could not be justified. She added that she did not believe that "the division of mankind into capitalists and hired labourers, and the regulation of the reward of labourers mainly by

demand and supply, will be for ever, or even much longer, the rule of the world."[27]

Most of the reforms to marriage law demanded by feminists in the nineteenth century have now been enacted. Nevertheless, contemporary feminists still emphasize that the marriage contract diverges in significant respects from other contracts. Some of their arguments resemble those of Thompson and Mill, others highlight yet further peculiarities of marriage as a contract.[28] For example, contemporary feminists point out that the marriage contract, unlike other valid contracts, requires that one party gives up the right to self-protection and bodily integrity. They have also pointed out that the marriage contract does not exist as a written document that is read and then signed by the contracting parties. Generally, a contract is valid only if the parties have read and understood its terms before they commit themselves. If very large amounts of property are involved in a marriage today, a contract will sometimes be drawn up that resembles much older documents, common when marriage was a matter for fathers of families and not the free choice of two individuals. The fact that most marriages lack any document of this kind, illustrates one of the most striking features of the marriage contract. There is no paper headed "The Marriage Contract" to be signed. Instead, the unwritten contract of marriage, to which a man and a woman are bound when they become husband and wife, is codified in the law governing marriage and family life.[29]

There is another reason, too, why there is no written document. A man and a woman do not become husband and wife by putting their signatures on a contract. Marriage is constituted through two different acts. First, a prescribed ceremony is performed during the course of which the couple undertake a speech act. The man and woman each say the words "I do." These words are a "performative utterance"; that is to say, by virtue of saying the words, the standing of the man and woman is transformed. In the act of saying "I do," a man becomes a husband and a woman becomes a wife. Bachelors and spinsters are turned into married couples by uttering certain words—but the marriage can still be invalidated unless another act performed. Second, the marriage must also be "consummated" through sexual intercourse.

The story of the sexual contract explains why a signature, or even a speech act, is insufficient for a valid marriage. The act that is required, the act that seals the contract, is (significantly) called *the sex act*. Not until a husband has exercised his conjugal right is the marriage contract complete.

Contemporary feminists have also emphasized the fact that a married couple cannot determine the terms of the marriage contract to suit their own circumstances. There is not even a choice available between several different contracts, there is only *the* marriage contract. A married couple cannot contract to change the "essentials" of marriage, which are seen as "the husband's duty to support his wife, and the wife's duty to serve her husband."[31] The general parameters are set by the law governing marriage, and feminist legal scholars often follow other legal authorities in arguing that, therefore, marriage is less a contract than a matter of *status*.

But "status" in which sense? Some discussions suggest that the old world of status has lingered on into the modern world. Thus, in *The Subjection of Women*, John Stuart Mill argues that "the law of servitude in marriage is a monstrous contradiction to all the principles of the modern world," and that women's subordination is "a single relic of an old world of thought and practice exploded in everything else." The "peculiar character of the modern world . . . [is] that human beings are no longer born to their place in life, . . . but are free to employ their faculties, and such favourable chances as offer, to achieve the lot which may appear to them most desirable."[33] At present this principle applies only to men; to be born a woman still entails that a place in life is already waiting. Marriage, Mill argues, must thus be brought into the modern world; the relics of status must be eliminated and marriage must be moved from status to contract. In the old world of status, men and women had no choice about the social positions they occupied as husbands and wives.

To argue for the assimilation of marriage to the model of economic contract in the heyday of freedom of contract (if such a period ever existed) is to assume that the public and private worlds can be assimilated and to ignore the construction of the opposition between the world of contract and its "natural foundation" within civil society. Contract appears as the solution to the problem of patriarchal right (status) because contract is seen as a universal category that can include women. Contract in the public world is an exchange between equals (between "individuals") so it appears that, if contract is extended into the private sphere, inequalities of status between men and women in marriage must disappear. The husband exercises political right over his wife, and only men can be "husbands." Status in yet another sense must also be replaced by contract.

Contemporary feminist critics have pointed out that, unlike other contracts, the marriage contract cannot be entered into by any two (or more) sane adults, but is restricted to two parties, one of whom must be a man and the other a woman (and who must not be related in certain prescribed ways). Not only does a "husband" obtain a certain power over his wife whether or not he wishes to have it, but the marriage contract is sexually ascriptive. A man is always a "husband" and a woman is always a "wife." But what follows from this criticism? The argument that marriage should become a properly contractual relation implies that sexual difference is also an aspect of "status." Legal writers argue that there has been a movement back from contract to status because substantive social characteristics of parties to contracts are treated as relevant matters in decisions whether certain contracts should be permitted or regulated. Freedom of contract (proper contract) demands that no account is taken of substantive attributes—such as sex. If marriage is to be truly contractual, sexual difference must become irrelevant to the marriage contract; "husband" and "wife" must no longer be sexually determined. Indeed, from the standpoint of contract, "men" and "women" would disappear.

The completion of the movement from status to contract entails that status as sexual difference should disappear along with "status" in its other senses. There can be no predetermined limits on contract, so none can be imposed by specifying the sex of the parties. In contract, the fact of being a man or a woman is irrelevant. In a proper marriage contract two "individuals" would agree on whatever terms were advantageous to them both. The parties to such a contract would not be a "man" and a "woman" but two owners of property in their persons who have come to an agreement about their property to their mutual advantage. Until recently, there was no suggestion that status in the sense of sexual difference would also give way to contract. To sweep away the last remnants of status in marriage can have consequences not foreseen by Thompson or Mill who did not object to the fact that *women* became wives; they strongly objected to what being a *wife* entailed. Earlier feminist attacks on the indissoluble marriage contract and its non-negotiable terms were directed at the husband's conjugal right, not at the sexually ascriptive construction of "wife" and "husband." The contemporary attack on sexual difference, apparently much more radical than older arguments, suffers from an insuperable problem; the "individual" is a patriarchal category. Contract may be the enemy of status, but it is also the mainstay of patriarchy. Marriage as a purely contractual relation remains caught in the contradiction that the subjection of wives is both rejected and presupposed.

One of Hegel's objections to marriage as a contract is that it leaves the relationship at the mercy of the whims and capricious wills of the contractors. Similarly, Durkheim emphasizes that the bond created by contract is both external and of short duration; it leads to "transient relations and passing associations."[70] A contract of mutual advantage and reciprocal use will last only as long as it appears advantageous to either party. A new contract with a different partner will always appear as a possible and enticing alternative. That is to say, exit from the marriage contract becomes as important as entry. Contemporary advocates of marriage contracting stress that one advantage is that the contract can be for a limited term, and run for, say, five years in the first instance. Nor is it accidental that current controversy over slave contracts and paternalism emphasizes the crucial importance of dissoluble contracts. The way in which popular advice-books on marriage and

sexual matters present divorce illustrates the influence of a contractual view of marriage; divorce is seen as something that can be pre-considered in terms of personal upward mobility, with stress . . . on what lies ahead that "may be incorporated into a new and better image."[71] When the contract is made only for mutual use and advantage, its real point becomes "to anticipate and provide for divorce."[72] To anticipate the termination of the marriage contract in the very act of contracting has become possible only quite recently. In England, for example, there was no divorce before 1700 (a divorce *a mensa et thoro* could be obtained from an ecclesiastical court but it did not permit remarriage) and until 1857 divorce could only be granted through a private Act of Parliament.[73] Not until 1969, when the ground for divorce became the irretrievable breakdown of the marriage, were divorces obtained relatively easily by both wives and husbands and by members of all social classes. Only recently, too, have divorce and divorced persons ceased to be a scandal. Many nineteenth-century feminists who favoured divorce, in particular as the best means for a wife to escape from a brutal husband, steered clear of the subject for fear of compromising their other goals; other feminists were opposed to divorce, fearing that the consequence would be to enable husbands to abandon their wives and children more readily. Divorce is usually seen as the opposite of marriage, but Christine Delphy argues that divorce today is, rather, the transformation of marriage. She argues that, since divorced wives almost always continue to look after the children of the marriage, "marriage and divorce can be considered as two ways of obtaining a similar result: the collective attribution to women of the care of children and the collective exemption of men from the same responsibility."[74] However, it is far from clear, from the standpoint of contract, whether such a responsibility would continue to arise.

The logic of contract, and of marriage as nothing more than a contract of mutual sexual use, is that "marriage" and "divorce" should be eliminated. The most advantageous arrangement for the individual is an endless series of very short-term contracts to use another's body as and when required. Other services presently provided within marriage would also be contracted for in the market. A universal market in bodies and services would replace marriage. The logic of contract is that marriage would be supplanted by contracts for access to sexual property. Marriage would give way to *universal prostitution*. Moreover, "individuals," and not "men" and "women," would enter these contracts. Contract would then have won the final victory over status (sexual difference). When negotiations about use of sexual property in the person can have no predetermined outcome, and individuals can contract as they see fit to use the property of another, sexual difference would be meaningless.

The Beatles used to sing that "All You Need is Love." The objection that contract will never be victorious because love will stand in the way has been anticipated already; love has been reduced to another external relation, or aspect of property in persons, and defined, for example, as a "particular non-marketable household commodity."[75] To draw attention to such arguments is not to imply that contract is invincible, but to illustrate the incongruous character of an alliance between feminism and contract. The victory of contract has a considerable appeal for feminists, given the long sway of coverture and the various social and legal means still used to deny women ownership of property in their persons. The conclusion is easy to draw that the denial of civil equality to women means that the feminist aspiration must be to win acknowledgment for women as "individuals." Such an aspiration can never be fulfilled. The individual is a patriarchal category. The individual is masculine and his sexuality is understood accordingly (if, indeed, "sexuality" is a term that can be used of a self that is externally related to the body and sexual property). The patriarchal construction of sexuality, what it means to be a sexual being, is to possess and to have access to sexual property. How access is gained and how the property is used is made clear in the story of the demand of the brothers for equal access to women's bodies. In modern patriarchy, masculinity provides the paradigm for sexuality; and masculinity means sexual mastery. The "individual" is a man who makes use of

a woman's body (sexual property); the converse is much harder to imagine.

Contemporary feminists (especially in the United States) often conclude that the only alternative to the patriarchal construction of sexuality is to eliminate sexual difference, to render masculinity and femininity politically irrelevant. At first sight, the complete elimination of status and its replacement by contract appears to signal the final defeat of patriarchy and the law of male sex-right. The realization of the promise of contract as freedom appears to be in sight, and the patriarchal construction of men and women, masculinity and femininity, appears to be breaking down. Feminists have campaigned for, and won, legal reforms that are couched in what are now usually called "gender neutral" terms. Such reforms can mean that women's civil rights are safeguarded, but this approach to reform can also lead to curious results when, for example, attempts are made to incorporate pregnancy into legislation that applies indifferently to men or women. Odd things happen to women when the assumption is made that the only alternative to the patriarchal construction of sexual difference is the ostensibly sex-neutral "individual."

The final victory of contract over status is not the end of patriarchy, but the consolidation of the modern form. The story of the sexual contract tells how contract is the medium through which patriarchal right is created and upheld. For marriage to become merely a contract of sexual use—or, more accurately, for sexual relations to take the form of universal prostitution—would mark the political defeat of women *as women*. When contract and the individual hold full sway under the flag of civil freedom, women are left with no alternative but to (try to) become replicas of men. In the victory of contract, the patriarchal construction of sexual difference as mastery and subjection remains intact but repressed. Only if the construction is intact can the "individual" have meaning and offer the promise of freedom to both women and men so that they know to what they must aspire. Only if the construction is repressed can women have such an aspiration. Heterosexual relations do not inevitably take the form of mastery and subjection, but free relations are impossible within the patriarchal opposition between contract and status, masculinity and femininity. The feminist dream is continuously subverted by entanglement with contract.

DISCUSSION QUESTIONS

1. What are William Thompson's criticisms of marriage as a contractual relation? How are J. S. Mill's criticisms of marriage less radical than Thompson's, from a feminist perspective?

2. What are some of the contemporary feminist arguments about how the marriage contract is unlike any other contract?

3. In what ways is marriage actually more a matter of status than of contract? Why does Pateman find this worrisome?

4. Explain Pateman's argument that because the concept of the "individual" is itself patriarchal, any feminist attempt to reform marriage that does not reject the model of contractarianism is doomed.

Minimal Marriage: What Political Liberalism Implies for Marriage Law

BY ELIZABETH BRAKE

Elizabeth Brake is a feminist philosopher whose work spans topics such as love, sex, marriage, amatonormativity, and procreative ethics. In this essay, Brake defends a minimal conception of marriage that abandons most of the constraints of traditional marriage, including the sex or number of spouses, the nature and purpose of caring relationships, and which marital rights are exchanged and whether they are exchanged reciprocally or asymmetrically.

Introduction

I open with a detailed proposal for a minimally restricted law of marriage. The central idea is that individuals can have legal marital relationships with more than one person, reciprocally or asymmetrically, themselves determining the sex and number of parties, the type of relationship involved, and which rights and responsibilities to exchange with each. For brevity, I call this "minimal marriage." This name for the proposal alludes to Nozick's minimal state (although the political framework here is liberal egalitarian, not libertarian). Just as Nozick describes the libertarian state as minimal in comparison with current welfare states, so minimal marriage has far fewer state-determined restrictions than current marriage. And just as Nozick's minimal state is, in his view, the most extensive state justifiable, these restrictions on marriage, so exiguous from the point of view of the current regime, are the most extensive which can be justified within political liberalism.

Discussions of marriage reform are met with the objection that they wrongly treat marriage as a constructed, not a natural or prepolitical, relationship. As I argue below, there are empirical and theoretical problems with claiming that a certain form of marriage is "natural." But even were marriage "natural" in some sense relevant to institutional design, natural features could not specify its legal framework. In the next section, I review some of the more than one thousand legal implications of marriage in the United States. What these suggest—among other things—is that a legal marriage framework makes many decisions about the boundaries of marriage and its constituent legal powers, responsibilities, entitlements, and so on, which cannot be read off "nature."

Minimal Marriage

Minimal marriage institutes the most extensive set of restrictions on marriage compatible with political liberalism. It is minimal in that limiting the institutional framework to only what is so compatible entails a significant reduction of the restrictions placed on marriage. It might also be described as marital pluralism or disestablishment. I argue that a liberal state can set no principled restrictions on the sex or number of spouses and the nature and purpose of their relationships, except that they be caring relationships (a concept I will specify below). Moreover, the state cannot require exchanges of marital rights (shorthand for various entitlements, powers, and obligations) to be reciprocal and complete, as opposed to asymmetrical and divided. Minimal marriage would also reduce the marital rights available.

To show what is at stake, I will review some of the numerous entitlements, liabilities, permissions, and powers currently exchanged reciprocally and as a complete package in marriage. In U.S. federal law alone, there are "1,138 federal statutory provisions . . . in which marital status is a factor in determining or receiving benefits, rights, and privileges."[1] Laws concerning property, inheritance, and divorce are additional, falling under state jurisdiction.

Marriage entails rights "to be on each others' health, disability, life insurance, and pension plans," "jointly [to] own real and personal property, an arrangement which protects their marital estate from each other's creditors," and to automatic inheritance if a spouse dies intestate. Spouses have rights in one another's property in marriage and on divorce. They are designated next of kin "in case of death, medical emergency, or mental incapacity" and for prison visitation and military personnel arrangements.[2] They qualify for special tax and immigration status and survivor, disability, Social Security, and veterans' benefits. Marital status is implicated throughout U.S. federal law— in "Indian" affairs, homestead rights, taxes, trade and commerce, financial disclosure and conflict of interest, federal family violence law, immigration, employment benefits, federal natural resources law, federal loans and guarantees, and payments in agriculture. Marital status also confers parental rights and responsibilities—assignment of legal paternity, joint parenting and adoption rights, and legal status with regard to step-children. Mary Anne Case argues that marriage's "principal legal function" is not to structure relationships between spouses "but instead to structure their relations with third parties" through the "designation, without elaborate contracting, of a single other person third parties can look to in a variety of legal contexts," especially in distributing benefits.[3] While this may be an efficient system, it is not, I argue, currently just.

The large array of marriage rights can be roughly taxonomized according to function. Some marriage rights are entitlements to direct financial assistance: West Virginia's cash payouts on marriage,[4] increased Social Security disability payments for married persons, and increased disability pensions for married veterans and federal employees. Married soldiers can receive family separation allowance and increased housing allowance.[5] Tax benefits "permit married couples to transfer substantial sums to one another, and to third parties, without tax liability in circumstances in which single people would not enjoy the same privilege." Old Age, Survivors, and Disability Insurance (Social Security) "is written in terms of the rights of husbands and wives," and spouses may qualify for Medicaid, housing assistance, loans, food stamps, and military commissary benefits.[6] Many of these entitlements appear to reflect an assumption of a "traditional" single-breadwinner model, in which one spouse depends on the other for health insurance and income.[7]

Other rights directly facilitate day-to-day maintenance of a relationship or enable spouses to play significant roles in one another's lives. Special consideration for immigration is an example: spouses cannot share daily life if they are in different countries. Civil service and military spouses may receive employment and relocation assistance and preferential hiring. Out-of-state spouses may qualify for in-state tuition.[8] Other examples are spousal immunity from testifying, spousal care leave entitlement, hospital and prison visiting rights, entitlement to burial with one's spouse in a veterans' cemetery, and emergency decision-making powers. Through such entitlements and through status designation, marriage allows spouses to express and act on their care for one another.

Another function of note is protection of the widowed through funeral and bereavement leave, pension and health care entitlements, indemnity compensation or the right to sue for a spouse's death, automatic precedence for life insurance payouts and final paychecks, control of copyright, and automatic rights to inherit if the spouse dies intestate and to make decisions about the disposal of the body. Marriage law also provides protection for spouses on divorce.

In an ideal liberal egalitarian society, minimal marriage would consist only in rights which recognize (e.g., status designation, burial rights, bereavement leave) and support (e.g., immigration rights, caretaking leave) caring relationships. Care, broadly construed, may involve physical or emotional caretaking or simply a caring attitude (an attitude of concern for a particular other). "Relationship," as I am using the term here, implies that parties know and are known to one another, have ongoing direct contact, and share a history. I will argue that a law performing the functions of designating, recognizing, and supporting caring relationships is justifiable, even required.

Unlike current marriage, minimal marriage does not require that individuals exchange marital rights reciprocally and in complete bundles: it allows their disaggregation to support the numerous relationships, or adult care networks, which people may have. Minimal marriage would allow a person to exchange all her marital rights reciprocally with one other person or distribute them through her adult care network. In an ideal liberal egalitarian society, law should not assume a dependency relationship between spouses, and so most marital entitlements to direct financial benefits would be eliminated (except for those, such as in state tuition eligibility, whose primary purpose is to enable relationship maintenance). Likewise, the compatibility of specific "insurance" provisions of marriage with justice will depend on their rationale.

As noted above, many current marriage rights would be eliminated in an ideal liberal egalitarian society. Such a society would not provide health care and basic income through marriage. Nor would it provide economic assistance on the assumption of dependency between spouses. Because the state would not assume the financial terms of the relationship, property arrangements would be contractualized, allowing parties to decide property division, alimony, and inheritance and to set conditional terms and specify penalties for default. Some currently protected marital "privacy" rights would be retained within minimal marriage, but others would not. "Privacy" rights which allow individuals to choose the terms of their relationships are, for the most part, entitlements under freedom of association. For example, as Mary Anne Case points out, marriage law, unlike most domestic partnership laws, does not require couples to cohabit or share finances; marriage thus protects spouses' "privacy" in these choices as the contrasting partnership laws do not.[9] But "privacy" rights within marriage may conflict with justice when they override legal rights in other domains. For example, marriage currently carries involuntary exemptions from contract law, labor law, and criminal law. But exceptions to criminal law (as in exemptions for sexual battery within marriage) conflict with justice. Moreover, as the state cannot assume the nature of marriage relationships, it cannot automatically remove spouses' entitlements under tort and labor law.

At this point, an objector might suggest as a reductio that minimal marriage will have to countenance immoral or ludicrous marriages.[10] However, as minimal marriage complies with criminal law, it cannot permit rights violations. Actual marriage law has overridden human rights—under the doctrine of coverture, a wife contracted away her civil and legal rights for life. Indeed, while marital rape is now a crime in all states, the marital rape exemption lingers in state criminal codes exempting spouses from sexual battery charges.[11] But minimal marriage, which respects criminal law, could not countenance such exemptions (or, a fortiori, marital slave contracts).[12] Pedophilia is ruled out on the same grounds. In addition, children and nonhuman animals cannot make marriage contracts because they cannot make any contracts. No one can marry unilaterally; minimal marriage status designations require consent from both parties, and minors are not legally competent to consent.[13]

Ludicrously large marriages are another potential reductio. Could Hugh Hefner marry his top fifty Playmates? Could a hundred cult members marry? No. Minimal marriage is a framework for caring relationships, and caring relationships require that parties are known personally to one another, share history, interact regularly, and have detailed knowledge of one another. These criteria impose practical limits, for there are psychological and material limits on the number of such relationships one can sustain.[14] However, should a surprisingly large number of people genuinely sustain caring relationships, there is no principled reason to deny them distributable benefits such as visiting rights (though they may be required to alternate, cut short visits, etc.), though other entitlements might be limited in number on grounds of feasibility. Minimal marriage could be implemented by giving prospective spouses a list of entitlements, which they could assign as desired, the form indicating numerical limits. For some rights, self-designation of a caring relationship would be feasible; for others, such as immigration eligibility, an interview to determine that parties do actually know each other well and (so far as can be determined!) care for one another may be appropriate.[15] Because minimal marriage rights differ in content and are implicated in different areas of law and policy, a general prescription as to their institutional design is undesirable; different rights will involve different specific considerations.

So far, the proposal might seem extravagantly removed from real life. But consider an example of how minimal marriage rights might be distributed. Rose lives with Octavian, sharing household expenses. To facilitate this ménage, Rose and Octavian form a legal entity for certain purposes—jointly owned property, bank account access, homeowner and car insurance, and so on. The arrangement is long term but not permanent. Octavian's company will relocate him in five years, and Rose will not move—but they agree to cohabit until then. They even discuss how to divide property when the household dissolves, and they agree that if either moves out sooner, the defaulter will pay the other compensation and costs. (The arrangement for default is not punitive but merely protective.)

Rose's only living relative, Aunt Alice, lives nearby. Alice lives in genteel poverty, and Rose feels a filial responsibility toward her. Rose's employer provides excellent pension and health care benefits, for which any spouse of Rose's is eligible (at a small cost), and other spousal perks, such as reduced costs for its products. Octavian is a well-off professional and does not need these benefits—he has his own—but Alice needs access to good health care and, should Rose die, she could use the pension that would go to Rose's spouse if she had one. Assuming that such entitlements comport

with justice, minimal marriage would allow Rose to transfer the eligibility for these entitlements to Alice.

While Rose enjoys Octavian's company and has affection for Alice, only Marcel truly understands her. Marcel is, like Rose, a bioethicist, and he understands her complex views on end-of-life decision making. Rose wants to transfer powers of executorship and emergency decision making to him. In addition, Marcel and Rose spend a lot of time together, discussing philosophy while enjoying recreational activities, and they would like eligibility for "family rates" at tourist attractions, health clubs, and resorts. Their local city gym, for instance, has a special rate for married couples, but they do not qualify.

There could be more people in Rose's life who occupy a role usually associated with spouses. Rose might share custody of a child with an ex. Or she might cohabit platonically with Octavian, living separately from the long-term love of her life, Stella. There is no single person with whom Rose wants or needs to exchange the whole package of marital rights and entitlements. In fact, doing so would be inconvenient, requiring her to make additional contracts to override the default terms of marriage. Even worse, marrying any one person would expose her to undesired legal liabilities, such as obligatory property division, and it could interfere with her eligibility for some loans and government programs. But Rose wants and needs to exchange some marital rights with several different people.

Rose's ménage might seem strange to some—though putting all one's eggs in one basket might seem equally strange to Rose! It is certainly not obvious that each person will find another with whom their major emotional, economic, and social needs permanently mesh. But minimal marriage does not take sides on this. It allows "traditionalists" to exchange their complete sets of marital rights reciprocally, while Rose and others like her distribute and receive marital rights as needed. Minimal marriage is a law of adult care networks, including "traditional" marriages.

Marriage, including same-sex marriage, currently recognizes a single central exclusive relationship of a certain priority and duration, often understood as "union." But this ignores alternative ideals of relationship: for instance, networks of multiple, significant, nonexclusive relationships which provide emotional support, caretaking, and intimacy and are not (all) romantic or sexual. Such adult care networks appear in the gay community, in African American communities, and among seniors, unmarried urbanites, and polyamorists.

This diversity reflects competing conceptions of valuable relationships. Some gay and lesbian theorists and critics of heterosexism have criticized the central, exclusive relationship ideal as a heterosexual paradigm. They point out that gays and lesbians often choose relationships which are less possessive, demanding, and insular and more flexible and open. They have challenged the desirability of same-sex marriage on the grounds that instead of affirming difference, it will assimilate lesbian and gay relationships into the heterosexual model.[16] But this concern rather implies that marriage law should be reframed to accommodate difference.

Different conceptions of good relationships are not, of course, exclusive to the gay and lesbian community. Polyamorists (gay, straight, and bisexual) promote polyamory—engaging in multiple love relationships—as involving less jealousy and more honesty than exclusive monogamy. They see marriage as promoting a psychologically unhealthy norm of possessiveness, what social theorist Laura Kipnis calls the "domestic gulag." Like the Romantics, Kipnis argues that exclusivity and monogamy destroy passion and spontaneity.[17] Kipnis, along with Anne Kingston and other critics of the "wedding-industrial complex," sees commodification of marriage as obscuring deeper problems in the institution, such as the instability of romantic love matches and the confusion over the nature of spousal roles and duties.[18]

In other ways, social critics have come to value "alternative" relationships as they found "traditional" marriage to be incompatible with more fundamental ideals such as equality. For example, Adrienne Rich argued that the exclusive, prioritized relationship of heterosexual marriage undermines strong relationships between women.[19]

Some feminists have criticized the idea of marriage as *union* insofar as women have lost their identity in the union. Marxists understand monogamous marriage as ownership of women and embodying pernicious aspects of capitalism.[20]

Toni Morrison writes: "Inevitably [feminist debates over marriage] led me to the different history of black women in this country—a history in which marriage was discouraged, impossible, or illegal; in which birthing children was required, but 'having' them, being responsible for them—being, in other words, their parent—was as out of the question as freedom."[21] This history may to some extent account for the "alternative" family models which bell hooks argues reflect working-class African American experience.[22] In minority communities strong intergenerational ties between women or extended family members help people to face economic challenges by combining paid work and child care. Race theorists argue that models of the family which rule out such relations are ethnocentric and racist. For example, Patricia Collins writes that the "imagined traditional family ideal" makes hierarchy seem natural, an idea which lends itself to racism.[23]

Despite such reports of alternative practices, some theorists write as if critiques of the central relationship ideal reflect academic theories removed from real life. Thus, Wedgwood admits that the exclusion of "alternative" "social meanings" of marriage would be discriminatory if anyone seriously wanted to enter them, but then he writes dismissively, "so far as I know, no one in modern Western society seriously wants to enter one of these alternative legal relationships."[24] As the examples he gives of "alternative" relationships are marrying one's foot, Shiite Muslim "temporary marriages," and forced marriage, his claim may well be true. However, he ignores widespread calls in the queer community for recognition of "adult care networks,"[25] as well as similar demands made by "quirky-alones" and urban tribalists. Many contemporaries live outside marriage, many in alternative care networks—and many by choice. Marriage rates have decreased; the *New York Times* reported that, according to census data, in 2005, 51 percent of women were "living without a spouse."[26]

Popular U.S. entertainment, such as *Friends* and *Will and Grace*, suggests that many identify with the unmarried main characters.

The monogamous central relationship ideal is only one contested ideal among many found within different comprehensive doctrines. Framing marriage law in a way which presupposes such a relationship fails to respect public reason and reasonable pluralism.[27] In the absence of a publicly justifiable reason for defining marital relationships as heterosexual, monogamous, exclusive, durable, romantic or passionate, and so on, the state must recognize and support all relationships—same-sex, polygamous, polyamorous, urban tribes—if it recognizes and supports any. Because it cannot assume that spouses must relate in a certain way, it also cannot assume one set of one-size-fits-all marital rights. What it can do is make available a number of rights which designate and support relationships which individuals can use as they wish.

I can now state the reason for calling the proposed legal framework "minimal *marriage.*" Nomenclature matters: political resistance to calling same-sex unions "marriages" is often an attempt to deny them full legitimacy. Extending the application of "marriage" is one way of rectifying past discrimination against homosexuals, bisexuals, polygamists, and care networks. While this departs from current usage, the reference of "marriage" need not be determined by past use (though there is precedent in "Boston marriage," probably originating from James's *Bostonians*, and referring to a companionate relationship between "spinsters"!). The objective is to rectify past state discrimination; such rectification might also take the form of an apology, reparations, or a monument to victims of discrimination on the basis of sexual orientation. If such measures were taken, it would be less important to retain the term "marriage," and in that case, it might be desirable to replace "marriage" as a legal term with "personal relationships" or "adult care networks."

Non-Ideal Theory

So far, I have been considering what justice would imply in an ideally just society. But we do not live in one. In non-ideal circumstances, it may be unjust to implement the results of ideal theory. Sexism, racism, and heterosexism are powerful forces which must be addressed by any political philosophy aspiring to relevance.

Although I cannot argue for this here, I believe it is a mistake to reject ideal theory completely. Instead, one can take the ideal as a guide and evaluate which steps toward it are just under current conditions. In this section, I briefly consider the justice of implementing minimal marriage.

It might be thought that minimal marriage, by promoting nontraditional arrangements, would exacerbate poverty. U.S. federal policy addresses the poverty of single mothers through marriage promotion.[28] It is difficult to summarize the problems with this approach, but here are a few. First, trying to address the poverty of single mothers through marriage is like trying to shove an escaped elephant back into a cage. The conditions which, according to Stephanie Coontz, undermined the "traditional family"—women's economic independence, birth control, and the idea that marriage should be emotionally satisfying—are persistent. One-third of U.S. children are now being reared outside marriage. Marriage promotion is an inefficient antipoverty program, a point which is even more obvious when one considers that poorer families have less to divide on divorce.[29] In contrast, minimal marriage—assuming that for a period benefits such as health care will be available in it—would provide women with greater access to benefits. While current marriage promotion aims to increase women's economic dependence on men, and so may exacerbate abuse, minimal marriage allows women more marriage options.

Second, justice, as well as efficiency, demands that society address real sources of poverty, such as economic disadvantage to child carers, the drop in working-class men's real wages, racism and the legacy of slavery and Jim Crow, the lack of decent affordable housing, and the gendered division of labor. Marriage promotion policy exaggerates the role of marriage and ignores many real contributors to poverty. For example, the African American Healthy Marriage Initiative targets African American persons but seems to ignore the effects—and causes—of extraordinarily high incarceration rates for black males.[30] Minimal marriage is no more an antipoverty program than marriage promotion, but it would benefit the worst-off more by increasing access to benefits.

Among feminists, marriage reform is controversial. Claudia Card has argued that marriage is unjust and should be abolished because marital access rights and incentives to get or stay married facilitate abuse and because distribution of health care and other benefits through marriage unjustly excludes the unmarried. The minimal marriage of ideal theory meets these criticisms, but immediate abolition of marital health care benefits—with no alternative provision—would harm many. While such benefits unjustly exclude the unmarried, providing health care unjustly to some comes closer to the requirement of justice than unjustly providing it to far fewer people. And while these benefits can constrain the choice to stay married, removing the benefits actually reduces options. Thus, immediate abolition is problematic; a transitional stage in which minimal marriage continues to carry such benefits would continue to exclude some unjustly, but it would address abuse and constraints on choice by increasing women's options and hence their bargaining power. In contrast to the difficulties of abolishing health care benefits, it would be entirely helpful and just to remove legal access rights and sexual assault exemptions from marriage immediately.

Susan Moller Okin and Mary Lyndon Shanley have argued against contractualizing marriage on the grounds that comparatively restrictive marriage law can protect economically vulnerable women in "traditional," gender-structured marriages through property division on divorce.[31] Okin documented how women become economically vulnerable through marriage by giving up careers or doing more housework. Likewise, Carole Pateman argues that contractualization will legitimize oppressive forms of marriage.[32] Freedom of contract is compatible with women being pressured to make disadvantageous choices.

These concerns may justify a transitional stage retaining alimony. But there are weaknesses to relying on alimony to protect the vulnerable.

One concerns efficiency. The amount of money received and the percentage who receive it are particularly low for poor women. Also, mothers earn less than childless women. ("Mothers earn about 70 percent of the mean wages of men, and childless women earn 80 to 90 percent.")[33] Thus, pursuing policies such as Anne Alstott's "caretaker resource account" or raising the minimum wage stand to do more good than alimony. Still, given that it is already in place, an inefficient program is better than none.

There is also a problem regarding the grounds for interpersonal obligation in mandatory alimony.[34] Addressing background problems of systematic gender discrimination in employment, including lower wages for "women's work," through marriage risks injustice to individual men. If the supposed reason for alimony is equal opportunity, why should individual men be held responsible for the inequities of the social system? This is especially pertinent because the husbands of the neediest women are likely to be poor themselves. Mandatory alimony based on equal opportunity needs to be sensitive to the position of both parties. However, spousal support liability on grounds of opportunities forgone and contributions to the other's career might be justified by appeal to induced reliance and verbal contracts—mechanisms independently available in contract law. Moreover, provisions preventing contracts from eventuating in one party's impoverishment and the other's enrichment are compatible with liberal egalitarianism. Finally, in non-ideal circumstances, the injustice of burdening a well-off husband with the costs of his ex-wife's job training may be less than the injustice of allowing her to enter poverty. If overall justice does require such transfers, then default rules governing property division on exit from intimate relationships can be enacted independently from marriage.[35]

I want to conclude by emphasizing the feminist attractions of minimal marriage. First, unlike current marriage, it involves informing prospective spouses of their rights, the terms of the agreement, and its implications. Basic principles of contract require that contractors understand terms. Arguably, equal opportunity and rectification for past discrimination require educating women about their potential economic vulnerability. Information about the likely consequences of their choices might lead women to resist exploitative relationships.

Second, and more distinctively, minimal marriage gives women more marriage options, increasing their bargaining power. Along these lines, economists who study "marriage markets" argue that polygamy, in a context of liberal rights, increases women's bargaining power.[36] Such ideal models do not speak to the real problems of exploitation of women and children in closed polygynous communities, and, once again, a liberal egalitarian state may be justified in enacting targeted measures to deal with these problems in context. However, even in unequal contexts, legal marital rights would benefit multiple wives. More generally, the increased marriage options of minimal marriage would open alternative, potentially more egalitarian, relationship models to women.

Finally, minimal marriage denormalizes heterosexual monogamy as a way of life. In this respect, I consider my position responsive and sympathetic to lesbian and queer critiques of marriage such as Claudia Card's, Paula Ettelbrick's, and Drucilla Cornell's. By extending marriage to all caring relationships, minimal marriage really does affirm difference. Minimal marriage does not mark some relationships as "legitimate." Its rationale is to support the caring relationships individuals choose, not to distinguish among them.

This has a further implication. Social pressures surrounding heterosexual monogamy contribute to women's economic vulnerability by promoting "traditional" wifehood. Minimal marriage removes state endorsement from "traditional" marriage, and over time this will change people's aspirations. One tension between liberalism and feminism results from skepticism about whether choice will serve women's interests in light of social pressures. This article has obliquely drawn attention to how state marriage promotion reinforces those social pressures and how political liberalism, properly implemented, might combat them.

The viability of a liberal feminist position on marriage is important because of the concerns of many feminists that liberal feminism is untenable, one reason being that liberal "neutrality" masks a nonneutral, gender-biased state. Such criticism of liberal neutrality (e.g., MacKinnon's) shows that the actual state is nonneutral and that "neutrality" has served bias. However, it is possible that, despite its biased implementation, the proper implementation of neutrality would benefit women. This article is one step toward showing that taking political liberalism seriously in light of feminist social theory has far-reaching implications often unrecognized by liberals and feminists. It requires the state to root out its own sexist and heterosexist assumptions. Minimal marriage is one example of the extensive change which that would require.

DISCUSSION QUESTIONS

1. Explain how minimal marriage is a "law of adult care networks." How does it differ from traditional marriage?
2. Describe the many "entitlements, liabilities, permissions, and powers" that are currently entailed by traditional marriage, and explain how minimal marriage could make them unbundled and unreciprocated.
3. Explain why minimal marriage would not countenance immoral or ludicrous marriages.
4. Describe the hypothetical case of Rose, a woman who distributes minimal marriage rights to Octavian, Aunt Alice, Marcel, and Stella.
5. Describe some of the many different kinds of adult care relationships people already engage in other than traditional marriage, and explain why Brake proposes including them under the umbrella of minimal marriage.

NOTES

1. At the end of 2003, reported by the General Accounting Office (GAO), Dayna K. Shaw, Associate General Counsel, in a letter of January 23, 2004, to Bill Frist. The letter accompanies the 2004 GAO report, labeled "GAO-04–353R Defense of Marriage Act." See also Enclosure I, "Categories of Laws Involving Marital Status," in a letter of January 31, 1997, by Barry R. Bedrick, Associate General Counsel, GAO, to Henry J. Hyde. The letter

accompanies the 1997 GAO report, labeled "GAO/OGC97-16 Defense of Marriage Act."

2. Craig Dean, "Gay Marriage: A Civil Right," *Journal of Homosexuality* 27 (1994): 111–115, at 112.

3. Mary Anne Case, "Marriage Licenses," *Minnesota Law Review* 89 (2004–5): 1758–1797, 1781, 1783.

4. See "State Policies to Promote Marriage," a report prepared for the U.S. Department of Health and Human Services, 2002, available from the USDHHS.

5. Department of Defense Web site (http://www.dfas.mil/); Nathan McIntire, "Marrying for Money," *L.A. Weekly*, April 20–26, 2007, 26–27.

6. Both quotations are from the 1997 GAO report, Enclosure I.

7. In *Marriage: A History* (London: Penguin, 2006), Stephanie Coontz shows how this "traditional" ideal developed over the past 150 years, how its flourishing in the 1950s and 1960s was exceptional, and how it failed to apply to large numbers of working-class families.

8. I include these forms of financial assistance here as they are directly targeted to allowing spouses to maintain a relationship.

9. Case, "Marriage Licenses," 1773. Where caretaking is involved, privacy rights may protect caretaker autonomy; see Martha Fineman, "Postscript," in her *The Autonomy Myth: A Theory of Dependency* (New York: New Press, 2004); and Harry Brighouse and Adam Swift, "Parents' Rights and the Value of the Family," *Ethics* 117 (2006): 80–108.

10. John Corvino, in "Homosexuality and the PIB Argument," *Ethics* 115 (2005): 501–534, responds at length to the "polygamy, incest, bestiality" argument against same-sex marriage, an argument made by John Finnis among others.

11. For example, Kansas Code §21–3517, Ohio Code §§2907.03.

12. On legal access rights, see Claudia Card, "Against Marriage and Motherhood," *Hypatia* 11 (1996): 1–23. On how equity, partnership, labor, and tort law might apply, see Fineman, *Autonomy Myth*, 134–135. Fineman argues for abolishing marriage as a legal category and replacing it with a legal framework for caretakers; thus her proposal would shift many relations now governed by marriage to the realm of contract, labor, and tort law.

13. Their exclusion is overdetermined: parents or guardians have rights regarding minors in their care, with which minimal marriage contracts might conflict. See Brighouse and Swift, "Parents' Rights."

14. How many close relationships can one have? Apparently the social networking site Facebook limits users to 5,000 "friends"; most of these would presumably be mere acquaintances. I suspect the actual number of sustainable caring relationships is much lower. It might be objected that this criterion raises the bar as contrasted with current marriage, which does not require a caring relationship. It might be responded that, in immigration cases, spouses are required to document their intimacy and shared history. Although it would be impractical and invasive for the state to undertake such investigations in every case, it does not seem undesirable, in theory, to make such a relationship a criterion for legal marriage (ruling out, for instance, mail-order brides).

15. "Beyond Conjugality: Recognizing and Supporting Close Personal Adult Relationships," a 2001 publication of the Law Commission of Canada, available at http://www.samesexmarriage.ca/docs/beyond_conjugality.pdf, examines the feasibility of self-designation (32–36) and other questions of institutional design. Thanks to Rachel Buddeberg for drawing my attention to this document.

16. Paula Ettelbrick, "Since When Is Marriage a Path to Liberation?" *Out/look: National Lesbian and Gay Quarterly* 6 (1989): 14–17, reprinted in Andrew Sullivan, ed., *Same-Sex Marriage: Pro and Con* (New York: Vintage, 2004), 122–128. See also Card, "Against Marriage"; and Drucilla Cornell, "The Public Supports of Love," in Shanley, *Just Marriage*, 81–86. Emma Goldman and Voltairine De Cleyre are earlier critics of state regulation of sexuality and the possessiveness and dependence of marriage.

17. Laura Kipnis, *Against Love* (New York: Pantheon, 2003); compare Friedrich von Schlegel's novel *Lucinde* (1799) and Eric M. Cave, "Marital Pluralism: Making Marriage Safer for Love," *Journal of Social Philosophy* 34 (2003): 331–347.

18. Anne Kingston, *The Meaning of Wife* (Toronto: HarperCollins, 2004).

19. Adrienne Rich [1980], "Compulsory Heterosexuality and Lesbian Existence," in *Adrienne Rich's Poetry and Prose*, ed. Albert Gelpi and Barbara Charlesworth Gelpi (London: Norton, 1993), 203–224.

20. John McMurtry, "Monogamy: A Critique," *Monist* 56 (1972): 587–599.

21. Toni Morrison, "Foreword," in *Beloved* (1987; rev. ed., New York: Vintage, 2004), xvi–xvii.

22. bell hooks, "Revolutionary Parenting," in her *Feminist Theory: From Margin to Center* (Boston: South End, 1984), 133–146.

23. Patricia Hill Collins, "It's All in the Family: Intersections of Gender, Race, and Nation," *Hypatia* 13 (1998): 62–82, 62. See also Enakahi Dua, "Beyond Diversity: Exploring the Ways in Which the Discourse of Race Has Shaped the Institution of the Nuclear Family," in *Scratching the Surface*, ed. Enakshi Dua and Angela Robertson (Toronto: Women's Press, 1999), 237–259.

24. Wedgwood, "The Fundamental Argument," 239.

25. Wellington reviews this literature in "Why Liberals Should Support," 17 ff.

26. "51% of Women Are Now Living without Spouse," *New York Times*, January 16, 2007; an editorial ("Can a 15-Year-Old Be a 'Woman without a Spouse'?" published February 11, 2007) criticized the data but acknowledged that revised calculations showed a majority of spouseless women.

27. Wellington, "Why Liberals Should Support," and Cave, "Harm Prevention," consider and reject harm-based arguments for restricting marriage; I direct the reader to their able refutations.

28. "State Policies to Promote Marriage," 1. See also the 1996 U.S. Personal Responsibility and Work Opportunity Reconciliation Act, Title I, Sec. 101 (findings and related congressional testimony asserting pressing public interest in maintaining our current understanding of marriage.)

29. Alstott, *No Exit,* 8; cf. Cave, "Harm Prevention."

30. See online documents at http://www.aahmi.net/.

31. Shanley, "Just Marriage."

32. See Carole Pateman, *The Sexual Contract* (Cambridge: Polity, 1988).

33. Alstott, *No Exit,* 24.

34. Lucinda Ferguson, "Interpersonal Obligation, Spousal Support, and the Social Nature of Intimacy," paper presented at the 2007 Applied Philosophy annual conference, Philosophy and the Family, Birmingham, June 29 to July 1.

35. Cass Sunstein and Richard Thaler, "Privatizing Marriage," *Monist* 91 (2008): 377–387, at 384.

36. See Gary Becker, "Polygamy and Monogamy in Marriage Markets," in his *A Treatise on the Family*, enlarged ed. (Cambridge, MA: Harvard University Press, 1993), 80–107.

Against Marriage and Motherhood

BY CLAUDIA CARD

> Claudia Card (1940–2015) was an American philosopher best known for her groundbreaking work on issues in feminist theory, LGBTQ theory, and the nature of evil. In this essay, Card rejects the institutions of marriage and motherhood as irredeemably corrupt and corrupting, arguing that LGBTQ people should direct their personal and political energies to forming new more egalitarian forms of association.

This essay argues that current advocacy of lesbian and gay rights to legal marriage and parenthood insufficiently criticizes both marriage and motherhood as they are currently practiced and structured by Northern legal institutions. Instead we would do better not to let the State define our intimate unions and parenting would be improved if the power presently concentrated in the hands of one or two guardians were diluted and distributed through an appropriately concerned community.

The title of this essay is deliberately provocative, because I fear that radical feminist perspectives on marriage and motherhood are in danger of being lost in the quest for equal rights. My concerns, however, are specific. I am skeptical of using the institution of motherhood as a source of paradigms for ethical theory. And I am skeptical of legal marriage as a way to gain a better life for lesbian and gay lovers or as a way to provide a supportive environment for lesbian and gay parents and their children. Of course, some are happy with marriage and motherhood as they now exist. My concern is with the price of that joy borne by those trapped by marriage or motherhood and deeply unlucky in the company they find there. Nevertheless, nothing that I say is intended to disparage the characters of many magnificent women who have struggled in and around these institutions to make the best of a trying set of options.

Backgrounds

My perspective on marriage is influenced not only by other's written reports and analyses but also by my own history of being raised in a lower-middle-class white village family by parents married (to each other) for more than three decades, by my firsthand experiences of urban same-sex domestic partnerships lasting from two and one half to nearly seven years (good ones and bad, some racially mixed, some white, generally mixed in class and religious backgrounds), and by my more recent experience as a lesbian feminist whose partner of the past decade is not a domestic partner. My perspective on child rearing is influenced not by my experience as a mother, but by my experience as a daughter reared by a full-time mother-housewife, by having participated heavily in the raising of my younger siblings, and by having grown to adulthood in a community in which many of the working-class and farming families exemplified aspects of what bell hooks calls "revolutionary parenting" (hooks 1984, 133–46).

When confronted with my negative attitudes toward marriage and motherhood, some recoil as though I were proposing that we learn to do without water and oxygen on the ground that both are polluted (even killing us). Often, I believe, this reaction comes from certain assumptions that the reader or hearer may be inclined to make, which I here note in order to set aside at the outset.

First, my opposition to marriage is not an opposition to intimacy, nor to long-term relationships of intimacy, nor to durable partnerships of many sorts.[1] I understand marriage as a relationship to which the State is an essential third party. Also, like the practices of footbinding and suttee, which, according to the researches of Mary Daly (1978, 113–52), originated among the powerful classes, marriage in Europe was once available only to those with substantial social power. Previously available only to members of propertied classes, the marriage relation has come to be available in modem Northern democracies to any adult heterosexual couple neither of whom is already married to someone else. This is what lesbian and gay agitation for the legal right to marry is about. This is what I find calls for extreme caution.

Second, my opposition to motherhood is neither an opposition to the guidance, education, and caretaking of children nor an opposition to the formation of many kinds of bonds between children and adults.[2] Nor am I opposed to the existence of homes, as places of long-term residence with others of a variety of ages with whom one has deeply committed relationships. When "the family" is credited with being a bulwark against a hostile world, as in the case of many families in the African and Jewish disaporas, the bulwark that is meant often consists of a variety of deeply committed personal (as opposed to legal) relationships and the stability of caring that they represent, or home as a site of these things. The bulwark is not the legitimation (often precarious or nonexistent) of such relationships through institutions of the State. The State was often one of the things that these relationships formed a bulwark against.

Marriage and motherhood in the history of modern patriarchies have been mandatory for and oppressive to women, and they have been criticized by feminists on those grounds. My concerns, however, are as much for the children as for the women that some of these children become and for the goal of avoiding the reproduction of patriarchy. Virginia Held, one optimist about the potentialities of marriage and motherhood, finds

motherhood to be part of a larger conception of family, which she takes to be constructed of noncontractual relationships. She notes that although Marxists and recent communitarians might agree with her focus on noncontractual relationships, their views remain uninformed by feminist critiques of patriarchal families. The family from which she would have society and ethical theorists learn, ultimately, is a postpatriarchal family. But what is a "postpatriarchal family"? Is it a coherent concept?

"Family" is itself a family resemblance concept. Many contemporary lesbian and gay partnerships, households, and friendship networks fit no patriarchal stereotypes and are not sanctified by legal marriage, although their members still regard themselves as "family."[3] But should they? Many social institutions, such as insurance companies, do not honor such conceptions of "family." Family, as understood in contexts where material benefits tend to be at stake, is not constituted totally by noncontractual relationships. At its core is to be found one or more marriage contracts. For those who would work to enlarge the concept of family to include groupings that are currently totally noncontractual, in retaining patriarchal vocabulary there is a danger of importing patriarchal ideals and of inviting treatment as deviant or "second class" at best.

"Family," our students learn in Women's Studies 101, comes from the Latin *familia*, meaning "household," which in turn came from *famulus*, which, according to the OED, meant "servant." The ancient Roman *paterfamilias* was the head of a household of servants and slaves, including his wife or wives, concubines, and children. He had the power of life and death over them. The ability of contemporary male heads of households to get away with battering, incest, and murder suggests to many feminists that the family has not evolved into anything acceptable yet. Would a household of persons whose relationships with each other transcended (as those of families do) sojourns under one roof continue to be rightly called "family" if no members had significant social support for treating other members abusively? Perhaps the postpatriarchal relationships envisioned by

Virginia Held and by so many lesbians and gay men should be called something else, to mark that radical departure from family history. But it is not just a matter of a word. It is difficult to imagine what such relationships would be.

In what follows, I say more about marriage than about motherhood, because it is legal marriage that sets the contexts in which and the background against which motherhood has been legitimated, and it defines contexts in which mothering easily becomes disastrous for children.

Lesbian (or Gay) Marriage?

The question whether lesbians and gay men should pursue the right to marry is not the same as the question whether the law is wrong in its refusal to honor same-sex marriages. What I have to say should apply to relationships between lovers (or parents) of different races as well as to those of same-sex lovers (or parents). The ways we have been treated are abominable. But it does not follow that we should seek legal marriage.

It is one thing to argue that others are wrong to deny us something and another to argue that what they would deny us is something we should fight for the right to have. I do not deny that others are wrong to exclude same-sex lovers and lovers of different races from the rights of marriage. I question only whether we should fight for those rights, even if we do not intend to exercise them. Suppose that slave-owning in some mythical society were denied to otherwise free women, on the ground that such women as slave-owners would pervert the institution of slavery. Women (both free and unfree) could (unfortunately) document empirically the falsity of beliefs underlying such grounds. It would not follow that women should fight for the right to own slaves, or even for the rights of other women to own slaves. Likewise, if marriage is a deeply flawed institution, even though it is a special injustice to exclude lesbians and gay men arbitrarily from participating in it, it would not necessarily advance the cause of justice on the whole to remove the special injustice of discrimination.

About same-sex marriage I feel something like the way I feel about prostitution. Let us, by all means, *decriminalize* sodomy and so forth.

Although marriage rights would be *sufficient* to enable lovers to have sex legally, such rights should not be *necessary* for that purpose. Where they *are* legally necessary and also available for protection against the social oppression of same-sex lovers, as for lovers of different races, there will be enormous pressure to marry. Let us not pretend that marriage is basically a good thing on the ground that durable intimate relationships are. Let us not be eager to have the State regulate our unions. Let us work to remove barriers to our enjoying some of the privileges presently available only to heterosexual married couples. But in doing so, we should also be careful not to support discrimination against those who choose not to marry and not to support continued state definition of the legitimacy of intimate relationships. I would rather see the state deregulate heterosexual marriage than see it begin to regulate same-sex marriage.

As noted above, my partner of the past decade is not a domestic partner. She and I form some kind of fairly common social unit which, so far as I know, remains nameless. Along with such namelessness goes a certain invisibility, a mixed blessing to which I will return. We do not share a domicile (she has her house; I have mine). Nor do we form an economic unit (she pays her bills; I pay mine). Although we certainly have fun together, our relationship is not based simply on fun. We share the sorts of mundane details of daily living that Mohr finds constitutive of marriage (often in her house, often in mine). We know a whole lot about each other's lives that the neighbors and our other friends will never know. In times of trouble, we are each other's first line of defense, and in times of need, we are each other's main support. Still, we are not married. Nor do we yearn to marry. Yet if marrying became an option that would legitimate behavior otherwise illegitimate and make available to us social securities that will no doubt become even more important to us as we age, we and many others like us might be pushed into marriage. Marrying under such conditions is not a totally free choice.

Because of this unfreedom, I find at least four interconnected kinds of problems with marriage. Three may be somewhat remediable in principle, although if they were remedied, many might no longer have strong motives to marry. I doubt that the fourth problem, which I also find most important, is fixable.

The first problem, perhaps easiest to remedy in principle (if not in practice) is that employers and others (such as units of government) often make available only to legally married couples benefits that anyone could be presumed to want, married or not, such as affordable health and dental insurance, the right to live in attractive residential areas, visitation rights in relation to significant others, and so forth. Spousal benefits for employees are a significant portion of many workers' compensation. Thus married workers are often, in effect, paid more for the same labor than unmarried workers (Berzon 1988, 266; Pierce 1995, 5). This is one way in which people who do not have independent access to an income often find themselves economically pressured into marrying. Historically, women have been in this position oftener than men, including, of course, most pre-twentieth-century lesbians, many of whom married men for economic security.

The second problem is that even though divorce by mutual consent is now generally permitted in the United States, the consequences of divorce can be so difficult that many who should divorce do not. This to some extent is a continuation of the benefits problem. But also, if one partner can sue the other for support or receive a share of the other's assets to which they would not otherwise have been legally entitled, there are new economic motives to preserve emotionally disastrous unions.

The third issue, which would be seriously troublesome for many lesbians, is that legal marriage as currently understood in Northern democracies is monogamous in the sense of one *spouse* at a time, even though the law in many states no longer treats "adultery" (literally "pollution") as criminal. Yet many of us have more than one long-term intimate relationship during the same time period. Any attempt to change the current understanding of marriage so as to allow plural marriage partners (with plural contracts) would have economic implications that I have yet to see anyone explore.

Finally, the fourth problem, the one that I doubt is fixable (depending on what "marriage" means) is

that the legal rights of access that married partners have to each other's persons, property, and lives makes it all but impossible for a spouse to defend herself (or himself), or to be protected against torture, rape, battery, stalking, mayhem, or murder by the other spouse. Spousal murder accounts for a substantial number of murders each year. This factor is made worse by the presence of the second problem mentioned above (difficulties of divorce that lead many to remain married when they should not), which provide motives to violence within marriages. Legal marriage thus enlists state support for conditions conducive to murder and mayhem.

The point is not that all marriages are violent. It is not about the frequency of violence, although the frequency appears high. The points are, rather, that the institution places obstacles in the way of protecting spouses (however many) who need it and is conducive to violence in relationships that go bad. Battery is, of course, not confined to spouses. Lesbian and gay battery is real (see Renzetti 1992; Lobel 1986; Island and Letellier 1991). But the law does not protect unmarried batterers or tend to preserve the relationships of unmarried lovers in the way that it protects husbands and tends to preserve marriages.

Why, then, would anyone marry? Because it is a tradition, glorified and romanticized. It grants status. It is a significant (social) mark of adulthood for women in patriarchy. It is a way to avoid certain hassles from one's family of origin and from society at large—hassles to oneself, to one's lover (if there is only one), and to children with whom one may live or whom one may bring into being. We need better traditions. And women have long needed other social marks of adulthood and ways to escape families of origin.

Under our present exclusion from the glories of legal matrimony, the usual reason why lesbians or gay men form partnerships and stay together is because we care for each other. We may break up for other kinds of reasons (such as one of us being assigned by an employer to another part of the country and neither of us being able to afford to give up our jobs). But when we stay together, that is usually because of how we feel about each other and about our life together. Consider how this basic taken-for-granted fact might change if we could marry with the State's blessings. There are many material benefits to tempt those who can into marrying, not to mention the improvement in one's social reputation as a reliable citizen (and for those of us who are not reliable citizens, the protection against having a spouse forced to testify against us in court).

Let us consider each of these four problems further. The first was that of economic and other benefits, such as insurance that employers often make available only to marrieds, the right of successorship to an apartment, inheritance rights, and the right to purchase a home in whatever residential neighborhood one can afford. The attachment of such benefits to marital status is a problem in two respects. First, because the benefits are substantial, not trivial, they offer an ulterior motive for turning a lover relationship into a marriage—even for pretending to care for someone, deceiving oneself as well as others. As Emma Goldman argued in the early twentieth century, when marriage becomes an insurance policy, it may no longer be compatible with love (1969). Second, the practice of making such benefits available only to marrieds discriminates against those who, for whatever reason, do not marry. Because of the first factor, many heterosexuals who do not fundamentally approve of legal marriage give in and marry anyhow. Because of the second factor, many heterosexual feminists, however, refuse legal marriage (although the State may regard their relationships as common law marriages).

Now add to the spousal benefits problem the second difficulty, that of the consequences of getting a divorce (for example, consequences pertaining to shared property, alimony, or child support payments and difficulties in terms of access to children), especially if the divorce is not friendly. Intimate partnerships beginning from sexual or erotic attraction tend to be of limited viability, even under favorable circumstances. About half of all married couples in the United States at present get divorced, and probably most of the other half should. But the foreseeable consequences of divorce provide motives to stay married for many

spouses who no longer love each other (if they ever did) and have even grown to hate each other. Staying married ordinarily hampers one's ability to develop a satisfying lover relationship with someone new. As long as marriage is monogamous in the sense of one *spouse* at a time, it interferes with one's ability to obtain spousal benefits for a new lover. When spouses grow to hate each other, the access that was a joy as lovers turns into something highly dangerous. I will return to this.

Third, the fact of multiple relationships is a problem even for relatively good marriages. Mohr, as noted, argues in favor of reforming marriage so as not to require sexual exclusiveness rather than officially permitting only monogamy. Yet he was thinking not of multiple *spouses* but of a monogamous marriage in which neither partner expects sexual exclusiveness of the other. Yet, one spouse per person is monogamy, however promiscuous the spouses may be. The advantages that Mohr enumerates as among the perks of marriage apply only to spouses, not to relationships with additional significant others who are not one's spouses. Yet the same reasons that lead one to want those benefits for a spouse can lead one to want them for additional significant others. If lesbian and gay marriages were acknowledged in Northern democracies today, they would be legally as monogamous as heterosexual marriage, regardless of the number of one's actual sexual partners. This does not reflect the relationships that many lesbians and gay men have or want.

Christine Pierce argues, in support of the option to legalize lesbian and gay marriages, that lesbian and gay images have been cast too much in terms of individuals—*The Well of Loneliness* (Hall 1950), for example—and not enough in terms of relationships, especially serious relationships involving long-term commitments (Pierce 1995, 13). Marriage gives visibility to people "as couples, partners, family, and kin," a visibility that lesbians and gay men have lacked and that could be important to dispelling negative stereotypes and assumptions that our relationships do not embody many of the same ideals as those of many heterosexual couples, partners, family, and kin (Pierce 1995). This is both true and important.

It is not clear, however, that legal marriage would offer visibility to our relationships as they presently exist. It might well change our relationships so that they became more like heterosexual marriages, loveless after the first few years but hopelessly bogged down with financial entanglements or children (adopted or products of turkey-baster insemination or previous marriages), making separation or divorce (at least in the near future) too difficult to contemplate, giving rise to new motives for mayhem and murder. Those who never previously felt pressure to marry a lover might confront not just new options but new pressures and traps.

In such a context, pointing out that many marriages are very loving, not at all violent, and proclaim to the world two people's honorable commitment to each other, seems to me analogous to pointing out, as many slave-owners did, that many slave-owners were truly emotionally bonded with their slaves, that they did not whip them, and that even the slaves were proud and honored to be the slaves of such masters.

Central to the idea of marriage, historically, has been intimate access to the persons, belongings, activities, even histories of one another. More important than sexual access, marriage gives spouses physical access to each other's residences and belongings, and it gives access to information about each other, including financial status, that other friends and certainly the neighbors do not ordinarily have. For all that has been said about the privacy that marriage protects, what astonishes me is how much privacy one gives up in marrying.

This mutual access appears to be a central point of marrying. Is it wise to abdicate legally one's privacy to that extent? What interests does it serve? Anyone who in fact cohabits with another may seem to give up similar privacy. Yet, without marriage, it is possible to take one's life back without encountering the law as an obstacle. One may even be able to enlist legal help in getting it back. In this regard, uncloseted lesbians and gay men presently have a certain advantage—which, by the way, "palimony" suits threaten to undermine by applying the idea of "common law" marriage to same-sex couples (see, e.g., Faulkner with Nelson 1993).

Among the trappings of marriage that have received attention and become controversial, ceremonies and rituals are much discussed. I have no firm opinions about ceremonies or rituals. A far more important issue seems to me to be the marriage *license*, which receives hardly any attention at all. Ceremonies affirming a relationship can take place at any point in the relationship. But a license is what one needs to initiate a legal marriage. To marry legally, one applies to the state for a license, and marriage, once entered into, licenses spouses to certain kinds of access to each other's persons and lives. It is a mistake to think of a license as simply enhancing everyone's freedom. One person's license, in this case, can be another's prison. Prerequisites for marriage licenses are astonishingly lax. Anyone of a certain age, not presently married to someone else, and free of certain communicable diseases automatically qualifies. A criminal record for violent crimes is, to my knowledge, no bar. Compare this with other licenses, such as a driver's license. In Wisconsin, to retain a driver's license, we submit periodically to eye exams. Some states have more stringent requirements. To obtain a driver's license, all drivers have to pass a written and a behind-the-wheel test to demonstrate knowledge and skill. In Madison, Wisconsin, even to adopt a cat from the humane society, we have to fill out a form demonstrating knowledge of relevant ordinances for pet-guardians. Yet to marry, applicants need demonstrate no knowledge of the laws pertaining to marriage nor any relationship skills nor even the modicum of self-control required to respect another human being. And once the marriage exists, the burden of proof is always on those who would dissolve it, never on those who would continue it in perpetuity.

Further disanalogies between drivers' and marriage licenses confirm that in our society there is greater concern for victims of bad driving than for those of bad marriages. You cannot legally drive without a license, whereas it is now in many jurisdictions not illegal for unmarried adults of whatever sex to cohabit. One can acquire the status of spousehood simply by cohabiting heterosexually for several years, whereas one does not acquire a driver's license simply by driving for years without one. Driving without the requisite skills and scruples is recognized as a great danger to others and treated accordingly. No comparable recognition is given the dangers of legally sanctioning the access of one person to the person and life of another without evidence of the relevant knowledge and scruples of those so licensed. The consequence is that married victims of partner battering and rape have less protection than anyone except children. What is at stake are permanently disabling and life-threatening injuries, for those who survive. I do not, at present, see how this vulnerability can be acceptably removed from the institution of legal marriage. Measures could be taken to render its disastrous consequences less likely than they are presently but at the cost of considerable state intrusion into our lives.

Thus I conclude that legalizing lesbian and gay marriage, turning a personal commitment into a license regulable and enforceable by the state, is probably a very bad idea and that lesbians and gay men are probably better off, all things considered, without the "option" (and its consequent pressures) to obtain and act on such a license, despite some of the immediate material and spiritual gains to some of being able to do so. Had we any chance of success, we might do better to agitate for the abolition of legal marriage altogether.

Nevertheless, many will object that marriage provides an important environment for the rearing of children. An appreciation of the conduciveness of marriage to murder and mayhem challenges that assumption. Historically, marriage and motherhood have gone hand in hand—ideologically, although often enough not in fact. That marriage can provide a valuable context for motherhood—even if it is unlikely to do so—as an argument in favor of marriage seems to presuppose that motherhood is a good thing. So let us consider next whether that is so.

Why Motherhood?

The term "mother" is ambiguous between a woman who gives birth and a female who parents, that is, rears a child—often but not necessarily the same woman. The term "motherhood" is ambiguous between the experience of mothers (in either sense, usually the second) and a social practice the rules of which structure child rearing. It is the latter that interests me here. Just as some today would stretch the concept of "family" to cover any committed partnership, household, or close and enduring network of friends, others would stretch the concept of "motherhood" to cover any mode of child rearing. That is not how I understand "motherhood." Just as not every durable intimate partnership is a marriage, not every mode of child rearing exemplifies motherhood. Historically, motherhood has been a core element of patriarchy. Within the institution of motherhood, mother's primary commitments have been to father and only secondarily to his children. Unmarried women have been held responsible by the State for the primary care of children they birth, unless a man wished to claim them. In fact, of course, children are raised by grandparents, single parents (heterosexual, lesbian, gay, asexual, and so on), and extended families, all in the midst of patriarchies. But these have been regarded as deviant parentings, with nothing like the prestige or social and legal support available to patriarchal mothers, as evidenced in the description of the relevant "families" in many cases as providing at best "broken homes."

Apart from the institution of marriage and historical ideals of the family, it is uncertain what characteristics mother-child relationships would have, for many alternatives are possible. In the good ones, mother-child relationships would not be as characterized as they have been by involuntary uncompensated caretaking. Even today, an ever-increasing amount of caretaking is being done contractually in day-care centers, with the result that a legitimate mother's relationship to her child is often much less a caretaking relationship than her mother's relationship to her was.

Much ink has been spilled debunking what passes for "love" in marriage. It is time to consider how much of the "love" that children are said to need is no more love than spousal attachments have been. Children do need stable intimate bonds with adults. But they also need supervision, education, health care, and a variety of relationships with people of a variety of ages. What the

State tends to enforce in motherhood is the child's access to its mother, which guarantees none of these things, and the mother's answerability for her child's waywardness, which gives her a motive for constant supervision, thereby removing certain burdens from others but easily also endangering the well-being of her child if she is ill supplied with resources. Lacking adequate social or material resources, many a parent resorts to violent discipline in such situations, which the State has been reluctant to prevent or even acknowledge. This is what it has meant, legally, for a child to be a mother's "own": her own is the child who has legal rights of access to her and for whose waywardness she becomes answerable, although she is largely left to her own devices for carrying out the entailed responsibilities.

By contrast, children raised by lesbian or gay parents today are much more likely to be in relationships carefully chosen and affirmed by their caretakers.[4] Even though that would no doubt continue to be true oftener of the children of lesbian and gay parents in same-sex marriages than of the children of heterosexual parents, marriage would involve the State in defining who really had the status of "parent." The State has been willing to grant that status to at most two persons at a time, per child. It gives the child legal rights of access to at most those two parties. And it imposes legal accountability for the child's waywardness on at most those two parties. Under the present system that deprives lesbian and gay parents of spousal status, many lesbian and gay couples do their best anyway to emulate heterosexual models, which usually means assuming the responsibilities without the privileges.[5] Others I have known, however, attempt to undermine the assumption that parental responsibility should be concentrated in one or two people who have the power of a child's happiness and unhappiness in their hands for nearly two decades. Children raised without such models of the concentration of power may be less likely to reproduce patriarchal and other oppressive social relationships.

The "revolutionary parenting" that bell hooks describes (1984) dilutes the power of individual parents. Although children retain special affectional ties to their "bloodmothers," accountability for children's waywardness is more widely distributed. With many caretakers (such as "othermothers"), there is less pressure to make any one of them constantly accessible to a child and more pressure to make everyone somewhat accessible. With many caretakers, it is less likely that any of them will get away with prolonged abuse, or even be tempted to perpetrate it.

In my childhood, many adults looked out for the children of my village. I had, in a way, a combination of both kinds of worlds. My parents, married to each other, had the legal rights and the legal responsibilities of patriarchal parents. Yet, some of those responsibilities were in fact assumed by "othermothers," including women (and men) who never married anyone. Because it could always be assumed that wherever I roamed in the village, I would never be among strangers, my parents did not think they always needed to supervise me, although they were also ambivalent about that, as they would be legally answerable for any trouble I caused. I used to dread the thought that we might move to a city, where my freedom would probably have been severely curtailed, as it was when we lived in a large, white middle-class urban environment during World War II. In the village, because everyone assumed (reasonably) that someone was watching us, we children often escaped the intensity of physical discipline that I experienced alone with my mother amid the far larger urban population.

There are both worse and better environments that can be imagined for children than stereotypical patriarchal families. Urban environments in which parents must work away from home but can neither bring their children nor assume that their children are being watched by anyone are no doubt worse. Children who have never had effective caretakers do not make good caretakers of each other, either. Feminism today has been in something of a bind with respect to the so-called postpatriarchal family. If both women and men are to be actively involved in markets and governments and free to become active members of all occupations and professions, when, where, and how is child care going to be done? The solution of many feminists has been, in practice, for two parents to take turns spending time with the children. There is an increasing tendency today for parents who divide responsibilities for the children to pay others to do the child care, if they can afford it, when their turn comes. To the extent that this works, it is evidence that "mothering" is not necessary for child care.

When one does in fact have a primary caretaker who has, if not the power of life and death, then the power of one's happiness and unhappiness in their hands for many years in the early stages of one's life, the influence of that experience on the rest of one's life is profound. It seems, for example, to affect one's ability to form good relationships with others in ways that are extremely difficult to change, if they are changeable at all. Yet, it may be misleading if it suggests that everyone really needs a single primary caretaker (or even two primary caretakers) who has the power of one's happiness and unhappiness in their hands for many years during the early stages of one's life. Perhaps people need that only in a society that refuses to take and share responsibility collectively for its own consciously and thought fully affirmed reproduction. In such a society, conscientious mothers are often the best protection a child has. But if so, it is misleading to say that such a relationship as the mother-child relationship is the, or even a, fundamental social relationship. It has been even less fundamental for many people, historically, than one might think, given how many children have been raised in institutions other than households or raised by a variety of paid caretakers with limited responsibilities.

Because mothers in a society that generally refuses to take collective responsibility for reproduction are often the best or even the only protection that children have, in the short run it is worth fighting for the right to adopt and raise children within lesbian and gay households. This is emergency care for young people, many of whom are already here and desperately in need of care. There is little that heterosexual couples can do to rebel as individual couples in a society in which their relationship is turned into a common law relationship after some years by the State and in which they are given the responsibilities and rights of parents over

any children they may raise. Communal action is what is required to implement new models of parenting. In the long run, it seems best to keep open the option of making parenting more "revolutionary" along the lines of communal practices such as those described by bell hooks. Instead of encouraging such a revolution, legal marriage interferes with it in a state that glorifies marriage and takes the marriage relationship to be the only truly healthy context in which to raise children. Lesbian and gay unions have great potentiality to further the revolution, in part because we *cannot* marry.

If motherhood is transcended, the importance of attending to the experiences and environments of children remains. The "children" if not the "mothers" in society are all of us. Not each of us will choose motherhood under present conditions. But each of us has been a child, and each future human survivor will have childhood to survive. Instead of finding that the mother-child relationship provides a valuable paradigm for moral theorizing, even one who has mothered might find, reflecting on both her experience as a mother and her experience of having been mothered, that mothering should not be necessary, or that it should be less necessary than has been thought, and that it has more potential to do harm than good. The power of mothers over children may have been historically far more detrimental to daughters than to sons, at least in societies where daughters have been more controlled, more excluded from well-rewarded careers, and more compelled to engage in family service than sons. Such a finding would be in keeping with the project of drawing on the usually unacknowledged historically characteristic experiences of women.

In suggesting that the experience of being mothered has great potential for harm to children, I do not have in mind the kinds of concerns recently expressed by political conservatives about mothers who abuse drugs or are sexually promiscuous. Even these mothers are often the best protection their children have. I have in mind the environments provided by mothers who in fact do live up to contemporary norms of ideal motherhood or even exceed the demands of such norms in the degree of attention and concern they manifest for their children in providing a child-centered home as fully constructed as their resources allow.

Everyone would benefit from a society that was more attentive to the experiences of children, to the relationships of children with adults and with each other, and to the conditions under which children make the transition to adulthood. Moral philosophy might also be transformed by greater attention to the fact that adult experience and its potentialities are significantly conditioned by the childhoods of adults and of those children's relationships to (yet earlier) adults. Whether or not one agrees with the idea that motherhood offers a valuable paradigm for moral theorizing, in getting us to take seriously the significance of the child's experience of childhood and to take up the standpoint of the "child" in all of us, philosophical work exploring the significance of mother-child relationships is doing feminism and moral philosophy a great service.

DISCUSSION QUESTIONS

1. Explain why Card distinguishes between the question of whether lesbians and gay men should pursue the right to marry and the question of whether the law is wrong in its refusal to honor same-sex marriages.
2. What does Card say are the four interconnected problems with marriage? Why does she think so many people choose to marry nevertheless?
3. Explain what Card means by characterizing motherhood as "involuntary uncompensated caretaking," then explain why "revolutionary parenting" is a superior model.
4. Explain why Card thinks gay and lesbian couples are particularly well situated to offer new models of romantic and parenting relationships.

NOTES

Thanks to Harry Brighouse, Vicky Davion, Virginia Held, Sara Ruddick, anonymous reviewers for *Hypatia*, and especially to Lynne Tirrell for helpful comments and suggestions and to audiences who heard ancestors of this essay at the Pacific and Central Divisions of the American Philosophical Association in 1995.

1. Betty Berzon claims that her book *Permanent Partners* is about "reinventing our gay and lesbian relationships" and "learning to imbue them with all the *solemnity* of marriage without necessarily imitating the heterosexual model" (1988, 7), and yet by the end of the book it is difficult to think of anything in legal ideals of the heterosexual nuclear family that she has not urged us to imitate.

2. Thus I am not an advocate of the equal legal rights for children movement as that movement is presented and criticized by Purdy (1992), namely, as a movement advocating that children have exactly the same legal rights as adults, including the legal right not to attend school.

3. See, for example, Weston (1991), Burke (1993), and Slater (1995). In contrast, Berzon (1988) uses the language of partnership, reserving "family" for social structures based on heterosexual unions, as in chap. 12, subtitled "Integrating Your Families into Your Life as a Couple."

4. An outstanding anthology on the many varieties of lesbian parenting is Arnup (1995). Also interesting is the anthropological study of lesbian mothers by Lewin (1993). Both are rich in references to many resources on both lesbian and gay parenting.

5. Lewin (1993) finds, for example, that lesbian mothers tend to assume all caretaking responsibilities themselves, or in some cases share them with a partner, turning to their families of origin, rather than to a friendship network of peers, for additionally needed support.

REFERENCES

Arnup, Katherine, ed. 1995. *Lesbian parenting: Living with pride and prejudice*. Charlotte-town, P.E.I.: Gynergy Books.

Baier, Annette C. 1994. *Moral prejudices: Essays on ethics*. Cambridge: Harvard University Press.

Berzon, Betty. 1988. *Permanent partnerships: Building lesbian and gay relationships that last*. New York: Penguin.

Blumenfeld, Warren J. 1996. Same-sex marriage: Introducing the discussion. *Journal of Gay, Lesbian, and Bisexual Identity* 1(1): 77.

Boswell, John. 1988. *The kindness of strangers: The abandonment of children in Western Europe from late antiquity to the Renaissance*. New York: Pantheon.

Boswell, John. 1994. *Same-sex unions in premodern Europe*. New York: Villard.

Brownworth, Victoria A. 1996. Tying the knot or the hangman's noose: The case against marriage. *Journal of Gay, Lesbian, and Bisexual Identity* 1(1): 91–98.

Burke, Phyllis. 1993. *Family values: Two moms and their son*. New York: Random House.

Card, Claudia. 1988. Gratitude and Obligation. *American Philosophical Quarterly* 25(2): 115–27.

Card, Claudia. 1990. Gender and Moral Luck. In *Identity, character, and morality: Essays in moral psychology*, ed. Owen Flanagan and Amelie Oksenberg Rorty. Cambridge: MIT Press.

Card, Claudia. 1995. *Lesbian choices*. New York: Columbia University Press.

Collins, Patricia Hill. 1991. *Black feminist thought: Knowledge, consciousness, and the politics of empowerment*. New York: Routledge.

Daly, Mary. 1978. *Gyn/Ecology: The metaethics of radical feminism*. Boston: Beacon.

Faulkner, Sandra, with Judy Nelson. 1993. *Love match: Nelson vs. Navratilova*. New York: Birch Lane Press.

Friedman, Marilyn. 1993. *What are friends for? Feminist perspectives on personal relationships and moral theory*. Ithaca: Cornell University Press.

Gilman, Charlotte Perkins. 1966. *Women and economics: The economic factor between men and women as a factor in social evolution*, ed. Carl Degler. New York: Harper.

Gilman, Charlotte Perkins. 1992. *Herland*. In *Herland and selected stories by Charlotte Perkins Gilman*, ed. Barbara H. Solomon. New York: Signet.

Goldman, Emma. 1969. Marriage and Love. In *Anarchism and other essays*. New York: Dover.

Hall, Radclyffe. 1950. *The well of loneliness*. New York: Pocket Books. (Many editions; first published 1928).

Held, Virginia. 1993. *Feminist morality: Transforming culture, society, and politics*. Chicago: University of Chicago Press.

Hoagland, Sarah Lucia. 1988. *Lesbian ethics: Toward new value*. Palo Alto, CA: Institute of Lesbian Studies.

hooks, bell. 1984. *Feminist theory from margin to center*. Boston: South End Press.

Island, David, and Patrick Letellier. 1991. *Men who beat the men who love them: Battered gay men and domestic violence*. New York: Harrington Park Press.

Lewin, Ellen. 1993. *Lesbian mothers*. Ithaca: Cornell University Press.

Lobel, Kerry, ed. 1986. *Naming the violence: Speaking out about lesbian battering*. Seattle: Seal Press.

Lorde, Audre. 1984. *Sister outsider: Essays and speeches*. Trumansburg: Crossing Press.

Mahmoody, Betty, with William Hoffer. 1987. *Not without my daughter*. New York: St. Martin's.

Mohr, Richard D. 1994. *A more perfect union: Why straight America must stand up for gay rights*. Boston: Beacon.

Newman, Leslea. 1989. *Heather has two mommies*. Northampton, MA: In Other Words Publishing.

Pierce, Christine. 1995. Gay marriage. *Journal of Social Philosophy* 28(2): 5–16.

Purdy, Laura M. 1992. *In their best interest? The case against equal rights for children*. Ithaca: Cornell University Press.

Renzetti, Clair M. 1992. *Violent betrayal: Partner abuse in lesbian relationships*. Newbury Park, CA: Sage Publications.

Rich, Adrienne. 1976. *Of woman born: Motherhood as experience and as institution*. New York: Norton.

Ruddick, Sara. 1989. *Maternal thinking: Toward a politics of peace*. Boston: Beacon.

Slater, Suzanne. 1995. *The lesbian family life cycle*. New York: Free Press.

Trebilcot, Joyce, ed. 1983. *Mothering: Essays in feminist theory*. Totowa, N.J.: Rowman and Allanheld.

Weston, Kath. 1991. *Families we choose*. New York: Columbia University Press.

Wolfson, Evan. 1996. Why we should fight for the freedom to marry: The challenges and opportunities that will follow a win in Hawaii. *Journal of Lesbian, Gay, and Bisexual Identity* 1(1): 79–89.

Do Black Men Have a Moral Duty to Marry Black Women?

BY CHARLES MILLS

Charles Mills (1951–2021) was a Jamaican philosopher of race whose pioneering work on racial critiques of the social contract revolutionized critical race theory. In this essay, Mills subjects the question raised in the title—long a major point of contention in the Black community—to rigorous yet accessible philosophical analysis.

It is a measure of the continuing social distance between the races that the average white liberal, I am sure, would automatically assume that only a racist could think that the answer to this question is anything but an obvious "No!" The answer may, of course, still be "No," but it might not be quite so obvious. At any rate, I want to suggest that this issue—a major point of contention in the black community for decades, particularly among black women—is worthy of philosophical investigation. What arguments could there be for such a duty? On what axiological foundation would it be based? How strong would it be?

I

That there could be such antipathies in the black community will come as a revelation to many whites, who will, of course, be used to thinking of the prohibitions going the other way. The famous line challenging would-be integrationists, after all, was always "But would you let one marry your daughter?" Indeed in the biracial coalitions of the civil rights movements, both communist and liberal, of the 1930s–1960s, acceptance of such relationships was often seen as a kind of ultimate test of good faith, a sign of whether or not whites had genuinely overcome their racist socialization.

This final intimacy (as the Klan warned: let 'em in the classroom and they'll end up in the bedroom) has assumed such significance because of the deep connection between racism and sex. Various theories have been put forward to explain white racism: that it is just "primordial" ethnocentrism writ large and backed by the differential technological and economic power of the European conquest (so *all* human groups would have been equally racist had they gotten the chance); the "culturalist" explanations that tie it, more specifically, to militant Christianity's *jihad* against non-European infidels and heathens, and the Manichaean white/good black/evil color symbolism in many European languages, particularly English; Marxist economic explanations that see it basically as an ideological rationalization of expansionist colonial capitalism (so that a naive ethnocentrism, and admitted cultural predispositions, would easily have been *overcome* had it not been for the need to justify conquest, expropriation, and enslavement); and psycho-sexual explanations' focusing on the anal and genital regions, with their powerful associations of desire and shame, and their perceived link with dirt, blackness, and the dark body. But all theories have had to come to grips—some more, some less, successfully—with the peculiar horror that black male/white female couplings have aroused in the European imagination, the fear, as in *Othello*, that "Even now . . . an old black ram/Is tupping your white ewe."[1]

For many this is truly, as some have called it, "the last taboo," and in a world where we're trying to eliminate racism, it would seem that interracial unions should be welcomed as a sign of progress.

Yet many blacks, particularly women, are hostile to such relationships.

In a class on African-American Philosophy I taught this year, this question came up in discussions, and, when I decided to pose it as an essay question, was far and away the most popular topic, the majority of students arguing for "Yes." If this notion seems strange and bizarre to most liberal white philosophers, then, this simply reflects the fact that, while the black male voice is still under-represented in the academy, the black female voice has until recently been silenced altogether.

This paper is, in part, an attempt to reconstruct—doubtless somewhat presumptuously—some of the possible arguments from this usually neglected perspective. So this is one for the sisters. I will go through what I take to be the most popular arguments, dealing with the weaker ones first and leaving the most interesting and challenging ones to the end.[2]

III

1. The Racial Purification, or "Let's Get the Cream Out of the Coffee," Argument

In its classic version, the Racial Purification Argument is straightforwardly biologistic, with culture, where it is invoked, being envisaged as tied to race by hereditarian links.

The claim here is that there is (i) such a thing as a "pure" race, (ii) racial "purity" is good, either in itself and/or as a means to other ends, such as cultural preservation and future racial achievement, and (iii) members of the race should therefore regard themselves as having a duty to foster purity, or—when it has already been vitiated—to girding up their loins to restore it.

The structure of the argument is unhappily familiar from its better-known white supremacist version, Klan or Nazi. This version will include corollary racist eugenic notions of degraded "mongrel" types produced by racial interbreeding. However, since blacks are the subordinated rather than dominant race, the boundaries here are perforce drawn so as to *include* rather than exclude

those of "mixed" race (the "one-drop" rule—some "black" blood makes you black, whereas some "white" blood *doesn't* make you white). For white racists, then, the emphasis would originally have been on *maintaining* purity against black and/or Jewish "pollution" (seen—in the times when black/Jewish relations were somewhat happier than they are now—as collaborating on this joint contaminatory project: bring on those white Christian virgins!). For blacks, on the other hand, because of the myriad rapes and economically-coerced sexual transactions of slavery and post-slavery, the emphasis is usually on *restoring* a lost purity, getting rid of the "pollution" of *white* blood. Those of mixed race are counted, sometimes reluctantly, as black, but the idea is that they should try to darken their progeny. (So for light-skinned black men, the injunction is sometimes put in the stronger terms of marrying *dark* black women.)

This argument is, of course, multiply vulnerable. To be convincing, it would really have to presuppose polygenism, the heretical hypothesis that popped up repeatedly in racist thought in the 18th and 19th centuries (and was endorsed by such Enlightenment luminaries as Hume and Voltaire) that, *contra* Christian orthodoxy, there were really separate creations for the races, so that blacks and whites were different species.[3] The theology of the black version will necessarily be different (for example, the original Black Muslim claim that whites were created by the evil scientist Yacub[4]), but the logic, with the terms inverted, is the same. In a post-Darwinian framework that assumes a common humanity, it is harder to defend (which has not, of course, stopped 20th-century white racists), though of course one can, and people still do, talk about "higher" and "lower," "more" and "less" evolved, races. However, most biologists and anthropologists would today agree that there are no such things as races in the first place, so that, *a fortiori*, there cannot be "pure" races (this is, to use old-fashioned Rylean language, a kind of "category mistake"). Instead what exists are "clines," gradients of continuously-varying (i.e., *not* discretely-differentiated) phenotypical traits linked with clumpings of genetic patterns.[5] Humans share most of their genes, and, as ironists have pointed out, if you go back far enough, it turns out that we're all originally African anyway, so that even those blond-haired, blue-eyed Nordic types just happen to be grandchildren who left the continent earlier.

Moreover, even if there were natural ontological divisions between different branches of humanity, an auxiliary argument would still obviously be needed to establish why maintaining these particular configurations of genes *would* be a good thing, and such a good thing that the duty to realize it overrides other claims. Culture is not tied to genotype—the familiar point that children of different "races" would, if switched at birth, take on the cultural traits of their new home. So the argument can only really plausibly get off the ground on the assumption, clearly racist whether in its white or black version, that moral character and/or propensity for intellectual achievement and/or aesthetic worth is genetically racially encoded, *and* of such a degree of difference that promoting it outweighs other considerations such as freedom of choice, staying with the person that you love, and so forth.

Finally, as a fallback position, there is the defiant assertion—what Anthony Appiah calls "intrinsic racism"[6]—that one race is better than another in complete *independence* of these contestable claims about ability and character, so that it is just good *in itself* that there be more pure whites (or more pure blacks). And here one would simply point out that this is not so much an argument, as a concession that there *is* no argument.

2. The Racial Caution, or "Don't Get the White Folks Mad," Argument

Another kind of consequentialist argument involves quite different kinds of considerations, not questionable claims about racial purity but pragmatic points about strategy. This rests on the uncontroversial factual claim that, as mentioned, many, indeed the majority, of whites are disturbed and angered by such unions,[7] so that entering into them will increase white hostility and opposition to integration. (As surveys during the period of civil rights activism showed, many whites were convinced that integration of the bedroom was

in fact the *main thing on* the minds of blacks who were pressing for "civil rights," so that this would just confirm their worst fears.) The principle would not, of course, be that one should avoid white anger at all costs (since the advance of the black liberation struggle will *necessarily* anger some whites, and this would certainly not be a moral reason for abandoning it). Rather, the idea would be that black-on-white relationships *unnecessarily* infuriate whites. So since such unions stir up great passion, and are not a necessary component of the struggle, they should be eschewed. (Some versions might then leave it open for them to be permissible in the future non-racist society, or at least when racism has considerably diminished.)

This argument is obviously somewhat more respectable. It does, however, rest on the assumption that either no point of moral principle is involved, or that breach of the principle is justified by the overwhelmingly negative consequences for achieving black liberation of stirring such passions. The reply to the first might take the anti-utilitarian, let-the-heavens-fall line that individual rights to choice trump such considerations, and that if two people love one another, they should not forsake their relationship for the sake of expediting a cause. (Or, less nobly, it might just take the in-your-face form of the joys of *épater-ing* Whitey.) It could also be argued that such an approach panders to racism, and as such is immoral in its failure to confront it, since asserting full black personhood means exercising all the rights white persons have. Alternatively, on the second point (that any such principle is in this case overridden by likely negative repercussions), it might be conceded that a greater good sometimes requires restraint, discretion, and so forth, but denied that at this particular time, the consequences are likely to be so horrendous (so the viability of the argument may be in part conjunctural, depending on the situation, e.g., 1920s Mississippi vs. 1990s New York). Or it might be claimed that those who will be infuriated by "miscegenation" will be infuriated by the civil rights struggle *anyway*, so that it is not clear that there is a discrete differential increment of outrage which can be placed in the consequential balance pan, or maybe it's not clear how big it will be. (And it could be argued that the allegations of interracial sex will be made whether it's taking place or not.) Nevertheless, I think it is clear that this argument, unlike the first, does have something to be said for it, though there could be debate over how much. Note that here, of course, it will be the negative prohibition ("stay away from white women!") rather than the positive duty that is involved.

3. The Racial Solidarity, or "No Sleeping with the Enemy," Argument

This argument usually accompanies, or is actually conflated with, the Racial Purification Argument, but it's obviously conceptually distinct. Both consequentialist and deontological version are possible, cast in terms of the imperative to promote black liberation (and the putatively inhibitory effect of such unions on this project) or one's general duty to the race (to be elaborated on later). Note that because of the *defensibility* of this consequentialist goal, the black version of the Racial Solidarity Argument is not as immediately and clearly flawed as the corresponding white version, with the goal of preserving white *supremacy*, would be.

Let me run through the important variants, moving, as before, from less to more plausible. To begin with, there are those resting on straightforwardly racist *innatist* theses, whether in theological guise (whites as "blue-eyed devils"—the reactive black counterpart to the traditional data that blacks are descendants of Ham's accursed son Canaan) or pseudo-scientific guise (whites as biologically evil "ice people" damned by melanin deficiency—the reactive black counterpart[8] to the post-Darwinian "scientific racism" of the late 19th–early 20th centuries). So the idea is that all whites are intrinsically evil, not to be associated with except out of necessity (e.g., in the workplace), and certainly not to be sought out as sexual partners. They are collectively, racially responsible for the enslavement of blacks (the thesis of innate evil implies that though *these* whites are not literally responsible, they would have acted just the same had they been around at the time), so that willingly sleeping with them is like Jews voluntarily sleeping with Nazis. Both for the consequences and for the

preservation of one's moral character, then, one has a duty not to enter interracial relationships.

Since moral character and responsibility are *not* genetically encoded in this way (even the claims of sociobiologists wouldn't stretch to this kind of reasoning), this variant is easily dismissable. The more interesting version need not make any such fantastic assumptions. The argument here readily, or maybe grudgingly, admits that whites are just humans like all of us, born as fairly plastic entities who will both be shaped by, and in turn shape, a particular socio-cultural environment. But it will be pointed out that their socialization in a white-supremacist society makes them ineluctably beneficiaries and perpetrators of the system of oppression responsible for keeping blacks down, so that they are all, or mostly (claims of differing strength can be made), the enemy, whether through active policy or passive complicity. Even if they seem to show good faith, the entering of a social "whiteness" into their personal identity means that they will never, or only very rarely (again, claims of differing strength can be made), be able to overcome their conditioning; sooner or later, their "true colors" are going to come out. If nothing else, because of the numerous affective and cognitive ties—family, friendship, cultural attachment—that link them to this white world, and help to constitute their being, they will naturally be less sensitive to its racist character, and more reluctant to confront the radical changes that have to be made to bring about a truly just society.

In the absence of hypotheses about innate evil, the deontological version gets less of a foothold (though argument #6 below can be seen as partially felling under this category), and the consequentialist version is the one which would have to be run. The idea would be that, given these empirical claims, blacks in such unions are likely to find their efforts to attack white supremacy subtly (maybe even unconsiously) resisted and diverted, so that the long-term consequences will be to compromise black struggles. Since it is often the more successful black men (prominent black businessmen, lawyers, entertainers, intellectuals) who marry white women, such unions usually lead to a departure from the black world of the elite who (at least on some theories) are precisely the most potentially threatening to the status quo, and their entry into an immensely seductive white world of wealth, comfort and glamour where black problems, e.g., the misery of the inner cities, will gradually seem more and more remote. (This inflection of the argument makes the class dimension of black oppression particularly salient. It has traditionally been claimed that blacks have a general duty to "uplift the race," and it is sometimes pointed out in addition that by marrying a white woman, the economic and status resources of the successful black male [material and cultural/symbolic capital] are likely to be removed from the black community.) Without even realizing it, and through familiar processes of self-deception and motivated inattention, one will gradually "sell out" to the white establishment.

Unlike the innatist version, with its dubious biology, or biotheology, this version has the merits of being more in touch with social reality, and indeed of telling a not-implausible psychological tale. One response is the blunt *denial* that blacks should regard themselves as having any particular duty to combat white supremacy, the individualist every-man-for-himself solution, though this will, of course, rarely be said out loud (as against secretly practiced). A more defensible approach might be to accept the existence of this duty while simultaneously arguing, as some contemporary ethicists have done, for a *restricted* role for consequentialist moral demands.[9] So the idea would be that of course you do have *some* free-floating obligation to resist racism, but this can't be a full-time job invading every aspect of one's life, and unless one's white wife is actually a Klan member or a Nazi (obviously somewhat unlikely), one's personal life is one's own business. (Often this is accompanied by the universalist/humanist claim that in the end, color doesn't matter, we're all just human beings, and so forth.)

Another tack would be to challenge the crucial empirical premise that whites cannot *ever* purge themselves of a whiteness committed to racial supremacy (or the weaker version that their doing so is rare enough that the injunction is warranted on Bayesian grounds). It would be pointed out that

people can resist and overcome their socialization, proving by their deeds that they are committed to eradicating racism. For those white women who are naive about the pervasiveness of racism, even among their own family and friends, embarking on an interracial relationship may actually have a salutary cognitive effect, the latter's hostile response awakening her to realities to which she would otherwise have been blind. An abstract opposition to racism might then assume a more visceral force, so that the net result would be a gain for the forces of anti-racism. Once the innatist framework has been abandoned, the biological link between race and character severed, and the Racial Solidarity Argument put on the consequentialist foundation of ending white supremacy, there is the danger (for its proponents) of the argument being turned on its head. Since not all *black* women will automatically be activist foes of racism (they may have succumbed to racist socialization, or, like the vast majority of human beings, just be trying to get along without heavy-duty political commitments), the question of which spouse will be of more assistance in fighting racism might then come down to simple empirical questions, rather than *a priori* assumptions. If other kinds of arguments are excluded, the foe of interracial marriages would then have to show why, in each case, the overall outcome is likely to be a debit for the anti-racism struggle.

4. The Racial Demographics, or "Where Are All the Black Men?" Argument

The Racial Demographics Argument is interesting because, of those we have looked at so far, it is least tied to the explicit political project of fighting white racism, with its accompanying ideological assumptions. This argument simply points to the relatively uncontroversial statistical fact that, because of the disproportionate numbers of black men in jail, unemployed, or dead at an early age (which may or may not be attributed to white racism), there is a significant imbalance of females to "marriageable" black males.[10] ("Marriageable" may itself, of course, seem to have classist overtones, and it is true that this complaint comes most often from middle-class, or upwardly-mobile, black women,[11] but the problem is more general.) William Julius Wilson is famous for his claim that this putative shortage is in part responsible for the perpetuation of the underclass, since single black women of poorer backgrounds will then fall into poverty if they have children.[12] (Some left critics have accused Wilson of sexism on this point arguing that the real political demand should be for women to get what is now reserved as a "male" wage.) The traditional race/gender status hierarchy in the United States is structured basically as: white men, white women, black men, black women. Because of this low prestige, black women have not generally been sought out as *respectable* partners (as against concubines, mistresses, prostitutes) by white men and men of other races. So if eligible black men differentially seek non-black, particularly white, women, then things will be made even worse for black women, who will then have been rejected both by their own men and the men of other races.[13]

If black men therefore have a duty arising out of this fact, what would its foundation be? Since we are considering arguments in isolation from one another, we need to differentiate this conceptually from the Racial Solidarity Argument as such, though it can obviously be seen in terms of racial solidarity. The argument would not be the *general* one, corollary of #3, to "sleep with the friend," but the claim that in *these* contingent circumstances black men have such a duty. This could be defended in deontological or utilitarian terms, i.e., as a remediable unhappiness which imposes some sort of obligation on us to relieve it. (So this, unlike the previous three arguments, does require more than just *not* marrying white women.)

How plausible is this? Note, to begin with that, as mentioned, no questionable racist claims about whites' innate characters are being made, so it is not vulnerable on that score. But one obviously unhappy feature it has is that, as a putative duty, it seems to be naturally assimilable to duties of *charity*, i.e., the standing obligations most moral theorists think we have (and invested with greater or lesser degrees of stringency) to relieve distress, e.g., through giving to the homeless, to Third World famine relief, and so forth. Isn't it insulting to the person to think that sexual relationships,

or marriages, should be generally entered into on these grounds? How would one react to the declaration, or inadvertent discovery, that one had been sought out as a *charitable* obligation? (The argument for endogamous marriage on the grounds of black self-respect is different, and will be discussed later.) So this seems a bit problematic from the start. There is also the question of how strong this putative obligation is supposed to be. For Kant and most other deontologists, charity is an "imperfect" duty, compliance with which leaves considerable latitude for choice (timing, beneficiary, extent of commitment, and so forth). In the case of something so central to one's life-plans as a choice of partner, rights of individual autonomy and personal freedom would easily override an alleged charitable claim of this sort. Utilitarianism is in general, of course, more demanding, with—depending on the variety—less or no room for what are sometimes called agent-relative "options," if welfare can be maximized through the policy in question. In this case, then, strategies of response would have to defend (non-black) commonsense morality against utilitarianism's demands, or make a case that such a policy, if taken seriously, would be more likely to promote net *un*happiness (through the constraints on the freedoms of black men, and the demeaning knowledge or uncertainty in the minds of black women as to why they had really been chosen). Nevertheless, it is clearly possible that some opponents of interracial marriage would be prepared to bite the bullet and insist on such a duty, arguing perhaps that the situation of black women is now so dire as to easily *outweigh* black male unhappiness at restriction of choice, and that as an entry in the welfare calculus, this unhappiness is not to be taken too seriously anyway, since it is likely, or necessarily, the result of a brainwashed preference for white women, and could be removed with a Brandtian "cognitive psychotherapy."[14] So this argument could be reinforced with considerations we shall look at later.

5. The Tragic Mulattos-to-Be, or "Burden on the Children," Argument

Another possible consequentialist argument is that the mixed racial and presumably (though not necessarily) cultural legacy of such unions will impose a differential burden on children of such households, who will be caught between two worlds and fully accepted by neither. This argument is often put forward hypocritically, with the actually-motivating considerations being along the lines of #1–4. Nevertheless, it should obviously still be examined.

To begin with, of course, it only gets off the ground if the couple *do* plan to have children. It could also be argued that it presupposes the continuation of racist attitudes, and that in a non-racist world such children would be completely accepted by both sides of the family. However, since there does not seem to be much likelihood of such a world coming into existence in the near future, this objection could not plausibly carry much weight.

One obvious reply would be that some parents-to-be will be able to speak with authority about the non-racist character of their side of the family. But what about those who can't? And even those who do sincerely give such assurances about others' feelings may, of course, be self-deceived, or even deceived by their relatives (whether through disingenuousness, and the fact that racism is no longer respectable, or by normal human self-opacity, and the genuine non-awareness of one's actual gut responses when faced with a flesh-and-blood "mixed" grandson or niece). The way to argue around this might be to insist that extra-loving parental care can make up for any family hostility. However, there is also the set of problems the child will face in the larger society, e.g., growing up in a school and neighborhood environment where racial polarization may lead to partial ostracism by other children of both races. So I think that this does raise genuine concerns, and even if they are outweighed by other factors, they should be given their due.

6. The Questionable Racial Motivations, or "Maybe You Can Fool That Stupid White Bitch, Nigger, and Maybe You Can Fool Yourself, But You're Not Fooling Anybody Else," Argument

I have left to the last what I consider to be the most interesting argument, or set of arguments.

This is the claim that black men who enter such unions, particularly with white women (as against women of other races), are either always, or usually (the claim can be made with differing strengths), motivated by questionable considerations. The argument tends to be deontological in form, the presumption being that some set of normative criteria can be imposed to assess the appropriate motivations for entering a marriage—these days, basically revolving around romantic love—and that, absent these motives, and/or present some other set, the decision to marry is wrong. Since motivation is unlikely ever to be pure, and we are not completely, or at all, self-transparent anyway, one might have to talk about the *preponderance*, and the *likelihood*, of certain kinds of motivations. In addition, there is the separate moral issue of the woman's awareness or non-awareness of the nature of the motivation. Thus one would have to distinguish cases of ignorance and deception, where the white woman doesn't know what is really driving her male spouse-to-be, from cases where both parties know what's going on.

Now obviously interracial marriages have no monopoly on questionable motivations, but the claim of opponents would be that they are *more* likely to be present (or, more strongly, *always* present) in such unions. What is the basis of this claim? The argument is that because of the central historic structuring of the American polity by white racism,[15] the psychology of both whites and blacks has been negatively affected, and that this has ramifications for human sexuality.

In a patriarchal society, sexuality is distorted by sexism as well as racism, so that male sexuality characteristically involves the notion of conquest, sexual competition, and a proving of one's manhood by securing the woman, or the series of women, more highly ranked in the established hierarchy of desirability. But *white women* will in general represent the female somatic ideal in our society: they are preeminently the beauty queens, fashion models, movie goddesses, magazine centerfolds, porn stars, whose images are displayed from a billion magazine covers, billboards, television screens, videos, and movie theaters.[16] Black males will inevitably be influenced by this, so that a wide range of potentially questionable motivations is generated:

(i)   sexual exoticism and forbidden fruit-picking,
(ii) racial revenge,
(iii) racially-differentiated aesthetic attraction, and
(iv) racial status-seeking and personhood by proxy.

(i) Sexual exoticism *per se*—the lure of the different—obviously has no intrinsic connection to black and white relations, and indeed need not involve *racial* difference at all, being felt across cultural, ethnic, and class lines. Moreover, on its own it would not really seem to raise any moral problems; people are sexually attracted to each other for all kinds of reasons, and if the strangeness of the Other is what is turning them on, there seems no harm in this—whatever gets you through the night, and so forth. The real concern here would be the prudential one that this is unlikely to prove a reliable foundation for a long-term relationship or marriage, exoticism rapidly being demystified in the quotidian domestic irritations of house-cleaning manias and toilet seats left up. It is really the coincidence of the exotic with the black-white racial taboo, the fact that this strange fruit is *forbidden*, that gives rise to what Spike Lee calls "jungle fever." But again, assuming a liberal view of sexuality, which would deny the legitimacy of such taboos, and taking for granted that both parties know what's going on, no moral, as against prudential, questions would really seem to be raised. I think when people advance this as a moral argument they are either unconsciously conflating it with one or more of the *other* possibilities ([ii] to [iv]), which we'll examine separately, or assuming that one party, e.g., the white woman, doesn't realize the real source of her appeal. So insofar as this is a successful moral

argument, it would really just be subsumable under the general proscription against deceit in interpersonal relationships, perhaps with the added *a priori* reminder that, given people's capacity for self-deception, black men are not likely to be willing to face the fact that this is really what's driving them (a point we'll encounter again). For (i), then, if there is a duty, it is derivable, given certain empirical assumptions, from the conventional set of duties to the other person, which can be founded either on welfare or Kantian grounds.

(ii) By contrast, racial revenge as a motivation is clearly and uncontroversially immoral. The idea here (though this will not usually be said out loud, or at least within earshot of whites) is that marriage to, or sometimes just sex with, a white woman (or, better, *many* white women), is an appropriate form of revenge, conscious or unconscious, upon white men. This is linked, obviously, to acceptance of a sexist framework in which male combat, here interracial, takes place in part across the terrain of the female body, so that masculinity and honor are fused with ability to appropriate the woman. Sex with the enemy's woman then becomes a symbolic retribution both specific—for the thousands of rapes and other sexual abuses visited upon black women over the hundreds of years of slavery and its aftermath, which black men were in general powerless to stop—and general—for the systematic humiliations of the denial to black men of their manhood in a society created by white men. Obviously black men who enter unions with white women for such purposes are just using them.

(iii), (iv) I will discuss these together since, though the details are different, the root issue is arguably the same. Thus far the duty, insofar as it exists, has been easily derivable from standard prohibitions against deceiving and using others. These final two subsets of allegedly questionable motives are to my mind the most interesting because they raise the possibility of duties to oneself and/or duties to the race.

First, the aesthetic question. As pointed out, in this country the white woman has traditionally represented the somatic norm of beauty.[17] White or light skin, long non-kinky hair, "fine" noses and narrow non-everted lips remain the norm, and as such are difficult or impossible to achieve without artificial assistance for black women of non-mixed heritage: hence the long-established cosmetic industry in the black community of skin bleaches, hair straighteners, wigs and hair extensions, and more recently (for those who can afford it) chemical peels, dermabrasion and plastic surgery. The argument is, then, that in choosing to marry white women, black men are admitting by this deed their acceptance of a white racist stereotype of beauty, and rejecting their own race.

The other set of motives is conceptually distinct, though in practice it will usually go with the aesthetic set, and the ultimate source of both is arguably the same.[18] This is the project of achieving social status through one's white wife. White women are then a kind of prize who can both affirm one's self-esteem, and help to provide an entree (at least in liberal circles) to the still largely white world of status and power of the upper echelons of society. Bluntly, a white woman on your arm shows that you have made it. As such, this is separate from the aesthetic argument, since the idea would be that even a white woman plain by conventional white standards of attractiveness will still provide the aura of social prestige radiating from white-skin privilege.

The more radical version of this accusation is that one is actually trying to achieve some kind of derivative personhood, personhood by proxy, in such marriages, insofar as black personhood is systematically denied in a racist society and the black man is likely to have internalized this judgment. (Personhood and status are linked, but separate, since obviously whites can have the former while still wanting to increase their ranking by some metric of the latter, e.g., through climbing the corporate hierarchy.)

For both these sets of motivations, then, duties would arise *in addition* to the obvious ones of not using the white partner. (The latter set of duties is still pertinent since, while people don't usually object to having been chosen at least in part on the basis of their looks, they would presumably *not* want to be chosen merely on the basis of being an abstract representative of an instrumental whiteness.) And these could perhaps be construed as duties to *oneself*, or duties to the *race* (or perhaps this could be collapsed into duties to oneself *insofar as* one is a member of the race, a subset of the more general duties we have to ourselves as humans). In modern moral theory, the notion of duties to oneself is found most famously, of course, in Kant. His idea was that in general we owe respect to all persons, a respect generating duties of differing degrees of stringency, and since we are persons ourselves, this means we have duties to *ourselves* (so that certain actions are wrong because we are *using* that self). So respecting ourselves precludes acting out of certain kinds of motivation. Applying this to the case of interracial marriage for reasons of types (iii) and (iv), then, the implication is that *even if the white woman is fully aware of, and has no problem with, the black man's motivation*, such marriage would be wrong because it endorses a racist set of values and as such implies a lack of respect for oneself and one's own race.

I think that, though the other arguments I have discussed are also employed, and taken seriously, this really captures the essential objection that many black women have to interracial relationships. And it coheres nicely with the interpretation of racism as an ideology which, in anti-Kantian fashion, systematically *denies* full personhood to certain groups of humans—in effect, the whole race is thought of as sub-persons, *Untermenschen*. The Jamaican activist Marcus Garvey, one of the most famous black leaders of the 20th century, is celebrated for his insight that white supremacy had left blacks as "a race without respect," and correspondingly the notion of "dissin" someone, so central to black popular culture, is arguably a recognition, on the level of folk wisdom, of the danger of this diminished moral standing.[19]

Could this then be seen as a friendly amendment to Kant? (I really mean "Kantianism" rather than Kant; in general Kant's own views on sexuality can't be taken seriously.) The immediate obstacle is that race is part of the phenomenal self deemed morally irrelevant, so how could we have duties to ourself based on racial membership? Or how could we have duties to the race that are differentiated from duties to abstract noumenal (and hence raceless) persons? But I think this objection can þe finessed in the following way. The claim is not that, *because* we're black (or white, or any other race) we're *differentially* deserving of respect; this would indeed be inconsistent with Kantian principles, presupposing hierarchy rather than equality of value for different persons. So the argument is not that race does enter at the noumenal level. The claim is rather that the historic legacy of white racism has been a social ontology in which race has *not* been abstracted from, but used as an indicator of one's personhood, so that those with a certain "phenomenal" phenotype have been seen as less than human and so undeserving of full (or any) respect. *Resistance* to this legacy therefore requires that one affirm one can be *both* black and a person, that the phenomenal does not correlate with a sub-par noumenal self. Retreat into typical philosophical abstraction ("we're all human—race doesn't matter") evades confronting this, since the terms on which humanity will have been defined will be *white* ones. So the "person" is tacitly constructed as white in the first place, which is why this hidden moral architecture, this colorlessness which is really colored white, has to be exposed to the light. Because of black socialization into this system of values, the fact is that marriage to a white woman *will* often be based on the continuing, if not consciously acknowledged, submission to this racist social ontology, and when it is, *will* imply a lack of racial self-respect, respect for one's race (as all other races) as equally entitled to take the full status of personhood. It is, finally, I believe, something like this moral perception which, even if not

always clearly articulated, underlies many black women's intuition that there is often something questionable about these relationships.

But what—the obvious reply will be—if one is quite sure, or as sure as one can be about anything, that one is *not* marrying for such motivations? Here, the opponent of interracial marriages has at least two interesting fallback positions (as distinct, that is, from any of the other arguments previously discussed). First, what the critic may do is introduce an auxiliary *epistemic* thesis (our knowledge of our motivation) as distinct front the *substantive* thesis itself (what our motivation is). The argument would then be that, though in some cases (a minority) black men's motivation might be pure, the combined effects of standard human self-opacity and the cognitive interference produced in these particular circumstances by the strong motivations for self-deception (who will want to admit to himself he's really trying to whiten his being?), mean that they can never *know* that it is pure, so the safest thing to do is to eschew such unions. If this fails, then there is, secondly, the ultimate fallback position of re-introducing a consequentialist framework to argue that even if (a) one's motivation is pure, *and* (b) one knows one's motivation is pure, there is always (c) the fact that, whatever one's motivation, one will be *perceived* by other blacks as having married out of racial self-contempt, thus reinforcing white superiority. And this (as one of my black female students coldly informed me when I was trying to defend a liberal position on the issue) will be "a slap in the face of black women everywhere." So the bottom line for critics is that one's actions will be perceived as being motivated by these self-despising beliefs, and—especially if one is a prominent black figure of high status, with a correspondingly enhanced range of racial spousal selection—this action will be sending a message to the world that, once you *do* have this option to choose: *black women just ain't good enough.*

IV

I have no neat, wrap-up conclusion to offer, since I think the issue is a complicated one about which a lot more could be said. Rather, my basic aim has been to demonstrate this complexity, and, as a corollary, to show the mistakenness of the knee-jerk white liberal (or, for that matter, black liberal) response that no defensible case could possibly be made for the existence of such a duty. Some of the arguments *are* obviously weak (e.g., #1), but others are stronger, though they may be of conjunctural strength (e.g., #2), involve empirical and normative claims which may or may not hold true (#3, 4, 5), or rest on speculative claims about motivation which are hard to disprove, with a consequentialist fallback line which may seem illegitimately to hold us hostage to others' perceptions (#6). Whether singly or in combination (to the extent that this is possible, bearing in mind that *different* normative frameworks have sometimes been used) they do yield at least a presumptive duty I will leave, perhaps somewhat evasively, for the reader to decide, and if so what kind of a duty it is. At the very least I think I have shown that—using conventional moral theories, and without making racist assumptions about whites, or even appealing to any controversial separatist ideology—an interesting case can in fact be built for a position quite widespread in the "commonsense morality" of the black community.

One common, misguided white liberal reaction to racism has been to move from the anthropological premise that "race" (in the biological sense) doesn't exist, to the conclusion that "race" (in the social sense) doesn't exist either, so that the solution is to proclaim an (ostensibly) colorless universalism in which we pay no attention to race. Sometimes this is expressed in the claim that race is "constructed" (true enough) and therefore unreal. But neither conclusion follows (try walking through the next constructed brick wall you encounter). As Aristotle pointed out long ago, treating people equally doesn't necessarily mean treating them the same, and one could argue analogously that genuine race-neutrality actually requires not *blindness* to race but close attention to the difference race makes.

DISCUSSION QUESTIONS

1. Discuss the racist explanations for why interracial relationships between black men and white women have been viewed as particularly fraught throughout history.

2. Describe the arguments Mills thinks fail to support the claim that black men have a moral duty to marry black women. Explain why these arguments fail.

3. Describe the arguments Mills thinks might successfully support the claim that black men have a moral duty to marry black women. Explain why these arguments succeed.

4. Discuss the role of a Kantian duty of self-respect in establishing the claim that black men have a moral duty to marry black women.

NOTES

1. For discussions of racism in general, and racism and sex in particular, see, for example: Winthrop D. Jordan, *White Over Black: American Attitudes Toward the Negro, 1550–1812* (1968; rpt. New York and London: W.W. Norton, 1977); St. Clair Drake, *Black Folk Here and There*, vol. I (Los Angeles: Center for Afro-American Studies, UCLA, 1987); John D'Emilio and Estelle B. Freedman, *Intimate Matters: A History of Sexuality in America* (New York: Harper & Row, 1988), chapter five; Calvin C. Hernton, *Sex and Racism in America* (1966; rpt. New York: Grove Press, 1988).

2. I should record here the fact that I have greatly benefited from exposure to, even when I have not always agreed with, the arguments put forward by my students in classroom discussion and essays submitted in the "African-American Philosophy" course I taught in Spring 1993.

3. For a discussion, see, for example, Stephen Jay Gould, *The Mismeasure of Man* (New York and London: W.W. Norton, 1981).

4. See, for example, chapter 10, "Satan," of *The Autobiography of Malcolm X*, as told to Alex Haley, (1965; rpt New York: Ballantine Books, 1973).

5. "There are no races, there are only clines." Frank B. Livingstone, "On the Nonexistence of Human

Races" (1962); rpt in Sandra Harding, ed., *The "Racial" Economy of Science: Toward a Democratic Future* (Bloomington and Indianapolis: Indiana University Press, 1993).

6. Kwame Anthony Appiah, *In My Father's House: Africa in the Philosophy of Culture* (New York and Oxford: Oxford University Press, 1992), pp. 13–15.

7. As late as 1978, a national survey showed that "70% of whites . . . rejected interracial marriage on principle": cited in Douglas S. Massey and Nancy A. Denton, *American Apartheid: Segregation and the Making of the Underclass* (Cambridge, Mass.: Harvard University Press, 1993), p. 95.

8. Though contemporary "melanin theory" is indigenous to the black community, the notion of "sun people" and "ice people" actually comes from the white Canadian author Michael Bradley's *The Iceman Inheritance: Prehistoric Sources of Western Man's Racism, Sexism, and Aggression* (New York: Kayode, 1978).

9. See, for example, Samuel Scheffler, *Human Morality* (New York: Oxford University Press, 1992).

10. Black unemployment rates in recent decades have been at least twice as high as white unemployment rates, and for the category of young black men in the inner cities the rate approaches catastrophic proportions. Another tragic figure frequently cited is the 1990 study that showed that, on any given day in 1989, nearly 1 in 4 black men from the ages of 20 to 29 were either in prison, on parole, or on probation. The leading cause of death for black men 15–34 is homicide. For some of these frightening statistics, see William Julius Wilson, *The Truly Disadvantaged: The Inner City, the Underclass, and Public Policy* (Chicago and London: The University of Chicago Press, 1987) and Andrew Hacker, *Two Nations: Black and White, Separate, Hostile, Unequal* (New York: Charles Scribner's Sons, 1992).

11. Terry McMillan's recent bestseller, *Waiting to Exhale* (1992; rpt. New York: Pocket Star books, 1993), revolves in large part around this theme.

12. Wilson, *The Truly Disadvantaged.*

13. I have worked throughout within a heterosexual, and, some gays might say, heterosexist, framework. Why, it may be asked, should black women wait for black, or any other, men? Why shouldn't they embrace their sisters? I certainly don't mean to impugn the legitimacy of lesbian relationships—I think that gay relationships and marriages should be recognized—but, on established assumptions about people's sexual orientation, there will still be a majority of *straight* women for whom this is not an attractive solution. If these assumptions are wrong, of course, so that the whole concept of a basic sexual orientation is misleading in the first place, and sexuality is radically plastic, then some of these I arguments won't work. But the *general* issue of racism and sex obviously isn't just an issue for straights.

14. See Richard Brandt, *A Theory of the Good and the Right* (New York: Oxford University Press, 1979).

15. And many other countries too, of course. Though I have implicitly focused on the United States throughout, many of these arguments would be applicable elsewhere also.

16. A quick riddle for the reader: name a black female movie star other than Whoopi Goldberg (pop singer Whitney Houston's one-shot appearance in *The Bodyguard* doesn't count). My guess is that the average white reader will come up empty. Now think how remarkable this is in a country where for most of the century movies have epitomized American popular culture, and blacks make up 12% of the population. (Goldberg, by the way, is the exception that proves the rule, in the original sense of that expression, now largely forgotten, of *testing* the rule so that an explanation for the anomaly is called for. At least until lately, she has standardly appeared as a de-sexed comic grotesque. After I completed the original draft of this article, Angela Bassett was nominated for a "Best Actress" Academy Award for her role as Tina Turner in *What's Love Got To Do With It.* So that's one more black actress the white reader is now likely to know. But my general point obviously still stands.)

17. The following discussion draws on *The Color Complex.* The notion of a racial "somatic norm" was first put forward by the Dutch sociologist Harmannus Hoetink; see, for example, *Caribbean Race Relations: A Study of Two Variants* (London: Oxford University Press, 1962).

18. It should be noted, though, that some researchers have argued, on anthropological evidence, that there is a pro-light skinned aesthetic bias in *all* societies, which pre-existed, though of course it will be reinforced by, colonialism and white racism.

19. Likewise, it is no accident that the work of black philosophers has so often focused on the particular importance of *self-respect* for blacks; see, for example, Laurence Thomas, "Self-Respect: Theory and Practice," and Bernard Boxill, "Self-Respect and Protest," both in Leonard Harris, ed., *Philosophy Born of Struggle: Anthology of Afro-American Philosophy from 1917* (Dubuque, Iowa: Kendall/Hunt Publishing Co., 1983).

Man on Man, Man on Dog, or Whatever the Case May Be

BY JOHN CORVINO

John Corvino, an American philosopher whose work focuses on ethical questions arising in the "culture wars," has written several books on the moral legitimacy of homosexual relationships and homosexual marriage. In this essay, Corvino attacks and successfully debunks each of the standard arguments against homosexuality, all of which are based on the idea that it is "unnatural" or contrary to sound religious doctrine.

Back in 2003, when Rick Santorum was the U.S. Senate's third ranking Republican, an Associated Press reporter asked his opinion on laws prohibiting homosexual conduct. (At the time, the U.S. Supreme Court was preparing to rule in *Lawrence v. Texas*, ultimately striking down such laws in a 6–3 majority.) The senator responded:

> I have a problem with homosexual acts . . . [I]f the Supreme Court says that you have the right to consensual sex within your home, then you have the right to bigamy, you have the right to polygamy, you have the right to incest, you have the right to adultery. You have the right to anything. Does that undermine the fabric of our society? I would argue yes, it does . . . .
>
> Every society in the history of man has upheld the institution of marriage as a bond between a man and a woman. . . In every society, the definition of marriage has not ever to my knowledge included homosexuality. That's not to pick on homosexuality. It's not, you know, man on child, man on dog, or whatever the case may be.[1]

Reaction to Santorum's now-infamous "man on dog" remarks was swift and sharp. Sex-advice columnist Dan Savage even launched a successful internet campaign to associate Santorum's name with a nasty byproduct of anal intercourse. Santorum, for his part, has never apologized for the remarks, although in recent years he has denied that he was comparing homosexuality with bestiality and child sexual abuse. During his 2012 Republican presidential campaign he told CNN's John King: "I said it's *not* those things. I didn't connect them. I specifically excluded them."[2] This denial sounds unconvincing. When Santorum said that it's *not* man on child, man on dog, and so on, the *not* was there to distinguish traditional heterosexual marriage from a list of bad things. In his view, homosexuality clearly belongs on the bad list.

That doesn't mean, of course, that Santorum sees these things as equally bad. Analogies compare things that are similar in some respects, which is not the same as saying that they're identical in all respects. If you're in a particularly charitable mood and willing to overlook some parts of the interview, you can read Santorum's remarks as making a claim about the logic of privacy rights: if people have the right to do *whatever* they want in the privacy of their own homes, then they have the right to bigamy, polygamy, incest, adultery, bestiality, and so on. Or at least, they have the prima facie or presumptive right, which could be overridden only by some stronger countervailing right, such as other people's right not to be harmed. (That countervailing right would quickly rule out "man on child" sex, not to mention many instances of other things on the list.)

Having said that, it's difficult to maintain a charitable mood when someone mentions your consensual adult relationships in the same breath as "man on child" and "man on dog" sex. Whatever anyone says about Santorum's remarks as a matter of logic—and I'll have plenty to say in this chapter—they were thoughtless and nasty as a political sound bite. Even some of his fellow Republicans thought he had gone too far.

It's not just Rick Santorum who invokes the slippery slope. U.S. Supreme Court Justice Antonin Scalia made a similar argument in his scathing dissent in *Lawrence v. Texas*, as did Justice Byron White in *Bowers v. Hardwick*, which *Lawrence* reversed.[3] So have William Bennett, Hadley Arkes, Charles Krauthammer, and a host of other prominent conservative writers. In the colorful words of John Finnis, those who defend gay sex "have no principled moral case to offer against . . . the getting of orgasmic sexual pleasure in whatever friendly touch or welcoming orifice (human or otherwise) one may opportunely find it."[4]

In the past I've referred to this slippery-slope argument as the "PIB" argument, short for "polygamy, incest, and bestiality," although other items sometimes make the list as well.[5] What got me interested in PIB, aside from my wanting to defend gay people against nasty smears, is that it isn't entirely clear what the argument is saying. Is it predicting that once homosexuality becomes more accepted (some of) these other things will become more accepted as well? Is it making a logical point, suggesting that even if the things won't ensue, in fact, they're somehow related in principle? Or is it primarily a rhetorical move, simply trying to scare people away from homosexuality by invoking a parade of horribles? In many ways, the PIB argument seems more like a question or a challenge than an argument proper: "Okay, Mr. or Ms. Sexual Liberal, explain to me why all these other things are wrong." Most people aren't prepared to do that on short notice, which makes the PIB point a debater's dream: It's a handy sound-bite argument that doesn't lend itself to a handy sound-bite response.

One way to approach the PIB argument is to turn the challenge around and ask, *What does one thing have to do with the other*? Polygamy can be heterosexual or homosexual, and the societies that practice it tend to be the least accepting of same-sex relationships. Incest can be heterosexual or homosexual. Bestiality, I suppose, can be heterosexual or homosexual, although like most folks I prefer not to think about it too carefully. Since there is no inherent reason to classify PIB with homosexuality rather than heterosexuality, we must ask, What's the connection?

There are two main answers to this question, and they give us the two broad versions of the PIB argument: a logical version and a causal version. (Note: calling one version the logical version does not mean that it is particularly reasonable or that the other version is illogical: it just means that the argument is based on logical connections rather than empirical ones.) Let's take each in turn.

PIB Argument: The Logical Version

The logical version of the PIB argument, which is the one that philosophers usually favor, says that the argument for same-sex relationships makes an equally good case for PIB relationships. In effect, it claims that the pro-gay argument "proves too much": if you accept it, you commit yourself to other, less palatable conclusions. So the logical PIB argument is what philosophers call a *reductio ad absurdum* ("reduction to absurdity"), a way of showing that certain premises—in this case, those establishing that same-sex relationships are morally permissible—have absurd implications. It doesn't matter whether approval of homosexuality actually leads to approval of these other things. The point is not to make a prediction: It's to indicate the alleged logical inconsistency of supporting homosexuality while opposing PIB.

But why would anyone think that supporting same-sex relationships logically entails supporting PIB? The answer, I think, is that some people misread the pro-gay position as resting on some version of the following premise: *People have a right to whatever kind of sexual activity they find fulfilling.* If that were true, then it would indeed follow that people have a right to polygamy, incest, "man on child, man on dog, or whatever the case may be." But no serious person actually believes this premise, at least not in unqualified form. That is, no serious person thinks that the right to sexual expression is absolute. The premise, thus construed, is a straw man.

A more reasonable premise suggests that sexual expression is an important feature of human life which must be morally balanced against other features of human life. For most people, sex is a key source of intimacy. It is a conduit of joy and sorrow, pride and shame, power and vulnerability, connection and isolation. Its absence—and especially its enforced denial—can be painful. On the other hand, there are good moral reasons for prohibiting some sexual relationships, either individually (say, because Jack's relationship with Jane breaks his vow to Jill) or as a class (say, because the relationship is unfaithful, or emotionally unhealthy, or physically harmful, or morally defective in some other way). So for any sexual relationship—and for that matter, any human action—we must ask: Are there good reasons for it? Are there good reasons against it? There is no reason to think that the answers to those questions will be the same for homosexuality as they are for polygamy, incest, or bestiality—which are as different from each other as each is from homosexuality. Each must be evaluated on its own evidence.

We have spent the last five chapters examining the moral evidence surrounding homosexuality. The basic case in favor of it is straightforward: For some people, same-sex relationships are an important source of genuine human goods, including emotional and physical intimacy, mutual pleasure, and so on. That positive case must be balanced against any negatives—although, as we have seen, the standard objections fall apart under scrutiny.

What about PIB? I don't doubt that *some* PIB relationships can realize genuine human goods. Polygamy is the most plausible candidate: It is quite common historically, and there may well have been circumstances (for example, a shortage of men due to war or other dangers) that made it work well in particular societies. But that's only half the story. The other half requires asking whether, despite these goods, there are overriding reasons for discouraging or condemning polygamy today. Polygamous societies are almost always *polygynous*, where one husband has multiple wives. (Polyandry—one wife with multiple husbands—is by contrast quite rare.) The usual result is a sexist and classist society where high-status males acquire multiple wives while low-status males become virtually unmarriageable. Thus, from a social-policy point of view, there are reasons to be wary of polygamy. Perhaps those reasons could be overcome by further argument, but the central point remains: Arguments about the morally appropriate *number* of sexual partners are logically distinct from arguments about the morally appropriate *gender* of sexual partners.

The same is true for incest arguments: whether people should have sex with close relatives (of either sex) is a distinct question from whether they should have sex with non-relatives of the same sex. Some might wonder whether the problem with incest is that it poses genetic risks for offspring, an objection that wouldn't apply to gay incest. But the reason for the incest taboo is not merely that offspring might have birth defects (a problem which can be anticipated via genetic testing, and which doesn't apply past childbearing age). It is also that sex has a powerful effect on the dynamics of family life. As Jonathan Rauch vividly puts it:

> Imagine being a fourteen-year-old girl and suspecting that your sixteen-year-old brother or thirty-four-year-old father had ideas about courting you in a few years. Imagine being the sixteen-year-old boy and developing what you think is a crush on your younger sister and being able to fantasize and talk about marrying her someday. Imagine being the parent and telling your son he can marry his sister someday, but right now he needs to keep his hands off her. . . . I cannot fathom all of the effects which the prospect of child-parent or sibling-sibling marriage might have on the dynamics of family life, but I can't imagine the effects would be good, and I can't imagine why anyone would want to try the experiment and see.[6]

These problems apply just as much to homosexual incest as to heterosexual incest.

There is another important disanalogy between the incest ban and the homosexuality ban. The incest ban means that every person is forbidden to have sex with *some* people—a relatively small group—whom he might find romantically appealing: his close relatives. By contrast, the homosexuality ban means that gay people are forbidden to have sex with *anyone* whom they might find romantically appealing. Unlike the incest ban, it reduces their pool of available romantic partners to zero—an infinitely greater restriction.[7] One could make a similar point about the polygamy ban: in principle, any man who can fall in love with two women can fall in love with one, and any woman who can fall in love with an already married man can fall in love with an unmarried one.

What about bestiality—Santorum's "man on dog" example? It's hard to know what to say here, except that I share most people's revulsion to it. Of course there's the issue of consent. On the other hand, we do plenty to animals without their consent, including many uncontroversial interactions. While bestiality is often harmful to animals, it need not be: there's an urban legend that comes to mind involving a woman, a dog, peanut butter, and a surprise party. (Feel free to Google it.) Ultimately, the problem with bestiality seems to be less about the effect on the animal than the effect on the person, damaging his or her capacity for appropriate human relationships.

I made this latter point in an article entitled "Homosexuality and the PIB Argument," which prompted a reply from Christopher Wolfe.[8] Wolfe agrees with me that bestiality is likely to damage a person's capacity for human relationships. But he worries that I appear to "back off" the argument and speculates that I must be afraid to say that any consensual act not harmful to others is immoral.[9] As you are probably aware by now, I have no such fear. To the extent that I back off the personal-damage argument, it's because I haven't done the relevant research and don't really care to. For all I know, zoophiles are some of the most psychologically healthy people in the world, have great sex with their (human) spouses, and so on. And if that

were so, Wolfe and I would have to find some other argument in order to maintain our objection, or else conclude that bestiality's wrongness is a fundamental moral fact.

Wolfe then contends that if I say that bestiality is intrinsically immoral, I open up a space for him to argue, analogously, that homosexuality is intrinsically immoral. This is wishful thinking at best, utter confusion at worst. The whole point of claiming that some action-type is *intrinsically* immoral is to say that its immorality does not depend on the wrongness of other action-types; its wrongness does not derive from some more general principle. It is entirely possible—and I would add, quite common—for someone consistently to believe that sex with animals (of any sex) is intrinsically immoral but that sex with persons of the same sex is not. Gay-rights advocates are as entitled to basic premises as anyone else. But basic premises about bestiality do not entail basic premises about homosexuality—or any about other behavior.

I'm reminded here of a funny story from Dan Savage. Savage was on a radio show with a man who sincerely claimed to have a romantic (including sexual) relationship with a horse. At the end of the interview, as the wrap-up music was playing, Savage offhandedly said, "Oh, I forgot to ask—is it a male horse or a female horse?" The man turned red, glared at Savage, and retorted indignantly, "I AM NOT GAY!!!" (I suppose people find comfort where they can.)

One might try arguing that since PIB and homosexuality have traditionally been grouped together as wrong, the burden of proof is on anyone who wants to take an item off the list. But this response fails twice over. First, the "tradition" that groups these things together is actually a relatively modern artifact: Polygamy, as noted, was a very common form of marriage historically, and it is accepted (indeed, encouraged) in various cultures today.[10] Homosexuality has been condemned in many cultures, but certainly not all.[11] Indeed, same-sex eroticism has been celebrated in the art and literature of great civilizations.[12]

The second problem with this response is that just because practices *have been* grouped together as wrong, it doesn't follow that they *should be*. This is especially obvious when we consider other things that were once common taboos, such as interracial sex. And while strict assignments of burden of proof may work in courtrooms, in everyday life the burden of proof (or at least, the burden of persuasion) is on whoever wants to prove something. Both sides are in the same boat there.

One might argue that homosexuality, like bestiality, is always non-procreative. That's true, but it doesn't explain why polygamy (which is abundantly procreative) and incest (which can be procreative, though often with disastrous results) land on the same list. Moreover . . . there is no good reason to think that all sex must be open to procreation. The more one examines the PIB argument, the more it appears that opponents just lump together things they don't like and then dare others to challenge the list. Of course, until one knows why the list members were initially grouped together, it's impossible to offer a reason why some item doesn't belong or to argue that the removal of one doesn't require the removal of others.

What if the PIB-plus-homosexuality list is simply a collection of morally wrong sexual practices, each one there for its own reasons? In that case, the logical form of the PIB argument would collapse: Its whole point is that PIB and homosexuality are logically related. If the various items are immoral, but for unrelated reasons, the following analogy would apply: it would be like putting various useful objects on my desk for different reasons—a pen for writing, a lamp for reading, a letter-opener, a stapler, a paperweight, and so on—and then arguing that if I remove the lamp I have to remove the stapler and the paperweight. Besides, as we have seen in previous chapters, the arguments for judging homosexual conduct immoral simply *don't work*. There was no good reason for putting homosexuality on the list in the first place.

I conclude that the best response to the logical version of the PIB argument remains the simple one we started with: *What does one thing have to do with the other?*

PIB Argument: The Causal Version

The foregoing discussion assumes that the PIB argument alleges some logical connection between PIB and homosexuality. There's another possibility, however. Perhaps the connection is not logical but empirical. That is, perhaps the endorsement of one item *will* lead to the endorsement of others, whether or not it logically should. For instance, maybe the wider acceptance of homosexuality will embolden polygamists and make it harder for others to resist their advocacy.

This is the causal version of the PIB argument. It typically ignores incest and bestiality—and from here on, so shall we. Because it focuses instead on polygamy, it usually refers to same-sex *marriage* rather than homosexual acts. (There is no such thing as a "polygamous act," strictly speaking, although one might refer to a pattern of behavior as polygamous *conduct*.) So our discussion will now focus more on public policy, and specifically marriage, than on the morality of relationships per se.

The best-known proponent of the causal PIB argument is Stanley Kurtz, who claims that the slippery slope to polygamy is "[a]mong the likeliest effects of gay marriage."[13] Kurtz has been predicting this pro-polygamy effect since the mid-1990s. But his evidence for it is thin, and his evidence for polygamy's connection with homosexuality is even thinner. He writes:

> It's getting tougher to laugh off the "slippery slope" argument—the claim that gay marriage will lead to polygamy, polyamory, and ultimately to the replacement of marriage itself by an infinitely flexible partnership system. We've now got a movement for legalized polyamory and the abolition of marriage in Sweden. The Netherlands has given legal, political, and public approval to a cohabitation contract for a polyamorous bisexual triad. Two out of four reports on polygamy commissioned by the Canadian government recommended decriminalization and regulation of the practice. And now comes *Big Love*, HBO's domestic drama about an American polygamous family.[14]

This paragraph nicely encapsulates the kinds of exaggerations and outright falsehoods that typify discussion of this issue.

First, in 2006, when Kurtz wrote the above paragraph, Sweden didn't have "gay marriage": it had "registered partnerships," the kind of "separate-but-equal" status most same-sex-marriage advocates typically oppose—as should anyone worried about an "infinitely flexible partnership system." Second, Kurtz's case of the "polyamorous bisexual triad" was not a marriage at all, but a private cohabitation contract signed by a Dutch notary public. The relationship was neither registered with nor sanctioned by the state: it was no more a legal polygamous marriage than a three-person lease agreement is a legal polygamous marriage. Third, the fact that some Canadian studies of polygamy recommended decriminalization and regulation is hardly evidence of widespread support for the practice. And fourth, the success of the HBO series *Big Love* signaled a wave of support for polygamy about as much as the success of *The Sopranos* signaled a wave of support for the Mafia.

Kurtz's deeper problem is that he fails to show any causal connection between these alleged phenomena and gay rights. He has tried to establish one by looking at marriage trends in Scandinavia, but his analysis falters on the fact that these trends substantially predated same-sex marriage there. (William Eskridge and Darren Spedale's *Gay Marriage for Better or for Worse?: What We've Learned from the Evidence* provides a book-length refutation.)

Kurtz has also tried to establish the connection by arguing that some of the same people who endorse polygamy also endorse same-sex marriage, and that they invoke the same "civil rights" language in both cases. This is true but entirely inconclusive. Some of the same people who oppose abortion also oppose capital punishment and invoke the same "sanctity of life" language, but that's no reason to conclude that one movement leads to the other. In fact, the vast majority of the world's polygamy supporters are religious fundamentalists who strenuously *oppose* homosexuality, and the practice tends to appear in U.S. states (like Utah, Nevada, and Texas) with the *lowest* support for gay rights. Indeed, to the extent that the gay-rights movement promotes an egalitarian view of

the sexes, it will likely undermine common forms of polygamy. Kurtz can link the two movements only by selective myopia.

Kurtz has also tried to connect the two issues via the issue of infidelity. He notes that polygamous societies tend to have high rates of infidelity, because they promote the idea that men "need" multiple women. Such infidelity is problematic because it causes instability for wives and for children, many of whom are born outside of marriage. How does Kurtz then connect this problem with homosexuality? His logic seems to go like this: Polygamous societies have high rates of infidelity; gay males have high rates of infidelity; therefore, the gay-rights movement will lead to polygamy—presumably by weakening the norms of fidelity that hitherto kept polygamy at bay. *If we let gays marry*, Kurtz seems to be saying, *then straight men will start cheating on their wives.* Even if this prediction were plausible—which it isn't—the conclusion hardly seems justified.

First, on the prediction's implausibility: Kurtz is basing his argument on the premise that gay male couples tend to be less sexually exclusive than either heterosexual couples or lesbian couples. Even Kurtz admits, "Lesbians, for their part, do value monogamy."[15] His worry seems to be that if we allow same-sex couples to marry, gay males' sexual infidelity will bleed into the general population. But he never explains how. Keep in mind that gay men and lesbians make up a relatively small minority of the general population.[16] Gay men make up about half of that minority, *coupled* gay men an even smaller subset, and *coupled gay males in open relationships* a smaller subset still. In Jonathan Rauch's words, "We might as well regard nudists as the trendsetters for fashion."[17]

While sexual exclusivity may be challenging, it's not so challenging that a sexually exclusive couple (straight or gay) can't look at a sexually open couple (straight or gay) and conclude, "Nope, that's not right for us." After all, people read the Bible without deciding to acquire concubines. More realistically, they often encounter neighbors with different cultural mores while still preferring—and sometimes having good reason to prefer—their own.

Then there's the fairness issue: The question of whether same-sex couples should be allowed to marry should no more hinge on the behavior of a subset of gay men than the question of whether Hollywood actors should be allowed to marry should hinge on the behavior of a subset of Hollywood actors. In terms of raw numbers, there are probably many more heterosexual "swingers" than there are gay men in open relationships, yet we still allow heterosexual couples (including swingers!) to marry. On what grounds, then, can we deny marriage to same-sex couples, including those who pledge and achieve sexual exclusivity? The argument works even less well against gay sex than it does against same-sex marriage: The moral status of one person's sexual acts does not hinge on what other members of his or her sexual orientation do.

In short, the causal version of the PIB arguments fails, both as a prediction and as a moral objection.

Taboos and Moral Reasons

There is still another way of understanding the PIB argument. Maybe there's no direct logical connection between endorsing homosexuality and endorsing PIB. And maybe the gay-rights movement won't have much effect, one way or another, on the polygamy movement. Still, the very process of challenging existing sexual mores invites the following concern: If we start questioning *some* sexual taboos, won't that make it more likely that we'll start questioning others? Perhaps some things are best left unquestioned.[18]

If that's the objection, then much of this chapter has missed the point. We've been comparing reasons for and against homosexuality with reasons for and against PIB. But some might worry that once we start demanding *reasons* for established moral claims, morality has already lost its essential majesty and force. This objection is a version of the argument from tradition, but it's more sophisticated than the simple assertion, "We've always done it this way, therefore we should continue doing it this way." Rather, the idea is that our moral traditions have an internal practical logic to them, even when it's not apparent on the surface. They evolved the way they did for a *reason*, and tinkering with them invites peril.[19]

It is worth noting that just because something evolved as it did for a reason, it does not follow that it evolved as it did for a *good* reason. One of my favorite stories comes from the late food critic Craig Claiborne: A woman received a ham and was disappointed that she didn't own a saw.[20] Although she had never cooked a whole ham, she knew that her mother always prepared hams for cooking by sawing off the end, and she assumed it had to be done this way. So she called her mother, who explained that she learned to cook from her mother, who always did it that way—she had no idea why. The perplexed pair then called Grandma: "Why did you always saw the ends off of hams before roasting them?" they asked her.

Surprised, the old woman replied, "Because I never had a roasting pan large enough to hold a whole ham!"

The problem with the argument from tradition, even in its more sophisticated form, is that it takes a good point too far. All else being equal, there's a good reason to favor "tried and true" practices, and it would be impractical, even foolhardy, for each generation to invent morality from scratch. So I would agree that we should proceed with caution when tampering with long-standing tradition. But it doesn't follow that we can *never* revisit moral traditions. Take, for example, the taboo against interracial relationships, which has appeared in many cultures to varying degrees. We can understand how this taboo might have arisen, from an overzealous collective instinct for group preservation. There may, indeed, be a further "internal logic" behind it. Yet somehow we also recognize that the taboo causes needless pain and that it ought to be discarded.

My point here is not to suggest a perfect analogy (no analogy is perfect) but to invoke some lessons from history.[21] When a taboo interferes with people's happiness with no apparent justification, it is probably time to rethink it. Traditions have value, but so too does the process of ongoing moral reflection. We should not confuse reasonable caution with obstinate complacency, which can sometimes be a cover for bigotry (one of the topics in our next chapter).

The process is challenging, to be sure, and there are no shortcuts. It's easy to draw lines around things we don't like and then condemn others for falling outside the lines; it's much harder to articulate a coherent, complete, and plausible sexual ethics. It's especially hard to do so when people keep changing the subject—which, in the end, seems to be the PIB argument's main function.

DISCUSSION QUESTIONS

1. What is Corvino's criterion for sex to be morally legitimate? What is the view he is arguing against?
2. Explain three of Corvino's arguments that there is nothing "unnatural" about gay sex. Do you agree or disagree? Why?
3. Gay sex is still illegal in many countries around the world, and those laws are usually justified by religious texts. Corvino was himself a devout Catholic. What do you think he might say to the people insisting on those laws? Use concrete examples (do a little research online) if you can.

NOTES

1. "Excerpts of Santorum's AP Interview," 2003.
2. http://transcripts.cnn.com/TRANSCRIPTS/1201/04/jkusa.01.html (emphasis added).
3. Justice Byron White used the analogy in the 1986 U.S. Supreme Court Decision *Bowers v. Hardwick* (478 U.S. 186 [1986]), and Justice Scalia used it in his dissent in the 2003 *Lawrence v. Texas* (539 U.S. 02-102 [2003]). See also Charles Krauthammer, "When John and Jim Say 'I Do,'" *Time*, July 22, 1996; William

Bennett, "Leave Marriage Alone," *Newsweek*, June 3, 1996; Hadley Arkes, "The Role of Nature," from the hearing of the House Judiciary Committee, May 15, 1996; all three are reprinted in Sullivan.
4. Finnis 1997, p. 34.
5. Corvino 2005.
6. Rauch, p. 132.
7. Rauch, p. 127.
8. Corvino 2005, Wolfe 2007.
9. Wolfe 2007, p. 101.
10. For an excellent history of marriage, including polygamy, see Coontz.
11. For a comprehensive discussion of homosexuality (and attitudes toward it) in history, see Crompton.
12. Again, see Crompton.
13. Kurtz 2003.
14. Kurtz 2006.
15. Kurtz 2003.
16. No one knows exactly how many, due to the problems of self-reporting among a stigmatized population. Most reasonable estimates are between 2 and 6%. See Laumann et al., ch. 8.
17. Rauch, p. 153.
18. I'm indebted to my colleague Brad Roth in the Wayne State Political Science department for pressing this reading of the PIB objection.
19. Rauch refers to this as a Hayekian argument. See Rauch, pp. 162–171.
20. Claiborne, p. 41.
21. See the conclusion of the previous chapter for some reflections on the race analogy.

Monogamy's Law: Compulsory Monogamy and Polyamorous Existence

BY ELIZABETH EMENS

Elizabeth Emens is a legal scholar whose work focuses on issues in disability law, family law, anti-discrimination law, contracts law, and law and sexuality. In this essay, Emens explores mainstream culture's unthinking acceptance of monogamy as the only morally and socially acceptable option, especially given the high prevalence of nonmonogamous practices such as adultery, divorce, and remarriage. Set in the context of a broader discussion of the same-sex marriage debate, Emens defends polyamory, or "ethical nonmonogamy," as an important alternative to compulsory monogamy.

[O]ne reason monogamy is so important to us is that we are so terror-ized by what we imagine are the alternatives to it. The other person we fear most is the one who does not believe in the universal sacredness of—usually heterosexual—coupledom.

—Adam Phillips

This article aims to understand why, at a time of serious debate about the different-sex requirement of marriage (one *man* and one *woman*), eliminating the numerosity requirement (*one* man and *one* woman) is so widely agreed to be undesirable. The article approaches this question as part of the larger puzzle of why mainstream culture seems to accept the numerosity requirement of marriage without question, even while so many people practice alternatives to lifelong monogamy either secretly (adultery) or serially (divorce and remarriage).

Perhaps because of this country's dramatic relationship to Mormon polygamy, when Americans hear the term "polygamy" or try to picture relationships of more than two, they typically think of traditional polygyny—one man in a hierarchical relationship to several wives. But there is another model—called "polyamory" by its increasingly vocal practitioners—which in principle eschews hierarchy and which encompasses various models of intimate relationships of more than two people.

The practice of polyamory as "ethical non-monogamy"[1] bears serious consideration at a moment when the terms and conditions of intimate relationships are such a focus of discussion. Polyamory is a lifestyle embraced by a minority of individuals who exhibit a wide variety of relationship models and who articulate an ethical vision that I understand to encompass five main principles: self-knowledge, radical honesty, consent, self-possession, and privileging love and sex over other emotions and activities such as jealousy.[2] Contrary to the common view of multiparty relationships as either oppressive or sexual free-for-alls, at least some set of individuals—polyamorists, or "polys" for short—seems to be practicing nonmonogamy as part of an ethical practice that shares some of its aspirations with more mainstream models of intimate relationships.

The societal resistance to the idea of polyamory may merely be an artifact of historical associations with patriarchal polygyny, which could be partially or completely ameliorated by contemporary accounts of egalitarian polyamorous relationships or of polygynous unions where the women feel they benefit from sharing their wifely duties with other women.[3] Alternatively, resistance to the idea of polyamorous relationships may stem from other concerns, about practical inefficiency of such relationships, negative physical or psychological effects, the equality or sufficiency of love among multiple partners, or associations with other taboos such as incest or homosexuality. While any of these may contribute to mainstream responses to the idea of polyamory, the article proposes that something else is also fueling that response.

I argue that a key reason for the opposition to polyamory is, somewhat paradoxically, the pervasive or potential failure of monogamy. This argument draws lessons from the theory and politics of homosexuality, which demonstrate that the "universalizing" possibilities of a particular minority practice may drive allies away, rather than creating the conditions for solidarity through common ground.[4] Many people engage in nonmonogamous behavior; many more have nonmonogamous fantasy lives. Indeed, one might go so far as to say that it is the rare person whose sexual thoughts only ever involve his or her partner in monogamy. Paradoxically, this mainstream impulse to nonmonogamy helps to explain the position of multiparty relationships beyond the pale of the marriage debates. Rather than prompting outsiders to identify with polyamorists, the potential of nearly everyone to imagine him or herself engaging in non-monogamous behavior leads outsiders to steel themselves against polyamory and to eschew the idea of legitimizing such relationships through law. This I call the paradox of prevalence.

Compulsory Monogamy

For many, the fantasy of monogamy is different from its reality. In the normative fantasy, exclusive relationships of two people are the romantic ideal that we should and do strive for. At times, this ideal is realized, but at other times, desire and behavior betray that ideal. That people sometimes behave nonmonogamously is not a novel proposition, but

the idea that love equals monogamy and jealousy equals love is so pervasive that it seems important to frame the overall analysis in the article with a brief and plain look at monogamy. This Part, therefore, uses statistical, legal, literary, and scientific sources to sketch the contemporary landscape of monogamy.

A. Monogamy's Mandate

The institutions of monogamy loom large in this nation's social landscape. According to the 2000 census, sixty percent of Americans over eighteen are married, and seventy-six percent of Americans over eighteen are or have been married. In addition, seventy percent of those who divorce will remarry, and over ninety percent of Americans say they want to marry. These numbers sketch the contours of our drive toward monogamy's core institution. A vivid picture of our romance with monogamy, however, requires richer sources. This section will adumbrate two prevailing discourses of monogamy: the western romance tradition and the scientific defense of monogamy.

1. The Western Romance Tradition

Psychoanalyst Adam Phillips articulates a perplexing aspect of love—the idea that in friendship the lack of jealousy is a virtue, even a prerequisite to true friendship, but in erotic love the presence of jealousy is a virtue, even an emblem of true love. Phillips writes:

> We may believe in sharing as a virtue—we may teach it to our children—but we don't seem to believe in sharing what we value most, our sexual partners. But if you really loved someone, wouldn't you want to give them the best thing you've got, your partner? It would be a relief not to be puzzled by this.[5]

Phillips offers a provocative answer to his own question: "Perhaps this is what friendship is for, perhaps this is the difference between friends and lovers. Friends can share, lovers have to do something else. Lovers dare not be too virtuous."[6] In Phillips' formulation, jealousy is a form of selfishness, a vice it might be brave and generous to overcome. But Phillips sees that his view is uncommon and that in reality lovers indulge jealousy; he is puzzled by this. He hypothesizes that lovers act out of fear, implying that they fear loss through abandonment. Like Phillips, literary theorist Roland Barthes seems to valorize the rejection of jealousy: "'When I love, I am very exclusive,' Freud says (whom we shall take here for the paragon of normality). To be jealous is to conform. To reject jealousy ('to be perfect') is therefore to transgress a law."[7]

Phillips and Barthes identify key aspects of monogamy: first, that jealousy is treated as evidence of love, and, second, that jealousy may be understood to define romantic love. Phillips highlights how friends and lovers are distinguished by their approach to sharing. Friends may share themselves and each other among many; lovers must possess one another.[8] This resonates with the romantic accounts of couples who were friends first and "discovered" their love only upon realizing their jealousy of one another's lovers. A key distinction between friends and lovers, then, lies in the possessive aspect of romantic love, in the presumption that romantic love is possessive but platonic love is not. The operation of jealousy between partners may be understood as a related tenet of monogamy's law: that one partner's jealousy trumps the other partner's desire for extracouple sexual experience.

Of course nonsexual relationships do involve jealousy sometimes. And people, especially children, sometimes speak of having one "best friend." The difference between friendship and romantic relationships lies in the normative response to the two forms of jealousy. Jealousy of a friend's other friends is generally considered a problem for the one who is jealous, who should thus overcome the jealousy. By contrast, jealousy of a lover's other lovers is generally considered a problem for the one who inspires the jealousy, who should overcome the impulse to be unfaithful to the lover. Our toleration of sexual jealousy may be seen vividly in the criminal law of homicide. For centuries, sexual jealousy over adultery has been treated as adequate provocation to mitigate murder to voluntary manslaughter; indeed, rage over adultery is viewed by many courts and commentators as the paradigmatic case of adequate provocation. As noted above, Phillips is puzzled by the divergence

between friendship and romantic love along the axis of sexual possession. But Barthes displays none of Phillips's wonder at the normality of jealousy. Drawing on Freud, Barthes states the situation simply: Monogamy is the law.

Condemnation of divorce, both historical and extant, points us towards another, stricter model of monogamy: the fantasy of "supermonogamy." Supermonogamy is the idea that only one "right" partner exists for each person. Though it pervades popular and high culture, the idea of supermonogamy is perhaps most vividly portrayed in a classical story, Aristophanes' tale of originary beings from Plato's *Symposium*. "[I]n the beginning . . . ," Plato writes in Aristophanes' speech, "[t]here were three kinds of human beings . . . male and female . . . [and] a third, a combination of those two . . . ." These beings were "completely round, with . . . four hands each, as many legs as hands, and two faces, exactly alike, on a rounded neck . . . There were two sets of sexual organs . . . ." Offended by these beings' ambitions to attack the gods, Zeus split them in two to diminish their strength. The result was pitiable. The beings ran around looking for their other halves, which they clung to, "wanting to grow together" again. "In that condition they would die from hunger and general idleness, because they would not do anything apart from each other," so Zeus took pity on them and moved their genitals around to the front. This allowed them consummation which in turn allowed them to "stop embracing, return to their jobs, and look after their other needs in life."

Plato first digests this originary myth in a quiet, conclusory tone, observing, "This, then, is the source of our desire to love each other. Love is born into every human being; it calls back the halves of our original nature together; it tries to make one out of two and heal the wound of human nature." He continues, "[e]ach of us, then, is a 'matching half' of a human whole." Plato matter-of-factly offers this story as the origin of three types of beings, which to a modern eye look like gay men, lesbians, and heterosexuals, in terms of the sex of their desired object.

As Plato proceeds again and again to describe the emotional legacy of this prelapsarian state, the romantic intensity of his writing increases. "And so," he writes:

> when a person meets the half that is his very own, whatever his orientation, whether it's to young men or not, then something wonderful happens: the two are struck from their senses by love, by a sense of belonging to one another, and by desire, and they don't want to be separated from one another, not even for a moment.[9]

2. Stories from Biological Anthropology

Biological anthropologists, evolutionary psychologists, and other scientists of human and nonhuman animal behavior have offered various deterministic explanations for "human monogamy." The basic story follows the selfish gene into unexpected territory. Darwinian and other adaptive explanations of animal behavior might seem to argue against monogamy. That is, would not adaptive creatures seek to reproduce as much and as widely as possible, giving their gene pool the best chance of survival? This view has its adherents, but various evolutionary scientists also offer explanations for why humans may pair up in order to promote the survival of their individual gene pools. These types of explanations of human behavior have been much criticized; they are of interest here primarily as examples of the kinds of stories we tell in support of monogamy.

The basic story of adaptive monogamy is quality over quantity. Due to the relatively lengthy human gestation period and childhood,[10] the story goes, women want the support and protection of men during this vulnerable period of child-bearing and child-rearing.[11] In addition, pairing with one provider helps females ensure the health, safety, and development of their offspring. Thus, it is advantageous for females "to develop a pairing tendency."

The male interest in monogamy is less clear, but writers offer three types of explanations of male monogamy. The first type focuses on the males' relations with each other, interpreting monogamy's equal distribution of the sexual resources (i.e., women) as advantageous to cooperative hunting

behavior among males, or as the result of democratic progress by the less wealthy men who have a harder time obtaining a wife under a polygamous system. The second type of explanation yokes the males' interests directly to the offspring, whom the males may want to protect or nourish in order to increase their chance of survival.

The third type of explanation focuses on male-female relations. Here, the males may stay close to home to make sure no other male is impregnating the female, and thereby diverting her resources or those of the primary male. Or, the males may be understood to develop pairing tendencies in order to be more sexually successful with the females who presumptively prefer males who will pair. This account presents sociobiological explanations of human love and jealousy. Under a refinement of this theory, males pair up because monogamy creates domestic bliss that is beneficial to offspring.

Because compelling counternarratives about nonmonogamy are also told from an adaptive perspective,[12] the accounts outlined here are particularly interesting for their dogged pursuit of an "encouraging"—which is to say, monogamous—explanation of human sexual behavior. One can almost hear the sighs of relief emitted by evolutionary theorists when they can conclude that humans are basically monogamous,[13] and even better yet, when they can supply explanations of why this trait is part of human evolutionary "success." Thus, Matt Ridley observes, "The nature of the human male, then, is to take opportunities, if they are granted him, for polygamous mating, and to use wealth, power and violence as means to sexual ends in the competition with other men—though usually not at the expense of sacrificing a secure monogamous relationship." Fortunately, it seems, the male interests in keeping the monogamous relationship secure—though less obvious than the female interests—outweigh his polygamous drive. And this is part of what makes humans special: "Even in the most despotic and polygamous moment of human history, mankind was faithful to the institution of monogamous marriage, quite unlike any other polygamous animal."

B. Monogamy's Reality

This foray into the romantic and scientific story of monogamy leads us back to the data. The numbers on actual relationship behavior illustrate the gap between theory and practice.

1. The Failures of Supermonogamy

The frequent failure of supermonogamy—the idea of one partner ever—is reflected in our high divorce rates. Rates of divorce in the United States have increased dramatically during the twentieth century, and studies indicate that forty percent of Americans get divorced[14] and that seventy percent of those who divorce remarry.[15]

Second, and more importantly here, adultery occurs often enough to undermine even the idea of simple, serial monogamy—the idea that people have one sexual partner at a time. "Researchers [of adultery in America] have reported lifetime prevalence rates from as low as 20 percent . . . to nearly 75 percent . . . ." The most comprehensive study of American sexual behavior to date offers figures on the low end of that scale. The National Health and Social Life Survey, released in 1994, claims that approximately twenty percent of married women and thirty-five percent of married men have had adulterous sex, and there is reason to think that levels of adultery among those studied are even higher. The American data on adultery are consistent with those of other major western nations. Dr. Judith Mackay, Senior Policy Advisor for the World Health Organization, reports that "40% of sexually active 16–45 year-old Germans admit to having been sexually unfaithful, compared with 50% of Americans, 42% of British, 40% of Mexicans, 36% of the French, and 22% of the Spanish." Bear in mind that these figures reflect only those subjects who admit to infidelity.

III. Contemporary Polyamory

Relationships among more than two partners may strike many people as "preposterous." As just discussed, however, monogamy often fails to achieve its goals. The failure of one model does not, in itself, make other models viable. But monogamy's frequent failure may give us reason to pause before dismissing as absurd the possibility of alternatives.

And as polyamory is not frequently in the public eye, we are rarely exposed to its reality.

This Part discusses the scope, terms, and structures of polyamory today. Since such skeletal information does little to enrich our understanding of a practice, this Part also portrays several polyamorous relationships. These portraits aim to capture something of the feeling and experience of living inside these relationships by weaving together structural aspects and mundane details. How much anyone can understand another's experience is a question beyond the scope of this article, but despite the sage advice that you have to "*go there t*[o] *know* there," this Part proceeds from the premise that words allow at least the possibility of seeing the world through the eyes of another. Finally, this Part discusses the ethical vision of polyamory, setting forth five ideas that I derive from writings by its practitioners.

Before proceeding to discuss polyamory, however, I want to address a certain confusion surrounding the term "polygamy." Charles Krauthammer has identified a key split in the responses to polygamy:

> [I]f marriage is redefined to include two men in love, on what possible principled grounds can it be denied to three men in love?
>
> This is traditionally called the polygamy challenge, but polygamy—one man marrying more than one woman—is the wrong way to pose the question. Polygamy, with its rank inequality and female subservience, is too easy a target. It invites exploitation of and degrading competition among wives, with often baleful social and familial consequences. (For those in doubt on this question, see Genesis: 26-35 on Joseph and his multimothered brothers.)
>
> The question is better posed by imagining three people of the same sex in love with one another and wanting their love to be legally recognized and socially sanctioned by marriage.

The distinction Krauthammer draws here is instructive. American ideas of multiparty relationships are shaped by this country's historical experience with Mormon polygamy, and I would go so far as to say this is what most Americans think of first when they think of polygamy. In addition, the image of polygamy as a Muslim practice undoubtedly adds to its negative public image, historically and also particularly in the wake of September 11, 2001. Arguably, one reason Americans oppose multiparty relationships is that these relationships evoke the image of a man sanctioned by a patriarchal religious society to have many wives as emblems of his power or chosen status. There is some disagreement among scholars as well as polygynists as to whether this model is necessarily bad for women, as discussed later, but certainly it is widely thought to be so. Thus, as Congressman Barney Frank has said about why people oppose plural marriage, "First, it's almost always polygamy and not polyamory. So a lot of women don't like it."

Frank's comment highlights a common problem of terminology. The term "polygamy" is often used to mean two different things: 1) marriage to more than one person, regardless of sex; and 2) the marriage of one man to more than one woman. As noted above, the latter—one man with multiple wives—is specifically called "polygyny." Polygyny is the opposite of "polyandry," one woman with multiple husbands. The elision of polygamy and polygyny is exemplified, with some acknowledgement of the confusion, by the *Oxford English Dictionary* definition of "polygamy": "Marriage with several, or more than one, at once; plurality of spouses; the practice or custom according to which one man has several wives (distinctively called *polygyny*), or one woman several husbands (*polyandry*), at the same time. *Most commonly used of the former.*" To avoid this confusion, the article uses the term "polygamy" to mean several spouses, regardless of sex. It is, however, significant that polygamy commonly refers to a man with many wives. I agree with Frank that this tendency to conflate polygamy and polygyny is one reason that people object to the idea of multiparty relationships. To pry these concepts apart, this article offers several examples of multiparty relationships that are not structured by institutionalized patriarchy.

A. Terms and Models

No studies or surveys estimate the number of people currently engaged in polyamory, but the national organization Loving More reports a rate of 1,000 hits per day on its website and a circulation of 10,000 readers for its eponymous magazine. Loving More provides the following general definition of polyamory:

> Polyamory (many loves) is a relatively new word created for relationships where an adult intimately loves more than one other adult. This includes forms like open couples, group marriage, intimate networks, triads and even people who currently have one or no partners, yet are open to the possibility of more. . . . People who describe themselves as polyamorous (or poly) also usually embrace the value of honesty in relationships. They do not want to have affairs or cheat on a loved one and are dedicated to growing beyond jealousy and possession in relationships.

This explanation conveys at least four things about polyamory. First, the word is "relatively new." Like "homosexuality," it is a mixture of Greek (poly) and Latin (amor). Second, the hybridity of the word points to a feature of polyamory represented in this definition: the wide variety of relationships that fall within its ambit. Third, the reference to polyamorous "people who currently have one or no partners" suggests that people not only practice polyamory, people can *be* "poly." Finally, the last two sentences point toward the philosophical interests of many of polyamory's practitioners: polys have well-articulated views of relationships and beliefs about interpersonal ethics.

One dispute about the boundaries of polyamory concerns whether traditional polygyny, as practiced by, most prominently, fundamentalist Mormons, "counts" as polyamory. The sex-based hierarchy of traditional Mormon polygyny seems incompatible with the typical poly dedication to principles of equality and individual growth, causing some polys and commentators to exclude Mormon polygyny from the umbrella of polyamory. In this article, one of the relationships profiled is a Mormon-type polygynous union, which none of the participants calls "polyamorous" but which blends elements of traditional hierarchy with modern feminist ideas of female solidarity, satisfaction, and work outside the home, according to the accounts given by the female participants. By including this relationship, I do not mean to resolve the question of whether this relationship "counts" as polyamorous, but mean merely to present it as a lesser-known type of the polygyny that most people picture when they think of multiparty relationships.

Because the number of people in poly relationships has no theoretical limit, the models of poly relationships are also theoretically limitless. Some of the more typical models have specific names. Definitions of these models often rely on the terms "primary relationship," "secondary relationship," and occasionally "tertiary relationship," although some polys object to the hierarchy implied by these terms. For example, according to Deborah Anapol, an "intimate network" comprises "several ongoing secondary relationships. . . . Sometimes all members of the group eventually become lovers. Sometimes individuals have only two or three partners within the group. The group can include singles only, couples only[,] or a mixture of both." The term "line marriage" identifies "a different form of familial immortality than the traditional one of successive generations of children"; rather, a line marriage is "a marriage that from time to time adds younger members, eventually establishing an equilibrium population (spouses dying off at the same rate as new ones are added)."

A term such as "polyfidelity" clarifies the type of commitment among the parties, and is defined as "[a] lovestyle in which three or more primary partners agree to be sexual only within their family. Additional partners can be added to the marriage with everyone's consent." The idea of polyfidelity brings us to a distinction between two aspects of polyamorists' transgression of monogamy, what I call the "exclusivity" axis and the "numerosity" axis.

Criminal law helps us to see the distinctiveness and the importance of these two axes.

"Exclusivity" refers to whether someone has sex with people outside a relationship. As in the common phrase "open relationship," exclusivity concerns whether a relationship is "open" or "closed." In the legal realm, adultery statutes target violations of the exclusivity norm. By contrast, "numerosity" concerns how many people are in a relationship. From the perspective of monogamy, the basic question here is whether a relationship involves two individuals or more than two individuals. Thus, bigamy statutes target violations of numerosity norms. Within polyamory, exclusivity and numerosity define aspects of individual relationship models, such as polyfidelity, which might be understood as a sexually exclusive model analytically distinct from monogamous relationships primarily in the number of the participants.

Some relationship models are specifically defined by the number of participants. For example, an "open marriage" is a "nonexclusive couple relationship[]" in which the two "partners have agreed that each can independently have outside sexualoving partners." A poly "triad" involves "[t]hree sexualoving partners who may all be secondary, all be primary, or two may be primary with a third secondary. It can be open or closed. A triad can be heterosexual or homosexual, but is often the choice of two same sex bisexuals and an opposite sex heterosexual." Two different types of triads are further distinguished by the types of bonds among the three partners: "vees" and "triangles," each of which may be diagrammed as the figure that names it:

Vee—Three people, where the structure puts one person at the bottom, or "hinge" of the vee, also called the pivot point. In a vee, the arm partners are not as commonly close to each other as each is to the pivot.

Triangle (or equilateral triangle)—relationship where three people are each involved with both of the others. Sometimes also called a triad.

As these examples indicate, diagrams may help to demonstrate the possible polyamorous configurations. These are just a few of the poly models with specific names, which are in turn only a small sample of the possible models.

C. Theory

Polyamory is not only a practice. For some, it is a theory of relationships. In an effort to organize and explain the contours of that theory, this Section sketches five principles espoused by contemporary polys. These principles, which I have extracted from a range of poly writings and comments, are presented by polys as both aspirational and descriptive. That is, experienced polys tend to present these principles as tools for making polyamorous relationships work (aspirational), based on their experience in and around functioning polyamorous relationships (descriptive). And the principles are aspirational in another way. They are offered by polys not only as functional tools for creating and sustaining intimacy among multiple people; they also represent an ethical vision of how those relationships should be conducted.

To my knowledge, there are no studies of the content of contemporary polyamorous relationships. For this and other reasons, such as the wide variety of poly relationships, my purpose in presenting these principles is not to say that poly relationships all successfully embody these ideas. Rather, my purpose is to show the seriousness with which some polys have considered the ethical and practical questions of how multiparty relationships should be conducted, and to convey some of the answers they have developed thus far.

These five principles come from no one source but instead represent my attempt to synthesize the content of many sources. The principles are self-knowledge, radical honesty, consent, self-possession, and privileging love and sex. These principles are of course not unique to polys; on the contrary, most of them are embraced by many monogamous couples. The poly privileging of more loving and sexual experiences over other activities and emotions, such as jealousy, is the most particular to polyamory, and the other principles have particular applications, meanings, and significance in the poly context. This Section considers each principle in turn.

1. Self-Knowledge

Self-knowledge is portrayed by polyamorists not only as valuable, but as necessary. In her foundational book, *Polyamory, the New Love Without Limits: Secrets of Sustainable Intimate Relationships*, Deborah Anapol outlines "Eight Steps to Successful Polyamory," the first of which is to "Know yourself." This dictate operates on two levels. The first level involves understanding one's own sexual identity. This no doubt comprises knowledge of one's "sexual orientation" as we typically use the term—as in heterosexual, bisexual, or homosexual—but also, more importantly, it encompasses self-knowledge about one's sexual identity with regard to monogamy. As discussed in Part IV, some polys embrace the view that you either are poly or you are not, whereas other poly writings characterize monogamy and polyamory more as choices or constructed identities. Regardless, whether they understand "poly" and "mono" identities as hardwired or chosen, polys call for an interrogation of one's own identity.

Polys also value self-knowledge as the core structural component, and the daily substrate, of healthy, successful relationships. Understanding oneself and listening to one's own feelings are vital to the process of working through the "baggage" of living in a monogamous world. Anapol instructs, as another of her eight steps to success, "Let jealousy be your teacher." Rather than deny the existence of emotions like jealousy, polys encourage an honest interrogation of these feelings. Individuals in any form of relationship may of course aspire to and attain self-knowledge. But polys, in order to do all that "processing," have a particularly strong need for constant access to their feelings and desires.

2. Radical Honesty

The poly ethic of honesty also operates on two levels: a broader philosophical position and a daily practice of living. The structural critique may be understood partly as a reaction to the gap between the fantasy and the reality of compulsory monogamy. The judge in the Divilbiss case criticized April for her "immoral" response to a man's attentions: "[W]hen some guy came to her and said I'm in love with you too although you are married, you know, most people would have said, well, hey, I'm married; forget it."[16] In response, a poly might assert instead: "The judge has it wrong. Most people would have said, 'Well, hey, I'm married, so we'll have to keep this a secret.'"[17]

One theory of polyamory views the entire culture as basically polyamorous but dishonest about it. In the words of Deborah Anapol, "Lies, deceit, guilt, unilateral decisions and broken commitments are so commonplace in classic American-style monogamy that responsible nonmonogamy may sound like an oxymoron."[18] The weak form of this claim is that serial monogamy is in a sense polyamory. That is, almost no one settles down with the first person she has sex with, no one is truly supermonogamous, and so everyone is really polyamorous. The stronger claim, however, is that many people are polyamorous in the sense that they feign simple monogamy while practicing nonmonogamy. They lie to their partners and to the world.[19] Thus, radical honesty is a philosophical and practical approach to living that involves admitting and embracing nonmonogamy. For many polys, honesty is so central to polyamory that they would object to the use of the term polyamory independent of honesty, protesting that honesty is a definitional element of polyamory. For example, one posting on a popular polyamory webpage says, "A great many people have secret affairs while they're in a supposedly monogamous relationship. I think those people might have the potential to be polyamorous, but I do not think they are practicing polyamory."[20]

Brad Blanton is a writer praised by some polys for his books on "radical honesty."[21] His books outline a philosophy of absolute honesty and of honesty as a revolutionary way to improve oneself and the world. Radical honesty, Blanton tells us, "involves not denying or avoiding anything, particularly anger that comes from attachment to the one true way we all seem to come up with every fifteen seconds, it involves clearing our way back to contact with each other through honesty about what we think and feel and do . . . ."[22] Many of the examples of life changes made by participants in Blanton's workshops include spouses who admit their affairs, prompting the couples either to turn a failed marriage into a positive honest one[23] or to split up and try to find new, more honest, relations elsewhere.[24]

Whether or not they particularly follow Blanton, polys tend to privilege honesty as the foundation of positive relationships.

Of course, polys are not alone in recognizing the value of honesty. But a heightened emphasis on communication is highly characteristic of polys, and openness about nonmonogamy is the most distinctive aspect of poly honesty. Indeed, the latter commitment prompts polys to describe their honesty as "radical." Note, however, that if society presumed nonmonogamy, then it might be radical to embrace and admit openly a commitment to monogamy. In this way, the radicalness of poly honesty is contingent.

3. Consent

Honesty is also something more than the transmission of information in polyamorous relationships. In this context, honesty forms the basis of consent. The ideal of consent—that partners in a relationship or a sexual encounter make an informed decision to participate in the relationship or the encounter, including knowing its polyamorous context—pervades poly writing, both implicitly and explicitly. For instance, Dr. Joy Davidson presents "Negotiating and making agreements" as one of the key relationship challenges for polyamorous relationships, emphasizing that "each agreement is a reminder that consent is at the heart of successful poly relating" and that "consent must be given at an explicit and detailed level." From her perspective as a clinical psychologist who works with polyamorous partners, Singer also emphasizes the importance of distinguishing between "true consent" and "[c]oerced consent," noting that "[t]herapists may see clients whose relationships reflect manipulation, dishonesty, or other dysfunctional patterns that are no more representative of healthy poly than healthy monogamy." Though individual poly relationships may not always embody true consent, this ideal is a vital part of the relationship models to which polys aspire.

Consent is also of vital importance in nonpoly relationships, of course. In a simple way, the poly emphasis on consent is another part of the poly critique of the secretive nonmonogamy practiced by some purported monogamists. But the poly attention to consent runs deeper than that. The prominence of the idea of consent also stems from the poly emphasis on freedom of choice about relationship norms and the importance of individual, rather than societal, relationship expectations. Because no one relationship model provides a blueprint for the number, shape, or type of bonds among individuals within and without poly relationships, polys must develop their own models through the agreement of the partners.

4. Self-Possession

A number of prominent poly writers describe their embrace of polyamory as fueled by their insights about power and possessiveness in monogamy and by their desire for autonomy within their relationships. This aspect of polyamory builds in part on a feminist understanding of monogamy as a historical mechanism for the control of women's reproductive and other labor. Judith Stelboum writes, "Feminist scholars state that the origins of monogamy have their source in patriarchal thinking. Viewed as the possessions of the male, women were used for barter and/or procreation. . . . Legitimacy of a child relates to acknowledgement of the child's father, not to the child's mother."[25] In light of these accounts of the patriarchal origins and functions of monogamy, Stelboum seeks to explain why so many contemporary lesbians adopt monogamy: "The implications of the historical prerogative of male inheritance have little relevance for the lesbian community, but the social values and behavioral modes of the dominant heterosexual community have been firmly implanted within most of the lesbian population."[26] In response, she offers several purposes of nonmonogamy in lesbian relationships, including as a political statement against the "confining heterosexual models of monogamy," and as "a way for two women to define autonomy within a coupled situation and avoid the intense bonding typical of some lesbian partners."[27]

For Dossie Easton and Deborah Anapol, realizations about the strictures of monogamy came through their experience or study of domestic violence. As described above, Easton devotes energy and emotion to preserving the independence made possible by polyamory because an abusive relationship opened her eyes to the control exerted in monogamous relationships.[28] Anapol, whose doctoral dissertation in clinical psychology focused on domestic violence, identifies connections between the possessive claims of monogamy and the cycles of abuse and violence in these relationships:

> I married for the second time, trying to fit myself into the traditional mold with an ambitious, personable husband and a house with a white picket fence. He too had unfinished business with an old lover, but while continued friendships were acceptable to him, extra-marital love affairs were not. I was researching domestic violence for my doctoral dissertation . . . and was horrified to realize that the dynamics of domination, control, jealousy and dependency that I'd observed in abusive marriages I was studying, existed, at a more moderate level, in my own marriage.

These realizations were one factor which led Anapol to reject traditional monogamy and pursue polyamory as a way to exercise greater personal autonomy in her relationships.

5. Privileging Love and Sex

A crucial aspect of poly thinking, and the one most particular to polyamory, is the idea that when it comes to sex and love, more expression and experience may truly be better than less. One source of this philosophy is the various free love movements of the 1960s. The science fiction writer Robert Heinlein famously said, "'Love is that condition wherein another person's happiness is essential to your own." One poly writer asserts that, in light of Heinlein's "foundational premise, jealousy and possessiveness become seen [by our community] not as symptoms of love, but as a pathology of insecurity." This idea, that more may be better, inspires the name of Loving More, as well as its mission statement, which explains that the organization has

[A] specific vision of relationships based on honesty, openness, respect for the individual, love as an infinite resource, the body and sexuality as sacred, and relationship as a path to personal & spiritual growth. In this vision, there's room for more love, more intimacy, more possibilities, and more people.

Accordingly, there is also more responsibility and challenge: a deeply personal challenge to transform ourselves, our lives, and our world into a more loving and responsible place.

Love and sex are of course widely valued. But poly relationships, to a greater extent than many monogamous relationships, privilege love and sex over other feelings and activities. Polys privilege love insofar as they tend to prioritize talking and other forms of creating and sustaining intimacy over other activities. They therefore devote much time to processing everyone's feelings.

Polys truly seem distinct from most monos when it comes to sexual beliefs and behavior. Rejecting the law of monogamy that allows one partner's jealousy to trump another's outside sexual desires and experiences, polys feel that jealousy should be overcome to make room for more sexual and loving possibilities. Rather than assuming that a philandering partner should curb her wandering impulse, then, polys more often proceed from the assumption that the jealous partner should work through his jealousy.

IV. The Paradox of Prevalence

Why is the possibility that same-sex marriage might lead to multiparty marriage such an effective rhetorical scare tactic for the opponents of same-sex marriage? In this Part, I argue that the widespread resistance to the idea of marriage among more than two people is actually the result of monogamy's frequent failure. In a sense, the threat of polyamory stems from its apparent prevalence.

B. The Problem of the Universalizing View of Polyamory

This Section takes its cue from insights into sexuality developed in the context of homosexuality.

In particular, the conceptual distinction between "universalizing" and "minoritizing" views of sexual identity, posed by sexuality theorist Eve Kosofsky Sedgwick, helps to pinpoint a crucial problem for polyamorists.

Sedgwick defines a "minoritizing" view of homosexuality as the view that "there is a distinct population of persons who 'really are' gay." By contrast, a "universalizing" view of homosexuality holds "that apparently heterosexual persons and object choices are strongly marked by same-sex influences and desires, and vice versa for apparently homosexual ones. . . ." The concept of minoritizing and universalizing discourses of identity encourages a focus on the ways that this aspect of identity is pervasively important in the lives of many people, even those who do not identify as sexual minorities. Rather than focusing our attention exclusively on some narrow idea of biologically essential identities—or some superficial assessment of identities as constructed and therefore deconstructable—the minoritizing/universalizing axis prompts us to ask: "'In whose lives is homo/heterosexual [or nonmonogamous/monogamous] definition an issue of continuing centrality and difficulty?'" Sedgwick's categories, therefore, urge a focus on the discourses and perceptions surrounding a particular identity category, rather than on the search for any inherent truth of sexual identities.

Sedgwick argues that "[m]ost moderately to well-educated Western people in this century seem to share a similar understanding of homosexual definition,"[29] one that is marked by "a radical and irreducible incoherence."[30] That is, Sedgwick claims that most people hold minoritizing and universalizing views of homosexuality simultaneously. For example, many people think that there is a distinct minority of people who are immutably gay, but many of these same people also do not want their children exposed to gay role models for fear that it could make their children gay. In this sense, I agree with Sedgwick about the incoherence in views of homosexuality. But I would also posit that the contemporary view of homosexuality is highly minoritizing relative to the general view of polyamory.

Unlike homosexuals, who are understood by many to possess a distinct and unalterable identity, polyamorists are rarely seen as having a distinct identity. In the words of Jonathan Rauch:

> Do homosexuals actually exist? I think so, and today even the Vatican accepts that some people are constitutively attracted only to members of the same sex. By contrast, no serious person claims there are people constitutively attracted only to relatives, or only to groups rather than individuals. Anyone who can love two women can also love one of them. People who insist on marrying their mother or several lovers want an additional (and weird) marital option. Homosexuals currently have no marital option at all. A demand for polygamous or incestuous marriage is thus frivolous in a way that the demand for gay marriage is not.[31]

Similarly, Andrew Sullivan claims, "Almost everyone seems to accept, even if they find homosexuality morally troublesome, that it occupies a deeper level of human consciousness than a polygamous impulse."[32] Without directly assessing the truth-value of their allegations about gays versus polys, both Rauch and Sullivan reflect the divergence in popular perceptions of the depth of these sexual identities. Gay identity is viewed by many to be a deeply rooted element of identity; poly identity is seen to be so superficial as to be frivolous. Because a desire to be involved with more than one person is not perceived to "occup[y] a deep[] level of human consciousness,"[33] nor to be a "constitutive[] attract[ion],"[34] polys are generally not seen as a discrete group of individuals. There is little sense of a distinct group of people who "really are" poly.

Rather, the desire to be sexually involved with more than one person, or with someone other than an existing partner, is viewed as nearly universal. To translate Sedgwick's definition of universalizing homosexuality into an observation about universalizing polyamory: "[A]pparently [monogamous] persons and object choices are strongly marked by [nonmonogamous] influences and desires. . . ." The universalizing account of nonmonogamy may seem obvious: Of course most people *want* to sleep with others; they just resist that impulse. From this perspective, polyamory may seem, like bisexuality, to be a form of greed or indulgence.

Much thinking and writing from within poly communities also sounds in a universalizing register. Most notably, the idea of radical honesty is universalizing about people's involvement in nonmonogamous activity, through serial monogamy and adultery. The poly ethic of honesty posits that many more people engage in nonmonogamous behavior than own up to it. From this perspective, polys seem less a distinct minority than outspoken representatives of the masses. Poly thinking thus shifts scrutiny to monogamy, asking how it is constructed and why people lie about their nonmonogamous behavior and desires.

The idea of privileging love and sex also seems to offer benefits to anyone willing and able to experience them. Rather than proposing that some small subset of people might grow and enrich their lives through further sexual and loving relationships, the poly commitment to experiencing love and sex seems a credo of expansiveness, a manifesto of living that has no obvious stopping point or confinement to those who espouse it. Moreover, the poly ethic of self-possession offers a resounding critique of the strictures of monogamy—of its jealousy, possessiveness, and patriarchy—a critique that implicates mainstream institutions.

Deborah Anapol boldly captures the universalizing challenge inherent in much poly talk:

> The fact is that most of us *are* polyamorists at heart whether we are willing to admit it to ourselves or not. It is no accident that "serial monogamy," which is not really monogamy at all, is currently the most common relationship form in our culture. Serial monogamy can be viewed as being one step closer to who we really are. Unlike lifelong monogamy, it allows us to express our polyamorous nature while maintaining a monogamous fiction in which our multiple mates are separated by linear time. For some people this marriage-divorce-remarriage cycle remains the best solution.

But divorce increasingly appears to be more stressful and disruptive than first thought. . . . Where infidelity or the desire for broader sexual expression is the primary cause for dissolution of a marriage, surely we can find more imaginative alternatives than divorce. . . .

. . . The point is that, ultimately, the clash between our nonmonogamous nature and our monogamous tradition must begin to be seen as a legitimate reason to develop new forms of relationships. . . .

. . . *Polyamory, a viable alternative for those who wish to expand their social horizons to include multipartner relationships, is a concept whose time has come.*[35]

This is classic universalizing language, and it challenges people to admit their own transgressions and violations of the law of monogamy, and to embrace an alternative open to everyone. Anapol's position is interesting because it locates polyamory as somehow essential, but essential in most everyone. In a gay context, this might be akin to saying that homosexuality is hardwired into everyone.

Notably, Anapol initially seems to blur the distinction between nonmonogamy and polyamory by suggesting that everyone might be a "polyamorist[] at heart." Arguably, though, she expresses herself in this way for rhetorical impact. By the end of the passage, polyamory reemerges as a practice distinct from other forms of nonmonogamy—such as "cheating"—because she describes "polyamory" as a "viable alternative" involving "multipartner relationships." This is consistent with the distinction I drew at the end of Part III, that polyamory is a subset of nonmonogamy distinguished primarily by its devotion to certain principles, such as honesty and privileging sexual and loving experiences over jealousy.

Nonetheless, as Anapol points out, polyamorists have something in common with much of the population: an impulse towards nonmonogamy. One might contrast the prevalence of the capacity to imagine nonmonogamy—to experience desire for someone other than one's primary partner—with the capacity to imagine homosexuality.

Arguably, many more people have nonmonogamous fantasies than have homosexual fantasies. Even according to Alfred Kinsey's findings, which have been widely criticized for overstating the extent of homosexual desire and activity because of problems such as sample bias, 50% of males reported no same-sex desires or experience after the onset of adolescence,[36] and 72% of females reported no same-sex desires at all.[37] By contrast, somewhere between 25% and 75% of Americans have engaged in adulterous sex, as discussed earlier.[38] The number of people who have felt nonmonogamous desires is, no doubt, much greater.

Indeed, it seems a fair assumption that almost everyone has at some time felt desire for more than one person. There certainly may be some small subset of people who have never experienced desire for anyone other than their current partner (if they have one). Nevertheless, the prevalence of serial monogamy (as indicated by divorce rates) suggests that it is an extremely rare person who cannot imagine feeling desire for more than one person, since he can at least think of two people that he has desired in sequence. Sexual variation is arguably infinite, so there may well be some people who exhibit supermonogamous desires par excellence—people who have desired one and only one person in their entire lives. However, it also seems fair to assume that such people are extremely rare.

In this light, polys would seem to have many potential allies because many people could seemingly empathize with at least some aspect of polys' desires. Although many people may not actually want multiple sexual partners in *love*, most can presumably empathize with the aspect of poly desire that means more than one *sexual* partner. The sheer ubiquity of nonmonogamous desire, and the prevalence of nonmonogamous behavior, could mean a larger constituency and more allies for pro-poly politics. I want to argue, however, based on certain lessons from gay theory and politics, that the universalizing possibilities suggested by Anapol's words form a basic stumbling block to public recognition of poly relationships.

Rather than empathizing with others who share one's traits, people often fear or shun the people they could become, particularly when the common traits are stigmatized.[39] This difficulty may be understood through the figure of the self-hating Jew, black, or homosexual.[40] Similarly, the principle behind "homophobia" is that the presence of homosexuality in one's self can create the fear of actual homosexuals. Pervasive homophobia may therefore be understood as a sign of the pervasiveness of same-sex fantasies or desires. Thus, one lesson from gay politics is that the universal potential of an identity trait may engender distance rather than empathy, resistance rather than support.

In addition, the difficulty of organizing and generating support for an "invisible" group has been a longstanding obstacle for gays. The challenge of identifying invisible gay allies, much less convincing them to be oppositional rather than to hide in the closet, has inspired political fantasies of all gays turning blue. That is, if all gays were blue, then gays would have the ability—and the need—to seek solidarity and to end the prisoner's dilemma of the closet. The invisibility of gays may also contribute to a lack of empathy from nongays, or a lack of avowed support from gay-friendly nongays, because those who support gays may be mistakenly deemed gay in a way that supporters of a race- or sex-based group can expect not to be. The impulse to shy away from those who are like oneself, rather than forming allegiances based on commonality, may also be seen in the different attitudes toward homosexuality and bisexuality. Bisexuals share with heterosexuals the common ground of a desire for the opposite sex, yet bisexuals are more marginalized than homosexuals. If one pictures a straight white politician who has the option of supporting the political agenda of African-Americans, gays, or bisexuals, he would have the most reason to fear being mistaken for a bisexual, and thus, the most reason to fear supporting the bisexual agenda, although he seems to have the most in common, along a salient identity axis, with the bisexuals.

As Joy Singer observes, "seeking broad societal tolerance for and acceptance of poly lifestyles appears to be more difficult than it was for the gay movement . . . [because] our message just hits too much 'closer to home' for the largely heterosexual,

married opinion leaders who run the country. . . . Because 'most people may in fact be "pre-poly,"'" Singer says, for them to acknowledge the viability of polyamory is to imperil their self-conception, and poly issues therefore "seem much more threatening" than gay or lesbian issues.[41] Singer's statement that "most people" may be "pre-poly" is, of course, a perfect example of the universalizing challenge of some poly talk.

Moreover, polys have another, related, problem. Not only might an outsider to polyamory worry that *she* is poly because the desire for nonmonogamy is so widespread; an outsider might worry that her *partner* is, or could become, polyamorous.

The mere possibility of her partner's interest in polyamory could cause someone to treat the idea of polyamory as absurd and avoid discussion that might increase its legitimacy.

Relatedly, the norm of compulsory monogamy can be useful to those who wish to have it both ways. If someone wants to be nonmonogamous but wants his partner to be monogamous, then in many cases, his only way to achieve that goal is to pretend to embrace monogamy but dishonestly to practice nonmonogamy. In other words, he can get what he wants only by cheating. Thus, cheaters may have an investment in disparaging the idea of polyamory.

In light of the above discussion, the rhetorical positioning of multiparty marriage at the end of the same-sex marriage slippery slope makes sense. The monogamous aspirations of the same-sex marriage campaigners fit well with the nation's deep cultural commitment to the fantasy of monogamy and its equally trenchant resistance to recognizing monogamy's frequent failure. The prevalence of the fantasy and the reality of nonmonogamy suggests, however, that the rhetorical slippery slope masks the real proximity of nonmonogamy to mainstream reality. For polyamory's practitioners, this paradox of prevalence stands in the way of mainstream social or political support.

VI. Conclusion

For same-sex couples who are now marrying, and those who will marry in greater numbers in coming years, this may be a uniquely fertile time to think critically about the kind of intimate relationships they are forming. The present moment may someday be revealed as the end of an era, the end of a period in which same-sex couples were not subject to precisely the same pressures of compulsory monogamy as straight couples. Moreover, for everyone, regardless of relationship views or status, this monumental debate about marriage presses the question of the proper components—both practical and emotional—of intimate relationships. It is the hope of this article that everyone will take this opportunity to question monogamy "as a 'preference' or 'choice' . . . and to do the intellectual and emotional work that follows. . . ." Monogamy may be both more of a choice and less of a choice than we think, but whether the paradox of prevalence persists in dictating our views of others' relationships is undoubtedly a choice. By depicting the ways that people frequently fail to achieve the ideal of compulsory monogamy, by tracing the ways that polyamorists openly embrace this failure rather than simply falling into it, and by beginning to imagine how the law might be used to encourage people to express monogamy-related preferences to their partners, this article has attempted to shed light on the practice of intimacy and on our conflicted relationship with monogamy's law.

DISCUSSION QUESTIONS

1. Describe the traditional romantic and scientific defenses of monogamy. How do these ideals of monogamy differ from reality?
2. What is polyamory? How is it different from the practice of polygamy (including both polygyny and polyandry)?
3. What are the five main principles of polyamory as "ethical nonmonogamy"?
4. What is the "paradox of prevalence" and how does it lead people to eschew nonmonogamous behavior?

NOTES

1. *E.g.*, Lana Tibbetts, Commitment in Monogamous and Polyamorous Relationships 1 (Spring 2001) (defining ethical nonmonogamy as "practicing extradyadic relationships with mutual consent among those involved") (unpublished manuscript, on file with author), *available at* http://www.prairienet,org/~star/polypaper.html.
2. *See infra* Section III.C.
3. *See infra* Section III.B.
4. *See infra* Part IV.
5. Phillips, *supra* note 2, at 15. Phillips' language of giving is perplexing here; it seems to imply that the partner is a possession available for transfer. In the context of Phillips' overall text, however, this gift metaphor is rare and thus seems to appear here to dramatize this particular question about generosity—as opposed to possessiveness—with regard to a beloved partner.
6. *Id.*
7. Roland Barthes, *A Lover's Discourse* 144, 145 (Richard Howard trans., 1979). Barthes's epigraph for the *Jealousy* essay is as follows: "'A sentiment which is born in love and which is produced by the fear that the loved person prefers someone else' (Littré)." *Id.* at 144.
8. *See, e.g.,* Joan Iversen, *Feminist Implications of Mormon Polygyny*, 10 Feminist Stud. 505, 515 (1984) (quoting nineteenth-century critic of polygamy Fanny Stenhouse as saying that plural marriage must mean the loss of "true love" because "where there is no jealousy there is very little love" (citing Mrs. T.B.H, Stenhouse, Exposé of Polygamy in Utah: A Lady's Life Among the Mormons 75, 123 (American News Co., 2d ed, 1872); Mrs. T.B.H. Stenhouse, Tell It All: The Tyranny of Mormonism, or, an Englishwoman in Utah 213 (Praeger, 1971))); Kenneth L. Karst, *The Freedom of Intimate Association*, 89 Yale L.J. 624, 629, n.26 (1980) (noting that "friendship does not involve the degree of exclusivity that is present in other kinds of linkage between intimates").
9. Plato, *supra* note 62, at 28.
10. These features of humans are said to allow the development of "better brains," which are necessary to survival through hunting. Morris, *supra* note 77, at 63.
11. *Id.*
12. *See supra* note 76.
13. Ridley, *supra* note 77, at 212 ("Even in the polygamous societies of pastoralists, the great majority of marriages are monogamous ones.").
14. Weis, *Supra* note 38.

15. *Id.*

16. For the full quotation, see *supra* text accompanying note 183.

17. *Cf., e.g.,* Stelboum, *supra* note 101, at 44 ("In those cultures that regard monogamy as ideal, non-monogamy is widely practiced, secretly.").

18. Anapol, *supra* note 127, at 3.

19. *See* Maillu, *supra* note 100, at 29–32 (making this point in an argument for structural polygamy).

20. Matthesen, *supra* note 130 (quoting a post to the alt.polyamory newsgroup by Stef).

21. *See* Thomas Burgio, *Coming Out Going In: True Confessions of a Polyamorous Bodyworker*, Loving More Mag., Fall 1998, at 13, 13. Blanton's books include Brad Blanton, *Radical Honesty: How to Transform Your Life by Telling the Truth* (1997), and Brad Blanton, *Practicing Radical Honesty: How To Complete the Past, Live in the Present, and Build a Future* (2000) [hereinafter Blanton, *Practicing Radical Honesty*]. The "About the Author" page at the back of Blanton's most recent book tells the reader:

> I've been married 4 times and divorced 3 times, and am currently separated from my most recent wife. We were together for 21 years. We are on somewhat amicable terms and do not know yet whether we will divorce. I am currently sexually and emotionally involved with several women and they all know about each other, and some of them know each other. I have 5 kids ranging in age from 7 years old to 31 years old. I love them with all of my heart. They are the teachers to whom I am most grateful and from whom I have learned the very most. They continue to teach me.

22. Blanton, *Practicing Radical Honesty, supra,* at 343–344.

22. Blanton, Practicing Radical Honesty, *supra* note 273, at 338.

23. *E.g., id.* at 24.

24. *E.g., id.* at 25 ("A woman diagnosed by physicians with arthritis told the truth to her husband about an affair she had been hiding for a long time. They eventually split up, but her 'arthritis' went away. Her next relationship was one of more honesty, less pain and illness, and more creativity in a shared life together.").

25. Stelboum, *supra* note 101, at 42.

26. *Id.* at 44.

27. *Id.* at 45.

28. *See supra* text accompanying notes 244–263.

29. *Id.*

30. *Id.*

31. Jonathan Rauch, *Marrying Somebody, in* Same-Sex Marriage: Pro and Con, *supra* note 10, at 286.

32. Sullivan, *supra* note 19, at 279. Sullivan neatly avoids the question of bisexuality here too.

33. *Id.*

34. Rauch, *supra* note 357, at 286.

35. Anapol, *supra* note 127, at viii–ix (emphasis in original).

36. Alfred Kinsey, Wardell B. Pomeroy & Clyde E. Martin, *Homosexual Outlet, in* Sexual Behavior in the Human Male 610, 650 (1948).

37. Alfred Kinsey, Wardell B. Pomeroy, Clyde E. Martin & Paul H. Gebhard, *Homosexual Responses and Contacts, in* Sexual Behavior in the Human Female 446, 453, 493 tbl. 131 (1953).

38. *See supra* notes 106–109.

39. *See, e.g.,* Yoshino, *supra* note 352, at 512.

40. *Id.*

41. *Id.*

A Critique of the Bionormative Concept of the Family

BY CHARLOTTE WITT

Charlotte Witt is a philosopher specializing in ancient philosophy, metaphysics, and feminist theory. In this essay, Witt argues that a bionormative understanding of the family—one that privileges families that are biologically related as either normal or as superior—unfairly stigmatizes certain families and thus should be rejected.

The last good-bye I ever said to my grandmother (on my Dad's side) was when I was ten years old and it was September 8th. She died September 12th. My grandmother, Jeannette Okrent, grew up and lived in New York. In Brooklyn to be exact. She was the typical Jewish mother; full of life, opinion, and care for those in her family. In a way I never felt like I would ever have to say good-bye to her . . . . Death was never imminent in my mind. Especially not about my grandmother. As long as I can remember my family and I always visited her in New York every summer. The city became a second home to me, and to this day I still feel at home only whenever I'm there.

(from "The Last Good-bye" by Anna Witt)

Introduction

Everyone knows that children like Anna, who was adopted from Vietnam in infancy, are family members in the full sense. Indeed, everyone knows that families with children can originate in several ways. They are formed through adoption (both formal and informal) and ART (assisted reproductive technologies) as well as via sexual intercourse. However, everybody knows something else as well, which is that families with children who are not genetically related to both their parents are not the gold standard or Platonic form of the family, even though it is hard to pinpoint exactly what is wrong with them. I call this the bionormative conception of the family. The two sides of what everyone knows work together to maintain the superiority of families with children genetically related to their parents by affirming both that all families are the same, and that some families are different (and lacking in some respect) (p. 50).

The bionormative conception of the family is so deeply embedded in our culture that we find it in unlikely places like the adoption world and ART communities, and even in individual families with children who are not genetically related to their parents. It is also highly resistant to change, despite the increasing pace of change in family formations. And, even though there is a large and growing literature on the ethical challenges surrounding the institutions and practices of both adoption and ART, there is relatively little that focuses on the idea central to the bionormative conception of the family, namely that families formed via biological reproduction (in which there is a genetic relationship between parents and children) are, *for that reason*, superior to families formed in other ways. The relative lack of explicit defence of this position might well be the consequence of two factors; namely, the widespread acceptance of the bionormative conception of the family, coupled with the psychological tendency to infer from what often happens to what ought to happen. Whatever the explanation, I think it is important to challenge the bionormative view of the family because it has negative social and political implications for the standing of families that originate in other ways. If there are no good reasons to accept the bionormative view of the family, then we can begin to undermine its widespread, tacit acceptance. Or so I hope.

Velleman's Argument from Family Resemblances

In a series of essays, J. David Velleman (2008) addresses the question of how we should understand our responsibilities to future persons. Velleman (2008: 249–50) endorses the Aristotelian idea that human flourishing requires the development of characteristic human abilities and capacities. But the child will not develop towards human flourishing inevitably; she requires support of various kinds. So parents have an obligation to support and facilitate the development of future children so that they can attain human flourishing. In this context Velleman argues that the practice of anonymous gamete vending is harmful to the resultant children and should be abandoned because it precludes or damages development towards human flourishing. Velleman's central and original argument in support of this claim is the argument from family resemblances, namely that we need direct acquaintance with biological relations in order (p. 52) to develop an adequate sense of self. Hence, children who live in families created by anonymous gamete vending are, by that fact alone, deliberately denied the materials necessary for development towards human flourishing. The same is true of children living in families formed through adoption of course, but for an already existing child this might be the best option available, preferable to institutional life or life with people who cannot provide adequate care (Velleman, 2008: 256). Since the argument from family resemblances is the centrepiece of Velleman's case for the bionormative family, we will begin with it.

In "Family History" Velleman reflects upon the significance that knowledge of his familial history—his ancestry—has had on his self-understanding. But Velleman (2005: 358) is particularly interested in the significance of his biological or genetic inheritance and how it factors into the significance of his ancestry:

> That I am the great-grandson of Russian Jewish immigrants, that I also enjoy the fruits of their strivings—this much I know with certainty. I also know that I inherited not just the fruits but the striving too. What I don't know is how to understand that latter piece of my inheritance. Was it passed down entirely through my mother's upbringing by her father, and my upbringing by her? Or is the push in my personality a genetic endowment, from great-grandparents who twice pushed on?

After several autobiographical vignettes, Velleman argues that the practice of anonymous gamete vending is morally wrong because it deliberately creates a child who will lack direct knowledge of one (or both) of his or her biological parents and hence will lack access to his or her biological ancestry. But what is the precise harm here?[1] Velleman (2005: 365, 368) thinks that self-understanding, knowing what one is like, is usually accomplished by seeing resemblances between oneself and one's biological relatives:

> In coming to know and define themselves, most people rely on their acquaintance with people who are like themselves by virtue of being their biological relatives.... If I want to see myself as another, however, I don't have to imagine myself as seen through other people's eyes: I just have to look at my father, my mother and my brothers, who show me by way of family resemblance what I am like.

In other words it is by virtue of seeing similarities between myself and other family members that I come to understand myself. So far, so good. But Velleman actually has a stronger view in two respects. He holds that directly observing familial similarities is *necessary* to form an adequate self-image (not just one way among many others), and that the enlightening similarities must hold between a self and his or her *biological* kin: "Not knowing any biological relatives must be like wandering in a world without reflective surfaces, permanently self-blind" (Velleman, 2005: 368). Velleman (2005: 366) also makes weaker claims: "I think that forming a useful (p. 53) family-resemblance concept of myself would be very *difficult* were I not acquainted with people to whom I bear a literal family resemblance" and "knowing one's relatives and especially one's parents provides a kind of self-knowledge that is of *irreplaceable value* in the life-task of identity formation" (2005: 357). Clearly for Velleman a literal family resemblance refers to a resemblance to biological relatives. And, even though *very difficult* is weaker than *impossible*, the clear sense of the three passages taken together is that, without direct acquaintance with biological relatives, a child would lose the central and irreplaceable resource for identity formation. That is the precise harm to children in families not formed via biological reproduction; it is avoidable in the case of anonymous gamete vending and unavoidable in the case of adoption. Since forming an adequate sense of self plausibly is required for a child to develop towards human flourishing, Velleman's argument from family resemblances supports a bionormative view of the family.

Is Velleman correct that, without direct acquaintance with biological relatives, a child would lose the central and irreplaceable resource for identity formation, and hence be thwarted in her progress towards human flourishing? Consider the epigraph to this chapter written by my daughter. My daughter Anna shares with her grandmother Jeannette the attribute of "only feeling at home in New York" whereas Mark, Jeannette's son and Anna's father, dislikes New York and never wanted to live there. We might say Anna resembles Jeannette in her attitude towards New York, but Mark does not. However, it is Mark who stands in the correct causal relationship to Jeannette and Anna who does not. Anna is our adopted daughter and Mark is Jeannette's biological son. It is just false that a family resemblance must be grounded in a biological kinship relation or that a biological kinship relation is sufficient to ground a similarity

between two individuals. It is also noteworthy that the resemblance is one that Anna employs in her self-description; it is an element in her self-understanding. As a New-York-o-phile Anna sees herself as like her grandmother.

However, perhaps all that Velleman wants to claim is that biological kinship results in similarities among individuals in some respects. This seems plausible. After all, we know that a number of the traits of individuals are heritable (via the gene) through biological reproduction. But the weaker claim does not provide what is needed to make Velleman's argument in support of the bio-centric concept of the family. Let's recall how the argument goes. Children who lack direct acquaintance with their biological relatives will for that reason lack the necessary ingredients to form an adequate self-image because the necessary ingredients are gathered from direct acquaintance with biological relatives who look like them or resemble them in personality, etc.

It is worth noting two preliminary points. First, many of us lack direct acquaintance with some or most of our biological relatives due to death, divorce, immigration, and other events. So, there is reason to doubt the degree to which even the family with children formed via traditional biological reproduction provides the raw materials for self-understanding as Velleman describes them. Second, although the statistics vary, a significant number of presumed biological fathers are not—in fact—the biological (p. 54) parent of their child. This presents Velleman with a dilemma. It seems that Velleman cannot say that it makes no difference whether the father is the biological parent of the child or not, because he holds that biological kin alone can play the appropriate role in a child's self-understanding. But it also seems very implausible to think that the fact that the child's father is not biologically related to her would make a difference in the child's psychological development.

But there is a more serious difficulty facing the weaker argument. There is a big gap between the premise and the conclusion that an individual's self-understanding will be seriously compromised without access to biological relatives. This is because the weaker claim loosens the connection between a biological relationship between individuals and the existence of observable similarities among them. It allows for there being no similarities between biologically related individuals on the one hand, and for the existence of similarities among non-biologically related individuals on the other. Recall the example of Anna and her grandmother. So, the problem with the weaker premise is that it does not establish the desired conclusion, which is that children need direct acquaintance with their biological relatives in order to form a psychologically adequate self-image. And without that conclusion Velleman's argument provides us with no reason to think that biocentred families are the gold standard or the Platonic form of the family.

Velleman (2005: 365) bolsters the family resemblance argument by connecting it to the philosophical concept of family resemblances coined by Wittgenstein:

> Philosophers should not have to be reminded that living things tend to resemble their biological relatives. After all the philosophical term for indefinable similarities is "family resemblance." Though much has been written by philosophers about family resemblance in this technical sense, little has been written about literal resemblance within families, which is after all the paradigm case of technical family resemblance.

Of course Velleman is referring to Wittgenstein's theory of family resemblance concepts, according to which a concept is unified by an overlapping and open-ended series of resemblances, which are not further analyzable. And Velleman assumes that the relevant resemblances hold among biological family members, who are paradigmatic exemplars of this kind of resemblance relation. Hence Velleman uses Wittgenstein's metaphor of family resemblance to reinforce the connection he draws between biological kinship and resemblances among family members.

But it is not at all clear that Wittgenstein's family relations concept supports Velleman's family resemblance argument. In an important article Hans Sluga (2006: 15) points out that

Wittgenstein's metaphor of family resemblance conflates two very different kinds of concepts: kinship concepts and similarity concepts. A kinship concept is one that maps real causal connections between individuals whether those connections are established by biology, culture, or law. The concept of nationality is an example of a kinship term. An individual can become a German biologically by being the offspring of a German or legally by immigration to Germany. Looking a lot like a (p. 55) German does not make you a German and conversely many Germans do not look like the stereotypical German. Family, like nationality, is a kinship term. "The conclusion I draw then is that 'family' in the human sense is a kinship and not a similarity term" (Sluga, 2006: 16). The concept of resemblance, pertinent to the notion of family resemblance, is a similarity term and not a kinship term. Similarity terms admit of degrees and they do not require a causal connection among individuals.

Where does Sluga's distinction between kinship terms and similarity terms leave Vellemans appeal to Wittgenstein's metaphor of family resemblances in support of a bionormative conception of family? Pretty clearly, if Sluga is correct, then there is no conceptual connection tying biological ancestry relations to resemblances as the metaphor of family resemblances might suggest. If a case for the biocentric conception of the family presupposes a conceptual connection between biological ancestry and similarity of appearance, we have good reason to reject it. Further, the example of Anna, Mark, and Jeannette shows that being a biological relative is neither necessary nor sufficient to establish a likeness between individuals. And, as we have seen, the weaker connection does not establish the conclusion that Velleman's position requires.

A third strand of Velleman's (2008: 255) argument makes an appeal to what he calls "universal common sense":

> I claim that a life estranged from its ancestry is already truncated in this way. This claim is no less than universal common sense—though it is also no more, I readily

admit. I cannot derive it from moral principles; I can at best offer some reflections on why we should trust rather than override common sense in this instance.

Of course, as Velleman notes, nothing of ethical significance follows from universal common sense. Moreover, some of the evidence Velleman (2008: 256) mentions is itself questionable, like the idea that it would be hard to understand great works of literature by Homer, Sophocles, and even the story of Moses in the Bible, without accepting his view about the necessity of direct acquaintance with biological kin for the development of a flourishing human life. Other evidence Velleman mentions, like the heritability of psychological characteristics based on twin studies, is controversial and, perhaps more importantly, its relevance to the argument from family resemblances is not entirely clear. At most it would establish that a child might be more likely to resemble her biological kin in some respects. But, as I explained earlier, it does not follow from this that the child could not find other sources of resemblance (and difference) in those around her sufficient to develop a sense of self as required for human flourishing.

Finally, Velleman points to the phenomenon of adoptees searching for their birth families, and the more recent movement by vendor-conceived children to search, as evidence that might be interpreted in support of the family resemblance argument.[2] According to a literature study (Muller and Perry, 2001) cited by Velleman (2005), up (p. 56) to 50 per cent of adoptees will search for their birth parents at some point in their lives. Velleman says that "we can only speculate why" and then provides his speculation, which is a version of the family resemblance argument. However, the literature study Velleman cites provides a different interpretation of the reasons for search, one that is not speculative but supported by the studies under review. For the estimated 50 per cent of adoptees who will undertake a search during their lifetimes, Muller and Perry describe a wide range of motives for search including: identity-related motives, the need for factual or medical information, the need to fill a gap in an individual's history, and just plain curiosity.

In addition to extensive description of studies that record considerable variation in motivation for search and in degree of intensity, Muller and Perry propose three theoretical frameworks for explaining adoptee search. The social interactionist and the normality models, some combination of which the authors find supported by the evidence, and the psychopathological model, a model not supported by the evidence. According to the normativity model, search is an expression of normal psychosocial development for an adoptee and the social interactionist model emphasizes that adoptees' searching may be a result of our culture's definition of kinship in terms of blood ties. Although it is not a perfect match the psychopathological model (sometimes called "genealogical bewilderment") is the closest to Velleman's view of how to understand adoptee searches. It is striking that this is the model that the study authors *reject* based on the evidence; "the vast majority of searchers appear to be rather well-adjusted" (Muller and Perry, 2001: 31). Furthermore, Velleman simply rejects the social interactionist model, which the survey authors find partially supported by the evidence. He comments: "But maybe they (adoptees who search) are simply confused, because they live in a culture that is itself confused about the importance of biological ties" (Velleman, 2005: 360). In sum, the study Velleman cites to support "what everyone knows" about adoptees, biological ancestry, and searching turns out not to support "universal common sense." Another study concludes: "The vast majority of children who are adopted are well within the normal range of adjustment and show behavioural patterns that are similar to their nonadopted peers" (Brand and Brinich, 1999: 30).[3]

Velleman develops the family resemblance argument in order to defend the bionormative conception of the family and to criticize what he calls "the new ideology of the family." According to Velleman (2005: 360), the new ideology of the family was "developed for people who want to have children but lack the biological means to 'have' them in the usual sense . . . It [the new ideology] says that these children will have families in the only sense that matters, or at least in a sense that is good enough." But, as we have seen,

Velleman's argument from family resemblances fails to establish its conclusion. And since he presents no other compelling evidence in support of the bionormative concept of the family, we have no reason to think that these families are the (p. 57) gold standard or Platonic form of the family. And so we have no reason to accept the bionormative concept of the family.

Conclusion

Velleman is interested in an individual's autobiography, or in how an individual human being charts her understanding of herself. What landmarks will she use? What story will she have available to her in this endeavour? Velleman's description of his family history and the way in which it informs his self-understanding is genuine and moving. But so is the story my daughter Anna tells of her connection to Jeannette Okrent, who was both her grandmother and someone different from her in race, (p. 62) religion, and ancestry. Nonetheless, Anna draws inspiration and self-understanding from her similarity to Grandma Jeannette. If family resemblances are central to our self-understanding and that is an important ingredient in human flourishing as Velleman believes, then Anna is all set. And, contra Velleman, the argument from family resemblances gives us no reason to consider families with children who are genetically related to their parents to be the gold standard and Platonic form of the family.

In this chapter I have focused fairly narrowly on the question of whether or not families formed via biological reproduction with children genetically related to their parents are, for that reason alone, superior to families formed in other ways. It might seem that I have achieved very little since I only reject two philosophical arguments that support the bionormative family concept. What about all the other reasons and arguments out there? The surprising fact is that there aren't any other persuasive arguments out there.[10] There is simply what everyone knows about families.

DISCUSSION QUESTIONS

1. What is the bionormative conception of the family?

2. How does bionormativity about the family unfairly stigmatize some families?
3. Describe J. David Velleman's arguments for how anonymous gamete vending is supposed to preclude or damage future children's potential flourishing.
4. Describe Charlotte Witt's criticisms of Velleman's arguments from family resemblances against what he calls "the new ideology of the family."

NOTES

1. It is important to note that Velleman does not argue that there is anything intrinsically wrong with the care provided in families not formed via biological reproduction. So, if there is a wrong here, it must be located elsewhere.
2. Velleman (2008: 261) allows that the connection he draws between the phenomenon of adoptee (and vendor-conceived) search and the argument from family resemblances is speculative.
3. Brand and Brinich (1999) is cited in Blake, Richards, and Golombok . . . which contains a nuanced and rich discussion of families formed via adoption and ART.

REFERENCES

Brand, A. E., and Brinich, P. M. (1999). Behavior Problems and Mental Health Contacts in Adopted, Foster, and Nonadopted Children. *Journal of Child Psychology and Psychiatry*, 40(8), 1221–1229.

Buller, D. J. (2005). *Adapting Minds: Evolutionary Psychology and the Persistent Quest for Human Nature*. Cambridge, MA: MIT Press.

Haslanger, S., and Witt, C. (eds) (2005). *Adoption Matters: Philosophical and Feminist Essays*. Ithaca, NY: Cornell University Press. (p. 63)

Muller, U., and Perry, B. (2001). Adopted Persons' Search for and Contact with Their Birth Parents: I. Who Searches and Why? *Adoption Quarterly*, 4(3), 5–34.

Pratten v British Columbia (Attorney General), 2011 BCSC 656. (2011). Retrieved July 2013 from http://www.courts.gov.bc.ca/jdb-txt/SC/11/06/2011BCSC0656corl.htm.

Sluga, H. (2006). Family Resemblance. *Grazer Philosophische Studien*, 71(1), 1–21.

Velleman, J. D. (2005). Family History. *Philosophical Papers*, 34(3), 357–378.

Velleman, J. D. (2008). Persons in Prospect. *Philosophy and Public Affairs*, 36(3), 221–288.

Wilson, R. (2008a). Blood is Thicker than Water, *nicht wahr?* Unpublished manuscript, Department of Philosophy, University of Alberta, Edmonton, AB, Canada. On file with author.

Wilson, R. (2008b). What is so Special about Kinship? Unpublished manuscript. Department of Philosophy, University of Alberta, Edmonton, AB, Canada. Retrieved July 2013 from http://www.artsrn.ualberta.ca/raw/5WhatsSpecialmay08.pdf.

Witt, C. (2005). Family Resemblances: Adoption, Personal Identity and Genetic Essentialism. In S. Haslanger and C. Witt (eds), *Adoption Matters* (pp. 135–145). Ithaca, NY: Cornell University Press.

What Do Grown Children Owe Their Parents?

BY JANE ENGLISH

Jane English (1947–1978) was a philosopher at the University of North Carolina. English proposes the controversial thesis that grown children have no debt to their parents ("What do grown children owe their parents? The answer is nothing"). We have been misled by ordinary language into supposing that we have debts to our parents. The love relationship between parents and grown children is best understood as one of deep, ongoing friendship.

Favors Create Debts

There are some cases, other than literal debts, in which talk of "owing," though metaphorical, is apt. New to the neighborhood, Max barely knows his neighbor, Nina, but he asks her if she will take in his mail while he is gone for a month's vacation. She agrees. If, subsequently, Nina asks Max to do the same for her, it seems that Max has a moral obligation to agree (greater than the one he would have had if Nina had not done the same for him), unless for some reason it would be a burden far out of proportion to the one Nina bore for him. I will call this *a favor*: when A, at B's request, bears some burden for B, then B incurs an obligation to reciprocate. Here, the metaphor of Max's "owing" Nina is appropriate. It is not literally a debt, of course, nor can Nina pass this IOU on to heirs, demand payment in the form of Max's taking out her garbage, or sue Max. Nonetheless, since Max ought to perform one act of a similar nature and amount of sacrifice in return, the term is suggestive. Once he reciprocates, the debt is "discharged"—that is, their obligations revert to the condition they were in before Max's initial request.

Contrast a situation in which Max simply goes on vacation and, to his surprise, finds upon his return that his neighbor has mowed his grass twice weekly in his absence. This is a voluntary sacrifice rather than a favor, and Max has no duty to reciprocate. It would be nice for him to volunteer to do so, but this would be supererogatory on his part. Rather than a favor, Nina's action is a friendly gesture. As a result, she might expect Max to chat over the back fence, help her catch her straying dog, or something similar—she might expect the development of a friendship, but Max would be chatting (or whatever) out of friendship, rather than in repayment for mown grass. If he did not return her gesture, she might feel rebuffed or miffed, but not unjustly treated or indignant, since Max has not failed to perform a duty. Talk of "owing" would be out of place in this case.

It is sometimes difficult to distinguish between favors and nonfavors, because friends tend to do favors for each other, and those who exchange favors tend to become friends, but one test is to ask how Max is motivated. Is it "to be nice to Nina" or "because she did *x* for me"? Favors are frequently performed by total strangers without any friendship developing. Nevertheless, a temporary obligation is created, even if the chance for repayment never arises. For instance, suppose that Oscar and Matilda, total strangers, are waiting in a long checkout line at the supermarket. Oscar, having forgotten the oregano, asks Matilda to watch his cart for a second. She does. If Matilda now asks Oscar to return the favor while she picks up some tomato sauce, he is obliged to agree. Even if she had not watched his cart, it would be inconsiderate of him to refuse, claiming he was too busy reading the magazines. He may have a duty to help others, but he would not "owe" it to her. However, if she has done the same for him, he incurs an additional obligation to help, and talk of "owing" is apt. It suggests an agreement to perform equal, reciprocal, canceling sacrifices.

The Duties of Friendship

The terms "owe" and "repay" are helpful in the case of favors, because the sameness of the amount of sacrifice on the two sides is important; the monetary metaphor suggests equal quantities of sacrifice. However, friendship ought to be characterized by *mutuality* rather than reciprocity: friends offer what they can give and accept what they need, without regard for the total amounts of benefits exchanged, and friends are motivated by love rather than by the prospect of repayment. Hence, talk of "owing" is singularly out of place in friendship.

For example, suppose Alfred takes Beatrice out for an expensive dinner and a movie. Beatrice incurs no obligation to "repay" him with a goodnight kiss or a return engagement. If Alfred complains that she "owes" him something, he is operating under the assumption that she should repay a favor, but on the contrary, his was a generous gesture done in the hopes of developing a friendship. We hope that he would not want her repayment in the form of sex or attention if this was done to discharge a debt rather than from friendship. Since, if Alfred is prone to reasoning in this way, Beatrice may well decline the invitation or request to pay for her own dinner, his attitude of expecting a "return" on his "investment" could hinder the development of a friendship. Beatrice should return the gesture only if she is motivated by friendship.

Another common misuse of the "owing" idiom occurs when the Smiths have dined at the Joneses' four times, but the Joneses at the Smiths' only once. People often say, "We owe them three dinners." This line of thinking may be appropriate between business acquaintances, but not between friends. After all, the Joneses invited the Smiths not in order to feed them or to be fed in turn, but because

of the friendly contact presumably enjoyed by all on such occasions. If the Smiths do not feel friendship toward the Joneses, they can decline future invitations and not invite the Joneses; they owe them nothing. Of course, between friends of equal resources and needs, roughly equal sacrifices (though not necessarily roughly equal dinners) will typically occur. If the sacrifices are highly out of proportion to the resources, the relationship is closer to servility than to friendship.[1]

Another difference between favors and friendship is that, after a friendship ends, the duties of friendship end. The party that has sacrificed less owes the other nothing. For instance, suppose Elmer donated a pint of blood that his wife Doris needed during an operation. Years after their divorce, Elmer is in an accident and needs one pint of blood. His new wife, Cora, is also of the same blood type. It seems that Doris not only does not "owe" Elmer blood, but that she should actually refrain from coming forward if Cora has volunteered to donate. To insist on donating not only interferes with the newlyweds' friendship, but it belittles Doris and Elmer's former relationship by suggesting that Elmer gave blood in hopes of favors returned instead of simply out of love for Doris. It is one of the heart-rending features of divorce that it attends to quantity in a relationship previously characterized by mutuality. If Cora could not donate, Doris's obligation would be the same as that for any former spouse in need of blood; it is not increased by the fact that Elmer similarly aided her. It is affected by the degree to which they are still friends, which, in turn, may (or may not) have been influenced by Elmer's donation.

In short, unlike the debts created by favors, the duties of friendship do not require equal quantities of sacrifice. Performing equal sacrifices does not cancel the duties of friendship, as it does the debts of favors. Unrequested sacrifices do not themselves create debts, but friends have duties regardless of whether they requested or initiated the friendship. Those who perform favors may be motivated by mutual gain, whereas friends should be motivated by affection. These characteristics of the friendship relation are distorted by talk of "owing."

Parents and Children

The relationship between children and their parents should be one of friendship characterized by mutuality rather than one of reciprocal favors. The quantity of parental sacrifice is not relevant in determining what duties the grown child has. The medical assistance grown children ought to offer their ill mothers in old age depends on the mothers' need, not on whether they endured a difficult pregnancy, for example. Nor do one's duties to one's parents cease once an equal quantity of sacrifice has been performed, as the phrase "discharging a debt" may lead us to think.

Rather, what children ought to do for their parents (and parents for children) depends on (1) their respective needs, abilities, and resources and (2) the extent to which there is an ongoing friendship between them. Thus, regardless of the quantity of childhood sacrifices, an able, wealthy child has an obligation to help his or her needy parents more than does a needy child. To illustrate, suppose sisters Cecile and Dana are equally loved by their parents, even though Cecile was an easy child to care for and was seldom ill, whereas Dana was often sick and caused some trouble as a juvenile delinquent. As adults, Dana is a struggling artist living far away, whereas Cecile is a wealthy lawyer living nearby. When the parents need visits and financial aid, Cecile has an obligation to bear a higher proportion of these burdens than her sister. This results from her abilities, rather than from the quantities of sacrifice made by the parents earlier.

Sacrifices have an important causal role in creating an ongoing friendship, which may lead us to assume incorrectly that it is the sacrifices that are the source of the obligation. That the source is the friendship instead can be seen by examining cases in which the sacrifices occurred, but the friendship, for some reason, did not develop or persist. For example, if a woman gives up her newborn child for adoption, and if no feelings of love ever develop on either side, it seems that the grown child does not have an obligation to "repay" her for her sacrifices in pregnancy. For that matter, if the adopted child has an unimpaired love relationship with the adoptive parents, he or she has the same obligations to help them as a natural child would have.

The filial obligations of grown children are a result of friendship, rather than owed for services rendered. Suppose that Vance married Lola despite his parents' strong wish that he marry within their religion, and that as a result, the parents refuse to speak to him again. As the years pass, the parents are unaware of Vance's problems, his accomplishments, and the birth of his children. The love that once existed between them, let us suppose, has been completely destroyed by this event and 30 years of desuetude. At this point, it seems, Vance is under no obligation to pay his parents' medical bills in their old age, beyond his general duty to help those in need. An additional, filial obligation would only arise from whatever love he may still feel for them. It would be irrelevant for his parents to argue, "But look how much we sacrificed for you when you were young," for that sacrifice was not a favor, but occurred as part of a friendship that existed at that time but is now, we have supposed, defunct. A more appropriate message would be, "We still love you, and we would like to renew our friendship."

I hope this helps to set the question of what children ought to do for their parents in a new light. The parental argument, "You ought to do x because we did y for you," should be replaced by, "We love you, and you will be happier if you do x," or "We believe you love us, and anyone who loved us would do x." If the parents' sacrifice had been a favor, the child's reply, "I never asked you to do y for me," would have been relevant; to the revised parental remarks, this reply is clearly irrelevant. The child can either do x or dispute one of the parents' claims: by showing that a love relationship does not exist, or that love for someone does not motivate doing x, or that he or she will not be happier doing x.

Seen in this light, parental requests for children to write home, visit, and offer them a reasonable amount of emotional and financial support in life's crises are well founded, so long as a friendship still exists. Love for others does call for caring about and caring for them. Some other parental requests, such as for more sweeping changes in the child's lifestyle or life goals, can be seen to be insupportable, once we shift the justification from debts owed to love. The terminology of favors suggests the reasoning, "Since we paid for your college education, you owe it to us to make a career of engineering, rather than becoming a rock musician." This tends to alienate affection even further, since the tuition payments are depicted as investments for a return rather than done from love, as though the child's life goals could be "bought." Basing the argument on love leads to different reasoning patterns. The suppressed premise, "If A loves B, then A follows B's wishes as to A's lifelong career" is simply false. Love does not even dictate that the child adopt the parents' values as to the desirability of alternative life goals. So the parents' strongest available argument here is, "We love you, we are deeply concerned about your happiness, and in the long run you will be happier as an engineer." This makes it clear that an empirical claim is really the subject of the debate.

The function of these examples is to draw out our considered judgments as to the proper relation between parents and their grown children, and to show how poorly they fit the model of favors. What is relevant is the ongoing friendship that exists between parents and children. Although that relationship developed partly as a result of parental sacrifices for the child, the duties that grown children have to their parents result from the friendship rather than from the sacrifices. The idiom of owing favors to one's parents can actually be destructive if it undermines the role of mutuality and leads us to think in terms of quantitative reciprocal favors.

DISCUSSION QUESTIONS

1. What does English think grown children owe their parents? What are the constraints on that debt? Do you agree?
2. Explain the distinction between mutuality and reciprocity. Now explain why it matters for her argument.
3. What do you feel you owe your parents? Why? Will your children have this same debt to you? Why or why not? Be as specific as possible.

NOTE

1. Cf T. E. Hill, Jr. (1973) Servility and self-respect. *Monist* 57, 87–104. Thus, during childhood, most of the sacrifices will come from the parents, since they have most of the resources, and the child has most of the needs. When children are grown, the situation is usually reversed.

Philosophy of Sex

Introduction

Sex sells, even for philosophers. Someone who doesn't see the point of most other philosophical speculation can usually be convinced to give a second thought to questions that come up in the philosophy of sex: What makes a sexual desire unnatural or perverted? If your lover lost their looks and charm, would you still love them? Is monogamy the ideal sexual relationship, or does polyamory better serve our deep human needs for sexual fulfillment and self-expression? Does watching pornography count as infidelity? And so on.

But there's a danger in this domain of treating the issues that arise primarily as topics of abstract conceptual analysis—more salacious, perhaps, but fundamentally no different than other philosophical questions about the fundamental nature of reality. And what's worse, the philosophy of sex tends to be treated as a fun game (or "gateway drug") that will, with any luck, tempt students to ultimately care about more important or respectable philosophical concerns.

We think the stakes in the philosophy of sex are too high to let ourselves fall prey to the temptations of prurient titillation, and that the philosophical questions that arise are legitimate in their own right. In selecting these readings we've been motivated by the recognition that sexuality can be the site of some of the most meaningful interactions and connections we can have with others, but also the source of some of the most traumatic abuses.

Sex is fundamentally connected to power—this, in large part, is what explains its enduring allure. But sex also opens up a vulnerability in us that is ripe for exploitation, and this exploitation can be implicated in some way in virtually every oppressive power dynamic that structures our social worlds. Rather than checking off a laundry list of "hot-button" issues, the readings we've included have been chosen through an anti-oppressive political lens that recognizes both the importance of sex in our lives *and* that the background social conditions in which we live structure what kind of sex is likely—and, indeed, what kind of sex is *possible*—for all of us.

We take seriously the significance of the philosophical questions we entertain, not as mere thought experiments or logical puzzles, but as live questions whose answers matter to our lived experiences. We hope you'll do the same. The sorts of questions we'll take up are: Whose interests are served when sexual intercourse is defined exclusively as penis-in-vagina? What do our experiences of our own racial and gender identities play in how we experience sexual attraction? Is sexual desire really best understood as a longing for something we lack? Is consent the only concept we need in our sexual morality? What do feminists mean when they argue that rape is about power, not sex? How should well-intentioned heterosexual men flirt with women after they've come to recognize that we live in a world full of sexualized violence? What should we do when our sexual desires come into conflict with our political principles? What moral issues arise when sex is sold? What is the difference between pornography and erotica? How do racialized sexual stereotypes perpetuate racism? How can better understandings of disability lead to better understandings of sex?

As a note for sophisticated readers, there are some philosophical questions we do not take up. For instance, this book contains no readings from TERFs—trans-exclusionary radical feminists, who argue that trans women's experiences of womanhood are fundamentally different from the supposedly universally shared experiences of cis women who were assigned female at birth. Some TERF philosophers present themselves as merely raising interesting philosophical questions or articulating coherent positions in conceptual space, but they inevitably end up treating trans people as test cases whose (supposedly confused) firsthand experiences of sex and gender can be mined to tell cis people about their (supposedly irrefutable) experiences. Other TERFs make their vitriol more explicit, insisting (without evidence) that trans women represent a threat to cis women in public bathrooms and other sex-segregated spaces.

What philosophical questions we're interested in asking is itself a political issue—one that has concrete material consequences. The bottom line, however, is that not everything is up for debate and not every position deserves space. Just as it would clearly be unconscionable to ask a Black student to take seriously the arguments of a white supremacist who denies their full humanity, or to ask a Jewish student to consider adopting the perspective of a Nazi "just for the sake of argument," we believe it is disrespectful and frankly inhumane to ask trans students to treat debates about whether they deserve to be taken at their word about their gender identity as a topic about which others might reasonably disagree.

Are We Having Sex Now, or What?

BY GRETA CHRISTINA

Greta Christina is an author and blogger who has written about issues ranging from atheism to polyamory and BDSM. In this accessible essay she shows that once we unshackle ourselves from the assumptions of heteronormativity (the assumption that heterosexuality is the normal and preferred sexual orientation for all people), even something as seemingly simple as defining what sex is can become surprisingly complicated.

When I first started having sex with other people, I used to like to count them. I wanted to keep track of how many there had been. It was a source of some kind of pride, or identity anyway, to know how many people I'd had sex with in my lifetime.

It got to the point where, when I'd start having sex with a new person for the first time, when he first entered my body (I was only having sex with men at the time), what would flash through my head wouldn't be "Oh, baby, baby you feel so good inside me," or "What the hell am I doing with this creep," or "This is boring, I wonder what's on TV." What flashed through my head was "Seven!"

Doing this had some interesting results.

Sometimes I'd try to determine what kind of person I was by how many people I'd had sex with. At eighteen, I'd had sex with ten different people. Did that make me normal, repressed, a total slut, a free-spirited bohemian, or what? Not that I compared my numbers with anyone else's—I didn't. It was my own exclusive structure, a game I played in the privacy of my own head.

Then the numbers started getting a little larger, as numbers tend to do, and keeping track became more difficult. I'd remember that the last one was *seventeen* and so this one must be *eighteen*, but then I'd start having doubts about whether I'd been keeping score accurately or not.

There was always a nagging suspicion that maybe I'd missed someone, some dreadful tacky little scumball that I was trying to forget about having invited inside my body. And as much as I maybe wanted to forget about the sleazy little scumball, I wanted more to get that number right.

It kept getting harder, though. I began to question what counted as sex and what didn't. There was that time with Gene, for instance. I was pissed off at my boyfriend, David, for cheating on me. It was a major crisis, and Gene and I were friends and he'd been trying to get at me for weeks and I hadn't exactly been discouraging him. I went to see him that night to gripe about David. He was very sympathetic of course, and he gave me a backrub, and we talked and touched and confided and hugged, and then we started kissing, and then we snuggled up a little closer, and then we started fondling each other, you know, and then all heck broke loose, and we rolled around on the bed groping and rubbing and grabbing and smooching and pushing and pressing and squeezing. He never did actually get it in. He wanted to, and I wanted to too, but I had this thing about being faithful to my boyfriend, so I kept saying, "No, you can't do that, Yes, that feels so good, No, wait that's too much, Yes, yes, don't stop, No, stop that's enough." We never even got our clothes off. Jesus Christ, though, it was some night. One of the best, really. But for a long time I didn't count it as one of the times I'd had sex. He never got inside, so it didn't count.

Later, months and years later, when I lay awake putting my list together, I'd start to wonder: Why doesn't Gene count? Does he not count because he never got inside? Or does he not count because I had to preserve my moral edge over David, my status as the patient, ever-faithful, cheated-on, martyred girlfriend, and if what I did with Gene counts then I don't get to feel wounded and superior?

Years later, I did end up fucking Gene and I felt a profound relief because, at last, he definitely had a number, and I knew for sure that he did in fact count.

Then I started having sex with women, and, boy, howdy, did *that* ever shoot holes in the system. I'd always made my list of sex partners by defining sex as penile-vaginal intercourse—you know, screwing. It's a pretty simple distinction, a straightforward binary system. Did it go in or didn't it? Yes or no? One or zero? On or off? Granted, it's a pretty arbitrary definition, but it's the customary one, with an ancient and respected tradition behind it, and when I was just screwing men, there was no compelling reason to question it.

But with women, well, first of all there's no penis, so right from the start the tracking system is defective. And then, there are so many ways women can have sex with each other, touching and licking and grinding and fingering and fisting—with dildoes or vibrators or vegetables or whatever happens to be lying around the house, or with nothing at all except human bodies. Of course, that's true for sex between women and men as well. But between women, no one method has a centuries-old tradition of being the one that counts. Even when we do fuck each other there's no dick, so you don't get that feeling of This Is What's Important, We Are Now Having Sex, objectively speaking, and all that other stuff is just foreplay or afterplay. So when I started having sex with women the binary system had to go, in favor of a more inclusive definition.

Which meant, of course, that my list of how many people I'd had sex with was completely trashed. In order to maintain it I would have had to go back and reconstruct the whole thing and include all those people I'd necked with and gone down on and dry-humped and played touchy-feely games with. Even the question of who filled the all-important Number One slot, something I'd never had any doubts about before, would have to be re-evaluated.

By this time I'd kind of lost interest in the list anyway. Reconstructing it would be more trouble than it was worth. But the crucial question remained: What counts as having sex with someone?

It was important for me to know. You have to know what qualifies as sex because when you have sex with someone your relationship changes. Right? *Right*? It's not that sex itself has to change things all that much. But knowing you've had sex, being conscious of a sexual connection, standing around making polite conversation with someone while thinking to yourself; "I've had sex with this person," that's what changes things. Or so I believed. And if having sex with a friend can confuse or change the friendship, think how bizarre things can get when you're not sure whether you've had sex with them or not.

The problem was, as I kept doing more kinds of sexual things, the line between *sex* and *not-sex* kept getting more hazy and indistinct. As I brought more into my sexual experience, things were showing up on the dividing line demanding my attention. It wasn't just that the territory I labeled *sex* was expanding. The line itself had swollen, dilated, been transformed into a vast gray region. It had become less like a border and more like a demilitarized zone.

Which is a strange place to live. Not a bad place, just strange. It's like juggling, or watchmaking, or playing the piano—anything that demands complete concentrated awareness and attention. It feels like cognitive dissonance, only pleasant. It feels like waking up from a compelling and realistic bad dream. It feels like the way you feel when you realize that everything you know is wrong, and a bloody good thing too, because it was painful and stupid and it really screwed you up.

But, for me, living in a question naturally leads to searching for an answer. I can't simply shrug, throw up my hands, and say, "Damned if I know." I have to explore the unknown frontiers, even if I don't bring back any secret treasure. So even if it's incomplete or provisional, I do want to find some sort of definition of what is and isn't sex.

I know when I'm *feeling* sexual. I'm feeling sexual if my pussy's wet, my nipples are hard, my palms are clammy, my brain is fogged, my skin is tingly and super-sensitive, my butt muscles clench, my heartbeat speeds up, I have an orgasm (that's the real giveaway), and so on. But feeling sexual with someone isn't the same as having sex with them. Good Lord, if I called it sex every time I was attracted to someone who returned the favor I'd be even more bewildered than I am now. Even *being* sexual with someone isn't the same as *having* sex with them. I've danced and flirted with too many people, given and received too many sexy, would-be-seductive backrubs, to believe otherwise.

I have friends who say, if you thought of it as sex when you were doing it, then it was. That's an interesting idea. It's certainly helped me construct a coherent sexual history without being a revisionist swine: redefining my past according to current definitions. But it really just begs the question. It's fine to say that sex is whatever I think it is; but then what do I think it *is*? What if, when I was doing it, I was *wondering* whether it counted?

Perhaps having sex with someone is the conscious, consenting, mutually acknowledged pursuit of shared sexual pleasure. Not a bad definition. If you are turning each other on and you say so and you keep doing it, then it's sex. It's broad enough to encompass a lot of sexual behavior beyond genital contact/orgasm; it's distinct enough *not* to include every instance of sexual awareness or arousal; and it contains the elements I feel are vital—acknowledgment, consent, reciprocity, and the pursuit of pleasure. But what about the situation where one person consents to sex without really enjoying it? Lots of people (myself included) have had sexual interactions that we didn't find satisfying or didn't really want and, unless they were actually forced on us against our will, I think most of us would still classify them as sex.

Maybe if *both* of you (or all of you) think of it as sex, then it's sex whether you're having fun or not. That clears up the problem of sex that's consented to but not wished-for or enjoyed. Unfortunately, it begs the question again, only worse: now you have to mesh different people's vague and inarticulate notions of what is and isn't sex and find the place where they overlap. Too messy.

How about sex as the conscious, consenting, mutually acknowledged pursuit of sexual pleasure of *at least one* of the people involved. That's better. It has all the key components, and it includes the situation where one person is doing it for a reason other than sexual pleasure—status, reassurance, money, the satisfaction and pleasure of someone they love, etc. But what if *neither* of you is enjoying it, if you're both doing it because you think the other one wants to? Ugh.

I'm having trouble here. Even the conventional standby—sex equals intercourse—has a serious flaw: it includes rape, which is something I emphatically refuse to accept. As far as I'm concerned, if there's no consent, it ain't sex. But I feel that's about the only place in this whole quagmire where I have a grip. The longer I think about the subject, the more questions I come up with. At what point in an encounter does it *become* sexual? If an interaction that begins nonsexually turns into sex, was it sex all along? What about sex with someone who's asleep? Can you have a situation where one person is having sex and the other isn't? It seems that no matter what definition I come up with, I can think of some real-life experience that calls it into question.

For instance, a couple of years ago I attended (well, hosted) an all-girl sex party. Out of the twelve other women there, there were only a few with whom I got seriously physically nasty. The rest I kissed or hugged or talked dirty with or just smiled at, or watched while they did seriously physically nasty things with each other. If we'd been alone, I'd probably say that what I'd done with most of the women there didn't count as having sex. But the experience, which was hot and sweet and silly and very, very special, had been created by all of us, and although I only really got down with a few, I felt that I'd been sexual with all of the women there. Now, when I meet one of the women from that party, I always ask myself: Have we had sex?

For instance, when I was first experimenting with sadomasochism, I got together with a really hot woman. We were negotiating about what we were going to do, what would and wouldn't be OK, and she said she wasn't sure she wanted to have sex. Now we'd been explicitly planning all kinds of fun and games—spanking, bondage, obedience—which I strongly identified as sexual activity. In her mind, though, *sex* meant direct genital contact, and she didn't necessarily want to do that with me. Playing with her turned out to be a tremendously erotic experience, arousing and stimulating and almost unbearably satisfying. But we spent the whole evening without even touching each other's genitals. And the fact that our definitions were so different made me wonder: Was it sex?

For instance, I worked for a few months as a nude dancer at a peep show. In case you've never been to a peep show, it works like this: the customer goes into a tiny, dingy black box, kind of like a phone booth, puts in quarters; and a metal plate goes up; the customer looks through a window at a little room/stage where naked women are dancing. One time, a guy came into one of the booths and started watching me and masturbating. I came over and squatted in front of him and started masturbating too, and we grinned at each other and watched each other and masturbated, and we both had a fabulous time. (I couldn't believe I was being paid to masturbate—tough job, but somebody has to do it . . .). After he left I thought to myself: Did we just have sex? I mean, if it had been someone I knew, and if there had been

no glass and no quarters, there'd be no question in my mind. Sitting two feet apart from someone, watching each other masturbate? Yup, I'd call that sex all right. But this was different, because it was a stranger, and because of the glass and the quarters. Was it sex?

I still don't have an answer.

DISCUSSION QUESTIONS

1. Christina argues that the conventional definition of sex as whether her partner "got inside" (i.e., sex as heterosexual intercourse) is flawed. Discuss some reasons to think that the heternormativity of this conventional definition is problematic even for those people who only engage in heterosexual sex.

2. Christina describes herself as initially being very interested in keeping track of the number of people she'd had sex with, in part because she thought it said something about the kind of person she was. Why do you think our culture encourages men and women to think very differently about how their "number" affects their identity?

3. The best definition of sex Christina thinks she can come up with is the "conscious, consenting, mutually acknowledged pursuit of sexual pleasure of at least one of the people involved." Explain the work being done by each of the elements of this definition, and explain why she thinks even this definition falls short.

Plain Sex

BY ALAN GOLDMAN

> Alan Goldman is a philosopher at William and Mary University. In this seminal essay, Goldman argues that we should recognize the moral importance of the simple but compelling idea that sex can be valued simply for the pleasure it produces.

. . .

Having criticized these analyses for the sexual ethics and concepts of perversion they imply, it remains to contrast my account along these lines. To the question of what morality might be implied by my analysis, the answer is that there are no moral implications whatever. Any analysis of sex which imputes a moral character to sex acts in themselves is wrong for that reason. There is no morality intrinsic to sex, although general moral rules apply to the treatment of others in sex acts as they apply to all human relations. We can speak of a sexual ethic as we can speak of a business ethic, without implying that business in itself is either moral or immoral or that special rules are required to judge business practices which are not derived from rules that apply elsewhere as well. Sex is not in itself a moral category, although like business it invariably places us into relations with others in which moral rules apply. It gives us opportunity to do what is otherwise recognized as wrong, to harm others, deceive them or manipulate them against their wills. Just as the fact that an act is sexual in itself never renders it wrong or adds to its wrongness if it is wrong on other grounds (sexual acts towards minors are wrong on other grounds, as will be argued below), so no wrong act is to be excused because done from a sexual motive. If a "crime of passion" is to be excused, it would have to be on grounds of temporary insanity rather than sexual context (whether insanity does constitute a legitimate excuse for certain actions is too big a topic to argue here). Sexual motives are among others which may become deranged, and the fact that they are sexual has no bearing in itself on the moral character, whether negative or exculpatory, of the actions deriving from them. Whatever might be true of war, it is certainly not the case that all's fair in love or sex.

Our first conclusion regarding morality and sex is therefore that no conduct otherwise immoral should be excused because it is sexual conduct, and nothing in sex is immoral unless condemned by rules which apply elsewhere as well. The last clause requires further clarification. Sexual conduct can be governed by particular rules relating only to sex itself. But these precepts must be implied by general moral rules when these are applied to specific sexual relations or types of conduct. The same is true of rules of fair business, ethical medicine, or courtesy in driving a car. In the latter case, particular acts on the road may be reprehensible, such as tailgating or passing on the right, which seem to bear no resemblance as actions to any outside the context of highway safety. Nevertheless their immorality derives from the fact that they place others in danger, a circumstance which, when avoidable, is to be condemned in any context. This structure of general and specifically applicable rules describes a reasonable sexual ethic as well. To take an extreme case, rape is always a sexual act and it is always immoral. A rule against rape can therefore be considered an obvious part of sexual morality which has no bearing on nonsexual conduct. But the immorality of rape derives from its being an extreme violation of a person's body, of the right not to be humiliated, and of the general moral prohibition against using other persons against their wills, not from the fact that it is a sexual act.

The application elsewhere of general moral rules to sexual conduct is further complicated by the fact that it will be relative to the particular desires and preferences of one's partner (these may be influenced by and hence in some sense include misguided beliefs about sexual morality itself). This means that there will be fewer specific rules in the area of sexual ethics than in other areas of conduct, such as driving cars, where the relativity of preference is irrelevant to the prohibition of objectively dangerous conduct. More reliance will have to be placed upon the general moral rule, which in this area holds simply that the preferences, desires, and interests of one's partner or potential partner ought to be taken into account. This rule is certainly not specifically formulated to govern sexual relations; it is a form of the central principle of morality itself. But when applied to sex, it prohibits certain actions, such as molestation of children, which cannot be categorized as violations of the rule without at the same time being classified as sexual. I believe this last case is the closest we can come to an action which is wrong *because* it is sexual, but even here its wrongness is better characterized as deriving from the detrimental effects such behavior can have on the future emotional and sexual life of the naive victims, and from the fact that such behavior therefore involves manipulation of innocent persons without regard for their interests. Hence, this case also involves violation of a general moral rule which applies elsewhere as well.

Aside from faulty conceptual analyses of sex and the influence of the Platonic moral tradition, there are two more plausible reasons for thinking that there are moral dimensions intrinsic to sex acts per se. The first is that such acts are normally intensely pleasurable. According to a hedonistic, utilitarian moral theory they therefore should be at least prima facie morally right, rather than

morally neutral in themselves. To me this seems incorrect and reflects unfavorably on the ethical theory in question. The pleasure intrinsic to sex acts is a good, but not, it seems to me, a good with much positive moral significance. Certainly I can have no duty to pursue such pleasure myself, and while it may be nice to give pleasure of any form to others, there is no ethical requirement to do so, given my right over my own body. The exception relates to the context of sex acts themselves, when one partner derives pleasure from the other and ought to return the favor. This duty to reciprocate takes us out of the domain of hedonistic utilitarianism, however, and into a Kantian moral framework, the central principles of which call for just such reciprocity in human relations. Since independent moral judgments regarding sexual activities constitute one area in which ethical theories are to be tested, these observations indicate here, as I believe others indicate elsewhere, the fertility of the Kantian, as opposed to the utilitarian, principle in reconstructing reasoned moral consciousness.

It may appear from this alternative Kantian viewpoint that sexual acts must be at least prima facie wrong in themselves. This is because they invariably involve at different stages the manipulation of one's partner for one's own pleasure, which might appear to be prohibited on the formulation of Kant's principle which holds that one ought not to treat another as a means to such private ends. A more realistic rendering of this formulation, however, one which recognizes its intended equivalence to the first universalizability principle, admits no such absolute prohibition. Many human relations, most economic transactions for example, involve using other individuals for personal benefit. These relations are immoral only when they are one-sided, when the benefits are not mutual, or when the transactions are not freely and rationally endorsed by all parties. The same holds true of sexual acts. The central principle governing them is the Kantian demand for reciprocity in sexual relations. In order to comply with the second formulation of the categorical imperative, one must recognize the subjectivity of one's partner (not merely by being aroused by her or his desire, as Nagel describes). Even in an act which by its nature "objectifies" the other, one recognizes a partner as a subject with demands and desires by yielding to those desires, by allowing oneself to be a sexual object as well, by giving pleasure or ensuring that the pleasures of the acts are mutual. It is this kind of reciprocity which forms the basis for morality in sex, which distinguishes right acts from wrong in this area as in others. (Of course, prior to sex acts one must gauge their effects upon potential partners and take these longer range interests into account.)

VII

I suggested earlier that in addition to generating confusion regarding the rightness or wrongness of sex acts, false conceptual analyses of the means-end form cause confusion about the value of sex to the individual. My account recognizes the satisfaction of desire and the pleasure this brings as the central psychological function of the sex act for the individual. Sex affords us a paradigm of pleasure, but not a cornerstone of value. For most of us it is not only a needed outlet for desire but also the most enjoyable form of recreation we know. Its value is nevertheless easily mistaken by being confused with that of love, when it is taken as essentially an expression of that emotion. Although intense, the pleasures of sex are brief and repetitive rather than cumulative. They give value to the specific acts which generate them, but not the lasting kind of value which enhances one's whole life. The briefness of these pleasures contributes to their intensity (or perhaps their intensity makes them necessarily brief), but it also relegates them to the periphery of most rational plans for the good life.

By contrast, love typically develops over a long term relation; while its pleasures may be less intense and physical, they are of more cumulative value. The importance of love to the individual may well be central in a rational system of value. And it has perhaps an even deeper moral significance relating to the identification with the interests of another person, which broadens one's possible relationships with others as well. Marriage is again important in preserving this relation between adults and children, which seems as important

to the adults as it is to the children in broadening concerns which have a tendency to become selfish. Sexual desire, by contrast, is desire for another which is nevertheless essentially self-regarding. Sexual pleasure is certainly a good for the individual, and for many it may be necessary in order for them to function in a reasonably cheerful way. But it bears little relation to those other values just discussed, to which some analyses falsely suggest a conceptual connection.

. . .

While my initial analysis lacks moral implications in itself, as it should, it does suggest by contrast a concept of sexual perversion. Since the concept of perversion is itself a sexual concept, it will always be defined relative to some definition of normal sex; and any conception of the norm will imply a contrary notion of perverse forms. The concept suggested by my account again differs sharply from those implied by the means-end analyses examined above. Perversion does not represent a deviation from the reproductive function (or kissing would be perverted), from a loving relationship (or most sexual desire and many heterosexual acts would be perverted), or from efficiency in communicating (or unsuccessful seduction attempts would be perverted). It is a deviation from a norm, but the norm in question is merely statistical. Of course, not all sexual acts that are statistically unusual are perverted—a three-hour continuous sexual act would be unusual but not necessarily abnormal in the requisite sense. The abnormality in question must relate to the *form of the desire* itself in order to constitute sexual perversion; for example, desire, not for contact with another, but for merely looking, for harming or being harmed, for contact with items of clothing. This concept of sexual abnormality is that suggested by my definition of normal sex in terms of its typical desire. However not all unusual desires qualify either, only those with the typical physical sexual effects upon the individual who satisfies them. These effects, such as erection in males, were not built into the original definition of sex in terms of sexual desire, for they do not always occur in activities that are properly characterized as sexual, say, kissing for the pleasure of it. But they do seem to bear a closer relation to the definition of activities as perverted. (For those who consider only genital sex sexual, we could build such symptoms into a narrower definition, then speaking of sex in a broad sense as well as "proper" sex.)

Solomon and Nagel disagree with this statistical notion of perversion. For them the concept is evaluative rather than statistical. I do not deny that the term "perverted" is often used evaluatively (and purely emotively for that matter), or that it has a negative connotation for the average speaker. I do deny that we can find a norm, other than that of statistically usual desire, against which all and only activities that properly count as sexual perversions can be contrasted. Perverted sex is simply abnormal sex, and if the norm is not to be an idealized or romanticized extraneous end or purpose, it must express the way human sexual desires usually manifest themselves. Of course not all norms in other areas of discourse need be statistical in this way. Physical health is an example of a relatively clear norm which does not seem to depend upon the numbers of healthy people. But the concept in this case achieves its clarity through the connection of physical health with other clearly desirable physical functions and characteristics, for example, living longer. In the case of sex, that which is statistically abnormal is not necessarily incapacitating in other ways, and yet these abnormal desires with sexual effects upon their subject do count as perverted to the degree to which their objects deviate from usual ones. The connotations of the concept of perversion beyond those connected with abnormality or statistical deviation derive more from the attitudes of those likely to call certain acts perverted than from specifiable features of the acts themselves. These connotations add to the concept of abnormality that of *sub*normality, but there is no norm against which the latter can be measured intelligibly in accord with all and only acts intuitively called perverted.

The only proper evaluative norms relating to sex involve degrees of pleasure in the acts and moral norms, but neither of these scales coincides with statistical degrees of abnormality, according to which perversion is to be measured. The three parameters operate independently (this was implied for the first two when it was held above that the pleasure of sex is a good, but not necessarily a moral good). Perverted sex may be more or less enjoyable to particular individuals than normal sex, and more or less moral, depending upon the particular relations involved. Raping a sheep may be more perverted than raping a woman, but certainly not more condemnable morally.[1] It is nevertheless true that the evaluative connotations attaching to the term "perverted" derive partly from the fact that most people consider perverted sex highly immoral. Many such acts are forbidden by long standing taboos, and it is sometimes difficult to distinguish what is forbidden from what is immoral. Others, such as sadistic acts, are genuinely immoral, but again not at all because of their connection with sex or abnormality. The principles which condemn these acts would condemn them equally if they were common and nonsexual. It is not true that we properly could continue to consider acts perverted which were found to be very common practice across societies. Such acts, if harmful, might continue to be condemned properly as immoral, but it was just shown that the immorality of an act does not vary with its degree of perversion. If not harmful, common acts previously considered abnormal might continue to be called perverted for a time by the moralistic minority; but the term when applied to such cases would retain only its emotive negative connotation without consistent logical criteria for application. It would represent merely prejudiced moral judgments.

To adequately explain why there is a tendency to so deeply condemn perverted acts would require a treatise in psychology beyond the scope of this paper. Part of the reason undoubtedly relates to the tradition of repressive sexual ethics and false conceptions of sex; another part to the fact that all abnormality seems to disturb and fascinate us at the same time. The former explains why sexual perversion is more abhorrent to many than other forms of abnormality; the latter indicates why we tend to have an emotive and evaluative reaction to perversion in the first place. It may be, as has been suggested according to a Freudian line,[2] that our uneasiness derives from latent desires we are loathe to admit, but this thesis takes us into psychological issues I am not competent to judge. Whatever the psychological explanation, it suffices to point out here that the conceptual connection between perversion and genuine or consistent moral evaluation is spurious and again suggested by misleading means-end idealizations of the concept of sex.

The position I have taken in this paper against those concepts is not totally new. Something similar to it is found in Freud's view of sex, which of course was genuinely revolutionary, and in the body of writings deriving from Freud to the present time. But in his revolt against romanticized and repressive conceptions, Freud went too far—from a refusal to view sex as merely a means to a view of it as the end of all human behavior, although sometimes an elaborately disguised end. This pansexualism led to the thesis (among others) that repression was indeed an inevitable and necessary part of social regulation of any form, a strange consequence of a position that began by opposing the repressive aspects of the means-end view. Perhaps the time finally has arrived when we can achieve a reasonable middle ground in this area, at least in philosophy if not in society.

DISCUSSION QUESTIONS

1. Explain Goldman's argument that sex is just for pleasure. How does the notion of "purpose" play into his argument?
2. Most of us tend to think that sex is often involved with emotional intimacy. How would Goldman respond?
3. What is the moral content of sex? What does Goldman think? What do you think? How might culture play a role? Be as specific as you can, and use examples.

NOTES

1. The example is like one from Sara Ruddick, "Better Sex," *Philosophy and Sex*, p. 96.
2. See Michael Slote, "Inapplicable Concepts and Sexual Perversion," *Philosophy and Sex*.

Confessions and On Christian Doctrine (selections)

BY ST. AUGUSTINE

> Augustine of Hippo (354–430), also known as Saint Augustine, was an early Christian theologian and philosopher. These selections from some of his major works illustrate his influential belief that carnal and corporeal desires must be subjugated to a desire for God.

The Confessions Book Two

He concentrates here on his sixteenth year, a year of idleness, lust, and adolescent mischief. The memory of stealing some pears prompts a deep probing of the motives and aims of sinful acts. "I became to myself a wasteland."

Chapter I

1. I wish now to review in memory my past wickedness and the carnal corruptions of my soul—not because I still love them, but that I may love you, O my God. For love of your love I do this, recalling in the bitterness of self-examination my wicked ways, that you may grow sweet to me, you sweetness without deception! You sweetness happy and assured! Thus you may gather me up out of those fragments in which I was torn to pieces, while I turned away from you, O Unity, and lost myself among "the many." [40] For as I became a youth, I longed to be satisfied with worldly things, and I dared to grow wild in a succession of various and shadowy loves. My form wasted away, and I became corrupt in your eyes, yet I was still pleasing to my own eyes—and eager to please the eyes of men.

Chapter II

2. But what was it that delighted me save to love and to be loved? Still I did not keep the moderate way of the love of mind to mind—the bright path of friendship. Instead, the mists of passion steamed up out of the puddly concupiscence of the flesh, and the hot imagination of puberty, and they so obscured and overcast my heart that I was unable to distinguish pure affection from unholy desire. Both boiled confusedly within me, and dragged my unstable youth down over the cliffs of unchaste desires and plunged me into a gulf of infamy. Your anger had come upon me, and I knew it not. I had been deafened by the clanking of the chains of my mortality, the punishment for my soul's pride, and I wandered farther from you, and you didst permit me to do so. I was tossed to and fro, and wasted, and poured out, and I boiled over in my fornications—and yet you didst hold your peace, O my tardy Joy! You didst still hold your peace, and I wandered still farther from you into more and yet more barren fields of sorrow, in proud dejection and restless lassitude.

3. If only there had been someone to regulate my disorder and turn to my profit the fleeting beauties of the things around me, and to fix a bound to their sweetness, so that the tides of my youth might have spent themselves upon the shore of marriage! Then they might have been tranquilized and satisfied with having children, as your law prescribes, O Lord—O you who dost form the offspring of our death and art able also with a tender hand to blunt the thorns which were excluded from your

paradise! [41] For your omnipotence is not far from us even when we are far from you. Now, on the other hand, I might have given more vigilant heed to the voice from the clouds: "Nevertheless, such shall have trouble in the flesh, but I spare you," [42] and, "It is good for a man not to touch a woman," [43] and, "He that is unmarried cares for the things that belong to the Lord, how he may please the Lord; but he that is married cares for the things that are of the world, how he may please his wife." [44] I should have listened more attentively to these words, and, thus having been "made a eunuch for the Kingdom of Heaven's sake," [45] I would have with greater happiness expected your embraces.

4. But, fool that I was, I foamed in my wickedness as the sea and, forsaking you, followed the rushing of my own tide, and burst out of all your bounds. But I did not escape your scourges. For what mortal can do so? You were always by me, mercifully angry and flavoring all my unlawful pleasures with bitter discontent, in order that I might seek pleasures free from discontent. But where could I find such pleasure save in you, O Lord—save in you, who dost teach us by sorrow, who wound us to heal us, and dost kill us that we may not die apart from you. Where was I, and how far was I exiled from the delights of your house, in that sixteenth year of the age of my flesh, when the madness of lust held full sway in me—that madness which grants indulgence to human shamelessness, even though it is forbidden by your laws—and I gave myself entirely to it? Meanwhile, my family took no care to save me from ruin by marriage, for their sole care was that I should learn how to make a powerful speech and become a persuasive orator.

On Christian Doctrine BOOK III.

Chap. 21.—David not lustful, though he fell into adultery

But when King David had suffered this injury at the hands of his impious and unnatural son, he not only bore with him in his mad passion, but mourned over him in his death. He certainly was not caught in the meshes of carnal jealousy, seeing that it was not his own injuries but the sins of his son that moved him. For it was on this account he had given orders that his son should not be slain if he were conquered in battle, that he might have a place of repentance after he was subdued; and when he was baffled in this design, he mourned over his son's death, not because of his own loss, but because he knew to what punishment so impious an adulterer and parricide had been hurried. For prior to this, in the case of another son who had been guilty of no crime, though he was dreadfully afflicted for him while he was sick, yet he comforted himself after his death.

31. And with what moderation and self-restraint those men used their wives appears chiefly in this, that when this same king, carried away by the heat of passion and by temporal prosperity, had taken unlawful possession of one woman, whose husband also he ordered to be put to death, he was accused of his crime by a prophet, who, when he had come to show him his sin set before him the parable of the poor man who had but one ewe-lamb, and whose neighbour, though he had many, yet when a guest came to him spared to take of his own flock, but set his poor neighbour's one lamb before his guest to eat. And David's anger being kindled against the man, he commanded that he should be put to death, and the lamb restored fourfold to the poor man; thus unwittingly condemning the sin he had wittingly committed. And when he had been shown this, and God's punishment had been denounced against him, he wiped out his sin in deep penitence. But yet in this parable it was the adultery only that was indicated by the poor man's ewe-lamb; about the killing of the woman's husband,—that is, about the murder of the poor man himself who had the one ewe-lamb,—nothing is said in the parable, so that the sentence of condemnation is pronounced against the adultery alone. And hence we may understand with what temperance he possessed a number of wives when he was forced to punish himself for transgressing in regard to one woman. But in his case the immoderate desire did not take up its abode

with him, but was only a passing guest. On this account the unlawful appetite is called even by the accusing prophet, a guest. For he did not say that he took the poor man's ewe-lamb to make a feast for his king, but for his guest. In the case of his son Solomon, however, this lust did not come and pass away like a guest, but reigned as a king. And about him Scripture is not silent, but accuses him of being a lover of strange women; for in the beginning of his reign he was inflamed with a desire for wisdom, but after he had attained it through spiritual love, he lost it through carnal lust.

DISCUSSION QUESTIONS

1. Augustine famously remarks in his *Confessions*: "Make me chaste, Lord . . . but not yet, Lord, not yet!" Why does he want to be chaste? If God wants us to be chaste, why did God make us sexual beings? Answer for Augustine, and also offer your own answer, please.

2. What are the differences between the love for a family member, the love for a friend, the love for a romantic partner, and the love of God?

3. How does the love of God inform our other styles of loving, according to Augustine? And how does freedom work in all of this?

The History of Sexuality (selections)

BY MICHEL FOUCAULT

Michel Foucault (1926–1984) was a French philosopher, historian of ideas, political activist, and literary critic. Selections from this influential work focus on Foucault's "repressive hypothesis"—his claim that despite the common presumption that sexuality was suppressed in western society from the seventeenth to the mid-twentieth century, discourse on sexuality actually proliferated during this time as sexuality came to be seen as something that could be examined in a scientific manner—and on his arguments about how these new understandings of sex made it something that could be controlled by power.

The seventeenth century, then, was the beginning of an age of repression emblematic of what we call the bourgeois societies, an age which perhaps we still have not completely left behind. Calling sex by its name thereafter became more difficult and more costly. As if in order to gain mastery over it in reality, it had first been necessary to subjugate it at the level of language, control its free circulation in speech, expunge it from the things that were said, and extinguish the words that rendered it too visibly present. And even these prohibitions, it seems, were afraid to name it. Without even having to pronounce the word, modern prudishness was able to ensure that one did not speak of sex, merely through the interplay of prohibitions that referred back to one another: instances of muteness which, by dint of saying nothing, imposed silence. Censorship.

Areas were thus established, if not of utter silence, at least of tact and discretion: between parents and children, for instance, or teachers and pupils, or masters and domestic servants. This almost certainly constituted a whole restrictive economy, one that was incorporated into that politics of language and speech—spontaneous on the one hand, concerted on the other—which accompanied the social redistributions of the classical period.

At the level of discourses and their domains, however, practically the opposite phenomenon occurred. There was a steady proliferation of discourses concerned with sex—specific discourses, different from one another both by their form and by their object: a discursive ferment that gathered momentum from the eighteenth century onward. More important was the multiplication of discourses concerning sex in the field of exercise of power itself: an institutional incitement to speak about it, and to do so more and more; a determination on the part of the agencies of power to hear it spoken about, and to cause it to speak through explicit articulation and endlessly accumulated detail.

While the language may have been refined, the scope of the confession—the confession of the flesh—continually increased. This was partly because the Counter Reformation busied itself with stepping up the rhythm of the yearly confession in the Catholic countries, and because it tried to impose meticulous rules of self-examination; but above all, because it attributed more and more importance in penance—and perhaps at the expense of some other sins—to all the insinuations of the flesh: thoughts, desires, voluptuous imaginings, delectations, combined movements of the body and the soul; henceforth all this had to enter, in detail, into the process of confession and guidance. According to the new pastoral, sex must not be named imprudently, but its aspects, its correlations, and its effects must be pursued down to their slenderest ramifications: a shadow in a daydream, an image too slowly dispelled, a badly exorcised complicity between the body's mechanics and the mind's complacency: everything had to be told. A twofold evolution tended to make the flesh into the root of all evil, shifting the most important moment of transgression from the act itself to the stirrings—so difficult to perceive and formulate—of desire. For this was an evil that afflicted the whole man, and in the most secret of forms: "Examine diligently, therefore, all the faculties of your soul: memory, understanding, and will. Examine with precision all your senses as well. . . . Examine, moreover, all your thoughts, every word you speak, and all your actions. Examine even unto your dreams, to know if, once awakened, you did not give them your consent. And finally, do not think that in so sensitive and perilous a matter as this, there is anything trivial or insignificant."[1] Discourse, therefore, had to trace the meeting line of the body and the soul, following all its meanderings: beneath the surface of the sins, it would lay bare the unbroken nervure of the flesh. Under the authority of a language that had been carefully expurgated so that it was no longer directly named, sex was taken charge of, tracked down as it were, by a discourse that aimed to allow it no obscurity, no respite.

It was here, perhaps, that the injunction, so peculiar to the West, was laid down for the first time, in the form of a general constraint. I am not talking about the obligation to admit to violations of the laws of sex, as required by traditional penance; but of the nearly infinite task of telling—telling oneself and another, as often as possible, everything that might concern the interplay of innumerable pleasures, sensations, and thoughts which, through the body and the soul, had some affinity with sex. This scheme for transforming sex into discourse had been devised long before in an ascetic and monastic setting. The seventeenth century made it into a rule for everyone. It would

seem in actual fact that it could scarcely have applied to any but a tiny elite; the great majority of the faithful who only went to confession on rare occasions in the course of the year escaped such complex prescriptions. But the important point no doubt is that this obligation was decreed, as an ideal at least, for every good Christian. An imperative was established: Not only will you confess to acts contravening the law, but you will seek to transform your desire, your every desire, into discourse. Insofar as possible, nothing was meant to elude this dictum, even if the words it employed had to be carefully neutralized.

This is the essential thing: that Western man has been drawn for three centuries to the task of telling everything concerning his sex; that since the classical age there has been a constant optimization and an increasing valorization of the discourse on sex; and that this carefully analytical discourse was meant to yield multiple effects of displacement, intensification, reorientation, and modification of desire itself. Not only were the boundaries of what one could say about sex enlarged, and men compelled to hear it said; but more important, discourse was connected to sex by a complex organization with varying effects, by a deployment that cannot be adequately explained merely by referring it to a law of prohibition. A censorship of sex? There was installed rather an apparatus for producing an ever greater quantity of discourse about sex, capable of functioning and taking effect in its very economy.

This technique might have remained tied to the destiny of Christian spirituality if it had not been supported and relayed by other mechanisms. In the first place, by a "public interest." Not a collective curiosity or sensibility; not a new mentality; but power mechanisms that functioned in such a way that discourse on sex—for reasons that will have to be examined—became essential. Toward the beginning of the eighteenth century, there emerged a political, economic, and technical incitement to talk about sex. And not so much in the form of a general theory of sexuality as in the form of analysis, stocktaking, classification, and specification, of quantitative or causal studies. This need to take sex "into account," to pronounce a discourse on sex that would not derive from morality alone but from rationality as well, was sufficiently new that at first it wondered at itself and sought apologies for its own existence. How could a discourse based on reason speak of *that*? "Rarely have philosophers directed a steady gaze to these objects situated between disgust and ridicule, where one must avoid both hypocrisy and scandal."[2] And nearly a century later, the medical establishment, which one might have expected to be less surprised by what it was about to formulate, still stumbled at the moment of speaking: "The darkness that envelops these facts, the shame and disgust they inspire, have always repelled the observer's gaze. . . . For a long time I hesitated to introduce the loathsome picture into this study."[3] What is essential is not in all these scruples, in the "moralism" they betray, or in the hypocrisy one can suspect them of, but in the recognized necessity of overcoming this hesitation. One had to speak of sex; one had to speak publicly and in a manner that was not determined by the division between licit and illicit, even if the speaker maintained the distinction for himself (which is what these solemn and preliminary declarations were intended to show): one had to speak of it as of a thing to be not simply condemned or tolerated but managed, inserted into systems of utility, regulated for the greater good of all, made to function according to an optimum. Sex was not something one simply judged; it was a thing one administered. It was in the nature of a public potential; it called for management procedures; it had to be taken charge of by analytical discourses. In the eighteenth century, sex became a "police" matter—in the full and strict sense given the term at the time: not the repression of disorder, but an ordered maximization of collective and individual forces: "We must consolidate and augment, through the wisdom of its regulations, the internal power of the state; and since this power consists not only in the Republic in general, and in each of the members who constitute it, but also in the faculties and talents of those belonging to it, it follows that the police must concern themselves with these means and make them serve the public welfare. And they can only obtain this result through the knowledge they have of those different assets."[4]

A policing of sex: that is, not the rigor of a taboo, but the necessity of regulating sex through useful and public discourses.

Of course, it had long been asserted that a country had to be populated if it hoped to be rich and powerful; but this was the first time that a society had affirmed, in a constant way, that its future and its fortune were tied not only to the number and the uprightness of its citizens, to their marriage rules and family organization, but to the manner in which each individual made use of his sex. Things went from ritual lamenting over the unfruitful debauchery of the rich, bachelors, and libertines to a discourse in which the sexual conduct of the population was taken both as an object of analysis and as a target of intervention; there was a progression from the crudely populationist arguments of the mercantilist epoch to the much more subtle and calculated attempts at regulation that tended to favor or discourage—according to the objectives and exigencies of the moment—an increasing birthrate. Through the political economy of population there was formed a whole grid of observations regarding sex. There emerged the analysis of the modes of sexual conduct, their determinations and their effects, at the boundary line of the biological and the economic domains. There also appeared those systematic campaigns which, going beyond the traditional means—moral and religious exhortations, fiscal measures—tried to transform the sexual conduct of couples into a concerted economic and political behavior. In time these new measures would become anchorage points for the different varieties of racism of the nineteenth and twentieth centuries. It was essential that the state know what was happening with its citizens' sex, and the use they made of it, but also that each individual be capable of controlling the use he made of it. Between the state and the individual, sex became an issue, and a public issue no less; a whole web of discourses, special knowledges, analyses, and injunctions settled upon it.

The situation was similar in the case of children's sex. It is often said that the classical period consigned it to an obscurity from which it scarcely emerged before the *Three Essays* or the beneficent anxieties of Little Hans. It is true that a longstanding "freedom" of language between children and adults, or pupils and teachers, may have disappeared. No seventeenth-century pedagogue would have publicly advised his disciple, as did Erasmus in his *Dialogues*, on the choice of a good prostitute. And the boisterous laughter that had accompanied the precocious sexuality of children for so long—and in all social classes, it seems—was gradually stifled. But this was not a plain and simple imposition of silence. Rather, it was a new regime of discourses. Not any less was said about it; on the contrary. But things were said in a different way; it was different people who said them, from different points of view, and in order to obtain different results. Silence itself—the things one declines to say, or is forbidden to name, the discretion that is required between different speakers—is less the absolute limit of discourse, the other side from which it is separated by a strict boundary, than an element that functions alongside the things said, with them and in relation to them within over-all strategies. There is no binary division to be made between what one says and what one does not say; we must try to determine the different ways of not saying such things, how those who can and those who cannot speak of them are distributed, which type of discourse is authorized, or which form of discretion is required in either case. There is not one but many silences, and they are an integral part of the strategies that underlie and permeate discourses.

Since the eighteenth century, sex has not ceased to provoke a kind of generalized discursive erethism. And these discourses on sex did not multiply apart from or against power, but in the very space and as the means of its exercise. Incitements to speak were orchestrated from all quarters, apparatuses everywhere for listening and recording, procedures for observing, questioning, and formulating. Sex was driven out of hiding and constrained to lead a discursive existence. From the singular imperialism that compels everyone to transform their sexuality into a perpetual discourse, to the manifold mechanisms which, in the areas of economy, pedagogy, medicine, and justice, incite, extract, distribute, and institutionalize the sexual discourse, an immense verbosity is what our civilization has required and organized. Surely no other type of society has ever accumulated—and in such a relatively short span of time—a similar quantity of discourses concerned with sex. It may well be that we talk about sex more than anything else; we set our minds to the task; we convince ourselves that we have never said enough on the subject, that, through inertia or submissiveness, we conceal from ourselves the blinding evidence, and that what is essential always eludes us, so that we must always start out once again in search of it. It is possible that where sex is concerned, the most long-winded, the most impatient of societies is our own.

But as this first overview shows, we are dealing less with *a* discourse on sex than with a multiplicity of discourses produced by a whole series of mechanisms operating in different institutions. The Middle Ages had organized around the theme of the flesh and the practice of penance a discourse that was markedly unitary. In the course of recent centuries, this relative uniformity was broken apart, scattered, and multiplied in an explosion of distinct discursivities which took form in demography, biology, medicine, psychiatry, psychology, ethics, pedagogy, and political criticism. More precisely, the secure bond that held together the moral theology of concupiscence and the obligation of confession (equivalent to the theoretical discourse on sex and its first-person formulation) was, if not broken, at least loosened and diversified: between the objectification of sex in rational discourses, and the movement by which each individual was set to the task of recounting his own sex, there has occurred, since the eighteenth century, a whole series of tensions, conflicts, efforts at adjustment, and attempts at retranscription. So it is not simply in terms of a continual extension that we must speak of this discursive growth; it should be seen rather as a dispersion of centers from which discourses emanated, a diversification of their forms, and the complex deployment of the network connecting them. Rather than the uniform concern to hide sex, rather than a general prudishness of language, what distinguishes these last three centuries is the variety, the wide dispersion of devices that were invented for speaking about it, for having it be spoken about, for inducing it to speak of itself, for listening, recording, transcribing, and redistributing what is said about it: around sex, a whole network of varying, specific, and coercive transpositions into discourse. Rather than a massive censorship, beginning with the verbal proprieties imposed by the Age of Reason, what was involved was a regulated and polymorphous incitement to discourse.

It would be a mistake to see in this proliferation of discourses merely a quantitative phenomenon, something like a pure increase, as if what was said in them were immaterial, as if the fact of speaking about sex were of itself more important than the forms of imperatives that were imposed on it by speaking about it. For was this transformation of sex into discourse not governed by the endeavor to expel from reality the forms of sexuality that were not amenable to the strict economy of reproduction: to say no to unproductive activities, to banish casual pleasures, to reduce or exclude practices whose object was not procreation? Through the various discourses, legal sanctions against minor perversions were multiplied; sexual irregularity was annexed to mental illness; from childhood to old age, a norm of sexual development was defined and all the possible deviations were carefully described; pedagogical controls and medical treatments were organized; around the least fantasies, moralists, but especially doctors, brandished the whole emphatic vocabulary of abomination. Were these anything more than means employed to absorb, for the benefit of a genitally centered sexuality, all the fruitless pleasures? All this garrulous attention which has us in a stew over sexuality, is it not motivated by one basic concern: to ensure population, to reproduce labor capacity, to perpetuate the form of social relations: in short, to constitute a sexuality that is economically useful and politically conservative?

Up to the end of the eighteenth century, three major explicit codes—apart from the customary regularities and constraints of opinion—governed sexual practices: canonical law, the Christian pastoral, and civil law. They determined, each in its own way, the division between licit and illicit. They were all centered on matrimonial relations.

These different codes did not make a clear distinction between violations of the rules of marriage and deviations with respect to genitality. Breaking the rules of marriage or seeking strange pleasures brought an equal measure of condemnation. On the list of grave sins, and separated only by their relative importance, there appeared debauchery (extramarital relations), adultery, rape, spiritual or carnal incest, but also sodomy, or the mutual "caress." As to the courts, they could condemn homosexuality as well as infidelity, marriage without parental consent, or bestiality. What was taken into account in the civil and religious jurisdictions alike was a general unlawfulness. Doubtless acts "contrary to nature" were stamped as especially abominable, but they were perceived simply as an extreme form of acts "against the law"; they were infringements of decrees which were just as sacred as those of marriage, and which had been established for governing the order of things and the plan of beings. Prohibitions bearing on sex were essentially of a juridical nature. The "nature" on which they were based was still a kind of law.

The discursive explosion of the eighteenth and nineteenth centuries caused this system centered on legitimate alliance to undergo two modifications. First, a centrifugal movement with respect to heterosexual monogamy. Of course, the array of practices and pleasures continued to be referred to it as their internal standard; but it was spoken of less and less, or in any case with a growing moderation.

On the other hand, what came under scrutiny was the sexuality of children, mad men and women, and criminals; the sensuality of those who did not like the opposite sex; reveries, obsessions, petty manias, or great transports of rage. It was time for all these figures, scarcely noticed in the past, to step forward and speak, to make the difficult confession of what they were. No doubt they were condemned all the same; but they were listened to; and if regular sexuality happened to be questioned once again, it was through a reflux movement, originating in these peripheral sexualities.

Whence the setting apart of the "unnatural" as a specific dimension in the field of sexuality. This kind of activity assumed an autonomy with regard to the other condemned forms such as adultery or rape (and the latter were condemned less and less): to marry a close relative or practice sodomy, to seduce a nun or engage in sadism, to deceive one's wife or violate cadavers, became things that were essentially different.

Similarly, in the civil order, the confused category of "debauchery," which for more than a century had been one of the most frequent reasons for administrative confinement, came apart. From the debris, there appeared on the one hand infractions against the legislation (or morality) pertaining to marriage and the family, and on the other, offenses against the regularity of a natural function (offenses which, it must be added, the law was apt to punish).

Although not without delay and equivocation, the natural laws of matrimony and the immanent rules of sexuality began to be recorded on two separate registers. There emerged a world of perversion which partook of that of legal or moral infraction, yet was not simply a variety of the latter. An entire sub-race race was born, different—despite certain kinship ties—from the libertines of the past. From the end of the eighteenth century to our own, they circulated through the pores of society; they were always hounded, but not always by laws; were often locked up, but not always in prisons; were sick perhaps, but scandalous, dangerous victims, prey to a strange evil that also bore the name of vice and sometimes crime. They were children wise beyond their years, precocious little girls, ambiguous schoolboys, dubious servants and educators, cruel or maniacal husbands, solitary collectors, ramblers with bizarre impulses; they haunted the houses of correction, the penal colonies, the tribunals, and the asylums; they carried their infamy to the doctors and their sickness to the judges. This was the numberless family of perverts who were on friendly terms with delinquents and akin to madmen. In the course of the century they successively bore the stamp of "moral folly," "genital neurosis," "aberration of the genetic instinct," "degenerescence," or "physical imbalance."

What does the appearance of all these peripheral sexualities signify? Is the fact that they could appear in broad daylight a sign that the code had become more lax? Or does the fact that they were given so much attention testify to a stricter regime and to its concern to bring them under close supervision? In terms of repression, things are unclear. There was permissiveness, if one bears in mind that the severity of the codes relating to sexual offenses diminished considerably in the nineteenth century and that law itself often deferred to medicine. But an additional ruse of severity, if one thinks of all the agencies of control and all the mechanisms of surveillance that were put into operation by pedagogy or therapeutics. It may be the case that the intervention of the Church in conjugal sexuality and its rejection of "frauds" against procreation had lost much of their insistence over the previous two hundred years. But medicine made a forceful entry into the pleasures of the couple: it created an entire organic, functional, or mental pathology arising out of "incomplete" sexual practices; it carefully classified all forms of related pleasures; it incorporated them into the notions of "development" and instinctual "disturbances"; and it undertook to manage them.

Perhaps the point to consider is not the level of indulgence or the quantity of repression but the form of power that was exercised. When this whole thicket of disparate sexualities was labeled, as if to disentangle them from one another, was the object to exclude them from reality? It appears, in fact, that the function of the power exerted in this instance was not that of interdiction, and that it involved four operations quite different from simple prohibition.

1. Take the ancient prohibitions of consanguine marriages (as numerous and complex as they were) or the condemnation of adultery, with its inevitable frequency of occurrence; or on the other hand, the recent controls through which, since the nineteenth century, the sexuality of children has been subordinated and their "solitary habits" interfered with. It is clear that we are not dealing with one and the same power mechanism. Not only because in the one case it is a question of law and penality, and in the other, medicine and regimentation; but also because the tactics employed is not the same. On the surface, what appears in both

cases is an effort at elimination that was always destined to fail and always constrained to begin again. But the prohibition of "incests" attempted to reach its objective through an asymptotic decrease in the thing it condemned, whereas the control of infantile sexuality hoped to reach it through a simultaneous propagation of its own power and of the object on which it was brought to bear. It proceeded in accordance with a twofold increase extended indefinitely.

The child's "vice" was not so much an enemy as a support; it may have been designated as the evil to be eliminated, but the extraordinary effort that went into the task that was bound to fail leads one to suspect that what was demanded of it was to persevere, to proliferate to the limits of the visible and the invisible, rather than to disappear for good. Always relying on this support, power advanced, multiplied its relays and its effects, while its target expanded, subdivided, and branched out, penetrating further into reality at the same pace. In appearance, we are dealing with a barrier system; but in fact, all around the child, indefinite *lines of penetration* were disposed.

This new persecution of the peripheral sexualities entailed an *incorporation of perversions* and a new *specification of individuals.* As denned by the ancient civil or canonical codes, sodomy was a category of forbidden acts; their perpetrator was nothing more than the juridical subject of them. The nineteenth-century homosexual became a personage, a past, a case history, and a childhood, in addition to being a type of life, a life form, and a morphology, with an indiscreet anatomy and possibly a mysterious physiology. Nothing that went into his total composition was unaffected by his sexuality.

The machinery of power that focused on this whole alien strain did not aim to suppress it, but rather to give it an analytical, visible, and permanent reality: it was implanted in bodies, slipped in beneath modes of conduct, made into a principle of classification and intelligibility, established as a *raison d'être* and a natural order of disorder. Not the exclusion of these thousand aberrant sexualities, but the specification, the regional solidification of each one of them. The strategy behind this dissemination was to strew reality with them and incorporate them into the individual.

3. The power which thus took charge of sexuality set about contacting bodies, caressing them with its eyes, intensifying areas, electrifying surfaces, dramatizing troubled moments. It wrapped the sexual body in its embrace. There was undoubtedly an increase in effectiveness and an extension of the domain controlled; but also a sensualization of power and a gain of pleasure. This produced a twofold effect: an impetus was given to power through its very exercise; an emotion rewarded the overseeing control and carried it further; the intensity of the confession renewed the questioner's curiosity; the pleasure discovered fed back to the power that encircled it. But so many pressing questions singularized the pleasures felt by the one who had to reply. They were fixed by a gaze, isolated and animated by the attention they received. Power operated as a mechanism of attraction; it drew out those peculiarities over which it kept watch. Pleasure spread to the power that harried it; power anchored the pleasure it uncovered.

The medical examination, the psychiatric investigation, the pedagogical report, and family controls may have the over-all and apparent objective of saying no to all wayward or unproductive sexualities, but the fact is that they function as mechanisms with a double impetus: pleasure and power. The pleasure that comes of exercising a power that questions, monitors, watches, spies, searches out, palpates, brings to light; and on the other hand, the pleasure that kindles at having to evade this power, flee from it, fool it, or travesty it. The power that lets itself be invaded by the pleasure it is pursuing; and opposite it, power asserting itself in the pleasure of showing off, scandalizing, or resisting. Capture and seduction, confrontation and mutual reinforcement: parents and children, adults and adolescents, educator and students, doctors and patients, the psychiatrist with his hysteric and his perverts, all have played this game continually since the nineteenth century. These attractions, these evasions, these circular incitements have traced around bodies and sexes, not boundaries not to be crossed, but *perpetual spirals of power and pleasure.*

Whence those *devices of sexual saturation* so characteristic of the space and the social rituals of the nineteenth century. People often say that modern society has attempted to reduce sexuality to the couple—the heterosexual and, insofar as possible, legitimate couple. There are equal grounds for saying that it has, if not created, at least outfitted and made to proliferate, groups with multiple elements and a circulating sexuality: a distribution of points of power, hierarchized and placed opposite to one another; "pursued" pleasures, that is, both sought after and searched out; compartmental sexualities that are tolerated or encouraged; proximities that serve as surveillance procedures, and function as mechanisms of intensification; contacts that operate as inductors. This is the way things worked in the case of the family, or rather the household, with parents, children, and in some instances, servants. Was the nineteenth-century family really a monogamic and conjugal cell? Perhaps to a certain extent. But it was also a network of pleasures and powers linked together at multiple points and according to transformable relationships. The separation of grown-ups and children, the polarity established between the parents' bedroom and that of the children (it became routine in the course of the century when working-class housing construction was undertaken), the relative segregation of boys and girls, the strict instructions as to the care of nursing infants (maternal breast-feeding, hygiene), the attention focused on infantile sexuality, the supposed dangers of masturbation, the importance attached to puberty, the methods of surveillance suggested to parents, the exhortations, secrets, and fears, the presence—both valued and feared—of servants: all this made the family, even when brought down to its smallest dimensions, a complicated network, saturated with multiple, fragmentary, and mobile sexualities. To reduce them to the conjugal relationship, and then to project the latter, in the form of a forbidden desire, onto the children, cannot account for this apparatus which, in relation to these sexualities, was less a principle of inhibition than an inciting and multiplying mechanism.

Nineteenth-century "bourgeois" society—and it is doubtless still with us—was a society of blatant and fragmented perversion. And this was not by way of hypocrisy, for nothing was more manifest and more prolix, or more manifestly taken over by discourses and institutions. Not because, having tried to erect too rigid or too general a barrier against sexuality, society succeeded only in giving rise to a whole perverse outbreak and a long pathology of the sexual instinct. At issue, rather, is the type of power it brought to bear on the body and on sex. In point of fact, this power had neither the form of the law, nor the effects of the taboo. On the contrary, it acted by multiplication of singular sexualities. It did not set boundaries for sexuality; it extended the various forms of sexuality, pursuing them according to lines of indefinite penetration. It did not exclude sexuality, but included it in the body as a mode of specification of individuals. It did not seek to avoid it; it attracted its varieties by means of spirals in which pleasure and power reinforced one another. It did not set up a barrier; it provided places of maximum saturation. It produced and determined the sexual mosaic. Modern society is perverse, not in spite of its puritanism or as if from a backlash provoked by its hypocrisy; it is in actual fact, and directly, perverse.

The manifold sexualities—those which appear with the different ages (sexualities of the infant or the child), those which become fixated on particular tastes or practices (the sexuality of the invert, the gerontophile, the fetishist), those which, in a diffuse manner, invest relationships (the sexuality of doctor and patient, teacher and student, psychiatrist and mental patient), those which haunt spaces (the sexuality of the home, the school, the prison)—all form the correlate of exact procedures of power. We must not imagine that all these things that were formerly tolerated attracted notice and received a pejorative designation when the time came to give a regulative role to the one type of sexuality that was capable of reproducing labor power and the form of the family. These polymorphous conducts were actually extracted from people's bodies and from their pleasures; or rather, they were solidified in them; they were drawn out, revealed, isolated, intensified, incorporated, by multifarious power devices. The growth of perversions is not a moralizing theme that obsessed the scrupulous minds of the Victorians. It is the real product of the encroachment of a type of power on bodies and their pleasures. It is possible that the West has not been capable of inventing any new pleasures, and it has doubtless not discovered any original vices. But it has defined new rules for the game of powers and pleasures. The frozen countenance of the perversions is a fixture of this game.

This implantation of multiple perversions is not a mockery of sexuality taking revenge on a power that has thrust on it an excessively repressive law. Neither are we dealing with paradoxical forms of pleasure that turn back on power and invest it in the form of a "pleasure to be endured." The implantation of perversions is an instrument-effect: it is through the isolation, intensification, and consolidation of peripheral sexualities that the relations of power to sex and pleasure branched out and multiplied, measured the body, and penetrated modes of conduct. And accompanying this encroachment of powers, scattered sexualities rigidified, became stuck to an age, a place, a type of practice. A proliferation of sexualities through the extension of power; an optimization of the power to which each of these local sexualities gave a surface of intervention: this concatenation, particularly since the nineteenth century, has been ensured and relayed by the countless economic interests which, with the help of medicine, psychiatry, prostitution, and pornography, have tapped into both this analytical multiplication of pleasure and this optimization of the power that controls it. Pleasure and power do not cancel or turn back against one another; they seek out, overlap, and reinforce one another. They are linked together by complex mechanisms and devices of excitation and incitement.

We must therefore abandon the hypothesis that modern industrial societies ushered in an age of increased sexual repression. We have not only witnessed a visible explosion of unorthodox sexualities; but—and this is the important point—a deployment quite different from the law, even if it is locally dependent on procedures of prohibition, has ensured, through a network of interconnecting mechanisms, the proliferation of specific pleasures and the multiplication of disparate sexualities. It is said that no society has been more prudish; never have the agencies of power taken such care to feign ignorance of the thing they prohibited, as if they were determined to have nothing to do with it. But it is the opposite that has become apparent, at least after a general review of the facts: never have there existed more centers of power; never more attention manifested and verbalized; never more circular contacts and linkages; never more sites where the intensity of pleasures and the persistency of power catch hold, only to spread elsewhere.

DISCUSSION QUESTIONS

1. Sketch out a basic understanding of how sex is related to power, according to Foucault. Can you explain Foucault's interconnections between sex and power to a friend?
2. What is the "repressive hypothesis," and how does it continue to operate in contemporary society, if it does?
3. How do power and freedom interact in the politics of our sexual relationships, according to Foucault? How have those changed over time? Give specific examples if possible.

NOTES

1. Segneri, *L'Instruction du pénitent*, pp. 301–302.
2. Condorcet, cited by Jean-Louis Flandrin, *Familles: parenté, maison, sexualité dans l'ancienne société*, (Paris: Hachette, 1976).
3. Auguste Tardieu, *Étude médico-légale sur les attentats aux moeurs* (1857), p. 114.
4. Johann von Justi, *Éléments généraux de police* (French trans. 1769), p. 20.

La Conciencia de la Mestiza: Towards a New Consciousness

BY GLORIA ANZALDÚA

Gloria Anzaldúa (1942–2004) was an American scholar of Chicana cultural theory, feminist theory, and queer theory. In this semiautobiographical work, she discusses the struggles of being a lesbian woman of color who is rejected by all her cultures for her sexuality. Anzaldúa introduces the influential concept of the "New Mestiza"—one whose identity does not fit neatly into any cultural category available to her and whose very existence thus undermines the legitimacy of these categories.

> *Por la mujer de mi raza*
> *hablará el espíritu.*[1]

Jose Vascocelos, Mexican philosopher, envisaged *una raza mestiza, una mezcla de razas afines, una raza de color—la primera raza síntesis del globo.* He called it a cosmic race, *la raza cósmica,* a fifth race embracing the four major races of the world.[2] Opposite to the theory of the pure Aryan, and to the policy of racial purity that white America practices, his theory is one of inclusivity. At the confluence of two or more genetic streams, with chromosomes constantly "crossing over," this mixture of races, rather than resulting in an inferior being, provides hybrid progeny, a mutable, more malleable species with a rich gene pool. From this racial, ideological, cultural and biological cross-pollinization, an "alien" consciousness is presently in the making— a new *mestiza* consciousness, *una conciencia de mujer.* It is a consciousness of the Borderlands.

Una lucha de fronteras / A Struggle of Borders

> Because I, a *mestiza,*
> continually walk out of one culture
> and into another,
> because I am in all cultures at the same time,
> *alma entre dos mundos, tres, cuatro,*
> *me zumba la cabeza con lo còntradictorio.*

> *Estoy norteada por todas las voces que me*
> *hablan*
> *simultáneamente.*

The ambivalence from the clash of voices results in mental and emotional states of perplexity. Internal strife results in insecurity and indecisiveness. The mestiza's dual or multiple personality is plagued by psychic restlessness.

In a constant state of mental nepantilism, an Aztec word meaning torn between ways, *la mestiza* is a product of the transfer of the cultural and spiritual values of one group to another. Being tricultural, monolingual, bilingual, or multilingual, speaking a patois, and in a state of perpetual transition, the *mestiza* faces the dilemma of the mixed breed: which collectivity does the daughter of a darkskinned mother listen to?

El choque de un alma atrapado entre el mundo del espiritu y el mundo de la técnica a veces la deja entullada. Cradled in one culture, sandwiched between two cultures, straddling all three cultures and their value systems, *la mestiza* undergoes a struggle of flesh, a struggle of borders, an inner war. Like all people, we perceive the version of reality that our culture communicates. Like others having or living in more than one culture, we get multiple, often opposing messages. The coming together of two self-consistent but habitually incompatible frames of reference[3] causes *un choque*, a cultural collision.

Within us and within *la cultura chicana*, commonly held beliefs of the white culture attack commonly held beliefs of the Mexican culture, and both attack commonly held beliefs of the indigenous culture. Subconsciously, we see an attack on ourselves and our beliefs as a threat and we attempt to block with a counterstance.

But it is not enough to stand on the opposite river bank, shouting questions, challenging patriarchal, white conventions. A counterstance locks one into a duel of oppressor and oppressed; locked in mortal combat, like the cop and the criminal, both are reduced to a common denominator of violence. The counterstance refutes the dominant culture's views and beliefs, and, for this, it is proudly defiant. All reaction is limited by, and dependent on, what it is reacting against. Because the counter stance stems from a problem with authority—outer as well as inner—it's a step towards liberation from cultural domination. But it is not a way of life. At some point, on our way to a new consciousness, we will have to leave the opposite bank, the split between the two mortal combatants somehow healed so that we are on both shores at once and, at once, see through serpent and eagle eyes. Or perhaps we will decide to disengage from the dominant culture, write it off altogether as a lost cause, and cross the border into a wholly new and separate territory. Or we might go another route. The possibilities are numerous once we decide to act and not react.

A Tolerance for Ambiguity

These numerous possibilities leave *la mestiza* floundering in uncharted seas. In perceiving conflicting information and points of view, she is subjected to a swamping of her psychological borders. She has discovered that she can't hold concepts or ideas in rigid boundaries. The borders and walls that are supposed to keep the undesirable ideas out are entrenched habits and patterns of behavior; these habits and patterns are the enemy within. Rigidity means death. Only by remaining flexible is she able to stretch the psyche horizontally and vertically. *La mestiza* constantly has to shift out of habitual

formations; from convergent thinking, analytical reasoning that tends to use rationality to move toward a single goal (a Western mode), to divergent thinking,[4] characterized by movement away from set patterns and goals and toward a more whole perspective, one that includes rather than excludes.

The new *mestiza* copes by developing a tolerance for contradictions, a tolerance for ambiguity. She learns to be an Indian in Mexican culture, to be Mexican from an Anglo point of view. She learns to juggle cultures. She has a plural personality, she operates in a pluralistic mode—nothing is thrust out, the good the bad and the ugly, nothing rejected, nothing abandoned. Not only does she sustain contradictions, she turns the ambivalence into something else.

She can be jarred out of ambivalence by an intense, and often painful, emotional event which inverts or resolves the ambivalence. I'm not sure exactly how. The work takes place underground—subconsciously. It is work that the soul performs. That focal point or fulcrum, that juncture where the mestiza stands, is where phenomena tend to collide. It is where the possibility of uniting all that is separate occurs. This assembly is not one where severed or separated pieces merely come together. Nor is it a balancing of opposing powers. In attempting to work out a synthesis, the self has added a third element which is greater than the sum of its severed parts. That third element is a new consciousness—a mestiza consciousness—and though it is a source of intense pain, its energy comes from continual creative motion that keeps breaking down the unitary aspect of each new paradigm.

En unas pocas centurias, the future will belong to the mestiza. Because the future depends on the breaking down of paradigms, it depends on the straddling of two or more cultures. By creating a new mythos—that is, a change in the way we perceive reality, the way we see ourselves, and the ways we behave—*la mestiza* creates a new consciousness.

As a *mestiza* I have no country, my homeland cast me out; yet all countries are mine because I am every woman's sister or potential lover. (As a lesbian I have no race, my own people disclaim me; but I am all races because there is the queer of me in all races.) I am cultureless because, as a feminist, I challenge the collective cultural/religious male-derived beliefs of Indo-Hispanics and Anglos; yet I am cultured because I am participating in the creation of yet another culture, a new story to explain the world and our participation in it, a new value system with images and symbols that connect us to each other and to the planet. *Soy un amasamiento*, I am an act of kneading, of uniting and joining that not only has produced both a creature of darkness and a creature of light, but also a creature that questions the definitions of light and dark and gives them new meanings.

"You're nothing but a woman" means you are defective. Its opposite is to be *un macho*. The modern meaning of the word "machismo," as well as the concept, is actually an Anglo invention. For men like my father, being "macho" meant being strong enough to protect and support my mother and us, yet being able to show love. Today's macho has doubts about his ability to feed and protect his family. His "machismo" is an adaptation to oppression and poverty and low self-esteem. It is the result of hierarchical male dominance. The Anglo, feeling inadequate and inferior and powerless, displaces or transfers these feelings to the Chicano by shaming him. In the Gringo world, the Chicano suffers from excessive humility and self-effacement, shame of self and self-deprecation. Around Latinos he suffers from a sense of language inadequacy and its accompanying discomfort; with Native Americans he suffers from a racial amnesia which ignores our common blood, and from guilt because the Spanish part of him took their land and oppressed them. He has an excessive compensatory hubris when around Mexicans from the other side. It overlays a deep sense of racial shame.

The loss of a sense of dignity and respect in the macho breeds a false machismo which leads him to put down women and even to brutalize them. Coexisting with his sexist behavior is a love for the mother which takes precedence over that of all others. Devoted son, macho pig. To wash down the shame of his acts, of his very being, and to handle the brute in the mirror, he takes to the bottle, the snort, the needle, and the fist.

Though we "understand" the root causes of male hatred and fear, and the subsequent wounding of women, we do not excuse, we do not condone, and we will no longer put up with it. From the men of our race, we demand the admission/acknowledgment/disclosure/testimony that they wound us, violate us, are afraid of us and of our power. We need them to say they will begin to eliminate their hurtful put-down ways. But more than the words, we demand acts. We say to them: We will develop equal power with you and those who have shamed us.

It is imperative that mestizas support each other in changing the sexist elements in the Mexican-Indian culture. As long as woman is put down, the Indian and the Black in all of us is put down. The struggle of the mestiza is above all a feminist one. As long as *los hombres* think they have to *chingar mujeres* and each other to be men, as long as men are taught that they are superior and therefore culturally favored over *la mujer*, as long as to be a *vieja* is a thing of derision, there can be no real healing of our psyches. We're halfway there—we have such love of the Mother, the good mother. The first step is to unlearn the *puta/virgen* dichotomy and to see *Coatlapopeuh-Coatlicue* in the Mother, *Guadalupe*.

Tenderness, a sign of vulnerability, is so feared that it is showered on women with verbal abuse and blows. Men, even more than women, are fettered to gender roles. Women at least have had the guts to break out of bondage. Only gay men have had the courage to expose themselves to the woman inside them and to challenge the current masculinity. I've encountered a few scattered and isolated gentle straight men, the beginnings of a new breed, but they are confused, and entangled with sexist behaviors that they have not been able to eradicate. We need a new masculinity and the new man needs a movement.

Lumping the males who deviate from the general norm with man, the oppressor, is a gross injustice. *Asombra pensar que nos hemos quedado en ese pozo oscuro donde el mundo encierra a las lesbianas. Asombra pensar que hemos, como feministas y lesbianas, cerrado nuestros corazónes a los hombres, a nuestros hermanos los jotos, desheredados y marginales como nosotros.* Being the supreme crossers of cultures, homosexuals have strong bonds with the queer white, Black, Asian, Native American, Latino, and with the queer in Italy, Australia and the rest of the planet. We come from all colors, all classes, all races, all time periods. Our role is to link people with each other—the Blacks with Jews with Indians with Asians with whites with extraterrestrials. It is to transfer ideas and information from one culture to another. Colored homosexuals have more knowledge of other cultures; have always been at the forefront (although sometimes in the closet) of all liberation struggles in this country; have suffered more injustices and have survived them despite all odds. Chicanos need to acknowledge the political and artistic contributions of their queer. People, listen to what your *jotería* is saying.

The mestizo and the queer exist at this time and point on the evolutionary continuum for a purpose. We are a blending that proves that all blood is intricately woven together, and that we are spawned out of similar souls.

DISCUSSION QUESTIONS

1. What is "mestiza consciousness"? Explain how this way of seeing the world arises out of a particular set of life experiences.

2. Explain how mestiza consciousness can offer new strategies for addressing the interconnected problems of sexist, racist, homophobic, and classist oppressions.

NOTES

1. This is my own "take off" on Jose Vasconcelos' idea. Jose Vasconcelos, *La Raza Cósmica: Misión de la Raza Ibero-Americana* (México; Aguilar S. A. de Ediciones, 1961).

2. Vasconcelos.

3. Arthur Koestler termed this "bisociation." Albert Rothenberg, *The Creative Process in Art, Science, and Other Fields* (Chicago, IL: University of Chicago Press, 1979), 12.

4. In part, I derive my definitions for "convergent" and "divergent" thinking from Rothenberg, 12–13.

When Selves Have Sex: What the Phenomenology of Trans Sexuality Can Teach About Sexual Orientation

BY TALIA MAE BETTCHER

Talia Mae Bettcher is an American philosopher who writes primarily about the political and practical impacts of issues of trans identity and inclusion. In this essay, Bettcher argues that the experience of trans people illustrates that we need to rethink our understanding of sexual attraction, replacing an exclusively other-directed notion of gendered attraction with one that includes the gendered eroticization of the self as an essential component.

The standard way of viewing sexual attraction has been inadequate for capturing the experiences of trans people. To this end, I propose we rethink sexual attraction in light of those experiences. The result is "erotic structuralism"—a theory that concerns sexual attraction in general (not just trans-specific attractions). My goal is to do the ground-clearing work necessary to outline and pro-visionally defend it. My methodological approach is principally that of a philosopher; I use analysis and argumentation. However, my own experience as a transsexual woman is relevant to my theori-zation, as is the fact that my experience is shaped by the subcultures I inhabit (along with my friends, past lovers, chosen family, and life partner).

Erotic structuralism maintains that the con-tent of arousal is often complex and structured. It endorses two general ideas. The first idea (the complexity of sexual attraction) is that sexual at-traction to a person possesses an internal, consti-tutive structure that includes the eroticized self as an element.[1] The second, closely related, idea (the interest/attraction distinction) is that erotic con-tent is not exhausted by the "source of attraction" (the person to whom one is attracted). To be eroti-cally interested in something (to be aroused by it) is not necessarily to be attracted to it.

The theory includes a specific "interactional account" according to which sexual attraction pos-sesses a structure comprising the eroticized other ("the source of attraction"), the eroticized self ("the locus of attraction"), and the erotic inter-actions between the two. Erotic experiences of self and of other are equally necessary, dynami-cally related, and mutually informing where they "mirror" each other through the mediating inter-action. While there can be different types of eroti-cized interaction, sheer increase in intimacy is the constitutive mode of interaction defining this dy-namic. And insofar as intimacy is fundamentally gendered, erotic experiences of self and other are likewise gendered.

Erotic structuralism has two important con-sequences. First, the controversial notion of "au-togynephilia" is rejected. To briefly summarize, "autogynephilia" is one name, among others, for a particular phenomenon—namely, an erotic inter-est in oneself (or in the thought or image of one-self) "as a woman" (Serano, 2010). We might call this "female embodiment eroticism." The term "autogynephilia" literally means "love of oneself as a woman," and it suggests that sexual attraction wrongly loops back around and targets oneself ("as a woman"). The concept of autogynephilia plays a key role in Blanchard's (1985) causal distinction between his two exclusive and exhaustive types of male-to-female (MtF) transsexuality—androphilic and autogynephilic. As it is used in Blanchard's theory (1992), it names a misdirected heterosexual orientation where "normal" heterosexual orientation and autogynephilia compete with each other.

According to erotic structuralism, defenders of the notion of autogynephilia err in assuming that sexual attraction is simple and in conflating erotic interest with sexual attraction. This leads them to identify the eroticized self with the source of attraction (and the effect of some imagined "target error"). In the interactive account of sexual attraction, by contrast, an eroticized self is a necessary component of attraction to another. Consequently, "attraction to oneself" is literally impossible and, therefore, so is autogynephilia. While there are indeed cases in which the eroticized gendered self can appear in isolation from the other erotic content required for attraction, this phenomenon is better viewed as a non-pathological "erotic fragment."[2]

The second consequence is that sexual orientation is re-understood to include a core erotic gendered self, and, consequently, the traditional distinction between gender identity and sexual orientation is blurred. Since sexual attraction to a gendered other necessitates a gendered self, gynephilic and androphilic attractions each come in two varieties—andro-reflexive and gyne-reflexive. In other words, sexual orientation is not merely determined by stable gendered "object preference" but also by stable "preference of gendered self." Consequently, orientation and gender identity are more closely related than the orientation/gender identity distinction maintains.

In the first part of this article, I provide an argument in support of the interest/attraction distinction. The argument also suggests that, at least in some cases, sexual attraction possesses a complex structure. In the second part of the article, I defend the interactional account of attraction. This hypothesizes that, in all cases, attraction possesses a complex structure. I conclude by considering the two major theoretical consequences mentioned above.

The Interest/Attraction Distinction and the Complexity of Attraction

Preliminaries

Consider David, who has little gynephilic attraction. He can still have sex with a woman, Wendy, through the use of extensive internal fantasies about sexual interaction with some man (say, Jeremy). By "running a movie in his mind," he might be able to "get involved in" the sexual encounter. In such a case, David is fantasizing *about* Jeremy. Nonetheless, the actual act of sexual movement with Wendy may be sexually stimulating him physiologically. While both erotic fantasy and experience of physical stimulation have a phenomenology (by which I mean that both "*feel* like something" specific) the latter is not included in the erotic content. He is not excited *about* his genital activity *with Wendy*, nor is he excited *about* her. One way to put this is to say that he does not have an erotic interest in Wendy, while he does have an erotic interest in Jeremy. Jeremy, not Wendy, is part of the erotic content (i.e., the content of arousal).

While David is not sexually attracted to Wendy, he may be attracted to his ex-lover, Jeremy. One says that David has sexual desire *for* Jeremy or else that he has sexual attraction *to* him. I shall use these two expressions interchangeably. Strictly speaking, the term "desire" is broader than "attraction." And it is also ambiguous. Does one desire sexual pleasure (and, ultimately, the achievement of orgasm), sexual activity, or the person one is with? I bypass these types of questions by focusing exclusively on attraction. To be clear, I am not interested in the mere cognitive assessment that a person is attractive, but the actual experience of sexual attraction *to* a person. Being sexually attracted *to* somebody *feels like something*. And I assume that when somebody says she experiences sexual desire *for* somebody, she refers to the experience of sexual attraction *to* them.

A natural assumption is that sexual attraction *to* a person is nothing more than an erotic interest *in* them. This assumption commits to the "simplicity of attraction" in that the erotic content of attraction is taken to include nothing but the source of attraction. That is, the erotic content is not subject to a complex structure of elements. For example, suppose David sees Jeremy without his shirt and gets excited. In such a case, it appears that Jeremy, alone, belongs to the erotic content. David is attracted *to* him, in this view, just because he is aroused *by* him. Blanchard (1985) appears to accept this view; he speaks of the "male physique" as the "effective erotic stimulus" in "normal homosexual attraction" (249). Attraction *to* somebody, in this view, includes the other's physique within the erotic content (and nothing else). The assumption is also implicit in the view that homosexual/heterosexual attractions can be fully captured by the replacement notions of gynephilic and androphilic attractions (e.g., Serano 2010). The underlying idea is that homo/hetero attractions are exhaustively characterized in terms of "gendered object preference."

The belief in the simplicity of attraction yields the related view that there is no distinction between erotic interest and sexual attraction. If to be attracted *to* a person involves nothing more than that person being (the only or the main) part of the erotic content, then it would seem that anything that is an important part of the content is basically a source of attraction (since there is no basis for a distinction). The effect of the first assumption is, therefore, a collapse of erotic content and source of attraction. By this I mean that to be aroused *by* something, in this view, is necessarily to be attracted *to* it; the experience of arousal *by* is, in all cases, the same as attraction *to*. This means that should anything other than the source of attraction occur prominently in the erotic content, it will seem to be nonnormative. It will seem that one is attracted to the "wrong" thing. This is Blanchard's (1992) view; he sees female embodiment eroticism as a kind of misdirected attraction. And once anything that occurs within the erotic content is viewed as an attraction, it is easy to see why one might see different attractions as competing with each other, as Blanchard (1992) does.

Erotic structuralism maintains, by contrast, that multiple objects of erotic interest are structured within a larger whole. This is obvious in the case of complex, narrative sexual fantasies.

It would be foolish to see each part of the fantasy as its own independent object of interest. But this is also fairly obvious in the case of sexual attraction. For while one can experience sexual attraction *to* somebody without having an explicit aim of doing something sexual *with* them, it is also the case that often one experiences doing something with the source of attraction as itself exciting. For example, one might find the prospect of being fellated by an attractive man sexually exciting. In this case, one is not merely sexually aroused by the thought *of* the man himself, one is also excited by the thought of doing something *with* him. In this case, it seems fair to say the act (fellatio) is part of the erotic content insofar as the thought of receiving fellatio from him is sexually exciting. One has an erotic interest in being fellated, one has an interest in the man, and the two interests are structurally connected.

While the preceding is largely unsurprising, note that many of these activities involve various forms of sexual interaction between bodies. So it seems to follow that one's own body is necessarily included in the erotic content. One is not merely attracted *to* him. One is excited *by* him as performing fellatio on one's own penis. How does one remove one's own penis from the fellatio? And how does one deny that one's own penis plays a significant part in the erotic content?[3] There is a natural response that makes it seem one's own penis should not be included. One is not attracted to one's own penis as one is attracted to the man fellating it. If that is correct, one might conclude that one's own penis cannot be part of the erotic content. The background assumption, of course, is that to be erotically interested *in* something is to be attracted *to* it. The argument below, however, shows that this assumption must be rejected.

The Argument

Imagine a trans man, Sam, who is gynephilically oriented (with little androphilic attraction). Suppose he is having sex with a woman, Kim. He does not have a penis, but he does have a strap-on dildo. Suppose Kim is fellating the dildo, and the dildo is eroticized by both participants as a flesh-and-blood penis. Sam fantasizes that his penis is being fellated (by Kim) and so does Kim herself. Now consider the following argument:

1. The fantasized penis is a significant part of Sam's erotic content.
2. Sam is not attracted to his fantasized penis.
3. Therefore, some significant erotic content is not reducible to "the source of attraction."

The argument is valid. If the premises are true, then it follows that there is an interest/attraction distinction. *Are* they true?

The sub-argument in favor of premise (1) is based on parity concerns. Reconsider David who, not attracted to women, fantasizes that he is with Jeremy when he is actually with Wendy. In this case, while he has feelings of stimulation from engaging in heterosexual intercourse, that activity, as such, is not eroticized. Rather, having sex with Jeremy is the content of his excitement. Were he with Jeremy, he would not be engaging in this fantasy; he would simply be excited by Jeremy (in the flesh). But this case is analogous to that of Sam. Sam fantasizes that he has a penis that is being fellated by Kim. While he has feelings of sexual stimulation from the base of the dildo pressing against him, the cause of the stimulation is not part of the fantasy. Rather, the fellated penis is part of the fantasy, and it is a very important part. Were he to have a flesh-and-blood penis, he would not be engaging in this fantasy at all. That is, the work of the sexual fantasy primarily concerns the fellated penis. The fellated penis is primarily *what the fantasy is about*. It is, therefore, an important part of the erotic content. But why should the flesh-and-blood penis then occupy a less important role in the erotic content once the need for fantasy has been eliminated? One does not think the gender of the sexual partner becomes any less important to the erotic content in the first case. Why should the fellated penis become less important in the second?

Consider the second premise. The fantasized penis, while a primary part of the erotic content, is not a source of sexual attraction. The other possibility is that Sam is literally attracted to himself as possessing a penis. One could say his attraction is "autophallophilic" (Serano, 2007). Instead of being attracted to another person, he is attracted to himself (as a man). The problem with this suggestion is obvious, however. Sam *is* attracted to another person, namely Kim, who is fellating the dildo and whom he fantasizes as fellating his penis. Nor does it make sense to say he is attracted to two people (Kim along with himself with a penis). First, it makes it seem he possesses both gynephilic and androphilic attractions. This distorts what seems to be a straightforward gynephilic attraction on his part. Second, and more important for my purposes, that his penis is part of the erotic content is obviously connected to his attraction to his partner. His sexual attraction *for* her, in this specific situation, has, as its eroticized aim, her fellating his penis. This is precisely what implicates his (fantasized) body in the erotic content. The view that he is merely attracted to two people—the woman and himself (as a man with a penis) distorts this evident structural connection that builds his fantasized penis into the complex of his aim-driven attraction to his partner.

So both premises are true. And by this argument, it follows that there is some important erotic content that is not identical to the source of attraction. Interest and attraction are distinct. Moreover, there is reason to accept that there are some cases in which attraction admits of a complex structure. In this case, Kim's attractiveness to Sam is temporarily mediated through the act of fellatio. He experiences her as attractive, in part, as one who is fellating him. Crucially, he likewise experiences *himself* erotically as one receiving the fellatio. His erotic experience of her is reflected in his erotic experience of self as his erotic experience of self is mirrored in his erotic experience of her.

This argument can be generalized by recognizing this example as merely one of various complex activities and fantasies in which some trans people engage in order to recode their bodies to lessen body dysphoria, while allowing certain body parts to become part of a sexual encounter (Bettcher, 2013; Hale, 1997; Serano, 2010). For example, if a trans woman (with a "penis") is receiving oral sex, it is possible for her and her partner to erotically re-understand the activity as a form of cunnilingus rather than fellatio, perhaps by eroticizing a component of her genitals as a "clit." Practices of this type involve two features. First, "recoding" can involve the reimagined body part being taken up into the erotic content. Second, that there is this erotic uptake does not undermine the capacity of the trans person to be sexually attracted *to* a partner. Indeed, the erotic uptake of the body part is structurally part of their sexual desire *for* the partner, where there is a specific eroticized activity. If one takes such common trans practices seriously, therefore, one must admit that erotic content is not exhausted by the source of attraction. Moreover, one must recognize that at least in some cases, sexual attraction admits of an interactive structure in which eroticized experience of self and other are mirrored through eroticized interactions.

The pressing question now is how to characterize the difference between erotic content that is the source of attraction and erotic content that is not. Given that being an erotic interest is insufficient to count as being a "source of attraction," what makes an erotic interest a source of attraction? According to erotic structuralism, an erotic interest is a "source of attraction" when it plays a certain structural role in "the complex of attraction." In the following section, I specify the exact nature of this structure. (Individual activities such as fellatio cannot provide that structure since they are variable and even altogether eliminable from attraction.)

I also address the following challenge: in cases of sexual attraction that do not have any explicit eroticized aim, it seems that sexual attraction *is* simple. Consider the case of a man looking at a naked woman. Suppose he experiences sexual attraction *to* her. In cases like this, it would appear that the self is not implicated in sexual attraction. The erotic content seems exhausted by the source of attraction (in this case, "the female physique" as Blanchard [1985] might term it). I show how the interactional account can explain such cases through analysis of physical intimacy. In particular, I show that even in cases that do not seem to implicate the self, the self is nonetheless involved.

The Interactional Account of Sexual Attraction

Overview

In outlining the interactional account, I assume that erotic content is highly variable. While there may be actual limits on what can be eroticized, this is not an assumption that can be made in a theoretical article. (Any limits that I suppose would most likely be failures of imagination on my part.) Moreover, given this assumption and the view that sexuality is social in nature, informed by cultural "scripts" (Gagnon & Simon, 2005 [1973]), it seems reasonable to assume that erotic content in a culture is significantly determined by the sociality of that culture. In other words, erotic content can vary cross-culturally. My goal in this section, then, is to understand sexual attraction as a culturally specific, well-defined, and structured form of erotic content. And an erotic interest, in this view, is not a source of attraction unless it plays a specific role in this specific structure.

The basic idea runs as follows: "sexual attraction" suggests a spatial metaphor whereby two entities are drawn closer together through a kind of "magnetic" (sexual) force. In the interactional account, to be sexual attracted *to* a person is to be aroused *by* increasing physical intimacy between the other (the source of attraction) and the self (the locus of attraction). Intimacy is understood according to a spatial metaphor of closeness and distance (Bettcher, 2012), and the increase in intimacy is understood as movement through interpersonal space whereby the locus and source are brought closer together ("intimization").[4]

This view brings the representation of self into the light of day. In order to eroticize the intimization of self and other, the self needs to be included as an important component of the eroticism (since the self is one of the things being drawn together). Moreover, it provides a structural distinction between the eroticized experience of self and the attraction to an other. In this view, it is impossible to be attracted to oneself insofar as there is no interpersonal distance between oneself and oneself, and, consequently, it makes no sense to speak of the eroticization of the intimization between one-self and oneself.[5] For the rest of the section, I elaborate this account in greater detail. First, I develop the idea of sexual attraction as the eroticization of intimization and show how this is relevant to gendered forms of attraction. Second, I show how a gendered experience of self is necessarily included in all forms of gendered attraction. Finally, I elaborate the idea of "mirroring" as central to the dynamics of gendered attraction.

Interpersonal Spatiality and Gendered Attraction

Physical intimacy primarily involves sensory access to bodies (Bettcher, 2012). It also implicates specific activities that require various types of sensory access to bodies as part of the activity's structure. For example, fellatio requires sensory access to a penis through the medium of a mouth and sensory access to a mouth through a penis. In this view, what is experienced as erotic is not merely a body but sensory access to that body. While sensory access is not an activity (although it can involve activities such as touching, undressing, and so forth), it involves both a subject and an object of sensory access.

Intimacy, however, does not merely involve increased sensory access. Rather, it requires interpersonal boundaries traversed in cases of mutuality and transgressed in cases of abuse (Bettcher, 2012). Certain body parts are deemed "intimate" where exposure draws down moral concerns (as evidenced by Janet Jackson's notorious "wardrobe malfunction"). Moreover, in order to traverse a boundary, a movement from one stage (of intimacy or non-intimacy) to another, more intimate, stage is necessary. Consequently, interpersonal boundaries are vaguely ordered sequentially so as to allow for socially recognized degrees of closeness (Bettcher, 2012). Different kinds of sensory access "occur earlier than others" (a woman's breasts are touched before her genitals) as do sexual activities (kissing comes before heterosexual intercourse). Indeed, nakedness, I have argued elsewhere, is a mode of self-presentation that is every bit as socially constituted as the clothed mode of self-presentation (Bettcher, 2012). In particular, it is

constituted through these interpersonal boundaries regulating visual access where the ordering of boundaries gives the body a moral structure.

As a result, attraction has a temporal aspect. What is arousing, in this view, is not merely sensory access to a body part, but to an intimate (private) body part that is part of a larger ordering of boundaries. Suppose Germaine is slowly undressing Sheena. Germaine's sexual attraction to Sheena takes the form of a continuous augmentation in arousal through a continuous increase in intimate visual access to Sheena. What is arousing is not merely seeing Sheena's breasts, for example, but the significance of that intimate access to private body within the larger context (actual or implied) of continuously increasing sensory access. The augmentation of arousal (as the experience of "building" excitement) tracks the growing intimacy (in this case, the steadily increasing visual exposure of Sheena). And although Germaine need not explicitly desire to increase intimacy in some specific way with Sheena, her present arousal is characterized by "erotic anticipation." In seeing Sheena's breasts, part of the eroticism, for Germaine, is the potential that this is "leading somewhere." This is because visual access to breasts is a stage of intimacy that can lead to closer stages, so part of the erotic significance of this visual access now is precisely its implied potential for greater intimacy later. This account has notable consequences in terms of how gynephilic and androphilic attractions ought to be understood. Suppose Germaine has only gynephilic attractions. According to the account, this is a feature of the way she experiences attraction and not merely what gender she experiences as attractive. Sex-differentiated bodies have distinct "boundary structures" applied to them, constituting nakedness differentially (Bettcher, 2012). In effect, there are two main types of nakedness—female and male.[6] One difference is that the former has a tiered structure, whereas the latter does not (i.e., female chests have moral significance). Since to be attracted *to* somebody is to be aroused *by* the traversal of structured boundaries, different types of sexual attraction can be distinguished on the basis of which structures of nakedness are in the erotic content. Contrary to the view that Germaine is aroused by the "female physique," then, Germaine is aroused by the female physique as implicated and structured within a system of ordered boundaries governing sensory access to it.

Erotic (Gendered) Experiences of Self

While attraction eroticizes the closing distance between self and other, there are multiple ways in which this can happen. One way is for the source of attraction to move closer to the self. I call this "subject-centered-attraction." This is what happens with Germaine's attraction. It pulls Sheena "in closer" (as an object of sensory access). However, consider Sheena's corresponding eroticism. She is also aroused by Germaine's increasing sensory access to her. She feels excited by the prospect of being undressed and viewed by Germaine, etc. And the fact that Sheena is aroused by her own exposure to Germaine does not rule out her attraction to Germaine. In this case, Sheena has object-centered attraction to Germaine-as-sensory-subject. Her attraction moves her own self closer to the source of attraction. This means Sheena necessarily has an eroticized self as part of her attraction to Germaine. That is, Sheena's own visually accessed body is part of her erotic content (even though she is not attracted to her own body). Moreover, Sheena's erotic self is given by the same boundary structure (to which Germaine is attracted). That is, a specific feature of her eroticization of the increasing transversal of boundaries between self and other is that her own boundaries be structured in a particular way, namely female. For example, her arousal at Germaine's visually accessing her breasts requires precisely that her own body have a female boundary structure.

Not only is Sheena's eroticized self structured according to gendered boundaries, however, so is her "eroticized other" (Germaine). She is not merely excited by her own exposure to another, but by exposure to *a woman*. The reason for this is that boundaries are gender-sensitive (Bettcher, 2012). How a boundary works depends on the gender of the person traversing it (as well as the person who has the boundary). Consider sex-segregation (in restrooms, changing rooms, congregate housing,

etc.). Same-sex intimacy is socially acceptable in such cases, while hetero intimacy is not. The reason for this is complicated. But note that visual intimacy is controlled in two ways. It is controlled by the object through self-presentation (naked or clothed) and by the subject (looking or not). In sex-segregated contexts, the boundaries concern the latter (where overtly looking is considered a violation of privacy). The implicit rationale for prohibiting hetero intimacy in such contexts takes "looking" for granted and focuses on the self-presentation. In such cases, the boundaries operate asymmetrically (Bettcher, 2012). A woman being in a state of undress with a man would constitute a privacy violation. A man being in a state of undress with a woman would constitute a decency offense (against the woman). In this case, the sheer threat of looking is sufficient for the arrangement to be considered boundary violating (always against the woman), thereby justifying sex-segregation.

The point is that the gender of the subject is relevant in cases in which one has an object-centered attraction. Even a straight man who is aroused by having his penis touched by woman will rarely experience a similar arousal by having his penis touched by a man. A man touching his penis is not part of that erotic content; a woman touching it is. An important feature of this is that the erotic object and the erotic subject are components on one and the same intimization track. It is not merely that Sheena erotizes a female other and a female self, for example, but, rather, she specifically eroticizes female-female intimacy.

In light of this, Germaine's subject-centered attraction to Sheena can be shown to contain an erotic gendered experience of self as well. While the erotic experience of self is somewhat obscured in this case, since her eroticized self is not in "intimate motion," it is nonetheless required as the fixed point toward which Sheena moves. This point is required in order for the intimate movement of Sheena to be erotized over time. She is the viewer to whom Sheena is increasingly exposed. Germaine, therefore, has an erotic experience of herself as the sensory subject toward which Sheena moves through interpersonal space. And insofar as Germaine eroticizes female-female intimacy specifically, this point of reference is necessarily gendered. For in eroticizing her increasing visual access to Sheena as an increase in female-female intimacy, she necessarily has an erotic experience of herself as a female subject.

Beyond this, however, note that a person typically possesses both object- and subject-centered attractions at once. In such cases, a person's attraction pulls both self and other together. Rather than the other moving toward the self or the self moving toward the other, the two move toward each other. Such cases bring out the relevance of the erotic self in a way that does not sharply distinguish subject and object. Consider David. The view that he is merely attracted to the male physique truncates a more complex homoeroticism of male-male intimacy. What he finds arousing is not just seeing a man's naked body, but *being two naked men together*, sexually experiencing each other's bodies (both seeing and being seen). This suggests that cases (like Germaine and Sheena) involving a strict asymmetry in intimate access also include this asymmetry itself as part of the erotic content. There is a differential distribution of vulnerability/invulnerability that provides even more content to Germaine's eroticized experience of self (namely, an eroticized contrast of Sheena as vulnerable and herself as not).[7]

Gendered Mirroring and the Attraction Dynamic

In light of the preceding, it is clear that a reductive focus on erotic interest in gendered physique is a restricted conception of a more complex attraction dynamic. This dynamic can be conceptualized in terms of "mirroring." In erotically experiencing Sheena, Germaine erotically experiences herself. And in erotically experiencing herself, Germaine erotically experiences Sheena. The dialectic is gendered insofar as the eroticized intimacy boundaries are gendered. Sheena's body is subject to gendered boundaries (her nakedness has a female moral structure), and Germaine traverses those gendered boundaries in a gendered way. In this case, the mirroring is "direct" (reflected through the lens of sameness). However, their dialectic also concerns differential distribution of subject and object positions. In erotically experiencing Sheena as vulnerable object, Germaine erotically experiences herself as a non-vulnerable subject, and in erotically experiencing herself as a non-vulnerable subject, she experiences Sheena as a vulnerable object. In this case, the mirroring is also "indirect" (reflected through the lens of difference).

Gender is the prime modality by which self and other are mirrored (either directly or indirectly) since sexual attraction eroticizes intimization and intimacy is essentially gender-differentiated. However, there is room for considerable complexity. First, gender is not monolithic, so sometimes different aspects can come apart. In butch/femme lesbian attractions, for example, both direct and indirect gender mirroring may occur (where sexed-bodies are similar, but gender presentations are differential). Second, it may not always be that gender is the basis for mirroring (as seen above with vulnerability). In sadomasochistic attractions, for example, the basis for mirroring may concern pain and/or power distribution. Third, different kinds of gender mirroring may themselves be eroticized. For example, some people might find only direct gendered mirroring erotic, while others might find only indirect mirroring erotic. This could offer one explanation why some trans people retain same-sex attractions through their transitions (moving from lesbian relations, for example, to gay male relations). Finally, the various structural components (self, other, modality and type of mirroring, etc.) may be more or less gender-specific within a given person's sexuality. Obviously, a full discussion of such complexity is best left for another article. My aim in considering it now is only to hint at the potential explanatory power of the account.

This sketch, however, is enough for my current purposes. I have outlined the structure of sexual attraction and have shown that even in cases in which attraction might seem simple, it is subject to a complex structure that includes the eroticized self. While I have not defended the interactional account of attraction in great detail, I have defended my views about intimacy and the social construction of nakedness elsewhere (Bettcher, 2012). And in light of them, it is difficult to believe that excitement at seeing a woman's breasts, for example, is not significantly shaped by their socially constituted "privatization," making it at least plausible to believe that sexual attraction is the eroticization of gendered intimization between self and other. Most importantly, however, the account provides an explanation of *why* some erotic content is "the source of attraction," and some is not. The interest/attraction distinction and the complexity of sexual attraction, recall, are significant features of trans "recoding" practices. For this reason, simpler conceptions of attraction cannot accommodate them and are therefore inadequate. The interactional account, by contrast, provides a viable alternative that elucidates these features and therefore successfully accommodates these practices. This is a powerful argument in its favor.

Consequences

Against Autogynephilia

There are two important consequences of adopting the logics of erotic structuralism. First, "autogynephilia" must be rejected. In saying this, I do not mean to critique the hypothesis that autogynephilia is causally responsible for MtF transsexuality or that it can be used to categorize MtFs into different "types." These claims have already been convincingly critiqued by Moser (2010) and Serano (2010). (Erotic Structuralism does have consequences for Blanchard's categorization scheme that I do not explore here.) Instead, I question the very framing of "female embodiment eroticism" in terms of "autogynephilia." That is, rather than critiquing Blanchard's theory of autogynephilia, I critique the very notion of female embodiment eroticism as autogynephilic in nature. There are two false assumptions involved. First, it is falsely assumed that attraction is simple (i.e., to be a source of attraction is merely to be a part of the erotic content). Second, interest and attraction are conflated. Once these assumptions have been rejected in favor of erotic structuralism, there is no longer any reason to construe female embodiment eroticism as a kind of "misdirected" attraction. Instead, an erotic interest in oneself as a gendered being can be recognized as a legitimate (indeed, necessary) part of all normally

directed sexual attraction to others. Indeed, the alleged misdirected attraction is actually impossible, according to erotic structuralism, insofar as a decrease in interpersonal distance between one and oneself is unintelligible (and therefore cannot be eroticized). "Autogynephilia" is, therefore, a seriously misleading term insofar it explicitly characterizes the nature of the phenomenon in a distorted way.

To be sure, there can be cases of arousal when this eroticized self appears by itself (without an "other"), particularly in solitary fantasy. And this is the phenomenon to which "autogynephilia" typically refers. But the question is whether this phenomenon is to be framed as "attraction to oneself as a woman." According to erotic structuralism, it cannot. There is, however, an alternative view. In fantasy, one can produce scenarios that, while arousing, do not constitute (or even replicate) attraction *per se*. In order for an erotic interest to be implicated in attraction, recall, it must be subject to the appropriate structure. Such interests, may, however, be replications of parts of the larger structure (from whence they derive their erotic power). For example, a woman may be erotically interested in a sexual scenario that does not include her own involvement as part of it. While the scenario may be arousing, this will not be a case of attraction since crucial elements of interpersonal interaction (the self, intimate access) have been omitted. Instead, it can be characterized as an "erotic fragment." Similarly, a woman might have erotic narratives about herself as a gendered being that do not include a well-defined "other" to whom she is attracted. In such cases, female embodiment eroticism is, rather than a misdirected attraction, an erotic fragment that abstracts (and yet gets its erotic force from) the interactional structure of attraction. This account predicts that "other-exclusive" fantasies will shade into ones with a more explicitly eroticized self (or at least implicit identifications) and that "self-exclusive" fantasies will shade into ones that involve (or imply) an other.

Of course, one might argue that "self-exclusive" female embodiment fantasies are still pathological since they involve a truncated eroticism that replicates only a fragment of sexual attraction to another. I do not see the value of such assessments, however. They are too detached from the health and happiness of the individual. And I suspect a host of different types of erotic fragments can be found in the fantasy lives of "normal" people. The important question is what role solitary fantasy plays in the overall well-being of the individual. And in light of the intersubjective "recoding" practices discussed earlier, it seems appropriate to regard such self-exclusive female-embodiment fragments occurring among trans women as likewise productively allowing them to "recode" their bodies (Serano, 2007, 2010). That view accords well with the transient nature of such fantasies, unlike Blanchard's (1992) theory in which they somehow constitute a permanent orientation (Moser, 2009; Serano, 2010).

Moreover, it is worth noting that if "self-exclusive" fantasies are viewed as pathological (on the grounds that they are erotic fragments), it follows that "other-exclusive" fantasies should be viewed as pathological as well. Yet such a result is surely implausible. And, indeed, in heterosexuality there tends to be a mutual emphasis on the objectification of the woman, suggesting that it is not unlikely the fantasies of heterosexual men will tend toward those that shade into "other-exclusive" ones (and that it is not unlikely the fantasies of heterosexual women will tend toward those that shade into self-exclusive ones).[8] One ironic result of the view that "self-exclusive" fantasies are pathological, therefore, is that much non-transgender, heterosexual male fantasies are similarly pathological. It is preferable, I think, to avoid this route of pathologization altogether.

Blurring the Gender Identity/Sexual Orientation Distinction

A second consequence of erotic structuralism is the rejection of a central assumption in transgender politics, namely that gender identity is entirely distinct from sexual orientation (e.g., Serano, 2010). For sexual orientation must be reconceptualized to include a core gender-inflected erotic self in addition to a persistent attraction to a type of gendered persons. Insofar as one can speak of gynephilic and androphilic attractions, one can also speak of andro-reflexive and gyne-reflexive

attractions. That is, in addition to distinguishing attractions on the basis of gendered "object choice," one can distinguish them on the basis of gendered erotic self as well. This means that hetero/homo attractions cannot be adequately captured by the replacement terms, "androphilic" and "gynephilic" attractions, since the latter include only gendered object preference.

Insofar as one speaks of a *stable* gynephilic/androphilic attraction, one ought to speak of a *stable* gendered erotic self. David, who only has androphilic attraction, can be said to possess a stable orientation toward men. And it follows, by parity, that Sam, who has only andro-reflexive attractions, likewise possesses a stable erotic male self.[9] Both exemplify two important parts of orientation. David is likewise andro-reflexive, while Sam is, unlike David, gynephilic. And while David eroticizes male-male intimacy, Sam eroticizes male-female intimacy. So while it is true that gendered self-identity and orientation are somewhat distinct, it is also true that orientation has an erotic gendered sense of self as a component.

To be clear, this theory does not reduce transsexual motivation to transition to a sexualized one. Such a view is implausible for many reasons, not least of which is the complete erasure of trans people's own accounts of their experiences and motivations. However, it *is* plausible to believe that gendered self-identity and erotic gendered self tend to correspond to each other. Given that a trans woman has the self-identity of a woman, it is little surprise she also has a core erotic self that is female. The consequence is that gender identity and sexual attraction are far more relevant to each other than one might have supposed, and in ways that are ultimately congenial to transgender politics.

DISCUSSION QUESTIONS

1. What does Bettcher mean by a "gendered eroticization of the self"? Do you experience yourself as erotic? What does that mean for you? What does Bettcher think it means for sexual equality?
2. Why does our traditional way of thinking about sexual attraction fail, according to Bettcher? Do you agree? Why or why not?

3. According to Bettcher, how does the sexual experience of trans people open new ways to think about our own sexual experience? Do you think we should broaden our sexual horizons? Why or why not?

NOTES

1. Thomas Nagel (1979) provides a classic account in which he claims that "self-perception" is involved in sexual desire. This is largely because he takes *ideal* desire to include desiring that "one's partner be aroused by the recognition of one's desire that he or she be aroused." I do not have the space to contrast my account with his. Suffice it to say that his account does not actually concern an eroticized *gendered* sense of self. Moreover, my account concerns "first-order" arousal, rather than the iterative stages of arousal that are necessary in Nagel's idealized account.

2. A related idea can be found in Nagel (1979).

3. Serano (2007) makes a related point (pp. 268–269). One worry is the putative contrast between one's body merely being important to the overall success of a fantasy and one's body actually being a significant source of arousal (Moser, 2009). If the former is the case, then one's body is not really part of the erotic content. If the latter is the case, however, it might seem the body is best viewed as the source of attraction. The argument I provide is designed to address this worry.

4. Thanks to Susan Forrest for this neologism.

5. This does not rule out thinking oneself to be attractive. But that is different from literally experiencing attraction to oneself.

6. This is far more complex in non-mainstream (non-dominant) contexts.

7. While I do not have the space to contrast my account with Gayle Salamon's (2010) illuminating reading of Merleau-Ponty's notion of the "sexual schema" in detail, let me note that in Salamon's view, the experience of self is not included *within* the content of sexual desire. It is simply the embodied experience of *desire itself*. This is because Salamon is principally concerned with the experience of sexual desire as "located" within the body (in a specific body part or spread throughout). In Merleau-Ponty's notion of "sexual transposition," sexual desire replaces and effectively becomes the body itself. In this way, awareness of self is a kind of virtual proprioceptive awareness of body *qua* desiring subject. By contrast, my account concerns the experience of the body as a subject *or object* of intimate sensory access *within the field of attraction*—where attraction is understood as complex, structured erotic content. Rather than experiencing herself as the *desiring subject*, Germaine experiences herself primarily as *sensory subject*. And rather than experiencing herself as the *desiring subject*, Sheena experiences herself primarily as the *sensory object*. What is at stake is not the location of desire itself within a body, but the *content* of desire—namely, intimate contact between self and other (as normatively bounded sensory access). In my view, therefore, the body is not primarily implicated *qua* desiring subject, but as that which is normatively bounded with respect to sensory access. Such boundaries are a precondition of sexual desire and hence prior to it.

8. Moser (2009) finds female embodiment eroticism among non-trans women, undermining Blanchard's view that this is an MtF-specific phenomenon.

9. There are interesting complexities raised by bisexuality. For example, just as a person may possess both gynephilic and androphilic attractions, it seems possible that a person may possess both andro-reflexive and gyne-reflexive attractions. I have not explored this issue here.

REFERENCES

Bettcher, T. M. (2012). Full frontal morality: The naked truth about gender. *Hypatia: A Journal of Feminist Philosophy*, 27(2), 319–337.

Bettcher, T. M. (2013). Trans women and "interpretive intimacy": Some initial reflections. In D. Castañeda (Ed.), *The essential handbook of women's sexuality: Diversity, health, and violence* (Vol. 2, pp. 51–68). Santa Barbara, CA: Praeger.

Blanchard, R. (1985). Typology of male-to-female transsexualism. *Archives of Sexual Behavior*, 14(3), 247–261.

Blanchard, R. (1992). Nonmonotonic relation of autogynephilia and heterosexual attraction. *Journal of Abnormal Psychology*, 101(2), 271–276.

Gagnon, J. H., & Simon, W. (2005 [1973]). *Sexual conduct: The social sources of human sexuality* (2nd ed.). New Brunswick, NJ: Aldine Transaction.

Hale, C. J. (1997). Leatherdyke boys and their daddies: How to have sex without women or men. *Social Text*, 16(3/4), 223–236.

Moser, C. (2009). Autogynephilia in women. *Journal of Homosexuality*, 56, 539–547.

Moser, C. (2010). Blanchard's autogynephilia theory: A critique. *Journal of Homosexuality*, 57, 790–809.

Nagel, T. (1979). Sexual perversion. In T. Nagel (Ed.), *Mortal questions* (pp. 39–52). Cambridge, MA: Cambridge University Press.

Salamon, G. (2010). *Assuming a body: Transgender and rhetorics of materiality*. New York, NY: Columbia University Press.

Serano, J. (2007). *Whipping girl: A transsexual woman on sexism and the scapegoating of femininity*. Emeryville, CA: Seal Press.

Serano, J. (2010). The case against autogynephilia. *International Journal of Transgenderism*, 12(3), 176–187.

Refiguring Lesbian Desire

BY ELIZABETH GROSZ

> Elizabeth Grosz is an Australian philosopher who uses the work of twentieth-century French theorists to focus on feminist issues in gender and sexuality. In this essay, Grosz rejects philosophical accounts that conceptualize desire as a longing for something one lacks as inadequate to explain lesbian desire, which she instead conceptualizes as a sort of fuel capable of creating or uniting things.

> I knew you'd be a good lover when I noticed you always smelt books before you read them—especially hardbacks . . . now make love to me.
>
> —Mary Fallon, *Working Hot*, 86

The Ontology of Lack

My problem is how to conceive of desire, particularly, how to think desire as a "proper" province of women. The most acute way in which this question can be formulated is to ask the question: How to conceive lesbian desire given that lesbian desire is the preeminent and most unambiguous exemplar of *women's* desires, women's desire(s) for other women? In what terms is desire to be understood so that it can be attributed to and conceived of in terms of women? This is not really an idle or perverse question though it may seem so at first sight. I am asking how it is that a notion like desire, which has been almost exclusively understood in male (and commonly heterocentric) terms, can be transformed so that it is capable of accommodating the very category on whose exclusion it has previously been based. Desire has up to now functioned only through the surreptitious exclusion of women (and hence lesbians). How can this concept be dramatically stretched to include as subject what it has previously designated only by the position of object, to make what is considered passivity into an activity?

There are, in my understanding, irresolvable problems associated with the notions of desire we have generally inherited in the West. These problems signal that desire must be thoroughly overhauled if it is to be capable of accommodating women's desires and those desires—whatever they might be—that specify and distinguish lesbianism. These I can indicate only briefly although they clearly warrant a much more thorough investigation.

In the first place, the concept of desire has had an illustrious history beginning with the writings of Plato, especially in *The Symposium*, where Plato explains that desire is a lack in man's being, an imperfection or flaw in human existence. For him, desire is both a shortcoming and a vindication of human endeavor. Desire is considered a yearning for access to the good and the beautiful, which man lacks. It is thus simultaneously the emblem of atrophy and of progress toward the Idea. Born of *penia* (poverty) and *poros* (wealth), of inadequacy and excess together, this Platonic understanding of desire remains the dominant one within our received history of thought, even today. This trajectory for thinking desire reaches a major, modern turning point in Hegel's understanding of desire in *The Phenomenology of Spirit*, where Hegel conceives of desire as a unique lack that, unlike other lacks, can function only if it remains unfilled. It is therefore a lack with a peculiar object all its own—its object is always another desire. The only object desire can desire is an object that will not fill the lack or provide complete satisfaction. To provide desire with its object is to annihilate it. Desire desires to be desired. Thus, for Hegel, the only object that both satisfies desire yet perpetuates, it is not an object but another desire. The desire of the other is thus the only appropriate object of desire.

Freud himself and the psychoanalytic theory following him are the heirs to this tradition of conceiving of desire in negative terms, in terms of an absence, and it is largely through psychoanalytic theory—in which, for example, Lacan reads Freud quite explicitly in terms of Hegel's understanding of desire—that this conception of desire continues to be the dominant one in feminist, lesbian, and gay studies. Freud modifies the Platonic understanding of desire while nonetheless remaining faithful to its terms: the lack constitutive of desire is not an inherent feature of the subject (as Hegel assumed) but is now a function of (social) reality. Desire is the movement of substitution that creates a series of equivalent objects to fill a primordial lack. In seeking to replace an (impossible) plenitude, a lost completion originating (at least in fantasy) in the early mother/child dyad, desire will create a realm of objects that can be substituted for the primal (lost, forbidden) object. Desire's endless chain is an effect of an oedipalizing process that requires that the child relinquishes its incestual attachments through creating an endless network of replacements, substitutes, and representations of the perpetually absent object.

Now this notion of desire as an absence, lack, or hole, an abyss seeking to be engulfed, stuffed to satisfaction, is not only uniquely useful in capitalist models of acquisition, propriety, and ownership (seeing the object of desire on the model of the consumable commodity), but it also inherently sexualizes desire, coding it in terms of the prevailing characteristics attributed to the masculine/feminine opposition, presence and absence. Desire, like female sexuality itself, is insatiable, boundless, relentless, a gaping hole that cannot be filled or can only be temporarily filled; it suffers an inherent dependence on its object(s), a fundamental incompletion without them. I would suggest that the metaphorics of desire on such models[1] are in

fact coded as a sexual polarization. Where desire is given a negative status, it is hardly surprising that it becomes or is coded in terms similar to the ones attributed to femininity. Moreover, it is precisely such a model, where desire lacks, yearns, seeks, without ever being capable of finding itself and its equilibrium, that enables the two sexes to be understood as (biological, sexual, social, and psychical) complements of each other—each is presumed to complete, to fill up, the lack of the other. The model of completion provided here corresponds to or is congruent with the logic regulating the goal posited by Aristophanes's hermaphrodite. Such a model, in other words, performs an act of violence: for any consideration of the autonomy of the two sexes, particularly the autonomy of women is rendered impossible within a model of complementarity. It feminizes, heterosexualizes, and binarizes desire at an ontological and epistemological level. The activity of this model of complementarity is merely a reaction to its perceived shortcomings, its own failure to sustain itself.

If this is the primary model of desire we in the West have inherited over millennia, this problem seems to me to be complicit with a second problem, a problem that can, this time, be more narrowly circumscribed and represented by a single corpus of writing. This second problem I see with the notion of desire as it is commonly understood can be most readily articulated with reference to a psychoanalytic account of desire, which in this context can be used as a shorthand version for—indeed, as a symptom of—a broader cultural and intellectual tradition. In such models—the most notable certainly being Freud's—desire is, as he describes it, inherently masculine. There is only male or rather masculine libido; there is only desire as an activity (activity being, for Freud, correlated with masculinity); in this case, the notion of female desire is oxymoronic.

Freud does get around this complication in a variety of ingenious ways: for him the so-called normal or heterosexual response on the part of woman is to give up the (masculine, phallic, anaclitic) desire to love and to substitute for it the passive aim of being loved and desired. This constitutes women's adult, secondary version of their primary narcissism;[2] by contrast, the woman suffering from the "masculinity complex" retains an active relation to desire at the cost of abandoning any self-representation as feminine or castrated. In exchange for the activity and phallic status she refuses to renounce—and while retaining the structure of virile desire—she abandons femininity. When she loves and desires, she does so not as a woman but as a man.

This understanding of female "inversion" (both literally and metaphorically) permeates the two case studies of female homosexuality Freud undertook—his study of Dora (1905) (which he recognized too late as a study of *homosexual* desire, that is, well after Dora had left him) and the study of the young female homosexual (1920), in which he can only represent the young woman's love relations to "her lady" on the model of the chivalrous male lover. In short, insofar as the woman occupies the feminine position, she can only take the place of the object of desire and never that of the subject of desire; insofar as she takes the position of the subject of desire, the subject who desires, she must renounce any position as feminine.[3] The idea of feminine desire or even female desire is contradictory.

It is now clear, I hope, why there may be a problem using theories like psychoanalysis—as many lesbian theorists have done[4]—to explain the psychic and sexual economies of lesbians even if psychoanalysis could provide an explanation/account of male homosexuality (which seems dubious to me, given Freud's presumption of the primitive, maternally oriented heterosexuality as the "origin" of male desire). In the terms we have most readily available, it seems impossible to think lesbian desire. To think desire is difficult enough: desire has never been thoroughly reconsidered as an intensity, innervation, positivity, or force. Women's desire is inconceivable within models attributing to desire the status of an activity: women function (for men) as objects of desire. To think lesbian desire thus involves surmounting both of these obstacles; while it is possible to experience it, to have/to be it, psychoanalysis, theories of interiority, and, indeed, sociological, literary, and representational accounts—accounts that attempt to explain or assess it—are all required to do so in the very terms and within the very frameworks making this unthinkable. For this reason I would propose a temporary abandonment of the attempt to understand and explain lesbian desire and instead propose the development of very different models by which to experiment with it, that is, to understand desire not in terms of what is missing or absent, not in terms of a depth, latency, or interiority but in terms of surfaces and intensities.

Refiguring Desire

If the dominant or received notions of desire from Plato to Freud and Lacan have construed desire as a lack or negativity, there is a minor or subordinated tradition within Western thought that has seen desire in quite different terms. In contrast to the negative model that dooms desire to consumption, incorporation, dissatisfaction, destruction of the object, there is a tradition—we may for our purposes date it from Spinoza[5]—of seeing desire primarily as production rather than as lack. Here, desire cannot be identified with an object whose attainment provides satisfaction but with processes that produce. In contrast to Freud, for Spinoza reality does not prohibit desire but is produced by it.[6] Desire is the force of positive production, the energy that creates things, makes alliances, and forges interactions between things. Where Hegelian desire attempts to internalize and obliterate its objects, Spinozist desire assembles things, joins, or unjoins them. Thus, on the one hand, desire is a pure absence striving for an impossible completion, fated evermore to play out or repeat its primal or founding loss; on the other hand, we have a notion of desire as a pure positivity, as production, forging connections, making things, as non-fantasmatic, as real. If Freud and psychoanalytic theory can act as representatives of the first and dominant understanding of desire as a lack, then Deleuze and Guattari can be seen to represent the second broad trajectory. And it is to some of their work I now wish to turn, acknowledging that in the space that I have here, I am unable to do justice to the richness and complexity of their works. What follows must therefore be considered as notes pointing toward a further investigation.

Following Nietzsche and Spinoza, Deleuze understands desire as immanent, positive, and productive, as inherently full. Instead of a yearning, desire is seen as an actualization, a series of practices, action, production, bringing together components, making machines, creating reality: "Desire is a relation of effectuation, not of satisfaction," as Colin Gordon put it ("The Subtracting Machine," 32). Desire is primary, not lack. It is not produced as an effect of frustration but is primitive and given; it is not opposed to or postdates reality, but it produces reality. It does not take a particular object for itself whose attainment provides it with satisfaction; rather, it aims at nothing in particular, above and beyond its own self-expansion, its own proliferation. It assembles things out of singularities and breaks down things, assemblages, into their singularities: "If desire produces, its product is real. If desire is productive, it can be so in reality, and of reality" (Deleuze and Guattari, *Anti-Oedipus*, 26).

As production, desire does not provide blueprints, models, ideals, or goals. Rather, it experiments, it makes: it is fundamentally aleatory, inventive. Such a theory cannot but be of interest for feminist theory insofar as women are the traditional repositories of the lack constitutive of desire and insofar as the oppositions between presence and absence, between reality and fantasy, have conventionally constrained women to occupy the place of men's other. Lack only makes sense to the (male) subject insofar as some other (woman) personifies and embodies it for him. Such a model of desire, when explicitly sexualized, reveals the impossibility of understanding lesbian desire. Any model of desire that dispenses with a reliance on lack seems to be a positive step forward and for that reason alone worthy of further investigation.

Lesbian Bodies and Pleasure

The terms by which lesbianism and lesbian desire are commonly understood seem to me problematic: it is no longer adequate to think them in terms of psychology, especially given that the dominant psychological models—psychoanalytic ones—are so inadequate for thinking femininity. So, in attempting to go the other way, I want to be able to provide a reading of lesbianism, or at least of lesbian sexuality and desire; in terms of bodies, pleasures, surfaces, intensities, as suggested by Deleuze and Guattari, Lyotard, and others.

There are a number of features of lesbian theory and of characterizations of lesbian desire that I would consequently like to avoid. In the first place, I wish to avoid the sentimentality and romanticism so commonly involved in thinking lesbian relationships. While I can understand the political need to validate and valorize lesbian relations in a culture openly hostile to lesbianism, I think it is also politically important to remain open to self-criticism and thus to change and growth. Lesbian relationships are no better, nor any worse, than the complexities involved in all sociosexual interrelations. Nor are they in any sense a solution to patriarchal forms of sexuality, because lesbianism and gay male sexuality are, as much as heterosexuality, products of patriarchy. There is no pure sexuality, no inherently transgressive sexual practice, no sexuality beyond or outside the limits of patriarchal models. This is not, however, to say that all forms of human sexuality are equally invested in patriarchal values, for there are clearly many different kinds of subversion and transgression, many types of sexual aberration that cannot be assimilated into historically determinate norms and ideals. It is not only utopian but also naive to take the moral high ground in proclaiming for oneself the right to judge the transgressive or other status of desire and sexuality: the function of moral evaluations of the sexual terrain can only be one of policing and prohibition, which does not deal with and does not explain the very desire for and energy of transgression.

In the second place, I would like to avoid seeing lesbian relations in terms of a binary or polarized model: this means abandoning many of the dominant models of sexual relations between women. In short, I want to avoid seeing lesbian sexual partners either as imaginary, mirror-stage duplicates, narcissistic doubles, self-reflections, bound to each other through mutual identification and self-recognition or in terms of complementarity with the lovers complementing each other's sexual style and role—butch-femme and bottom-top couplings.

In the third place, I would also like to avoid models that privilege genitality over other forms of sexuality. While it is clear that genitality remains a major site of intensity, in a phallic model it is the only true sexuality. I would like to use a model or framework in which sexual relationships are contiguous with and a part of other relationships—those of the writer to pen and paper, of the body-builder to weights; of the bureaucrat to files. The bedroom is no more the privileged site of sexuality than any other space; sexuality and desire are part of the intensity and passion of life itself.

In the fourth place, I want to avoid the kinds of narrow judgmentalism that suggest that any kind of sexuality or desire is better, more political, more radical, more transgressive than another and the kinds of feminist analysis that seek to judge the morality and ethics of the sexual practices of others, adjudicating what is wrong if not what is right.

And fifth, I want to look at lesbian relations and, if possible, at all social relations in terms of bodies, energies, movements, and inscriptions rather than in terms of ideologies, the inculcation of ideas, the transmission of systems of belief or representations, modes of socialization, or social reproduction, flattening depth, reducing it to surface effects.

Sexuality and desire, then, are not fantasies, wishes, hopes, aspirations (although no doubt these are some of their components), but they are energies, excitations, impulses, actions, movements, practices, moments, pulses of feeling. The sites most intensely invested always occur at a conjunction, an interruption, a point of machinic connection; they are always surface effects between one thing and another—between a hand and a breast, a tongue and a cunt, a mouth and food, a nose and a rose. In order to understand this notion, we have to abandon our habitual understanding of entities as the integrated totality of parts, and instead we must focus on the elements, the parts, outside their integration or organization; we must look beyond the organism to the organs comprising it. In looking at the interlocking of two such parts—fingers and velvet, toes and sand—there is not, as psychoanalysis suggests, a predesignated

erotogenic zone, a site always ready and able to function as erotic. Rather, the coming together of two surfaces produces a tracing that imbues both of them with eros or libido, making bits of bodies, its parts, or particular surfaces throb, intensify, for their own sake and not for the benefit of the entity or organism as a whole: In other words, they come to have a life of their own, functioning according to their own rhythms, intensities, pulsations, and movements. Their value is always provisional and temporary, ephemeral and fleeting; they may fire the organism, infiltrate other zones and surfaces with their intensity, but they are unsustainable—they have no memory. They are not a recorded or a recording activity.

These body relations are not (as much of gay male culture presumes) anonymous, quick encounters; rather, each is a relation to a singularity or particularity, always specific, never generalizable. Neither anonymous nor yet entirely personal; each is still an intimacy of encounter, a pleasure/unpleasure of and for itself. Encounters, interfaces between one part and another of bodies or bodies and things, produce the erotogenic surface, inscribe it as a surface, linger on and around it for their evanescent effects: like torture, diet, clothing, and exercise, sexual encounters mark or inscribe the body's surface, and in doing so they produce an intensity that is in no way innate or given. Probably one of the most interesting and undervalued theorists of the erotic and of desire is Alphonso Lingis, whose wonderful texts shimmer with the very intensity he describes:

> The libidinal excitations do not invest a pregiven surface; they extend a libidinal surface. This surface is not the surface of a depth, the contour enclosing an interior. The excitations do not function as signals, as sensations. Their free mobility is horizontal and continually annexes whatever is tangent to the libidinal body. On this surface exterior and interior are continuous; its spatiality that of a Moebius strip. The excitations extend a continuity of convexities and concavities, probing fingers, facial contours, and orifices, swelling thighs and mouths, everywhere glands surfacing, and

what was protuberance and tumescence on the last contact can now be fold, cavity, squeezed breasts, soles of feet forming, still another mouth. Feeling one's way across the outer face of this Moebius strip one finds oneself on the inner face—all surface still and not inwardness. (Lingis, *Libido*, 76)

To relate through someone to something else, or to relate through something to someone: not to relate to some one and only one, without mediation. To use the machinic connections a body part forms with another, whether it be organic or inorganic, to form an intensity, an investment of libido, is to see desire and sexuality as productive. Productive, though in no way reproductive, for this pleasure can serve no other purpose, can have no other function than its own augmentation, its own proliferation: a production, then, that makes but reproduces nothing—a truly nomad desire unfettered by anything external, for anything can form part of its circuit and be absorbed into its operations.

If we are looking at intensities and surfaces rather than latencies and depths, then it is not the relation between an impulse and its absent other—its fantasies, wishes, hoped-for objects—that interests us; rather, it is the spread or distribution, the quantity and quality of intensities relative to each other, their patterns, their contiguities that are most significant. It is their effects rather than any intentions that occupy our focus, what they make and do rather than what they mean or represent. They transform themselves, undergo metamorphoses, become something else, never retain an identity or purpose. Others, human subjects, women, are not simply the privileged objects of desire: through women's bodies to relate to other things to make connections.

While I cannot give a "real life illustration," I can at least refer to one of Australia's few postmodern lesbian writers, Mary Fallon:

Stroking my whole body all night long until your fingers became fine sprays of white flowers until they became fine silver wires

electrifying my epidermis until they became delicate instruments of torture and the night wore on for too many hours and I loved you irritably as dawn reprieved us we are two live-wire women wound and sprung together we are neither of us afraid of the metamorphoses transmogrifications the meltings the juices squelching in the body out of the body—a split fruit of a woman we are neither of us is afraid to sink our teeth into the peach it's not love or sex it's just that we are collaborating every night on a book called The Pleasures of the Flesh Made Simple. (Fallon, *Working Hot*, 87)

One "thing" transmutes into another, becomes something else through its connections with something or someone outside. Fingers becoming flowers, becoming silver, becoming torture instruments. This is precisely what the Deleuzian notion of "becoming" entails: entry into an arrangement, an assemblage of other fragments, other things, becoming bound up in some other production, forming part of a machine, becoming a component in a series of flows and breaks, of varying speeds and intensities. To "become animal" (or, more contentiously, to "become woman") does not involve imitating, reproducing, or tracing the animal (woman) and becoming like it. Rather, it involves entering into relation with a third term and with it to form a machine that enters into relations with a machine composed of "animal" components.[7] Becomings then are not a broad general trajectory of development but always concrete and specific, becoming something, something momentary, provisional, something inherently unstable and changing. It is not a question of being (animal, woman, lesbian), of attaining a definite status as a thing, a permanent fixture, nor of clinging to, having an identity, but of moving, changing, being swept beyond one singular position into a multiplicity of flows or into what Deleuze and Guattari have described as "a thousand tiny sexes": to liberate the myriad of flows, to proliferate connections, to intensify.

Becoming lesbian, if I can put it this way, is thus no longer or not simply a question of being lesbian, of identifying with that being known as a lesbian, of residing in a position or identity. The question is not am I—or are you—a lesbian but, rather, what kinds of lesbian connections, what kinds of lesbian-machine, we invest our time, energy, and bodies in, what kinds of sexuality we invest ourselves in, with what other kinds of bodies, with what bodies of our own, and with what effects? What it is that together, in parts and bits and interconnections, we can make that is new, that is exploratory, that opens up further spaces, induces further intensities, speeds up, enervates, and proliferates production (production of the body, production of the world)?

While what I am putting forth here is a positive view, it is not, in my opinion, a utopian one: it is not a prophecy of the future, a vision of things to come, an ideal or goal to aspire to. It is a way of looking at things and doing things with concepts and ideas in the same ways we do them with bodies and pleasures, a way of leveling, of flattening the hierarchical relations between ideas and things, qualities and entities, of eliminating the privilege of the human over the animal, the organic over the inorganic, the male over the female, the straight over the "bent"—of making them level and interactive, rendering them productive and innovative, experimental and provocative. That is the most we can hope for from knowledge. Or desire.

DISCUSSION QUESTIONS

1. Describe the traditional understanding of desire in negative terms, as found in the work of Plato, Hegel, and Freud. Explain how this negative understanding of desire enables a model of the sexes as complementary, then explain how this model of complementarity can be problematic for feminist purposes.

2. Describe the contrasting understanding of desire in positive terms, as found in the work of Spinoza, Nietzsche, Deleuze, and Guattari. Explain why this positive understanding of desire offers a more promising alternative for understanding lesbian desire.

3. Explain what it means to understand desire and sexuality as productive, rather than reproductive. What sorts of things can be produced?

NOTES

1. Such models are of course not the only ones spawned by Western thought; alternative models, which see desire as a positivity, a production or making, while considerably rarer in our received history, nonetheless still develop and have exerted their influence in the writings of, among others, Spinoza, Nietzsche, Deleuze, and Lyotard, as I will discuss in more detail below.

2. I have tried to elaborate in considerable detail the differences between masculine, anaclitic forms of love/desire and feminine/narcissistic forms in *Jacques Lacan: A Feminist Introduction*, ch. 5.

3. This idea has been effectively explored in Jacqueline Rose's penetrating analysis of Freud's treatment of Dora (1985).

4. See the works of Butler, De Lauretis, and Fuss.

5. I am grateful to Moira Gatens for her research on Spinoza, which has been invaluable to me in this paper and in reconceiving corporeality. See Gatens, *Feminism and Philosophy*.

6. The mind endeavours to persist in its being for an indefinite period, ... This endeavour ... when referred to the mind and the body in conjunction ... is called *appetite*; it is, in fact, nothing else but man's essence, from the nature of which necessarily follow all those results which tend to its preservation. ... Further, between appetite and desire, there is no difference ... we deem a thing to be good, because we strive for it, wish for it, long for it or desire it. (Spinoza, *The Ethics*, 3:ix).

7. "The actor Robert De Niro walks 'like' a crab in a certain sequence: but, he says, it is not a question of his imitating a crab; it is a question of making something that has to do with the crab enter into composition with the image, with the speed of the image" (Deleuze and Guattari, *A Thousand Plateaus*, 274).

REFERENCES

Braidotti, Rosi. *Patterns of Dissonance: A Study of Women in Contemporary Philosophy*. Translated by Elizabeth Guild. Cambridge: Polity Press, 1991.

Butler, Judith. *Gender Trouble: Feminism and the Subversion of Identity*. New York and London: Routledge, 1990.

Butler, Judith. "Imitation and Gender Insubordination." In Diana Fuss, ed., *Inside/Out: Lesbian Theories, Gay Theories*, pp. 13–31. New York and London: Routledge, 1991.

Creet, Julia. "Daughter of the Movement: The Psychodynamics of Lesbian S/M Fantasy." *differences* 5(2) (1991): 135–159.

de Lauretis, Teresa. "The Female Body and Heterosexual Presumption." *Semiotica* 67(3–4) (1987).

de Lauretis, Teresa. "Sexual Indifference and Lesbian Representation," *Theatre Journal* 40(2) (1988).

Deleuze, Gilles. *Masochism: Coldness and Cruelty.* Translated by Jean McNeil. New York: Zone Books, 1989.

Deleuze, Gilles, and Felix Guattari. *Anti-Oedipus: Capitalism and Schizophrenia.* Vol. 1. Translated by Mark Seem. Minneapolis: University of Minnesota Press, 1977.

Deleuze, Gilles, and Felix Guattari. *A Thousand Plateaus: Capitalism and Schizophrenia.* Vol. 2. Translated by Brian Massumi. Minneapolis: University of Minnesota Press, 1987.

Fallon, Mary. *Working Hot.* Melbourne: Sybella Press, 1989.

Freud, Sigmund. "Fragment of an Analysis of a Case of Hysteria." In *The Standard Edition of the Complete Psychological Works of Sigmund Freud.* Translated and edited by James Strachey. Vol. 7 (1905), pp. 1–122. London: Hogarth Press, 1953–1974.

Freud, Sigmund. "The Psychogenesis of a Case of Homosexuality in a Woman." In *The Standard Edition of the Complete Psychological Works of Sigmund Freud.* Translated and edited by James Strachey. Vol. 18 (1920), pp. 145–172, London: Hogarth Press, 1953–1974.

Frye, Marilyn. *The Politics of Reality: Essays in Feminist Theory.* Trumansburgh, N.Y.: Crossings Press, 1984.

Fuss, Diana. *Essentially Speaking: Feminism, Nature, and Difference.* New York and London: Routledge, 1989.

Fuss, Diana, ed. *Inside/Out: Lesbian Theories, Gay Theories.* New York and London: Routledge, 1991.

Gatens, Moira. *Feminism and Philosophy: Perspectives in Equality and Difference.* Cambridge: Polity Press, 1991.

Gordon, Colin. "The Subtracting Machine." *I & C* 8 (1981).

Grosz, Elizabeth. *Sexual Subversions: Three French Feminists.* Sydney: Alien and Unwin, 1989.

Grosz, Elizabeth. *Jacques Lacan: A Feminist Introduction.* New York and London: Routledge, 1990.

Grosz, Elizabeth. "Lesbian Fetishism?" *differences* 5(2) (1991): 39–54.

Grosz, Elizabeth. (Forthcoming) "A Thousand Tiny Sexes: Feminism and Rhizomatics." In Constantin Boundas and Dorothea Olkowski, eds., *Gilles Deleuze: The Theater of Philosophy.*

Irigaray, Luce. *This Sex Which Is Not One.* Translated by Catherine Porter. Ithaca: Cornell University Press, 1985.

King, Katie. "Producing Sex, Theory, and Culture: Gay/Straight Remappings in Contemporary Feminism." In Marianne Hirsch and Evelyn Fox Keller, eds., *Conflicts in Feminism*, pp. 82–101. New York and London: Routledge, 1990.

Lingis, Alphonso. *Libido: The French Existential Theories.* Bloomington: Indiana University Press, 1985.

Rose, Jacqueline. "Dora: Fragment of an Analysis." In Charles Bertheimer and Claire Kahane, eds., *Dora's Case; Freud—Hysteria—Feminism*, pp. 128–147. New York: Columbia University Press, 1985.

Whitford, Margaret. *Luce Irigaray: Philosophy in the Feminine.* London and New York: Routledge, 1991.

The Meaning of Consent

BY VERA BERGELSON

> Vera Bergelson is a Russian legal scholar who has written about consent, provo-
> cation, self-defense, necessity, victimless crime, and human trafficking. In this
> essay, she surveys the legal/philosophical literature on "the moral magic of con-
> sent" and proposes adding a new rule that treats consent differently depending
> on whether the perpetrator is prima facie wrong in acting.

In view of these complicated and often politically charged discussions, it has become particularly important to clarify and define the basic terms. Specifically: What is *consent*? What does it mean to say that Jill consented to having sex with Jack? As we know, criminal law is largely driven by the goal of protecting people's autonomy. The state justifies employing the harshest and most intrusive powers against an individual by the overarching need to enforce the rights and obligations of all members of society. Consent involves changing the balance of those rights and corresponding obligations.[1] By consenting to having sex with Jack, Jill temporarily waives her right to physical inviolability. She relieves Jack of his obligation not to cross the boundaries of her sexual autonomy, and in most instances, simultaneously relieves the state of its obligation to protect her from Jack's boundary-crossing conduct. Moreover, by consenting to having sex with Jack, Jill not only *relieves* the state of its obligation to protect Jill—Jill *demands* that the state not intervene (e.g., by punishing Jack) in this consensual transaction because such intervention would violate both Jack's and Jill's autonomy.[2]

In short, consent is a crucial, game changing mechanism in a relationship between individuals as well as between an individual and the state. So, what exactly has to happen between Jack and Jill in order to make their intercourse consensual? Is it Jill's internal state of mind or her external expression of acquiescence that magically changes the moral and legal character of Jack's actions? Naturally, if it is the latter, we will need to determine what actions by Jill (passive non-resistance; non-verbal cooperation; or verbal approval) should suffice for granting Jack a valid license. However, before we reach that point, we have a more fundamental question to resolve: Should normative consent be based on the internal or external reality?

Those who believe in the former argue that consent means one's subjective state of mind, "attitudinal" consent. Heidi Hurd, for example, maintains that to consent is to intend another's act of crossing what otherwise would be a moral boundary.[3] Larry Alexander is somewhat less restrictive: for him, to consent to certain conduct is not to *intend* it but rather to *waive an objection* to it.[4] I tend to agree with the latter interpretation but, irrespective of this difference, both Hurd and Alexander focus on one's internal attitude towards the action of another. If Jill tacitly welcomes Jack's sexual advances, Jack is not guilty of committing sexual assault. He is not guilty of sexual assault regardless of Jill's external conduct.

This theory of consent is exemplified in *People v. Bink.*[5] In that case, a young prison inmate complained to a correction officer that another inmate, Bink, had implicitly threatened him and forced him to perform certain sexual acts on Bink.[6] The new encounter was to take place the following morning. The complainant declined offers of physical protection but instead requested that the correction officers watch him closely the next day.[7] As the complainant later testified, "he wanted [the] defendant and himself to be caught 'in the act.'"[8] Bink was convicted of forcible sodomy but his conviction was reversed on appeal. The appellate court did not deny that initially the complainant could have been acting under intimidation; however, during the observed encounter the complainant was driven by the desire to capture the defendant, and in that sense he "wanted to be assaulted,"[9] and thus lacked the required attitudinal non-consent.

Another way to look at consent is called performative or expressive or communicative. For scholars like Nathan Brett or Stephen Schulhofer, normative consent implies explicit permission by words or conduct to another's act.[10] In the stronger form of this viewpoint, explicit permission is a sufficient condition of (otherwise valid) consent. Internal thoughts and desires of the consent-giver are irrelevant. In a weaker, hybrid form, explicit permission is at least necessary for valid consent, albeit the subjective mental acquiescence of the consent-giver is also required.[11]

A classic example of the performative theory of consent is *People v. Burnham*.[12] In that case, a severely beaten woman agreed, under the threat of further beating by her husband, to engage in sexual intercourse with strangers.[13] Fearing her husband, she feigned willingness and desire.[14] The husband was prosecuted and convicted of spousal rape but no charges were filed against the victim's sex partners because they had no knowledge of the threats, and—for them—her expression of consent defeated the required element of non-consent.[15]

So, which theory of consent reflects our moral sense more accurately? To test them further, let me suggest a few hypotheticals:

1. Polly is secretly in love with Mick and would like to have sex with him. At a party at Mick's home, she sneaks into his bedroom, and pretends to be completely drunken and asleep. Mick finds Polly in his bed and has sex with her under the mistaken impression that she is not aware of his actions. In the end, both are quite happy. Did Mick commit sexual assault?

2. Polly is in love with Mick. At a party, she pulls him into a bedroom and suggests that she perform a certain sexual act on him. Mick finds the idea repulsive and (in his mind) strongly objects to it; however, he is afraid of losing Polly's companionship, so he pretends to welcome Polly's advances and goes along with her wishes. Did Polly commit sexual assault?

3. Polly hates her long nose. She would love to have a nose job but she is too proud to openly admit that. In fact, she has a secret wish that her fiancé Mick (who is a plastic surgeon) singlehandedly put her under anesthesia and fix her nose. Mick also hates Polly's nose but he is not aware of Polly's inner thoughts. Nevertheless, one day he puts Polly under anesthesia and performs a surgery on her. Outraged by his conduct, his nurse reports him to the authorities. Is Mick guilty of battery?

4. Polly's dentist insists that she have her wisdom teeth removed. Polly disagrees with the dentist believing (quite correctly) that there is no need for the surgery. However, being an obedient young woman, she does not express her objections, and the dentist removes her wisdom teeth. Is the dentist guilty of battery?

These examples are meant to demonstrate the gap between one's internal feelings (welcoming an act by another or at least waiving moral objections to that act) and one's expressive conduct (by words or actions). Clearly the two do not always go hand in hand.

- In the first example, Polly may be said to have granted Mick attitudinal but not performative consent to sex.
- In the second case, conversely, Mick gave Polly performative consent to sex but (arguably) not attitudinal.
- In the third example, Polly may have granted Mick attitudinal consent to surgery but not performative.

– And finally, in the fourth, Polly may have granted her dentist performative but not attitudinal consent to the oral surgery.

What consent (attitudinal or performative) should lie in the foundation of a legal rule that defines the boundaries of permissive conduct?

Advocates of the attitudinal approach usually argue that criminal law should rely on the subjective acquiescence of the parties.[16] After all, it is their subjective attitudes that make the whole difference between right and wrong. How can we say that Jack raped Jill when Jill tacitly welcomed their intimacy? These advocates would argue that expression of one's acquiescence is neither sufficient nor necessary for valid consent. For instance, if Jill expressed her willingness to have sex with Jack merely because she felt threatened by him, her consent would be invalid. Thus, expressing consent is not sufficient for making it valid. Similarly, expressing consent is not necessary. Consent, they argue, is like a belief—and a belief may be present or absent regardless of its expression.[17] Accordingly, Jack is not guilty of rape regardless of what Jill did—enthusiastically welcomed Jack's advances, passively accepted them, or even desperately fought—as long as she mentally, at a minimum, did not object, freely and voluntarily, to Jack's actions.

The opponents of the attitudivists, the adherents of the performative theory of consent, disagree. In their view, consent is an act, not a belief. It is like "I do" in the exchange of marital vows. For them, consent does not describe the state of events but rather *creates* a new normative reality. Like a promise, it is an illocutionary act that changes the moral meaning of the applicable conduct only by communication. It would be ridiculous to say that Polly agreed to have her nose fixed by Mick by simply having positive thoughts about that surgery. In the same way, it is ridiculous to think that Polly consented to sex with Mick without communicating her acquiescence. As Alan Wertheimer phrased it:

[T]here is no moral magic to consent that has to be explained. B's consent is morally transformative because it changes A's reasons for

action. If we ask what could change A's reasons for action, the answer must be that B performs some token of consent. It is hard to see how B's mental state—by itself—can do the job.[18]

It appears, therefore, that the dividing line between the attitudivists and performativists lies in the reasons *why* each group considers consent important. The attitudivists focus on the victim. If the rational and responsible putative victim, B, mentally gave his free and voluntary approval (even without expressing it) to A's act, then B was not wronged. B was not wronged, even if he was objectively harmed, i.e. his interests were set back (say, upon B's request, A destroyed B's valuable stamp collection). And if the putative victim was not wronged, no crime was committed, and the state may not punish the perpetrator for it.[19]

In contrast, the performativists focus not on the victim but on the perpetrator and his relationship with the state/society. For them, consent is relevant mainly because it changes the perpetrator's reasons for action; i.e. for them, the essence of the crime is not the violation of rights of an individual victim but rather the perpetrator's moral and political transgression. Regardless of the victim's idiosyncratic choices, *we, all of us*, are harmed when the perpetrator acts for a wrong reason. The fact that Jill happened to welcome intimacy with Jack is just a matter of luck and should not change Jack's culpability. He was not aware of Jill's inner thoughts and acted, at a minimum, with reckless disregard for Jill's consent. He is, therefore, subjectively culpable (wrong) and is as dangerous and deserving of punishment as any other perpetrator who was not so atypically lucky with respect to his victim's feelings.

Both models capture some of our important moral intuitions and yet both are flawed. Their flaw, in my view, lies in their absolutist approach to the role of consent in drastically different circumstances. The supporters of both the attitudinal and the performative theories aspire to explain very different moral realities with one overarching model. In contrast, I suggest that we should not be selecting one theory over the other to cover all cases, but instead we should establish a rule that would assign the attitudinal model to one group of cases and the expressive model to the other. Let's look again at the possible combinations of the attitudinal and expressive consent.

Attitudinal Consent	Expressive Consent
present	present
present	absent
absent	present
absent	absent

The present/present (the victim consented) and the absent/absent (the victim did not consent) scenarios pose little problem, so we should be concerned only about the present/absent and the absent/present paradigms. I suggest that different models of consent should be used depending on whether the role of consent in a particular case is inculpatory or exculpatory.

It is inculpatory if non-consent is an element of an offense; it is exculpatory if consent is a defense.

In the first instance, the perpetrator's act is prima facie morally neutral; it becomes criminal due to the attending circumstances (non-consent). Theft, rape, trespass, and kidnapping provide examples of the inculpatory non-consent. Absent the victim's non-consent, there is nothing wrongful or regrettable in the act of taking the property of another or having sex or visiting someone's home. Therefore, from the policy perspective, there is no need to inquire into the actor's motives. From the legal perspective too, the actor's motives for acting in this non-wrongful and non-regrettable fashion are largely irrelevant: the actor may not be convicted of a completed crime in the absence of a required element of the offense (non-consent).[20] If I had sent my neighbor an invitation for a tea party but the neighbor forgot to open it yet decided to crash my tea party in order to embarrass me, he would still not be guilty of trespass regardless of his lapse of memory and judgment.

In contrast, when consent plays an exculpatory role, the perpetrator's act is prima facie wrongful (there would be no need for exculpation if it were not). Homicide, maiming, and battery are examples of such conduct. Causing death, injury or pain is prima facie bad and should be avoided. A prima facie bad act may of course lose its wrongful character due to the defense of justification.[21] For example, the perpetrator may not be blamed or punished for killing a deadly aggressor if the killing was necessary in order to protect the perpetrator's life or the lives of other innocent people. To be entitled to that defense, the perpetrator (at a minimum) would have to show:

(1) the basis for the defense (the deadly attack by an unprovoked aggressor),
(2) a positive balance of harms and evils (innocent lives were saved at the cost of the aggressor's life), and
(3) the perpetrator's subjective awareness of the justifying circumstances (the deadly attack and the need to use deadly force in order save innocent lives).

If conditions (1) or (2) were not satisfied due to the perpetrator's mistake (including a reasonable mistake), the perpetrator should not be entitled to justification, even though he may be entitled to an excuse. If condition (3) was not satisfied (i.e. the defendant was not aware of the aggressor's impending attack and attacked him out of sheer hatred), the defendant would not be entitled to any defense whatsoever.[22]

Why do we have this discrepancy between the knowledge required to defeat a prima facie case (none; the case of my party-crashing neighbor) and to plead successfully a defense (self-defense)? Mainly because we view a defense of justification as a limited license to commit an otherwise prohibited act in order to achieve a socially and morally desirable outcome. Justification is invoked when a prima facie wrongful act has been committed and the actor seeks to explain it. No surprise, the defense requires "clean hands" and must be deserved whereas a morally neutral act may be done for any reason.[23]

Applying the same justificatory logic to the defense of consent, we should only grant complete justification to the perpetrator who, in addition to having the true attitudinal consent of the victim (the basis for the defense), also achieved a better balance of harms and evils, and was aware of the victim's consent and motivated by the desire to achieve a better result.

In practical terms, that means that the objective presence of consent (attitudinal consent) precludes even a prima facie case of rape or theft, regardless of whether the consensual act brings about more good than harm and regardless of whether the defendant is aware of the victim's consent. However, full knowledge of the justifying circumstances (victim's consent) should be required for a successful defense to the charge of homicide or battery.[24] And full knowledge is impossible without the victim's expressive consent. So, Mick in the first sex hypothetical is not guilty of sexual assault (but is most likely guilty of attempted sexual assault). But Mick the plastic surgeon in the first medical scenario is guilty of battery.

What about those cases in which there is no attitudinal consent; however, the expressive consent is present, or at least the perpetrator is reasonably mistaken about the presence of consent? Take, for instance, Mick and Polly in hypotheticals 2 and 4. In hypothetical number 2, Mick gives Polly expressive consent authorizing her to perform a certain sexual act on him although deep inside he strongly objects to that. In hypothetical number 4, Polly externally goes along with her dentist's decision to remove her wisdom teeth although deep inside she disagrees. In both hypotheticals, the objective, attitudinal, consent is lacking, therefore, the perpetrators are not entitled to justification. But is their conduct criminal? Certainly not. Neither the proactive Polly who initiates sex in hypothetical number 2, nor the wisdom-teeth-hating dentist in hypothetical number 4 is guilty of any wrongdoing. Their mistakes were innocent; each of them acted with the prudence of a reasonable person. We may not ask more of an average citizen.

At the same time, we cannot say that the victims (Mick in hypothetical number 2 and Polly in hypothetical number 4) were not wronged—objectionable physical intrusion is certainly a wrong. What we can say, however, is that the perpetrators were not culpable: through no fault of theirs, they lacked the accurate understanding of the situation. They should be entitled to the complete defense of excuse.

Conclusion

The proposed rule has the advantage of recognizing that consent should be treated differently depending on whether the act of the perpetrator is prima facie wrong or not. The different models of consent are required by the doctrine of criminal harm. Traditionally, criminal harm is defined through wrongful violation of rights. This definition is sometimes interpreted rather simplistically—by looking only at the victim and the victim's rights and interpreting the "wrongful" component as "unauthorized" or "unwarranted." Naturally, such interpretation makes criminalization of consensual killing or hurting problematic: being a waiver of rights, consent defeats any rights violation. However, if we focus not only on the victim but also on the actor, not only on the result but also on the act itself, we will see that criminal law has a strong deontological component. Committing a prima facie wrongful act requires an explanation, and the explanation brings in the perpetrator's reason for acting in a harmful way. Thus, wrongfulness of an act is not reducible to a breach of the victim's rights; it also includes a poor reason for action. And when consent defeats the former element of wrongfulness, there still may remain the latter.

Therefore, when the act is prima facie morally neutral, we do not need to question the actor's reasons for action, and attitudinal consent is enough to defeat criminal harm. However, when the act is prima facie wrong (as in cases of intentional infliction of physical harm), and it requires an explanation (defense), the actor's reasons for action become crucial. To invoke the defense of consent, the perpetrator needs to be aware of the victim's consent. And the only way the perpetrator may be aware of consent is if the victim has expressed it; i.e., for a successful defense of consent, consent must be performative.

DISCUSSION QUESTIONS

1. Explain Bergelson's new rule for consent. How does it work? Do you think it is helpful?

2. Detail Bergelson's analysis of the concept of consent. What are the four or five key elements of her analysis?

3. How does power change consent, according to Bergelson? What do you think? Use a contemporary example or two to illustrate your view.

NOTES

1. Judith Jarvis Thomson, The Realm of Rights 322–374 (1990).
2. Markus Dirk Dubber, *Toward a Constitutional Law of Crime and Punishment*, 55 Hastings L. J. 509, 569 (2004). In the presence of consent, invoking the criminal law is inappropriate not only because the conduct is harmless in the relevant sense—so that punishing the "offender" would violate his autonomy without vindicating the autonomy of the "victim"—but also because doing so would violate the autonomy of the "victim." The *victim*, in other words, has a *right to consent*. *Id.* (citation omitted).
3. Hurd, *supra* note 1, at 124.
4. Alexander, *supra* note 4, at 166. "One consents to an act when, acting with the capacity necessary for autonomous, responsible agency, one chooses to forego valid rights-based moral objections to the act." *Id.* at 172.
5. 84 A.D.2d 607 (N.Y. App. Div. 1981).
6. *See id.*
7. *Id.* at 608.
8. *Id.*
9. Kimberly Kessler Ferzan, *Clarifying Consent: Peter Westen's "The Logic of Consent,"* 25 Law & Phil. 193, 214 (2006).
10. Nathan Brett, *Sexual Offenses and Consent*, 11 Can. J. L. & Juris. 69, 69 (1998); Stephen J. Schulhofer, *Rape in the Twilight Zone: When Sex is Unwanted But Not Illegal*, 38 Suffolk U. L. Rev. 415, 422 (2005)

11. Hurd, *supra* note 1, at 135.
12. 176 Cal. App. 3d 1134 (Ct. App. 1986).
13. *See id.* at 1142; Wertheimer, *supra* note 5, at 149.
14. *See Burnham*, 176 Cal. App. 3d at 1143; Wertheimer, *supra*, note 5, at 149.
15. Both cases, *People v. Bink* and *People v. Burnham*, were aptly discussed in Westen, *supra* note 5, at 139–140.
16. Alexander, *supra* note 4; Hurd, *supra* note 1.
17. Brett, *supra* note 15, at 80–88 (1998); Wertheimer, *supra* note 5, at 144–162.
18. Wertheimer, *supra* note 5, at 146.
19. Whether the crime was attempted and whether the state may have reasons to punish inchoate crimes is a separate question.
20. For an excellent discussion of the difference between a definition and a defense, see George P. Fletcher, *The Right Deed for the Wrong Reason: A Reply to Mr. Robinson*, 23 UCLA L. Rev. 293, 308–321 (1975).
21. *See also* Vera Bergelson, *The Right to Be Hurt: Testing the Boundaries of Consent*, 75 Geo. Wash. L. Rev. 165, 203 (2007).
22. *See also* Vera Bergelson, *Consent to Harm, in* The Ethics of Consent: Theory and Practice, *supra* note 5, at 173–174.
23. George Fletcher raises similar points in his groundbreaking work, *Rethinking Criminal Law*. *See* George P. Fletcher, Rethinking Criminal Law 705 (1986).
24. I am not suggesting that consent of the victim is all that should be required for the successful defense. My point is that consent of the victim should be a necessary condition of such a defense.

The Harms of Consensual Sex

BY ROBIN WEST

Robin West is an American legal scholar best known for her work on the ethics of care and feminist legal theory. In this essay, West offers a critique of the tendency of some feminists to focus on consent in the law, arguing that even when consensual heterosexual encounters can frequently be harmful to women.

Are consensual, non-coercive, non-criminal, and even non-tortious, heterosexual transactions ever harmful to women? I want to argue briefly that many (not all) consensual sexual transactions are, and that accordingly we should open a dialogue about what those harms might be. Then I want to suggest some reasons those harms may be difficult to discern, even by the women sustaining them, and lastly two ways in which the logic of feminist legal theory and practice itself might undermine their recognition.

Let me assume what many women who are or have been heterosexually active surely know to be true from their own experience, and that is that some women occasionally, and many women quite frequently, consent to sex even when they do not desire the sex itself, and accordingly have a good deal of sex that, although consensual, is in no way pleasurable. Why might a woman consent to sex she does not desire? There are, of course, many reasons. A woman might consent to sex she does not want because she or her children are dependent upon her male partner for economic sustenance, and she must accordingly remain in his good graces. A woman might consent to sex she does not want because she rightly fears that if she does not her partner will be put into a foul humor, and she simply decides that tolerating the undesired sex is less burdensome than tolerating the foul humor. A woman might consent to sex she does not want because she has been taught and has come to believe that it is her lot in life to do so, and that she has no reasonable expectation of attaining her own pleasure through sex. A woman might consent to sex she does not want because she rightly fears that her refusal to do so will lead to an outburst of violent behavior some time following—only if the violence or overt threat of violence is *very* close to the sexual act will this arguably constitute a rape. A woman may consent to sex she does not desire because she *does* desire a friendly man's protection against the very real threat of non-consensual violent rape by other more dangerous men, and she correctly perceives, or intuits, that to gain the friendly man's protection, she needs to give him in exchange for that protection, the means to his own sexual pleasure. A woman, particularly a young woman or teenager, may consent to sex she does not want because of peer expectations that she be sexually active, or because she cannot bring herself to hurt her partner's pride, or because she is uncomfortable with the prospect of the argument that might ensue, should she refuse.

These transactions may well be rational—indeed in some sense they all are. The women involved all trade sex for something they value more than they value what they have given up. But that doesn't mean that they are not harmed. Women who engage in unpleasurable, undesired, but consensual sex may sustain real injuries to their sense of selfhood, in at least four distinct ways. First, they may sustain injuries to their capacities for self-assertion: the "psychic connection," so to speak, between pleasure, desire, motivation, and action is weakened or severed. *Acting* on the basis of our own felt pleasures and pains is an important component of forging our own way in the world—of "asserting" our "selves." Consenting to *un*pleasurable sex—acting in spite of displeasure—threatens that means of self-assertion. Second, women who consent to undesired sex may injure their sense of self-*possession*. When we consent to undesired penetration of our physical bodies we have in a quite literal way constituted ourselves as what I have elsewhere called "giving selves"—selves who cannot be violated, because they have been defined as (and define themselves as) being "for others." Our bodies to that extent no longer belong to ourselves. Third, when women consent to undesired and unpleasurable sex because of their felt or actual dependency upon a partner's affection or economic status, they injure their sense of autonomy; they have thereby neglected to take whatever steps would be requisite to achieving the self-sustenance necessary to their independence. And fourth, to the extent that these unpleasurable and undesired sexual acts are followed by contrary to fact claims that they enjoyed the whole thing—what might be called "hedonic lies"—women who engage in them do considerable damage to their sense of integrity.

These harms—particularly if multiplied over years or indeed over an entire adulthood—may be quite profound, and they certainly may be serious enough to outweigh the momentary or day-to-day benefits garnered by each individual transaction. Most debilitating, though, is their circular, self-reinforcing character: the more thorough the harm—the deeper the injury to self-assertiveness, self-possession, autonomy and integrity—the greater the likelihood that the woman involved will indeed *not* experience these harms as harmful, or as painful. A woman utterly lacking in self-assertiveness, self-possession, a sense of autonomy, or integrity will not experience the activities in which she engages that reinforce or constitute those qualities *as harmful*, because she, to that degree, lacks a self-asserting, self-possessed self who *could* experience those activities as a threat to her selfhood. But the fact that she does not experience these activities as harms certainly does

not mean that they are not harmful. Indeed, that they are not felt as harmful is a consequence of the harm they have already caused. This phenomenon, of course, renders the "rationality" of these transactions tremendously and even tragically misleading. Although these women may be making those calculations in the context of the particular decision facing them, they are by making those calculations, sustaining deeper and to some degree unfelt harms that undermine the very qualities that constitute the capacity for rationality being exercised.

Let me quickly suggest some reasons that these harms go so frequently unnoticed—or are simply not taken seriously—and then suggest in slightly more detail some ways that feminist legal theory and practice may have undermined their recognition. The first reason is cultural. There is a deep-seated U.S. cultural tendency to equate the legal with the good, or harmless: we are, for better or worse an anti-moralistic, anti-authoritarian, and anti-communitarian people. When combined with the sexual revolution of the 1960s, this provides a powerful cultural explanation for our tendency to shy away from a sustained critique of the harms of consensual sex. Any suggestion that legal transactions to which individuals freely consent may be harmful, and hence *bad*, will invariably be met with skepticism—*particularly* where those transactions are sexual in nature. This tendency is even further underscored by more contemporary postmodern skeptical responses to claims asserting the pernicious consequences of false consciousness.

Second, at least our legal-academic discourses, and no doubt academic political discourses as well, have been deeply transformed by the "exchange theory of value," according to which, if I exchange A for B voluntarily, then I simply must be better off after the exchange than before, having, after all, agreed to it. If these exchanges *are* the source of value, then it is of course impossible to ground a *value* judgment that some voluntary exchanges are harmful. Although stated baldly this theory of value surely has more critics than believers, it nevertheless in some way perfectly captures the modem zeitgeist. It is certainly, for example, the starting and ending point of nonnative analysis for many, and perhaps most, law students. Obviously, given an exchange theory of value, the harms caused by consensual sexual transactions simply fade away into definitional oblivion.

Third, the exchange theory of value is underscored, rather than significantly challenged, by the continuing significance of liberal theory and ideology in academic life. To the degree that liberalism still rules the day, we continue to valorize individual choice against virtually anything with which it might seem to be in conflict from communitarian dialogue to political critique, and continue to perceive these challenges to individual primacy as somehow on a par with threats posed by totalitarian statist regimes.

Fourth and perhaps most obvious, the considerable harms women sustain from consensual but undesired sex must be downplayed if the considerable pleasure men reap from heterosexual transactions is morally justified—*whatever* the relevant moral theory. Men do have a psycho-sexual stake in insisting that voluntariness alone ought be sufficient to ward off serious moral or political inquiry into the value of consensual sexual transactions.

Let me comment in a bit more detail on a further reason why these harms seem to be underacknowledged, and that has to do with the logic of feminist legal theory, and the efforts of feminist practitioners, in the area of rape law reform. My claim is that the theoretical conceptualizations of sex, rape, force, and violence that underscore both liberal and radical legal feminism undermine the effort to articulate the harms that might be caused by consensual sexuality. I will begin with liberal feminism and then turn to radical feminism.

First, and entirely to their credit, liberal feminist rape law reformers have been on the forefront of efforts to stiffen enforcement of the existing criminal sanction against rape, and to extend that sanction to include non-consensual sex which presently is not cognizable legally as rape but surely should be. This effort is to be applauded, but it has the *almost* inevitable consequence of valorizing, celebrating, or, to use the critical term, "legitimating" consensual sexual transactions. If rape is bad *because* it is non-consensual—which is increasingly the dominant liberal-feminist position

on the badness of rape—then it seems to follow that *consensual* sex must be good because it is consensual. But appearances can be misleading, and this one certainly is. That non-consensual transactions—rape, theft, slavery—are bad because nonconsensual does *not* imply the value, worth or goodness of their consensual counterparts—sex, property, or work. It only follows that consensual sex, property, or work are not bad in the ways that non-consensual transactions are bad; they surely may be bad for some other reason. We need to explore, in the case of sex (as well as property and work) what those other reasons might be. Non-consensuality does not exhaust the types of harm we inflict on each other in social interactions, nor does consensuality exhaust the list of benefits.

That the liberal-feminist argument for extending the criminal sanction against rape to include non-consensual sex *seems* to imply the positive value of consensual sex is no doubt in part simply a reflection of the powers of the forces enumerated above—the cultural, economic, and liberal valorization of individualism against communal and authoritarian controls. Liberal feminists can obviously not be faulted for that phenomenon. What I want to caution against is simply the ever present temptation to *trade* on those cultural and academic forces in putting forward arguments for reform of rape law. We need not trumpet the glories of consensual sex *in order to* make out a case for strengthening the criminal sanction against coercive sex. Coercion, violence, and the fear under which women live because of the threat of rape are sufficient evils to sustain the case for strengthening and extending the criminal law against those harms. We need not and should not supplement the argument with the unnecessary and unwarranted celebration of consensual sex—which whatever the harms caused by coercion, does indeed carry its own harms.

Ironically, radical feminist rhetoric—which *is* aimed at highlighting the damage and harm done to women by ordinary, "normal" heterosexual transactions—*also* indirectly burdens the attempt to articulate the harms done to women by consensual heterosexual transactions, although it does so in a very different way. Consider the claim, implicit in a good deal of radical feminist writing, explicit in some, that "all sex is rape," and compare it for a moment with the rhetorical Marxist claim that "all property is theft." Both claims are intended to push the reader or listener to a reexamination of the ordinary, and both do so by blurring the distinction between consent and coercion. Both seem to share the underlying premise that which is coerced—and perhaps *only* that which is coerced—is bad, or as a strategic matter, is going to be perceived as bad. Both want us to reexamine the value of that which we normally think of as good or at least unproblematic because of its apparent consensuality—heterosexual transactions in the first case, property transactions in the second—and both do so by putting into doubt the reality of that apparent consensuality.

But there is a very real difference in the historical context and hence the practical consequences of these two rhetorical claims. More specifically, there are two pernicious, or at least counterproductive consequences of the feminist claim which are not shared, at least to the same degree, by the marxist. First, and as any number of liberal feminists have noted, the radical feminist equation of sex and rape runs the risk of undermining parallel feminist efforts in a way not shared by the marxist equation of property and theft. Marxists are for the most part not engaged in the project of attempting to extend the existing laws against *theft* so as to embrace nonconsensual market transactions that are currently not covered by the laws against larceny and embezzlement. Feminists, however, *are* engaged in a parallel effort to extend the existing laws against rape to include all nonconsensual sex, and as a result, the radical feminist equation of rape and sex is indeed undermining. The claim that all sex is in effect non-consensual runs the real risk of "trivializing," or at least confusing, the feminist effort at rape reform so as to include all truly non-consensual sexual transactions.

There is, though, a second cost to the radical feminist rhetorical claim, which I hope these comments have by now made clear. The radical feminist equation of rape and sex, no less than the liberal rape reform movement, gets its rhetorical force by trading on the liberal, normative-economic, and cultural assumptions that whatever is coercive is bad, and whatever is non-coercive is morally non-problematic. It has the effect, then, of further burdening the articulation of harms caused by consensual sex by forcing the characterization of those harms into a sort of "descriptive funnel" of non-consensuality. It requires us to say, in other words, that consensual sex is harmful, if it is, only because or to the extent that it shares in the attributes of nonconsensual sex. But this might not be true—the harms caused by consensual sex might be just as important, just as serious, but nevertheless *different* from the harms caused by nonconsensual sex. If so, then women are disserved, rather than served, by the equation of rape and sex, even were that equation to have the rhetorical effect its espousers clearly desire.

Liberal feminist rape reform efforts and radical feminist theory both, then, in different ways, undermine the effort to articulate the distinctive harms of consensual sex; the first by indirectly celebrating the value of consensual sex, and the latter by at least rhetorically denying the existence of the category. Both, then, in different ways, underscore the legitimation of consensual sex effectuated by non-feminist cultural and academic forces. My conclusion is simply that feminists could counter these trends in part by focusing attention on the harms caused women by consensual sexuality . . .

DISCUSSION QUESTIONS

1. What are the harms of consensual sex, according to West?
2. Why are the harms of consensual sex often not taken seriously?
3. Have you suffered harms as a consequence of consensual sex? Have you inflicted harms? Can you think of examples?

Feminist Theories of Rape: Sex or Violence?

BY ANN J. CAHILL

Ann J. Cahill is an American philosopher who writes on issues in feminist philosophy, phenomenology, and philosophy of the body. In this essay, Cahill surveys and critiques the dominant strands of feminist theorizing about rape—including thinking of rape as gendered domination, as sexualized violence, as threat to the feminine body, as enforcement of sexual inequality, and as manifestation of heterosexuality.

Where feminism and feminist theory have approached the problem of rape, it has almost always been described as paradigmatic of women's larger oppression. That is, the crime of rape has been understood not primarily as a specific, singular crime, but rather as the most blatant example of systematic misogyny and masculine dominance.

The following discussion will describe and analyze two distinct feminist approaches to the problem of rape. While neither approach will prove ultimately satisfactory, it is important to recognize that both achieved important feminist insights. They brought to light the social and political nature of rape at a time when it was assumed to be not the symptom of a larger pattern of oppression, but a mere aberration among the normally pleasant interactions of the sexes. They raised sexual violence as a political and philosophical question, and in doing so they affirmed and highlighted aspects of women's oppression that had remained veiled and mystified. They spoke the unspeakable, and their efforts encouraged women to be more open and less self-blaming about the violence that had been so unjustly imposed upon them.

Susan Brownmiller and the Second Wave

The first school of feminist thought regarding rape developed in the second wave of U.S. feminism. In many ways, this aspect of liberal feminism, best represented by the work of Susan Brownmiller, is often perceived as *the* feminist perspective on rape and so has been influential in the development of reforms concerning rape law.[1]

In Brownmiller's book *Against Our Will: Men, Women, and Rape* (1975), she seeks, as she claims in the work's penultimate sentence, "to give rape its history" (404). Brownmiller endeavors to place the phenomenon of rape within the context of social and biological realities, to unveil its political purposes, and to counter the persistent myths surrounding it. Above all, she seeks to counter the perception that rape is a sexual act. Until now, Brownmiller claims, rape has been understood as an act that serves primarily sexual (that is, natural and biological) needs and is a response to sexual stimuli. To the contrary, rape is inspired not by sexual stimuli, but by political motivations to dominate and degrade. Moreover, in refusing the primacy of sexuality in the phenomenon of rape, Brownmiller denies its individualistic nature. The meaning of rape cannot be elucidated by mere reference to individual cases, because rape is, in her startling phrase, "nothing more or less than a conscious process of intimidation by which *all men* keep *all women* in a state of fear" (15).[2]

Although Brownmiller does not distinguish them clearly in her work, it would appear that for her, rape has two primary political functions. First, it ensures the continued and necessary protection of women by men. Hampered by the fear of rape—not a paranoia, but a reasonable fear grounded in empirical reality—women are incapable of moving in the social and political world without the accompanying arm of a male. Such vulnerability has produced, among other things, the institution of marriage:

> Female fear of an open season of rape, and not a natural inclination toward monogamy, motherhood or love, was probably the single causative factor in the original subjugation of woman by man, the most important key to her historic dependence, her domestication by protective mating. . . . The earliest form of permanent, protective conjugal relationship, the accommodation called mating that we now know as marriage, appears to have been institutionalized by the male's forcible abduction and rape of the female. (Brownmiller 1975, 16–17)

In the institution of marriage, as codified by patriarchal law, the woman abdicates any possibility of an independent being; one symbol of this abdication is the fact that the wife takes her husband's name.[3] The married woman's social status and being are thereby rendered solely derivative of her husband's; she adopts his name, prestige and most importantly, his protection. As Brownmiller describes, given the threat of contract that women can hope to keep their persons safe. In addition, women's fundamental dependence on men for their physical safety justified their socially inferior status by presenting them as a priori lesser beings, as, in fact, beings who are profoundly incomplete by themselves (in a way that men are not). In Brownmiller's analysis, the very social existence of a woman, as well as her economic survival, was directly linked to her institutionalized relationship to a man, whether father or husband. Women's vulnerability, along with the fact that they do not *in and of themselves* have the power to retaliate or resist, translates into a consistently inferior social status. The fact of rape, according to Brownmiller, inspired a host of social institutions that render women necessarily derivative of men, dependent in the most profound ways, and lacking any sense of independent value or self-worth.

The second function of rape, although linked importantly to the first, considers the role of women in the context of conflicts among men. Brownmiller cites act after act of rape in the context of political strife, from world wars to urban racial violence. In every instance, she notes, the particular physical appearance of the victim was utterly irrelevant. What mattered was her status as the property of the enemy:

> It is worth noting the similarity of experience, as far as women were concerned, between such disparate events in time and place as the Ukrainian pogroms and, for example, the Mormon persecutions in this country and the periodic outbreaks of white mob violence against blacks. In each historic interlude a mob of men, sometimes an official militia, armed itself with an ideology that offered a moral justification—"for the public good"—to commit acts of degradation upon women. In each interlude a campaign of terror, and a goal that included the annihilation of a people, provided a license to rape. In each interlude the symbol of the man's hatred and contempt became its exuberant destruction of *other men's property*, be it furniture, cattle, or women. Further, it mattered little to the rapists acting under the cover of a mob whether or not their victims were "attractive." This, too, is significant, since it argues that sexual appeal, as we understand it, has little to do with the act of rape. A mob turns to rape as an expression of power and dominance. Women are used almost as inanimate objects, to prove a point among men. (Brownmiller 1975, 124–25)

Here women are used as political pawns, as symbols of the potency of the men to whom they belong. To rape a woman in the context of war or other violent conflicts, Brownmiller suggests, is not (according to the ultimate intention and motivation of the rapist) an act against the woman herself. Indeed, such a formulation would demand that the woman is someone *herself*, which she clearly is not. Rather, the act is a direct threat to the ownership of the man who is the rapist's enemy. This model too can account for the phenomenon of rape during slavery, where the forcible taking of slave women as sexual partners was an assertion of the slave owner's power as well as a demonstration of the powerlessness of the male slave. Under this rubric, the *male* slave is emasculated (and therefore dehumanized, rendered powerless) by being denied sole access to the slave women.

Brownmiller asserts that rape in all its forms is primarily political. The political motivation of rape predominant in contemporary society is directly linked with the first political purpose. Given a context wherein the institutions by which men dominate women are well established, rape is an act that expresses a political dominance that is already, by and large, accepted. It is an act by which individual men can enact and personally impose the dominant status that society has endowed on them.

Rape is thus "a deliberate, hostile, violent act of degradation and possession on the part of a would-be conqueror, designed to intimidate and inspire fear" (391). By raping a woman, the rapist degrades and denies her being and her autonomy and in doing so (thinks he) elevates his own. The act therefore becomes an echo and an imposition of a social structure by which the full personhood of women is not recognized. Yet Brownmiller's point here is that, even in the context of an individual case, the meaning of rape is never individualistic. Rapists do not rape individuals, but members of a class; the act of rape, then, becomes a reminder to both assailant and victim that membership in one of these classes is the defining element of identity. To be a man is to be a member of the dominant class and thus to have nearly limitless power, or at least power extensive enough to include the power over the bodies of women; to be a woman is to be constantly subject to that dominant power and unable to protect oneself from its reach.

This motivation to rape allows Brownmiller to claim so persuasively that the attractiveness of the rape victim is utterly irrelevant to the rapist's motives, contrary to societal myths of a male sexuality that cannot help but respond to the stimulus of a beautiful woman. The claim that a rape makes

is generic: men in general (whether attractive or not, wealthy or not, educated or not) have power over women in general (whether attractive or not, etc.). Rape is not inspired by the shapely leg or the exposed cleavage of the victim, but by the desire for power and dominance of the assailant. Rape is not primarily sexual, but violent.

Brownmiller's account of rape represented a significant leap forward in feminist thought and politics. However, it also contained some significant gaps and difficulties. For example, neither of the two political functions of rape that Brownmiller describes (to ensure the continued dependence of women on men by necessitating male protection, and to allow men to express their dominance and hatred of each other through the bodies of women) can sufficiently account for the pervasive phenomenon of rape in present-day Western culture.[4] Despite Brownmiller's questionable claim that the process of intimidation is "conscious," one can hardly presume that individual men rape so that men as a class will retain their protective roles and so that those institutions dependent on women's social inferiority will remain impervious to claims of women's autonomy. While Brownmiller clearly states that the combined actions of individual rapists have precisely those effects ("Rather than society's aberrants or 'spoilers of purity,' men who commit rape have served in effect as front-line masculine shock troops, terrorist guerrillas in the longest sustained battle the world has ever known" [1975, 209]), she does not claim that those effects provide the individual motivation for rape. Nor is the present-day United States engaged in a full-out war; unless, as the above quote suggests, one chooses to perceive everyday Western culture as literally in a state of war, gender pitted against gender. However, even in such an extreme model, the conflict would be between men and women, and thus the model discussed above—where women are precisely denied a participatory role in the conflict, but are rather mute, powerless representations of the warring factions—would be inaccurate. Even more strikingly, Brownmiller does not address, with the exception of a discussion concerning the legal status of marital rape, the phenomenon of rape within the context of familial and/or sexual relationships. Yet the majority of women raped in the United States know their attacker in a social context.

The Politics of Sexuality

Brownmiller's defense of the essentially political, and therefore primarily violent, nature of rape is largely dependent on the irrelevance of the attractiveness of the victim. In this aspect of her work, she is responding directly to the prevalent understanding of rape as essentially a crime of passion. Men rape, so the theory went (and sadly, in some cases, still goes), because they find themselves at the mercy of their sexual desires. They view an attractive woman and find it difficult, if not impossible, to control themselves. This model implied that because of this hormonal reaction on the part of men, the women who provided the men with the stimuli that resulted in such a reaction were themselves responsible for the ensuing assault. Hence the socially accepted relevance of the "appropriateness" of the victim's attire.

Such an understanding of rape, Brownmiller avers, is utterly mistaken. The motivation for rape is not to be found in the goal of sexual satisfaction, nor can it be reduced to the visual stimuli that rape victims present. It is rather to be discovered in the will to dominate, to degrade, to possess: motivations that relate directly to a male-dominated culture. Brownmiller's motivations in redefining rape as primarily political (that is, as a matter of power and domination) are clear and certainly honorable, although the specifics of her argument are at times difficult to determine and therefore demand some interpolation.

When rape was understood as primarily sexual, women were perceived as inciting the crime on the basis of their appearance. In order to free women from this assumption of guilt, Brownmiller must eradicate sexuality as a motivation, or at the very least, render it subject to the political structure by which women are dominated by men. That feminism needed to answer the law's implicit assumption of the victim's guilt is obvious, and Brownmiller's theory achieved much to that end. However, Brownmiller's particular answer to this problem presents at least two difficulties.

First, this model of rape places women strictly over and against the political and social structures that underscore the phenomenon of rape, or at the very least understands women as merely objectified by them. In an attempt to undermine the prevailing assumption that women actively provoke the act of rape, Brownmiller paradoxically threatens the possibility of any female agency. She claims that women are acted on by these political dynamics, constructed as rape victims, and forbidden the freedom and mobility granted to men. Yet while all these claims are true, it is inaccurate to understand women as *only* acted on and never acting. In other words, to say that the political and social structure acts in such a way as to perpetuate rape and the threat of rape, and thus to construct women as rape victims by definition and training, is to assume that that same structure does not in some important way include women as acting subjects themselves. Political dynamics are set in direct opposition to women and are perceived as relentlessly hostile to the possibility of female autonomy, when in fact those dynamics are far more complex and are not immune to the influences of actual, particular women.

Second, Brownmiller's own work does not sufficiently take into account the complex interplay between sexuality and politics. In her claim that rape is not primarily sexual but political, she sets up a false distinction between the two domains.

It is striking that the feminine culpability often invoked in rape cases can be answered only by an eradication of any and all sexual significance. Yet the mere presence of sexual significance need not include the vilification and blame of women. It is both possible and necessary to understand rape as a particularly sexual crime as well as a politically and socially meaningful one.

The sexuality of rape differentiates it from other forms of violence and assault. The quality of the assault is marked indelibly by its invocation of not only the sexuality of the assailant, but also that of the victim. Simply put, it *matters* that sexuality is the medium of the power and violence that are imposed on the victim. It matters that the act of rape constructs male sexuality in a particular way such that it constitutes a way of imposing harm, pain, and powerlessness. It matters that the act of rape constructs female sexuality in terms of passivity, victimhood, and lack of agency.

It matters too that in the context of the assault, the rapist is sexually aroused. Brownmiller is correct to argue that the appearance of the victim is not to be blamed for the attack. However, that the rapist's actions are not an automatic, essentially understandable response to the sexualized appearance of the victim does not indicate the total absence of sexual stimuli. The rapist's sexuality *is* engaged: he experiences an erection and, frequently, orgasm. That these sexual experiences may be the result of the violence and the asymmetric power relations inherent in the assault makes them no less sexual in nature.[5]

Brownmiller's theory attempts to separate the effects of power (the violence, the victimization) from their means (sexuality), but such a separation seriously misrepresents the phenomenon. It is not only the case that a victim's body and mind are assaulted. Her sexuality is also assaulted, such that rape victims often find it difficult to return to the sexual behavior in which they engaged prior to the assault. To assume that the realms of sexuality and politics are easily demarcated and separable is to ignore that the violence of rape is peculiarly sexual, that the sexuality on which the phenomenon of rape feeds is peculiarly violent, and that the complex relationship between the two cannot be reduced to one factor.

Nowhere, however, does Brownmiller seriously address the question of the sexuality present within the act of rape. In stressing the political motivations of rapists—the desire to dominate, degrade, humiliate, and control—she at times seems to forget that the rapist usually also achieves a sexual climax. The crime of rape finds its source at the cross-section of these motivations.

Other Second Wave Views of Rape

For the most part, feminist theorists writing in the 1970s echoed and developed the insights of Brownmiller's *Against Our Will*. While some anticipated an alternative model, developed in more detail by Catharine MacKinnon, that emphasized the similarities between rape and "normal"

heterosexual intercourse, most were concerned with expanding on the definition of rape as violence and aggression to the exclusion of sexual motivations. Susan Griffin, however found the social acceptance of rape to be rooted in familiar gender stereotypes and a refusal to see things sexual as things political:

> That the basic elements of rape are involved in all heterosexual relationships may explain why men often identify with the offender in this crime. But to regard the rapist as the victim, a man driven by his inherent sexual needs to take what will not be given him, reveals a basic ignorance of sexual politics. For in our culture heterosexual love finds an erotic expression through male dominance and female submission. A man who derives pleasure from raping a woman clearly must enjoy force and dominance as much or more than the simple pleasures of the flesh. . . . If a man can achieve sexual pleasure after terrorizing and humiliating the object of his passion, and in fact while inflicting pain upon her, one must assume he derives pleasure directly from terrorizing, humiliating, and harming a woman. (318)

Griffin here addresses what Brownmiller does not, the curious but fundamental interplay of pleasure and power of which rape consists. Yet her analysis too falls short. Although she later defines rape as "an act of aggression in which the victim is denied her self-determination. It is an act of violence" (331), the larger quotation above clearly describes the sexual moment inherent in rape. A rapist not only succeeds in physically harming a woman, in degrading and humiliating her, he also derives sexual satisfaction. Rape provides what the "simple pleasures of the flesh" cannot; but in turn, it also provides what a simple act of violence cannot. Griffin's explanation of the phenomenon of rape invokes a socially specific male sexuality that is based upon the erotic value of dominance, and as such it suggests the possibility of other ways of shaping masculinity such that dominance and degradation no longer hold erotic sway. However, her analysis still cannot account for this particular marriage of sexuality and dominance. Griffin can persist in defining rape as primarily violent only insofar as she defines culturally imposed heterosexuality itself as primarily violent (an argument that differs from that of MacKinnon in subtle but significant ways). That is, she is able to reduce the sexuality in rape to the violence in sexuality.

Although Griffin claims that "heterosexual love finds an erotic expression through male dominance and female submission," we cannot infer from her analysis that the eroticization of male dominance and female submission is merely one among many moments that heterosexuality, as currently constructed, offers. The sexual politics that Griffin invokes is one that insists on the fundamental nature of this domination; that is, it takes the oppression of women by men as socially, and therefore sexually, necessary. Indeed, it is only insofar as this domination is largely accepted that the phenomenon of rape, despite ostensible public outrage at individual cases, is even possible.

The faults in Griffin's argument foreshadow the difficulties that the theories of Catharine MacKinnon and Andrea Dworkin faced some years later. However, the real difficulty for Griffin is not the mere overdetermination of compulsory heterosexuality or the valorization of masculine dominance, but rather the failure to articulate specifically the complexity of sexual politics. Given her analysis of the erotic role of masculine dominance, it is difficult to accept her ultimate definition of rape as violence. As much as Griffin appears at first glance to be in agreement with Brownmiller, her analysis does not, in fact, eradicate sexuality from rape; quite to the contrary, it places sexuality at the very root of the phenomenon. While Griffin does not make the mistake of assuming that sexuality is defined by biological realities, nevertheless she describes a patriarchal sexual politics so pervasive that it seems hardly less potent or fixed than the allegedly necessary biological facts that have justified women's social inferiority. Like Brownmiller, Griffin is aware of the inevitably oppressive effects of sexual politics on women; unlike Brownmiller, she cannot avoid defining rape in terms of sexuality, and so

her conclusion that rape is primarily violent rings hollow.

Whereas Brownmiller's tactic risks defining women out of any and all agency, Griffin's strategy risks subsuming all that is sexual under the strict delineation of the political. This is not a necessary outcome of her analysis, which initially includes a recognition of both the sexual and the violent factors of rape. However, in choosing to define rape by its violent, rather than its sexual, content, she reduces the latter to the former. As a "classic act of domination," rape is essentially viewed by Griffin as yet another method of male supremacy, perhaps the most extreme tool in the patriarchal arsenal. But rape is not just another tool, and its significance in women's lives and experience cannot be exhausted by a reference to violence, precisely because its particular violence is so explicitly and indelibly sexualized.

Catharine MacKinnon and the Radical Feminist Strategy

If the liberal feminist perspective on rape risked defining any and all terms of sexuality out of rape in favor of its violent characteristics, the arguments of radical feminists such as Catharine MacKinnon and Andrea Dworkin reverse the emphasis. The theoretical positions of MacKinnon and Dworkin place the phenomenon of rape squarely within the confines of so-called normal, but imposed, heterosexuality. Such a strategy raises important questions concerning the violence inherent in imposed heterosexuality, the erotic centrality of dominance to such an imposed heterosexuality, and the relation between what is perceived as "normal" heterosexual sex and rape. However, my analysis of MacKinnon and Dworkin will demonstrate that their position depends on a theory of power and social construction that does not allow for the possibility of female sexual agency. The radical feminist strategy is correct in drawing links between compulsory heterosexuality and rape, but as exemplified in the writings of MacKinnon and Dworkin, it overestimates the influence and coherence of the patriarchal construction of heterosexuality such that it identifies that construction with the impossibility of feminine agency.

MacKinnon approaches rape directly in a chapter from her work *Toward a Feminist Theory of the State* (1989). Her analysis questions the legal perspective on rape that defines it as nonconsensual, forced, and coerced sex. MacKinnon notes that it is not legally sufficient to define rape as merely forced, but that the crime must be marked by a distinct and proven lack of consent as well. Such a demand "assumes the sadomasochistic definition of sex: intercourse with force or coercion can be or become consensual" (172). In legal, political, and social realms, that is, a certain level of force or coercion can be expected in "normal" heterosexual sex, or at least the presence of force does not necessarily indicate a lack of consent. Thus the demonstration that force was used will not necessarily convince a judge or jury that rape occurred; because the scope of what is considered "normal" heterosexual sex includes the use of (only male) force, the judge or jury may well assume that the alleged (female) victim may have consented to the use of force.

Moreover, for MacKinnon it is not merely the case that heterosexuality as currently constructed allows for the possibility of the mutual coexistence of force and consent. What lies at the heart of the problem of rape is a construction of heterosexuality wherein the use of force is at the very least prevalent, and perhaps endemic. She notes that "rape is not less sexual for being violent. To the extent that coercion has become integral to male sexuality, rape may even be sexual to the degree that, and because, it is violent" (1989, 173). Given the central and privileged place that (male) force (utilized against females) has in the construction of compulsory heterosexuality, the question becomes not how to distinguish between rape and "normal" heterosexual intercourse, but whether the two are in any significant way distinguishable.

> The convergence of sexuality with violence, long used at law to deny the reality of women's violation, is recognized by rape survivors with a difference: where the legal system has seen the intercourse in rape, victims see the rape in intercourse. The uncoerced context for sexual expression becomes as elusive as the physical acts come to feel indistinguishable. Instead of asking what is the violation of rape, their experience suggests that the more relevant question is, what is the nonviolation of intercourse? To know what is wrong with rape, know what is right about sex. If this, in turn, proves difficult, the difficulty is as instructive as the difficulty men have in telling the difference when women see one. Perhaps the wrong of rape has proved so difficult to define because the unquestionable starting point has been that rape is defined as distinct from intercourse, while for women it is difficult to distinguish the two under conditions of male dominance. (174)

Because women are hard pressed to describe sexual encounters that are not coerced, rape appears not as an exception to, but merely a variation on, normal heterosexual activity. This indicates that forced sex is not merely possible within the scope of women's experiences of heterosexual sex, but that, given male dominance and compulsory heterosexuality, intercourse is virtually always accompanied by a degree of coercion or force. "If sexuality is central to women's definition and forced sex is central to sexuality, rape is indigenous, not exceptional, to women's social condition" (172). Given the central nature of force to heterosexuality itself, women are already implicated in terms contrary to their interests (assuming those interests include physical well-being and the freedom from both rape and the fear of rape) as soon as they enter and participate in the heterosexual world.

The violence in rape, then, is virtually indistinguishable (that is to say, indistinguishable in kind) from the violent imposition of compulsory heterosexuality that serves the needs of male supremacy.[6] Indeed, MacKinnon suggests that it is precisely in rape's sexual meanings that one finds its violence embedded. To define rape solely or primarily by its violent characteristics to the exclusion of its sexual qualities, then, is paradoxically to miss the specific violence that rape represents. "Considering rape as violence not sex evades, at the moment it most seems to confront, the issue of who controls women's sexuality and the dominance/submission dynamic that has defined it" (1989, 178).

MacKinnon is making two distinct points about heterosexuality as currently constructed, although she does not always delineate the two explicitly. First, heterosexuality itself is forced, that is, socially compulsory. One cannot speak of women freely choosing a heterosexual identity (or, more poignantly yet, a "lifestyle") in a culture where alternative sexualities are not equally valued, accepted, or institutionalized. By means of social pressure, encouragement, and at times crass manipulation, women are both urged and expected to be heterosexual. If they respond positively to the various means of persuasion (which are themselves veiled and subtle, for compulsory heterosexuality must be portrayed as natural and inevitable), they receive social rewards that are barred to those who resist. When it comes to heterosexuality, there is no moment of "true choice."

Second, heterosexuality is defined primarily as a dynamic of masculine domination and feminine submission. Specifically, heterosexual intercourse and the social rituals and habits pertaining to it are constructed in such a way as to endow the male with the role of conqueror and the female with the role of the conquered. Women are properly courted, and they risk a loss of their feminine appeal should they appear overly aggressive or even active; men are properly the pursuers who seek to convince women, by whatever means necessary, to surrender the sought prize. Feminine sexuality is thus constructed as primarily reactive or derivative of masculine desire. It has no independent ontological status of its own, but is a means to an end (that end being, for women, among other things, social status and/or financial security). Feminine sexuality, MacKinnon writes, is "socially, a thing to be stolen, sold, bought, bartered, or exchanged by others. But women never own or possess it. . . . The moment women 'have' it—'have sex' in the dual gender/sexuality sense— it is lost as theirs" (1989, 172).

MacKinnon is here emphasizing the erotic role of the dominant/submissive structure. Given the twin and intertwined demands of compulsory heterosexuality and male privilege, domination itself must ground erotic experience. Women are implicated in the system of their own domination

precisely as they participate in a constructed heterosexuality that assumes, even requires, that they respond erotically to masculine aggression. Indeed, the possibility of women's positive sexual response to sexually and otherwise physically aggressive men (a response that is socially expected and accepted) is directly linked to their inferior social status.

For MacKinnon, then, if women inhabit a world where their (hetero) sexuality is already and always predicated on an assumption of the regular use of force and coercion, then to blithely invoke the omnipotence of consent in references to matters sexual is nothing short of farcical. Virtually every aspect of the heterosexual woman's experience is pervaded by a valorization of her submissive position. She has no true choice in becoming heterosexual; moreover, once constructed as heterosexual, she is automatically subject to a discourse that defines both her appeal and her desire in terms of her passivity and vulnerability (men, of course, are also subject to compulsory heterosexuality; however, in their case the imposed sexuality reiterates their socially endowed superiority over women by defining their desire in terms of control and activity). She cannot choose to redefine her sexuality according to some alternative paradigm without risking literal social nonexistence. A failure to accept her passive, submissive role is a sure indication of antisocial and perhaps pathological behavior, and at the very least it places her at odds with the dominant heterosexual institutions and behaviors.[7] Thus the consent that women believe they wield—the illusion that they actually have choices with regard to sexuality and sexual encounters—serves to obscure the extensive degree to which women's sexuality is imposed. Valid consent has no place in this model of constructed heterosexuality, where there are only various types of force and coercion, the most explicit and blatant being the pervasive phenomenon of rape.

According to MacKinnon, rape varies from normal heterosexual intercourse only in quantity (its violence is more palpable, its level of coercion more blatant and explicit), not in quality. The law's confusion in determining the difference between rape and consensual sex is due to its masculinist assumption that sex is, by definition, consensual, and that most women, most of the time, freely consent to heterosexual intercourse. That assumption reflects the expectation on the part of heterosexual men that women win, even as—and perhaps because—they desire sex, protest it. The more force, the sexier the encounter; hence, women's protests can easily, and sincerely, be read as implicit consent, and perhaps even encouragement:

> Many women are raped by men who know the meaning of their acts to their victims perfectly well and proceed anyway. But women are also violated every day by men who have no idea of the meaning of their acts to the women. To them it is sex. Therefore, to the law it is sex. . . . [T]he law assumes that, because the rapist did not perceive that the woman did not want him, she was not violated. She had sex. Sex itself cannot be an injury. Women have sex every day. Sex makes woman a woman. Sex is what women are for. (MacKinnon 1989, 180–81)

MacKinnon's response to this legal perspective is, in essence, a pithy one. The truth that the law and the institutions that produce and support compulsory heterosexuality and male dominance refuse to recognize is that sex itself can be an injury to women. In fact, virtually every detail surrounding the social construct of heterosexuality—its alleged naturalness, its assumption and celebration of masculine aggression, its institutional and social incarnations—is a blow to female autonomy. Until sex, as currently constructed, can be understood as contrary to women's social and political independence, the law will remain forever confused as to the line between heterosexual sex and rape.

MacKinnon's analysis indicates that it is not the violence surrounding a particular act of rape (the threatening weapon, the bodily weight that immobilizes the victim, or the threat of worse violence if the victim does not submit) that gives rape its peculiar character. Rather, the violence of rape is to be found in its (hetero)sexual characteristics. Rape is violent insofar as it is a moment on the continuum of heterosexual experience, which is pervaded through and through by the presence of coercion and force. Its sexual nature is not set against its violent nature, but the latter is equated with the former.

Andrea Dworkin too invokes the relentlessly coercive nature of socially constructed heterosexuality when she writes that "[a]ny so-called choice for [heterosexual] sex is a choice for prostitution" (Dworkin 1989, 151). Like MacKinnon, Dworkin defines the phenomenon of rape as predicated upon a wholly derivative feminine sexuality. Pornography, which Dworkin considers to be directly and causally linked to the occurrence of rape, serves to veil this derivative nature of feminine sexuality even as it is proclaiming it. That is, although pornography explicitly portrays women solely as sexual objects created for the consumption of masculine desire, at the same time it insists that the women it portrays voluntarily choose such a status, and that in fact, most women make identical choices. Although pornography demonstrates in the clearest way the dominance inherent in heterosexuality, its power demands that the agency of the women involved be assumed:

> The essence of rape, then, is in the conviction that no woman, however clearly degraded by what she does, is a victim. If the harlot nature of the female is her true nature, then nothing that signifies or reveals that nature is either violating or victimizing. The essence of rape is in the conviction that such [pornographic] photographs—in any way, to any degree—show a female sexuality independent of male power, outside the bounds of male supremacy, uncontaminated by male force. (138)

Dworkin asserts that the feminine sexual identity portrayed by pornography and assumed implicitly or explicitly in various defenses or understandings of the phenomenon of rape is not in fact independent of male power, but rather is the most blatant expression of the extent of masculine dominance. Not only do women not choose to be degraded or violated, but in fact, according to Dworkin, (heterosexual) women cannot choose anything when it comes to sexuality. The two concepts are mutually exclusive, for women's sexual experiences, the contexts in which those experiences occur, and the social meanings and ramifications produced by those experiences are all manifestations of and elaborations on women's social inferiority and powerlessness. Women cannot choose to have (heterosexual) sex for physical pleasure, as a demonstration of affection, or for any other reason. Their heterosexuality can only be used for other purposes, traded for social status, bartered for other, nonsexual goods; insofar as they are heterosexual, they are necessarily prostitutes.

The theories of MacKinnon and Dworkin effectively served to caution feminist thought against presuming that women's sexuality, sexual preferences, and sexual practices are somehow unconnected to, and therefore protected from, larger discourses of sexual inequality. They pushed the envelope of the insight that "the personal is political" by linking what seemed to be the most private and personally held desires to a political system so comprehensive as to be virtually transparent. In doing so, they encouraged feminists to challenge more deeply their assumptions concerning the criteria that must be met in order for women's sexual choices to be truly freely made. One of the strengths of compulsory heterosexuality as a political institution is its ability to conceal itself, such that women believe that their desire for marriage, for example, is authentically their own, untainted by coercive forces. MacKinnon and Dworkin undermine that concealment, and thus expand the scope of the visible effects of patriarchy. However, their theories tend to overstate the power of patriarchal discourse to such an extent that they actually serve to render impossible women's subjectivity. By defining rape as essentially similar to other heterosexual practices, their theories assume not only that women's sexual desires are affected by compulsory heterosexuality, but that they are wholly constituted by it.

For both MacKinnon and Dworkin, rape is virtually (or, at the very least, importantly) indistinguishable from "normal" heterosexual intercourse. MacKinnon has vehemently refuted those who interpret her theory as a claim that "all sex is rape"

(1997). Clearly, to reduce her complex theory to such an oversimplified statement is inaccurate and perhaps ambiguous, as David Estlund notes (1997, 167). Yet it is clear that the theoretical perspectives of MacKinnon and Dworkin are compelled by the fundamental similarities between rape and consensual intercourse; those similarities are emphasized so strongly and are so central to the theories being developed that they render those theories incapable of accounting for a differentiation between the two phenomena. Perhaps more exactly, the theories cannot account for such a differentiation within the context of sexual inequality, and MacKinnon's analysis certainly states that such a context is pervasive in contemporary Western society. As Estlund remarks, "It is certainly possible that the view attributed to MacKinnon under the phrase 'all sex is rape' is the view that all intercourse under present conditions is rape. And that is pretty close to her view" (1997, 167).

In reducing the violence of rape to the violence inherent in compulsory heterosexuality, both MacKinnon and Dworkin full prey to theoretical dichotomies that ultimately cannot hold. The first clue to the weakness of their position is that it renders virtually all heterosexuality misogynistic. While noting this implication does not in and of itself constitute a sufficient argument against their theory, it does ring some fairly serious warning bells. If we are to give women's experience any credence in a theory of rape, it must be acknowledged that for most women, in most cases, to be raped is a strikingly different experience than to engage in voluntary heterosexual sex. Even women who are involved in relationships that have consistently included forced sex can, for the most part, conceive of heterosexual encounters that are enjoyable and centered around their sexual pleasure. Some women, it is true, may learn to associate dominance with eroticism and may in fact eroticize their own submission and inferior status. But MacKinnon and Dworkin assert that such eroticization is fundamental to any and all heterosexual experiences on the part of women; it is just as theoretically significant that in fact, heterosexuality and women's heterosexual experiences are far more varied and complex than their account allows.

Moreover, such a theory of rape pits female sexuality and female agency strictly against each other. Given that, as MacKinnon herself notes, sexuality is integral to identity, the denial of the possibility of heterosexuality in favor of the possibility of autonomy seems a poor choice indeed. If MacKinnon is correct, if heterosexuality as currently constructed is hopelessly pervaded by notions of female inferiority and by the valorization of masculine dominance, it is impossible for women to be both actively heterosexual and actively pursuing their equality and autonomy. Nowhere in her account is there an emphasis on, or even the hope for, reconstructing heterosexuality in such a way as to rid it of its insistently misogynistic values. If we take her theory to its ultimate application, even assuming that such a reconfiguring of heterosexuality was possible, it is difficult to imagine how it would be undertaken, or, more significantly, who would undertake it. Women, insofar as their heterosexual identities were formed contrary to their own desires and interests (so much so that even their desires are not their own), could hardly be capable of envisioning an alternative, for they have virtually no capabilities outside those determined by the masculinist paradigms. Considering the privileges that accompany the present system of compulsory heterosexuality and male dominance, the possibility of a masculine undermining of the system is far-fetched indeed. It would appear that insofar as women participate in the heterosexual paradigm, they themselves are undermining the possibility of their own agency; and yet if that paradigm is as powerful and pervasive as MacKinnon and Dworkin imply, to exist outside it is not to exist socially at all.

Again, that such ramifications are merely distasteful or pessimistic does not, as some seem to think, in and of itself constitute a sufficient answer to the theories of MacKinnon and Dworkin. After all, it is theoretically possible that feminine agency is a literal impossibility. However, such implications should give us pause. Is the power of patriarchy unlimited? Where, in this model, is the possibility of resistance?

The theoretical structure outlined by MacKinnon and Dworkin cannot, ultimately, account sufficiently for the possibility of resistance precisely because it endows male dominance with a potency that is virtually infinite. It adopts a dichotomous model of power dynamics whereby, by definition, women are victims and men are oppressors. For this reason, Drucilla Cornell (1995, 104, 125) argues that MacKinnon's perspectives on male and female sexuality correspond to, rather than contradict, the rigid gender identities that mainstream heterosexual pornography portrays. For MacKinnon and Dworkin, power is a strictly straightforward matter, a means wielded by men to dominate women, a force that infuses all aspects of social interaction and is therefore inescapable. In this model of power, women are only acted on, not acting; they are at the whims of a society that studiously ignores their true desires and even goes so far as to construct those desires that women (perhaps foolishly) believe to be their own. Yet if women are so diligently constructed, how is it possible that some women end up questioning their own situations? How do we have a history of feminist consciousness existing within (even as it is sometimes opposed to) Western culture? As Cornell observes, "In MacKinnon's account . . . nothing of women's personhood is left over with which we could organize so as to begin the feminist process of becoming 'for ourselves.' There is in MacKinnon's account of silencing no space at all for the woman's aspiration to become a person. We have been effectively shut off from ourselves by the imposed fantasies of others" (1995, 144).

In the process of overstating their case, MacKinnon and Dworkin fall prey to some philosophically traditional dichotomies. Because power is, for MacKinnon and Dworkin, an essentially repressive force, with a single source (men) and a well-defined target (women), it is theoretically impossible to construct women as anything other than the victims of that power. The very existence of women, and certainly any possibility of feminine agency, will, or desire, is pitted directly against the overwhelming authority of society. Were a woman to insist on the validity of her heterosexual desires, for example, a theory such as MacKinnon's would dismiss such a defense on the basis of false consciousness. Such a dismissal of the empirical experience of the disempowered group, namely, women, is not identical to the patriarchal stereotype of the lying, untrustworthy woman, but it is uncomfortably close. Moreover, it rests upon a dichotomy of power versus powerlessness that is altogether too simple.

The point is not that MacKinnon and Dworkin are incorrect about the deep links between compulsory heterosexuality and masculine dominance. The point is rather that they assert that those links are bonds of identity, to the extent that heterosexuality (and therefore any participation in heterosexual activity) is *identified strictly* with misogyny. That heterosexuality is not constituted as a true choice (that is, an option among other equally valid options) in contemporary Western society is clear; however, the absence of absolute choice does not necessarily indicate the presence of totalizing coercion. West's (1991a) analysis of radical legal feminist theory notes that it shares with liberal feminism an essential belief in the possibility of autonomy, and indeed a view of the human being as essentially autonomous (given a just political structure). Indeed, the autonomy that the radical legal feminist position seeks is an all-or-nothing affair; hence MacKinnon's implicit claim that heterosexuality can be a valid, real choice or experience only in the context of the eradication of all sexual dominance and hierarchy. However, as West (1991a) points out, the concept of a profound autonomy, the ability to act in complete independence from the influence of others and of society as a whole, is faulty, not to mention deeply masculinist. A belief in profound autonomy or utterly free choice is an illusory one that ignores the real and complex matrix of relationships, social and political as well as familial, sexual, and so forth, that constitute the context of any decision. If autonomy and valid choice are not the all-or-nothing affairs that MacKinnon implies, then the choices and sexual experiences that women make and have, *even within the context of sexual hierarchies*, cannot be dismissed as invalid.

To claim that free choice, understood in an absolutist sense, is illusory is not to claim that any agency is impossible. Rather, it is to situate agency within a defining context; while I am not

free to choose anything at any time (precisely because my context is specific, and therefore limited), nevertheless my context is never, or rarely, so limited as to preclude any options whatsoever. Compulsory heterosexuality does indicate that women especially do not have unmitigated choice in terms of their sexual orientation or experience, and MacKinnon and Dworkin are quite correct to articulate the various ways society imposes limitations on those choices. However, that women's choices are limited does not necessarily indicate that women are precluded from making any choices whatsoever; that particular extension of the argument assumes a polarity (choice versus coercion) that is more properly a continuum. Defending herself against critics, on both the left and the right, who claim that her analysis implies that all sex is rape, MacKinnon pithily sums up her position by stating that "sexuality occurs in a context of gender inequality" (MacKinnon 1997, 103), and indeed, that is an irrefutable claim. However, that sexuality takes place in such a context does not indicate that (hetero)sexuality and women's experiences of (hetero)sexuality are wholly derivative of or strictly reducible to that inequality.

In seeking to describe the very real ways women's experiences are formulated and determined by and with patriarchy, MacKinnon and Dworkin have risked portraying women as solely derivative of masculine power. In terms of their theory of rape, this has resulted in a necessarily wholesale condemnation of heterosexuality, at least for the present time; and indeed, if the power of compulsory heterosexuality and masculine dominance is as fundamental and pervasive as MacKinnon and Dworkin indicate, it would be a long, hard, and perhaps even impossible road to its undermining. In this way their attempt to define rape as primarily sexual by reducing the violence of rape to its sexual nature serves to call into question the possibility of a female agency that includes sexuality. By pitting women's agency strictly against the social agenda of masculine dominance, and by assuming that the presence of force and coercion necessarily includes the absence of the possibility of choice, they assume dichotomies that are philosophically dubious. Their attempt to reduce the phenomenon of rape to only one of its aspects does not, ultimately, elucidate the full social and political meanings of rape; nor does it serve the interests of women, who, although certainly subject to discourses hostile to their experiences, abilities, and desires, nevertheless are not utterly devoid of agency.

Power and the Body

Both attempts to theorize rape discussed above can be accurately termed reductive. The definition of rape as primarily violent seeks to rid the crime of sexual significance and meaning, and redefine it solely within the existing legal framework of assault. The definition of rape as primarily sexual claims that the violence inherent in the crime is directly due to its particularly sexual nature, and that its wrong is to be found in the context of an overarching system of compulsory heterosexuality and masculine dominance. Neither theory sufficiently accounts for the significance of rape, and the threat of rape, in women's lives.

Indeed, it is the specificity of rape that both theories fail to approach. This failure is essentially due to faulty, or perhaps simply absent, understandings of the intersection of political power and female bodies. It is striking indeed that in both of these theories there is a marked lack of attention paid to the role of the body in agency and social and political being. Although MacKinnon gestures toward the formation of feminine sexual desire in relation to patriarchy's valorization of masculine dominance, the details of this formation are decidedly murky. Likewise, Brownmiller's attempt to distinguish strictly between things sexual (i.e., biologically determined) and things political leaves unaskable the question of the body as politically and socially constructed. Finally, neither theory speaks substantially to the role of rape in the formation of the feminine body, and to the implications of that role in the experience and phenomenon of rape itself.

To begin to locate the place of the body not only in relation to the phenomenon of rape, but also in relation to the dynamics of power, agency, and politics, involves its own potential hazards as well. The body is notoriously difficult to theorize, and the dangers of assuming it to be natural or clearly determined are well documented. Yet the politics of the body and the politics of gender are deeply intertwined, and rape, as a crime against specifically female bodies, takes place at the intersection of the two. Before we can articulate the ethical relevance of rape, its phenomenological significance, or its social and political functions, we need a detailed analysis of the social, political, and phenomenological aspects of the body.

Moreover, given the deep implication of the body and gender politics, this analysis must retain sex and gender as central to its questioning. Insofar as the body and embodiment are significant, sexual difference cannot be far behind, and indeed, any allegedly sex-neutral theories of the body are rightfully suspect. Men's and women's bodies are accorded radically different social significance, subject to radically different discourses, and presented with radically different demands. It is likely, then, that men and women experience their bodies in radically different ways. Class, race, sexual orientation: these axes also distinguish bodies and produce different bodily experiences; therefore, those axes produce differences in the experience of rape and the threat of rape.

By understanding the role of the body in sexual and social politics, we will gain a clearer and more nuanced understanding of rape as that bodily assault that is a disproportionate threat to women. Rather than reducing rape to either sexuality or violence, a coherent and detailed analysis of the body will elucidate the relation of both factors, while also serving to articulate the sex-specific meanings of rape. Most important, it will articulate the relation between the body and agency, thus serving to argue against theories that preclude the possibility of feminine subjectivity, even as, or perhaps precisely because, subjectivity itself becomes redefined.

The theories of Brownmiller and MacKinnon fail on the basis of their inattention to the body. What tools, then, do current feminist theories of the body have to offer to the task of unraveling this knot of violence, embodiment, masculinity, and sexual difference? If those previous theories imply problematic definitions of women, usually to the extent that feminine agency is exposed as a necessary contradiction, what can feminist theories of the body tell us about the subjectivity of those beings subjected to a pervasive threat of rape?

Who are the beings being raped? What is the status and quality of their being? What can their being tell us of the phenomenon of rape?

DISCUSSION QUESTIONS

1. Describe Brownmiller's liberal feminist account of rape as a fundamentally political, not sexual, act. Focus in particular on the claim that rape ensures women's continued dependence on men by making male protection necessary, and on the claim that rape allows men to use women's bodies to express their dominance over each other.

2. Describe MacKinnon and Dworkin's radical feminist account of rape as inevitable in a culture in which heterosexuality is compulsory and gendered roles of dominance and submission are eroticized.

3. Explain Cahill's concern that both Brownmiller's and MacKinnon's accounts, in different ways, paradoxically undermine the possibility of women's agency.

NOTES

1. Spohn and Horney (1992) analyze the effects of rape law reform in several cities. One important reform undertaken by several jurisdictions that was clearly inspired by Brownmiller and others was definitional: "[M]any states replaced the crime of rape and other traditional sex crimes with a series of gender-neutral graded offenses with commensurate penalties. . . . [M]any states eliminated the term rape and substituted sexual assault, sexual battery, or criminal sexual content" (Spohn and Horney 1992, 22). In evaluating the effectiveness of these definitional changes, Spohn and Horney write: Changing the name of the crime from rape to sexual assault, criminal sexual conduct, or sexual battery also may have had unintended consequences. Reformers reasoned that the change would emphasize that rape is an assault and a crime of violence. Criminal justice officials in the

three jurisdictions that changed the name of the crime disagreed. They pointed out that the term "rape" has a strong connotation and "conjures up a much more inflammatory image in the mind of the jury." A judge in Houston stated that changing the name of the offense from rape to sexual assault "sugarcoated" the offense. A prosecutor in Chicago charged that the new terminology was confusing to jurors, "who often wondered why we didn't just charge the guy with rape." (161). In general, the authors find to their disappointment that the rape law reforms did not result an increase in convictions or in an increase in the reporting of rapes.

2. This statement is strikingly ambiguous. Brownmiller's analysis of rape, as discussed below, describes it as essentially a political means of the repression of one class (women) by another (men). In this sense, it makes sense that the threat of rape benefits all men. However, this does not necessarily entail that all men consciously participate in this process of intimidation, as the quote suggests. The distinction between men as a class and real, particular men (as well as that between women as a class and real, particular women) is difficult to trace in Brownmiller's thought, as exemplified by this quote.

3. For certain cultures and historical periods, of course, even the term "abdicates" is overly strong, as women, or usually young girls, are literally "given away" by their father to their husband, without any degree of consent or participation on the part of the bride. Brownmiller would link this type of extremely female social dependence with the possibility of rape and the need for constant male protection (not to mention the social currency of female virginity).

4. For surveys and comparative studies of various sociological theories (not always feminist) concerning the occurrence of rape, see Ellis (1989) and Baron and Strauss (1989). Sunday and Tobach (1985) provide a collection of essays criticizing the sociobiological theory of rape, which asserts that rape is the result of evolutionary selection and can therefore be understood as a reproductive strategy of men who would otherwise not reproduce.

5. A. Nicholas Groth, in support of just such an understanding of rape as primarily violent rather

than sexual, claimed that "rape is in fact serving primarily nonsexual needs. It is the sexual expression of power and anger . . . Rape is a pseudosexual act, complex and multidetermined, but addressing issues of hostility (anger) and control (power) more than passion (sexuality)" (1979, 2). However, it is worth noting that the rapists Groth studied were, by his own admission, representative only of those who "come to the attention of criminal justice and mental health agencies and with whom law enforcement officials and providers of social services are expected to deal in some effective manner" (xiii); not surprisingly, therefore, the anecdotal examples Groth quotes refer almost exclusively to stranger rape and do not address the phenomena of acquaintance rape and marital rape. Moreover, although Groth claims that only 25 percent of identified rapists experience no erective or ejaculatory dysfunction (88), the types of sexual dysfunction he does find prevalent do not indicate a complete lack of sexual arousal on the part of the rapist (for example, premature ejaculation, or temporary or conditional impotency, which refers to an inability to achieve an erection except by imposing a certain set of actions or scenarios).

6. Note that MacKinnon's argument differs here, albeit slightly, from Griffin's. Griffin reduced the sexuality in rape primarily to the eroticized violence inherent in heterosexuality, thus in general reducing the sex in rape to violence. MacKinnon, while recognizing the centrality of the eroticization of violence, is also stressing the violent imposition of heterosexuality, that is, its socially compulsory aspect, which limits or negates the possibility of feminine sexual autonomy, thus essentially reducing the violence in rape to sex.

7. See Barbara Ehrenreich and Deirdre English (1979) for a history of the medical institution's interpretation and treatment of women's bodies and women's health. Especially interesting is the discussion of the "rejection of the feminine" (270–74), a diagnosis that conveniently accounted for all aspects of that particularly feminine illness of hysteria—an illness that, Ehrenreich and English claim, utilized the feminine virtues of passivity and weakness to avoid the imposed duties of wifehood and motherhood (133–40). The real problem, as far as the medical institution was concerned, was not so much the suffering of the hysterical patient, but her failure to fulfill her various social duties.

Creepers, Flirts, Heroes, and Allies: Four Theses on Men and Sexual Harassment

BY BONNIE MANN

Bonnie Mann is an American philosopher whose work focuses on issues in feminist phenomenology. Rather than focusing on sexual harassment primarily from the perspective of its female victims, in this essay Mann discusses how men in a sexist society should respond to sexual harassment. Laying out the potential pitfalls—from feeling creepily entitled to annex women's sexuality, to swooping in to rescue the damsel in the distress—Mann presents an alternative, feminist-friendly picture of male sexuality for men to aspire to.

What Does "Creepy" Mean?

"Wow! What a creeper!" my sixteen-year-old daughter often says, breezing in the door, referring to some encounter she's just had taking the city bus home from school, or walking through the park down the street. Her three teenage sisters say it too. When they have occasion to remind each other of the unpleasant experiences they've already started to collect walking down the streets, standing at the bus-stop, in the cars of boys they have dated, and with one or two of their male teachers, the reminder starts, as often as not, with "Remember that creeper who. . . ." When I ask, "What do you mean by that?" they just say, "You know, a creeper . . . as in *creepy*," and roll their eyes at their philosopher-mother's efforts to get them to think more about something so self-evident. And the truth is, I *do* know what they mean. In fact, I've taken to calling out to them in their very own vernacular, "Watch out for creepers!" as they head out of the house on some teenage errand.

But perhaps they resist my efforts to get them to talk about what they mean in part because it isn't so easy to *say* what "creeper" means, when you really sit down to do it. Even for me, after years working in organizations for battered women, managing the crisis hotline, training hundreds of volunteers and staff members to work the crisis hotline, advocating for women and training others to advocate for women in the counseling room and in courts of law—I really need my philosophical training in order to say what "creeper" means. After all, a creeper doesn't necessarily engage in the blatant and (for the most part) more easily defined behavior that we have in mind when we say "battery" or "rape" or "sexual assault," and the words change if he does. He's no longer just a "creeper" but something even worse. Whatever he is doing that makes him a creeper seems to carry the threat or possibility of these other forms of abuse,[1] but he needn't ever cross those lines to earn the name "creeper." Feminists had to fight long and hard to get the more overt forms of abuse recognized by the police and the courts (and even more importantly to recognize them ourselves), and that battle still isn't over. But "creepy" is something that doesn't necessarily rise to the level of more overt abuse.

Let's start by paying attention to the words: "creepy," "creeper." Something that creeps sneaks up on you, threatens to catch you unaware. In the garden, bindweed is the clear example. It is actually a rather pretty plant, even delicate, with triangular leaves and seductive, cone-shaped white flowers. It looks like a morning glory. It camouflages itself against the green leaves of the host plant. Yet bindweed is viciously invasive. If you don't stop it, it wraps itself around the host plant again and again. Its tendrils get thicker and stronger. If you pull it out of the ground, any bit of root left will bring it back to life, and the roots are actually invigorated by your resistance. If you allow it to seed, the seeds stay viable for 30 years. If it were to choose you as its host, you can imagine it wrapping you up while you were napping, and waking up unable to move.

Keeping the bindweed in mind, let's consider Sartre's famous (and creepy) example of a woman on a date, whose bad faith dictates her response to her date's sexual overtures.

> She knows very well the intentions which the man who is speaking to her cherishes regarding her. She knows also that it will be necessary sooner or later for her to make a decision. But she does not want to realize the urgency . . . She does not apprehend [her date's] conduct as an attempt to achieve what we call "the first approach"; . . . she does not wish to read in the phrases which he addresses to her anything other than their explicit meaning. If he says to her, "I find you so attractive!" she disarms this phrase of its sexual background . . . The man who is speaking to her appears to her sincere and respectful as the table is round or square . . . This is because she is not quite sure what she wants . . . she refuses to apprehend the desire for what it is; she does not even give it a name; she recognizes it only to the extent that it transcends itself toward admiration, esteem, respect . . . But then suppose he takes her hand. This act of her companion risks changing the situation by calling for an immediate decision. To leave the hand there is to consent to flirt, to engage herself . . . To withdraw it is to break the troubled and unstable harmony which gives the hour its charm . . . We know what happens next, the young woman leaves her hand there, but she does not notice that she is leaving it . . . she is at this moment all intellect. She draws her companion up to the most lofty regions of sentimental speculation . . . the hand rests inert

between the warm hands of her companion—neither consenting nor resisting—a thing.[2]

What makes this an example of "bad faith" for Sartre is that the woman "has disarmed the actions of her companion by reducing them to being only what they are," rather than recognizing that these actions point beyond themselves. When he says, "I find you so attractive!" for example, she recognizes this phrase only in its immanence (only as being what it is), and refuses to "know" that this means he wants to have sex with her. On the other hand, she recognizes his desire only in its mode of transcendence (only as not being what it is), in other words, the brute bodily desire *to fuck* is only apprehended as a kind of admiration or esteem. She doesn't hold transcendence and immanence together in her responses, but is continually fragmenting them—thus refusing to assume her freedom. When her date presses the moment of decision by taking her hand, Sartre complains, she refuses to be forced into a decision. Leaving her hand alive and animated in his would be to consent. Withdrawing it would be to refuse.

Of course, this scenario might not happen on a date. A feminist consciously misreading this scene as autobiographical (and knowing Sartre's particular history, such a misreading is too tempting to resist) might well wonder whether the young woman—no doubt one of Sartre's philosophy students—even though she was on a date. Maybe she thought she had been presented with the opportunity to discuss existentialism with one of the great minds of her time because she had impressed the professor with her intelligence in class. Or maybe she had just approached him with a question about Brentano's notion of intentionality; walked boldly up to his table at the café and been asked to sit down. And maybe she was so shocked to find that *for him*, even such student-like behavior was apprehended as "a date," she froze—needing time to formulate a response, but finding that he had already stolen time from her.

And this is one characteristic of creepers. They steal your time. They are already in the mode of "I-regard-you-as-fuckable" by the time you've taken your seat or walked by on the street, before you've even properly introduced yourself. If your sense is that *any* human relation—erotic or not— is an open structure, the very first requirement of which is curiosity, and the very second requirement of which is a certain humility, which in turn demands hesitation, approach, retreat, listening, playfulness, responsiveness, self-protection, self-disclosure, etc.; in other words, if any human relation requires *time*, then one knows one has encountered a creeper when one experiences the sexualized theft of time. The approach of the creeper reduces this whole complex temporality of the encounter by *already* having decided its meaning, by already having framed it exclusively in terms of his own needs and desires, by already knowing who-you-are-for-him before you get your coffee.

But then again, maybe the young woman *did* think it was a date, naively hoping that the old professor's sexual interest in her was an opening toward full-fledged curiosity and fascination, rather than just another effort to get laid. Maybe she was open to the possibility that he would encounter her as a living value in a complex erotic situation, as an end-in-herself (to throw in the relevant Kantian language)—rather than as a mere use value, a means to the old professor's narcissistic, urgent ends. Maybe she discovers, and is disappointed to discover, that he's really just another creeper. Or maybe she's not sure, or not sure yet.

When I imagine one of my daughters sitting in the café with the old professor, though, or even sharing a bottle of wine, I don't interpret the lifeless hand in the same way Sartre (who has a hard time being curious about what women know) does. Instead, I read her lifeless hand as evidence of a kind of knowledge. What this young woman-on-a-date knows, at least what her hand knows, even if she couldn't articulate this to you, is that she is with someone whose epistemic arrogance poses a threat. The creeper has already started to wrap her up in the tendrils of his intentionality— which in phenomenology isn't about conscious intentions. Intentionality is understood as the *of* in consciousness-of, or the *about* in knowing-about, or the *for* in wishing-for. It is a directedness toward an object of consciousness. This directedness is always shaded by a certain mood—one can

be *conscious-of* someone in a mood of curiosity, or fear, or love; and one can be *conscious-of* someone in a mood of contempt. The intentional mood saturates the whole interaction. The creeper's dominant intentional mood, when he is in the presence of certain women, is entitlement to acquisition. (Picture the bindweed.) He has already embarked on a kind of *capture*. His *way* of having a world is relentlessly acquisitive, in other words he seeks to seduce or compel certain others into a relation characterized primarily by use.

On the other side of the table, the young woman finds herself reduced to a feature of his having-a-world. This is not to say that he is merely objectifying her, relating to her as if she were a thing, although feminists have often used this language to try and express the harm of what is happening. It is, more significantly, that the expansiveness of his own agency demands that the agency of certain others be *annexed* to and consumed in his— it is not that her body is put to use as an object, though it well might be, but that the woman as body-*subject* is put to use.[3]

His creepiness is a kind of demand expressed in the mood of entitlement. When a demand is expressed in this mood, the possibility of real refusal or consent is effectively short-circuited, since both will be read through the fog of entitlement. He demands that she employ her agency (through flirtation, or feeling flattered, or expressing outrage) in the project of his sexual self-aggrandizement, but he communicates in the demand his *entitlement* to the demand. She discovers that the use *is already underway* in the demand, since he already confirms his entitlement by acting as one who is in a position to make such demands. His whole approach to her is saturated by a mood of sexual entitlement, so that *before she can even respond,* his enactment of the approach has already confirmed his status as entitled. Her blistering refusal feeds his way of having a world as much as her active acquiescence, since both confirm his authority to compel her subjective capacities to be-in-relation to him in a field whose possibilities he effectively controls.

We now see that leaving one's hand dead and numb on the table is a refusal, though not likely a consciously chosen one.[4] She refuses not just the demand, but the whole *scene* in which the world gets structured as a place where he demands and she responds, in which the possibilities of her agency are reduced to a response to his demand. She resists the creeping vines wrapping round her ankles and her wrists, so that every motion is a confirmation of the creeper's power, by remaining completely still. It may seem as though she will be strangled if she moves. If he is going to grasp her hand, as an expression of his entitlement to annex her agency, then she' will refuse to manifest freedom in her hand. In other words, she resists a world in which her own world-shaping capacity is preempted, by refusing to participate.

If the first harm of creepiness is the theft of time, the second harm is the pre-emption of her very way-of-having-a-world. This is why encounters with creepers, especially if they hold positions of respect or power or authority, have the potential to derail a woman's sense of self, to disrupt her ability to act. And indeed, the actions of creepers seem to be designed for this purpose, more than for the purposes of sexual titillation (except insofar as seeing a woman so derailed is titillating).

Of course, it is important to remind ourselves why it is that creepers seem to have such power, before they actually do anything to hurt you in the material sense of the word. Again, if the creeper starts threatening your grade or your employment or your professional reputation—that's already beyond creepy and, mostly, there are remedies for that. But certainly, not every other who approaches me in a mood of entitlement or acquisition undermines me so effectively as the creeper does, at least sometimes.

What makes creepiness so *effectively* creepy is that the mood of entitlement and acquisition that characterizes creepers is backed up by and taps into a whole world of imagery, language, and material relations that echo and amplify the creeper's demands.[5] A creeper in a context not saturated with images and stories of women as use-values for men, in a language which did not provide terms for referring to women as use-values for men, or in a material context in which women were not systematically disadvantaged, would simply be an annoyance—like a mosquito in a place where the fear of mosquito-borne illnesses has been eliminated. This whole complex is shored up by the fact that men often carry with them "a sense of implicit (and often unconscious) ownership of public space and its definitions and values—a sense of ownership that women typically do not feel."[6] This sense of ownership is backed up by the structure of material relations as well as the content of dominant cultural narratives. It is the total concrete situation, to use Beauvoir's important phrase, in which the creeper creeps that makes his creepiness so efficacious.

Creepiness, then, is not something teenage girls make up, nor something that a young woman philosophy student just imagines, sitting across from her old professor. Creepers pose an epistemic threat that closes time and pre-empts—with the collusion of an entire culture, with the complicity of social power arrangements—young women's world-making capacities. It is the enactment of a creepy kind of capture; it's already wrapped around your throat before you can start paying attention and threatens to close off your airway entirely if you dare to move.

Thesis #1: "Creepy" is an entitled and acquisitive mood of intentionality, nourished by broader misogynist social arrangements, through which a narcissistic subject steals your time, annexes your subjective powers, and pre-empts your world-making capacities.

What About Flirtation?

It is important to distinguish creepiness from flirtation, as some will object that my analysis is taking the fun out of everything. Flirtation, of course, has its proper place, though I will say that I think it is best left out of most hierarchical relationships most of the time—especially those characterized by significant imbalances of power—as between professors and their students, or supervisors and their employees, or adults and children. In these relations it is mostly not possible to flirt without being creepy. But it would be a sad mistake to misread all erotically charged interactions as "creepy," and I am not advocating anything of the sort. One of the crucial preconditions for flirtation will be power that is *equal enough* so that the vulnerability of the two parties stands a chance of being more or less the same, at least at the start.

One of my favorite examples of flirtation is that scene in the old feminist film *Thelma and Louise*, where the cowboy-hitchhiker-robber played by Brad Pitt flirts with Thelma (Geena Davis) in the car, and later in her hotel room. For those who don't know the story, Thelma and Louise are two friends on the lam, after the innocent Thelma (whose long marriage to her high school sweetheart has been a disaster) encounters a real creeper, who turns out to be a rapist, in a bar. Louise (Susan Sarandon) rescues Thelma from rape at gunpoint, then shoots the would-be rapist in the parking lot. Convinced they will never be believed, the two women head for the border in Thelma's old convertible. On the way they meet J. D. (Brad Pitt), and Thelma is smitten. Even though J. D. turns out to be quite a jerk, stealing Louise's life savings, which was to finance their escape—you couldn't call him a creeper *sexually*. His compliments to and playfulness with Thelma enact a kind of delighted, respectful invitation. When Thelma hesitates, he backs off and waits for her approach, clearly open to the possibility that her hesitation is the final word on the encounter. He waits to see if her *desire* is there to meet his. After hours of playful flirtation infused with intense curiosity in Thelma's hotel room, the two have wildly passionate sex. But even here, when Thelma says "wait" he listens. She emerges from the encounter having experienced herself as a sexual agent for the first time. When they discover their money is gone, she borrows a narrative J. D. recounted to her when he told her about his chosen profession, and robs a convenience store with Louise's gun. The film is, in large part, the story of Thelma's transformation from victim (of her abusive husband, of the rapist) to a woman conscious of her own world-shaping capacities, even in the context of a broader misogyny that she can't completely undo. Her empowerment is symbolized by her handiness with a gun, her ability to make things happen—as in one dramatic scene in which she and Louise blow the oil-tanker truck of another creeper sky high.

What one notices is that the structure of time is different, in flirtation, then in an encounter with a creeper. Her hesitation is met by his giving-space to that hesitation; his urgency is put out of play (by him) if not met by her responding urgency. In other words, a field of possibility is kept wide *open* in flirtation, at least insofar as I must leave open the possibility that you will respond, or you won't, that you will desire, or you won't, or that we will desire differently. Flirtation is acute curiosity about such possibilities, which doesn't, therefore, immediately close them all up; it is intensified attention to the details and particularities of a unique existent with an ability to enjoy surprises. In flirtation time opens, stretches out, luxuriates. Flirtation, especially if it is welcome, is a gift of time.

In flirtation, the mood of intentionality that saturates the encounter implies a way of having a world that has an open structure as well, so that I invite you to curiosity about my way of having a world, to enter in, but I refuse to make any assumptions about who you will be to me, even as my wonder or hope about the question infuses the whole encounter with a kind of intensity. There is no threat of unwilling capture before I've even had time to let myself wonder, so there is no threat of being locked into a world where my-meaning-for-you is already sealed up and decided, without my having played an active part in it. My world-shaping capacities are not pre-empted, but attended to intensively at the very heart of the encounter. This attention is reciprocal if the flirtation is.

The mood of intentionality in flirtation is nearly the opposite of the mood of intentionality in entitled acquisition. It is the animation of curiosity in an intensified, erotically charged field. It is invitation and appeal, not demand. It requires vigilance against acquisitiveness and entitlement. What distinguishes flirtation from creepiness is this open structure of time in an opened-up world, a sensitivity to refusal and consent, a willingness to retreat or approach. Frankly, the world we live in stacks the cards against flirtation, in favor of creepiness—which is why we need to think about the difference.

Thesis #2: Flirtation is a kind of erotic attention which opens the structure of time and intensifies wonder and curiosity between two subjects, in an opened-up world, in which one appeals to the world-making capacities of the other.

Beware of Male Heroes!

It bothers me a great deal that those same teenage daughters of mine who, I've just argued, take epistemic charge of a situation that is stacked against them by declaring, "What a creeper!" are also addicted to stories of male heroes. It hit me hardest when the older three, a few years ago, passed around the *Twilight* novels, huge, fat, 700-page monsters—and read each of them with a kind of breathless urgency. Wondering what all the fuss was about, I spent a few weeks reading the whole four-volume set myself.[7] I met Bella, the teenaged protagonist, and watched her be rescued—again and again and again. Edward Cullen, the vampire hero of the series, is the main rescuer, and his rival, Jacob, is rescuer number two. Bella's world-shaping capacities are reduced to choosing between them on occasion, though just as often they collaborate to save her despite their animosity to one another, or her half-hearted resistance, passing her back and forth like a rag doll. Though finally, at the end of volume four, she is actually able to effect a major rescue herself, the tone and tenor of the texts is dominated by images of Bella threatened by some really over-the-top creepers, then whisked away, draped over Edward's overly developed forearms as he carries her to safety.

Heroes are, it seems, overwhelmingly seductive to the current generation of young women. One teenage girl I know flushes with pride when she reports that her (well-meaning) boyfriend has just told her, for example, that she is "not allowed to walk alone in that area anymore." His urgency to protect her somehow disguises the fact that he takes it upon himself to "allow" or "not allow" certain actions—and this girl, who is not generally fond of people's authority to allow or not allow her things, virtually melts with delight as she recounts the story.

The problem is, there is a long patriarchal tradition of protectionism that is easily re-animated when women are victimized. The notion that men need to protect women from other men is, after all, an integral part of masculinist thinking. Just as girls grow up with stories and images of Prince Charming, or Edward Cullen, running around kissing them back to life or scooping them, in the nick of time, out of danger—boys grow up with stories and images of such rescues saturating their cultural space. Even cognitive scientists say that the rescue narrative is deeply culturally entrenched.[8] Rescuing women is, in fact, a necessary part of the life-story a manly man imagines for himself in a masculinist culture. It's part of what makes you a manly man, if you think you are one. And in a world in which women really *are* in danger of being victims of sexual violence, and also grow up with the rescue narrative all around them, this kind of chivalry can seem friendly, welcome, even necessary.

But what's going on, upon philosophical reflection, in the relation between the hero and the victim he sets out to rescue? First, as in any encounter, this meeting is characterized by a particular mood. We might call the mood, at first glance, before reflection, hyperbolic responsibility. I mean by this that he feels himself to be responsible for her in the way that a parent necessarily feels herself to be responsible for an infant or young child. This is an extreme existential responsibility, in that the very life or death of the child is in the parent's hands. In fact, a parent who brings a child into the world gives the child both life and *time*, in that the life-story of an individual starts at birth. Similarly, the hero imagines himself to occupy a certain position and to enjoy a certain status in the victim's world. He is the one without whom she ceases to exist. He is the one whom she waits for. He imagines the victim to exist in a state of *temporal suspension* in anticipation of his arrival, and that his arrival will bring her (as with Prince Charming and Snow White) back to life. He is the one who gives her back *time*, in other words. The hero thinks he restarts the life story of the victim at the moment of rescue, which he tends to mistakenly believe actually makes him the *author* of her story.

The problem with this impassioned fantasy is that it actually requires the victim's passivity, the victim's vulnerability, in order to keep itself going. There is only one agent in the rescue narrative, and it's not the victim. The hero can be recognized, in fact, by his tendency toward obsessive and hyperbolic displays of agency. Wherever women are victimized, if male heroes appear, they speak very loudly and flail around a lot. Their form of rescue tends to leave a great deal of destruction in its wake. Sometimes male heroes even appear in the absence of victims, as when white supremacists set out to save white womanhood from black rapists by lynching, though in the vast majority of lynching cases based on an accusation of insult to or assault on a white woman, no victim had come forward or was even named.[9] When there *are* victims, heroes constantly make the mistake of replacing the victim's agency with their own, violating a central principle of victim advocacy.

Since no victim *chooses* to be victimized or has control over a violent act committed against him or her, the ability for victims to *regain control* over their lives, and *make decisions* affecting their lives, becomes very important."[10] The worst hero will capture the entire story of a victim of harassment or abuse to animate his own agenda, whether that agenda consists of simple self-aggrandizement, a destructive war of aggression, or some other passionate mission to which he has linked his identity.

Commonly, this is more or less unconsciously motivated—and comes with a certain epistemic incapacity; the narcissistically driven personality cannot get enough distance from itself to recognize that it is self-obsessed, after all. While heroes claim to be knowers of women, they enjoy the hero-role to such an extent, and are so committed to their status as heroes, that they end up being aggressively ignorant about women's experiences and perspectives. In fact, that women might *have* perspectives that differ from theirs, might actually interpret or resist abuse rather than merely suffer it, is in itself a threat to the hero's status as the sole agent of the scene. What we first interpreted as an intentional mood of hyperbolic responsibility now shows itself to be something else: obsessive self-aggrandizement disguised as selfless devotion. Just as the devoted parent becomes the weight which holds a maturing child captive, the hero's heroism becomes an obsession which pins the victim to her victimization.

This is why male heroes are unable to accept leadership from women. They are very comfortable with women who are victimized, who are vulnerable—but they get very uncomfortable when women gain power. The hero will not ally himself with women who are likely to challenge his version of events, or who are perhaps more qualified for leadership when it comes to redressing the victimization of women than he is. More than this the male hero will need to systematically discredit those feminists who have been doing the work in the trenches all along, in order to present himself as the sole savior of vulnerable women. He will forget to mention the years of work that feminists have done to redress the harm in question. The work that women have done fighting for and writing sexual harassment policies and law, for example, may be entirely erased. The hero takes credit where he can, as if he's done all the work that mattered all by himself—women who are or have been world-shaping agents pose a danger to his ego. He will warn victims to stay away from those women whose self-definition is not heavily focused on victimization, because if the victims who feed his ego cease to see themselves primarily as such, and instead understand themselves to be capable of world-shaping activity, his status as the savior of vulnerable women will be punctured like an oversized hot-air balloon.

In relation to other men, the hero operates on the principle that the bigger and meaner the dragon-to-be-slayed, the more valiant will be the charming prince. The fact is, *the hero needs the creeper* in order to tell his story. He is as committed to a world in which women are victimized as the creeper is. His wish to exaggerate the differences between himself and other men creates the need to portray men who harass or abuse women as pathological monsters, rather than simply as men whose behavior is "an expression of the norms of the culture, not violations of those norms."[11] Heroes tend to exaggerate stories of abuse in order to add glory to their own heroism. Even men who stand against the abuse of women, but in a quieter, less dramatic way, are in for a slaying. The paradigm of hyperbolic manhood doesn't have room for sissies, whose agency is not obsessively on display. The problem is, of course, that men who harass and abuse women are not, by and large, pathological. They simply take the entitlements offered to them in a misogynist culture quite seriously. Portraying them as monsters lets the culture of masculinism, which includes the very dynamic of protectionism the hero enacts, off the hook. It also lets the hero off the hook—he needn't ever reflect on how he benefits from the arrangements as they are. A focus on individual monsters who need to be slayed distorts the truth of sexual harassment, which is rooted in a total concrete situation that is structured to pre-empt women's world-making capacities, through masculinist violence *and* masculinist protectionism.

And here it becomes clear that heroes and creepers have something in common. Both are epistemically arrogant. Both live their relations to women in a posture of entitlement, in which they relate to the women around them primarily as players-of-parts in their own stories. They are incapable of recognizing women as authors or potential authors of perception and meaning. Their posture toward women is, in other words, acquisitive. They are "creepy" in the way that certain invasive vines are creepy, in that the intentional threads that anchor their actions in the world, which their female interlocutors also inhabit, perform a kind of capture. Both the creeper's and the hero's way of having a world pre-empts women's world-making capacities. These capacities are already siphoned off and harnessed to the hero's grand narrative before she sits down across the table from him, opening a conversation, or looking for help.

Thesis #3: A hero is a narcissistic subject, whose hero story, nourished by broader misogynist social arrangements, requires victims to rescue; the hero's obsessive displays of agency preempt and undermine the world-making capacities of the ones he sets out to save.

How to Know an Ally When You See One

Allies are very different sorts of men, and I'm happy to say I've had the opportunity to know and work with a good number of them. They aren't loud or flashy. They don't obsessively display their self-sacrifice, and they don't talk endlessly about their heroic efforts on behalf of women. In fact, on subjects like this one, they do more listening than talking. They are aware that in the world we have inherited, their voices will tend to command some authority, at least in their own communities, just because they are men, and they are circumspect about this—thinking hard about when it is appropriate to deploy that authority strategically, and when it is not. Allies tend to work more than they talk. They are the ones who support women's events by taking over the child-care or volunteering to be on the clean-up team, rather than appointing themselves to be key-note speaker. To put the point more philosophically, an ally is someone who respects the epistemic authority of women in relation to women's experiences and concerns.

More than this, an ally remains cognizant of the ways that he is implicated in the very culture and structures of power that are the backdrop for and the animating force for individual acts of abuse or harassment. In encounters with an ally one is immediately aware of an intentional mood that might best be described as *circumspect*. He practices epistemic humility in relation to women and women's concerns, without giving up his responsibility to know and to act. He understands that self-reflection, when one holds power, can be both painful and difficult, even as it is necessary. Here, the temporal mood is one of hesitation first, then care. When confronted with a feminist criticism or demand, he will not necessarily accept it, but he will respond first with curiosity, wondering what he might have missed, or what he is not understanding yet.

When women are victimized, allies don't sit on their hands, but neither do they rush to seal up a definition of the situation, the agenda, or the path out—knowing that space needs to be left, and created, for women to do those things. When advocating for victims of male violence or exploitation, they are very careful not to replace the victims' voices with their own. They are very careful not to replace the victims' agendas with their own. Allies are aware of the need to *create space* for women to come to a definition of the situation, to set agendas, and to decide on strategies for redress. They will employ their privilege or institutional power, if they have it, to make such space. In addition to exercising epistemic humility then, allies are space-makers.

One clear difference between a hero and an ally is that while heroes demonize male perpetrators of harassment or abuse in order to exalt themselves, allies challenge the behavior of other men, often forcefully, as *peers*.[12] Allies do not shy away from face-to-face conversations in which they challenge their male peers to behave better. They recognize that exaggerating stories of harassment or abuse by portraying the men who practice these things as "crazed rapists," even if they know that the public at large will have a hard time recognizing the harms in more "subtle" forms of harassment, serves no one's interest but their own. In fact such portrayals serve to distort the reality of sexual harassment and other abuses, including rape, which are enacted most often by men who *comply* with dominant cultural norms, rather than deviating from them. Understanding that portraying certain men (often racially coded) as monsters amounts to engaging in a kind of public relations campaign for masculinism as a whole, allies avoid such portrayals. Instead, they are careful to point out how the most subtle sexist behavior, often unconsciously enacted, plays its part in the whole cultural scene, in which harassment and abuse emerge as intensified moments of the same structure. They will not approach the harasser as an individual monster, then, but as a co-beneficiary of a system that is not of their own, individual, making—knowing that they, too, have to be vigilant against enacting its privileges. While allies will not hesitate to avail themselves of policy and law to assist women who seek redress from particular harms, their sense of responsibility will be much broader, extending most importantly to the constitution of male peer culture. Allies are not princes in shining armor, they are culture critics.

Allies are not threatened by women who have power, though they may not always agree with them. They understand how important it is for women who have been harmed to find and talk with other women who have experienced similar harms. They understand that sexual harassment and other abuses that fall along traditional gender lines nourish themselves on a world that is saturated with messages and images of women as use-values for men, and that is often structured materially to women's collective disadvantage relative to men of their race and social class. They realize that feminism is the emancipatory movement that has undertaken resistance to these arrangements, and that, consequently, *the promotion of feminism is itself a form of resistance to the harms of sexual harassment or abuse.*

Thesis #4: An ally is a hard-working and epistemically humble culture critic, who is circumspect about his unwilling or unwitting participation in misogynist social arrangement, without being immobilized by his own circumspection.

Conclusion

The real men in our lives are not always so neatly divided up, of course, either creepers or flirts, heroes or allies. One man might be any or all of these characters over the course of a lifetime, and the boundaries between them, even in a single moment, are not always clear cut. Creepiness, flirtation, heroism, and alliance are all, ultimately, modes of intersubjective engagement rather than typologies of character. While some men will so wholeheartedly affirm and so passionately commit themselves to one of these modes that the character of the person becomes dominated and saturated by the mode of engagement, mostly, things will be more confusing than that. All of us know that, often enough, we discover ourselves to be in the grip of a certain intentional mood when already in the midst of an encounter, *before* having made a reflective commitment to it.

By teasing these four modes apart, we see more clearly the possibilities of harm and the potential goods that come with different modes of intentional engagement. For those who are men of good will, reflecting on the intentional structures of the kinds of intersubjective engagement that are enacted by "creepers, flirts, heroes, and allies" might make it possible to change the direction of an encounter, or change the tone of one's dominant mode of engagement with certain women, so that women's world-shaping capacities are engaged rather than undermined. It might also make it possible to challenge male peers on the less overtly coercive forms of sexual harassment, to recognize the harms of those forms of harassment, without having to resort to the slash-and-bum strategies deployed by heroes.

In fact, taking responsibility for male peer culture would entail challenging both creepers and heroes, where creepers invigorate the backdrop of fear and the threat of sexual violence that allows heroes to come to the rescue. The distance provided by critical reflection allows us to recognize that both postures implicitly affirm and rely on a culture in which facing sexual harm and depending on rescue are rigidified as necessary facets of the condition of being female. Both postures preempt women's world-making capacities by reifying these conditions. The only way out of this "male protection racket," as feminists called it in the 70s, is for women collectively, in the company of allies, to reshape the social world so that it is not structured in terms of these two possibilities.

For those of us who are women, if we are to live our way through the complex dynamics we encounter in the work place, at the mall, or on the street, we need to be aware of and skilled at recognizing the signs of each of these intentional modes. Naming creepers, flirts, heroes, and allies is part of assuming epistemic authority over a situation. Reflecting on what it is that we know when we use such names is one task of feminist criticism. What is at stake, in the daily gifts and thefts of space and time, in our ability to accept the gifts and resist the thefts in each case, is the status of our world-shaping capacities. What is at stake is our ability to insist on a world in which those capacities might flourish.

DISCUSSION QUESTIONS

1. Explain the differences between creepers, flirts, heroes, and allies. Which of these two archetypes should men strive to model their behavior after, and which two should they avoid?
2. If creepiness were to occur in a society that was not sexist, it would at most be annoying. Explain how the background conditions in a sexist society transform this behavior into something far more sinister.
3. Where Sartre diagnoses a woman on a date as exhibiting "bad faith" for refusing to either accept

or refuse her partner's sexual demands, Mann reinterprets Sartre's story to defend this woman's actions as existentially responsible. Explain how Mann's defense of this woman involves a rejection of masculine sexual entitlement.
4. Explain what Mann means when she argues that "the hero needs the creeper in order to tell his story. He is as committed to a world in which women are victimized as the creeper is."

NOTES

1. Especially, but not only in the case of street harassment, many feminists have noted how the threat of sexual violence is evoked by and backgrounds the harassment, so that such harassment, in the words of June Larkin, "contributes to the moulding of young women's subordinate status . . . because so much of their energy is geared to securing their own safety. When a young woman is continually reminded of the risks that accompany her developing body, when she is constantly under the scrutiny and surveillance of males, and when she lives in a state of constant vigilance, it's unlikely that she'll ever develop a sense of herself as a powerful and autonomous person." See June Larkin, "Sexual Terrorism on the Streets: The Moulding of Young Women into Subordination," in *Sexual Harassment: Contemporary Feminist Perspectives*, edited by Alison M. Thomas and Celia Kitzinger (Buckingham and Philadelphia: Open University Press, 1997), 115–130.
2. Jean Paul Sartre, *Being and Nothingness: A Phenomenological Essay on Ontology* (New York: Washington Square Press, 1992), 96–97.
3. Beauvoir was the first to understand this structure of acquisition, which she called "inessential otherness" in *The Second Sex*. For a more contemporary exploration, see Ann Cahill, *Overcoming Objectification: A Carnal Ethics* (Hoboken: Taylor and Francis, 2010).
4. Kathleen Cairns wonders, "How can we explain the frequency with which otherwise assertive and self-confident women experience this paralysis of the will that makes it impossible for them to say no to unwanted sexual activity?" "'Femininity' and Women's Silence in Response to Sexual Harassment and Coercion," in *Sexual Harassment: Contemporary Feminist Perspectives*, op. cit., p. 92.

She argues, citing Kaschak, that "Masculine meanings organize social and personal experience, so that women are constantly imbued with meanings, not of their own making," p. 95.

5. I am accepting, here, what MacKinnon calls the "social" position on sexual harassment, described by Crouch as the idea that "sexual harassment is a manifestation of the basic inequality of men and women as "men" and "women" are constructed in our society. Crouch, p. 10.

6. *Ibid.*, p. 232.

7. An article resulted from this exercise. See my "Vampire Love: The Second Sex Negotiates the 21st Century," in *Twilight and Philosophy: Vampires, Vegetarians, and the Pursuit of Immortality*, edited by Rebecca Housel and Jeremy Wisnewski (Blackwell Press, 2009). Excerpted in The Philosopher's Magazine 47, 4th Quarter (2009). Reprinted in *Introducing Philosophy through Popular Culture*, edited by William Irwin and David Kyle Johnson (Wiley-Blackwell 2010).

8. George Lakoff, George. *The Political Mind: Why You Can't Understand 21st Century Politics with an 18th Century Brain*. New York: Viking Press, 2008.

9. Angela Davis, "Rape, Racism and the Myth of the Black Rapist," in *Women, Race and Class* (New York: Vintage Books, 1983).

10. Justice Solutions: A Website by Crime Victim Professionals for Crime Victim Professionals. http://www.iusticesoiutions.org/artj3ub_communicating_with_victims.pdf (November 4, 2011).

11. Jackson Katz, *The Macho Paradox: Why Some Men Hurt Women and How All Men Can Help* (Naperville, Illinois: Sourcebooks, 2006), 149. Jackson Katz gives a convincing account of why both men and women are reassured by images of men who harm women as "crazed rapists" rather than as regular guys, whose behavior is broadly supported by the culture. See his analysis of this phenomenon beginning on p. 149.

12. Katz proposes that men take responsibility for building a male peer culture that is intolerant of the abuse of women generally, rather than dividing men into the "good guys" and the "bad guys" (i.e., the "crazed rapists"), a strategy which means, "men who do not rape can easily distance themselves from the problem" (150).

Sexual Objectification: From Kant to Contemporary Feminism

BY EVANGELIA PAPADAKI

Evangelia Papadaki is a Greek philosopher who writes on issues in Kantian philosophy. This essay explores the ways that many influential feminist accounts of sexual objectification—from Catharine MacKinnon and Andrea Dworkin to Martha Nussbaum—have their roots in the philosophy of Immanuel Kant. Papadaki explains both the surprising similarities and the important differences between these accounts, including a contrast of Kant's argument that marriage provides the solution to the problem of sexual objectification with the feminist argument that marriage, with its historical connotations of ownership and domination, is not a solution but rather part of the problem.

Introduction

Sexual objectification is a common theme in contemporary feminist theory. Catharine MacKinnon and Andrea Dworkin have famously argued that due to men's consumption of pornography women as a group are objectified. More recently, Martha Nussbaum has done some remarkable work exploring the negative, as well as the positive, aspects involved in the notion of objectification. Interestingly, those feminists' views on sexuality and objectification have their foundations in the philosophy of Immanuel Kant.

Within sexual relationships outside monogamous marriage, as Kant has argued, the risk of objectification is always present.

> Sexual love makes of the loved person an Object of appetite; as soon as that appetite has been stilled, the person is cast aside as one casts away a lemon which has been sucked dry . . . as soon as a person becomes an Object of appetite for another, all motives of moral relationship cease to function, because as an Object of appetite for another a person becomes a thing and can be treated and used as such by every one (Kant, 1963, 163).

The loved person, Kant holds in this passage from the *Lectures on Ethics*, is made into an "object of appetite"; a thing.[1]

My purpose in this paper is, first, to provide a focused study of Kant's views on sexual objectification. It is my belief that Kant gave us a coherent theory of objectification. Yet his views on this issue are often blurred and, at times, even sound contradictory. They therefore deserve a close and careful examination. This is done in the next three sections. I then proceed in further sections, to some contemporary feminist discussions on sexual objectification, showing how influential Kant's ideas have been for thinkers like MacKinnon, Dworkin, and Nussbaum. My analysis of these feminists' work focuses on the striking similarities, as well as the differences, that exist between their views on what objectification is, how it is caused, and how it can be eliminated and Kant's.

That Kant's ideas on sex and its dangers find application today in the work of these prominent scholars is an important observation. It shows that we do indeed have an additional reason to take Kant's views on these issues, which have been criticized harshly by many as puritanical, conservative, even incomprehensible, more seriously.

At the same time, being able to discover the Kantian elements in the work of these feminists is essential in order to comprehend their views on sexuality and objectification.

Kant and the Process of Objectification

I will start my investigation of Kant's views on sexual objectification by dealing with some apparently contradictory views he has about persons and sex. The following two passages from the *Lectures on Ethics* are crucial in our understanding of the objectification process:

> (1) Amongst our inclinations there is one which is *directed towards other human beings. They themselves*, and not their work and services, are its Objects of enjoyment. It is true that man has no inclination to enjoy the flesh of another—except, perhaps, in the vengeance of war, and then it is hardly a desire—but none the less there does exist an inclination which we may call *an appetite for enjoying another human being*. We refer to sexual impulse (Kant, 1963, 162–163. *My italics*).
>
> Because sexuality *is not an inclination which one human being has for another as such*, but is an *inclination for the sex of another*, it is a principle of the degradation of human nature, in that it gives rise to the preference of one sex to the other, and to the dishonouring of that sex through the satisfaction of desire. The desire which a man has for a woman *is not directed towards her because she is a human being*, but because she is a woman; *that she is a human being is of no concern to the man; only her sex is the object of his desires* (Kant, 1963, 164. *My italics*).

A first glance at the above passages may give one the impression that they involve two contradictory ideas. In the first passage, Kant says that sexual desire is an appetite for enjoying another *human being*.[2] She as a human being is the object of the man's enjoyment, and not her "work" or "services." According to passage (1), then, sexual desire is directed towards a human being, in a way that makes the latter an object of her partner's enjoyment, and so a thing.[3]

In the second passage, Kant seems to locate the problem elsewhere; sexual desire is directed towards a *human being's sex* (towards her eroticized body or genitalia), *not* towards a *human being as such*. In fact, according to passage (2), what seems to be wrong with sexual desire is that it does not pay any attention to the other as a human being. When sexuality is involved, all the attention is directed towards the other's sex. Reading those passages leaves us wondering whether the problem with sexuality is that it is directed towards the individual as a human being or, rather, that it is directed towards her sex only.

Later on, in the *Lectures on Ethics*, Kant explains that a human being is constituted by a body and a self, or rational personhood (Herman, 1993, 61). An individual's body and self are integrally bound together, in a way that the two cannot be separated (Kant, 1963, 166). At this point, we begin to get a clearer grasp of his view in passage (1), that sexual desire is directed towards a *human being*. The inseparability between body and self makes it simply impossible that sexual desire is directed towards an individual's *body only*. It is necessarily directed towards an individual as a whole. However, passage (2) sounds even more puzzling now. Kant writes in this passage that sexual desire is directed towards *sex only*, not towards a *human being as such* (Kant, 1963, 164). How can this be possible given his view on the inseparable unity between body and self in human beings?

There is, I believe, a possible way to read passages (1) and (2) which removes the apparent contradiction between them. There seem to be two ways in which Kant uses the term "human being" in the passages in question: (a) human being as a unity between body and self, and (b) human being as an individual with humanity, a being with dignity, an absolute value that a person has *qua* person, and that must always be respected in moral choice and action.[4] Use (a) describes the fact that a human being is constituted by a body and a self. I will call it the *neutral use*. Use (b) refers to the morally correct way to treat one's partner, which is, for Kant, to respect her humanity. I will call this second use of the term "human being" the *moral use.*

Let us go back to the two passages in question with the above in mind. When Kant says, in passage (1), that sexual desire is directed towards a human being he employs the neutral use of this term. It is inevitably directed towards another human being, in the sense that is directed towards an individual's body and self. In passage (2), now, when Kant writes that sexuality is not directed towards a human being as such but towards her sex, he employs the moral use of the term. He wants to emphasize the fact that in exercising his sexuality, a person does not respect his partner's humanity. Rather, he regards her as a being of the opposite sex with whom he only wishes to interact sexually.

We can conclude from the above that Kant's views in passages (1) and (2) are not contradictory. Both these passages are crucial in our understanding of how Kant thought sexual desire can objectify: sexual desire is directed towards an individual's person (body and self) in a way that the individual in question is regarded as an object of appetite, a thing. This means that she is not regarded as a person in the moral sense; her humanity is not respected. Consequently, for Kant, the individual becomes (she is made into) an object of appetite.

Why Is Sex in Marriage Morally Permissible?

Kant admits in the *Lectures on Ethics* that sexuality is indeed very important for people. Without it, he writes, an individual is incomplete, imperfect as a human being (Kant, 1963, 164). According to him, the *only* context where people can exercise their sexuality "without degrading humanity and breaking the moral laws" is that of monogamous marriage (Kant, 1963, 167). My aim in this section is to explain Kant's reasons for thinking that sex within this context is morally permissible.

To begin with, Kant strongly believed that monogamous marriage is an objectification-free relationship. First of all, there is no financial gain involved in marriage, unlike in prostitution; the spouses do not use each other sexually in exchange for money. Secondly, unlike concubinage, a relationship of inequality in the surrender of persons, Kant conceived of marriage as a relationship of perfect equality and reciprocity in the surrender of the two spouses' persons. Neither of them, therefore, is in danger of losing his or her person and getting objectified.

In the *Lectures on Ethics*, Kant describes this equality and reciprocity in the giving and taking of the two spouses' persons: ". . . if I yield myself completely to another and obtain the person of the other in return, I win myself back; I have given myself up as the property of another, but in turn I take that other as my property, and so win myself back again in winning the person whose property I have become. In this way the two persons become a unity of will" (Kant, 1963, 167). Barbara Herman calls this mutual exchange of the spouses' persons a "romantic blending" (Herman, 1993, 61). Figure 1 explains how Kant thought it works.

Kant emphasizes that this equality and reciprocity in the giving and taking of the two spouses must be *legally* enforced. Marriage is, Kant states, "sexual union in accordance with law" (Kant, 1996, 62); it is a legal contract, which obligates the two parties to surrender their persons completely (in the sense of exclusively) to one another, each allowing the other to completely own his or her person (to become the other's property). Kant wants something external, the law, to guarantee this lifelong ownership of the two parties' persons. The two spouses simply do not have the right to stop surrendering their persons to one another in this way.

This legal obligation to surrender one's person to one's spouse is what makes marriage different from a relationship between two unmarried partners. The latter may surrender their persons completely to one another, as long as they feel like it, but there is nothing external to guarantee that such reciprocal surrender will last. In the absence of a legal obligation to keep surrendering their persons to one another for life, there is always the risk that one of the two partners will leave the other. The legal nature of the marital relationship, then, gives to each of the two parties security in the ownership of the other's person: since each spouse is owned by the other, neither of them has the right to leave or be unfaithful to his or her spouse (Kant, 1996, 62). Within marriage, then, each party can safely surrender his or her person completely to the other, reassured that the latter will do the same. In this way, the reciprocity of surrender is maintained.

In marriage, then, as Kant describes it, the two parties have equal rights to own and dispose of each other's persons (Kant, 1963, 167). The two spouses' right to use each other's persons, includes the right to use each other's bodies (sexually and otherwise). As Kant explains, "If I have the right over the whole person, I have also the right to use that person's *organa sexualia* for the satisfaction of sexual desire" (Kant, 1963, 167). The two spouses in marriage, then, can rightfully make use of each other's sexual attributes.

Within monogamous marriage, furthermore, the two spouses are not only allowed but also required to use each other sexually, according to Kant, and not only for the purposes of procreation (Kant, 1996, 62). If one or both spouses are incapable of intercourse, or have agreed for some other reason to refrain from it, Kant says that their contract is simulated and, therefore, institutes no marriage (Kant, 1996, 63). This is because Kant thought that the reciprocal ownership of the two spouses' persons, which is so crucial in order for his conception of marriage to work, "is realized only through the use of their sexual attributes by each other" (Kant, 1996, 64). So, in order for the two spouses to be able to own each other's persons (bodies and selves) they must, according to Kant, make sexual use of each other's bodies.[5] The spouses' using each other sexually, then, is absolutely essential for the very functioning of Kantian marriage.

So far, we have seen why Kant thought that monogamous marriage is an objectification-free context: in equally and reciprocally owning each other's persons, neither of the two spouses is in danger of losing his or her person and getting objectified. Surprisingly, however, instances of animality are present within marriage. Even within this context, sex itself remains, for Kant, nothing more than an animal inclination. He characterizes marital sex as the ". . . permitted bodily union of the sexes . . . (a union which is in itself merely an animal union)" (Kant, 1996, 179). Sexual desire is by its nature dehumanizing in this sense. So, when having sex, the two spouses do surrender to their sexual animal inclinations.

Such moments of animality, however, do not seem to bother Kant when occurring within monogamous marriage. Sex within this context is an animal inclination, yet it is permissible. There is an air of paradox in this claim. However, it is indeed possible to explain why Kant allows such instances of animality within marriage. To put it very simply, Kant, who does acknowledge the fact that is very important for people to satisfy their sexual inclinations, must come up with a context in which people can do this in a morally unproblematic way. Of all sexual relationships Kant discusses, monogamous marriage clearly stands out as a morally safe and unproblematic context. Within this relationship, the two parties in general respect and deeply value each other's humanity. So, those instances of animality, which inevitably occur when people exercise their sexuality, are, when taking place within such a morally sound context, benign. That is, they constitute no threat to the two spouses' status as agents with dignity.

Sexual Objectification: The Feminists

It has been argued, in the previous sections, that objectification, for Kant, involves the reduction of a person to the level of an object for use; a mere sexual instrument. Objectification, therefore, constitutes the loss of an individual's humanity; she no longer has a dignity, an absolute value, but only a relative or instrumental value. As Kant puts it: "as an object of appetite, a person becomes a thing, and can be treated and used as such by everyone . . . used by all and sundry as an instrument for the satisfaction of sexual inclination . . . [humanity] is thereby sacrificed to sex" (Kant, 1963, 163–165).

MacKinnon and Dworkin describe objectification in strikingly similar terms. Like Kant, these feminists take objectification to involve treating a person as an object, a mere instrument for someone else's purposes, in such a way that the person in question is reduced to the status of an object for use. Dworkin, using very Kantian language, writes about the phenomenon of sexual objectification: "Objectification occurs when a human being . . . is made less than human, turned into a thing or commodity, bought or sold. When objectification occurs, a person is depersonalized . . . those who can be used as if they are not fully human are no longer fully human in social terms; their humanity is hurt by being diminished" (Dworkin, 2000, 30–31).

MacKinnon too uses Kantian language in her description of sexual objectification. She writes: "A sex object is defined on the basis of its looks, in terms of its usability for sexual pleasure . . . A person, in one Kantian view, is a free and rational agent whose existence is an end in itself, as opposed to instrumental. In pornography women exist to the *end* of male pleasure" (MacKinnon, 1987, 173, 158). Kant compares the objectified individual to a lemon, used and discarded afterwards, and elsewhere to a steak consumed by people for the satisfaction of their hunger (Kant, 1963, 163, 165). In a similar manner, MacKinnon holds that due to men's consumption of pornography women become comparable to cups, and as such they are valued only for how they can be used by men (MacKinnon, 1987, 138).

For Kant, Dworkin, and MacKinnon, then, objectification involves treating a person as an object (a mere sexual tool), in a way that leads to the reduction of the individual in question to the status of a thing for use (a lemon, a steak, a cup). Objectification, therefore, for all these thinkers constitutes a serious harm to an individual's humanity.

Nussbaum conceives of objectification in a much broader way than Kant, MacKinnon, and Dworkin. She believes that seven notions are involved in the idea of objectification: instrumentality, denial of autonomy, inertness, fungibility, violability, ownership, and denial of subjectivity (Nussbaum, 1995, 257). Nussbaum aims to challenge the idea shared by Kant, as well as by MacKinnon and Dworkin, that objectification should be conceived as a phenomenon that necessarily harms an individual's humanity. A person, Nussbaum suggests, can be treated as an object in one or more of these seven ways, without such treatment posing a threat to her humanity. Objectification, she believes, can possibly constitute a harmless or even a "wonderful" element of sexual life (Nussbaum, 1995, 251).

Nussbaum, however, does acknowledge the fact that objectification often takes negative forms, constituting a serious harm to people's humanity. For example, Nussbaum agrees with MacKinnon, Dworkin, and Kant that objectification in the form of treating an individual as a mere instrument for another's purposes is deeply problematic morally. She states: "It would appear that Kant, MacKinnon, and Dworkin are correct in one central insight: that the instrumental treatment of human beings, the treatment of human beings as tools of the purposes of another, is always morally problematic" (Nussbaum, 1995, 289).

Sexual objectification, then, as described by Kant, involving the treatment of a person as a mere sexual instrument, is still recognized as a deeply worrying phenomenon by contemporary feminists. Nussbaum, MacKinnon, and Dworkin, furthermore, agree with Kant that the phenomenon of objectification is tightly linked to inequality. In concubinage, Kant thought, because of the inequality in the possession of the two parties' persons, the woman eventually loses her person and becomes a thing. In marriage, by contrast, there is no objectification taking place precisely because the two spouses are equal in the ownership of each other's persons.

Nussbaum follows Kant in arguing that within sexual contexts characterized by inequality and lack of mutuality between the parties involved, people's humanity is at risk. Objectification within such contexts, Nussbaum argues, is of a negative kind. She mentions three such examples of negative objectification, in her article: a passage from Hankinson's novel, *Isabelle and Veronique*, in which the heroine Isabelle is raped and physically hurt by a man; an example from *Playboy*, in which the woman depicted in the magazine is treated by men as a mere sexual tool; and, finally, a passage taken from James' *The Golden Bowl*, where the two heroes, Adam and the Maggie, treat their spouses as antique furniture (Nussbaum, 1995, 252–253, 353–354, respectively). In all three of these cases, characterized by inequality and lack of reciprocity, the powerless individuals' humanity, as Nussbaum acknowledges, is deeply hurt.

MacKinnon and Dworkin also take inequality of power to be closely bound up with objectification. The feminists in question, however, believe that the phenomenon of inequality is much more widespread and pervasive than Kant and Nussbaum take it to be. MacKinnon and Dworkin emphasize that we live in a world of *gender inequality*. A person's *gender* is, for MacKinnon, clearly distinguished from a person's *sex*. Gender, being a man or a woman, is socially constructed, whereas sex, being male or female, is biologically defined. Within our patriarchal societies, men and women have very clearly defined roles: women (all women, women as a group) are objectified, whereas men (all men, men as a group) are their objectifiers (MacKinnon, 1987, 6, 32–45, 50; MacKinnon, 1989, 113–114, 128, 137–140; Haslanger, 1993, 98–101).

For MacKinnon and Dworkin, then, women are by definition the objectified. Moreover, the feminists in question believe that pornography is responsible for creating and sustaining this unfortunate reality.[6] Kant, by contrast, did not take women's objectification to be a necessary fact. Even though he did acknowledge the fact that women are the most common victims of objectification, Kant did not exclude the possibility of a woman objectifying a man if she happens to be in a position of power within a certain relationship. Furthermore, Kant, unlike MacKinnon and Dworkin, thought that men's humanity is also at risk when engaging in problematic sexual contexts, even when they do not get objectified. For instance, within prostitution and concubinage, Kant believed that men's humanity is threatened by the danger of animality.

Interestingly, Kant and the anti-pornography feminists in question agree that a person's consent to allow herself to be sexually used by others as an object is not enough to make such use permissible. However, their attitude towards the objectified individual is completely different. According to Kant, it is the responsibility of a person to refrain from offering herself as a sexual instrument outside the contexts of monogamous marriage, in order to protect her own humanity and avoid her objectification. If she does allow others to make sexual use of her, then she is responsible and blameworthy for the harm done to her humanity (Kant, 1963, 165). Kant is admittedly very harsh towards the objectified individual who, according to him, chooses to dishonour her humanity in offering her person as a thing to be sexually used by others.

MacKinnon and Dworkin, on the other hand, believe that women consent to be sexually used by men, not because they truly want to be used in this way, but simply out of lack of options available to them within our patriarchal societies. Their consent is, therefore, not true consent. As MacKinnon notes: "The sex is not chosen for the sex. Money is the medium of force and provides the cover for consent" (MacKinnon, 1993, 28). MacKinnon and Dworkin, then, do not take women to be truly blameworthy for their reduction to objects of merely instrumental value. Women's objectification, according to them, is demanded and inflicted by men in our societies. As Dworkin characteristically writes: ". . . those who dominate you get you to take the initiative in your own human destruction . . ." (Dworkin, 1997, 143).

DISCUSSION QUESTIONS

1. Explain Immanuel Kant's account of what is wrong with sexual objectification.
2. Explain why Kant thinks monogamous marriage is the condition under which morally acceptable sexual relations can occur. Given that procreation is explicitly not the only factor here, do you think this argument could be used to defend the permissibility of same-sex marriage?
3. How does Kant's understanding of sexual objectification bear on the accounts of feminists such as Catharine MacKinnon, Andrea Dworkin, and Martha Nussbaum?
4. Explain why feminists such as MacKinnon, Dworkin, and Nussbaum argue that heterosexual monogamous marriage is not the solution to sexual objectification, but rather part of the problem.

NOTES

1. This paper focuses on sexual objectification occurring within heterosexual relationships. Objectification, however, the lowering of person to the level of an object, is not, for Kant, the only moral danger involved in the exercise of sexuality. He is also worried that "sexuality . . . exposes mankind to the danger of equality with the beasts" (Kant, 1963, 164). Here, Kant is concerned that sex will engage the human predisposition to animality, which John Rawls describes as a, "Physical and 'purely mechanical' self-love by which [Kant] means that it does not require the exercise of reason and is generally guided by instinct and by acquired tendencies and habits" (Rawls, 2000, 292).

2. Kant uses the German terms "mensch" ("human being") and "person" ("person") interchangeably when talking about sexual desire in the *Lectures on Ethics* (Kant, 1963, 162–168). In this paper, I also use these two terms in an interchangeable manner.

3. Since women, according to Kant, generally have fewer rights and less power than men within sexual relationships outside monogamous marriage, they are the most likely victims of objectification. Even though, in theory, for Kant, a woman can objectify a man, this does not very often happen in practice, as his discussions of concubinage and polygamous marriage reveal. I have decided, therefore, to use the female pronoun for the "loved person" (the objectified) and the male pronoun for the "lover" (the objectifier) throughout this paper.

4. "Every human being has a legitimate claim to respect from his fellow human beings and is *in turn* bound to respect every other. Humanity itself is a dignity; for a man cannot be used merely as a means by any man (either by others or even by himself) but must always be used at the same time as an end. It is just in this that his dignity (personality) consists, by which he raises himself above all other beings in the world that are not men and yet can be used, and so over all *things*" (Kant, 1996, 209).

5. This is a quite striking view; in order for the spouses to be able to own each other's persons, it is necessary not only that they *own* each other's bodies, but also that they *use* each other's bodies sexually.

6. As MacKinnon explains: "Men treat women as who they see women as being. Pornography constructs who that is. Men's power over women means that the way men see women defines who women can be. Pornography is that way. Pornography is not imagery in some relation to a reality elsewhere constructed. It is not a distortion, reflection, projection, expression, fantasy, representation, or symbol either. It is sexual reality" (MacKinnon, 1987, 172–173).

REFERENCES

Dworkin, A. (1989) *Pornography: Men Possessing Women*, New York: EP Dutton.

Dworkin, A. (1997) *Intercourse*, New York: Free Press Paperbacks.

Dworkin, A. (2000) "Against the Male Flood: Censorship, Pornography, and Equality," in D. Cornell (ed.) *Oxford Readings in Feminism: Feminism and Pornography*, Oxford: Oxford University Press.

Haslanger, S. (1993) "On Being Objective and Being Objectified," in L. M. Antony and C. Witt (eds.) *A Mind of One's Own: Feminist Essays on Reason and Objectivity*, Boulder, San Francisco, Oxford: Westview Press.

Herman, B. (1993) "Could It Be Worth Thinking About Kant on Sex and Marriage?," in L. M. Antony and C. Witt (eds.) *A Mind of One's Own: Feminist Essays on Reason and Objectivity*, Boulder, San Francisco, Oxford: Westview Press.

Kant, I. (1963) "Trans," in L. Infield (ed.) *Lectures on Ethics*, New York: Harper and Row.

Kant, I. (1996) "Trans," in M. Gregor (ed.) *The Metaphysics of Morals*, Cambridge: Cambridge University Press.

Korsgaard, C. (1996) *Creating the Kingdom of Ends*, Cambridge: Cambridge University Press.

MacKinnon, C. (1987) *Feminism Unmodified*, Cambridge, MA and London, England: Harvard University Press.

MacKinnon, C. (1989) *Towards a Feminist Theory of the State*, Cambridge, MA: Harvard University Press.

MacKinnon, C. (1993) *Only Words*, Cambridge, MA: Harvard University Press.

Nussbaum, M. (1995) "Objectification," *Philosophy and Public Affairs* 24(4): 249–291.

Rawls, J. (2000) "The Moral Psychology of the Religion," Book I, The Three Predispositions, in B. Herman (ed.) *Lectures on the History of Moral Philosophy*, Cambridge, MA, London: Harvard University Press.

The Obligation to Resist Oppression

BY CAROL HAY

Carol Hay is a Canadian philosopher whose work focuses on issues in analytic feminism, liberal social and political philosophy, oppression studies, Kantian ethics, and the philosophy of sex and love. In this essay, Hay takes up the question of whether a woman who has been sexually harassed has an obligation to confront her harassers. In the end, she argues, such a woman has a duty to resist her oppression, but because this duty is best understood as an imperfect Kantian duty of self-respect there are multiple ways it may be fulfilled.

In 1944, the year after the Great Bengal Famine, 45.6 per cent of widowers surveyed ranked their health as either "ill" or "indifferent." Only 2.5 per cent of widows made the same judgement. This subjective ranking belied their actual situations since, as group, the widows' basic health and nutrition tended to be particularly abysmal. These women were starving and yet most of them claimed not to be sick. One explanation for this unwarranted stoicism is that, unlike men who were similarly situated, these women reacted to the scarcity of food by coming to believe that what little food there was should not be wasted on them.[1] This is (literally) a textbook case of the problem of adaptive preferences; the reason the Bengali women formed these desires while the men did not is that they had already internalized prevalent sexist social mores that granted women's interests less importance than men's.[2] Because these women did not believe their interests mattered as much as others', they did not experience their starvation as worth complaining about.

It is a terrible thing that, to satisfy the less dire needs of the men around them, these women were willing to give up the food that they needed to live. And it is a terrible thing that this happened because these women came to believe that their own needs were unimportant when compared to those of men. But I also think that the women had something to answer for. Rather than standing up for themselves, they accepted starvation. And, when they were being conditioned by sexist social norms to think that this was right, they did not (or did not effectively) reject this idea. In short, while these women were terribly wronged by an oppressive society, they also wronged themselves by failing to resist this oppression.

That it is wrong to oppress others, to take the food they need or deny them the social conditions necessary for the self-respect they deserve, is hardly controversial. But that those who are oppressed can also do wrong in not resisting their oppression is rather more so.[3] In this chapter I defend this claim; I argue that people have an obligation to resist their own oppression and that this obligation is rooted in an obligation to protect their rational nature.

The Obligation to Resist One's Oppression

The usual reason to think that someone's acquiescence in her or his oppression is morally problematic is other-oriented. By acquiescing in oppression, one might argue, someone is at least failing to help, and quite possibly actually *harming*, other people.[4] This idea has merit. After all, no one is oppressed in a social vacuum. The extent to which an individual goes along with her own oppression typically affects the oppression of others who share her social category. Accepting one's oppression can make oppression appear acceptable, or, even worse, it can make oppression appear not to be oppression at all.[5] And doing this is no better than endorsing oppression: sending the message that it is permissible to treat me in these ways in virtue of my being a woman sends the message that it is permissible to treat others in these ways in virtue of their being women as well.

But there is also a self-directed account of the obligation to resist one's oppression. Someone who is oppressed should stick up for herself, you might think, because, by acquiescing in her oppression, she is behaving in a way that is wrong regardless of how others are affected.

I argue that this obligation is best thought of as akin to a Kantian obligation of respect for one's own rational nature.

Kant's case for our obligations to ourselves, like his case for our obligations to others, begins with the value of our rational nature. Kant's argument for why rational nature in general is valuable relies on his second formulation of the Categorical Imperative, also known as the *Formula of Humanity*. This formulation of the Categorical Imperative famously commands you to "Act so that you use humanity in your own person, as well as in the person of every other, always at the same time as an end, never merely as a means" (*G* 4:429). The ground, or explanatory justification, of this moral principle, according to Kant, is that "[r]ational nature exists as an end in itself" (*G* 4:429). Kant says that insofar as we are rational we must conceive of ourselves as having a rational nature, and we must recognize that our rational nature confers upon us a value that requires that we always be treated as an end and never merely as a means. That is, insofar as we are rational we must view our rational nature as conferring on us a value that restricts the ways we may be treated. The obligation of self-respect, then, is an obligation to recognize the value of the rational nature within us and to respond accordingly. This obligation is an instance of the more general obligation to respect rational nature, wherever one finds it.

If Kant is right and our rational nature has ultimate value, then we ought to protect this nature by protecting all of it, including our capacity to act rationally. Oppression can harm rational capacities in a number of ways, we will see. Because one has an obligation to prevent harm to one's rational nature, and because oppression can harm one's capacity to act rationally, one has an obligation to resist one's oppression.

Of the various things that might be controversial about this line of thought, one that might stand out at this point is the claim that oppression harms one's capacity to act rationally (or at least often does so in familiar contexts of oppression). The goal of what comes next, then, is to show how oppression harms oppressed people's capacity to act rationally.

How Oppression Harms Rational Nature

Departing somewhat from many interpretations of Kant, I contend that we should think of our capacity for practical rationality as an ordinary human capacity, as susceptible to harm as many other human capacities.[6] Our capacity for practical rationality can be harmed when damage is done to either our capacities to form reasonable practically relevant beliefs, or to our capacities to form reasonable—that is, consistent—intentions on the basis of these beliefs, or to our capacities to practically deliberate from beliefs to intentions. Our capacity for practical rationality can also be harmed when we face illegitimate restrictions on the full and proper exercise of these capacities. For clarity's sake, I will refer to the former sort of harm—when one's rational capacities are prevented from functioning in a way that also threatens their future functioning—as *damage* to one's rational nature, and the latter sort of harm—when one encounters an unfair temporary interference with the full exercise of one's rational capacities—as a *restriction* on one's rational nature. The line between these two sorts of harm will not always be completely clear, but this vagueness is unimportant given our purposes here because both sorts of harm are seriously morally problematic.

Now, if development through childhood builds our rational capacities, and trauma or neglect tears them down, then why not think that other forces are capable of affecting them as well? Oppression is one such force, I argue; it can damage someone's rational capacities so thoroughly that her ability to act rationally is severely, sometimes permanently, compromised. And oppressed people face restrictions on their ability to exercise their rational capacities even more frequently than they face full-fledged damage to these capacities. There are a number of different ways that oppression can affect our capacity for practical rationality. I discuss several of them next.

Oppression Can Cause Self-Deception

A classic form of practical irrationality occurs when someone acts irrationally because she is deceiving herself. Oppression can cause self-deceptive behaviour because oppressive social systems create incentives for oppressed people to believe certain falsehoods about themselves, contrary to their own evidence. A particularly interesting example of this is given by Elizabeth Anderson, who shows how contradictory sexist norms of femininity and sexuality can cause women to become "radically self-deceived" about their motivations for some of their actions.[7] Anderson focuses on the case of women who seek abortions after having failed to use contraception. Despite not wanting to become pregnant, these women do not use contraception, Anderson argues, because doing so would force them to see themselves as "sexually active, receptive to sexual advances from strange men, taking sexual initiatives, [and] exercising agency with respect to their sexual choices."[8] And these women do not want to see themselves in these ways because they are in the grip of other norms of femininity that are inconsistent with this picture of sexual agency. These women are "caught between contradictory norms of femininity: one that tells them it isn't nice to have sex without intimacy; another that tells them it isn't nice to refuse their date's sexual demands unless they have a good excuse; [they are thus] heteronomous agents self-destructively caught between contradictory external norms."[9] To put the point more concretely, these women deceive themselves about the likelihood that they will have sex and so do not take steps to provide for contraception. But this is irrational behaviour since they do not want to become pregnant and they also do not take abortion to be as good a method for dealing with unwanted pregnancy as contraception. This irrational behaviour is evidence that these women have undergone harm to their rational nature.

Oppression Can Harm Capacities for Rational Deliberation

Another way oppression can harm people's capacity to act rationally is by harming their capacities for rational deliberation. This sort of harm can affect someone's capacity for determining which means will allow her to achieve the ends she has set, or it can affect her capacity for determining which ends to set in the first place.[10]

Harm to someone's capacity for instrumental rational deliberation could result, for example, from depriving her of the basic educational resources needed at key developmental stages to fully develop these skills.[11] This sort of harm could also result from the long-term cognitive damage that results from malnutrition—something possibly experienced by some of the Bengali women we considered earlier—or, in extreme cases, from language deprivation in early childhood. Members of oppressed groups are significantly more likely to be deprived of these various resources. The terror or trauma oppressed people can experience when they face violence, or even the threat of violence, can also impair their rational capacities. Harm to rational capacities can also result when someone is institutionalized, medicated, or lobotomized, or from extreme cases of depression. Oppressed people are more likely to face such adversities.[12]

Harm to an oppressed person's capacity to use means-ends reasoning could result if her independence is not fostered; if someone is always dependent on others to do things for her, her ability to figure out how to do things for herself can become impaired. If the means to your ends must always be to ask someone else to do it for you because you are unable to do it yourself, this could eventually permanently impair your capacity to determine how to do things on your own. And even in cases where one's rational capacities are not permanently damaged, insofar as this lack of independence places unfair limits on the means that are available to someone in the pursuit of her ends it is a restriction on the exercise of these capacities.

When oppression takes the form of infantilization, these harms can happen all too easily.

Harm to someone's rational capacity to choose certain valuable ends in the first place can result from oppression because oppression can make it less likely that the oppressed will imagine or conceive of various choices as live options for people like them. This, we have seen, occurs when internalized oppression results in the problem of adaptive preferences. Internalized oppression can damage or restrict people's sense of self-worth, so they do not set certain worthwhile ends for themselves because they do not think they deserve them. This can also happen when someone internalizes social roles that rule out various lifestyle choices as inappropriate or undesirable for people like her. In a related manner, when an oppressed person has internalized the belief that she is inferior to others, she can be more likely to set ends that fail to protect her future well-being; such ends, many philosophers think, are irrational because it is a requirement of practical reason that people have prudential regard for their future well-being.[13]

Oppression Can Cause Weakness of Will

Weakness of will—*akrasia*—is a matter of deciding what one has reason to do in a given situation, deciding to do it, but then doing something else instead because one has given in to countervailing pressures that have been brought on by various nonrational considerations. One way oppression might cause someone to do this turns on the self-fulfilling prophecies that can result when people who are oppressed internalize derogatory stereotypes that depict people like them as lazy or impetuous or irresponsible. Someone who has internalized such stereotypes just might not hold herself to very high standards of rationality and thus might be more susceptible to succumbing to weakness of will in various circumstances. If you know that others expect people like you to succumb to certain temptations, you might eventually come to expect yourself to succumb, and it can be that much harder to resist such temptations when they arise.

Another example of how oppression can cause weakness of will can be found in the case of the abortion-seeking women we considered earlier. At least some of these women consent to unwanted sex, Anderson claims, because they cannot see how to say "no." One explanation of what has gone on here is that they suffer from weakness of will inculcated by having internalized social norms that fail to teach women to stand up for themselves. These women recognize that they have good reason to refrain from having sex but succumb to their partners' sexual demands nevertheless. And engaging in this irrational behaviour is evidence that their rational nature has been harmed in some way.

Four Objections from Demandingness

We have just seen that oppression can damage or restrict one's capacity for practical rationality in a number of ways, and thus harm one's rational nature. Because there is an obligation to protect one's rational nature, in cases where oppression harms rational nature, one has an obligation to protect oneself from these harms. But what exactly does this obligation require? In most circumstances the most practical way to protect one's rational nature from the harms of oppression is to *resist* this oppression. What, then, is someone obligated to do when she is obligated to resist her own oppression, and when is she so obligated? Just how demanding is this obligation? Given the moral seriousness of these harms, there is good reason to think that someone is obligated to resist her oppression whenever she is oppressed. But, if this is the case, then, given the ubiquity of oppression and the resilience of the systems that produce it, the obligation to resist one's own oppression would be very demanding. Probably too demanding, in fact.

There is a real concern, I concede, that my account might be guilty of demanding too much of people. We just cannot be obligated to resist our oppression at *every available opportunity*, the thought might be. Nor can we be obligated to do *whatever it takes* to resist oppression. In many oppressive contexts, actively resisting oppression can be dangerous or counterproductive; resistance can be exhausting, victimizing, and can subject someone to retribution from others. In these sorts of cases, it looks like *not* resisting your oppression is a better way to protect your rational capacities from oppression's harms than resisting it is. In other cases, resistance might simply be impossible and, given the ubiquity of oppression, it is probably not logistically possible to resist its every manifestation; given the severity of some oppressive harms, a victim might be rendered incapable of resistance; given the social nature of oppression, resistance might require the cooperation of others who are unwilling to help; given the mystification of oppression, someone might not even realize she is oppressed and, as we all well know, if someone *cannot* do something then it cannot be that she *ought* to do it. And in virtually every case, defending an obligation to resist oppression seems to be tantamount to blaming the victim. If there is an obligation to resist oppression, after all, then it seems that those who fail to resist their oppression will be the appropriate subjects of blame. Finally, one might argue that resisting one's oppression is supererogatory rather than obligatory. Resisting one's own oppression is heroic, certainly, but it is simply not reasonable to say that failing to resist makes someone immoral or blameworthy.

These various objections can be classified into four broad categories: (1) *the objection from risk*; (2) *the objection from blaming the victim*; (3) *the objection from ought implies can*; and (4) *the objection from supererogation*. Let us now consider these four objections in more detail.

The Objection from Risk

According to the objection from *risk*, there cannot be a general obligation to resist oppression because resisting oppression can sometimes endanger the victim. The thought here is that, because in certain oppressive contexts taking action to protect one's rational capacities can be dangerous or counterproductive, *refraining* from acting to protect one's rational capacities might actually be the best way to *protect* them, sometimes *not* resisting your oppression can be a better way to protect your rational capacities from oppression's harms than resisting it. The dangers of resisting oppression could take the form of harms that are purely mental, or they could take the form of mental harms that are physically induced. These dangers could come from being made to experience feelings of exhaustion or

victimization, or they could come from facing the retribution of others. All of these possibilities have to do with this obligation's apparent requirement to resist oppression in every instance, whenever one is able.

For example, attempting to resist *every* instance of oppression—by, say, attempting to neutralize or dismantle every oppressive social institution, or by attempting to change the behaviour of every single oppressor—could be potentially exhausting or could lead to a sense of victimization that could leave oppressed people unable to appreciate their own potential for resisting oppression. Feelings of exhaustion or victimization could, in effect, damage oppressed people's rational capacities by leading to depression or feelings of helplessness that could undermine their ability to set or pursue their ends. This might be what Native Companion . . . has in mind when she expresses her desire to do nothing to resist her oppression at the hands of the carnies. Perhaps she recognizes on some level that, because oppressive situations like this one are so common, being required to mount resistance to every situation like it would be exhausting or victimizing. This exhaustion could, for example, make it difficult for someone to do what she judges to be best because she lacks the energy or inner strength to act effectively on her judgements; this kind of exhaustion would thus be conducive to a kind of practical irrationality. This victimization could, for example, make it difficult for someone to do what she judges to be best because her trust in her ability to make her own decisions has been undermined; this kind of victimization would thus be conducive to a kind of practical irrationality.

Perhaps what Native Companion is chafing against, then, is the implication that she could be obligated to do something that would subject her to these sorts of harms. In cases like this, it seems, resisting oppression does not necessarily protect one's rational capacities. So, because obligating people to resist their oppression would sometimes be obligating them to undergo a particular kind of harm to their rational capacities, and because the obligation here is supposed to be an obligation to *protect* these capacities, there cannot be a general obligation to resist oppression.

In addition to the harms that result from having to resist oppression in *every instance*, there are other harms that could result from attempting to resist certain *specific* instances of oppression. The cases I have in mind are those where resistance could expose oppressed people to severe physical harm, to death, or to expulsion from their only community. Should the Bengali women discussed above resist their oppression they could face serious consequences. If these women were to stand up for themselves—by, say, vocally demanding their fair share of the limited resources available to them—they could be perceived as disobedient or unruly and could face retribution from people keen to remind them of their place. They could risk beatings, expulsion from their community, even murder. Their external actions could subject their children to these risks. These retributive harms could, among other things, damage these women's rational capacities. So, again, because obligating people to resist their oppression would sometimes be obligating them to undergo harms to their rational capacities, and because the obligation here is supposed to be an obligation to *protect* these capacities, there cannot be a general obligation to resist oppression that is based on the obligation to defend one's rational capacities.

The Objection from Blaming the Victim

According to the objection from *blaming the victim*, an obligation to resist oppression is unfair because the victim has not done anything wrong. Given that someone who has been oppressed has been subjected to a moral harm, I admit that it seems strange to suggest that this imposes moral obligations on the victim, instead of the perpetrator. After all, an oppressed person has already suffered harms in virtue of her oppression; obligating her to resist this oppression would seem to unfairly impose further burdens upon her. Anita Superson makes such an argument. She argues that women who acquiesce in their oppression by conforming to patriarchal gender roles ought not to be blamed for this acquiescence. Superson thinks this is the case even though she admits that this acquiescence contributes not only to the oppression of those who conform, but also to the oppression of all women.

She argues that it is unfair to say that these women have an obligation to resist oppression because "their choice of lifestyle, and the values and beliefs accompanying it, . . . takes place in the context of severe restrictions of their freedom caused mainly by patriarchy. Their lifestyle, in turn, significantly limits their choices further."[14] To say that they have an obligation to change is to "expect them to act in ways that restrict their choices even further," and would be tantamount to blaming the victim.

But what, exactly, is wrong with blaming the victim? Jean Harvey argues that all morally objectionable practices of blaming the victim share three features in common: first, someone (the victim) is harmed in some way; second, in attempting to explain the harm, the victim is focused on in an "inappropriate and typically unflattering way"; and third, the act of blaming the victim is itself damaging to the victim.[15] Victim-blaming can be morally objectionable in a number of ways, Harvey argues. It is morally objectionable to blame a victim who is innocent, for example, whether the accusation is one of negligence or something worse. It is morally objectionable to shift some or all of the moral accountability away from the perpetrator who has actually harmed the victim. It is morally objectionable to claim that some nonmoral falling on the victim's part played a major role in the situation. It is morally objectionable to pretend that a victim has the power to do something safely about the situation, when she does not. It is morally objectionable to urge a victim into problematic relationships with other people or into a diminished moral status within her community at large. And it is morally objectionable to urge a victim to do things that will ultimately diminish her self-respect.

If an obligation to resist oppression results in the victims of oppression being blamed in any of these morally objectionable ways, that would be reason to reject the existence of such an obligation. And there is certainly a danger of this happening. If there is an obligation to resist oppression, after all, then those who fail to resist their oppression will be the appropriate subjects of blame. This would be to blame the victims of oppression for failing to live up to certain of their obligations.

The concern, then, is that failing to live up to the obligation to resist oppression would result in oppressed people being blamed in one or more of these morally objectionable ways.

The Objection from Ought Implies Can

According to the objection from *ought implies can*, the obligation to resist oppression founders on logistical considerations. In many different oppressive social situations, for any one of a number of different reasons, an oppressed person simply cannot resist her oppression. And, the argument goes, if someone *cannot* resist her oppression then it cannot be that she *ought* to.

One reason it might be logistically impossible to resist oppression has to do with how prevalent oppressive social institutions are. Frye's bird-cage analogy . . . illustrates just how ubiquitous oppression is; the harms of oppression surround a victim like the wires in a cage. Oppression infects virtually every aspect of its victims' lives: it is present in institutional structures, in interpersonal interactions, and even in the very ways they are able to think, speak, and feel. Its effects are present in the family, in the academy, in religion, in popular culture, in the workplace. Given this ubiquity, one might hold that it is just not logistically possible for someone to resist oppression by attempting to neutralize or dismantle every oppressive social institution. There simply are not enough hours in the day. And so, if one cannot resist oppression then it cannot be that she ought to.

Another reason it is sometimes not logistically possible to resist oppression is that in some cases resisting oppression requires the cooperation of others. Sometimes there is literally nothing one can do to resist one's oppression unless other members of one's oppressed group are willing to resist as well. Cudd gives an example of this sort of case:

> If you are the only worker at the plant who is willing to strike, then it cannot be a duty for you to strike, since your action will likely be ineffective even in sending a message of revolt (for example, if you just look like a shirker). And if striking (when others strike) is the only course of resistance in this case, then it cannot be a duty to resist.[16]

Because an individual worker cannot strike alone—because her actions *will not count* as striking unless other people take similar actions—her successful resistance is, in an importance sense, contingent on the actions of others. The point here, to be clear, is not simply that *effective* resistance requires solidarity from others; the point is that regardless of how effective your actions are in affecting an oppressive institution, the actions will not even *qualify* as resistance unless others are resisting with you. In such a case, if others are unwilling to cooperate, then one cannot resist her oppression. So it cannot be that she ought to.

A final reason it is sometimes not logistically possible to resist oppression is that the harms of oppression can damage someone's rational capacities so severely that she is incapable of resisting. Severe harms to someone's capacity for rational deliberation, of the sort we considered above, could have this effect. Deprivation of the basic educational resources needed at key developmental stages; long-term cognitive damage resulting from malnutrition at key developmental stages; extreme dependence resulting from infantilization; internalized feelings of worthlessness; depression; incapacitation resulting from being institutionalized, medicated, or lobotomized: these, and other, effects of oppression could render someone literally unable to resist. Severe cases of oppression can so thoroughly damage an oppressed person's rational capacities that acts of resistance are not merely *difficult* for her but are actually *impossible*. And, again, if one cannot resist oppression then it cannot be that she ought to.

The Objection from Supererogation

According to the final objection I want to consider, resisting oppression is *supererogatory* rather than obligatory. The objection from supererogation shares with my account the recognition that resisting one's oppression is sometimes possible, and when so, is a morally good thing to do. But, instead of characterizing resisting oppression as an obligation, a proponent of this view contends that resisting oppression is, in general, better thought of as supererogatory. This is because such a proponent thinks there are various reasons to think that there cannot be a general obligation to resist oppression. The clearest proponent of the supererogatory view of resisting oppression is Cudd.[17] Cudd explicitly denies that resistance to oppression is always obligatory. Instead, she argues that one has an obligation to resist oppression *only* when failing to do so harms other members of one's oppressed group. When there is a duty to resist oppression, then, this is a duty one has to others, not a duty one has to oneself. In cases where acquiescing in one's oppression harms only oneself, resistance is *supererogatory* rather than obligatory.

Cudd's justification for finding it implausible that people could have an obligation to resist their own oppression appeals to certain practical considerations. Many of these considerations are actually versions of the other objections we have just considered. Cudd argues, for example, that because oppressed people are often not in a position to know that they are oppressed—because "it is often a part of their oppression that it is hidden from them under the guises of tradition or divine command or the natural order of things"[18,19]—it will be difficult for these people to know how to go about resisting their oppression. She also points out that the pervasiveness of oppression means that it is impossible for someone who is oppressed to resist all of it simultaneously. And, as we just saw, she points out that because effective resistance to oppression is sometimes only possible in concerted effort with others, individual members of oppressed groups are powerless to resist unless other members of their oppressed group act in solidarity with them. These are all versions of the objection from *ought implies can*. Furthermore, Cudd argues that the coercive nature of oppression—the fact that oppressed people are put in oppressive circumstances through no fault of their own—should mitigate oppressed people's responsibility to ameliorate the situation. This is a version of the objection from *blaming the victim*.

These practical considerations are sufficient to undermine the possibility of there being a general obligation to resist one's oppression, Cudd thinks.

But she admits that resisting one's own oppression is usually still a good thing, despite being unwilling to argue that oppressed people are obligated to resist. In general, then, she thinks resisting one's oppression is, at most, *supererogatory*. There are certain cases of oppression, however, for which Cudd doesn't think the obligation to resist is merely supererogatory. The cases she has in mind are not those where failing to resist oppression harms oneself—these seem to be harms Cudd is willing to let people undergo willingly—but those cases where failing to resist oppression harms *others*:

> In [certain cases of] oppression ... the alternative to resistance is participation in the oppressive institution. *By participating in an oppressive situation, one lends some strength and stability to it, perhaps even legitimates it to some degree.* . . . One has only two options in such cases: resist or strengthen the unjust institution. Thus, in [these] cases of oppression . . . *failing to resist harms others.*[20]

Resistance to oppression in cases like these is not supererogatory, Cudd thinks. When failing to resist oppression amounts to participation in and legitimization of oppressive social structures that harm all members of an oppressed group, each individual member of that group has an obligation to resist. But it is important to notice that the obligation here is one oppressed people have to each other, not one they have to themselves. Insofar as an act of resisting oppression stands to benefit only the individual performing it, the resistance is perhaps morally praiseworthy but it is never morally required. So, even for the overlapping cases where both Cudd and I agree that people have an obligation to resist oppression, Cudd's account of *why* they have this obligation differs from mine. For her, the duty to resist oppression is a duty one has to prevent harms to others, not a duty to prevent harms to oneself. Cudd thinks resistance to one's own oppression is, in general, *supererogatory*.

To address these various lines of objection, in what follows I argue that the obligation to resist one's own oppression is an *imperfect duty* and that, as a result, someone is not obligated to do whatever it takes to resist her oppression; and it might be that she is not obligated to resist at every available opportunity either.

Imperfect Duties

I will argue below that there are many different forms that resistance to oppression can take. Thinking about the obligation to resist one's oppression in this way—as an obligation that can be fulfilled by more than one kind of action—makes this obligation what Kantians call an *imperfect duty*. The distinguishing characteristic of imperfect duties is that they permit a wider range of acceptable actions in fulfilling them than is the case for perfect duties.[21] This is because (unlike perfect duties) imperfect duties are not, strictly speaking, duties to perform specific *actions*. Rather, imperfect duties are duties to adopt certain *general maxims*, or principles of action. These maxims can be satisfied by more than one action. Imperfect duties thus allow a latitude of choice that perfect duties do not. To say that the duty to resist one's oppression is imperfect, however, is not to suggest that it is less stringent or less important than other duties. Instead, calling this duty imperfect means there is a strict duty to set the end of resisting one's own oppression, but there can be more than one way to go about pursuing this end. What the imperfect duty to resist one's oppression rules out is the refusal to do anything to resist one's oppression. That is, it rules out acquiescing in one's own oppression.

That imperfect duties permit latitude in action is not a matter of dispute. But exactly how much and what kind of latitude these duties have is very much up in the air. Kant says that imperfect duties "cannot specify precisely in what way one is to act" (*MM* 6:390) and "cannot specify precisely . . . how much one is to do" (*MM* 6:390). This might lead us to think that there is nothing more specific to be said about the particular actions prescribed by the different imperfect duties or about how often we have to act or how much we have to do to fulfil them. What is clear is that there is no general story to be told about the latitude that various imperfect duties have. Instead, we have to look at the duties individually since different imperfect duties have different kinds and degrees of latitude.

In what follows, I will focus on two different kinds of latitude in action that can be permitted by imperfect duties.[22] One kind of latitude someone might have is latitude to decide between various different ways of acting in a particular situation to satisfy the maxim required by an imperfect duty. Call this kind of latitude *latitude in which action to take*. Someone could fulfil the imperfect duty to be beneficent, for example, by working at a soup kitchen or by donating to Planned Parenthood or by giving used clothing to the Goodwill. The duty of beneficence does not require any of these acts in particular; it just requires that one do *something* that is beneficent. Because imperfect duties are duties to adopt general maxims, not duties to perform specific actions, all imperfect duties permit this kind of latitude. A second kind of latitude someone might have is latitude to choose either to perform, or to refrain from performing, an action on a particular occasion, so long as she stands ready to perform the given sort of action on at least some other occasions. Call this kind of latitude *latitude in refraining from action*. Someone could count as fulfilling the imperfect duty to be beneficent, for example, even if she refrained from performing all of the above-mentioned beneficent actions on a given occasion, as long as she does not always refrain from acting beneficently.

Before we consider whether, and to what extent, the imperfect duty to resist oppression permits these two different kinds of latitude, I want to take a step back to consider a potential objection to my characterization of this duty as imperfect. Remember, I am characterizing the obligation to resist one's oppression as an obligation to protect one's rational capacities from the harms of oppression. Given that the obligation to respect these capacities is supposed to be the duty that grounds all others in the Kantian picture, it might come as a surprise that I characterize the duty to resist one's oppression as an *imperfect*, rather than a *perfect*, duty; one might think that the fundamental importance of rational nature should mean that we have a strict, exceptionless duty to protect it.

It is fairly clear that Kant himself would insist that the duty to respect humanity is perfect. In the *Doctrine of Virtue*, for example, he says that we have a perfect duty to ourselves to preserve our animal nature, that is, to avoid "*depriving* oneself (permanently or temporarily) of one's *capacity* for the natural (and so indirectly for the moral) *use of* one's powers (*MM* 6:421)." This duty to not deprive yourself of your rational capacities is a *perfect duty*, Kant says. Allowing your rational capacities to be damaged is a kind of self-mutilation, which is a failing akin to suicide. This passage alone fairly definitively rules out the possibility that Kant himself would be happy to call the duty to resist one's oppression (as I have characterized it, as a duty to protect one's rational capacities) an imperfect rather than a perfect duty. Depriving yourself of the capacity for the use of your rational powers is, for all intents and purposes, the very harm we have been concerned with here: it is letting your rational capacities be damaged. A second example that bolsters the case for thinking that Kant would characterize the duty to resist oppression as perfect rather than imperfect can be found in what he says about the duty to avoid servility. The vice of servility, remember, amounts to a public and systematic willingness to disavow one's equal moral status; I argued . . . in favour of a duty to resist these failures of self-respect that are brought about under oppression. Kant says explicitly that the duty to avoid the vice of servility is perfect (*MM* 6:434–436). Given that Kant is so clear about both these points, I am forced to concede that Kant would think the duty to resist one's oppression is a perfect duty. Nevertheless, while Kant himself would characterize this duty as perfect, I hope to make a case for a Kant*ian* to be able to characterize it as imperfect.

The first consideration that supports interpreting this duty as imperfect has to do with how Kant characterizes the difference between perfect and imperfect duties. Much of what Kant says suggests that he thinks of the difference between perfect and imperfect duties as a matter of *degree* rather than *kind*. Kant compares various duties as wider or narrower relative to each other. He says, for example, that the duty to respect others is "*narrow* in comparison with the duty of love, and it is the latter that is considered a *wide* duty" (*MM* 6:449–450). He also says, for example, that,

"[t]he wider the duty, . . . the more imperfect is a man's obligation to action" (*MM* 6:390). In general, Kant speaks of duties as "wid*er*" and "narrow*er*," not "wide" or "narrow." This picture is one where duties fall on a scale of wideness and narrowness and where the line between perfect and imperfect is not necessarily a clean one. Certain duties are clearly perfect and permit no latitude in action; others are clearly imperfect and permit a great deal of latitude. But some duties are somewhere in between. Given that I will end up characterizing the duty to resist oppression as a relatively narrow imperfect duty—permitting quite a bit of latitude in which actions fulfil it, but relatively little latitude in refraining from action—my account of this duty should count as Kantian, even if Kant himself would characterize things slightly differently. Interpreting the difference between perfect and imperfect duties as one of degree rather than kind means that the difference between Kant's perfect duty to protect one's rational capacities from mutilation and my relatively narrow imperfect duty to protect these capacities from the harms of oppression need not amount to a repudiation of my Kantian approach.

A second consideration that supports interpreting this duty as imperfect has to do with what Kant says about other imperfect duties we have toward rational nature. While we cannot avoid interpreting Kant as saying we have a perfect duty *not to harm* rational capacities, we can still, at the same time, interpret him as saying we have an imperfect duty to *foster* these capacities. We just saw that Kant says we have a perfect duty not to harm our rational capacities; he thinks depriving oneself of the capacity to use one's rational powers is akin to murdering oneself and that we have a perfect duty to ourselves not to let this happen (*MM* 6:421). Elsewhere, however, Kant says that we have various *imperfect* duties with respect to our rational capacities: an imperfect duty to perfect these capacities in ourselves (*MM* 6:387, 393, 445–447); and an imperfect duty to beneficently encourage the development of these capacities in others (*MM* 6:388, 449–450). The imperfect duties of self-perfection and beneficence can be thought of as duties to *foster* rational capacities, in ourselves and others. We can thus show that the duty to resist oppression can be an imperfect duty by showing that *protecting* rational capacities is closer, in terms of the latitude it permits, to *fostering* them than it is to *not harming* them.

We can interpret beneficence as a duty to foster the rational capacities of others by focusing on how it requires taking the ends of another as your own (*MM* 6:449–450). Taking another's ends as your own—being concerned with their happiness and well-being—involves helping them achieve whatever it is they have decided they want to achieve (*MM* 6:388). But this is usually, among other things, to help them foster their rational capacities.[23] We saw above that Kant characterizes the duty of beneficence as a *wide* imperfect duty that permits latitude in which actions to take (because which actions you take to fulfil this duty will depend, in part, on what the other person's ends are) and in not having to act in every instance (because, at the very least, one is not bound by beneficence to expend so many of his resources that "he himself would finally come to need the beneficence of others" (*MM* 6:454)). If the duty of beneficence is, in part, a duty to foster others' rational capacities, then it follows that Kant thinks that our duty to foster others' rational capacities is imperfect. From this, we can infer that he could agree that our duty to *protect* others' rational capacities— at least in cases where only a small, incremental harm is at stake—is similarly imperfect. For the same reasons that he thinks there should be many ways we can act to fulfil the duty to foster others' rational capacities, and for the same reasons that he thinks we do not have to act in every instance to fulfil the duty to foster others' rational capacities, Kant could agree that the duty to protect others' rational capacities permits these kinds of latitude. But I will leave this claim undefended, because the duties we are most interested in are duties one has to oneself. It is enough here to notice that there is room for a Kantian to defend the view that the duty to protect other people's rational nature permits as much latitude in action as the duty to foster their rational nature.

Let us move on, then, to consider what Kant says about the duties we have to foster our own rational nature. It is reasonable to think that the imperfect duty of self-perfection includes, as one aspect, a duty to foster one's own rational capacities. This interpretation makes sense if we think of the duty of self-perfection as a matter of cultivating our various powers for the sake of our rational nature. Kant says there are two kinds of duties of self-perfection: the duty to perfect our *natural talents* and the duty to increase our *moral perfection*. The duty to perfect our natural talents requires us to develop our mental and physical capacities— everything; from analytical skills, memory, and imagination, to powers of the body—so that we are as well-prepared as possible to do that which makes us distinctively valuable (that is, to set ends) (*MM* 6:392, 445). The duty to increase our moral perfection requires us to strive to act always from duty—to have the incentive of our actions be only the moral law, to do what is right for its own sake (*MM* 6:393). Kant characterizes both of these duties of self-perfection as imperfect, and thus both as permitting latitude in action. When it comes to the duty to develop our natural talents, we have latitude in which action to take because which capacities we cultivate will depend on which ends we have, and we have latitude in refraining from action because we do not need to act in every possible instance to cultivate our powers (*MM* 6:392,446). When it comes to the I duty to increase our moral perfection, we might not have much latitude in refraining from action, but we have at least some latitude in which action to take because there is no one way to go about becoming a better person that will work for all people (*MM* 6:393,447).

If this interpretation of the duty of self-perfection as, in part, a duty, to foster our rational capacities fits plausibly within a Kantian framework, then a Kantian can characterize our duty to foster our rational capacities as imperfect. This opens up the possibility that our duty to *protect* our rational capacities could be similarly imperfect. Just as the imperfect duties of *fostering* our rational capacities can permit latitude both in which action to take and which to refrain from, the imperfect duty of *protecting* our rational capacities can permit a similar degree and kind of latitude. I will argue next that there are many different ways to protect our rational capacities in oppressive contexts, and thus many different actions that count as fulfilling the duty to protect them. There might even be reason to think that we can protect rational capacities in oppressive contexts without acting in every instance, and can thus fulfil the duty to protect them while refraining from action on occasion.

Latitude in Which Action to Take

What are the different sorts of actions one could take to fulfil the obligation to resist oppression? One could resist oppression by participating in some form of *activism* intended to engage with, and ultimately change, the social norms, roles, and institutions that make up an oppressive system. In at least some cases oppressed people can directly confront the individuals who are actively oppressing them. Oppressed people can also give time or money to organizations that are dedicated to dismantling oppressive social institutions. Sometimes oppressed people can both empower themselves and undermine the effectiveness of oppressive social roles by reappropriating derogatory stereotypes or language. People have attempted to do this (not uncontroversially[24]) with words like "bitch," "nigger," and "faggot." In some cases oppressed people can take part in oppressive social institutions in ways that demonstrate that such institutions need not necessarily be oppressive. One could, for example, enter into a marriage of mutual respect (one where both partners were committed to ensuring that each partner had an equal opportunity to pursue meaningful life projects and that the inevitable sacrifices and compromises of family life did not unfairly disadvantage one partner over the other) and thereby show that the institution of marriage itself is not necessarily oppressive, even if its most conventional forms function to entrench sexist oppression. In other cases activist resistance can take the form of sabotage from within an oppressive institution. Activism can also be a matter of publicly refusing to accept humiliation from one's oppressors, as in the following incident described by Nelson Mandela about the beginning of his incarceration at the hands of the apartheid South African government:

As we walked toward the prison, the guards shouted "Two—two! Two—two!"—meaning we should walk in pairs. . . . I linked up with Tefu. The guards started screaming, "Haas! . . . Haas!" The word haas means "move" in Afrikaans, but it is commonly reserved for cattle.

The wardens were demanding that we jog, and I turned to Tefu and under my breath said that we must set an example; if we give in now we would be at their mercy. . . .

I mentioned to Tefu that we should walk in front, and we took the lead. Once in front, we actually decreased the pace, walking slowly and deliberately. The guards were incredulous [and said] . . . we will tolerate no insubordination here. Haas! Haas! But we continued at our stately pace. [The head guard] ordered us to halt and stood in front of us: "Look, man, we will kill you, we are not fooling around. . . . This the last warning. Haas! Haas!"

To this I said: "You have your duty and we have ours." I was determined that we would not give in, and we did not, for we were already at the cells.[25]

Activist resistance such as this not only preserves one's dignity by refusing to accept the subhuman identity imposed by one's oppressors; it can also set an example for others.

Another way to resist oppression is to *opt out* of oppressive social norms, roles, and institutions. Oppressed people could boycott an oppressive institution, for example. Or they could opt out of oppressive social norms by refusing to conform to conventional modes of dress or behaviour as, for example, when someone refuses to identify with conventional gender norms and instead presents herself as androgynous or as opposite to the gender she has been assigned. Another option for oppressed people is to isolate themselves from their oppressors to foster solidarity with other members of their oppressed group. This sort of opting out could be as radical as lesbian separatism or as moderate as creating a women's-only space on a college campus. Opting out can also occur when oppressed people refuse to behave in ways considered appropriate to their social group such as, for example, when women are assertive, confident, or opinionated. Opting out like this can be particularly effective for women, since many of the kinds of practical irrationality to which many women are especially prone in virtue of their oppression are those that involve a lack of confidence, or a lack of willingness to make a scene, or a lack of willingness to make someone else uncomfortable.

Both engaging in activism and opting out are *external* forms of resisting oppression. But resistance to oppression could be *internal* as well; someone could, at least theoretically, fulfil the obligation to respect her rational nature by becoming the sort of person whose rational nature was simply not damaged by oppression, perhaps by building up mental walls against many of the harms. She could educate herself about the potential risks of these harms and be wary of their effects. She could simply refuse to believe what oppressive social messages were telling her about the character or worth of people like her. Insofar as these and other forms of internal resistance succeed in protecting one's rational capacities from the harms of oppression, they would qualify as actions that successfully fulfil the obligation to resist one's oppression. And insofar as these and other forms of internal resistance manifest self-respect, they are probably morally required for other reasons as well. . . .

In some cases, when every other form of resistance would subject her to harm (or the serious risk of harm), some form of internal resistance might be the only resistance available to an oppressed person. The Bengali widows we saw earlier could be an example. If risks like the ones faced by these women are attached to resisting externally, one has every reason not to resist externally. But even if these women would be risking harm by resisting oppression externally, they could still tell themselves that they *deserve* the food they are giving up as much as anyone else does and that their survival is as important as anyone else's.

In some cases, there might be nothing an oppressed person can do to resist her oppression other than simply *recognizing that something is*

wrong with her situation. This is, in a profound sense, better than nothing. It means she has not acquiesced to the innumerable forces that are conspiring to convince her that she is the sort of person who has no right to expect better. It means she recognizes that her lot in life is neither justified nor inevitable. It means she has resisted internalizing her oppression and resisted forming badly adaptive preferences. There is something importantly self-respecting about engaging in internal resistance, and the possibility of this sort of resistance captures the intuition that there are actions someone can engage in to fulfil the duty to resist oppression even when external resistance is imprudent or impossible.

Admittedly, in many cases it might be difficult to tell whether someone is resisting her oppression internally. Consider the case of Native Companion. . . . Native Companion, remember, argued that there was no point in confronting the carnival workers who harassed her:

> "So if I noticed or I didn't, why does it have to be *my* deal? What, because there's assholes in the world I don't get to ride on The Zipper? I don't get to ever spin? Maybe I shouldn't ever go to the pool or ever get all girled up, just out of fear of assholes?" . . .
>
> "Assholes are just assholes. What's getting hot and bothered going to do about it except keep me from getting to have fun?" . . .
>
> "They might ought to try just climbing on and spinning and ignoring assholes and saying Fuck 'em. That's pretty much all you can do with assholes."[26]

The question is how we should best understand Native Companion's responses here. Is she claiming that she has no obligation to resist her oppression in this situation? Or, by refusing to let the carnies get to her, is she actually resisting her oppression internally? We could argue that by refusing to feel humiliated, by refusing to let the carnies dictate when and how she can have fun, and by refusing to believe that their sexually objectifying her demeans her moral status as a person in any way, Native Companion is protecting her rational capacities from the harms of oppression and so is, in effect, resisting her oppression internally. This is a plausible interpretation of what has gone on in this situation, I think. Native Companion is portrayed in this story as someone who is feisty, confident, and self-secure; there is every reason to think she is the sort of person whose rational capacities are not endangered by an isolated incident of sexual harassment.

But an alternative interpretation of what has gone on here that is just as plausible, I think, is that Native Companion is exhibiting either bad faith or ignorance resulting from internalized oppression. She might be unaware of how the systematic nature of oppression means that its harms are likelier to occur corrosively than discretely, and thus that the full extent of its harms cannot be appreciated when looking only at isolated incidents. She might resist characterizing herself as oppressed because she does not want to think of herself as a victim or the men in her life as victimizers. She might be unwilling to give up the few benefits afforded to her by the oppressive status quo. She might have simply accepted the sexist status quo—a status quo where men are free to objectify and harass women and face relatively few consequences—as not merely inevitable but actually not unjust. Native Companion's hypothetical ignorance or bad faith here might be blameless. But she would be mistaken, nevertheless. If this interpretation of the situation is the right one, then Native Companion is not resisting her oppression internally by refusing to let the carnies get under her skin. Rather, she is exhibiting exactly the bad faith or ignorance that we should expect of someone in her circumstances.

The point here is that the very nature of oppression can make it difficult or impossible to tell whether someone is resisting internally or is acquiescing. So, if the only resistance someone is putting up is internal, we might have no way of knowing whether she is fulfilling the obligation to resist her oppression. There will be a fact of the matter here, but we might not have access to it. (To be clear: this is an epistemic point about whether we can know that internal resistance has taken place, not a metaphysical point about whether internal resistance has in fact taken place.) Notice

that this possibility holds not only when attempting to determine whether someone else is resisting her oppression; it also holds when attempting to determine whether we ourselves are resisting. You might think that you are resisting your oppression internally—or, if, like Native Companion, you are not inclined to think about things in terms of oppression, you might think you are being self-respecting or some such thing—but you could be fooling yourself. You could be engaging in *self-deception*, one of the forms of practical irrationality encouraged by oppression. This oppressive harm to our rational capacities can make it difficult to know whether we are fulfilling the obligation to resist oppression if we only resist internally. This gives us good reason to err on the side of caution, to not necessarily trust our gut when we think we are resisting internally, and to resist oppression externally whenever possible, to be sure we are successfully fulfilling this obligation.

Furthermore, internal resistance might be able to protect one's rational nature from the harms of oppression, but it would leave oppressive social structures intact. As I argued above, there are good reasons to think that someone who is oppressed has obligations to other members of her oppressed group to not acquiesce in oppressive social structures, even if these structures are not currently harming her personally. This means that internal resistance, even if successful in protecting one's own rational nature, would usually be insufficient to fulfil every moral obligation of resistance an oppressed person has.

On top of all this, it is psychologically implausible to suggest that successfully protecting one's rational nature solely by means of engaging in internal resistance is a live possibility for most oppressed people. Most people's psychologies are simply not oppression-proof. This is why the harms of oppression are so extensive. So, again, while the obligation to respect one's rational nature in the face of oppressive harms could theoretically be satisfied solely by resisting oppression internally rather than externally, there are epistemic, moral, arid practical reasons to think that, in all but the most extreme cases, some degree of external resistance to oppression will remain necessary.

Insofar as these different forms of resistance—internal and external—function to protect one's rational nature while destabilizing or undermining oppressive social structures, they all count as resisting one's oppression. They are thus *sufficient* to fulfil the obligation to resist one's own oppression. (By calling these actions "sufficient" I do not mean to imply that someone merely has to perform one of them and then she will have successfully fulfilled her obligation to resist her oppression and can go on her merry way and never have to bother resisting ever again. Rather, I mean that they count as one sort of action which, when performed in conjunction with other actions of this sort, successfully fulfil this obligation.) But are any of these forms of resistance *necessary*? Does the obligation to resist one's oppression *require* any of these actions? I contend that, while each of these actions counts as resisting one's oppression, none of these actions in particular is required by the obligation to resist.

Latitude in Refraining from Action

We have just seen that the imperfect duty to resist oppression permits a great deal of latitude in which action one can take to fulfil it. The question now is whether this obligation ever permits latitude in refraining from acting at all. All imperfect duties have the kind of latitude just discussed; because they are specified quite generally, there will always be more than one action someone can undertake to fulfil an imperfect duty. But some imperfect duties also have a different kind of latitude; it is sometimes permissible to refrain from acting to fulfil some imperfect duties, as long as one does not refrain all the time. The paradigm cases of imperfect duty found in Kant—beneficence and developing one's talents—have this land of latitude (*MM* 6:392–394, 444–446). But Kant thinks other imperfect duties—respecting others and increasing one's moral perfection—do not have this latitude (*MM* 6:393–394, 446–447). The question here, then, is whether the imperfect duty to resist one's oppression has this kind of latitude. The question is whether, just as someone counts as fulfilling the duty of beneficence even if she does not act to fulfil this duty at every available opportunity, she also counts as fulfilling the duty of resisting her

oppression if she does not act to fulfil this duty at every available opportunity. The question, in other words, is whether it is permissible to sometimes sit by and let oneself be oppressed.

To see why a Kantian might think the imperfect duty to resist one's oppression should permit latitude in refraining from action, think for a moment about the erosive effects of water dripping on stone. Just as individual droplets of water that seem not to have any effect on a piece of stone can cumulatively wear it away, rational nature can be harmed in almost invisible increments. So too for oppression. What might seem to be merely the harmless slights or annoyances or inconveniences of oppression can have a cumulative effect on people's rational nature. This analogy illustrates not only how the effects of oppression are as likely to be gradual and cumulative as they are discrete; it also presents us with a case for arguing that people are not obligated to resist *every* instance of their oppression. If you have a piece of stone that has to be protected only from *detectable* erosion, then you obviously cannot let water run over it for any period of time, but any individual drop splashing on it here and there will not be a problem as long as you are careful to not let it happen for too long or too often. So too for the corrosive effects of oppression on one's rational nature; many individual instances of oppression can be borne without discernibly harming one's rational nature, but eventually they will accumulate and discernible harm will occur. This means that the obligation to protect one's rational nature from being harmed by oppression could allow one to refrain from resisting at least once in a while. Because rational nature is so valuable, one needs to err on the side of caution, obviously, and be careful not to let the corrosive effects of oppression accumulate. But it is compatible with an obligation to protect one's rational nature to occasionally fail to resist individual instances of oppression that would end up harming one's rational nature were one to fail to resist them all the time. None of us is so fragile that we cannot bear the stress of an occasional instance of oppression.

This result suggests that the obligation to resist one's oppression might permit at least some latitude in refraining from action. Remember, imperfect duties are duties to adopt a general principle of action, not duties to perform a particular action; this generality means that one can fulfil some imperfect duties without necessarily acting on them at every available opportunity. And it looks like the obligation to resist one's oppression might allow this sort of latitude. Someone can protect her rational nature, and thus fulfil the obligation to protect it, without resisting her oppression at every opportunity, so long as she does not do this so often that the corrosive effects of oppression are allowed to accumulate. This means, for example, that someone like Native Companion could, on occasion, be morally permitted to not do everything in her power to resist her oppression. She could be morally permitted to do nothing in this instance; she could not bother confronting the carnies, and even not bother reporting the incident to their boss. If the erosion analogy is apt, it turns out that "climbing on and spinning and ignoring assholes and saying Fuck 'em"[27] might be okay, at least once in a while. Maybe sometimes it is true that this is "pretty much all you can do with assholes."[28] The erosion analogy suggests that Native Companion's imperfect duty to resist her oppression should permit her at least some latitude in refraining from action.

To be clear, what this duty does not permit her to do is resist so rarely that the harms of oppression accumulate and damage her rational nature. Because rational nature is so fundamentally valuable, the duty to protect it by resisting one's oppression would obviously have less of this sort of latitude than imperfect duties like the duty of beneficence and the duty to develop one's talents. But unlike, say, the imperfect duty to increase one's moral perfection, which Kant says permits no latitude in refraining from action, it is possible that the imperfect duty to resist one's oppression *could* permit *some* latitude in refraining from action. And, to be clear, this latitude is a possibility because the obligation here is not merely to *respect* one's rational nature, but to *protect* it.

To determine whether the obligation to resist oppression should permit latitude in refraining from action, we need to examine why Kant thinks

some other imperfect duties permit this latitude. Kant points out that there are countless ways to fulfil the imperfect duties of beneficence and of developing one's talents, and so we must recognize that our finite, limited nature forces us to choose among these options. It is simply impossible to pursue all the different ways in which we might develop our talents, and if we were to attempt to pursue every one of them we would fail to succeed at developing any of our talents at all. So too for beneficence; we could not successfully act beneficently were we to attempt to help every single other person achieve their ends in every instance. These two imperfect duties permit latitude in refraining from action because the possibility of successfully fulfilling them actually *requires* not acting at every available opportunity. The imperfect duties of respecting others and increasing our moral perfection, on the other hand, do not permit latitude in refraining from action because it is possible to successfully fulfil them while acting at every available opportunity.

Is the obligation to resist oppression like this? Is it impossible to fulfil this obligation if we must act on it at every available opportunity? What most strongly motivates the attractiveness of thinking that the obligation to resist oppression should permit latitude in refraining from action, I think, is the very same line of thinking that motivated the *objection from risk* that we considered above, that is, a recognition that there are situations where resisting one's oppression in the wrong way can be dangerous (or at least counterproductive). Because certain actions taken to protect rational capacities can be dangerous or counter-productive if they are taken all the time or in the wrong circumstances, *refraining* from acting to protect one's rational capacities might actually be the best way to *protect* them in certain circumstances. Fair enough. But it would be a mistake to categorize the latitude in question here as latitude in refraining from action. This is because the explanation for why someone is not required to *act* (or is permitted to not act) in these sorts of circumstances is that successfully fulfilling the duty to protect one's rational capacities requires (or permits) that one *not act* in these circumstances. One's failure to act here is thus actually better described as a failure to act *outwardly* or *externally*. One is still acting, in the relevant sense. One has still set the maxim to protect one's rational capacities, and one's behaviour is still in accord with this maxim. It is just that in these circumstances the best way to achieve this end is to refrain from doing anything outward. One recognizes this, and acts accordingly. One is, in short, resisting one's oppression *internally*. It is latitude in which action to take to fulfil the duty to protect rational capacities—the *other* kind of latitude—that explains why one is required (or permitted) to fulfil this duty by refraining from acting externally in these circumstances. Were this to be a case of latitude in refraining from action, one would set the maxim to protect her rational capacities, recognize that the best way to achieve this end in these circumstances would be to take a certain course of action, but then *refrain* from taking this course of action. And that is not what one has done here.

The possibility of internal resistance means that, unlike the imperfect duties of beneficence and developing one's talents, practical considerations do not make the obligation to resist one's oppression impossible to fulfil if acted on at every opportunity. Perhaps this should lead us to say that, because internal resistance is always a possibility, the duty to resist oppression permits *no* latitude in refraining from action.

But why, exactly, must we say that the duty to resist oppression always requires at least internal resistance? Why can we not say that refraining from even internal resistance is sometimes permissible? The erosion analogy establishes as a possibility that there could be cases where someone may not have to do *anything* to resist her oppression because it shows that many individual instances of oppression can be borne without discernibly damaging one's rational nature. But, given that we can account for the most intuitive cases of when it seems that resistance should not be required with the possibility of engaging in internal resistance, the burden of proof is on the person who wants to claim that not even internal resistance is required in a given circumstance. Notice that any argument attempting to claim that not even internal

resistance is required in a given circumstance is, in effect, going to be an argument for why someone does not have to be self-respecting in this circumstance. This will not be an easy argument to make. Saying, "I just don't feel like it," or, "It's just not that big a deal," is nowhere near sufficient to establish that one should not have to be self-respecting.

Think again of the other imperfect duties that permit latitude in refraining from action. Even when one permissibly refrains from engaging in a particular action that would fulfil the imperfect duties to be beneficent or to develop one's talents, one must retain a latent recognition that engaging in such an action is a possibility for oneself and that insofar as it would fulfil the duty it would be a good thing to do. One must not deny that such an action would fulfil the duty (even if someone chooses not to volunteer at a soup kitchen she must be willing to recognize that doing so would fulfil the duty of beneficence). And, importantly, one must not deny that the duty is important and that one remains subject to it (even if someone chooses not to be beneficent in this particular instance she must be willing to recognize that beneficence is important and that she is still bound by the duty).

So, if the obligation to resist one's oppression permits latitude in refraining from action, someone who avails herself of this latitude must still be willing to recognize the importance of the obligation to protect her rational nature from the harms of oppression. She must recognize that she remains subject to this obligation. And she must recognize that various actions are open to her to fulfil this obligation, and that they would be good to do, even if she chooses not to engage in them in a particular instance.

Take the case of Native Companion. If her expressed desire to do nothing to resist her oppression at the hands of the carnies is actually a form of internal resistance—perhaps because she recognizes on some level that being required to mount external resistance to every situation like this would be exhausting or victimizing—then she is in the clear. She is fulfilling the duty to protect her rational nature by reserving her energy for more important matters. She is respecting herself by resisting her oppression internally. If, on the other hand, by doing nothing to resist her oppression she is actually refraining from engaging in any sort of resistance, then if this is to be a permissible instance of latitude in refraining from action she must be willing to uphold the importance of resisting oppression, she must recognize that she is subject to the obligation to resist oppression, and she must recognize that the actions she is choosing not to engage in would count as fulfilling this obligation: So, if Native Companion wants to do nothing here because she is unwilling to recognize that she has been subject to oppression, because she is unwilling to recognize that she has an obligation to resist her oppression, or because she is unwilling to recognize the importance of resisting oppression, then this is not a permissible instance of latitude in refraining from action and she has not fulfilled the obligation to resist her oppression. If these are her reasons for refraining from action in this oppressive situation, she is likely to make a similar judgement about the permissibility of refraining from action in other oppressive situations.

Taking claims such as, "I just don't feel like it," or, "It's just not that big a deal," to be good reasons to refrain from action is evidence that one does not properly appreciate the gravity of the situation; it is evidence that one does not properly appreciate the value of her rational nature or the risks her rational nature faces under oppression. And failing to appreciate this will inevitably lead to harms to one's rational capacities. Refraining from internal resistance is thus likely to result in erosive harms to one's rational nature because it is likely that an unwillingness to resist oppression, at least internally, manifests either as a lack of appreciation of the seriousness of the moral harms of oppression or, worse, a lack of self-respect. Cases where one is permitted latitude in refraining from internal resistance will thus be exceedingly rare.

In spite of the evocativeness of the erosion analogy, it is extremely difficult to find practical cases where the imperfect duty to resist one's oppression does permit latitude in refraining from action. Here are a few final possibilities, all motivated by the considerations we looked at above in the objection from *ought implies can*. This objection, remember, contends that the obligation to resist oppression cannot accommodate certain logistical considerations. One of these logistical considerations has to do with how prevalent oppressive social situations are. Given this prevalence, it is simply impossible to resist oppression by attempting to neutralize or dismantle every oppressive social institution. Another consideration is that resisting oppression can be impossible when it has already severely damaged one's rational capacities to the point where acts of resistance are not merely difficult but are actually impossible. Yet another arises when we consider that the obligation to resist oppression seems to require that one is aware of her oppression and of the harm that it poses to her rational nature; in cases where someone does not have this knowledge, then, ignorance of one's oppression should presumably vitiate the obligation to resist it.[29] A proponent of the *ought implies can* objection claims that if one cannot resist her oppression then it cannot be that she ought to resist it. Perhaps these are the sorts of cases where the obligation to resist oppression might permit latitude in refraining from action.

The first logistical consideration—that it is impossible for any one person to single-handedly dismantle oppression—can be dispensed with relatively quickly. This is because the obligation to resist oppression, as I have characterized it here, is not an obligation to dismantle oppression. Rather, the obligation here is to protect one's rational capacities from the harms of oppression. And, while it might not be logistically possible for one person to fix every oppressive institution, it *is* possible for her to at least attempt to protect her rational capacities from the harms of these institutions.

The problem with the next consideration—that oppression can harm people's rational capacities to the point where it is not merely difficult but impossible for them to resist—is illustrated by a concern that Boxill raises about Frye's birdcage metaphor. What is wrong with this metaphor, he argues, is that it can encourage us to think of the victims of oppression as completely incapable of resisting their oppression.

All similes and metaphors have their limitations and this one is no exception. Birds in a cage flutter futilely against its bars until they drop in exhaustion. The simile invites us to think of the oppressed like those birds, fluttering piteously against their bars until they too drop in exhaustion. Like those birds they can do nothing to resist their oppression and consequently there is no point in posing the question whether they have a responsibility to resist it. But oppressed people are not really like birds in a cage. Perhaps caged birds are condemned to dash themselves against the bars of their cage until they give up, but humans are not.[30]

Instead, people can, and often do, resist their oppression. Of course, we should concede that if severely oppressed people, such as the Bengali women, have had their rational capacities harmed to the point where they are actually *incapable* of resisting their oppression, then clearly it cannot be that they have an obligation to resist. But we need to be careful not to arrive too quickly at the judgement that an individual is incapable of resistance. For example, the case of the Bengali women comes from a larger body of work in which Nussbaum shows how many oppressed people *do* resist their oppression, despite the tremendous odds. Much of Nussbaum's work focuses on highlighting the ways that even severely oppressed people can band together successfully to resist their oppression. Nussbaum concludes, in response to these sorts of cases, that oppressed people can "overcome the greatest of obstacles, showing an amazing courage and resourcefulness."[31] Because they *can* resist, even many people who are severely oppressed are obligated to resist. Of course, we should willingly concede that resistance is not always possible in severe cases of oppression, and if someone is so oppressed that she is literally *incapable* of resisting then she cannot be obligated to do so. But this is a virtue of my account, for it fits with the intuition both that we should hold people responsible for fulfilling their obligations when they are able to fulfil them, and that we should not hold them responsible when they are unable.

The possibility of this consideration vitiating the obligation to resist oppression is farther undermined in light of a discussion from Marcia Baron. People often misinterpret Kant's point of the "ought implies can" doctrine, Baron claims. According to her, "ought implies can" does not mean that morality ought not require too much of us; instead, it means that anything that morality requires of us is something we *are able* actually to do. This fits well with a familiar theme in Kant's ethics, that we are often far too quick to find excuses for making exceptions of ourselves from the requirements of morality.

> Kant's famous principle is often cited as support for a claim that we must not regard too much as our duty, but his point was not the contraposition of the dictum—that if we cannot do x, we have no duty to do x—but rather that if we ought to do it, we *can* do it. "When the moral law commands that we *ought* now to be better men, it follows inevitably that we must *be able* to be better men" (*R* 50–51/46). . . . Far from endorsing the assumption that acts that are very difficult for us should be regarded as optional, Kant's principle emphasizes that *difficult* does not mean *impossible*.[32]

Baron warns against thinking of acts that are *difficult* for us to perform as if they are *impossible* for us to perform because doing so threatens to undermine our freedom. If we pretend as if our particular inclinations—our "fears, desires, and aversions"—make it utterly impossible for us to perform certain acts, then we are acting as if we are not free. This is clearly something Kant would be loath to accept. Baron refers here to a passage where Kant discusses a person whose Sovereign threatens to kill him unless he makes

> a false deposition against an honourable man whom the ruler wished to destroy under a plausible pretext: "that it would be possible for him [to refuse] he would certainly admit without hesitation. He judges, therefore, that he can do something because he knows that he ought, and he recognizes that he is free—a fact which, without the

moral law, would have remained unknown to him" (*CPR* 5:30).

Knowing that we *ought* to do something can be what tells us that we are *able* to do it, Kant thinks. We should not pretend, then, that acts that are difficult for us are actually impossible for us. This further undermines the objection that acts that are difficult for us cannot be required by duty. "Ought implies can" means not that morality ought not be too demanding, but that it ought not be too lenient. So, then, as long as it has been established that an individual is actually *capable* of misting her oppression, the mere fact that this resistance will be *difficult* for her is, by itself, insufficient to excuse her from the obligation or to permit latitude in refraining from action to fulfil it.

The final consideration—that if someone does not know that she is oppressed, then it cannot be that she is obligated to resist—also fails to permit latitude in refraining from action to fulfil the obligation to resist oppression. Ignorance of an obligation does not make that obligation disappear. However, this does not prevent us from saying that at least some of the people who are ignorant of their oppression should not have to resist it. Notice that saying that someone who is ignorant of her oppression "should not have to resist it" does not necessarily mean that she is not *obligated* to resist. It might mean, instead, that she has an *excuse* for failing to fulfil this obligation. She might . . . not be *culpable* for this failure. The obligation to resist one's oppression exists whether someone is aware of her oppression or not. Ignorance of one's oppression can, however, affect whether someone is blameworthy for failing to fulfil the obligation to resist. This is a familiar moral phenomenon—when an agent does something wrong but, for one reason or another, we do not hold her culpable for her offense—and it shows that failing to fulfil the obligation to resist one's oppression does not necessarily mean that one is blameworthy for such a failure. To be clear, the latitude in refraining from action that characterizes some imperfect duties does not amount to permission to fail to fulfil these duties in situations where one *should* fulfil them. We should not try to explain these failures to fulfil

the obligation to resist oppression that result from ignorance as permissible instances of latitude in refraining from action. Instead, we should explain failures to resist that result from nonculpable ignorance as cases of nonculpable failure to fulfil the obligation, and failures to resist that result from culpable ignorance as cases of culpable failure to fulfil the obligation. So, for example, if Native Companion's ignorance of her oppression is not her fault, then neither is it her fault that she fails to resist this oppression. But her lack of blameworthiness for failing to fulfil this obligation does not mean the obligation itself goes away. It just means she should not be held morally responsible for her failure to fulfil it.

The erosion analogy shows that it might be compatible with an obligation to protect one's rational nature to occasionally fail to resist individual instances of oppression that would end up harming one's rational nature were one to fail to resist them all the time. But I think it is clear that if the erosion analogy is apt it gets us a really quite limited amount of latitude in refraining from action: because rational nature is so fundamentally valuable one needs to be very careful to not let the corrosive effects of oppression accumulate. This discussion emphasizes just how little latitude in refraining from action this duty should permit. Because the most compelling cases that seem to require latitude in refraining from action are actually addressed by the possibility of internal resistance, even if this duty does permit some of this latitude there is not much reason to want it to permit much of it. Still, because there are many different ways to protect our rational capacities in oppressive contexts, and thus many different actions that count as fulfilling the obligation to protect them, this obligation permits a great deal of latitude in which action to take.

Conclusion

My goal in this [essay] was to establish that oppressed people have an obligation to resist their oppression. I set out to do this first by defending the Kantian tenet that the fundamental moral importance of our rational nature means we have an obligation to protect it from harm. Then I showed how the systemic harms of oppression can damage people's rational natures, and showed how this often happens in nearly invisible increments. So, I argued, that under oppressive social circumstances the obligation to protect our rational nature translates into an obligation to resist oppression. And, if we understand this obligation as one that permits different kinds of latitude in action, we need not worry that imposing it on oppressed people would be too onerous.

DISCUSSION QUESTIONS

1. Explain how Hay's Kantian argument that people who are oppressed have a self-directed duty to resist their oppression might bear on a woman like Native Companion, who has been sexually harassed.
2. Describe some of the ways Hay argues that oppression can damage or restrict people's capacity for practical rationality.
3. Explain how Hay uses Kant's account of imperfect duties to respond to the objection that a self-directed duty to resist oppression would make unfair demands on victims of oppression.
4. What is the difference between internal and external forms of resistance to oppression? Explain the sorts of considerations that can arise in oppressive circumstances that tell in favor of preferring one form of resistance over the other.

NOTES

1. There might be other ways of explaining the results of this survey; I am merely speculating that the Bengali women held these beliefs about their relative worth. But, given that at least some oppressed people do internalize their oppression in this way—and, as we have seen, this phenomenon is so ubiquitous that most people internalize at least some aspects of their oppression—this speculation is unfortunately neither unreasonable nor unrealistic. There is a philosophical issue here, I contend, regardless of whether my speculations are right in this particular case.
2. See Sen, "Gender Inequality and Theories of Justice," and "Rights and Capabilities."
3. This, of course, is not to suggest that it is *worse* to fail to resist one's own oppression than it is

to oppress others. I mean only to argue that it is a moral failing to fail to resist one's own oppression.
4. For example, as we will see in more detail below, Ann Cudd argues that what is wrong when women acquiesce in their own oppression is that doing so strengthens sexist institutions that harm all women. See Cudd, *Analyzing Oppression*, 198–200. Also see her "Strikes, Housework, and the Moral Obligation to Resist," and her "Oppression by Choice."
5. Thanks to an anonymous reviewer for this second point.
6. It might be that Kant himself would not accept the idea that our practical rationality as such is something that admits of improvements or impairments. After all, the very idea suggests that one is not metaphysically free. If this is right, then my view differs from Kant's in this respect; I contend that practical rationality itself can be both harmed and improved. These harms and improvements are analogous to harms and improvements to our memory, imagination, and so on.
7. Elizabeth Anderson, "Should Feminists Reject Rational Choice Theory?," *A Mind of One's Own: Feminist Essays on Reason and Objectivity*, Antony and Witt (eds) (Boulder: Westview, 2002), 369–397.
8. Anderson, "Should Feminists Reject Rational Choice Theory?," 385.
9. Anderson, "Should Feminists Reject Rational Choice Theory?," 386.
10. In characterizing rationality as a matter that concerns not merely the means one uses to achieve one's ends, but also what one's ends themselves are, I am committing myself to the view that certain ends are intrinsically rational and others intrinsically irrational. For an account of how this sort of reason can be involved in determining what ends we set, see Henry Richardson, *Practical Reasoning About Final Ends* (Cambridge: Cambridge University Press, 1997). One implication of committing myself to this view is that my

account of rationality is set apart from those that would equate rationality with adaptive behaviour. Such adaptive accounts of rationality would suggest that members of the oppressed act rationally when they "play along" with their own subjugation. The ethical point I would like to advance, however, maintains that such complicity can compromise our rationality by undermining our capacity to set ends for ourselves and to pursue these ends in a purposeful manner.

11. There is evidence to suggest that various factors that bear on people's capacity for rational deliberation—things such as people's talents and their ability to see the value in delayed gratification—are highly dependent on education or training in one way or another. See, for example, J. Currie, "Early Childhood Education Programs," *Journal of Economic Perspectives* 15 (2001): 213–238; J. Currie and D. Thomas, "Does Head Start Make a Difference?," *American Economic Review* 85 (1995): 341–364; E. Zigler and S. J. Styfco (eds.) *The Head Start Debates*, (Baltimore: Brookes, 2004). For evidence that what is generally thought of as inborn talent is often actually highly socially determined, see Ericsson (ed.) *Cambridge Handbook of Expertise and Expert Performance* (New York: Cambridge University Press, 2006).

12. For example, performing the kind of work that women are traditionally held responsible for—work such as routine, repetitive housework—is associated with higher rates of depression. See, for example, R. C. Barnett and Y. C. Shen, "Gender, High- and Low-Schedule-Control Housework Tasks, and Psychological Distress," *Journal of Family Issues* 18 (1997): 403–428; J. Glass and T. Fukimoto, "Housework, Paid Work, and Depression among Husbands and Wives," *Journal of Health and Social Behavior* 35 (1994): 179–191; R. W. Larsen, M. H. Richards, and M. Perry-Jenkins, "Divergent Worlds: The Daily Emotional Experience of Mothers and Fathers in the Domestic and Public Spheres," *Journal*

of Personality and Social Psychology 67 (1994): 1034–1046. For discussions of how being oppressed increases one's likelihood of institutionalization, see, for example, R. T. Roth and J. Lerner, "Sex-Based Discrimination in the Mental Institutionalization of Women," *California Law Review* 62 (1974): 789–815; Licia Carlson, "Cognitive Ableism and Disability Studies: Feminist Reflections on the History of Mental Retardation," *Hypatia* 16 (2001): 124–146, and *The Faces of Intellectual Disability: Philosophical Reflections* (Bloomington: Indiana University Press, 2009).

13. See, for example, Thomas Nagel, *The Possibility of Altruism* (Princeton: Princeton University Press, 1970).

14. Superson, "Right-Wing Women," 40.

15. Jean Harvey, *Civilized Oppression* (Lanham: Rowman and Littlefield, 1999), 79–80.

16. Cudd, *Analyzing Oppression*, 199.

17. Cudd, *Analyzing Oppression*, 187–221.

18. Cudd, *Analyzing Oppression*, 198.

19. Cudd clearly has in mind here something like Sandra Bartky's concept of *mystification*, "the systematic obscuring of both the reality and agencies of psychological oppression so that its intended effect, the depredated self, is lived out as destiny, guilt, or neurosis." See Bartky, "On Psychological Oppression," 23.

20. Cudd, *Analyzing Oppression*, 199–200.

21. Kant says imperfect duties leave "a [wiggle-room] (*latitudo*) for free choice in following (complying with) the law, that is, that the law cannot specify precisely in what way one is to act and how much one is to do by the action for an end that is also a duty" (*MM* 6:390).

22. Thomas Hill's account of the different kinds of latitude that could be permitted by Kant's imperfect duties is probably the best accepted in the literature. The two kinds of latitude I focus on here are both articulated by Hill. See Thomas Hill, "Kant on Imperfect Duty and Supererogation," *Dignity and Practical Reason in Kant's Moral Theory* (Ithaca: Cornell University Press, 1992), 147–175.

23. In certain circumstances, helping someone else might actually harm her rational capacities, by encouraging dependence or a lack of self-confidence, for example. Nevertheless, the existence of such cases does not undermine the more general point that, in most cases, the result of beneficently helping other people is that their rational capacities are fostered.

24. There are a number of reasons why this way of resisting oppression could be problematic. One is that attempts at reappropriation might just *reinforce* derogatory stereotypes. Another is that it might be difficult to tell whether someone has really reappropriated derogatory stereotypes, or whether they have merely *internalized* (and thus endorsed) them. A third is that the use of epithets like these might be harmful to other members of the oppressed groups who are either not aware of, or take issue with, the ironic way in which the terms are being used. Thanks to an anonymous reviewer for these suggestions.

25. Nelson Mandela, *A Long Walk to Freedom: The Autobiography of Nelson Mandela* (London: Little Brown, 1994), 297–299. As cited in Morton Deutch, "Overcoming Oppression with Power," March, 2005 http://www.beyondintractability .org/bi essay/oppression-power (accessed 24 January 2013).

26. Wallace, "Getting Away from Already Pretty Much Being Away From It All," 101.

27. Wallace, "Getting Away from Already Pretty Much Being Away From It All," 101.

28. Wallace, "Getting Away from Already Pretty Much Being Away From It All," 101.

29. Thanks to two anonymous reviewers for pressing me to answer versions of this question.

30. Boxill, "The Responsibility of the Oppressed to Resist Their Own Oppression," 7.

31. Nussbam, Sex *and Social Justice*, 18.

32. Baron, *Kantian Ethics Almost Without Apology*, 44–45.

Kant and Kinky Sex

BY JORDAN PASCOE

Jordan Pascoe is a Canadian philosopher who writes on issues in feminist epistemology, Kantian political philosophy, and critical race philosophy. Addressing Kant's notoriously pessimistic views on sexual desire, in this essay Pascoe argues that Kant's mistake lies in mistaking all sex for what she calls "kinky" sex—admittedly "morally dangerous" sex whose pleasure lies in the precise fact that involves various forms of objectification. Even kinky sex can be undertaken in morally responsible ways, she argues, but only under the sorts of background conditions—those characterized by equality and mutual respect, where dynamics of trust, open communication, and consent are paramount—that Kant (mistakenly) thought marriage would secure.

Kantian Cannibalism

There are two things about Kant's moral philosophy that may encourage us to think about his views on sex, no matter how skewed they might be. First, Kant's moral philosophy is centrally concerned with the relationship between our reason and our desires. Second, Kant is concerned about our tendency to use other people. Morality, he says, is the obligation to treat others as ends in themselves, and never merely as a means. And we act morally when we're guided by our reason, not our desires.

This isn't to say that our desires are *bad*—they're just morally irrelevant. Sometimes our desires lead us to do good things: we're nice to people we love, and we occasionally save adorable puppies. But Kant thought that, to be moral, an action had to be motivated by reason and respect for persons as ends, not just a desire to be nice.

Think about it this way: if we choose good deeds for no reason other than that we enjoy them, we can't be counted on to choose good deeds when we don't feel like it. So, if my only reason for caring about you is the pleasure it brings me, what's to stop me from using or abandoning you when the mood suits me? Kant's moral philosophy, in other words, is concerned with constancy and reliability, which are important questions in sexual relationships.

Given this brief account of Kant's moral philosophy, it's easy to see what Kant might have to say about your relationship with your lover. He might say that this relationship presents a conflict between reason and desire, and that our natural sexual desires conflict with our moral obligations to respect each other as persons and ends in ourselves. Sex may lead us to care deeply for our lover, to desire to bring them great pleasure, and to do nice things for them because doing so adds to our pleasure. But if sexual desire is only about pleasure, then it won't make me a reliable or trustworthy lover: I can't be relied on to care for my lover when doing so won't bring me pleasure, and I can't be relied on to treat my lover as an end in himself.

But that's not the end of the story. No, Kant thought sex was much worse than other desires, and that it posed a uniquely dangerous moral problem. Kant, remember, called sex "cannibalistic": sex, he said, is the *only* case where I use another person directly as an object to satisfy my desires, and it's the only case where my desire is so graphically appetitive. My sexual desire for my lover, says Kant, is likely to be at odds with my moral concern for my lover, and even the best moral intentions are likely to be corrupted by the appetitive nature of sexuality.

Kant thinks sex deserves special attention because it leads us to objectify both others and ourselves. This seems hyperbolic, of course: we don't commonly think that our sexual relationships are necessarily morally corrupted. But I don't think we should dismiss Kant that easily. Kant is concerned that, when we move through the world as sexual objects, motivated by sexual appetite, we treat ourselves and others differently.

When we're "on the prowl," we present ourselves differently and we engage with others differently, and too often we think and behave in ways that are contrary to our moral obligation to treat others—and ourselves—as persons possessing dignity and deserving respect. Sexual impulse is a particular kind of orientation towards the world, and if unrestrained, it threatens to undermine our duties to ourselves and others. The trick, then, is to find a way of restraining sexual impulse so that we are not tempted to objectify ourselves and others.

Kant's proposed solution to the moral dangers of sex is, at first glance, predictable: we must only engage in sex within a legally sanctioned marriage. Which, sure, sounds like exactly the sort of thing an eighteenth-century moral philosopher *would* say. But, we might ask: if sex is such a thorny moral problem, can even marriage redeem sex? Why does Kant think that marriage can radically transform the cannibalistic nature of sexuality?

How Not to Cannibalize Your Lover

Kant's account of marriage is a tricky thing. Here's what he *does* say about marriage: it's a monogamous, equal, legal agreement that produces an exchange of equal and reciprocal rights that gives partners shared ownership of all their stuff, and it must occur through public law rather than private contract. Here's what he *doesn't* say about marriage: he says nothing about love, or about how partners ought to treat each other, beyond the basic, universal requirement that they are bound to respect each other as persons. He says a lot about what makes

marriage a useful legal institution, but almost nothing about what makes a marriage "good."

The puzzle, then, is this: how, exactly, does marriage as a carefully defined legal institution transform impermissible, cannibalistic sex into principled, morally permissible sex? What kind of transformation is marriage supposed to create? One argument is that marriage "blocks" sexual objectification: if sex is just one part of a relationship in which partners are legally required to respect each other as persons, and to take each others' ends and goals as their own, I am less likely to objectify or dehumanize my partner. Or, to put it differently, marriage creates a kind of "psychological transformation" where sex becomes a respectful encounter with my lover, rather than a dehumanizing one.

But if what we need is a "psychological transformation" of our relationship with our lovers, why is marriage necessary? Wouldn't a loving, committed relationship be enough to block the urge to cannibalize? There are two criticisms to make here: first, if respect brings about this transformation, and respect characterizes any loving, committed, monogamous relationship, why is sex only permissible within marriage? And second, if Kant defines marriage as a legal relationship and tells us nothing about what makes a marriage good, why assume that marriage *per se* will be loving, committed, and respectful enough to bring about this transformation?

To answer these criticisms, philosophers have argued that we need something more than marriage to bring about the transformation of sex that Kant describes: we need an account of a morally robust, committed relationship. This relationship doesn't need to be marriage, but it might benefit from some of the qualities that Kant ascribes to marriage: it should be equal and committed, and require partners to respect each other and take one another's ends as their own.

Within such a relationship, we can easily imagine that sex, like other parts of the relationship, would be concerned with equality and respect. Cannibalistic sex is humanized: my vampiric desire to consume my partner becomes a moral desire to love, respect, and enjoy my partner.

The idea is that sexual desires themselves are transformed so that my tendency to objectify my partner is checked by the deep respect that our loving, committed relationship has instilled in me.

Kant discusses just this kind of relationship in his *Metaphysics of Morals*, where he describes moral friendship. Moral friendship, he says, has the following characteristics: it is a friendship between equals with a genuine concern for one another as persons (rather than a friendship of "mutual advantage"). It's a relationship characterized by respect.

Kant says that moral friendship is based on "mutual respect" rather than on feelings (since feelings have a pesky tendency to change) and that true friendship involves limited intimacy, since too much intimacy tends to undermine respect. Respect, in this way, counteracts love: while love draws two people closer, Kant argues, respect urges them to maintain a reasonable distance from each other.

Curiously, though, Kant didn't think moral friendship was compatible with a sexual relationship. He thought this for a number of reasons, not all of which are good—for example, he didn't think this kind of friendship was possible with women, who lacked equality and tended to be emotional rather than reasonable. But more basically, I suspect, Kant thought sex was incompatible with the respect moral friendship requires. And this is not simply because sex involves objectification and debasement, but because it involves too much intimacy. The intimacy of a sexual relationship threatens to undermine the respect required to maintain a moral friendship.

The respect that characterizes a moral friendship requires distance, and so Kant tells us that friends shouldn't become too familiar with each other. Friends don't need or depend on each other: they can't care for one another when they're sick, for example, because doing so might create a troubling intimacy. And, by the same token, friends can't have sex with friends, since this kind of basic, consuming need would conflict with the distance that friendship requires.

This lets us see Kant's argument about marriage in a different light. Sex involves an unacceptable kind of intimacy, and intimacy necessarily undermines respect. Marriage doesn't make sex any less cannibalistic, but it creates a legal space in which we are allowed to indulge in sexual cannibalism. It's not that sex itself is morally transformed. Instead, it's quarantined: I'm no longer "on the prowl" with my rampant desire to cannibalize others. I'm now legally required to cannibalize only one other person, who has agreed to a lifetime of reciprocal cannibalization (which is exactly how wedding vows ought to put it), and we engage in this thorny sexual behavior behind closed doors.

The "behind closed doors" bit is critical to Kant's argument. If we take Kant's concerns about objectification and dehumanization seriously, sex undermines respect in a bunch of ways. When I present myself as a sexual creature, Kant suggests, I present myself as an object of desire, and in doing so I make myself unworthy of respect.

I want my lover to see me as a sexual creature and an object of desire, but I would rather my students and colleagues not think of me that way. I want to be free to explore my sexuality in one part of my life without it spilling into all the other parts.

Marriage, as Kant defines it, performs precisely this kind of quarantining function by legally allowing one person to objectify me, and simultaneously demanding that everyone else stop objectifying me (coveting your neighbor's wife and all that) and respect my relationship with my spouse (cannibalism and all). Only a legal institution, he thinks, can publicly compartmentalize my life so that I'm free to be sexual and intimate in one part of it, and deserving of dignity and respect in all the other parts.

Kant focused on marriage as a legal institution that quarantines sex rather than as a form of moral friendship. Kant didn't think sex could be morally transformed in the straightforward way that we might think it can. In other words, Kant thinks that sex is *always* cannibalistic. There's no such thing as morally unproblematic sex. And given this, his solution is simply to contain it, and to allow just one relationship in a person's life to be contaminated by it, which in turn allows that person to engage in all kinds of other relationships without fear of cannibalizing or being cannibalized.

Kant and Kink

There's one way in which Kant was rather radical about sex. Unlike many other philosophers and religious figures of his day, he rejected the idea that sex was about procreation and that sex was permissible only if it was procreative. Kant understood that sex was about pleasure and pleasure alone. This still totally freaked him out, as we've seen. Kant thought that sex was about the heedless pursuit of pleasure at the expense of one's own humanity and the humanity of one's lover. He thought it was the desire to objectify and be objectified, to debase and be debased, and an appetite so consuming as to be cannibalistic.

Kant thought sex was unimaginably kinky. And, given that he knew very little about sex, this is not surprising. He's wrong to think that sex is inherently kinky, cannibalistic, and debasing in this way. Lots of sex is loving and respectful and even (imagine!) motivated by an appreciation for the humanity of yourself and your lover. Lots of sex is totally consistent with dignity and respect and moral friendships as Kant understands them, and in this sense, Kant's concerns about sexuality seem like hyperbolic relics of another age.

But we can think about this in another way: some sex *is* unimaginably kinky. Some sex is about hunger and devouring and debasement and objectification. So Kant is right, in a sense: sex is about pleasure, and some pleasure is kinky. And the trouble with kinky sex is that (much like vampire sex) it's awesome and consuming and highly pleasurable—and totally morally dangerous. Often, it means seeking out scenarios in which we are debased and dehumanized just because this is pleasurable. Sometimes, what we want is precisely to be used, to be dominated and devoured, and to take a break from all that respect and dignity. So I suggest that we *can* take Kant's thoughts on sex seriously, as long as we understand that he's taking on the moral perils of unimaginably kinky sex.

And if we read Kant's concerns about sex is this way, his claim that kinky sex can't be *transformed*, but only *quarantined*, seems more reasonable. After all, we don't want to transform kinky sex and make it all moral and respectful and stuff. That would completely defeat the point of kinky sex. And, by the same token, we may not want the dehumanizing elements of our kinky sex lives to spill into other parts of our lives.

A relationship that's consistent with kinky sex isn't one that transforms our kinky urges, but one that creates a space in which we can explore them. A kinky sex life requires us to design relationships with the capacity to compartmentalize sexual cannibalism on the one hand, and moral respect for our lovers and ourselves on the other.

I'm not suggesting, as Kant does, that marriage is the solution to the untransformable kink that sex entails. But I think he may be on to something when he emphasizes the quarantining function of successful relationships, which allow us intimate spaces in which to explore our most cannibalistic urges within a broader relationship characterized by mutual trust and respect.

Moreover, by emphasizing the moral dangers of kinky sex, Kant suggests that we need to think carefully about the kinds of structures that would allow us to explore the rampant, morally troubling pleasures of uninhibited sex lives while maintaining loving, moral, and respectful relationships. The very presence of the moral dangers of sex requires us to think more carefully about our relationships with our lovers—which is a good thing, because it's likely to make us better lovers. I have to be *more* careful to respect my lover than the other people in my life, precisely because we often also objectify each other, devour each other, and allow ourselves to be consumed by each other. Sex poses a useful challenge to our relationship by forcing us to construct a relationship that can maintain respect in the face of intimacy, desire, and even kink.

DISCUSSION QUESTIONS

1. How do Kant's views on the relationship between reason and desire in general bear on his views about sexual desire in particular?
2. What is the relationship between Kant's characterization of sexual desire as "cannibalistic" and his account of objectification?
3. Why does Kant think sex is morally permissible only within the context of marriage?
4. Explain how Pascoe revises Kant's arguments to explain when kinky sex is, and is not, morally permissible.

Feminine Masochism and the Politics of Personal Transformation

BY SANDRA LEE BARTKY

Sandra Lee Bartky (1935–2016) was an American philosopher best known for her work in feminist phenomenology. In this provocative essay, Bartky raises the question of what we should do when our sexual desires come into conflict with our moral and political principles. Through an examination of a hypothetical woman who is a self-identified feminist who has sadomasochistic fantasies, she argues that sometimes internalized oppression cannot be undone, and the best one can hope for is to feel "entitled to their shame" about desires they know to be beneath them.

To be at once a sexual being and a moral agent can be troublesome indeed: no wonder philosophers have wished that we could be rid of sexuality altogether. What to do, for example, when the structure of desire is at war with one's principles? This is a difficult question for any person of conscience, but it has a particular poignancy for feminists. A prime theoretical contribution of the contemporary feminist analysis of women's oppression can be captured in the slogan "the personal is political." What this means is that the subordination of women by men is pervasive, that it orders the relationship of the sexes in every area of life, that a sexual politics of domination is as much in evidence in the private spheres of the family, ordinary social life, and sexuality as in the traditionally public spheres of government and the economy. The belief that the things we do in the bosom of the family or in bed are either "natural" or else a function of the personal idiosyncracies of private individuals is held to be an "ideological curtain that conceals the reality of women's systematic oppression."[1] For the feminist, two things follow upon the discovery that sexuality too belongs to the sphere of the political. The first is that whatever pertains to sexuality—not only actual sexual behavior, but sexual desire and sexual fantasy as well—will have to be understood in relation to a larger system of subordination; the second, that the deformed sexuality of patriarchical culture must be moved from the hidden domain of "private life" into an arena for struggle, where a "politically correct" sexuality of mutual respect will contend with an "incorrect" sexuality of domination and submission.

A number of questions present themselves at once. What is a politically correct sexuality, anyhow? What forms would the struggle for such a sexuality assume? Is it possible for individuals to prefigure more liberated forms of sexuality in their own lives now, in a society still marked by the subordination of women in every domain? Finally, the question with which we began, the moral worry about what to do when conscience and sexual desire come into conflict, will look like this when seen through the lens of feminism: What to do when one's own sexuality is "politically incorrect," when desire is wildly at variance with feminist principles? I turn to this question first.

The Story of P.

If any form of sexuality has a *prima facie* claim to be regarded as politically incorrect, it would surely be sadomasochism. I define sadomasochism as any sexual practice that involves the eroticization of relations of domination and submission. Consider the case of P., a feminist, who has masochistic fantasies. If P. were prepared to share her secret life with us, this is what she might say:

> For as long as I can remember (from around age six . . .), my sexual fantasies have involved painful exposure, embarrassment, humiliation, mutilation, domination by Gestapo-like characters.[2]

P. regarded her fantasies as unnatural and perverse until she discovered that of all women who have sexual fantasies, 25 percent have fantasies of rape.[3] Indeed, much material which is often arousing to women, material not normally regarded as perverse, is thematically similar to P.'s fantasies. Many women of her mother's generation were thrilled when the masterful Rhett Butler overpowered the struggling Scarlett O'Hara and swept her triumphantly upstairs in an act of marital rape: "treating 'em rough" has enhanced the sex appeal of many a male film star ever since.[4] The feminine taste for fantasies of victimization is assumed on virtually every page of the large pulp literature produced specifically for women. Confession magazines, Harlequin romances, and that genre of historical romance known in the publishing trade as the "bodice-ripper" have sales now numbering in the billions, and they can be bought in most drugstores and supermarkets across the land. The heroes of these tales turn out to be nice guys in the end, but only in the end; before that they dominate and humiliate the heroines in small "Gestapo-like" ways. In the Harlequin romance *Moth to the Flame* (she the moth, he the flame), the hero, Santino, "whose mouth, despite its sensual curve looked as if it had never uttered the word 'compromise' in its life," insults the heroine, Juliet, mocks her, kidnaps her, steals her clothes, imprisons her in his seaside mansion in Sicily, and threatens repeatedly to rape her."[5] Ginny, the heroine of *Sweet Savage Love* is "almost raped, then almost seduced, then deflowered— half by rape and half by seduction, then alternately raped and seduced"—all this by Steve, who is by turns her assailant and lover.[6] The purity and constancy of women like Juliet and Ginny finally restrain the brutality of their lovers and all ends

happily in marriage, but one cannot escape the suspicion that the ruthlessness of these men constitutes a good part of their sex appeal. When at last brutality recedes and the couple is reconciled, the fantasy ends; *the story is over.*[7]

It might be ventured that standard heterosexual desire in women has often a masochistic dimension, though such desire would fall out far lower on a continuum of masochistic desire than P.'s fantasies or the average Harlequin romance. Essential to masochism is the eroticization of domination. Now women are regularly attracted by power, its possession and exercise. Male power manifests itself variously as physical prowess, muscular strength, intellectual brilliance, worldly position, or the kind of money that buys respect. One or another of these kinds of power may become erotically charged for a woman depending on her values, her history, or her personal idiosyncrasies. In a sexually inegalitarian society, these manifestations of male power are precisely the instruments by which men are able to accomplish the subordination of women. Hence, insofar as male power is eroticized, male dominance itself becomes erotically charged.

One might object that there is nothing masochistic in the female attraction to power at all, that because the possession of power is a source of status for men, a woman who can attach herself to a powerful man will thereby enhance her own status. But this implies that the woman attracted by the athlete is aware only that his muscular prowess can protect her or gain him the esteem of his fellows, not that he can use it to restrain her if he wants, or that the student who idolizes her professor is unaware that he can use his stinging wit as much to put her down as to overawe his classes. I suggest instead that there is contained in the very apprehension of power the recognition that it can overwhelm and subdue as well as protect and impress. Power can raise me from my lowly status and exalt me; it is also that *before which I tremble.*

P. is deeply ashamed of her fantasies. Shame, according to John Deigh, is typically expressed in acts of concealment; it is a reaction to the threat of demeaning treatment one would invite in appearing to be a person of lesser worth.[8] P. would be mortified if her fantasies were somehow to be made public. But she suffers a continuing loss of esteem in her own eyes as well. While one of Schlafly's lieutenants might be embarrassed by such fantasies, too, P.'s psychic distress is palpable, for she feels obliged to play out in the theater of her mind acts of brutality which are not only abhorrent to her but which, as a political activist, she is absolutely committed to eradicating. She experiences her own sexuality as doubly humiliating; not only does the content of her fantasies concern humiliation but the very having of such fantasies, given her politics, is humiliating as well. Two courses of action seem open to someone in P.'s predicament; she can either get rid of her shame and keep her desire, or else get rid of her desire. I shall discuss each of these alternatives in turn.

Sadomasochism and Sexual Freedom

Sadomasochism has been roundly denounced in feminist writing, in particular the sadism increasingly evident in much male-oriented pornography.[9] Feminists have argued that sadomasochism is one inevitable expression of a women-hating culture. It powerfully reinforces male dominance and female subordination because, by linking these phenomena to our deepest sexual desires—desires defined by an ideologically tainted psychology as instinctual—it makes them appear natural. To participate willingly in this mode of sexuality is thus to collude in women's subordination.

I agree entirely with the demand that feminists defend sexual freedom, most tested in the case of sexual minorities, against a newly militant Right. But a political movement may defend some type of erotic activity against prudery or political conservatism without implying in any way that the activity in question is mandated by or even consistent with its own principles. Prostitution is a case in point. There are reasons, in my view, why feminists ought to support the decriminalization of prostitution. If prostitution were legalized, prostitutes would no longer be subject to police or Mafia shakedowns or to the harassment of fines and imprisonment, nor would they need the protection of pimps who often brutalize them. However, none of this implies approval of prostitution as

an institution or an abandonment of the feminist vision of a society without prostitutes.

The most convincing defense of sadomasochism, no doubt, is the claim that since sexual satisfaction is an intrinsic good, we are free to engage in any sexual activities whatsoever, provided of course that these activities involve neither force nor fraud. But this is essentially a *liberal* response to a *radical* critique of sexuality and, as such, it fails entirely to engage this critique. As noted earlier, one of the major achievements of contemporary feminist theory is the recognition that male supremacy is perpetuated not only openly, through male domination of the major societal institutions, but more covertly, through the manipulation of desire. Moreover, desires may be produced and managed in ways which involve neither force nor fraud nor the violation of anyone's legal rights.

The "normal" and the "perverse" have in common the sexualization of domination and submission, albeit to different degrees. Feminine masochism, like femininity in general, is an economical way of embedding women in patriarchy through the mechanism of desire, and while the eroticization of relations of domination may not lie at the heart of the system of male supremacy, it surely perpetuates it. The precise mechanisms at work in the sexualization of domination are unclear, and it would be difficult to show in every case a connection between a particular sexual act or sexual fantasy and the oppression of women in general. While it would be absurd to claim that women accept less pay than men because it is sexually exciting to earn sixty-two cents for every dollar a man earns, it would be equally naive to insist that there is no relationship whatever between erotic domination and sexual subordination. Surely women's acceptance of domination by men cannot be entirely independent of the fact that for many women, *dominance in men is exciting*.

The right, staunchly defended by liberals, to desire what and whom we please and, under certain circumstances, to act on our desire, is not an issue here; the point is that women would be better off if we learned when to refrain from the exercise of this right. A thorough overhaul of desire is clearly on the feminist agenda: the fantasy that we are overwhelmed by Rhett Butler should be traded in for one in which we seize state power and reeducate him. P. has no choice, then, except to reject the counsel that, unashamed, she make space in her psyche for the free and full enjoyment of every desire. This counsel in effect advises P. to ignore in her own life a general principle to which, as a feminist, she is committed and which she is therefore bound to represent to all other women: the principle that we struggle to decolonize our sexuality by removing from our minds the internalized forms of oppression that make us easier to control.

In their enthusiasm for sexual variation, liberals ignore the extent to which a person may experience her own sexuality as arbitrary, hateful, and alien to the rest of her personality. Each of us is in pursuit of an inner integration and unity, a sense that the various aspects of the self form a harmonious whole. But when the parts of the self are at war with one another, a person may be said to suffer from self-estrangement. That part of P. which is compelled to produce sexually charged scenarios of humiliation is radically at odds with the P. who devotes much of her life to the struggle against oppression. Now perfect consistency is demanded of no one, and our little inconsistencies may even lend us charm. But it is no small thing when the form of desire is disavowed by the personality as a whole. The liberal is right to defend the value of sexual satisfaction, but the struggle to achieve an integrated personality has value too and the liberal position does not speak to those situations in which the price of sexual satisfaction is the perpetuation of self-estrangement.

Phenomenologists have argued that affectivity has a cognitive dimension, that emotions offer a certain access to the world. P.'s shame, then, is the reflection in affectivity of a recognition that there are within her deep and real divisions. Insofar as these divisions cannot be reconciled—the one representing stubborn desire, the other a passionate political commitment—there is a sense in which P. is entitled to her shame. Now this is *not* to say that P. *ought* to feel shame: Profound existential contradictions are not uncommon and our response to them may vary. But it seems equally mistaken to claim that P. ought not to feel what she feels.

Her desires are not worthy of her, after all, nor is it clear that she is a mere helpless victim of patriarchal conditioning, unable to take any responsibility at all for her wishes and fantasies.

It is often the case that the less unwanted desires are acknowledged as belonging to the self and the more they are isolated and compartmentalized, the more psychic distress is minimized. The more extreme the self-estrangement, in other words, the less intense the psychic discomfort. P.'s shame and distress may well be a sign that she is *not* reconciled to her lack of inner harmony and integration and that she clings to the hope that the warring factions within her personality will still somehow be reconciled.

Let us suppose that P., determined to bring her desires into line with her ideology, embarks upon a course of traditional psychotherapy, and let us further suppose that her psychotherapy is unsuccessful. As part of her political education, P. is now exposed to a radical critique of psychotherapy: Psychotherapy is sexist; it is authoritarian and hierarchical; it is mired in the values of bourgeois society. P. now resolves to consult a "politically correct" therapist, indeed, a feminist therapist. In order to bring our discussion forward, let us suppose that this second attempt is unsuccessful too, for in spite of its popularity there is evidence that therapy fails as often as it succeeds, whatever the theoretical orientation of the therapist.[10] P. is finding it no simple thing to change her desires. Ought she to try again? In a society with little cohesiveness and less confidence in its own survival, an obsessional preoccupation with self has come to replace more social needs and interests. For many people, there is no higher obligation than to the self—to get it "centered," to realize its "potentialities," to clear out its "hangups"—and little to life apart from a self-absorbed trek through the fads, cults, and therapies of our time. But how compatible is such a surrender to the "new narcissism" (the old "bourgeois individualism") with a serious commitment to radical reform? Few but the relatively privileged can afford psychotherapy anyhow, and the search for what may well be an unrealizable ideal of mental health can absorb much of a person's time, energy, and money. It is not at all clear that the politically correct course of action for P. is to continue in this way whatever the cost; perhaps she is better advised to direct her resources back toward the women's movement. She is, after all, not psychologically disabled; within the oppressive realities of the contemporary world, her life is richer and more effective than the lives of many other people, and she is reconciled to her life—in every respect but one.

Paradise Lost and Not Regained: The Failure of a Politics of Personal Transformation

The view is widespread among radical feminists, especially among certain lesbian separatists, that female sexuality is malleable and diffuse and that a woman can, if she chooses, alter the structure of her desire. Here then is a new source of moral instruction for P. Without the help of any paid professional—for no such help is really needed—P. is now to pull herself up by her own psychological bootstraps.

The idea that we can alter our entire range of sexual feelings I shall call "sexual voluntarism." Sexual voluntarism has two sources: first, the fact that for many women, thoroughgoing and unforeseen personal changes, including the rejection of heterosexuality for lesbian sexuality, have often accompanied the development of a feminist politics; second, a theory of sexuality that relies heavily on Skinnerian-style behaviorism. While it is a fact that many women (and even some men) have been able to effect profound personal transformations under the influence of feminist ideas, a theory of sexuality I believe to be both false and politically divisive has taken this fact as evidence for the practicability of a willed transformation of self.

For the sexual voluntarist, individuals are thought to be blank tablets on which the culture inscribes certain patterns of behavior. Sexual norms are embedded in a variety of cultural forms, among them "common sense," religion, the family, books, magazines, television, films, and popular music. Individuals are "positively reinforced," i.e., rewarded, when they model their behavior on images and activities held out to them as normal and desirable, "negatively reinforced," i.e.,

punished, when their modeling behavior is done incorrectly or not done at all.

> If we come to view male-dominated heterosexuality as the only healthy form of sex, it is because we are bombarded with that model for our sexual fantasies long before we experience sex itself. Sexual images of conquest and submission pervade our imagination from an early age and determine how we will later look upon and experience sex.[11]

The masters of patriarchal society make sure that the models set before us incorporate their needs and preferences: All other possibilities become unspeakable or obscene. Thus, the pervasiveness of propaganda for heterosexuality, for female passivity, and male sexual aggressivity are responsible not only for ordinary heterosexuality but for sadomasochism as well. Sadomasochists reveal to the world, albeit in an exaggerated form, the inner nature of heterosexuality and they are stigmatized by the larger society precisely because they tear the veil from what patriarchal respectability would like to hide.[12] Sadomasochism is

> a conditioned response to the sexual imagery that barrages women in this society. . . . It is not surprising that women respond physically and emotionally to sadomasochistic images. Whether a woman identifies with the dominant or submissive figure in the fantasy, she is still responding to a model of sexual interaction that has been drummed into us throughout our lives.[13]

The language of these passages is graphic and leaves little doubt as to the theory of sexuality which is being put forward. Models of sexual relationship bombard us: they are drummed into our heads: the ideological apparatus of patriarchal society is said to condition the very structure of desire itself.

What is valuable in this view is the idea that sexuality is socially constructed. But are the voluntarists right about the mode of its construction? And those patterns of desire which may have been present in a person's psyche from the virtual dawn of consciousness: Are voluntarists perhaps too sanguine about the prospects of radically altering these patterns in adult life?

One can deviate from a feminist standard of sexual behavior as well as from the obligatory heterosexuality of the larger society. Given their theoretical commitments, feminist sexual voluntarists are unable to regard departure from feminist sexual norms as due to anything but a low level of political understanding on the one hand, or to weakness of will on the other or, of course, to a little of both.[14] They reason that if our sexuality is in fact a product of social conditioning, then we can become ourselves our own social conditioners and programmers, substituting a feminist input for a patriarchal one. Failure to do this is made out to fear, or insufficient determination, or not trying hard enough, i.e., to some form of *akrasia* or else to an inability to comprehend the extent to which certain patterns of sexual behavior—for example, sadomasochism or heterosexuality—support the patriarchal order. The feminist analysis of sexuality has, quite correctly, been a major theoretical achievement of the Second Wave; crucial to this analysis is an understanding of the extent to which our sexuality has been colonized. Hence, the refusal or inability of a woman to bring her sexuality into conformity is a serious matter indeed and may tend, in the eyes of many, to diminish her other contributions to the women's movement, whatever they may be. This kind of thinking has led to painful divisions within the radical women's movement. The accused, guilt-ridden heterosexuals or closeted masochists, stand charged with lack of resolve, inconsistency, or even collusion with the enemy, while their accusers adopt postures of condescension or self-righteousness.

"Any woman can"—such is the motto of voluntarism. Armed with an adequate feminist critique of sexuality and sufficient will power, any women should be able to alter the pattern of her desires. While the feminist theory needed for this venture is known to be the product of collective effort, and while groups of women—even, in the case of lesbian separatism, organized communities of women—may be waiting to welcome the reformed pervert, the process of transformation is seen, nonetheless, as something a woman must accomplish alone. How can it be otherwise, given the fact that no tendency within the contemporary women's liberation movement has developed a genuinely collective *praxis* which would make it possible for women like P. to bring their desires into line with their principles? (I shall return to this point later.) A pervasive and characteristic feature of bourgeois ideology has here been introduced into feminist theory, namely, the idea that the victims, the colonized, are responsible for their own colonization and that they can change the circumstances of their lives by altering their consciousness. Of course, no larger social transformation can occur unless individuals change as well, but the tendency I am criticizing places the burden for effecting change squarely upon the individual, an idea quite at variance with radical feminist thinking generally.

One final point, before I turn to another mode of theorizing about sexuality—one not as subject to moralism and divisiveness. Those who claim that any woman can reprogram her consciousness if only she is sufficiently determined hold a shallow view of the nature of patriarchal oppression. Anything done can be undone, it is implied; nothing has been permanently damaged, nothing irretrievably lost. But this is tragically false. One of the evils of a system of oppression is that it may damage people in ways that cannot always be undone. Patriarchy invades the intimate recesses of personality where it may maim and cripple the spirit forever. No political movement, even a movement with a highly developed analysis of sexual oppression, can promise an end to sexual alienation or a cure for sexual dysfunction. Many human beings, P. among them, may have to live with a degree of psychic damage that can never be fully healed.

Instead of a Conclusion

P. will search the foregoing discussion in vain for practical moral advice. The way out of her predicament seemed to be the abandonment either of her shame or of her desire. But I have suggested that there is a sense in which she is "entitled" to her shame, insofar as shame is a wholly understandable response to behavior which is seriously at variance with principles. In addition, I have argued that not every kind of sexual behavior, even behavior that involves consenting adults or is played out in the private theater of the imagination, is compatible with feminist principles, a feminist analysis of sexuality, or a feminist vision of social transformation. To this extent, I declare the incompatibility of a classical liberal position on sexual freedom with my own understanding of feminism.

P.'s other alternative, getting rid of her desire, is a good and sensible project if she can manage it, but it turns out to be so difficult in the doing that to preach to her a feminist code of sexual correctness in the confident anticipation that she will succeed would be a futility—and a cruelty. Since many women (perhaps even most women) are in P.'s shoes, such a code would divide women within the movement and alienate those outside of it. "Twixt the conception and creation," writes the poet, "falls the shadow." Between the conception of a sexuality in harmony with feminism and the creation of a feminist standard of political correctness in sexual matters, fall not one but two shadows: first, the lack of an adequate theory of sexuality; the second the lack of an effective political practice around issues of personal transformation. The second shadow need not wait upon the emergence of the first, for to take seriously the principle of the inseparability of theory and practice is to see that a better theoretical understanding of the nature of sexual desire might well begin to emerge in the course of a serious and sustained attempt to alter it.

I am not suggesting that human sexuality is entirely enigmatic. Quite the contrary. There have been revolutionary advances in our knowledge of human sexual psychology over the last ninety years, and the work of feminist theorists promises to extend our understanding still further. Nor do I want to substitute a sexual determinism for sexual voluntarism. Some people try to reorganize their erotic lives and they succeed. Others, caught up in the excitement of a movement that calls for the radical transformation of every human institution, find that they have changed without even trying. But more often than not, sexuality is mysterious and opaque, seemingly unalterable because its meaning is impenetrable. The significance of a particular form of desire as well as its persistence may lie in a developmental history only half-remembered or even repressed altogether. However embarrassing from a feminist perspective, a tabooed desire may well play a crucial and necessary role in a person's psychic economy.

The order of the psyche, here and now, in a world of pain and oppression, is not identical to the ideal order of a feminist political vision. We can teach a woman how to plan a demonstration, how to set up a phone bank, or how to lobby. We can share what we have learned about starting up a women's studies program or a battered women's shelter. But we cannot teach P. or the women of Samois or even ourselves how to decolonize the imagination: This is what I meant earlier by the claim that the women's movement has an insufficiently developed practice around issues of sexuality. The difficulties which stand in the way of the emergence of such a practice are legion; another paper would be required to identify them and also to examine the circumstances in which many women and some men have been able to effect dramatic changes in their lives. But in my view, the prevalence in some feminist circles of the kind of thinking I call "sexual voluntarism," with its simplistic formulas, moralism, intolerance, and refusal to acknowledge the obsessional dimension of sexual desire, is itself an obstacle to the emergence of an adequate practice.

Those who find themselves in the unfortunate situation of P. are living out, in the form of existential unease, contradictions which are present in the larger society. I refer to the contradiction between our formal commitment to justice and equality on the one hand—a commitment that the women's movement is determined to force the larger society to honor—and the profoundly authoritarian character of our various systems of social relationships on the other. Those who have followed my "Story of P." will have to decide whether P. is in fact caught in a historical moment which we have not as yet surpassed or whether I have merely written a new apology for a very old hypocrisy.

DISCUSSION QUESTIONS

1. Explain how Bartky uses the feminist arguments that the personal is political and that oppression is systemic to justify the appropriateness of analyzing the content of P.'s sexual fantasies.

2. Explain how sadomasochism reinforces male domination and female subordination, according to feminists like Bartky.

3. Explain how the liberal defense of sadomasochism fails to engage with the radical feminist critique of these desires, according to Bartky.

4. Explain what Bartky means when she says that P. is "entitled to her shame."

NOTES

1. Alison Jaggar, *Feminist Politics and Human Nature* (Totowa, N.J.: Rowman and Allanheld, 1983), p. 122.

2. *Ms.*, July–August 1982, p. 35.

3. Maria Marcus, *A Taste for Pain: On Masochism and Female Sexuality* (New York: St. Martin's Press, 1981), p. 46. Needless to say, the having of a fantasy, every detail of which the woman orchestrates herself, is not like a desire for actual rape. The pervasive fear of rape hangs like a blight over the lives of women, where it may severely restrict spontaneity and freedom of movement. Even if a woman escapes impregnation, venereal disease, or grave bodily injury during a rape, the psychological consequences to her may be devastating. The aftermath of rape, only recently documented by feminist scholars, may include nightmares, excessive fearfulness, phobic behavior, loss of sexual desire, and the erosion of intimate relationships. None of this is part of the typical rape fantasy.

4. A recent history of women in Hollywood film sets out at some length the increasingly brutal treatment of women in the movies, movies made by men to be sure, but patronized and enjoyed by large numbers of women. See Molly Haskell, *From Reverence to Rape* (New York: Penguin Books, 1974).

5. Sara Craven, *Moth to the Flame* (Toronto: Harlequin Books, 1979).

6. Beatrice Faust, *Women, Sex and, Pornography* (New York: Macmillan, 1980), p. 147. "Sweet Savagery girls cede a great deal of the responsibility to the heroes, saying no until virile and sometimes vicious men force them to say yes. Much of the time the relationship between heroines and heroes is that of master and slave, teacher and pupil, leader and the led. The heroines achieve autonomy only to relinquish it in marriage." Ibid., p. 156.

7. For a penetrating analysis of the Harlequin-type romance, see Ann Barr Snitow, "Mass Market Romance: Pornography for Women Is Different," *Radical History Review*, Vol. 20, Spring-Summer, 1979, pp. 141–161.

8. John Deigh, "Shame and Self-Esteem: A Critique," *Ethics*, Vol. 93, January 1983, pp. 225–245.

9. Laura Lederer, ed., *Take Back the Night: Women on Pornography* (New York: William Morrow, 1980).

10. See H. J. Eysenck, "The Effects of Psychotherapy: An Evaluation," *Journal of Consulting Psychology*, Vol. 16, 1952, pp. 319–324. For further discussion of this topic, see A. J. Fix and E. Haffke, *Basic Psychological Therapies: Comparative Effectiveness* (New York: Human Sciences Press, 1976).

11. Linda Phelps, "Female Sexual Alienation," in Jo Freeman, ed., *Women: A Feminist Perspective*, 2d ed. (Palo Alto, Calif.: Mayfield, 1979).

12. See Sarah Lucia Hoagland, "Sadism, Masochism and Lesbian-Feminism," in *Against Sadomasochism*.

13. Jeannette Nichols, Darlene Pagano, and Margaret Rossoff, "Is Sadomasochism Feminist?" in *Against Sadomasochism*. Many feminists, especially those in the anti-pornography movement, believe that men in particular will want to imitate the images of sexual behavior with which they are now being bombarded; this accounts for the urgency of these feminists' attack on male-oriented violent pornography. See Laura Lederer, ed., *Take Back the Night*, esp. Ann Jones, "A Little Knowledge," pp. 179 and 183, and Diana E. H. Russell, "Pornography and Violence: What Does the New Research Say?" p. 236.

14. The literature of lesbian separatism, in particular, is replete with examples of sexual voluntarism: "'Do what feels good. Sex is groovy. Gay is just as good as straight. I don't care what you do in bed, so you shouldn't care what I do in bed.' This argument assumes that Lesbians have the same lifestyle and sexuality as straight women. But we don't—straight women choose to love and fuck men. Lesbians have

commitments to women. Lesbians are not born. We have made a conscious choice to be Lesbians. We have rejected all that is traditional and accepted, and committed ourselves to a lifestyle that everybody ... criticizes." Barbara Solomon, "Taking the Bullshit by the Horns," in Nancy Myron and Charlotte Bunch, eds., *Lesbianism and the Women's Movement* (Baltimore: Diana Press, 1975), p. 40. For similar statements, see in the same volume, pp. 18, 36, and 70.

Markets in Women's Sexual Labor

BY DEBRA SATZ

Debra Satz is an American philosopher whose work focuses on issues such as the ethical limits of markets, the place of equality in political philosophy, theories of rational choice, democratic theory, feminist philosophy, and issues of international justice. After rejecting standard philosophical and feminist criticisms of sex work, in this essay Satz argues that sex work is wrong only insofar as it derives from and contributes to a cultural context that promotes inegalitarian relations between men and women.

There is a widely shared intuition that markets are inappropriate for some kinds of human endeavor: that some things simply should not be bought and sold. For example, virtually everyone believes that love and friendship should have no price. The sale of other human capacities is disputed, but many people believe that there is something about sexual and reproductive activities that makes their sale inappropriate. I have called the thesis supported by this intuition the asymmetry thesis.[1] Those who hold the asymmetry thesis believe that markets in reproduction and sex are asymmetric to other labor markets. They think that treating sexual and reproductive capacities as commodities, as goods to be developed and exchanged for a price, is worse than treating our other capacities as commodities. They think that there is something wrong with commercial surrogacy and prostitution that is not wrong with teaching and professional sports.

The intuition that there is a distinction between markets in different human capacities is a deep one, even among people who ultimately think that the distinction does not justify legally forbidding sales of reproductive capacity and sex. I accept this intuition, which I continue to probe in this article. In particular, I ask: What justifies taking an asymmetric attitude toward markets in our sexual capacities? What, if anything, is problematic about

a woman selling her sexual as opposed to her secretarial labor? And, if the apparent asymmetry can be explained and justified, what implications follow for public policy?

In this article, I sketch and criticize two popular approaches to these questions. The first, which I call the economic approach, attributes the wrongness of prostitution to its consequences for efficiency or welfare. The important feature of this approach is its treatment of sex as a morally indifferent matter: sexual labor is not to be treated as a commodity if and only if such treatment fails to be efficient or welfare maximizing. The second, the "essentialist" approach, by contrast, stresses that sales of sexual labor are wrong because they are inherently alienating or damaging to human happiness. In contrast to these two ways of thinking about the immorality of prostitution, I will argue that the most plausible support for the asymmetry thesis stems from the role of commercialized sex and reproduction in sustaining a social world in which women form a subordinated group. Prostitution is wrong insofar as the sale of women's sexual labor reinforces broad patterns of sex discrimination. My argument thus stresses neither efficiency nor sexuality's intrinsic value but, rather, equality. In particular, I argue that contemporary prostitution contributes to, and also instantiates, the perception of women as socially inferior to men.

On the basis of my analysis of prostitution's wrongness, there is no simple conclusion as to what its legal status ought to be. Both criminalization and decriminalization may have the effect of exacerbating the inequalities in virtue of which I claim that prostitution is wrong. Nonetheless, my argument does have implications for the form of prostitution's regulation, if legal, and its prohibition and penalties, if illegal. Overall, my argument tends to support decriminalization.

The argument I will put forward here is qualified and tentative in its practical conclusions, but its theoretical point is not. I will argue that the most plausible account of prostitution's wrongness turns on its relationship to the pervasive social inequality between men and women. If, in fact, no causal relationship obtains between prostitution and gender inequality, then I do not think that prostitution is morally troubling.[2] This is a controversial claim. In my evaluation of prostitution, consideration of the actual social conditions which many, if not most, women face plays a crucial role. It will follow from my analysis that male prostitution raises distinct issues and is not connected to injustice in the same way as female prostitution.

On my view, prostitution is not wrong irrespective of its cultural and economic context. Moreover, prostitution is a complex phenomenon. I begin, accordingly, with the question, Who is a prostitute?

Who Is a Prostitute?

While much has been written on the history of prostitution, and some empirical studies of prostitutes themselves have been undertaken, the few philosophers writing on this subject have tended to treat prostitution as if the term referred to something as obvious as "table."[3] But it does not. Not only is it hard to draw a sharp line between prostitution and practices which look like prostitution, but as historians of the subject have emphasized, prostitution today is also a very different phenomenon from earlier forms of commercial sex.[4] In particular, the idea of prostitution as a specialized

occupation of an outcast and stigmatized group is of relatively recent origin.[5]

While all contemporary prostitutes are stigmatized as outsiders, prostitution itself has an internal hierarchy based on class, race, and gender. The majority of prostitutes—and all those who walk the streets—are poor. The majority of streetwalkers in the United States are poor black women. These women are a world apart from prostitution's upper tier. Consider three cases: a streetwalker in Boston, a call girl on Park Avenue, and a male prostitute in San Francisco's tenderloin district. In what way do these three lives resemble one another? Consider the three cases:

1. A fourteen-year-old girl prostitutes herself to support her boyfriend's heroin addiction. Later, she works the streets to support her own habit. She begins, like most teenage streetwalkers, to rely on a pimp for protection. She is uneducated and is frequently subjected to violence in her relationships and with her customers. She also receives no social security, no sick leave or maternity leave, and—most important—no control as to whether or not she has sex with a man. The latter is decided by her pimp.

2. Now imagine the life of a Park Avenue call girl. Many call girls drift into prostitution after "run of the mill promiscuity," led neither by material want nor lack of alternatives.[6] Some are young college graduates, who upon graduation earn money by prostitution while searching for other jobs. Call girls can earn between $30,000 and $100,000 annually. These women have control over the entire amount they earn as well as an unusual degree of independence, far greater than in most other forms of work. They can also decide who they wish to have sex with and when they wish to do so.[7] There is little resemblance between their lives and that of the Boston streetwalker.

3. Finally, consider the increasing number of male prostitutes. Most male prostitutes (but not all) sell sex to other men.[8] Often the men who buy such sex are themselves married.

Unfortunately, there is little information on male prostitutes; it has not been well studied as either a historical or a contemporary phenomenon.[9] What we do know suggests that like their female counterparts, male prostitutes cover the economic spectrum. Two important differences between male and female prostitutes are that men are more likely to work only part time and that they are not generally subject to the violence of male pimps; they tend to work on their own.

Are these three cases distinct? Many critics of prostitution have assumed that all prostitutes were women who entered the practice under circumstances which included abuse and economic desperation. But that is a false assumption: the critics have mistaken a part of the practice for the whole.[10] For example, although women who walk the streets are the most visible, they constitute only about 20 percent of the prostitute population in the United States."[11]

The varying circumstances of prostitution are important because they force us to consider carefully what we think may be wrong with prostitution. For example, in the first case, the factors which seem crucial to our response of condemnation are the miserable background conditions, the prostitute's vulnerability to violence at the hands of her pimp or client, her age, and her lack of control over whether she has sex with a client. These conditions could be redressed through regulation without forbidding commercial sexual exchanges between consenting adults.[12] The second class of prostitution stands in sharp contrast. These women engage in what seems to be a voluntary activity, chosen among a range of decent alternatives. Many of these women sell their sexual capacities without coercion or regret. The third case rebuts arguments that prostitution has no other purpose than to subordinate women.

In the next section, I explore three alternative explanations of prostitution's wrongness, which I refer to respectively as economic, essentialist, and egalitarian.

What Is Wrong with Prostitution?

The Economic Approach

Economists generally frame their questions about the best way to distribute a good without reference to its intrinsic qualities. They tend to focus on the quantitative features of a good and not its qualities.[13] Economists tend to endorse interference with a market in some good only when the results of that market are inefficient or have adverse effects on welfare.

An economic approach to prostitution does not specify a priori that certain sales are wrong: no act of commodification is ruled out in advance.[14] Rather, this approach focuses on the costs and benefits that accompany such sales. An economic approach to contracts will justify inalienability rules—rules which forbid individuals from entering into certain transactions—in cases where there are costly externalities to those transactions and in general where such transactions are inefficient. The economic approach thus supports the asymmetry thesis when the net social costs of prostitution are greater than the net social costs incurred by the sale of other human capacities.

What are the costs of prostitution? In the first place, the parties to a commercial sex transaction share possible costs of disease and guilt.[15] Prostitution also has costs to third parties: a man who frequents a prostitute dissipates financial resources which might otherwise be directed to his family; in a society which values intimate marriage, infidelity costs a man's wife or companion in terms of mistrust and suffering (and therefore prostitution may sometimes lead to marital instability); and prostitutes often have diseases which can be spread to others. Perhaps the largest third-party costs to prostitution are "moralisms":[16] many people find the practice morally offensive and are pained by its existence. (Note that 'moralisms' refers to people's preferences about moral issues and not to morality as such.)

The economic approach generates a contingent case for the asymmetry thesis, focusing on prostitution's "moral" costs in terms of public opinion or the welfare costs to prostitutes or the population as a whole (e.g., through the spread of diseases).

Consideration of the limitations on sexual freedom which can be justified from a welfare standpoint can be illuminating and forces us to think about the actual effects of sexual regulations.[17] Nevertheless, I want to register three objections to this approach to justifying the asymmetry thesis.

First, and most obvious, both markets and contractual exchanges function within a regime of property rights and legal entitlements. The economic approach ignores the background system of distribution within which prostitution occurs. Some background systems, however, are unjust. How do we know whether prostitution itself is part of a morally acceptable system of property rights and entitlements?

Second, this type of approach seems disabled from making sense of distinctions between goods in cases where these distinctions do not seem to reflect mere differences in the net sum of costs and benefits. The sale of certain goods seems to many people simply unthinkable—human life, for example. While it may be possible to justify prohibitions on slavery by appeal to costs and benefits (and even count moralisms in the sum), the problem is that such justification makes contingent an outcome which reasonable people do not hold contingently. It also makes little sense, phenomenologically, to describe the moral repugnance people feel toward slavery as "just a cost."[18]

Let me elaborate this point. There seems to be a fundamental difference between the "goods" of my person and my external goods, a difference whose nature is not completely explained by appeal to information failures and externalities. "Human capital" is not just another form of capital. For example, my relationship with my body and my capacities is more intimate than my relationship with most external things. The economic approach fails to capture this distinction.

Richard Posner—one of the foremost practitioners of the economic approach to law—illustrates the limits of the economic approach when he views a rapist as a "sex thief."[19] He thus overlooks the fact that rape is a crime of violence and assault.[20] He also ignores the qualitative differences between my relationship with my body and my car. But that there are such differences is obvious.

The circumstances in which I sell my capacities have a much more profound effect on who I am and who I become—through effects on my desires, capacities, and values—than the circumstances in which I sell my Honda Civic. Moreover, the idea of sovereignty over body and mind is closely related to the idea of personal integrity, which is a crucial element of any reasonable scheme of liberty. The liberty to exercise sovereignty over my car has a lesser place in any reasonable scheme of liberties than the liberty to be sovereign over my body and mind.[21]

Third, some goods seem to have a special status which requires that they be shielded from the market if their social meaning or role is to be preserved. The sale of citizenship rights or friendship does not simply produce costs and benefits: it transforms the nature of the goods sold. In this sense, the market is not a neutral mechanism of exchange: there are some goods whose sale transforms or destroys their initial meaning. These objections resonate with objections to prostitution for which its wrongness is not adequately captured by summing up contingent welfare costs and benefits.

These objections resonate with moralist and egalitarian concerns. Below I survey two other types of arguments which can be used to support the asymmetry thesis: (1) essentialist arguments that the sale of sexual labor is intrinsically wrong because it is alienating or contrary to human flourishing and happiness; and (2) my own egalitarian argument that the sale of sex is wrong because, given the background conditions within which it occurs, it tends to reinforce gender inequality. I thus claim that contemporary prostitution is wrong because it promotes injustice, and not because it makes people less happy.

The Essentialist Approach

Economists abstract from the qualities of the goods that they consider. By contrast essentialists hold that there is something intrinsic to the sphere of sex and intimacy that accounts for the distinction we mark between it and other types of labor. Prostitution is not wrong simply because it causes harm; prostitution constitutes a harm. Essentialists hold that there is some intrinsic property of sex which makes its commodification wrong. Specific arguments differ, however, in what they take this property to be. I will consider two popular versions of essentialism: the first stresses the close connection between sex and the self; the second stresses the close connection between sex and human flourishing.[22]

Some feminist critics of prostitution have argued that sexual and reproductive capacities are more crucially tied to the nature of our selves than our other capacities.[23] The sale of sex is taken to cut deeper into the self, to involve a more total alienation from the self. As Carole Pateman puts it, "When a prostitute contracts out use of her body she is thus selling *herself* in a very real sense. Women's selves are involved in prostitution in a different manner from the involvement of the self in other occupations."[24] The realization of women's selfhood requires, on this view, that some of the capacities embodied in their persons, including their sexuality, remain "market-inalienable."[25]

Consider an analogous strategy for accounting for the value of bodily integrity in terms of its relationship to our personhood. It seems right to say that a world in which the boundaries of our bodies were not (more or less) secure would be a world in which our sense of self would be fundamentally shaken. Damage to, and violation of, our bodies affects us in a "deeper" way, a more significant way, than damage to our external property. Robbing my body of a kidney is a violation different in kind than robbing my house of a stereo, however expensive. Distributing kidneys from healthy people to sick people through a lottery is a far different act than using a lottery to distribute door prizes.[26]

But this analogy can only be the first step in an argument in favor of treating either our organs or sexual capacities as market-inalienable. Most liberals think that individual sovereignty over mind and body is crucial for the exercise of fundamental liberties. Thus, in the absence of clear harms, most liberals would reject legal bans on voluntary sales of body parts or sexual capacities. Indeed, the usual justification of such bans is harm to self: such sales are presumed to be "desperate exchanges" that the individual herself would reasonably want

to foreclose. American law blocks voluntary sales of individual organs and body parts but not sales of blood on the assumption that only the former sales are likely to be so harmful to the individual that given any reasonable alternative, she herself would refrain from such sales.

Whatever the plausibility of such a claim with respect to body parts, it is considerably weaker when applied to sex (or blood). There is no strong evidence that prostitution is, at least in the United States, a desperate exchange. In part this reflects the fact that the relationship people have with their sexual capacities is far more diverse than the relationship they have with their body parts. For some people, sexuality is a realm of ecstatic communion with another, for others it is little more than a sport or distraction. Some people will find consenting to be sexually used by another person enjoyable or adequately compensated by a wage. Even for the same person, sex can be the source of a range of experiences.

Of course, the point cannot simply be that, as an empirical matter, people have differing conceptions of sexuality. The critics of prostitution grant that. The point is whether, and within what range, this diversity is desirable.[27]

Let us assume, then, in the absence of compelling counterargument, that an individual can exercise sovereignty through the sale of her sexual capacities. Margaret Radin raises a distinct worry about the effects of widespread prostitution on human flourishing. Radin's argument stresses that widespread sex markets would promote inferior forms of personhood. She says that we can see this is the case if we "reflect on what we know now about human life and choose the best from among the conceptions available to us."[28] If prostitution were to become common, Radin argues, it would have adverse effects on a form of personhood which itself is intrinsically valuable. For example, if the signs of affection and intimacy were frequently detached from their usual meaning, such signs might well become more ambiguous and easy to manipulate. The marks of an intimate relationship (physical intimacy, terms of endearment, etc.) would no longer signal the existence of intimacy. In that case, by obscuring the nature of sexual relationships, prostitution might undermine our ability to apply the criteria for coercion and informational failure.[29] Individuals might more easily enter into damaging relationships and lead less fulfilling lives as a result.

Radin is committed to a form of perfectionism which rules out the social practice of prostitution as incompatible with the highest forms of human development and flourishing. But why should perfectionists condemn prostitution while tolerating practices such as monotonous assembly line work where human beings are often mere appendages to machines? Monotonous wage labor, moreover, is far more widespread than prostitution.[30] Can a consistent perfectionist give reasons for differentiating sexual markets from other labor markets?

It is difficult to draw a line between our various capacities such that only sexual and reproductive capacities are essential to the flourishing self. In a money economy like our own, we each sell the use of many human capacities. Writers sell the use of their ability to write, advertisers sell the use of their ability to write jingles, and musicians sell the use of their ability to write and perform symphonies. Aren't these capacities also closely tied to our personhood and its higher capacities?[31] Yet the mere alienation of the use of these capacities, even when widespread, does not seem to threaten personal flourishing.

An alternative version of the essentialist thesis views the commodification of sex as an assault on personal dignity.[32] Prostitution degrades the prostitute. Elizabeth Anderson, for example, discusses the effect of commodification on the nature of sex as a shared good, based on the recognition of mutual attraction. In commercial sex, each party now values the other only instrumentally, not intrinsically. And, while both parties are thus prevented from enjoying a shared good, it is worse for the prostitute. The customer merely surrenders a certain amount of cash; the prostitute cedes her body: the prostitute is thus degraded to the status of a thing. Call this the degradation objection.

I share the intuition that the failure to treat others as persons is morally significant; it is wrong to treat people as mere things. But I am skeptical as to whether this intuition supports the conclusion

that prostitution is wrong. Consider the contrast between slavery and prostitution. Slavery was, in Orlando Patterson's memorable phrase, a form of "social death": it denied to enslaved individuals the ability to press claims, to be—in their own right—sources of value and interest. But the mere sale of the use of someone's capacities does not necessarily involve a failure of this kind, on the part of either the buyer or the seller.[33] Many forms of labor, perhaps most, cede some control of a person's body to others. Such control can range from requirements to be in a certain place at a certain time (e.g., reporting to the office), to requirements that a person (e.g., a professional athlete) eat certain foods and get certain amounts of sleep, or maintain good humor in the face of the offensive behavior of others (e.g., airline stewardesses). Some control of our capacities by others does not seem to be ipso facto destructive of our dignity.[34] Whether the purchase of a form of human labor power will have this negative consequence will depend on background social macrolevel and microlevel institutions. Minimum wages, worker participation and control, health and safety regulations, maternity and paternity leave, restrictions on specific performance, and the right to "exit" one's job are all features which attenuate the objectionable aspects of treating people's labor as a mere economic input. The advocates of prostitution's wrongness in virtue of its connection to selfhood, flourishing and degradation have not shown that a system of regulated prostitution would be unable to respond to their worries. In particular, they have not established that there is something wrong with prostitution irrespective of its cultural and historical context.

There is, however, another way of interpreting the degradation objection which draws a connection between the current practice of prostitution and the lesser social status of women.[35] This connection is not a matter of the logic of prostitution per se but of the fact that contemporary prostitution degrades women by treating them as the sexual servants of men. In current prostitution, prostitutes are overwhelmingly women and their clients are almost exclusively men. Prostitution, in conceiving of a class of women as needed to satisfy male sexual desire, represents women as sexual servants to men. The degradation objection, so understood, can be seen as a way of expressing an egalitarian concern since there is no reciprocal ideology which represents men as servicing women's sexual needs. It is to this egalitarian understanding of prostitution's wrongness that I turn in the next section.

The Egalitarian Approach

While the essentialists rightly call our attention to the different relation we have with our capacities and external things, they overstate the nature of the difference between our sexual capacities and our other capacities with respect to our personhood, flourishing, and dignity.[36] They are also insufficiently attentive to the background conditions in which commercial sex exchanges take place. A third account of prostitution's wrongness stresses its causal relationship to gender inequality. I have defended this line of argument with respect to markets in women's reproductive labor.[37] Can this argument be extended to cover prostitution as well?

The answer hinges in part on how we conceive of gender inequality. On my view, there are two important dimensions of gender inequality, often conflated. The first dimension concerns inequalities in the distribution of income, wealth, and opportunity. In most nations, including the United States, women form an economically and socially disadvantaged group. The statistics regarding these disadvantages, even in the United States, are grim.

1. *Income inequality.*—In 1992, given equal hours of work, women in the United States earned on average sixty-six cents for every dollar earned by a man.[38] Seventy-five percent of full-time working women (as opposed to 37 percent of full-time working men) earn less than twenty thousand dollars.[39]
2. *Job segregation.*—Women are less likely than men to fill socially rewarding, high-paying jobs. Despite the increasing entrance of women into previously gender-segregated occupations, 46 percent of all working women are employed in service and administrative

support jobs such as secretaries, waitresses, and health aides. In the United States and Canada, the extent of job segregation in the lowest-paying occupations is increasing.[40]
3. *Poverty.*—In 1989, one out of five families were headed by women. One-third of such women-headed families live below the poverty line, which was $13,359 for a family of four in 1990.[41] In the United States, fathers currently owe mothers 24 billion dollars in unpaid child support.[42]
4. *Unequal division of labor in the family.*— Within the family, women spend disproportionate amounts of time on housework and rearing children. According to one recent study, wives employed full time outside the home do 70 percent of the housework; full-time housewives do 83 percent.[43] The unequal family division of labor is itself caused by and causes labor market inequality: given the lower wages of working women, it is more costly for men to participate in household labor.

Inequalities in income and opportunity form an important part of the backdrop against which prostitution must be viewed. While there are many possible routes into prostitution, the largest number of women who participate in it are poor, young, and uneducated. Labor market inequalities will be part of any plausible explanation of why many women "choose" to enter into prostitution.

The second dimension of gender inequality does not concern income and opportunity but status.[44] In many contemporary contexts, women are viewed and treated as inferior to men. This inferior treatment proceeds via several distinct mechanisms.

1. *Negative stereotyping.*—Stereotypes persist as to the types of jobs and responsibilities a woman can assume. Extensive studies have shown that people typically believe that men are more dominant, assertive, and instrumentally rational than women. Gender shapes beliefs about a person's capacities: women are thought to be less intelligent than their male equals.[45]

2. *Unequal power.*—Men are able to asymmetrically sanction women. The paradigm case of this is violence. Women are subjected to greater amounts of violence by men than is the reverse: every fifteen seconds a woman is battered in the United States. Battering causes more injury (excluding deaths) to women than car accidents, rape, and muggings combined.[46] Four million women a year are physically assaulted by their male partners.[47]

3. *Marginalization.*—People who are marginalized are excluded from, or absent from, core productive social roles in society—roles which convey self-respect and meaningful contribution.[48] At the extremes, marginalized women lack the means for their basic survival: they are dependent on state welfare or male partners to secure the basic necessities of life. Less severely marginalized women lack access to central and important social roles. Their activities are confined to peripheral spheres of social organization. For example, the total number of women who have served in Congress since its inception through 1992 is 134. The total number of men is 11,096. In one-third of governments worldwide, there are no women in the decision-making bodies of the country.[49]

4. *Stigma.*—A woman's gender is associated, in some contexts, with stigma, a badge of dishonor. Consider rape. In crimes of rape, the complainant's past behavior and character are central in determining whether a crime has actually occurred. This is not true of other crimes: "mail fraud" (pun intended) is not dismissed because of the bad judgment or naïveté of the victims. Society views rape differently, I suggest, because many people think that women really want to be forced into sex. Women's lower status thus influences the way that rape is seen.

Both forms of inequality—income inequality and status inequality—potentially bear on the question of prostitution's wrongness. Women's decisions to enter into prostitution must be viewed against the background of their unequal life chances and their unequal opportunities for income and rewarding work. The extent to which women face a highly constrained range of options will surely be relevant to whether, and to what degree, we view their choices as autonomous. Some women may actually loathe or judge as inferior the lives of prostitution they "choose." Economic inequality may thus shape prostitution.

We can also ask, Does prostitution itself shape employment inequalities between men and women? In general, whenever there are significant inequalities between groups, those on the disadvantageous side will be disproportionately allocated to subordinate positions. What they do, the positions they occupy, will serve to reinforce negative and disempowering images of themselves. In this sense, prostitution can have an effect on labor-market inequality, associating women with certain stereotypes. For example, images reinforced by prostitution may make it less likely for women to be hired in certain jobs. Admittedly the effect of prostitution on labor-market inequality, if it exists at all, will be small. Other roles which women disproportionately occupy—secretaries, housecleaners, babysitters, waitresses, and saleswomen—will be far more significant in reinforcing (as well as constituting) a gender-segregated division of labor.

I do not think it is plausible to attribute to prostitution a direct causal role in income inequality between men and women. But I believe that it is plausible to maintain that prostitution makes an important and direct contribution to women's inferior social status. Prostitution shapes and is itself shaped by custom and culture, by cultural meanings about the importance of sex, about the nature of women's sexuality and male desire.[50]

If prostitution is wrong it is because of its effects on how men perceive women and on how women perceive themselves. In our society, prostitution represents women as the sexual servants of men. It supports and embodies the widely held belief that men have strong sex drives which must be satisfied—largely through gaining access to some woman's body. This belief underlies the mistaken idea that prostitution is the "oldest" profession, since it is seen as a necessary consequence of human (i.e., male) nature. It also underlies the traditional conception of marriage, in which a man owned not only his wife's property but her body as well. It should not fail to startle us that until recently, most states did not recognize the possibility of "real rape" in marriage.[51] (Marital rape remains legal in two states: North Carolina and Oklahoma.)

Why is the idea that women must service men's sexual needs an image of inequality and not mere difference? My argument suggests that there are two primary, contextual reasons:

First, in our culture, there is no reciprocal social practice which represents men as serving women's sexual needs. Men are gigolos and paid escorts—but their sexuality is not seen as an independent capacity whose use women can buy. It is not part of the identity of a class of men that they will service women's sexual desires. Indeed, male prostitutes overwhelmingly service other men and not women. Men are not depicted as fully capable of commercially alienating their sexuality to women; but prostitution depicts women as sexual servants of men.

Second, the idea that prostitution embodies an idea of women as inferior is strongly suggested by the high incidence of rape and violence against prostitutes, as well as the fact that few men seek out or even contemplate prostitutes as potential marriage partners. While all women in our society are potential targets of rape and violence, the mortality rates for women engaged in streetwalking prostitution are roughly forty times higher than that of nonprostitute women.[52]

My suggestion is that prostitution depicts an image of gender inequality, by constituting one class of women as inferior. Prostitution is a "theater" of inequality—it displays for us a practice in which women are subordinated to men. This is especially the case where women are forcibly controlled by their (male) pimps. It follows from my conception of prostitution that it need not have such a negative effect when the prostitute is male. More research needs to be done on popular images and conceptions of gay male prostitutes, as well as

on the extremely small number of male prostitutes who have women clients.

The negative image of women who participate in prostitution, the image of their inferior status, is objectionable in itself. It constitutes an important form of inequality—unequal status—based on attitudes of superiority and disrespect. Unfortunately, this form of inequality has largely been ignored by political philosophers and economists who have focused instead on inequalities in income and opportunity. Moreover, this form of inequality is not confined to prostitutes. I believe that the negative image of women prostitutes has third party effects: it shapes and influences the way women as a whole are seen. This hypothesis is, of course, an empirical one. It has not been tested largely because of the lack of studies of men who go to prostitutes. Most extant studies of prostitution examine the behavior and motivations of the women who enter into the practice, a fact which itself raises the suspicion that prostitution is viewed as "a problem about the women who are prostitutes ... [rather than] a problem about the men who demand to buy them."[53] In these studies, male gender identity is taken as a given.

To investigate prostitution's negative image effects on female prostitutes and on women generally we need research on the following questions: (1) What are the attitudes of men who visit women prostitutes toward prostitutes? How do their attitudes compare with the attitudes of men who do not visit prostitutes toward women prostitutes? (2) What are the attitudes of men who visit women prostitutes toward women generally? What are the attitudes of men who do not visit women prostitutes toward women generally? (3) What are the attitudes of women toward women prostitutes? (4) What are the attitudes of the men and women involved in prostitution toward themselves? (5) Given the large proportion of African-American women who participate in prostitution, in what ways does prostitution contribute to male attitudes toward these women? (6) Does prostitution contribute to or diminish the likelihood of crimes of sexual violence? (7) What can we learn about these questions through cross-national studies? How do attitudes in the United States about women prostitutes compare with those in countries with more egalitarian wage policies or less status inequality between men and women?

The answers to these questions will reflect social facts about our culture. Whatever plausibility there is to the hypothesis that prostitution causally contributes to gender status inequality, it gains this plausibility from its surrounding cultural context.

I can imagine hypothetical circumstances in which prostitution would not have a negative image effect, where it could mark a reclaiming of women's sexuality. Margo St. James and other members of Call Off Your Old Tired Ethics (COYOTE) have argued that prostitutes can function as sex therapists, fulfilling a legitimate social need as well as providing a source of experiment and alternative conceptions of sexuality and gender.[54] I agree that in a different culture, with different assumptions about men's and women's gender identities, prostitution might not have unequalizing effects. But I think that St. James and others have minimized the cultural stereotypes that surround contemporary prostitution and their power over the shape of the practice. Prostitution, as we know it, is not separable from the larger surrounding culture which marginalizes, stereotypes, and stigmatizes women. Rather than providing an alternative conception of sexuality, I think that we need to look carefully at what men and women actually learn in prostitution. I do not believe that ethnographic studies of prostitution would support COYOTE's claim that prostitution contributes to images of women's dignity and equal standing.

If, through its negative image of women as sexual servants of men, prostitution reinforces women's inferior status in society, then it is wrong. Even though men can be and are prostitutes, I think that it is unlikely that we will find such negative image effects on men as a group. Individual men may be degraded in individual acts of prostitution: men as a group are not.

Granting all of the above, one objection to the equality approach to prostitution's wrongness remains. Is prostitution's negative image effect greater than that produced by other professions in which women largely service men, for example, secretarial labor? What is special about prostitution?

The negative image effect undoubtedly operates outside the domain of prostitution. But there are two significant differences between prostitution and other gender-segregated professions.

First, most people believe that prostitution, unlike secretarial work, is especially objectionable. Holding such moral views of prostitution constant, if prostitution continues to be primarily a female occupation, then the existence of prostitution will disproportionately fuel negative images of women.[55] Second, and relatedly, the particular image of women in prostitution is more of an image of inferiority than that of a secretary. The image embodies a greater amount of objectification, of representing the prostitute as an object without a will of her own. Prostitutes are far more likely to be victims of violence than are secretaries: as I mentioned, the mortality rate of women in prostitution is forty times that of other women. Prostitutes are also far more likely to be raped: a prostitute's "no" does not, to the male she services, mean no.

My claim is that, unless such arguments about prostitution's causal role in sustaining a form of gender inequality can be supported, I am not persuaded that something is morally wrong with markets in sex. In particular, I do not find arguments about the necessary relationship between commercial sex and diminished flourishing and degradation convincing. If prostitution is wrong, it is not because of its effects on happiness or personhood (effects which are shared with other forms of wage-labor); rather, it is because the sale of women's sexual labor may have adverse consequences for achieving a significant form of equality between men and women. My argument for the asymmetry thesis, if correct, connects prostitution to injustice. I now turn to the question of whether, even if we assume that prostitution is wrong under current conditions, it should remain illegal.

Should Prostitution Be Legalized?

It is important to distinguish between prostitution's wrongness and the legal response that we are entitled to make to that wrongness. Even if prostitution is wrong, we may not be justified in prohibiting it if that prohibition makes the facts in virtue of which it is wrong worse, or if its costs are too great for other important values, such as autonomy and privacy. For example, even if someone accepts that the contemporary division of labor in the family is wrong, they may still reasonably object to government surveillance of the family's division of household chores. To determine whether such surveillance is justified, we need to know more about the fundamental interests at stake, the costs of surveillance and the availability of alternative mechanisms for promoting equality in families. While I think that there is no acceptable view which would advocate governmental surveillance of family chores, there remains a range of plausible views about the appropriate scope of state intervention and, indeed, the appropriate scope of equality considerations.[56]

It is also important to keep in mind that in the case of prostitution, as with pornography and hate speech, narrowing the discussion of solutions to the single question of whether to ban or not to ban shows a poverty of imagination. There are many ways of challenging existing cultural values about the appropriate division of labor in the family and the nature of women's sexual and reproductive capacities—for example, education, consciousness-raising groups, changes in employee leave policies, comparable worth programs, etc. The law is not the only way to provide women with incentives to refrain from participating in prostitution. Nonetheless, we do need to decide what the best legal policy toward prostitution should be.

I begin with an assessment of the policy which we now have. The United States is one of the few developed Western countries which criminalizes prostitution.[57] Denmark, the Netherlands, West Germany, Sweden, Switzerland, and Austria all have legalized prostitution, although in some of these countries it is restricted by local ordinances.[58] Where prostitution is permitted, it is closely regulated.

Suppose that we accept that gender equality is a legitimate goal of social policy. The question is whether the current legal prohibition on prostitution in the United States promotes gender equality. The answer I think is that it clearly does not. The current legal policies in the United States arguably exacerbate the factors in virtue of which prostitution is wrong.

The current prohibition on prostitution renders the women who engage in the practice vulnerable. First, the participants in the practice seek assistance from pimps in lieu of the contractual and legal remedies which are denied them. Male pimps may protect women prostitutes from their customers and from the police, but the system of pimp-run prostitution has enormous negative effects on the women at the lowest rungs of prostitution. Second, prohibition of prostitution raises the dilemma of the "double bind": if we prevent prostitution without greater redistribution of income, wealth, and opportunities, we deprive poor women of one way—in some circumstances the only way—of improving their condition.[59] Analogously, we do not solve the problem of homelessness by criminalizing it.

Furthermore, women are disproportionately punished for engaging in commercial sex acts. Many state laws make it a worse crime to sell sex than to buy it. Consequently, pimps and clients ("Johns") are rarely prosecuted. In some jurisdictions, patronizing a prostitute is not illegal. The record of arrests and convictions is also highly asymmetric. Ninety percent of all convicted prostitutes are women. Studies have shown that male prostitutes are arrested with less frequency than female prostitutes and receive shorter sentences. One study of the judicial processing of 2,859 male and female prostitutes found that judges were more likely to find defendants guilty if they were female.[60]

Nor does the current legal prohibition on prostitution unambiguously benefit women as a class because the cultural meaning of current governmental prohibition of prostitution is unclear. While an unrestricted regime of prostitution—a pricing system in women's sexual attributes—could have negative external consequences on women's self-perceptions and perceptions by men, state prohibition can also reflect a view of women which contributes to their inequality. For example, some people support state regulation because they believe that women's sexuality is for purposes of reproduction, a claim tied to traditional ideas about women's proper role.

There is an additional reason why banning prostitution seems an inadequate response to the problem of gender inequality and which suggests a lack of parallel with the case of commercial surrogacy. Banning prostitution would not by itself—does not—eliminate it. While there is reason to think that making commercial surrogacy arrangements illegal or unenforceable would diminish their occurrence, no such evidence exists about prostitution. No city has eliminated prostitution merely through criminalization. Instead, criminalized prostitution thrives as a black market activity in which pimps substitute for law as the mechanism for enforcing contracts. It thereby makes the lives of prostitutes worse than they might otherwise be and without clearly counteracting prostitution's largely negative image of women. If we decide to ban prostitution, these problems must be addressed.

If we decide not to ban prostitution (either by legalizing it or decriminalizing it), then we must be careful to regulate the practice to address its negative effects. Certain restrictions on advertising and recruitment will be needed in order to address the negative image effects that an unrestricted regime of prostitution would perpetuate. But the current regime of prostitution has negative effects on the prostitutes themselves. It places their sexual capacities largely under the control of men. In order to promote women's autonomy, the law needs to ensure that certain restrictions—in effect, a Bill of Rights for Women—are in place.[61]

1. No woman should be forced, either by law or by private persons, to have sex against her will. (Recall that it is only quite recently that the courts have recognized the existence of marital rape.) A woman who sells sex must be able to refuse to give it; she must not be coerced by law or private persons to perform.

2. No woman should be denied access, either by law or by private persons, to contraception or to treatment for sexually transmitted diseases, particularly AIDS, or to abortion (at least in the first trimester).

3. The law should ensure that a woman has adequate information before she agrees to sexual intercourse. The risks of venereal and other sexually transmitted diseases, the risks of pregnancy, and the laws protecting a woman's right to refuse sex should all be generally available.

4. Minimum age of consent laws for sexual intercourse should be enforced. These laws should ensure that woman (and men) are protected from coercion and do not enter into sexual relationships until they are in a position to understand what they are consenting to.

5. The law should promote women's control over their own sexuality by prohibiting brokerage. If what is wrong with prostitution is its relation to gender inequality, then it is crucial that the law be brought to bear primarily on the men who profit from the use of women's sexual capacities. Each of these principles is meant to establish and protect a woman's right to control her sexual and reproductive capacities and not to give control of these capacities to others.

Each of these principles is meant to protect the conditions for women's consent to sex, whether commercial or not. Each of these principles also seeks to counter the degradation of women in prostitution by mitigating its nature as a form of female servitude. In addition, given that a woman's choices are shaped both by the range of available opportunities and by the distribution of entitlements in society, it is crucial to attend to the inferior economic position of women in American society and those social and economic factors which produce the unequal life chances of men and women.

Conclusion

If the arguments I have offered here are correct, then prostitution is wrong in virtue of its contributions to perpetuating a pervasive form of inequality. In different circumstances, with different assumptions about women and their role in society, I do not think that prostitution would be especially troubling—no more troubling than many other labor markets currently allowed. It follows, then, that in other circumstances, the asymmetry thesis would be denied or less strongly felt. While the idea that prostitution is intrinsically degrading is a powerful intuition (and like many such intuitions, it persists even after its proponents undergo what Richard Brandt has termed "cognitive therapy," in which errors of fact and inference are corrected), I believe that this intuition is itself bound up with well-entrenched views of male gender identity and women's sexual role in the context of that identity.[62] If we are troubled by prostitution, as I think we should be, then we should direct much of our energy to putting forward alternative models of egalitarian relations between men and women.

DISCUSSION QUESTIONS

1. Is prostitution moral or immoral, according to Satz? Why? Could it ever be moral? Can you think of ways?
2. What is the moral asymmetry between sex work and other kinds of bodily work?
3. For Satz, is prostitution about unhappiness, the diminishment of one's self-worth, or injustice? Explain in detail.

NOTES

1. Debra Satz, "Markets in Women's Reproductive Labor," *Philosophy and Public Affairs* 21 (1992): 107–131.

2. What would remain troubling would be the miserable and unjust background circumstances in which much prostitution occurs. That is, if there were gender equality between the sexes but a substantial group of very poor men and women were selling sex, this would indeed be troubling. We should be suspicious of any labor contract entered into under circumstances of desperation.

3. Laurie Shrage, "Should Feminists Oppose Prostitution?" *Ethics* 99 (1989): 347–361, is an important exception. See also her new book, Moral Dilemmas of Feminism: Prostitution, Adultery and Abortion (New York: Routledge, 1994).

4. The fact that monetary exchange plays a role in maintaining many intimate relationships is a point underscored by George Bernard Shaw in Mrs. Warren's Profession (New York: Garland, 1981).

5. Compare Judith Walkowitz, Prostitution and Victorian Society (Cambridge: Cambridge University Press, 1980); Ruth Rosen, Prostitution in America: 1900–1918 (Baltimore: Johns Hopkins University Press, 1982); B. Hobson, Uneasy Virtue: The Politics of Prostitution and the American Reform Tradition (Chicago: University of Chicago Press, 1990).

6. John Decker, Prostitution: Regulation and Control (Littleton, Colo.: Rothman, 1979), p. 191.

7. Compare Harold Greenwald, The Elegant Prostitute: A Social and Psychoanalytic Study (New York: Walker, 1970), p. 10.

8. For discussion of male prostitutes who sell sex to women, see H. Smith and B. Van der Horst, "For Women Only—How It Feels to Be a Male Hooker," Village Voice (March 7, 1977). Dictionary and common usage tends to identify prostitutes with women. Men who sell sex to women are generally referred to as "gigolos," not "prostitutes." The former term encompasses the sale of companionship as well as sex.

9. Male prostitutes merit only a dozen pages in John Decker's monumental study of prostitution. See also D. Drew and J. Drake, Boys for Sale: A Sociological Study of Boy Prostitution (Deer Park, N.Y.: Brown Book Co., 1969); D. Deisher, "Young Male Prostitutes," *Journal of American Medical Association* 212 (1970): 1661–1666; Gita

Sereny, The Invisible Children: Child Prostitution in America, West Germany and Great Britain (London: Deutsch, 1984). I am grateful to Vincent DiGirolamo for bringing these works to my attention.

10. Compare Kathleen Barry, Female Sexual Slavery (New York: Avon, 1979). If we consider prostitution as an international phenomenon, then a majority of prostitutes are desperately poor and abused women. Nevertheless, there is a significant minority who are not. Furthermore, if prostitution were legalized, it is possible that the minimum condition of prostitutes in at least some countries would be raised.

11. Priscilla Alexander, "Prostitution: A Difficult Issue for Feminists," in Sex Work: Writings by Women in the Sex Industry, ed. P. Alexander and F. Delacoste (Pittsburgh: Cleis, 1987).

12. Moreover, to the extent that the desperate background conditions are the problem it is not apparent that outlawing prostitution is the solution. Banning prostitution may only remove a poor woman's best option: it in no way eradicates the circumstances which led her to such a choice. See M. Radin, "Market-Inalienability," on the problem of the "double bind," Harvard Law Review 100 (1987): 1849–1937.

13. Sometimes the qualitative aspects of a good have quantitative effects and so for that reason need to be taken into account. It is difficult, e.g., to establish a market in used cars given the uncertainties of ascertaining their qualitative condition. Compare George Akerlof, "The Market for Lemons: Qualitative Uncertainty and the Market Mechanism," Quarterly Journal of Economics 84 (1970): 488–500.

14. For an attempt to understand human sexuality as a whole through the economic approach, see Richard Posner, Sex and Reason (Cambridge, Mass.: Harvard University Press, 1992).

15. Although two-thirds of prostitutes surveyed say that they have no regrets about choice of work. Compare Decker, pp. 165–166. This figure is hard to interpret, given the high costs of thinking that one has made a bad choice of occupation and the lack of decent employment alternatives for many prostitutes.

16. See Guido Calabresi and A. Douglas Melamed, "Property Rules, Liability Rules and Inalienability: One View of the Cathedral," Harvard Law Review 85 (1972): 1089–1128.

17. Economic analysis fails to justify the laws we now have regarding prostitution. See below.

18. See Radin, pp. 1884 ff.

19. Posner, Sex and Reason, p. 182. See also R. Posner, "An Economic Theory of the Criminal Law," Columbia Law Review 85 (1985): 1193–1231. "The prohibition against rape is to the sex and marriage 'market' as the prohibition against theft is to explicit markets in goods and services" (p. 1199).

20. His approach in fact suggests that rape be seen as a "benefit" to the rapist, a suggestion that I think we should be loathe to follow.

21. I do not mean to claim however that such sovereignty over the body is absolute.

22. This section draws from and enlarges upon Satz.

23. Prostitution is, however, an issue which continues to divide feminists as well as prostitutes and former prostitutes. On the one side, some feminists see prostitution as dehumanizing and alienating and linked to male domination. This is the view taken by the prostitute organization Women Hurt in Systems of Prostitution Engaged in Revolt (WHISPER). On the other side, some feminists see sex markets as affirming a woman's right to autonomy, sexual pleasure, and economic welfare. This is the view taken by the prostitute organization COYOTE.

24. Carole Pateman, The Sexual Contract (Stanford, Calif.: Stanford University Press, 1988), p. 207; emphasis added.

25. The phrase is Radin's.

26. J. Harris, "The Survival Lottery," Philosophy 50 (1975): 81–87.

27. As an example of the ways in which the diversity of sexual experience has been culturally productive, see Lynn Hunt, ed., The Invention of Pornography (New York: Zone, 1993).

28. Radin, p. 1884.

29. An objection along these lines is raised by Margaret Baldwin ("Split at the Root: Feminist Discourses of Law Reform," *Yale Journal of Law and Feminism* 5 [1992]: 47–120). Baldwin worries that prostitution undermines our ability to understand a woman's capacity to consent to sex. Baldwin asks, Will a prostitute's consent to sex be seen as consent to a twenty dollar payment? Will courts determine sentences in rape trials involving prostitutes as the equivalent of parking fine violations (e.g., as another twenty dollar payment)? Aren't prostitutes liable to have their fundamental interests in bodily integrity discounted? I think Baldwin's worry is a real one, especially in the context of the current stigmatization of prostitutes. It could be resolved, in part, by withholding information about a woman's profession from rape trials.

30. Radin is herself fairly consistent in her hostility to many forms of wage labor. She has a complicated view about decommodification in nonideal circumstances which I cannot discuss here.

31. Also notice that many forms of labor we make inalienable—e.g., bans on mercenaries—cannot be justified by that labor's relationship to our personhood.

32. Elizabeth Anderson, *Value in Ethics and Economics* (Cambridge, Mass.: Harvard University Press, 1993), p. 45.

33. Actually, the prostitute's humanity is a part of the sex transaction itself. Whereas Posner's economic approach places sex with another person on the same scale as sex with a sheep, for many people the latter is not a form of sex at all (*Sex and Reason*). Moreover, in its worst forms, the prostitute's humanity (and gender) may be crucial to the john's experience of himself as superior to her. See Catherine MacKinnon, *Toward a Feminist Theory of the State* (Cambridge, Mass.: Harvard University Press, 1989).

34. Although this statement might have to be qualified in the light of empirical research. Arlie Hochschild, e.g., has found that the sale of "emotional labor" by airline stewardesses and insurance salesmen distorts their responses to pain and frustration (*The Managed Heart: The Commercialization of Human Feeling* [New York: Basic, 1983]).

35. I owe this point to Elizabeth Anderson, who stressed the need to distinguish between different versions of the degradation objection and suggested some lines of interpretation (conversation with author, Oxford University, July 1994).

36. More generally, they raise questions about the desirability of a world in which people use and exploit each other as they use and exploit other natural objects, insofar as this is compatible with Pareto improvements.

37. See Satz.

38. U.S. Department of Labor, Women's Bureau (Washington, D.C.: Government Printing Office, 1992).

39. D. Taylor, "Women: An Analysis," in *Women: A World Report* (London: Methuen, 1985). Taylor reports that while on a world scale women "perform nearly two-thirds of all working hours [they] receive only one tenth of the world income and own less than one percent of world resources."

40. J. David-McNeil, "The Changing Economic Status of the Female Labor Force in Canada," in *Towards Equity: Proceedings of a Colloquium on the Economic Status of Women in the Labor Market*, ed. Economic Council of Canada (Ottawa: Canadian Government Publication Centre, 1985).

41. S. Rix, ed., *The American Woman, 1990–91* (New York: Norton, 1990), cited in Woman's Action Coalition, ed., *WAC Stats: The Facts about Women* (New York: New Press, 1993), p. 41.

42. Report of the Federal Office of Child Support Enforcement, 1990.

43. Rix, ed. Note also that the time women spend doing housework has not declined since the 1920s despite the invention of labor saving technologies (e.g., laundry machines and dishwashers).

44. My views about this aspect of gender inequality have been greatly clarified in discussions and correspondence with Elizabeth Anderson and Elisabeth Wood during 1994.

45. See Paul Rosenkrantz, Susan Vogel, Helen Bees, Inge Broverman, and David Broverman, "Sex-Role Stereotypes and Self-Concepts in College

Students," *Journal of Consulting and Clinical Psychology* 32 (1968): 286–295.

46. L. Heise, "Gender Violence as a Health Issue" (Violence, Health and Development Project, Center for Women's Global Leadership, Rutgers University, New Brunswick, N.J., 1992).

47. L. Heise, "Violence against Women: The Missing Agenda," in *Women's Health: A Global Perspective* (New York: Westview, 1992), cited in Woman's Action Coalition, ed., p. 55. More than one-third of female homicide victims are killed by their husbands or boyfriends.

48. I am indebted here to the discussion of Iris Young in *Justice and the Politics of Difference* (Princeton, N.J.: Princeton University Press, 1990).

49. Ruth Leger Sivard, *Women . . . a World Survey* (Washington, D.C.: World Priorities, 1985).

50. Shrage ("Should Feminists Oppose Prostitution?) argues that prostitution perpetuates the following beliefs which oppress women: (1) the universal possession of a potent sex drive; (2) the "natural" dominance of men; (3) the pollution of women by sexual contact; and (4) the reification of sexual practice.

51. Susan Estrich, *Real Rape* (Cambridge, Mass.: Harvard University Press, 1987).

52. Baldwin, p. 75. Compare the Canadian Report on Prostitution and Pornography; also M. Silbert, "Sexual Assault on Prostitutes," research report to the *National Center for the Prevention and Control of Rape*, November 1980, for a study of street prostitutes in which 70 percent of those surveyed reported that they had been raped while walking the streets.

53. Carole Pateman, "Defending Prostitution: Charges against Ericsson," *Ethics* 93 (1983): 561–565, p. 563.

54. See also, S. Schwartzenbach, "Contractarians and Feminists Debate Prostitution," *New York University Review of Law and Social Change* 18 (1990–91): 103–130.

55. I owe this point to Arthur Kuflik.

56. For example, does the fact that racist joke telling reinforces negative stereotypes and perpetuates racial prejudice and inequality justify legal bans on such joke telling? What are the limits on what we can justifiably use the state to do in the name of equality? This is a difficult question. I only note here that arguments which justify state banning of prostitution can be consistent with the endorsement of stringent protections for speech. This is because speech and expression are arguably connected with basic fundamental human interests—with forming and articulating conceptions of value, with gathering information, with testifying on matters of conscience—in a way that prostitution (and some speech, e.g., commercial speech) is not. Even if we assume, as I think we should, that people have fundamental interests in having control over certain aspects of their bodies and lives, it does not follow that they have a fundamental interest in being free to sell themselves, their body parts, or any of their particular capacities.

57. Prostitution is legalized only in several jurisdictions in Nevada.

58. These countries have more pay equity between men and women than does the United States. This might be taken to undermine an argument about prostitution's role in contributing to income inequality. Moreover, women's status is lower in some societies which repress prostitution (such as those of the Islamic nations) than in those which do not (such as those of the Scandinavian nations). But given the variety of cultural, economic, and political factors and mechanisms which need to be taken into account, we need to be very careful in drawing hasty conclusions. Legalizing prostitution might have negative effects on gender equality in the United States, even if legal prostitution does not correlate with gender inequality in other countries. There are many differences between the United States and European societies which make it implausible to think that one factor can alone be explanatory with respect to gender inequality.

59. Radin, pp. 1915 ff.

60. J. Lindquist et al., "Judicial Processing of Males and Females Charged with Prostitution," *Journal of Criminal Justice* 17 (1989): 277–291. Several state laws banning prostitution have been challenged

on equal protection grounds. These statistics support the idea that prostitution's negative image effect has disproportionate bearing on male and female prostitutes.

61. In this section, I have benefited from reading Cass Sunstein, "Gender Difference, Reproduction and the Law" (University of Chicago Law School, 1992, unpublished manuscript). Sunstein believes that someone committed to gender equality will, most likely, advocate a legal ban on prostitution.

62. Richard B. Brandt, A Theory of the Good and the Right (Oxford: Clarendon, 1979).

Whether from Reason or Prejudice: Taking Money for Bodily Services

BY MARTHA NUSSBAUM

Martha Nussbaum is an American philosopher whose influential work spans areas as diverse as ancient Greek and Roman philosophy, political philosophy, existentialism, feminism, and ethics, including animal rights. Comparing sex work to six other examples of jobs where people uncontroversially take money for bodily services, in this essay Nussbaum argues that there are no morally relevant differences between sex work and most other forms of paid work.

I. Body Sellers

All of us, with the exception of the independently wealthy and the unemployed, rake money for the use of our body. Professors, factory workers, lawyers, opera singers, prostitutes, doctors, legislators—we all do things with parts of our bodies, for which we receive a wage in return.[1] Some people get good wages and some do not; some have a relatively high degree of control over their working conditions and some have little control; some have many employment options and some have very few. And, some are socially stigmatized and some are not.

The stigmatization of certain occupations may be well founded, based on convincing, well-reasoned arguments. But it may also be based on class prejudice, or stereotypes of race or gender. Stigma may also change rapidly, as these background beliefs and prejudices change.

Today few professions are more honored than that of opera singer, and yet only two hundred years ago, that public use of one's body for pay was taken to be a kind of prostitution. Looking back at that time, we now think that the judgments and emotions underlying the stigmatization of singers were irrational and objectionable, like prejudices against members of different classes and races. Nor do we see the slightest reason to suppose that the unpaid artist is a purer and truer artist than the paid artist. We think it entirely right and reasonable that high art should receive a high salary. If a producer of opera should take the position that singers should not be paid, on the grounds that receiving money for the use of their talents involves an illegitimate form of commodification and even market alienation of those talents, we would think that this producer was a slick exploiter, out to make a profit from the ill treatment of vulnerable and impressionable artists. On the whole we think that far from cheapening or ruining talents, the presence of a contract guarantees conditions within which the artist can develop her art with sufficient leisure and confidence to reach the highest level of artistic production.[2]

It is widely believed, however, that taking money or entering into contracts in connection with the use of one's sexual and/or reproductive capacities is genuinely bad. Feminist arguments about prostitution, surrogate motherhood, and even marriage contracts standardly portray financial transactions in the area of female sexuality as demeaning to women and as involving a damaging commodification and market alienation of women's sexual and reproductive capacities.[3] The social meaning of these transactions is said to be both that these capacities are turned into objects for the use and control of men and also that the activities themselves are being turned into commodities, and thereby robbed of the type of value they have at their best.

My aim in this essay will be to investigate the question of sexual "commodification" by focusing on the example of prostitution.[4] I argue that a fruitful debate about the morality and legality of prostitution should begin from a twofold starting point: from a broader analysis of our beliefs and practices with regard to taking pay for the use of the body, and from a broader awareness of the options and choices available to poor working women. The former inquiry suggests that at least some of our beliefs about prostitution are as irrational as the beliefs about singers; it will therefore help us to identify the elements in prostitution that are genuinely problematic. Most, though not all, of the genuinely problematic elements turn out to be common to a wide range of activities engaged in by poor working women, and the second inquiry suggests that many of women's employment choices are so heavily constrained by poor options that they are hardly choices at all. I think that this should bother us—and that the fact that a woman with plenty of choices becomes a prostitute should not bother us provided there are sufficient safeguards against abuse and disease, safeguards of a type that legalization would make possible.

It is therefore my conclusion that the most urgent issue raised by prostitution is that of employment opportunities for working women and their control over the conditions of their employment. The legalization of prostitution, far from promoting the demise of love, is likely to make things a little better for women who have too few options to begin with.[5] The really helpful thing for feminists to ponder, if they deplore the nature of these options, will be how to promote expansion in the option set, through education, skills training, and job creation. These unsexy topics are not common themes in U.S. feminist philosophy, but they are inevitable in any practical project dealing with prostitutes and their female children.[6] This suggests that at least some of our feminist theory may be insufficiently grounded in the reality of working-class lives and too focused on sexuality as an issue in its own right, as if it could

be extricated from the fabric of poor people's attempts to survive.

. . .

III. Six Types of Bodily Service

Prostitution is not a single thing. It can only be well understood in its social and historical context. Ancient Greek *hetairai*, such as Pericles's mistress Aspasia, have very little in common with a modern call girl.[7] Even more important, within a given culture there are always many different types and levels of prostitution: In ancient Greece, the *hetaira*, the brothel prostitute, the streetwalker; in modern America, the self-employed call girl, the brothel prostitute, the streetwalker (and each of these at various levels of independence and economic success). It is also evident that most cultures contain a continuum of relations between women and men (or between same-sex pairs) that have a commercial aspect—ranging from the admitted case of prostitution to cases of marriage for money, going on an expensive date when it is evident that sexual favors are expected at the other end, and so forth. In most cultures, marriage itself has a prominent commercial aspect: The prominence of dowry murder in contemporary Indian culture, for example, testifies to the degree to which a woman is valued, above all, for the financial benefits one can extract from her family. Let us, however, focus for the time being on contemporary America (with some digressions on India), on female prostitution only, and on explicitly commercial relations of the sort that are illegal under current law.

It will be illuminating to consider the prostitute by situating her in relation to several other women who take money for bodily services:

1. A factory worker in the Perdue chicken factory, who plucks feathers from nearly frozen chickens.
2. A domestic servant in a prosperous upper-middle-class house.
3. A nightclub singer in middle-range clubs, who sings (often) songs requested by the patrons.
4. A professor of philosophy, who gets paid for lecturing and writing.

5. A skilled masseuse, employed by a health club (with no sexual services on the side).

6. A person whom I'll call the "colonoscopy artist": She gets paid for having her colon examined with the latest instruments, in order to test out their range and capability.[8]

By considering similarities and differences between the prostitute and these other bodily actors, we will make progress in identifying the distinctive features of prostitution as a form of bodily service.

Note that nowhere in this comparison am I addressing the issue of child prostitution or non-consensual prostitution (e.g., young women sold into prostitution by their parents, forcible drugging and abduction, etc). Insofar as these features appear to be involved in the international prostitution market, I do not address them here, although I shall comment on them later. I address only the type of choice to be a prostitute that is made by a woman over the age of consent, frequently in a situation of great economic duress.

The Prostitute and the Factory Worker

Both prostitution and factory work are usually low-paid jobs, but in many instances a woman faced with the choice can (at least over the short haul) make more money in prostitution than in this sort of factory work. (This would probably be even more true if prostitution were legalized and the role of pimps thereby restricted, though the removal of risk and some stigma might at the same time depress wages, to some extent offsetting that advantage for the prostitute.) Both face health risks, but the health risk in prostitution can be very much reduced by legalization and regulation, whereas the particular type of work the factory worker is performing carries a high risk of nerve damage in the hands, a fact about it that appears unlikely to change. The prostitute may well have better working hours and conditions than the factory worker; especially in a legalized regime, she may have much more control over her working conditions. She has a degree of choice about which clients she accepts and what activities she performs, whereas the factory worker has no choices but must perform the same motions again and again for years. The

prostitute also performs a service that requires skill and responsiveness to new situations, whereas the factory worker's repetitive motion exercises relatively little human skill[9] and contains no variety.

On the other side, the factory worker is unlikely to be the target of violence, whereas the prostitute needs—and does not always get—protection against violent customers. (Again, this situation can be improved by legalization: Prostitutes in the Netherlands have a call button wired up to the police.) This factory worker's occupation, moreover, has no clear connection with stereotypes of gender—though this might not have been the case. In many parts of the world, manual labor is strictly segmented by sex, and more routinized, low-skill tasks are given to women.[10] The prostitute's activity does rely on stereotypes of women as sluttish and immoral, and it may in turn perpetuate such stereotypes. The factory worker suffers no invasion of her internal private space, whereas the prostitute's activity involves such (consensual) invasion. Finally, the prostitute suffers from social stigma, whereas the factory worker does not—at least among people of her own social class. (I shall return to this issue, asking whether stigma too can be addressed by legalization.) For all these reasons, many women, faced with the choice between factory work and prostitution, choose factory work, despite its other disadvantages.

The Prostitute and the Domestic Servant

In domestic service as in prostitution, one is hired by a client and one must do what that client wants, or fail at the job. In both, one has a limited degree of latitude to exercise skills as one sees fit, and both jobs require the exercise of some developed bodily skills. In both, one is at risk of enduring bad behavior from one's client, although the prostitute is more likely to encounter physical violence. Certainly both are traditionally professions that enjoy low respect, both in society generally and from the client. Domestic service on the whole is likely to have worse hours and lower pay than (at least many types of) prostitution, but it probably contains fewer health risks. It also involves no invasion of intimate bodily space, as prostitution (consensually) does.

Both prostitution and domestic service are associated with a type of social stigma. In the case of domestic service, the stigma is, first, related to class: It is socially coded as an occupation only for the lowest classes.[11] Domestic servants are in a vast majority of cases female, so it becomes coded by sex. In the United States, domestic service is very often racially coded as well. Not only in the South, but also in many parts of the urban North, the labor market has frequently produced a clustering of African-American women in these low-paying occupations. In my home in suburban Philadelphia in the 1950s and 1960s, the only African Americans we saw were domestic servants, and the only domestic servants we saw were African American. The perception of the occupation as associated with racial stigma ran very deep, producing difficult tensions and resentments that made domestic service seem to be incompatible with dignity and self-respect. (It need not be, clearly, and I shall return to this.)

The Prostitute and the Nightclub Singer

Both of these people use their bodies to provide pleasure, and the customer's pleasure is the primary goal of what they do.[12] This does not mean that a good deal of skill and art is not involved, and in both cases it usually is. Both have to respond to requests from the customer, although (in varying degrees depending on the case) both may also be free to improvise or to make suggestions. Both may be paid more or less and have better or worse working conditions, more or less control over what they do.

How do they differ? The prostitute faces health risks and risks of violence not faced by the singer. She also allows her bodily space to be invaded, as the singer does not. It may also be that prostitution is always a cheap form of an activity that has a higher better form, whereas this need not be the case in popular vocal performance (though of course it might be).[13] The nightclub singer, furthermore, does not appear to be participating in, or perpetuating, any type of gender hierarchy—although in former times this would not have been the case, singers being seen as "a type of publick prostitute" and their activity associated, often,

with anxiety about the control of female sexuality. Finally, there is no (great) moral stigma attached to being a nightclub singer, although at one time there certainly was.

The Prostitute and the Professor of Philosophy

These two figures have a very interesting similarity: Both provide bodily services in areas that are generally thought to be especially intimate and definitive of selfhood. Just as the prostitute takes money for sex, which is commonly thought to be an area of intimate self-expression, so the professor takes money for thinking and writing about what she thinks—about morality, emotion, the nature of knowledge, whatever—all parts of a human being's intimate search for understanding of the world and oneself. It was precisely for this reason that the medieval thinkers I have mentioned saw such a moral problem about philosophizing for money: It should be a pure spiritual gift, and it is degraded by the receipt of a wage. The fact that we do not think that the professor (even one who regularly holds out for the highest salary offered) thereby alienates her mind, or turns her thoughts into commodities— even when she writes a paper for a specific conference or volume—should put us on our guard about making similar conclusions in the case of the prostitute.

There are other similarities: In both cases, the performance involves interaction with others, and the form of the interaction is not altogether controlled by the person. In both cases there is at least an element of producing pleasure or satisfaction (note the prominent role of teaching evaluations in the employment and promotion of professors), although in philosophy there is also a countervailing tradition of thinking that the goal of the interaction is to produce dissatisfaction and unease. (Socrates would not have received tenure in a modern university.) It may appear at first that the intimate bodily space of the professor is not invaded—but we should ask about this. When someone's unanticipated argument goes into one's mind, isn't this both intimate and bodily (and far less consensual, often, than the penetration of prostitute by customer)? Both performances involve skill. It might plausibly be argued that the professor's involves a more developed skill, or at least a more expensive training—but we should be cautious here. Our culture is all too ready to think that sex involves no skill and is simply "natural," a view that is surely false and is not even seriously entertained by many cultures.[14]

The salary of the professor, and her working conditions, are usually a great deal better than those of (all but the most elite) prostitutes. The professor has a fair amount of control over the structure of her day and her working environment, although she also has fixed mandatory duties, as the prostitute, when self-employed, does not. If the professor is in a nation that protects academic freedom, she has considerable control over what she thinks and writes, although fads, trends, and peer pressure surely constrain her to some extent. The prostitute's need to please her customer is usually more exigent and permits less choice. In this way, she is more like the professor of philosophy in Cuba than like the U.S. counterpart[15]—but the Cuban professor appears to be worse off, because she cannot say what she really thinks even when off the job. Finally, the professor of philosophy, if a female, both enjoys reasonably high respect in the community and also might be thought to bring credit to all women in that she succeeds at an activity commonly thought to be the preserve only of males. She thus subverts traditional gender hierarchy, whereas the prostitute, while suffering stigma herself, may be thought to perpetuate gender hierarchy.

The Prostitute and the Masseuse

These two bodily actors seem very closely related. Both use a skill to produce bodily satisfaction in the client. Unlike the nightclub singer, both do this through a type of bodily contact with the client. Both need to be responsive to what the client wants, and to a large degree take direction from the client as to how to handle his or her body. The bodily contact involved is rather intimate, although the internal space of the masseuse is not invaded. The type of bodily pleasure produced by the masseuse may certainly have an erotic element, although in the type of "respectable" masseuse I am considering, it is not directly sexual.

The difference is primarily one of respectability. Practitioners of massage have fought for, and have to a large extent won, the right to be considered dignified professionals who exercise a skill. Their trade is legal; it is not stigmatized. And people generally do not believe that they degrade their bodies or turn their bodies into commodities by using their bodies to give pleasure to customers. They have positioned themselves alongside physical therapists and medical practitioners, dissociating themselves from the erotic dimension of their activity. As a consequence of this successful self-positioning, they enjoy better working hours, better pay, and more respect than most prostitutes. What is the difference, we might ask? One is having sex, and the other is not. But what sort of difference is this? Is it a difference we want to defend? Are our reasons for thinking it so crucial really reasons, or vestiges of moral prejudice? A number of distinct beliefs enter in at this point: the belief that women should not have sex with strangers; the belief that commercial sex is inherently degrading and makes a woman degraded woman; the belief that women should not have to have sex with strangers if they do not want to, and in general should have the option to refuse sex with anyone they do not really choose. Some of these beliefs are worth defending and some are not. (I shall argue that the issue of choice is the really important one.) We need to sort them out and to make sure that our policies are not motivated by views we are not really willing to defend.

The Prostitute and the Colonoscopy Artist

I have included this hypothetical occupation for a reason that should by now be evident: It involves the consensual invasion of one's bodily space. (The example is not so hypothetical, either: Medical students need models when they are learning to perform internal exams, and young actors do earn a living playing such roles.[16]) The colonoscopy artist uses her skill at tolerating the fiber-optic probe without anesthesia to make a living. In the process, she permits an aperture of her body to be penetrated by another person's activity—and, we might add, far more deeply penetrated than is generally the case in sex. She runs some bodily risk, because she is being used to rest untested instruments, and she will probably have to fast and empty her colon regularly enough to incur some malnutrition and some damage to her excretory function. Her wages may not be very good—for this is probably not a profession characterized by what Smith called "the beauty and rarity of talents," and it may also involve some stigma given that people are inclined to be disgusted by the thought of intestines.

And yet, on the whole, we do not think that this is a base trade, or one that makes the woman who does it a fallen woman. We might want to ban or regulate it if we thought it was too dangerous, but we would not be moved to ban it for moral reasons. Why not? Some people would point to the fact that it does not either reflect or perpetuate gender hierarchy, and this is certainly true. (Even if her being a woman is crucial to her selection for the job—they need to study, for example, both male and female colons—it will not be for reasons that seem connected with the subordination of women.) But surely a far greater part of the difference is made by the fact that most people do not think anal penetration by a doctor in the context of a medical procedure is immoral,[17] whereas lots of people do think that vaginal or anal penetration in the context of sexual relations is (except under very special circumstances) immoral, and that a woman who goes in for that is therefore an immoral and base woman.

IV. Sex and Stigma

Prostitution, we now see, has many features that link it with other forms of bodily service. It differs from these other activities in many subtle ways, but the biggest difference consists in the fact that it is, today, more widely stigmatized. Professors no longer get told that selling their teaching is a *turpis quaestus*. Opera singers no longer get told that they are unacceptable in polite society. Even the masseuse has won respect as a skilled professional. What is different about prostitution? Two factors stand out as sources of stigma. One is that prostitution is widely held to be immoral; the other is that prostitution (frequently at least) is bound up with gender hierarchy, with ideas that women and their sexuality are in need of male domination and

control, and the related idea that women should be available to men to provide an outlet for their sexual desires. The immorality view would be hard to defend today as a justification for the legal regulation of prostitution, and perhaps even for its moral denunciation. People thought prostitution was immoral because they thought nonreproductive and especially extramarital sex was immoral; the prostitute was seen, typically, as a dangerous figure whose whole career was given over to lust. But female lust was (and still often is) commonly seen as bad and dangerous, so prostitution was seen as bad and dangerous. Some people would still defend these views today, but it seems inconsistent to do so if one is not prepared to repudiate other forms of nonmarital sexual activity on an equal basis. We have to grant, I think, that the most common reason for the stigma attaching to prostitution is a weak reason, at least as a public reason: a moralistic view about female sexuality that is rarely consistently applied (to premarital sex, for example), and that seems unable to justify restriction on the activities of citizens who have different views of what is good and proper. At any rate, it seems hard to use the stigma so incurred to justify perpetuating stigma through criminalization unless one is prepared to accept a wide range of morals laws that interfere with chosen consensual activities, something that most feminist attackers of prostitution rarely wish to do.

More promising as a source of good moral arguments might be the stigma incurred by the connection of prostitution with gender hierarchy. But what is the connection, and how exactly does gender hierarchy explain pervasive stigma? It is only a small minority of people for whom prostitution is viewed in a negative light because of its collaboration with male supremacy; for only a small minority of people at any time have been reflective feminists, concerned with the eradication of inequality. Such people will view the prostitute as they view veiled women, or women in *purdah*: with sympathetic anger, as victims of an unjust system. This reflective feminist critique, then, does not explain why prostitutes are actually stigmatized and held in disdain—both because it is not pervasive enough and because it leads to sympathy rather than to disdain.

The way that gender hierarchy actually explains stigma is a very different way, a way that turns out in the end to be just another form of the immorality charge. People committed to gender hierarchy, and determined to ensure that the dangerous sexuality of women is controlled by men, frequently have viewed the prostitute, a sexually active woman, as a threat to male control of women. They therefore become determined either to repress the occupation itself by criminalization or, if they also think that male sexuality needs such an outlet and that this outlet ultimately defends marriage by giving male desire a safely debased outlet, to keep it within bounds by close regulation. (Criminalization and regulation are not straightforwardly opposed; they can be closely related strategies. Similarly, prostitution is generally conceived as not the enemy but the ally of marriage: The two are complementary ways of controlling women's sexuality.) The result is that social meaning is deployed in order that female sexuality will be kept in bounds carefully set by men. The stigma attached to the prostitute is an integral part of such bounding.

A valuable illustration of this thesis is given by Alain Corbin's valuable and careful study of prostitutes in France in the late nineteenth century.[18] Corbin shows that the interest in legal regulation of prostitution was justified by the alleged public interest in reining in and making submissive a dangerous female sexuality that was always potentially dangerous to marriage and social order. Kept in carefully supervised houses known as *maisons de tolérance*, prostitutes were known by the revealing name of *filles soumises*, a phrase that most obviously designated them as registered, "subjugated" to the law, but that also connoted their controlled and confined status. What this meant was that they were controlled and confined so that they themselves could provide a safe outlet for desires that threatened to disrupt the social order. The underlying aim of the regulationist project, argues Corbin (with ample documentation), was "the total repression of sexuality."[19] Regulationists tirelessly cited St. Augustine's dictum: "Abolish the prostitutes and the passions will overthrow the world; give them the rank of honest women and infamy and dishonor will blacken the universe" (*De ordine* 2.4.12). In

other words, stigma has to be attached to prostitutes because of the necessary hierarchy that requires morality to subjugate vice, and the male the female, seen as an occasion and cause of vice. Bounding the prostitute off from the "good woman," the wife whose sexuality is monogamous and aimed at reproduction, creates a system that maintains male control over female desire.[20]

This attitude to prostitution has modern parallels. One instructive example is from Thailand in the 1950s, when Field Marshal Sarit Thanarat began a campaign of social purification, holding that "uncleanliness and social impropriety . . . led to the erosion of social orderliness. . . . "[21] In theory, Thanarat's aim was to criminalize prostitution by the imposition of prison terms and stiff fines; in practice, the result was a system of medical examination and "moral rehabilitation" that shifted the focus of public blame from the procurers and traffickers to prostitutes themselves. Unlike the French system, the Thai system did not encourage registered prostitution, but it was similar in its public message that the problem of prostitution is a problem of "bad" women, and in its reinforcement of the message that female sexuality is a cause of social disruption unless tightly controlled.

In short, sex hierarchy causes stigma, commonly, not through feminist critique but through a far more questionable set of social meanings, meanings that anyone concerned with justice for women should call into question. For it is these same meanings that are also used to justify the seclusion of women, the veiling of women, the genital mutilation of women. The view boils down to the view that women are essentially immoral and dangerous and will be kept in control by men only if men carefully engineer things so that they do not get out of bounds. The prostitute, being seen as the uncontrolled and sexually free woman, is in this picture seen as particularly dangerous, both necessary to society and in need of constant subjugation. As an honest woman, a woman of dignity, she will wreck society. As a *fille soumise*, her reputation in the dirt, she may be tolerated for the service she provides (or, in the Thai case, she may provide an engrossing public spectacle of "moral rehabilitation").

All this diverts attention from some very serious crimes, such as the use of kidnapping, coercion, and fraud to entice women into prostitution. For these reasons, international human rights organizations, such as Human Rights Watch and Amnesty International, have avoided taking a stand against prostitution as such and have focused their energies on the issue of trafficking and financial coercion.[22]

It appears, then, that the stigma associated with prostitution has an origin that feminists have good reason to connect with unjust background conditions and to decry as both unequal and irrational, based on a hysterical fear of women's unfettered sexuality. There may be other good arguments against the legality of prostitution, but the existence of widespread stigma all by itself does not appear to be among them. As long as prostitution is stigmatized, people are injured by that stigmatization, and it is a real injury to a person not to have dignity and self-respect in her own society. But that real injury (as with the comparable real injury to the dignity and self-respect of interracial couples, or of lesbians and gay men) is not best handled by continued legal strictures against the prostitute and can be better dealt with in other ways (e.g., by fighting discrimination against these people and taking measures to promote their dignity). As the Supreme Court said in a mixed-race custody case, "Private biases may be outside the reach of the law, but the law cannot, directly or indirectly, give them effect."[23]

V. Criminalization: Seven Arguments

Pervasive stigma itself, then, does not appear to provide a good reason for the continued criminalization of prostitution, any more than it does for the illegality of interracial marriage. Nor does the stigma in question even appear to ground a sound *moral* argument against prostitution. This is not, however, the end of the issue. There are a number of other significant arguments that have been made to support criminalization. With our six related cases in mind, let us now turn to those arguments.

(1) *Prostitution involves health risks and risks of violence.* To this we can make two replies.

First, insofar as this is true, as it clearly is, the problem is made much worse by the illegality of prostitution, which prevents adequate supervision, encourages the control of pimps, and discourages health checking. As Corbin shows, regimes of legal but regulated prostitution have not always done well by women: The health checkups of the *filles soumises* were ludicrously brief and inadequate.[24] But there is no reason why one cannot focus on the goal of adequate health checks, and some European nations have done reasonably well in this area.[25] The legal brothels in Nevada have had no reported cases of AIDS.[26] Certainly risks of violence can be far better controlled when the police are the prostitute's ally rather than her oppressor.

To the extent to which risks remain an inevitable part of the way of life, we must now ask what general view of the legality of risky undertakings we wish to defend. Do we ever want to rule out risky bargains simply because they harm the agent? Or do we require a showing of harm to others (as might be possible in the case of gambling, for example)? Whatever position we take on this complicated question, we will almost certainly be led to conclude that prostitution lies well within the domain of the legally acceptable, for it is certainly far less risky than boxing, another activity in which working-class people try to survive and flourish by subjecting their bodies to some risk of harm. There is a stronger case for paternalistic regulation of boxing than of prostitution, and externalities (the glorification of violence as example to the young) make boxing at least as morally problematic and probably more so. And yet I would not defend the criminalization of boxing, and I doubt that very many Americans would either. Sensible regulation of both prostitution and boxing, by contrast, seems reasonable and compatible with personal liberty.

In the international arena, many problems of this type stem from the use of force and fraud to induce women to enter prostitution, frequently at a very young age and in a strange country where they have no civil rights. An especially common destination, for example, is Thailand, and an especially common source is Burma, where the devastation of the rural economy has left many young women an easy mark for promises of domestic service elsewhere. Driven by customers' fears of HIV, the trade has focused on increasingly young girls from increasingly remote regions. Human rights interviewers have concluded that large numbers of these women were unaware of what they would be doing when they left their country and are kept there through both economic and physical coercion. (In many cases, family members have received payments, which then become a "debt" that the girl has to pay off.)[27] These circumstances, terrible in themselves, set the stage for other forms of risk and/or violence. Fifty to seventy percent of the women and girls interviewed by Human Rights Watch were HIV positive; discriminatory arrests and deportations are frequently accompanied by abuse in police custody. All these problems are magnified by the punitive attitude of the police and government toward these women as prostitutes or illegal aliens or both, although under both national and international law trafficking victims are exempt from legal penalty and are guaranteed safe repatriation to their country of origin. This situation clearly deserves both moral condemnation and international legal pressure, but it is made worse by the illegality of prostitution itself.

(2) *The prostitute has no autonomy; her activities are controlled by others.* This argument[28] does not distinguish prostitution from very many types of bodily service performed by working-class women. The factory worker does far worse on the scale of autonomy, and the domestic servant no better. I think this point expresses a legitimate moral concern: A person's life seems deficient in flourishing if it consists only of a form of work that is totally out of the control and direction of the person herself. Marx rightly associated that kind of labor with a deficient realization of full humanity and (invoking Aristotle) persuasively argued that a flourishing human life probably requires some kind of use of one's own reasoning in the planning and

execution of one's own work.[29] But that is a pervasive problem of labor in the modern world, not a problem peculiar to prostitution as such. It certainly does not help the problem to criminalize prostitution—any more than it would be to criminalize factory work or domestic service. A woman will not exactly achieve more control and "truly human functioning" by becoming unemployed. What we should instead think about are ways to promote more control over choice of activities, more variety, and more general humanity in the types of work that are actually available to people with little education and few options. That would be a lot more helpful than removing one of the options they actually have.

(3) *Prostitution involves the invasion of one's intimate bodily space.* This argument[30] does not seem to support legal regulation of prostitution, provided that as the invasion in question is consensual; that is, that the prostitute is not kidnapped, or fraudulently enticed, or a child beneath the age of consent, or under duress against leaving if she should choose to leave. In this sense prostitution is quite unlike sexual harassment and rape, and far more like the activity of the colonoscopy artist—not to everyone's taste, and involving a surrender of bodily privacy that some will find repellant—but not for that reason necessarily bad, either for self or others. The argument does not even appear to support a moral criticism of prostitution unless one is prepared to make a moral criticism of all sexual contact that does not involve love or marriage.

(4) *Prostitution makes it harder for people to form relationships of intimacy and commitment.* This argument is prominently made by Elizabeth Anderson, in defense of the criminalization of prostitution.[31] The first question we should ask is, Is this true? People still appear to fall in love in the Netherlands and Germany and Sweden; they also fell in love in ancient Athens, where prostitution was not only legal but also, probably, publicly

subsidized.[32] One type of relationship does not, in fact, appear to remove the need for the other—any more than a Jackie Collins novel removes the desire to read Proust. Proust has a specific type of value that is by no means found in Jackie Collins, so people who want that value will continue to seek out Proust, and there is no reason to think that the presence of Jackie Collins on the bookstand will confuse Proust lovers and make them think that Proust is really like Jackie Collins. So, too, one supposes, with love in the Netherlands: People who want relationships of intimacy and commitment continue to seek them out for the special value they provide, and they do not have much trouble telling the difference between one sort of relationship and another, despite the availability of both.

Second, one should ask which women Anderson has in mind. Is she saying that the criminalization of prostitution would facilitate the formation of love relationships on the part of the women who were (or would have been) prostitutes? Or, is she saying that the unavailability of prostitution as an option for working-class women would make it easier for romantic middle-class women to have the relationships they desire? The former claim is implausible, because it is hard to see how reinforcing the stigma against prostitutes, or preventing some poor women from taking one of the few employment options they might have would be likely to improve their human relations.[33] The latter claim might possibly be true (though it is hardly obvious), but it seems a repugnant idea, which I am sure Anderson would not endorse, that we should make poor women poorer so that middle-class women can find love. Third, one should ask Anderson whether she is prepared to endorse the large number of arguments of this form that might plausibly be made in the realm of popular culture—and, if not, whether she has any way of showing how she could reject those as involving an unacceptable infringement of liberty and yet allowing the argument about prostitution that she endorses. For it seems plausible that making

rock music illegal would increase the likelihood that people would listen to Mozart and Beethoven; that making Jackie Collins illegal would make it more likely that people would turn to Joyce Carol Oates; that making commercial advertising illegal would make it more likely that we would appraise products with high-minded ideas of value in our minds; that making television illegal would improve children's reading skills. What is certain, however, is that we would and do utterly reject those ideas (we do not even seriously entertain them) because we do not want to live in Plato's *Republic*, with our cultural options dictated by a group of wise guardians, however genuinely sound their judgments may be.[34]

(5) *The prostitute alienates her sexuality on the market; she turns her sexual organs and acts into commodities.*[35] Is this true? It seems implausible to claim that the prostitute alienates her sexuality just on the grounds that she provides sexual services to a client for a fee. Does the singer alienate her voice, or the professor her mind? The prostitute still has her sexuality; she can use it on her own, apart from the relationship with the client, just as the domestic servant may cook for her family and clean her own house.[36] She can also cease to be a prostitute, and her sexuality will still be with her, and hers, if she does. So she has not even given anyone a monopoly on those services, far less given them over into someone else's hands. The real issue that separates her from the professor and the singer seems to be the degree of choice she exercises over the acts she performs. But is even this a special issue for the prostitute, any more than it is for the factory worker or the domestic servant or the colonoscopy artist—all of whom choose to enter trades in which they will not have a great deal of say over what they do or (within limits) how they do it? Freedom to choose how one works is a luxury, highly desirable indeed, but a feature of few jobs that nonaffluent people perform.

As for the claim that the prostitute turns her sexuality into a commodity, we must ask what that means. If it means only that she accepts a fee for sexual services, then that is obvious, but nothing further has been said that would show us why this is a bad thing. The professor, the singer, the symphony musician—all accept a fee, and it seems plausible that this is a good state of affairs, creating spheres of freedom. Professors are more free to pursue their own thoughts now, as money makers, than they were in the days when they were supported by monastic orders; symphony musicians playing under the contract secured by the musicians' union have more free time than nonunionized musicians, and more opportunities to engage in experimental and solo work that will enhance their art. In neither case should we conclude that the existence of a contract has converted the abilities into things to be exchanged and traded separately from the body of the producer; they remain human creative abilities, securely housed in their possessor. So, if to "commodify" means merely to accept a fee, we have been given no reason to think that this is bad.

If, on the other hand, we try to interpret the claim of "commodification" using the narrow technical definition of "commodity" used by the Uniform Commercial Code,[37] the claim is plainly false. For that definition stresses the "fungible" nature of the goods in question, and "fungible" goods are, in turn, defined as goods "of which any unit is, by nature or usage of trade, the equivalent of any other like unit." Although we may not think that the soul or inner world of a prostitute is of deep concern to the customer, she is usually not regarded as simply a set of units fully interchangeable with other units.[38] Prostitutes are probably somewhat more fungible than bassoon players but not totally so. (Corbin reports that all *maisons de tolérance* standardly had a repertory of different types of women, to suit different tastes, and this should not surprise us.) What seems to be the real issue is that the woman is not attended to as an individual, not considered a special, unique being. But that is true of many ways people treat one another in many areas of life, and it seems implausible that we should use that kind of disregard as a basis for criminalization. It may not even be immoral, for surely we cannot deeply know all the

people with whom we have dealings in life, and many of those dealings are just fine without deep knowledge. So our moral question boils down to the question, Is sex without deep personal knowledge always immoral? It seems to me officious and presuming to use one's own experience to give an affirmative answer to this question, given that people have such varied experiences of sexuality.

In general, then, there appears to be nothing baneful or value debasing about taking money for a service, even when that service expresses something intimate about the self. Professors take a salary, artists work on commision under contract—frequently producing works of high intellectual and spiritual value. To take money for a production does not turn either the activity or the product (e.g., the article or the painting) into a commodity in the baneful sense in which that implies fungibility. If this is so, there is no reason to think that a prostitute's acceptance of money for her services necessarily involves a baneful conversion of an intimate act into a commodity in that sense. If the prostitute's acts are, as they are, less intimate than many other sexual acts people perform, that does not seem to have a great deal to do with the fact that she receives money, given that people engage in many intimate activities (painting, singing, writing) for money all the time without loss of expressive value. Her activity is less intimate because that is its whole point; it is problematic, to the extent that it is, neither because of the money involved nor because of the nonintimacy (which, as I have said, it seems officious to declare bad in all cases) but because of features of her working conditions and the way she is treated by others.

Here we are left with an interesting puzzle. My argument about professors and painters certainly seems to imply that there is no reason, in principle, why the most committed and intimate sex cannot involve a contract and a financial exchange. So why doesn't it, in our culture? One reply is that it quite frequently does, when people form committed relationships that include an element of economic dependence, whether one-sided or mutual; marriage has frequently had that feature, not always for the worse. But to the extent that we do not exchange money for sex, why don't we? In a number of other cultures, courtesans, both male and female, have been somewhat more common as primary sexual partners than they are here. Unlike quite a few cultures, we do not tend to view sex in intimate personal relationships the way we view an artist's creation of a painting, namely, as an intimate act that can nonetheless be deliberately undertaken as the result of an antecedent contract-like agreement. Why not? I think there is a mystery here, but we can begin to grapple with it by mentioning two features. First; there is the fact that sex, however, prolonged, still takes up much less time than writing an article or producing a painting. Furthermore, it also cannot be done too often; its natural structure is that it will not very often fill up the entire day. One may therefore conduct an intimate sexual relationship in the way one would wish, not feeling that one is slighting it, while pursuing another line of work as one's way of making a living. Artists and scholars sometimes have to pursue another line of work, but they prefer not to. They characteristically feel that to do their work in the way they would wish, they ought to spend the whole day doing it. So they naturally gravitate to the view that their characteristic mode of creative production fits very well with contract and a regular wage.

This, however, still fails to explain cultural differences. To begin to grapple with these we need to mention the influence of our heritage of romanticism, which makes us feel that sex is not authentic if not spontaneous, "natural," and to some degree unplanned. Romanticism has exercised a far greater sway over our ideas of sex than over our ideas of artistic or intellectual production, making us think that any deal or antecedent arrangement somehow diminishes that characteristic form of expression.

Are our romantic ideas about the difference between sex and art good, or are they bad? Some of each, I suspect. They are problematic to the extent that they make people think that sex happens naturally, does not require complicated adjustment and skill, and flares up (and down) uncontrollably.[39] Insofar as they make us think that sex fits badly with reliability, promise keeping, and

so forth, these ideas are certainly subversive of Anderson's goals of "intimacy and commitment," which would be better served, probably, by an attitude that moves sex in intimate personal relationships (and especially marriages) closer to the activity of the artist or the professor. On the other hand, romantic views also promote Anderson's goals to some degree, insofar as they lead people to connect sex with self-revelation and self-expression rather than prudent concealment of self. Many current dilemmas concerning marriage in our culture stem from an uneasy struggle to preserve the good in romanticism while avoiding the dangers it poses to commitment. As we know, the struggle is not always successful. There is much more to be said about this fascinating topic. But since (as I've argued) it leads us quite far from the topic of prostitution, we must now return to our primary line of argument.

(6) *The prostitute's activity is shaped by, and in turn perpetuates, male dominance of women.*[40] The institution of prostitution as it has most often existed is certainly shaped by aspects of male domination of women. As I have argued, it is shaped by the perception that female sexuality is dangerous and needs careful regulation; that male sexuality is rapacious and needs a "safe" outlet; that sex is dirty and degrading, and that only a degraded woman is an appropriate sexual object.[41] Nor have prostitutes standardly been treated with respect, or given the dignity one might think proper to a fellow human being. They share this with working-class people of many types in many ages, but there is no doubt that there are particular features of the disrespect that derive from male supremacy and the desire to lord it over women, as well as a tendency to link sex to (female) defilement that is common in the history of Western European culture. The physical abuse of prostitutes and the control of their earnings by pimps—as well as the pervasive use of force and fraud in international marts—are features of male dominance that are extremely harmful and do not have direct parallels in other types of

low-paid work. Some of these forms of conduct may be largely an outgrowth of the illegality of the industry and closely comparable to the threatening behavior of drug wholesalers to their—usually male—retailers. So there remains a question how far male dominance as such explains the violence involved. But in the international arena, where regulations against these forms of misconduct are usually treated as a joke, illegality is not a sufficient explanation for them.

Prostitution is hardly alone in being shaped by, and reinforcing, male dominance. Systems of patrilineal property and exogamous marriage, for example, almost certainly do more to perpetuate not only male dominance but also female mistreatment and even death. There probably is a strong case for making the giving of dowry illegal, as has been done since 1961 in India and since 1980 in Bangladesh[42] (though with little success), for it can be convincingly shown that the institution of dowry is directly linked with extortion and threats of bodily harm, and ultimately with the deaths of large numbers of women.[43] It is also obvious that the dowry system pervasively conditions the perception of the worth of girl children: They are a big expense, and they will not be around to protect one in one's old age. This structure is directly linked with female malnutrition, neglect, noneducation, even infanticide, harms that have caused the deaths of many millions of women in the world.[44] It is perfectly understandable that the governments of India, Bangladesh, and Pakistan are very concerned about the dowry system, because it seems very difficult to improve the very bad economic and physical condition of women without some structural changes. (Pakistan has recently adopted a somewhat quixotic remedy, making it illegal to serve food at weddings—thus driving many caterers into poverty.) Dowry is an institution affecting millions of women, determining the course of almost all girl children's lives pervasively and from the start. Prostitution as such usually does not have either such dire or such widespread implications. (Indeed, it is frequently the product of the dowry system, when parents take payment for prostituting a female child for whom they would otherwise have to pay dowry.) The case for making it illegal on grounds of subordination seems weaker than the case for making dowry, or even wedding feasts, illegal, and yet these laws are themselves of dubious merit and would probably be rightly regarded as involving undue infringement of liberty under our constitutional tradition. (It is significant that Human Rights Watch, which has so aggressively pursued the issue of forced prostitution, takes no stand one way or the other on the legality of prostitution itself.)

More generally, one might argue that the institution of marriage as most frequently practiced both expresses and reinforces male dominance. It would be right to use law to change the most inequitable features of that institution—protecting women from domestic violence and marital rape, giving women equal property and custody rights and improving their exit options by intelligent shaping of the divorce law. But to rule that marriage as such should be illegal on the grounds that it reinforces male dominance would be an excessive intrusion upon liberty, even if one should believe marriage irredeemably unequal. So, too, I think, with prostitution: What seems right is to use law to protect the bodily safety of prostitutes from assault, to protect their rights to their incomes against the extortionate behavior of pimps, to protect poor women in developing countries from forced trafficking and fraudulent offers, and to guarantee their full civil rights in the countries where they end up—to make them, in general, equals under the law, both civil and criminal. But the criminalization of prostitution seems to pose a major obstacle to that equality.

Efforts on behalf of the dignity and self-respect of prostitutes have tended to push in exactly the opposite direction. In the United States, prostitutes have long organized to demand greater respect, though their efforts are hampered by prostitution's continued illegality. In India, the National Federation of Women has adopted various strategies to give prostitutes more dignity in the public eye. For example, on National Women's Day, they selected a prostitute to put a garland on the head of the prime minister. Similarly, UNICEF in India's

Andhra Pradesh has been fighting to get prostitutes officially classified as "working women" so that they can enjoy the child-care benefits local government extends class. As with domestic service, so here: Giving workers greater dignity control can gradually change both the perception and the fact of dominance.

(7) *Prostitution is a trade that people do not enter by choice; therefore the bargains people make within it should not be regarded as real bargains.* Here we must distinguish three cases. First is the case in which the woman's entry into prostitution is caused by some type of conduct that would otherwise be criminal: kidnapping, assault, drugging, rape, statutory rape, blackmail, a fraudulent offer. Here we may certainly judge that the woman's choice is not a real choice, and that the law should take a hand in punishing her coercer. This is a terrible problem currently in developing countries; international human rights organizations are right to make it a major focus.[45]

Closely related is the case of child prostitution. Child prostitution is frequently accompanied by kidnapping and forcible detention; even when children are not stolen from home, their parents have frequently sold them without their own consent. But even where they have not, we should judge that there is an impermissible infringement of autonomy and liberty. A child (and, because of clients' fears of HIV, brothels now often focus on girls as young as ten[46]) cannot give consent to a life in prostitution; not only lack of information and of economic options (if parents collude in the deal) but also absence of adult political rights makes such a "choice" no choice at all.

Different is the case of an adult woman who enters prostitution because of bad economic options: because it seems a better alternative than the chicken factory, because there is no other employment available to her, and so on. This too, we should insist, is a case in which autonomy has been infringed but in a different way. Consider Joseph Raz's vivid example of "the hounded woman," a woman on a desert island who is constantly pursued by a man-eating animal.[47] In one sense, this woman is free to go anywhere on the island and do anything she likes. In another sense, of course, she is quite unfree. If she wants not to be eaten, she has to spend all her time and calculate all her movements in order to avoid the beast. Raz's point is that many poor people's lives are nonautonomous in just this way. They may fulfill internal conditions of autonomy, being capable of making bargains, reflecting about what to do, and so on. But none of this counts for a great deal, if in fact the struggle for survival gives them just one unpleasant option, or a small set of (in various ways) unpleasant options.

This seems to me the truly important issue raised by prostitution. Like work in the chicken factory, it is not an option many women choose with alacrity, when many other options are on their plate.[48] This might not be so in some hypothetical culture, in which prostitutes have legal protection, dignity and respect, and the status of skilled practitioner, rather like the masseuse.[49] But it is true now in most societies, given the reality of the (albeit irrational) stigma attaching to prostitution. But the important thing to realize is that this is not an issue that permits us to focus on prostitution in isolation from the economic situation of women in a society generally. Certainly it will not be ameliorated by the criminalization of prostitution, which reduces poor women's options still further. We may grant that poor women do not have enough options, and that society has been unjust to them in not extending more options while nonetheless respecting and honoring the choices they actually make in reduced circumstances.

How could it possibly be ameliorated? Here are some things that have actually been done in India, where prostitution is a common last-ditch option for women who lack other employment opportunities. First, both government and private groups have focused on the provision of education to women, to equip them with skills that will enhance their options. One group I recently visited in Bombay focuses in particular on skills training for the children of prostitutes; who are at especially high risk of becoming prostitutes themselves unless some action increases their options.

Second, nongovernmental organizations have increasingly focused on the provision of credit to women, in order to enhance their employment options and give them a chance to "upgrade" in the domain of their employment. One such project that has justly won international renown is the Self-Employed Women's Association (SEWA), centered in Ahmedabad in Gujerat, which provides loans to women pursuing a variety of informal-sector occupations,[50] from tailoring to hawking and vending to cigarette rolling to agricultural labor.[51] With these loans, they can get wholesale rather than retail supplies, upgrade their animals or equipment, and so forth. They also get skills training and, frequently, the chance to move into leadership roles in the organization itself. Such women are far less likely to need to turn to prostitution to supplement their income. Third, they can form labor organizations to protect women employed in low-income jobs and to bargain for better working conditions—once again making this work a better source of income and diminishing the likelihood that prostitution will need to be selected. (This is the other primary objective of SEWA, which is now organizing hawkers and vendors internationally.) Fourth, they can form groups to diminish the isolation and enhance the self-respect of working women in low-paying jobs; this was a ubiquitous feature of both government and nongovernment programs I visited in India, and a crucial element of helping women deliberate about their options if they wish to avoid prostitution for themselves or their daughters.

These four steps are the real issue, I think, in addressing the problem of prostitution. Feminist philosophers in the United States do not write many articles about credit and employment;[52] they should do so far more. Indeed, it seems a dead end to consider prostitution in isolation from the other realities of working life of which it is a part, and one suspects that this has happened because prostitution is a sexy issue and getting a loan for a sewing machine appears not to be. But feminists had better talk more about getting loans, learning to read, and so forth if they want to be relevant to the choices that are actually faced by working women, and to the programs that are actually doing a lot to improve such women's options.

VI. Truly Human Functioning

The stigma traditionally attached to prostitution is based on a collage of beliefs most of which are not rationally defensible, and which should be especially vehemently rejected by feminists: beliefs about the evil character of female sexuality, the rapacious character of male sexuality, and the essentially marital and reproductive character of "good" women and "good" sex. Worries about subordination more recently raised by feminists are much more serious concerns, but they apply to many types of work poor women do. Concerns about force and fraud should be extremely urgent concerns of the international women's movement. Where these conditions do not obtain, feminists should view prostitutes as (usually) poor working women with few options, not as threats to the intimacy and commitment that many women and men (including, no doubt, many prostitutes) seek. This does not mean that we should not be concerned about ways in which prostitution as currently practiced, even in the absence of force and fraud, undermines the dignity of women, just as domestic service in the past undermined the dignity of members of a given race or class. But the correct response to this problem seems to be to work to enhance the economic autonomy and the personal dignity of members of that class, not to rule off limits an option that may be the only livelihood for many poor women and to further stigmatize women who already make their living this way.

In grappling further with these issues, we should begin from the realization there is nothing per se wrong with taking money for the use of one's body. That's the way most of us live, and formal recognition of that fact through contract is usually a good thing for people, protecting their security and their employment conditions. What seems wrong is that relatively few people in the world have the option to use their body, in their work, in what Marx would call a "truly human" manner of functioning, by which he meant (among other things) having some choices about the work to be performed, some reasonable measure of control over its conditions and outcome, and also the chance to use thought and skill rather than just to function as a cog in a machine. Women in many parts of the world are especially likely to be stuck at a low level of mechanical functioning, whether as agricultural laborers or as factory workers or as prostitutes. The real question to be faced is how to expand the options and opportunities such workers face, how to increase the humanity inherent in their work, and how to guarantee that workers of all sorts are treated with dignity. In the further pursuit of these questions, we need, on balance, more studies of women's credit unions and fewer studies of prostitution.

DISCUSSION QUESTIONS

1. Describe Nussbaum's six hypothetical cases of women who take money for bodily services, and explain how these cases compare to prostitution.
2. Explain how prostitution and marriage are two sides of the same coin, both of which aim to control women's sexuality.
3. Describe the seven arguments in favor of criminalizing prostitution that Nussbaum considers, and explain how she rejects each one.

NOTES

1. Even if one is a Cartesian dualist, as I am not, one must grant that the human exercise of mental abilities standardly requires the deployment of bodily skills. Most traditional Christian positions on the soul go still further: Aquinas, for example, holds that souls separated from the body have only a confused cognition and cannot recognize particulars. So my statements about professors can be accepted even by believers in the separable soul.
2. The typical contract between major U.S. symphony orchestras and the musicians' union, for example, guarantees year-round employment to symphony musicians, even though they do not play all year; this enables them to use summer months to play in low-paying or experimental settings in which they can perform contemporary music and chamber music, do solo and concerto work, and so forth. It also restricts hours of both rehearsal and performance during the performing season, leaving musicians free to teach students, attend classes, work on chamber music with friends, and in other ways to enrich their work. It also mandates blind auditions (i.e., players play behind a curtain)—with the result that the employment of female musicians has risen dramatically over the past twenty or so years since the practice was instituted.

3. See Elizabeth Anderson, *Value in Ethics and Economics* (Cambridge, MA: Harvard University Press, 1993); and Anderson, "Is Women's Labor a Commodity?" *Philosophy and Public Affairs* 19 (1990), 71–92; Margaret Jane Radin, *Contested Commodities: The Trouble with the Trade in Sex, Children, Bodily Parts, and Other Things* (Cambridge, MA: Harvard University Press, 1996); and Radin, "Market-Inalienability," *Harvard Law Review* 100 (1987), 1849–1937; Cass R. Sunstein, "Neutrality in Constitutional Law (with Special Reference to Pornography, Abortion, and Surrogacy)," *Columbia Law Review* 92 (1992), 1–52; and Sunstein, *The Partial Constitution* (Cambridge, MA: Harvard University Press, 1993), 257–290. For contrasting feminist perspectives on the general issue of contract, see Jean Hampton, "Feminist Contractarianism," in *A Mind of One's Own: Feminist Essays on Reason and Objectivity* (Boulder, CO: Westview, 1993), 227–255; Susan Moller Okin, *Justice, Gender, and the Family* (New York: Basic Books, 1989).

4. I use this term throughout because of its familiarity, although a number of international women's organizations now avoid it for reasons connected to those in this essay, preferring the term "commercial sex worker" instead. For one recent example, see Report of the Panel on Reproductive Health, National Research Council, *Reproductive Health in Developing Countries: Expanding Dimensions, Building Solutions*, ed. Amy O. Tsui, Judith N. Wasserheit, and John G. Haaga (Washington, DC: National Academy Press, 1997), 30, stressing the wide variety of practices denoted by the term "commercial sex" and arguing that some studies show economic hardship as a major factor but some do not.

5. Among feminist discussions of prostitution, my approach is close to that of Sibyl Schwarzenbach, "Contractarians and Feminists Debate Prostitution," *New York University Review of Law and Social Change* 18 (1990–1), 103–129, and to Laurie Shrage, "Prostitution and the Case for Decriminalization," *Dissent* (Spring 1996), 41–45 (in which Shrage criticizes her earlier view expressed in "Should Feminists Oppose Prostitution?," *Ethics* 99 [1989]: 347–361).

6. To give just one example, the Annapurna Mahila Mandel project in Bombay offers job training and education to the daughters of prostitutes, in a residential school setting; they report that in five years they have managed to arrange reputable marriages for 1,000 such girls.

7. Aspasia was a learned and accomplished woman who apparently had philosophical and political views; she is said to have taught rhetoric and to have conversed with Socrates. On the other hand, she could not perform any of the functions of a citizen, both because of her sex and because of her foreign birth. On the other hand, her son Pericles was subsequently legitimated and became a general. More recently, it has been doubted whether Aspasia was in fact a *hetaira*, and some scholars now think her a well-born foreign woman. But other *hetairai* in Greece had good education and substantial financial assets; the two women recorded as students in Plato's Academy were both *hetairai*, as were most of the women attested as students of Epicurus, including one who was apparently a wealthy donor.

8. As far as I know, this profession is entirely hypothetical, though not by any means far-fetched. It is clear, at any rate, that individuals' abilities to endure colonoscopy without anesthesia and without moving vary considerably, so one might well develop (or discover) expertise in this area.

9. It is probably, however, a developed skill to come to work regularly and to work regular hours each day.

10. Consider, for example, the case of Jayamma, a brick worker in Trivandrum, Kerala, India, discussed by Leela Gulati, *Profiles of Female Poverty* (Delhi: Hindustan Publishing Corp., 1981) and whom I met on March 21, 1997, when she was approximately sixty-five years old. For approximately forty years, Jayamma worked as a brick carrier in the brick-making establishment, carrying heavy loads of bricks on her head all day from one place to another. Despite her strength, fitness, and reliability, she could never advance beyond that job because of her sex, whereas men were quickly promoted to the less physically demanding and higher-paying tasks of brick molding and truck loading.

11. Indeed, this appears to be a ubiquitous feature: In India, the mark of "untouchability" is the performance of certain types of cleaning, especially those dealing with bathroom areas. Mahatma Gandhi's defiance of caste manifested itself in the performance of these menial services.

12. This does not imply that there is some one thing, pleasure, varying only by quantity, that they produce. With Mill (and Plato and Aristotle), I think that pleasures differ in quality, not only in quantity.

13. This point was suggested to me by Elizabeth Schreiber. I am not sure whether I endorse it: It all depends on whether we really want to say that sex has one highest goal. Just as it would have been right, in an earlier era, to be skeptical about the suggestion that the sex involved in prostitution is "low" because it is nonreproductive, so too it might be good to be skeptical about the idea that prostitution sex is "low" because it is nonintimate. Certainly nonintimacy is involved in many noncommercial sexual relationships and is sometimes desired as such.

14. Thus the *Kama Sutra*, with its detailed instructions for elaborately skilled performances, strikes most Western readers as slightly comic, because the prevailing romantic ideal of "natural" sex makes such contrivance seem quite unsexy.

15. We might also consider the example of a skilled writer who writes advertising copy.

16. See Terri Kapsalis, *Public Privates: Performing Gynecology from Both Ends of the Speculum* (Durham: Duke University Press, 1997); and Kapsalis, "In Print: Backstage at the Pelvic Theater," *Chicago Reader*, April 18, 1997, 46. While a graduate student in performance studies at Northwestern, Kapsalis made a living as a "gynecology teaching associate," serving as the model

patient for medical students learning to perform pelvic and breast examinations.

17. The same goes for vaginal penetration, according to Kapsalis: She says that the clinical nature of the procedure more than compensates for "society's queasiness with female sexuality."

18. *Women for Hire: Prostitution and Sexuality in France after 1850,* trans. Alan Sheridan (Cambridge, MA: Harvard University Press, 1990).

19. Ibid., 29. Representative views of the authors of regulationism include the view that "[d]ebauchery is a fever of the senses carried to the point of delirium; it leads to prostitution (or to early death) . . ." and that "[t]here are two natural sisters in the world: prostitution and riot." Ibid., 373.

20. For a more general discussion of the relationship between prostitution and various forms of marriage, see Richard Posner, *Sex and Reason* (Cambridge, MA: Harvard University Press, 1992), 130–133.

21. Sukanya Hantrakul, "Thai Women: Male Chauvinism a la Thai," *The Nation*, November 16, 1992, cited with further discussion in Asia Watch Women's Rights Project, *A Modern Form of Slavery: Trafficking of Burmese Women and Girls into Brothels in Thailand* (New York: Human Rights Watch, 1993).

22. See *A Modern Form of Slavery; the Human Rights Watch Global Report on Women's Human Rights* (New York: Human Rights Watch, 1995), 196–273, esp. 270–273. The pertinent international human rights instruments take the same approach, including the International Covenant on Civil and Political rights, the Convention on the Elimination of All forms of Discrimination against Women, and the Convention for the Suppression of Traffic in Persons and the Exploitation of the Prostitution of Others.

23. *Palmore v. Sidoti*, 466 U.S. 429 (1984).

24. See Corbin, 90: In Paris, Dr. Clerc boasted that he could examine a woman every thirty seconds, and estimated that a single practitioner saw 400 women in a single twenty-four-hour period. Another practitioner estimated that the average number of patients per hour was fifty-two.

25. For a more pessimistic view of health checks, see Posner, *Sex and Reason*, 209, pointing out that they frequently have had the effect of driving prostitutes into the illegal market.

26. See Richard Posner, *Private Choices and Public Health: The AIDS Epidemic in an Economic Perspective* (Cambridge, MA: Harvard University Press, 1993), 149, with references.

27. See *Human Rights Watch Global Report*, 1–7.

28. See Anderson, *Value in Ethics and Economics*, 156: "Her actions under contract express not her own valuations but the will of her customer."

29. This is crucial in the thinking behind the "capabilities approach" to which I have contributed in *Women, Culture, and Development* and other publications. For the connection between this approach and Marx's use of Aristotle, see Martha C. Nussbaum, "Aristotle on Human Nature and the Foundations of Ethics," in *World, Mind, and Ethics: Essays on the Philosophy of Bernard Williams*, ed. J. E. J. Altham and R. Harrison (Cambridge: Cambridge University Press, 1993).

30. Made frequently by my students, not necessarily to support criminalization.

31. *Value in Ethics and Economics*, 150–158; Anderson pulls back from an outright call for criminalization, concluding that her arguments "establish the legitimacy of a state interest in prohibiting prostitution, but not a conclusive case for prohibition," given the paucity of opportunities for working women.

32. See K. J. Dover, *Greek Homosexuality*, 2nd ed. (Cambridge, MA: Harvard University Press, 1978); and David Halperin, "The Democratic Body," in *One Hundred Years of Homosexuality and Other Essays on Greek Love* (New York: Routledge, 1990). Customers were all males, but prostitutes were both male and female. The evidence that prostitution was publicly funded is uncertain because it derives from comic drama, but it is clear that both male and female prostitution enjoyed broad public support and approval.

33. For a similar point, see M. J. Radin, "Market-Inalienability," 1921–25; and *Contested Commodities*, 132–136; Anderson refers to this claim of Radin's,

apparently as the source of her reluctance to call outright for criminalization.

34. I would not go quite as far as John Rawls, however, in the direction of letting the market determine our cultural options. He opposes any state subsidy to opera companies, symphony orchestras, museums, and so on, on the grounds that this would back a particular conception of the good against others. I think, however, that we could defend such subsidies, within limits, as valuable because they preserve a cultural option that is among the valuable ones, and that might otherwise cease to exist. Obviously much more argument is needed on this entire question.

35. See Radin, "Market-Inalienability"; and Anderson, 156: "The prostitute, in selling her sexuality to a man, alienates a good necessarily embodied in her person to him and thereby subjects herself to his commands."

36. On this point, see also Schwarzenbach, with discussion of Marx's account of alienation.

37. See Richard Epstein, "Surrogacy: The Case for Full Contractual Enforcement," *Virginia Law Review 81* (1995), 2327.

38. Moreover, the UCC does not cover the sale of services, and prostitution should be classified as a service rather than a good.

39. It is well-known that these ideas are heavily implicated in the difficulty of getting young people, especially young women, to use contraception.

40. See Shrage's earlier article; Andrea Dworkin, "Prostitution and Male Supremacy, "*Life and Death* (New York: The Free Press, 1997).

41. An eloquent examination of the last view, with reference to Freud's account (which endorses it) is in William Miller, *The Anatomy of Disgust* (Cambridge, MA: Harvard University Press, 1997), chap. 6.

42. The Dowry Prohibition Act of 1961 makes both taking and giving of dowry illegal; in Bangladesh, demanding, taking, and giving dowry are all criminal offenses. . . .

43. It is extremely difficult to estimate how many women are damaged and killed as a result of this practice; it is certainly clear that criminal offenses are vastly underreported, as is domestic violence in India generally, but that very problem makes it difficult to form any reliable idea of the numbers involved. See Indira Jaising, *Justice for Women* (Bombay: The Lawyers' Collective, 1996). . . .

44. See Amartya Sen and Jean Dreze, *Hunger and Public Action* (Oxford: Clarendon Press, 1989), 52. . . . Kerala, the only Indian state to have a matrilineal property tradition, also has an equal number of men and women (contrasted with a 94/100 sex ratio elsewhere), and 97% both male and female literacy, as contrasted with 32% female literacy elsewhere.

45. See, for example, A *Modern Form of Slavery: Trafficking of Burmese Women; Human Rights Watch Global Report*, 1296–1373; Amnesty International, *Human Rights Are Women's Right* (London: Amnesty International, 1995), 53–56.

46. See *Human Rights Watch Global Report*, 197, on Thailand.

47. Joseph Raz, *The Morality of Freedom* (Oxford: Clarendon Press, 1986), 374.

48. See Posner, *Sex and Reason*, 132 n. 43 on the low incidence of prostitution in Sweden, even though it is not illegal; his explanation is that "women's opportunities in the job market are probably better there than in any other country."

49. See Schwarzenbach.

50. An extremely high proportion of the labor force in India is in the informal sector.

51. SEWA was first directed by Ela Bhatt, who is now involved in international work to improve the employment options of informal-sector workers. For a valuable description of the movement, see Kalima Rose, *Where Women Are Leaders: The SEWA Movement in India* (Delhi: Sage Publications, 1995).

52. But see, here, Schwarzenbach and Shrage (op. cit.). I have also been very much influenced by the work of Martha Chen, *A Quiet Revolution: Women in Transition in Rural Bangladesh* (Cambridge, MA: Schenkman, 1983); Chen, "A Matter of Survival: Women's Right to Work in India and Bangladesh," in *Women, Culture, and Development*, ed. M. Nussbaum and J. Glover (Oxford: Clarendon

Press, 1995); and Bina Agarwal, *A Field of One's Own: Gender and Land Rights in South Asia* (Cambridge: Cambridge University Press, 1994); and also "Bargaining" and Gender Relations: Within and Beyond the Household," FCND Discussion Paper No. 27, Food Consumption and Nutrition Division, International Food Policy Research Institute, Washington, DC.

Why Sex Work Isn't Work

BY LORI WATSON

> Lori Watson is an American philosopher who writes on issues in political and moral philosophy, feminism, and philosophy of law. In this clever and provocative essay, Watson takes issue with the argument that there are no fundamental differences between sex work and any other form of work, arguing that the existing American legal frameworks governing worker health and safety, sexual harassment, and civil rights are insufficient to deal with the particularities of the buying and selling of sex.

Many in favor of the legalization of prostitution refer to it as "sex work" and employ concepts such as "consent," "agency," "sexual freedom," "the right to work," and even "human rights" in the course of making their defense.[1] Consider some of the common claims defenders of legalization advance: sex work is work just like any other form of work, only the social shame and stigma around sex prevent people from seeing it as such;[2] many (most) women[3] who sell sex chose to be there, so we should respect their choice and agency, after all they are in no different a position than someone who chooses a minimum wage job without better alternatives;[4] women choosing to sell sex is an example of sexual freedom and rejecting repressive norms that limit women's sexuality,[5] so we should respect their sexually autonomous choices to sell sex for a living. Other defenders are more circumspect in their defense of legalization, arguing that prostitution is "the oldest profession," isn't going away, and so we are better off adopting a "harm reduction model." That is, they argue that many of the harms associated with the buying and selling of sex are harms that are either a product of its illegality or can be reduced by a program of regulation that would be required if prostitution were legalized.[6] For example, they claim that legalization will reduce trafficking for purposes of sexual exploitation; they claim that legalization will increase the health and safety of women (the workers); they claim that legalization will reduce death, violence, and other abuses.[7]

There is an abundance of literature rebutting these claims. Study after study shows that the primary reason that women begin selling sex for money is out of economic desperation.[8] Moreover, many women in prostitution began before the age of 18;[9] many feel trapped and feel they have no other realistic opportunities for economic survival.[10] Legalization does not come with many of the benefits its proponents suggest: it does not reduce trafficking (assuming a distinction can be made);[11] "indoor prostitution" is not necessarily safer than "outdoor" prostitution or streetwalking, as it is called;[12] it does not provide a solution to the most vulnerable women in prostitution—immigrants—who are often excluded from regulatory procedures and licensing; it does not necessarily increase the health and safety of women—buyer's health and STD status is not tested under legalization; legalization does not remove social stigma for the women in prostitution.[13] However, legalization does likely remove some of the social stigma for the buyers in addition to making access to women easier and less dangerous (for the buyer). Moreover, despite the common refrain calling prostitution "sex work," many of the women in prostitution, both actively and exited, refer to it as "the life" or "a lifestyle"— the emphasis on "the life" as describing a way of being in the world, a description of the whole of one's existence, not as something one leaves at "the office."[14] Finally, the violence—the potential for assault, rape, and even death—endemic to prostitution exceeds the level of danger accompanying even those most dangerous of other forms of work.[15]

Many of these arguments have been made and are gaining more and more traction against the legalization (regulatory) position. More and more nation-states and international bodies are recognizing that the options for addressing prostitution aren't simply legalization or criminalization[16]— neither of which does anything for the women in prostitution.[17] The Nordic model, in which the selling of sex is decriminalized and the buying of sex criminalized, alongside social services for increasing the exit options of the women, is being increasingly adopted and considered as the best approach to combating the harms of prostitution, empowering persons in prostitution, all the while affirming a commitment to sex equality.

However, in this paper, rather than defend the Nordic Model further, I wish to take seriously the claim that selling sex is "work like any other kind of work" and examine what taking this claim on its face as true would entail in the United States. In my view, there are serious problems with the regulatory approach that aims to treat women selling sex ("sex work" in their lingo) as simply a form of work like any other. To take the claim that "sex work" should be treated/regulated like any other form of work seriously, the following, at minimum, would have to be addressed:

1. Worker safety
2. Sexual harassment
3. Civil rights

In what follows, I draw on the laws of the United States regarding workers safety, sexual harassment, and civil rights to show that the claim that selling sex is work just like any other form of work is indefensible. It's indefensible because if we apply the regulations currently applied to other forms of work to the selling and buying of sex, the acts intrinsic to the "job" can't be permitted; they are simply inconsistent with regulations governing worker safety, sexual harassment laws, and civil rights.

OSHA (Occupational Safety and Health Administration) is responsible for overseeing worker safety and health in the U.S. They specify the standards for worker safety regarding in employment contexts that include exposure to blood borne pathogens and other potentially infectious materials (of which sperm counts),[18] as they are concerned with the potential transmission of HIV or Hepatitis, or other infectious diseases. The sexual acts that form the necessary working conditions for (persons) women selling sex means that routine "Occupational Exposure" is intrinsic to the "job." Occupational exposure "means reasonably anticipated skin, eye, mucous membrane, or parenteral contact with blood or other potentially infectious materials that may result from the performance of an employee's duties."[19] Employers must "list . . . all tasks and procedures or groups of closely related task and procedures in which occupational exposure occurs . . ." and "[t]his exposure determination shall be made without regard to the use of personal protective equipment."[20] So, presumably, every potential sex act would need to be on the list, as "tasks," in which occupational exposure occurs, and the list needs to be made without reference to condom use because the list is required list exposure threat without reference to personal protective equipment.

Condom use certainly would be a minimum requirement for compliance with OSHA standards. However, condom use will not be sufficient to meet OSHA regulations, for: "All procedures involving blood or other potentially infectious materials shall be performed in such a manner as to minimize splashing, spraying, spattering, and generation of droplets of these substances."[21] Condoms break, they are not foolproof. Condoms, while reducing risk, does not eliminate it, nor arguably does it "minimize risk" per the OSHA standard; Condoms also don't protect against all sexually transmitted infections (STIs). The CDC makes clear that, though condoms can reduce some STIs, they are not effective for all STIs, HPV and genital ulcers occur in places that condoms don't cover, and hence condom use is not necessarily an effective prophylactic in all cases.[22] Moreover, we know that even where condoms are required by law, "clients" often prefer not to use them.[23] We also know that the most vulnerable among persons selling sex are the least likely to use condoms (to have the power to require purchasers of sex to use them), for example, transgendered persons and "migrant sex-workers."[24]

Other relevant OSHA regulations that clearly would govern worker safety in a "sex work" environment:

1. "Mouth pipetting/suctioning of blood or other potentially infectious materials is prohibited." Note this doesn't say is permitted with protective gear. It says prohibited. So, oral sex seems to be inconsistent with OSHA worker safety standards as applied to every other form of work. Will "sex work regulations" allow an exception? And if so, what could possibly be the rationale? Will we say that worker safety is less of a concern in this industry?

2. "Gloves. Gloves shall be worn when it can be reasonably anticipated that the employee may have hand contact with blood, other potentially infectious materials, mucous membranes, and non-intact skin . . ." This regulation seems to entail that "sex workers" must wear latex gloves while performing any "work task" in which their hands may come in contact with potentially infectious materials (i.e., sperm). Moreover, in other fields in which exposure is possible or likely, notably medical fields, glove wearing is mandatory. Small cuts or abrasions to the skill are potential transmission sites and "minimizing risks" surely seems to demand gloves be worn at all times for all "tasks" in which exposure is possible.

3. "Masks, Eye Protection, and Face Shields. Masks in combination with eye protection devices, such as goggles or glasses with solid side shields, or chin-length face shields, shall be worn whenever splashes, spray, spatter, or droplets of blood or other potentially infectious materials may be generated and eye, nose, or mouth contamination can be reasonably anticipated."[25] Ejaculation on the face of women in pornography is routine. Data for how widespread this practice is among men who buy sex is unknown. However, we can safely assume it's not zero. However, this practice would either be prohibited (under the OSHA minimize risk standard) or if permitted worker protection demands masks, eye protection, and face shields. If this sounds absurd, consider that among porn performers gonorrhea and Chlamydia is frequent, including such infections in the eyes.[26]

4. "Gowns, Aprons, and Other Protective Body Clothing. Appropriate protective clothing such as, but not limited to, gowns, aprons, lab coats, clinic jackets, or similar outer garments shall be worn in occupational exposure situations. The type and characteristics will depend upon the task and degree of exposure anticipated." While this may indeed sound absurd in the context of "sex work," it goes to the point that the kinds of worker protections deemed necessary in every other work context, in which exposure to infection materials is possible or likely, cannot be maintained in the context in which the work is sex. One can argue that an exception can be carved out for this type of "work," but then what does that say about the relative value of these "workers" as opposed to every other worker who is entitled to such protection? Moreover, exceptions are permitted only in "rare and extraordinary circumstances" where it is judged that health and safety are put in jeopardy by the use of personal protective equipment.[27] Even further, as noted above not all STIs can be protected against by condom use, or even gloves. "Syphilis can be transmitted through skin-to-skin contact and does not require exposure to semen or vaginal fluids." The same is true of herpes, molluscum contagiosum, and HPV, among

other infectious diseases.[28] Direct skin on skin contact puts "workers" at risk. Hence, direct skin-to-skin contact is not compatible with OSHA regulations governing exposure to potentially infectious materials.

5. In the event of exposure OHSA requires: "The source individual's blood shall be tested as soon as feasible and after consent is obtained in order to determine HBV and HIV infectivity. If consent is not obtained, the employer shall establish that legally required consent cannot be obtained. When the source individual's consent is not required by law, the source individual's blood, if available, shall be tested and the results documented."[29] This means that if any employee is exposed to a potentially infectious material, despite using personal protective equipment, the source individual (the buyer in the case of "sex" work) needs to be tested for HIV and HBY. In all of the places in which prostitution is legal it is the sellers not the buyers that are mandated for testing, which of course protects the buyer to an extent, but does nothing to protect the seller/worker.

Obviously the OSHA standards were not created with sex work in mind, however that is irrelevant to the key point being made here—namely, if these are the regulations deemed necessary to protect worker safety in every other work environment in which exposure to potentially infectious material is a risk of the job, why should they not apply in the context of "sex work"? If selling sex is work like any other form of work, then the safety of these workers is just as important to protect as the safety of workers in other contexts. The retort that condom use will be required by law and that is sufficient to protect the health and safety of "sex workers" is simply not true. Condoms may reduce risk in some cases, as noted above, however they do not "minimize" risk nor do they protect against all potentially infections transmissions (STIs) as noted above. Moreover, where the selling and buying of sex is currently legal and condoms required by law—New Zealand, Australia, the Netherlands, parts of Nevada, e.g.—there is ample evidence of

clients preferring sex without condoms, offering to pay more for sex without condoms, and a lack of enforcement among "management."[30]

The attempt to draw attention to worker safety in the sex industry is not new. In 2012, voters in Los Angeles voted for "Measure B"—a law requiring condom use in the pornography industry as a means of protecting worker health and safety. The result of the law was not, in fact, increased worker safety. The result was that applications for permits to film in L.A. County dropped 90%; porn production companies either stopped filming in L.A. County or stopped filing for permits and continued to film illegally.[31]

The fact is the buyers drive the market, as is true generally in commercial exchanges. If the buyers don't want to use condoms or follow other "worker safety protocols" as would be necessary to protect the safety and health of workers, then we have little reason to be confident that legalization and regulation will effectively protect those who sell sex.

Sexual Harassment

Sexual harassment is defined as "unwelcome sexual conduct that is a term or condition of employment."[32] Such harassment can take the form of a quid pro quo (when "submission to or rejection of such conduct by an individual is used as the basis for employment decisions affecting such individual") or in subjecting the employee to a hostile work environment.[33] The standard kinds of cases of sexual harassment involve a supervisor or co-worker harassing, in one form or another, a co-worker. Presumably, in the context of "sex work" a supervisor or co-worker demanding sex as a condition of employment or creating a hostile work environment could be adjudicated similarly to other work contexts. A more difficult kind of case to consider in the context of "sex work" is harassment by a client. Hence, it is important to note: "The harasser can be the victim's supervisor, a supervisor in another area, a co-worker, or someone who is not an employee of the employer, such as a client or customer."[34] So, "clients" or "customers"—purchasers of sex in this discussion—can also be found to have sexually harassed someone from whom they are purchasing sex, under the current legal standards.

It is a serious question as to how sexual harassment laws can possibly be enforced in a context in which sex is a commercial exchange. Where every "job task" potentially involves unwelcome sexual conduct as a condition of employment, because sex is the job, how can we possibly enforce sexual harassment law? Will we carve out an exception for commercial sex—sexual harassment laws don't apply in this context? Or will we continue to stand by our judgments that sexual harassment is a form of sex inequality, from which employees deserve protection? In which case, legalization of prostitution is simply incompatible with sexual harassment legislation that protects "all workers."

To see precisely how the legalization of the buying and selling of sex is inconsistent with the logic of sexual harassment law, consider the following. First, as noted above "unwelcomeness" is the legal standard for whether some act constitutes sexual harassment. Whether the victim of the harassment voluntarily complied is not a defense to sexual harassment. "[T]he fact that sex-related conduct was 'voluntary,' in the sense that the complainant was not forced to participate against her will, is not a defense to a sexual harassment suit brought under Title VII. . . . The correct inquiry is whether [the victim] by her conduct indicated that the alleged sexual advances were unwelcome, not whether her actual participation in sexual intercourse was voluntary."[35] "The Eleventh Circuit provided a general definition of "unwelcome conduct": the challenged conduct must be unwelcome "in the sense that the employee did not solicit or incite it, and in the sense that the employee regarded the conduct as undesirable or offensive."[36] In the context of commercial sex, what will count at "soliciting" or "inciting" sexual conduct? Will it be because she agreed to do acts x, y, and z, she will have been found to "inciting" the acts she finds objectionable, refuses, or declares unwelcome? In other words, suppose she does agree to oral sex, vaginal sex, but refuses anal sex. Suppose the client then demands anal sex and conditions payment upon agreement. Suppose she complies—she

views the overture and the act as unwelcome, it was in fact a condition of employment (payment), whether it was voluntary is immaterial to whether she was sexually harassed. She was. But why should we exempt the first acts, the prior agreed upon acts, from sexual harassment? They were unwelcome in the sense that they were done for the money—and not for reciprocal sexual enjoyment—and they were a condition of getting the money (the employment). Submitting to unwelcome sexual acts as a condition of employment—getting paid for sex—is sexual harassment; submitting to sexual harassment is the job.

Moreover, there are legal grounds for thinking that the fact that she works in the sex industry and may have welcomed some acts but not others is irrelevant to whether some specific act was unwelcomed and so harassment. Legally, the fact that someone works in the sex industry is irrelevant as to whether any specific act of harassment was unwelcome. So, we can imagine an attempted defense along the lines that "well, she works as a prostitute. So, the behavior in question could not have been unwelcomed." However, "any past conduct of the charging party that is offered to show 'welcomeness' must relate to the alleged harasser." In other words, the only past conduct of the charging party that is relevant is conduct related to the specific individual alleged to have harassed her.

The EEOC acknowledges "a more difficult situation occurs when an employee first willingly participates in conduct of a sexual nature but then ceases to participate and claims that any continued sexual conduct has created a hostile work environment. Here the employee has the burden of showing that any further sexual conduct is unwelcome, work-related harassment. The employee must clearly notify the alleged harasser that his conduct is no longer welcome. If the conduct still continues, her failure to bring the matter to the attention of higher management or the EEOC is evidence, though not dispositive, that any continued conduct is, in fact, welcome or unrelated to work . . . In any case, however, her refusal to submit to the sexual conduct cannot be the basis for denying her an employment benefit or opportunity; that would constituted a 'quid pro quo' violation."[37] Assume for the moment that in the context of "sex work" agreeing to accept money for specific sex acts constitutes welcomeness—insofar as doing so can be understood to "solicit" or "incite" the agreed to acts. Under this assumption, the employee has the burden of showing that any further—unwelcome acts—are, in fact, unwelcome. Moreover, the employee must clearly notify the harasser that the conduct is unwelcome, and notify management. If we adopt the language of some of those who defend legalization, and see sex workers as "consumer service agents" engaged in "customer relations," how realistic is it to think that the sex worker is going to be in a position to make meaningful refusals? To notify the customer that is conduct is unwelcome? To report to management continued harassment? We know that economic survival is the reason that people do this "work." We also know that in work environments that aren't sexual, sexual harassment is underreported due to fear of sanction or loss of job. Moreover, what possible sense can it make to say that "refusal to submit to the sexual conduct cannot be a basis for denying her an employment benefit or opportunity" when sex is the condition of employment?

Consider further that Courts have found the presence of "pornographic magazines." "vulgar sexual comments" "sexually oriented pictures in a company sponsored movie and slide presentation," "sexually oriented pictures and calendars in the workplace," all relevant to hostile work environment claims.[38] In *Barbetta*, the court held that the proliferation of pornography and demeaning comments, if sufficiently continuous and pervasive "may be found to create an atmosphere in which women are viewed as men's sexual playthings rather than as their equal coworkers."[39] How could such a ruling have effect in a brothel: where pornography is used as an accompaniment to sex? Where "vulgar sexual comments" are the eroticized language of clients? Where sex is the job?

Of course, these rulings and regulations are premised upon the fact that sex isn't the job itself. If the sex is the job, what sense can we make of the claim that treating (unwelcome) sex as a condition of employment is an instance of sexual harassment, and so sex inequality? Legalizing prostitution is not compatible with the legal recognition of sexual harassment as a form of sex inequality. And, supposing advocates argue for a carve out, an exception, for this form of "work," what message does that convey? Some women are deserving of protection from, or legal recourse in the event of, unwanted sexual harassment while some women are not? And those that aren't are the least advantaged of all "workers"? This reeks of the all too common view that women that prostitute themselves are whores by nature and deserve whatever they get.

Civil Rights

Although those advocating for legalization (or decriminalization) often frame their arguments in terms of the civil or human rights of "sex workers," once sex is a regulated commercial activity the civil rights of the "clients" are legally enforceable. Businesses may not refuse service to a person on the basis of race, color, national origin/ancestry, sex/gender, religion/creed and disability (physical and mental), as a matter of Federal Law. Some U.S. states have further legislation prohibiting discrimination on the basis of sexual orientation, gender identity and expression. What this means is that businesses that provide "public accommodation" are not free to deny service to anyone who is a member of such a protected classes because they are member of the protected class. To do so is to infringe upon the civil rights of the relevant person. So far, so good. But, how are we to understand this in the context of providing sex, as a commercial service, and so "public accommodation"?

If sexual autonomy is to mean anything, it has to mean the right to refuse sex with anyone, at anytime, for any reason. We may think in one's personal life refusing to entertain the possibility of dating or becoming sexually involved with someone solely on the basis of their race, religion or disability is an undesirable preference, especially if such preferences are rooted in prejudice or animus more broadly speaking. Nonetheless, everyone has the right to choose their sexual partners on whatever grounds they subjectively judge to be relevant, including the sex and gender of any potential partner. If someone thinks they absolutely don't want to have sex with anyone over 65, it is absolutely their right to act (or refuse to act) on that preference. We are under no obligation to have sex with someone who might be interested in sex with us. The right to refusal for any reason, whether an "admirable" reason, or not is absolute.

However, where sex is a commercial activity, considered to be work just like any other form of work, it's hard to see any rationale for defending the "rights of workers" to refuse service to someone based on their subjective preferences. Should "clients" have the right to sue brothels or particular women for "refusing service" based on their membership in a protected class? If this sounds absurd, consider the evidence New Zealand's Prostitution Reform Act (PRA) offers: In a report following up on the PRA, five years after its passage, the Review Committee queries, among other things, the ability of "sex workers" to refuse sexual services to a particular client. They found that 60% of "sex workers" felt more able to refuse sex with a particular client than prior to the passage of the PRA, which, of course, means 40% did not feel more able to refuse sex with a particular client.[40] In interviewing both brothel owners and "sex workers," the Committee reports that although "workers" have "right" to refuse a particular client both "workers" and owners held that refusal was acceptable "only with a good reason." One brothel owner is quoted as saying, "We won't allow nationality to be the reason—they [the women selling sex] don't have a right to discriminate."[41]

Hence, where sex is a "job like any other," a regulated commercial exchange, the "providers" cannot be legally free to refuse clients in protected classes on grounds of their membership in the protected class. Refusing to have sex with anyone over 65 is age discrimination, where sex is a job like any other. Similarly, refusing to have sex with someone because of their sex (or gender or transgender status, where protected) is also potentially a civil

rights violation of the client. This argument, more than any other, I think exposes the fault lines of the "sex work is work like any other form of work" argument. Refusing sex is not like refusing to serve someone dinner, do their nails, cut their hair, or other forms of "personal service." Refusing to give someone a manicure on grounds of their race, age, sex, etc. is a gross refusal to treat them as an equal person. It is, in fact, to treat them unequally and to deny their basic civil rights. Refusing to have sex with someone, on any grounds, is simply not parallel. Refusing to have sex with someone does not make them unequal, civilly or otherwise.

Beyond the arguments I have presented here there are further questions raised by a system of legalization. Where it is legal to include sex as a condition of employment (in sex work), other types of job descriptions may be redefined to include sex. How will we draw the line? Or is sex potentially legitimate part of any job description? Where welfare or unemployment benefits require recipients to accept available work, will sex work be required of people (women) in lieu of public assistance? Under current contract law, failure to perform agreed upon services is a violation of the terms of the contract and may demand compensation or penalties for the party refusing to fulfill the contract: will this extend to "sex work" contracts?[42] Simply extending the regulations that currently cover employment law, contracts, and other public benefits to "sex work" reveals the implausibility of the slogan "its work *just* like any other form of work."

One of the primary motivations for the legalization argument is the desire to reduce harm among persons in prostitution, although as noted above many of the harms associated with the selling of sex will not be removed or reduced with legalization, and some, indeed may be exacerbated. However, the harms associated with the criminalization of the selling of sex—arrest, incarceration, inability to report the crimes of rape, assault, and other forms of violence need to be addressed. Even worse, under systems of criminalization of the selling of sex, vulnerable persons (largely, women) are made more vulnerable to assault and coercion into sex by police officers, the very people charged with "protecting" them against such abuses.[43] The answer to these harms is not legalization. Rather, it is the full decriminalization of the selling of sex. However, a commitment to sex equality, to the full social, civil, and political equality of prostituted persons does not entail providing buyers full, unfettered legal access through a system of legalization. The buyers—the demand—fuel the system of inequality that keeps prostitution flourishing. Criminalization of the buying of sex is an essential element of addressing the harms of prostitution, and the harm that is prostitution. We need the kind of Copernican Revolution the Nordic Model embodies.

DISCUSSION QUESTIONS

1. Describe the safety regulations, sexual harassment laws, and civil rights concerns that Watson argues could not be straightforwardly applied in the contexts in which sex work occurs.
2. Watson argues that if we treat sex work as work like any other kind of work then either it must be subject to the same regulatory control as these other forms of work, or a "carve out," or exception, to these regulations must be justified for sex work.
   a. Why does it strike us as absurd to think that sex workers would be legally required to, for example, wear sexy hazmat suits or legally forbidden from refusing to have sex with a client based on their membership in a protected class?
   b. Explain Watson's concern with the message that would be conveyed by permitting carve outs to these regulations and laws.
3. What is the Nordic Model? How does it minimize the harms and risks of sex work?

NOTES

1. For a history of the "Sex Worker" movement, see: Chateauvert, Melinda. *Sex Workers Unite: A History of the Movement from Stonewall to SlutWalk* (Boston, MA: Beacon Press, 2013). For an example of arguments in favor of legalization, see: Weitzer, Ronald. *Legalizing Prostitution: From Illicit Vice to Lawful Business* (New York: New York University Press, 2012).
2. See, for example, Nussbaum, Martha. "'Whether from Reason or Prejudice': Taking Money for Bodily Services," in *Prostitution and Pornography: Philosophical Debate about the Sex Industry* (Stanford, CA: Stanford University Press, 2006), edited by Jessica Spector, pp. 175–208.
3. Men, boys, and transgendered persons also sell sex for money. However, I refer to women throughout the text when I refer to the sellers of sex. I do this because, overwhelmingly, the persons who sell sex are women or girls. The fact that women are the overwhelming sellers, and men are the vast majority of buyers is relevant to discussing prostitution its harms and who would benefit from legalization. Moreover, it makes clear that it is a socially gender institution, which is crucial to an accurate engagement with the issues at stake.
4. Weitzer (2012).
5. Various groups such as C.O.Y.O.T.E (Call Off Your Old Tired Ethics) make this claim, see *Sex Workers Unite* for discussion. Weitzer also makes this argument of some women in prostitution. For example in a table defining "Selected Types of Prostitution" he classifies "Independent Call Girl/Escort" as having "None" under the category of "Exploitation by Third Parties" (Table 1.1, p. 17). And, later in discussing the benefits of prostitution, he cites job satisfaction higher among indoor workers including the benefits of "feeling 'sexy,' 'beautiful,' and 'powerful'" (*Legalizing Prostitution*, p. 29).
6. The best examples of these claims can be found in the *Occupational Health and Safety Handbook* published by St. James Infirmary (edited by Naomi Akers and Cathryn Evans, 2013, 3rd edition). St. James Infirmary "is an Occupational Saftey & Health Clinic for Sex Workers founded by activists from COYOTE (Call Off Your Old Tired Ethics) and the Exotic Dancers Alliance in collaboration with the STD Prevention and Control Section of the San Francisco Department of Public Health." They are a private, non-profit. The entire

handbook has been archived at http://perma
.cc/o2CetqGsJMU?type=live.

7. This was part of the argument relied on in *Bedford
v. Canada* (2013), the Canadian Supreme Court
Case in which the Court struck down the avails
and bawdy house provisions of the Canadian
criminal code (provisions which made it illegal to
live off the avails of prostitution of another person
and to maintain a bawdy house or place of prostitution, respectively). For a thorough analysis of
the Bedford case, see: Waltman, Max. "Assessing
Evidence, Arguments, and Inequality in Bedford
v. Canada," *Harvard Journal of Law & Gender*,
Summer 2014, Vol. 37, pp. 459–544, available
online at http://harvardjlg.com/wp-content/
uploads/2014/07/Waltman.pdf.

8. A variety of sources confirm this, across a range
of perspectives on whether prostitution should
be legalized, decriminalized, or criminalized in
some form. See for example: A study conducted
by the Policy Department on Citizen's Rights
and Constitutional Affairs for the European
Parliament titled, "Sexual Exploitation and
Prostitution and its impact on gender equality,"
completed in January 2014, available online at
http://www.europarl.europa.eu/RegData/
etudes/etudes/join/2014/493040/IPOL-FEMM_
ET(2014)493040_EN.pdf; see also, "Behind
Closed Doors," a report by the Sex Workers Rights
Project, available at http://sexworkersproject.org/
downloads/BehindClosedDoors.pdf, citing "financial vulnerability" and "economic deprivation"
as the overwhelming reason for entry into prostitution in a study of "indoor" sex work in New York
City; see also, "Shifting the Burden: Inquiry to
assess the operation of the current legal settlement
on prostitution in England and Wales," a March
2014 report prepared by an All-Party Parliament
Group on Prostitution and the Global Sex Trade,
available at http://appgprostitution.files.wordpress
.com/2014/04/shifting-the-burden1.pdf, citing
"poverty" as the primary reason for entry into
prostitution for 74% of indoor workers. Other
routes into prostitution cited by the report include: experience of sexual abuse as a child, drugs

and alcohol abuse, being in the foster care system
as a female child; they conclude "More often than
not, prostitution is entered out of desperation arising from a number of situation-specific factors."

9. The FBI reports the average age of entry for girls
into prostitution (in the U.S.) at between 13–14, see:
http://www.fbi.gov/stats-services/publications/
law-enforcement-bulletin/march_2011/human_
sex_trafficking; see also, "Myths and Facts about
Trafficking for Legal and Illegal Prostitution"
(March 2009) http://www.prostitutionresearch
.com/pdfs/Myths%20&%20Facts%20Legal
%20&%20Illegal%20Prostitution%203-09
.pdf.

10. Melissa Farley's extensive study of prostitution across nine countries, reports that 89% of
those women in prostitution interviewed for the
study "wanted to escape prostitution but did not
have other means for survival." See: Farley, et al.
"Prostitution and Trafficking in Nine Countries:
An Update on Violence and Posttraumatic Stress
Disorder," available at http://www.prostitutionre
search.com/pdf/Prostitutionin9Countries.pdf.

11. See: MacKinnon, Catharine A. "Trafficking,
Prostitution, and Inequality," *Harvard Civil Rights-
Civil Liberties Law Review*, 2011, Vol. 46, No. 2,
pp. 271–293, available at http://harvardcrcl.org/
wp-content/uploads/2011/08/MacKinnon.pdf.

12. See, Waltman. See also, *Behind Closed Doors: An
Analysis of Indoor Sex Work in New York City*, published by Sex Workers Project at the Urban Justice
Center (2005), available at http://sexworkers
project.org/downloads/BehindClosedDoors.pdf.

13. See, Waltman and MacKinnon (2011). See also,
Moran, Rachel. *Paid For: My Journey Through
Prostitution* (Dublin: Gil & Macmillan, 2013).

14. As one example, see Moran, *Paid For* (2013).

15. According to the National Bureau of Labor
Statistics report on fatal job injuries in 2011, fishers and logging are the most dangerous jobs in
the U.S. (as measured by fatalities). "In 2011, the
fatal injury rates of fishers (127.3) and loggers
(104.0) were approximately 25 times higher than
the national fatal occupational injury rate of 3.5
per 100,000 full-time equivalent workers. Pilots,

farmers, roofers, and drivers/sales workers and truck drivers also had fatal injury rates that exceeded the all-worker rate of 3.5 fatal occupational injuries per 100,000 full-time equivalent workers." See: http://www.bls.gov/opub/btn/volume-2/death-on-the-job-fatal-work-injuries-in-2011.htm. By contrast, the death rate of women in prostitution is 40 times higher than women not in prostitution. In a study of women in prostitution in Colorado, researchers calculated a crude morality rate of 391 per 100,000 and a homicide rate among active "prostitutes" as 229 per 100,000. See, "Morality in a Long-Term Open Cohort of Prostitute Women," *American Journal of Epidemiology* (2004), Vol. 159, no. 8, pp. 778–785. Based on this study, the death rate of women in prostitution is just over 3 times higher than that of fishers, and nearly 4 times higher than loggers, the two most dangerous jobs in the U.S.

16. Increasingly States and International Bodies are considering or advocating for the Nordic Model, which recognizes that the criminalization of the selling of sex harms women, and other prostituted persons, and so decriminalizes the selling of sex while continuing to criminalize the buying of sex. Norway, Sweden, Iceland all have adopted this model of legislation. France's parliament recently voted affirmatively in favor the Nordic Model, as did the European Parliament. It is currently being considered in the U.K. as well as Canada. In Germany, trauma experts are organizing against the current system of decriminalization and advocating for the Nordic model as well as claiming: "Prostitution is in no way a job like any other. It is degrading, torturous, exploitive. On the side of the prostituted, there is a lot of horror and disgust at play, which they have to repress in order to get through it at all." So says Michaela Huber, psychologist and head of the German Society for Trauma and Dissociation. See: http://www.emma.de/artikel/traumatherapeutinnen-gegen-prostitution-317787, see the English translation here: http://www.sabinabecker.com/2014/09/german-psychologists-and-the-scientific-case-against-prostitution.html.

17. Persons, women, in prostitution are not a monolithic group. The more inequality persons, women, face generally with regard to race, national origin, age, ability, economic status the more unequal they are within systems of prostitution. To the extent that legalization would benefit anyone currently in prostitution, it would benefit the most well-off, the women with the most choice, the most safety, and the most freedom within. Just like any other industry regulated by a capitalist market, there will be (and are) tiers of employment hierarchies within the industry. There is no reason to think that legalization will equalize the hierarchies within the sex industry any more than in any other industry.

18. "Other Potentially Infectious Materials means (1) The following human body fluids: semen, vaginal secretions, cerebrospinal fluid, synovial fluid, pleural fluid, pericardial fluid, peritoneal fluid, amniotic fluid, saliva in dental procedures, any body fluid that is visibly contaminated with blood, and all body fluids in situations where it is difficult or impossible to differentiate between body fluids; (2) Any unfixed tissue or organ (other than intact skin) from a human (living or dead); and (3) HIV-containing cell or tissue cultures, organ cultures, and HIV- or HBV-containing culture medium or other solutions; and blood, organs, or other tissues from experimental animals infected with HIV or HBV." See: Occupational Safety and Health Standards, Code of Federal Regulations, Standards, Part 1910, Toxic and Hazardous Substances, Blood Borne Pathogens, (hereinafter, OSHA regulations) available on line at, https://www.osha.gov/pls/oshaweb/owadisp.show_document?p_table=STANDARDS&p_id=10051.

19. OSHA regulations, https://www.osha.gov/pls/oshaweb/owadisp.show_document?p_table=STANDARDS&p_id=10051.

20. Ibid.

21. Ibid.

22. See, http://www.cdc.gov/condomeffectiveness/brief.html.

23. "Throughout the world, study after study documents that about half of all johns request or insist

that condoms are not used when they buy sex. Many factors militate against condom use: the need of women to make money; older women's decline in attractiveness to men; competition from places that do not require condoms; pimp pressure on women to have sex with no condom for more money; money needed for a drug habit or to pay off the pimp; and the general lack of control that prostituted women have over their bodies in prostitution venues. Even though sex businesses had rules that required men to wear condoms, men nonetheless attempted to have sex without condoms. According to an economic analysis of condom use in India, when extremely poor women used condoms, they were paid 66%-79% less by johns." See: http://www.prostitution research.com/pdfs/Myths%20&%20Facts%20 Legal%20&%20Illegal%20Prostitution%203-09 .pdf.

24. In a Special Report "Thematic Report: Sex Workers. Monitoring implementation of the Dublin Declaration on Partnership to Fight HIV/AIDS in Europe, Central Asia" prepared by . . . reports, "Overall, condom use by female sex workers with clients is relatively high. Reported data suggest that condom use may be lower among male sex workers than among female sex workers but it is difficult to draw firm conclusions as relatively few countries reported data on condom use by male sex workers and sample sizes were generally not representative. Reported data do not provide any information about use of condoms by other sub-groups of sex workers, such as migrant sex workers. http://www.ecdc.europa.eu/en/ publications/Publications/dublin-declaration-sex-workers.pdf.

25. OSHA regulations, https://www.osha.gov/pls/ oshaweb/owadisp.show_document?p_ table=STANDARDS&p_id=10051.

26. http://www.dir.ca.gov/dosh/DoshReg/ comments/STD%20and%20HIV%20Disease%20 and%20Health%20Risks%20Los%20Angeles%20 County%20DPH.pdf.

27. OSHA Regulations: "Use. The employer shall ensure that the employee uses appropriate personal protective equipment unless the employer shows that the employee temporarily and briefly declined to use personal protective equipment when, under rare and extraordinary circumstances, it was the employee's professional judgment that in the specific instance its use would have prevented the delivery of health care or public safety services or would have posed an increased hazard to the safety of the worker or coworker. When the employee makes this judgment, the circumstances shall be investigated and documented in order to determine whether changes can be instituted to prevent such occurrences in the future. OSHA regulations, https://www.osha .gov/pls/oshaweb/owadisp.show_document?p_ table=STANDARDS&p_id=10051.

28. St. James Infirmary, *Occupational Health and Safety Handbook*, pp. 21–30.

29. OSHA regulations, https://www.osha.gov/ pls/oshaweb/owadisp.show_document?p_ table=STANDARDS&p_id=10051.

30. See: Waltman (2013); Farley, Melissa. *Prostitution and Trafficking in Nevada Making the Connections* (San Francisco, CA: Prostitution Research & Education, 2007); Malarek, Victor. *The Johns: Sex for Sale and The Men Who Buy It* (New York: Arcade, 2009), esp. p. 232, where he writes: "The WHO failed to understand that the very request to wear a condom can get a woman beaten or even killed."

31. http://www.latimes.com/opinion/editorials/la-ed-condoms-porn-20140810-story.html.

32. http://www.eeoc.gov/policy/docs/currentissues .html.

33. Ibid.

34. Ibid.

35. http://www.eeoc.gov/policy/docs/currentissues .html.

36. Henson v. City of Dundee, 682 F.2d at 903.

37. http://www.eeoc.gov/policy/docs/currentissues .html.

38. Ibid.

39. Ibid.

40. http://www.justice.govt.nz/policy/commercial-property-and-regulatory/prostitution/

prostitution-law-review-committee/publications/
plrc-report/documents/report.pdf, p. 45.

41. Ibid.

42. For a thorough development and analysis of these questions, see: Anderson, Scott, Prostitution and

Sexual Autonomy," in *Prostitution and Pornography*, ed. Spector (cf. fn. 2).

43. See, "Behind Closed Doors," available at http://sexworkersproject.org/downloads/ BehindClosedDoors.pdf.

Pornography, Civil Rights, and Speech

BY CATHARINE MACKINNON

Catharine MacKinnon is an American legal scholar and activist whose influential work examines women's rights and sexual abuse and exploitation, including sexual harassment, rape, prostitution, sex trafficking, and pornography. In this groundbreaking and controversial feminist criticism of pornography, MacKinnon argues that insofar as it is responsible for eroticizing (and thus creating and sustaining) our culture's gendered relations of dominance and submission, pornography constitutes harmful speech and should thus be censored.

My formal agenda has three parts. The first treats pornography by connecting epistemology—which I understand to be about theories of knowing—with politics—which I will take to be about theories of power. For instance, when Justice Stewart said of obscenity, "I know it when I see it," that is even more interesting than it is usually taken to be, if viewed as a statement connecting epistemology—what he knows through his way of knowing, in this case, seeing—with the fact that his seeing determines what obscenity *is* in terms of what he sees it to be, because of his position of power.

Beneath this, though, the world is not entirely the way the powerful say it is or want to believe it is. If it appears to be, it is because power constructs the appearance of reality by silencing the voices of the powerless, by excluding them from access to authoritative discourse. Powerlessness means that when you say "this is how it is," it is *not* taken as being that way. This makes articulating silence, perceiving the presence of absence, believing those who have been socially stripped of credibility, critically contextualizing what passes for simple fact, necessary to the epistemology of a politics of the powerless.

My second thematic concern is jurisprudential. It is directed toward identifying, in order to change, one dimension of liberalism as it is embodied in law: the definition of justice as neutrality between abstract categories. The liberal view is that abstract categories—like speech or equality—define systems. Every time you strengthen free speech in one place, you strengthen it everywhere. Strengthening the free speech of the Klan strengthens the free speech of Blacks. Getting things for men strengthens equality for women. Getting men access to women's schools strengthens women's access to education. What I will be exploring is the way in which substantive systems, made up of real people with social labels attached, are *also systems*. You can reverse racism abstractly, but white supremacy is unfudgeably substantive. Sexism can be an equal abstraction, but male supremacy says who is where. Substantive systems like white supremacy do substantively different things to people of color than they do to white people. To say they are *also systems* is to say that every time you score one for white supremacy in one place, it is strengthened every place else.

In this view, the problem with neutrality as the definition of principle in constitutional adjudication is its equation of substantive powerlessness with substantive power, and calling treating these the same, "equality." The neutrality approach understands that abstract systems are systems, but it seems not to understand that substantive systems are also systems.

This criticism frames a problem that is the same problem for equal protection law under the sex-blind/color-blind rubric as it is for the first amendment under the absolutist rubric—the systematic defense of those who own the speech because they can buy it or have speech to lose because they have the power to articulate in a way that counts.

When these two frames converge—epistemology and politics on the one hand with the critique of neutrality on the other—they form a third frame of political philosophy. Here is how they converge. Once power constructs social reality, as I will show pornography constructs the social reality of gender, the force behind sexism, the subordination in gender inequality, is made invisible; dissent from it becomes inaudible as well as rare. What a woman is, is defined in pornographic terms; this is what pornography *does*. If the law then looks neutrally on the reality of gender so produced, the harm that has been done *will not be perceptible as harm*. It becomes just the way things are. Refusing to look at what has been substantively done will institutionalize inequality in law and it will look just like principle.

In the philosophical terms of classical liberalism, an equality-freedom dilemma is produced: Freedom to make or consume pornography weighs against the equality of the sexes. Some people's freedom hurts other people's equality. There is something to this, but my formulation, as you might guess, comes out a little differently. If one asks whose freedom pornography represents, a tension emerges that is not a dilemma among abstractions so much as it is a conflict between groups. Substantive interests are at stake on *both* sides of the abstract issues, and women are allowed to matter in neither. If women's freedom is as incompatible with pornography's construction of our freedom as our equality is incompatible with pornography's construction of our equality, we get neither freedom nor equality under the liberal calculus. Equality for women is incompatible with a definition of men's freedom that is at our expense. What can freedom for women mean, so long as we remain unequal? Why should men's freedom to use us in this way be purchased with our second-class civil status?

I.

Substantively considered, the situation of women is *not really like anything else*. Its specificity is due not only to our numbers—we are half the human race—and our diversity, which at times has obscured that we are a group with an interest at all. It is, in part, that our status as a group relative to men has almost never, if ever, been much changed from what it is. Women's roles do vary enough that gender, the social form sex takes, cannot be said to be biologically determined. Different things are valued in different cultures, but whatever is valued, women are not that. If bottom is bottom, look across time and space and women are who you will find there. Together with this, you will find in as varied forms as there are cultures, the belief that women's social inferiority to men is not that at all, but is merely the sex difference.

There is a belief that this is a society in which women and men are basically equals. Room for marginal corrections is conceded, flaws are known to exist, attempts are made to correct what are conceived as occasional lapses from the basic condition of sex equality. Sex discrimination law has centered most of its focus on these occasional lapses. It is difficult to overestimate the extent to which this belief in equality is an article of faith to most people, including most women, who wish to live in self-respect in an internal universe, even (perhaps especially) if not in the world. It is also partly an expression of natural law thinking: If we are inalienably equal, we can't "really" be degraded.

This is a world in which it is worth trying. In this world of presumptive equality, people make money based on their training or abilities or diligence or qualifications. They are employed and advanced on the basis of merit. In this world of just deserts, if someone is abused, it is thought to violate the basic rules of the community. If it doesn't, that person is seen to have done something she could have chosen to do differently, by exercise of will or better judgment. Maybe such people have placed themselves in a situation of vulnerability to physical abuse. Maybe they have done something provocative. Or maybe they were just unusually unlucky. In such a world, if such a person has an experience, there are words for it. When they speak and say it, they are listened to. If they write about it, they will be published. If there are certain experiences that are never spoken, or certain people or issues seldom heard from, it is supposed that silence has been chosen. The law, including much of the law of sex discrimination and the first amendment, operates largely within the realm of these beliefs.

Feminism is the discovery that women do not live in this world, that the person occupying this realm is a man, so much more a man if he is white and wealthy. This world of potential credibility, authority, security, and just rewards, recognition of one's identity and capacity, is a world that some people do inhabit as a condition of birth, with variations *among them*. It is not a basic condition accorded humanity in this society, but a prerogative of status, a privilege, among other things, of gender.

I call this a discovery because it has not been an assumption. Feminism is the first theory, the first practice, the first movement, to take seriously the situation of all women from the point of view of all women, both on our situation and on social life as a whole. The discovery has therefore been made that the implicit social content of humanism, as well as the standpoint from which legal method has been designed and injuries have been defined, has not been women's standpoint. Defining feminism in a way that connects epistemology with power as the politics of women's point of view, this discovery can be summed up by saying that women live in another world: specifically, a world of *not* equality, a world of inequality.

Looking at the world from this point of view, a whole shadow world of previously invisible silent abuse has been discerned. Rape, battery, sexual harassment, forced prostitution, and the sexual abuse of children emerge as common and systematic. We find rape happens to women in all contexts, from the family, including rape of girls and babies, to students and women in the workplace, on the streets, at home, in their own bedrooms by men that they do not know, and by men that they do know, by men they are married to, men they have had a social conversation with, or, least often, men

they have never seen before.[1] Overwhelmingly, rape is something that men do or attempt to do to women (forty-four percent according to a recent study) at some point in our lives. Sexual harassment of women by men is common in workplaces and educational institutions. Up to eighty-five percent of women in one study report it, many in physical forms. Between a quarter and a third of women are battered in their homes by men. Thirty-eight percent of little girls are sexually molested inside or outside the family. Until women listened to women, this world of sexual abuse was *not spoken* of. It was the unspeakable. What I am saying is, if you *are* the tree falling in the epistemological forest, your demise doesn't make a sound if no one is listening. Women did not "report" these events, and overwhelmingly do not today, because no one is listening, because no one believes us. This silence does not mean nothing happened, and it does not mean consent.

Believing women who say we are sexually violated has been a radical departure, both methodologically and legally. The extent and nature of rape, marital rape, and sexual harassment itself, were discovered in this way. Domestic battery as a syndrome, almost a habit, was discovered through refusing to believe that when a woman is assaulted by a man to whom she is connected, that is not an assault. The sexual abuse of children was uncovered, Freud notwithstanding, by believing that children were not making up all this sexual abuse. Now what is striking is that when each discovery is made, and somehow made real in the world, the response has been: It happens to men too. If women are hurt, men are hurt. If women are raped, men are raped. If women are sexually harassed, men are sexually harassed. If women are battered, men are battered. Symmetry must be reasserted. Neutrality must be reclaimed. Equality must be reestablished.

The only places where the available evidence supports this, where anything like what happens to women also happens to men, are with children— little boys are sexually abused—and in prison. The liberty of prisoners is restricted, their freedom restrained, their humanity systematically diminished, their bodies and emotions confined, defined, and regulated. If paid at all, they are paid starvation wages. They can be tortured at will, and it is passed off as discipline or as means to an end. They become compliant. They can be raped at will, at any moment, and nothing will be done about it. When they scream, nobody hears. To be a prisoner means to be defined as a member of a group for whom the rules of what can be done to you, of what is seen as abuse of you, are reduced as part of the definition of your status. To be a woman is also that kind of definition and has that kind of meaning.

Men *are* damaged by sexism. (By men, I am referring to the status of masculinity which is accorded to males on the basis of their biology, but is not itself biological.) But whatever the damage of sexism is to men, the condition of being a man is not defined as subordinate to women by force. Looking at the facts of the abuses of women all at once, you see that a woman is socially defined as a person who, whether or not she is or has been, *can at any time* be treated in these ways by men, and little, if anything, will be done about it. This is what it means when feminists say that maleness is a form of power and femaleness is a form of powerlessness.

Now why are these basic realities of the subordination of women to men, such that for example only 7.8 percent of women have never been sexually assaulted, not effectively believed, not perceived as real in the face of all this evidence? Why don't *women* believe our own experiences? In the face of all this evidence, especially of systematic sexual abuse—subjection to violence with impunity is one extreme expression, although not the only expression, of a degraded status—the view that basically the sexes are equal in this society remains unchallenged and unchanged. The day I got this was the day I understood its real message, its real coherence: *This is equality for us.*

I could describe this but I couldn't explain it until I started studying a lot of pornography. In pornography, there it is, in one place, all of the abuses that women had to struggle so long even to begin to articulate, all the *unspeakable* abuse: the rape, the battery, the sexual harassment, the prostitution, and the sexual abuse of children. Only in the pornography it is called something else: sex, sex, sex, sex, and sex, respectively. Pornography sexualizes rape, battery, sexual harassment, prostitution, and child sexual abuse; it thereby celebrates, promotes, authorizes, and legitimizes them. More generally, it eroticizes the dominance and submission that is the dynamic common to them all. It makes hierarchy sexy and calls that "the truth about sex" or just a mirror of reality. Through this process, pornography constructs what a woman is as what men want from sex. This is what the pornography means. (I will talk about the way it works behaviorally, with the evidence on it, when I talk about the ordinance itself.)

Pornography constructs what a woman is in terms of its view of what men want sexually, such that acts of rape, battery, sexual harassment, prostitution, and sexual abuse of children become acts of sexual equality. Pornography's world of equality is a harmonious and balanced place. Men and women are perfectly complementary and perfectly bipolar. Women's desire to be fucked by men is equal to men's desire to fuck women. All the ways men love to take and violate women, women love to be taken and violated. The women who most love this are most men's equals, the most liberated; the most participatory child is the most grown-up, the most equal to an adult. Their consent merely expresses or ratifies these preexisting facts.

The content of pornography is one thing. There, women substantively desire dispossession and cruelty. We desperately want to be bound, battered, tortured, humiliated, and killed. Or, to be fair to the soft core, merely taken and used. This is erotic to the male point of view. Subjection itself with self-determination ecstatically relinquished is the content of women's sexual desire and desirability. Women are there to be violated and possessed, men to violate and possess us either on screen or by camera or pen on behalf of the consumer. On a simple descriptive level, the inequality of hierarchy, of which gender is the primary one, seems necessary for the sexual arousal to work. Other added inequalities identify various pornographic genres or sub-themes, although they are always added through gender: age, disability, homosexuality, animals, objects, race (including anti-semitism), and so on. Gender is never irrelevant.

What pornography *does* goes beyond its content: It eroticizes hierarchy, it sexualizes inequality. It makes dominance and submission sex. Inequality is its central dynamic; the illusion of freedom coming together with the reality of force is central to its working. Perhaps because this is a bourgeois culture, the victim must look free, appear to be freely acting. Choice is how she got there. Willing is what she is when she is being equal. It seems equally important that then and there she actually be forced and that forcing be communicated on some level, even if only through still photos of her in postures of receptivity and access, available for penetration. Pornography in this view is a form of forced sex, a practice of sexual politics, an institution of gender inequality.

From this perspective, pornography is neither harmless fantasy nor a corrupt and confused misrepresentation of an otherwise natural and healthy sexual situation. It institutionalizes the sexuality of male supremacy, fusing the erotization of dominance and submission with the social construction of male and female. To the extent that gender is sexual, pornography is part of constituting the meaning of that sexuality. Men treat women as who they see women as being. Pornography constructs who that is. Men's power over women means that the way men see women defines who women can be. Pornography is that way. Pornography is not imagery in some relation to a reality elsewhere constructed. It is not a distortion, reflection, projection, expression, fantasy, representation, or symbol either. It is a sexual reality.

In Andrea Dworkin's definitive work on pornography, sexuality itself is a social construct gendered to the ground. Male dominance here is not an artificial overlay upon an underlying inalterable substratum of uncorrupted essential sexual being. Dworkin's *Pornography: Men Possessing Women*[2] presents a sexual theory of gender inequality of which pornography is a constitutive practice. The way in which pornography produces its meaning constructs and defines men and women as such. Gender has no basis in anything other than the social reality its hegemony constructs. Gender is what gender means. The process that gives

sexuality its mate supremacist meaning is the same process through which gender inequality becomes socially real.

In this approach, the experience of the (overwhelmingly) male audiences who consume pornography is therefore not fantasy or simulation or catharsis but sexual reality, the level of reality on which sex itself largely operates. Understanding this dimension of the problem does not require noticing that pornography models are real women to whom, in most cases, something real is being done; nor does it even require inquiring into the systematic infliction of pornography and its sexuality upon women, although it helps. The way in which the pornography itself provides what those who consume it want matters. Pornography *participates* in its audience's eroticism through creating an accessible sexual object, the possession and consumption of which *is* male sexuality, as socially constructed; to be consumed and possessed as which, *is* female sexuality, as socially constructed; and pornography is a process that constructs it that way.

The object world is constructed according to how it looks with respect to its possible uses. Pornography defines women by how we look according to how we can be sexually used. Pornography codes how to look at women, so you know what you can do with one when you see one. Gender is an assignment made visually, both originally and in everyday life. A sex object is defined on the basis of its looks, in terms of its usability for sexual pleasure, such that both the looking—the quality of the gaze, including its point of view—and the definition according to use become eroticized as part of the sex itself. This is what the feminist concept "sex object" means. In this sense, sex in life is no less mediated than it is in art. One could say men have sex with *their image* of a woman. It is not that life and art imitate each other; in this sexuality, they *are* each other.

To give a set of rough epistemological translations, to defend pornography as consistent with the equality of the sexes is to defend the subordination of women to men as sexual equality. What in the pornographic view is love and romance looks a great deal like hatred and torture to the feminist.

Pleasure and eroticism become violation. Desire appears as lust for dominance and submission. The vulnerability of women's projected sexual availability, that acting we are allowed (i.e. asking to be acted upon), is victimization. Play conforms to scripted roles. Fantasy expresses ideology, is not exempt from it. Admiration of natural physical beauty becomes objectification. Harmlessness becomes harm. Pornography is a harm of male supremacy made difficult to see because of its pervasiveness, potency, and, principally, because of its success in making the world a pornographic place. Specifically, its harm cannot be discerned, and will not be addressed, if viewed and approached neutrally, because it *is* so much of "what is." In other words, to the extent pornography succeeds in constructing social reality, it becomes invisible as harm. If we live in a world that pornography creates through the power of men in a male dominated situation the issue is not what the harm of pornography is, but how that harm is to become visible.

II.

Obscenity law provides a very different analysis and conception of the problem. In 1973, the legal definition of obscenity became that which

> the average person, applying contemporary community standards, would find that, taken as a whole, appeals to the prurient interest; that which depicts and describes in a patently offensive way [You feel like you're a cop reading someone's *Miranda* rights] sexual conduct as defined by the applicable state law; and that which, taken as a whole, lacks serious literary, artistic, political or scientific value.

Feminism doubts whether the average gender-neutral person exists; has more questions about the content and process of defining what community standards are than it does about deviations from them; wonders why prurience counts but powerlessness does not, and why sensibilities are better protected from offense than women are from exploitation; defines sexuality, and thus its violation and expropriation, more broadly than does state law; and questions why a body of law which has not in practice been able to tell rape from intercourse should, without further guidance, be entrusted with telling pornography from anything less. Taking the work "as a whole" ignores that which the victims of pornography have long known: Legitimate settings diminish the injury perceived to be done to those whose trivialization and objectification it contextualizes. Besides, and this is a heavy one, if a woman is subjected, why should it matter that the work has other value? Maybe what redeems the work's value is what enhances its injury to women, not to mention that existing standards of literature, art, science, and politics, examined in a feminist light, are remarkably consonant with pornography's mode, meaning, and message. And finally—first and foremost, actually—although the subject of these materials is overwhelmingly women, their contents almost entirely comprised of women's bodies, our invisibility has been such, our equation as a sex *with* sex has been such, that the law of obscenity has never even considered pornography a woman's issue.

Obscenity, in this light, is a moral idea; an idea about judgments of good and bad. Pornography, by contrast, is a political practice, a practice of power and powerlessness. Obscenity is ideational and abstract; pornography is concrete and substantive. The two concepts represent two entirely different things. Nudity, excess of candor, arousal or excitement, prurient appeal, illegality of the acts depicted, and unnaturalness or perversion are all qualities that bother obscenity law when sex is depicted or portrayed. Sex forced on real women so that it can be sold at a profit to be forced on other real women; women's bodies trussed and maimed and raped and made into things to be hurt and obtained and accessed and this presented as the nature of women in a way that is acted on and acted out over and over; the coercion that is visible and the coercion that has become invisible—this and more bothers feminists about pornography. Obscenity as such probably does little harm. Pornography is integral to attitudes and behaviors of violence and discrimination which define the treatment and status of half the population.

III.

At the request of the city of Minneapolis, Andrea Dworkin and I conceived and designed a local human rights ordinance in accordance with our approach to the pornography issue. We define pornography as a practice of sex discrimination, a violation of women's civil rights, the opposite of sexual equality. Its point is to hold accountable, to those who are injured, those who profit from and benefit from that injury. It means that women's injury—our damage, our pain, our enforced inferiority—should outweigh their pleasure and their profits, or sex equality is meaningless.

We define pornography as the graphic sexually explicit subordination of women through pictures or words that also includes women dehumanized as sexual objects, things, or commodities, enjoying pain or humiliation or rape, being tied up, cut up, mutilated, bruised, or physically hurt, in postures of sexual submission or servility or display, reduced to body parts, penetrated by objects or animals, or presented in scenarios of degradation, injury, torture, shown as filthy or inferior, bleeding, bruised, or hurt in a context that makes these conditions sexual. Erotica, defined by distinction as not this, might be sexually explicit materials premised on equality. We also provide that the use of men, children, or transsexuals in the place of women is pornography. The definition is substantive in that it is sex-specific, but it covers everyone in a sex-specific way, so is gender neutral in overall design.

Pornography is a practice of discrimination on the basis of sex, on one level because of its role in creating and maintaining sex as a basis for discrimination. It harms many women one at a time and helps keep all women in an inferior status by defining our subordination as our sexuality and equating that with our gender. It is also sex discrimination because its victims, including men, are selected for victimization on the basis of their gender. But for their sex, they would not be so treated.

The harm of pornography, broadly speaking, is the harm of the civil inequality of the sexes made invisible as harm because it has become accepted as the sex difference. If you see women as just different, even or especially if you don't know that you do, subordination will not look like subordination at all, much less like harm. It will merely look like an appropriate recognition of the sex difference.

Pornography does treat the sexes differently, so the case for sex differentiation can be made here. Men as a group do not tend to be (although some individuals may be) treated like women are treated in pornography. But as a social group, men are not hurt by pornography the way women as a social group are. Their social status is not defined as *less* by it.

Received wisdom seems to be that because there is so little difference between convicted rapists and the rest of the male population in levels and patterns of exposure, response to, and consumption of pornography, pornography's role in rape is insignificant. A more parsimonious explanation of this data is that knowing exposure to, response to, or consumption of pornography will not tell you who will be reported, apprehended, and convicted for rape. But the commonalities such data reveal between convicted rapists and other men are certainly consistent with the fact that only a tiny fraction of rapes ever come to the attention of authorities. It does not make sense to assume that pornography has no role in rape simply because little about its use or effects distinguishes convicted rapists from other men, when we know that a lot of those other men *do* rape women; they just never get caught. In other words, the significance of pornography in acts of forced sex is one thing if sex offenders are considered deviants and another if they are considered relatively nonexceptional except for the fact of their apprehension and incarceration. Professionals who work with that tiny percentage of men who get reported and convicted for such offenses, a group made special only by our ability to assume they once had sex by force in a way that someone (in addition to their victim) eventually regarded as serious, made the following observations about the population they work with. "Pornography is the permission and direction and rehearsal for sexual violence." "[P]ornography is often used by sex offenders as a stimulus to their sexually acting out." It is the "tools of sexual assault," "a way in which they practice" their crimes, "like a loaded gun," "like drinking salt water," "the chemical of sexual addiction." They hypothesize that pornography leads some men to abusiveness out of fear of loss of control that has come to mean masculinity when real women won't accept sex on the one-sided terms that pornography gives and from which they have learned what sex is. "[Because pornography] is reinforcing, [and leads to sexual release, it] leads men to want the experience which they have in photographic fantasy to happen in 'real' life." "They live vicariously through the pictures. Eventually, that is not satisfying enough and they end up acting out sexually." "[S]exual fantasy represents the hope for reality." These professionals are referring to what others are fond of terming "just an idea."

To reach the magnitude of this problem on the scale it exists, our law makes trafficking in pornography—production, sale, exhibition, or distribution—actionable. Under the obscenity rubric, much legal and psychological scholarship has centered on a search for the elusive link between pornography defined as obscenity and harm. They have looked high and low—in the mind of the male consumer, in society or in its "moral fabric," in correlations between variations in levels of antisocial acts and liberalization of obscenity laws. The only harm they have found has been one they have attributed to "the social interest in order and morality." Until recently, no one looked very persistently for harm to women, particularly harm to women through men. The rather obvious fact that the sexes *relate* has been overlooked in the inquiry into the male consumer and his mind. The pornography doesn't just drop out of the sky, go into his head and stop there. Specifically, men rape, batter, prostitute, molest, and sexually harass women. Under conditions of inequality, they also hire, fire, promote, and grade women, decide how much or whether or not we are worth paying and for what, define and approve and disapprove of women in ways that count, that determine our lives.

If women are not just born to be sexually used, the fact that we are seen and treated as though that is what we are born for becomes something in need of explanation. If we see that men relate to women in a pattern of who they see women as being, and that forms a pattern of inequality, it becomes important to ask where that view came from or, minimally, how it is perpetuated or escalated. Asking this requires asking different questions about pornography than the ones obscenity law made salient.

Now I'm going to talk about causality in its narrowest sense. Recent experimental research on pornography shows that the materials covered by our definition cause measurable harm to women through increasing men's attitudes and behaviors of discrimination in both violent and nonviolent forms. Exposure to some of the pornography in our definition increases normal men's immediately subsequent willingness to aggress against women under laboratory conditions. It makes normal men more closely resemble convicted rapists attitudinally, although as a group they don't look all that different from them to start with. It also significantly increases attitudinal measures known to correlate with rape and self-reports of aggressive acts, measures such as hostility toward women, propensity to rape, condoning rape, and predicting that one would rape or force sex on a woman if one knew one would not get caught. This latter measure, by the way, begins with rape at about a third of all men and moves to half with "forced sex."

As to that pornography covered by our definition in which normal research subjects seldom perceive violence, long-term exposure still makes them see women as more worthless, trivial, nonhuman, and object-like, i.e., the way those who are discriminated against are seen by those who discriminate against them. Crucially, all pornography by our definition acts dynamically over time to diminish one's ability to distinguish sex from violence. The materials work behaviorally to diminish the capacity of both men and women to perceive that an account of a rape is an account of a rape. X-only materials, in which subjects perceive no force, also increase perceptions that a rape victim is worthless and decrease the perception she was harmed. The overall direction of current research suggests that the more expressly violent materials accomplish on less exposure what the less overtly violent—that is, the so-called "sex only materials"—accomplish over the longer term. Women are rendered fit for use and targeted for abuse. The only thing that the research cannot document is which individual women will be next on the list. (This cannot be documented experimentally because of ethics constraints on the researchers—constraints which do not operate in life.) Although the targeting is systematic on the basis of sex, it targets individuals at random. They are selected on the basis of roulette. Pornography can no longer be said to be just a mirror. It does not just reflect the world or some people's perceptions. It *moves* them. It increases attitudes that are lived out, circumscribing the status of half the population.

What the experimental data predict would happen, actually does happen in women's real lives. You know, it's fairly frustrating that women have known that these things do happen for some time. As Ed Donnerstein, an experimental researcher in this area, often puts it, "we just quantify the obvious." It is women, primarily, to whom the research results have been the obvious, because we live them. But not until a laboratory study predicts that these things *would* happen, do people begin to believe you when you say they *did* happen to you. There is no—*not any*—inconsistency between the patterns the laboratory studies predict and the data on what actually happens to real women. Show me an abuse of women in society, I'll show it to you made sex in the pornography. If you want to know who is being hurt in this society, go see what is being done and to whom in pornography and then go look for them other places in the world. You will find them being hurt in just that way. We did in our hearings.

In our hearings, women spoke, to my knowledge for the first time in history in public, about the damage pornography does to them. We learned that pornography is used to break women, to train women to sexual submission, to season women, to terrorize women, and to silence their dissent. It is this that has previously been termed "having no effect." Men inflict on women the sex that they experience through the pornography in a way that gives women no choice about seeing the pornography or doing the sex.

Men also testified about how pornography hurts them. One young gay man who had seen *Playboy* and *Penthouse* as a child said of heterosexual pornography:

> It was one of the places I learned about sex and it showed me that sex was violence. What I saw there was a specific relationship between men and women. . . . [T]he woman was to be used, objectified, humiliated and hurt; the man was in a superior position, a position to be violent. In pornography I learned that what it meant to be sexual with a man or to be loved by a man was to accept his violence.

For this reason, when he was battered by his first lover, which he described as "one of the most profoundly destructive experiences of my life," he accepted it.

Pornography also hurts men's capacity to relate to women. One young man spoke about this in a way that connects pornography—not the prohibition on pornography—with fascism.

He spoke of his struggle to repudiate the thrill of dominance, of his difficulty finding connection with a woman to whom he is close. He said:

> My point is that if women in a society filled by pornography must be wary for their physical selves, a man, even a man of good intentions, must be wary for his mind. . . . I do not want to be a mechanical, goose stepping follower of the Playboy bunny, because that is what I think it is . . .

Pornography stimulates and reinforces, it does not cathect or mirror, the connection between one-sided freely available sexual access to women and masculine sexual excitement and sexual satisfaction. The catharsis hypothesis is fantasy. The fantasy theory is fantasy. Reality is: Pornography conditions male orgasm to female subordination. It tells men what sex means, what a real woman is, and codes them together in a way that is behaviorally reinforcing. This is a real five-dollar sentence but I'm going to say it anyway: Pornography is a set of hermeneutical equivalences that work on the epistemological level. Substantively, pornography defines the meaning of what a woman is by connecting access to her sexuality with masculinity through orgasm. The behavioral data show that what pornography means *is* what it does.

So far, opposition to our ordinance centers on the trafficking provision. This means not only that it is difficult to comprehend a group injury in a liberal culture—that what it *means* to be a woman is defined by this and that it is an injury for all women, even if not for all women equally. It is not only that the pornography has got to be accessible, which is the bottom line of virtually every objection to this law. It is also that power, as I said, is when you say something, it is taken for reality. If you talk about rape, it will be agreed that rape is awful. But rape is a conclusion. If a victim describes the facts of a rape, maybe she was asking for it, or enjoyed it, or at least consented to it, or the man might have thought she did, or maybe she had had sex before. It is now agreed that there is something wrong with sexual harassment. But describe what happened to you, and it may be trivial or personal or paranoid, or maybe you should have worn a bra that day. People are against discrimination. But describe the situation of a real woman, and they are not so sure she wasn't just unqualified. In law, all these disjunctions between women's perspective on our injuries and the standards we have to meet go under dignified legal rubrics like burdens of proof, credibility, defenses, elements of the crime, and so on. These standards all contain a definition of what a woman is in terms of what sex is and the low value placed on us through it. They reduce injuries done to us to authentic expressions of who we are. Our silence is written all over them. So is the pornography.

By contrast, we have as yet encountered comparatively little objection to the coercion, force, or assault provisions of our ordinance. I think that's partly because the people who make and approve laws may not yet see what they do as that. They *know* they use the pornography as we have described it in this law, and our law defines that, the reality of pornography, as a harm to women. If they suspect that they might on occasion engage in or benefit from coercion or force or assault, they may think that the victims won't be able to

prove it—and they're right. Women who charge men with sexual abuse are not believed. The pornographic view of them is: They want it; they all want it. When women bring charges of sexual assault, motives such as veniality or sexual repression must be invented, because we cannot really have been hurt. Under the trafficking provision, women's lack of credibility cannot be relied upon to negate the harm. There's no woman's story to destroy, no credibility-based decision on what happened. The hearings establish the harm. The definition sets the standard. The grounds of reality definition are authoritatively shifted. Pornography is bigotry, *period*. We are now—*in* the world pornography has decisively defined—having to meet the burden of proving, once and for all, for all of the rape and torture and battery, all of the sexual harassment, all of the child sexual abuse, all of the forced prostitution, *all* of it that the pornography is part of and that is part of the pornography, that the harm *does happen* and that when it happens it looks like this. Which may be why all this evidence never seems to be enough.

IV.

It is worth considering what evidence has been enough when other harms involving other purported speech interests have been allowed to be legislated against. By comparison to our trafficking section, analytically similar restrictions have been allowed under the first amendment, with a legislative basis far less massive, detailed, concrete, and conclusive. Our statutory language is more ordinary, objective, and precise, and covers a harm far narrower than its legislative record substantiates. Under *Miller*, obscenity was allowed to be made criminal in the name of the "danger of offending the sensibilities of unwilling recipients, or exposure to juveniles." Under our law, we have direct evidence of harm, not just a conjectural danger, that unwilling women in considerable numbers are not simply offended in their sensibilities, but are violated in their persons and restricted in their options. Obscenity law also suggests that the applicable standard for legal adequacy in measuring such connections may not be statistical certainty. The Supreme Court has said that it is not their job to resolve empirical uncertainties that underlie state obscenity legislation. Rather, it is for them to determine whether a legislature could reasonably have determined that a connection might exist between the prohibited material and harm of a kind in which the state has legitimate interest. Equality should be such an area. The Supreme Court recently recognized that prevention of sexual exploitation and abuse of children is, in their words, "a governmental objective of surpassing importance." This might also be the case for sexual exploitation and abuse of women, although I think a civil remedy is initially more appropriate to the goal of empowering adult women than a criminal prohibition would be.

Other rubrics provide further support for the argument that this law is narrowly tailored to further a legitimate governmental interest consistent with the interests underlying the first amendment. Exceptions to the first amendment—you may have gathered from this—exist. The reason they exist is that the harm done by some speech outweighs its expressive value, if any. In our law, a legislature recognizes that pornography, as defined and made actionable, undermines sex equality. One can say—and I have—that pornography is a causal factor in violations of women; one can also say that women will be violated so long as pornography exists; but one can also say simply that pornography violates women. *Chaplinsky v. New Hampshire* recognizes the ability to restrict as "fighting words" speech which, "by [its] very utterance inflicts injury. . . ." Perhaps the only reason that pornography has not been "fighting words"—in the sense of words which by their utterance tend to incite immediate breach of the peace—is that women have seldom fought back, yet.

Some concerns close to those of this ordinance underlie group libel laws, although the differences are equally important. In group libel law, as Justice Frankfurter's opinion in *Beauharnais* illustrates, it has been understood that individuals' treatment and alternatives in life may depend as much on the reputation of the group to which such a person belongs as on their own merit. Not even a partial analogy can be made to group libel doctrine without examining the point made by Justice Brandéis, and recently underlined by Larry Tribe: Would

more speech, rather than less, remedy the harm? In the end, the answer may be yes, but not under the abstract system of free speech, which only enhances the power of the pornographers while doing nothing substantively to guarantee the free speech of women, for which we need civil equality. The situation in which women presently find ourselves with respect to the pornography is one in which more *pornography* is inconsistent with rectifying or even counterbalancing its damage through speech, because so long as the pornography exists in the way it does there *will not be more speech by women*. Pornography strips and devastates women of credibility, from our accounts of sexual assault to our everyday reality of sexual subordination. We are deauthoritized and reduced and devalidated and silenced. Silenced here means that the purposes of the first amendment, premised upon conditions presumed and promoted by protecting free speech, do not pertain to women because they are not our conditions. Consider them: individual self-fulfillment—how does pornography promote our individual self-fulfillment? How does sexual inequality even permit it? Even if she can form words, who listens to a woman with a penis in her mouth? Facilitating consensus—to the extent pornography does so, it does so one-sidedly by silencing protest over the injustice of sexual subordination. Participation in civic life—central to Professor Meiklejohn's theory—how does pornography enhance women's participation in civic life? Anyone who cannot walk down the street or even lie down in her own bed without keeping her eyes cast down and her body clenched against assault is unlikely to have much to say about the issues of the day, still less will she become Tolstoy. Facilitating change—*this law* facilitates the change the existing first amendment theory has been used to throttle. Any system of freedom of expression that does not address a problem where the free speech of men silences the free speech of women, a real conflict between speech interests as well as between people, is not serious about securing freedom of expression in this country.

For those of you who still think pornography is only an idea, consider the possibility that obscenity law got one thing right. Pornography is more act-like than thought-like. The fact that pornography, in a feminist view, furthers the idea of the sexual inferiority of women, which is a political idea, doesn't make the pornography itself into a political idea. One can express the idea a practice embodies. That does not make that practice into an idea. Segregation expresses the idea of the inferiority of one group to another on the basis of race. That does not make segregation an idea. A sign that says "Whites Only" is only words. Is it therefore protected by the first amendment? Is it not an act, a practice, of segregation because of the inseparability of what it means from what it does? *Law* is only words.

The issue here is whether the fact that the central link in the cycle of abuse that I have connected is words and pictures will immunize that entire cycle, about which we cannot do anything without doing something about the pornography. As Justice Stewart said in *Ginsburg*, "When expression occurs in a setting where the capacity to make a choice is absent, government regulation of that expression may coexist with and *even implement* First Amendment guarantees." I would even go so far as to say that the pattern of evidence we have closely approaches Justice Douglas' requirement that "freedom of expression can be suppressed if, and to the extent that, it is so closely brigaded with illegal action as to be an inseparable part of it." Those of you who have been trying to separate the acts from the speech—that's an act, that's an act, there's a law against that act, regulate that act, don't touch the speech—*notice here* that the fact that the acts involved are illegal doesn't mean that the speech that is "brigaded with" *it, cannot* be regulated. It is when it *can* be.

I take one of two penultimate points from Andrea Dworkin, who has often said that pornography is not speech for women, it is the silence of women.

The most basic assumption underlying first amendment adjudication is that, socially, speech is free. The first amendment says Congress shall not abridge the freedom of speech. Free speech, get it, *exists.* Those who wrote the first amendment *had* speech—they wrote the Constitution. *Their* problem was to keep it free from the only power that realistically threatened it: the federal government. They designed the first amendment to prevent government from constraining that which if unconstrained by government was free, meaning *accessible to them.* At the same time, we can't tell much about the intent of the Framers with regard to the question of women's speech, because I don't think we crossed their minds. It is consistent with this analysis that their posture to freedom of speech tends to presuppose that whole segments of the population are not systematically silenced, socially, prior to government action. If everyone's power were equal to theirs, if this were a non-hierarchical society, that might make sense. But the place of pornography in the inequality of the sexes makes the assumption of equal power untrue.

This is a hard question. It involves risks. Classically, opposition to censorship has involved keeping government off the backs of people. Our law is about getting some people off the backs of other people. The risks that it will be misused have to be measured against the risks of the status quo. Women will never have that dignity, security, compensation that is the promise of equality so long as the pornography exists as it does now. The situation of women suggests that the urgent issue of our freedom of speech is not primarily the avoidance of state intervention as such, but getting affirmative access to speech for those to whom it has been denied.

DISCUSSION QUESTIONS

1. Why does MacKinnon think people tend to react to claims about women's abuse—rape, harassment, battery—with claims that men can undergo these harms as well?

2. What is MacKinnon's definition of pornography? Given this definition, how does pornography harm women in ways that it does not harm men?

3. Explain MacKinnon's argument that pornography eroticizes gendered relationships of dominance and submission.

4. Why does MacKinnon think existing obscenity laws are insufficient and inappropriate to address the harms of pornography?

5. Explain MacKinnon's argument that because pornography silences women, it is mistaken to presuppose that women have free speech, and thus mistaken to think that the solution to the harms of pornography is to encourage competing speech rather than to censor pornographic speech.

NOTES

1. *See* M. Amir, Patterns in Forcible Rape, 229–252 (1971); *See also* N. Gager & C. Schurr, Sexual Assault: Confronting Rape in America (1976); D. Russell, Sexual Exploitation *supra* note 20.
2. A. Dworkin, Pornography: Men Possessing Women (1981).

Erotica and Pornography: A Clear and Present Difference

BY GLORIA STEINEM

Gloria Steinem is an American journalist whose influential feminist activism made her one of the leaders of the American second wave feminist movement. In this influential and accessible essay, Steinem provides a practical test for distinguishing erotica from pornography, arguing that erotica features mutually pleasurable and consensual sexual expression premised on equality, while pornography features violent or dominating sexual expression intended to create or reinforce inequality.

No wonder the concepts of "erotica" and "pornography" can be so crucially different, and yet so confused. Both assume that sexuality can be separated from conception, and therefore can be used to carry a personal message. That's a major reason why, even in our current culture, both may be called equally "shocking" or legally "obscene," a word whose Latin derivative means "dirty, containing, filth." This gross condemnation of all sexuality that isn't harnessed to childbirth and marriage has been increased by the current backlash against women's progress. Out of fear that the whole patriarchal structure might be upset if women really had the autonomous power to decide our reproductive futures (that is, if we controlled the most basic means of production), right-wing groups are not only denouncing prochoice abortion literature as "pornographic," but are trying to stop the sending of all contraceptive information through the mails by invoking obscenity laws. In fact, Phyllis Schlafly recently denounced the entire Women's Movement as "obscene."

Not surprisingly, this religious, visceral backlash has a secular, intellectual counterpart that relies heavily on applying the "natural" behavior of the animal world to humans. That is questionable in itself, but these Lionel Tiger-ish studies make their political purpose even more clear in the particular animals they select and the habits they choose to emphasize.[1] The message is that females should accept their "destiny" of being sexually dependent and devote themselves to bearing and rearing their young.

Defending against such reaction in turn leads to another temptation: to merely reverse the terms, and declare that *all* nonprocreative sex is good. In fact, however, this human activity can be as constructive or destructive, moral or immoral, as any other. Sex as communication can send messages as different as life and death; even the origins of "erotica" and "pornography" reflect that fact. After all, "erotica" is rooted in *eros* or passionate love, and thus in the idea of positive choice, free will, the yearning for a particular person. (Interestingly, the definition of erotica leaves open the question of gender.) "Pornography" begins with a root meaning "prostitution" or "female captives," thus letting us know that the subject is not mutual love, or love at all, but domination and violence against women. (Though, of course, homosexual pornography may imitate this violence by putting a man in the "feminine" role of victim.) It ends with a root meaning "writing about" or "description of" which puts still more distance between subject and object, and replaces a spontaneous yearning for closeness with objectification and a voyeur.

The difference is clear in the words. It becomes even more so by example.

Look at any photo or film of people making love; really making love. The images may be diverse, but there is usually a sensuality and touch and warmth, an acceptance of bodies and nerve endings. There is always a spontaneous sense of people who are there because they *want* to be, out of shared pleasure.

Now look at any depiction of sex in which there is clear force, or an unequal power that spells coercion. It may be very blatant, with weapons of torture or bondage, wounds and bruises, some clear humiliation, or an adult's sexual power being used over a child. It may be much more subtle: a physical attitude of conqueror and victim, the use of race or class difference to imply the same thing, perhaps a very unequal nudity, with one person exposed and vulnerable while the other is clothed. In either case, there is no sense of equal choice or equal power.

The first is erotic: a mutually pleasurable, sexual expression between people who have enough power to be there by positive choice. It may or may not strike a sense-memory in the viewer, or be creative enough to make the unknown seem real; but it doesn't require us to identify with a conqueror or a victim. It is truly sensuous, and may give us a contagion of pleasure.

The second is pornographic: its message is violence, dominance and conquest. It is sex being used to reinforce some inequality, or to create one, or to tell us the lie that pain and humiliation (ours or someone else's) are really the same as pleasure. If we are to feel anything, we must identify with conqueror or victim. That means we can only experience pleasure through the adoption of some degree of sadism or masochism. It also means that we may feel diminished by the role of conqueror, or enraged, humiliated, and vengeful by sharing identity with the victim.

Perhaps one could simply say that erotica is about sexuality, but pornography is about power and sex-as-weapon—in the same way we have come to understand that rape is about violence, and not really about sexuality at all.

Yes, it's true that there are women who have been forced by violent families and dominating men to confuse love with pain; so much so that they have become masochists. (A fact that in no way excuses those who administer such pain.) But the truth is that, for most women—and for men with enough humanity to imagine themselves into the predicament of women—true pornography could serve as aversion therapy for sex.

Of course, there will always be personal differences about what is and is not erotic, and there may be cultural differences for a long time to come. Many women feel that sex makes them vulnerable and therefore may continue to need more sense of personal connection and safety before allowing any erotic feelings. We now find competence and expertise erotic in men, but that may pass as we develop those qualities in ourselves. Men, on the other hand, may continue to feel less vulnerable, and therefore more open to such potential danger as sex with strangers. As some men replace the need for submission from childlike women with the pleasure of cooperation from equals, they may find a partner's competence to be erotic, too.

Such group changes plus individual differences will continue to be reflected in sexual love between people of the same gender, as well as between women and men. The point is not to dictate sameness, but to discover ourselves and each other through sexuality that is an exploring, pleasurable, empathetic part of our lives; a human sexuality that is unchained both from unwanted pregnancies and from violence.

But that is a hope, not a reality. At the moment, fear of change is increasing both the indiscriminate repression of all nonprocreative sex in the religious and "conservative" male world, and the pornographic vengeance against women's sexuality in the secular world of "liberal" or "radical" men. It's almost futuristic to debate what is and is not truly erotic, when many women are again being forced into compulsory motherhood, and the number of pornographic murders, tortures, and woman-hating images are on the increase in both popular culture and real life.

It's a familiar division: wife or whore, "good" woman who is constantly vulnerable to pregnancy or "bad" woman who is unprotected from violence. *Both* roles would be upset if we were to control our own sexuality. And that's exactly what we must do.

In spite of all our atavistic suspicions and training for the "natural" role of motherhood, we took up the complicated battle for reproductive freedom. Our bodies had borne the health burden of endless births and poor abortions, and we had a greater motive for separating sexuality and conception.

Now we have to take up the equally complex burden of explaining that all nonprocreative sex is *not* alike. We have a motive: our right to a uniquely human sexuality, and sometimes even to survival. As it is, our bodies have too rarely been enough our own to develop erotica in our own lives, much less in art and literature. And our bodies have too often been the objects of pornography and the woman-hating, violent practice that it preaches. Consider also our spirits that break a little each time we see ourselves in chains or full labial display for the conquering male viewer, bruised or on our knees, screaming a real or pretended pain to delight the sadist, pretending to enjoy what we don't enjoy, to be blind to the images of our sisters that really haunt us—humiliated often enough ourselves by the truly obscene idea that sex and the domination of women must be combined.

Sexuality *is* human, free, separate—and so are we.

But until we untangle the lethal confusion of sex with violence, there will be more pornography and less erotica. There will be little murders in our beds—and very little love.

DISCUSSION QUESTIONS

1. What are the etymological roots of the words "erotica" and "pornography"? Describe the roles of choice and coercion in differentiating between erotica and pornography.

2. Explain how cultural forces can influence what people find erotic, and how Steinem hopes the women's movement might change this for the better.

3. Explain how both the "religious and 'conservative' male world" and the "secular world of 'liberal' or 'radical' men" fail to address feminist concerns about pornography.

NOTE

1. See "The Law of the Jungle (Revised)," *by* Cynthia Moss, Ms., January, 1978.

Pornutopia

BY NANCY BAUER

Nancy Bauer is an American philosopher specializing in feminist philosophy, existentialism and phenomenology, and the work of Simone de Beauvoir. In this essay, Bauer argues that pornography constructs its own world—the pornutopia— with its own rules about respectful interactions. Within this fictional world, she argues, there is no sexual objectification. Instead, respecting another person involves treating them like a sex object. Instead of wringing their hands about the content of pornography, Bauer argues, feminists should work to articulate how this fictional world affects us in the real world.

My fellow feminist philosophers have produced an enormous literature on what's wrong with sexual objectification. Their abiding faith in reason's ability to quash desire has resulted in a certain consensus on how to condemn these urges. The standard tactic is to define objectification as "treating a person like an object." You give an analysis of what an "object" is (something that can be owned and therefore used or transformed or destroyed), and sometimes what "treating" comes to (not just conceiving of a person as a thing, but reducing her to that status). Then you argue that people are not like objects in certain important ways (because people are autonomous, for example) and that to treat people in these ways is to violate their humanity.

There's nothing particularly controversial in this analysis. That's precisely the problem with it. No one argues that people are the same as things and so can always be treated in the same way. We don't need a philosopher's help to grasp that to the extent that pornography objectifies people, and to the extent that this objectification is dehumanizing, it's morally problematic.

No philosophical analysis of pornographic objectification will enlighten us unless it proceeds not from the outside, from the external standpoint of academic moralism, but from the inside, from a description of pornography's powers to arouse. Such a description reveals that, within the pornographic mise-en-scène, there is no space for the concept of objectification. The world as pornography depicts it is a utopia in which the conflict between reason and sexual desire is eliminated, in which to use another person solely as a means to satisfy one's own desire is the ultimate way to respect that person's humanity and even humanity in general.

In the real world, the unbridled expression of sexual desire is fundamentally incompatible with civilization, and in every culture there are harsh punishments for those whose lust gets the better of them. Most of us, the lucky ones, can discipline ourselves, more or less, not to act on our sexual urges when we don't think we should. We sublimate, harnessing our sexual vitality in the service of advancing civility and civilization.

In pornographic representation, civilization, though it sometimes gamely tries to assert itself, always ultimately surrenders to lust. But sexual desire is shown to be a gentlemanly victor: rather than destroy civilization, it repatriates it. Civilization pledges to uphold the laws of the pornutopia, in which the ordinary perils of sexual communion simply don't exist. Everyone has sex whenever the urge strikes, and civilization hums along as usual: people go to work and school, the mail gets delivered, commerce thrives. The good citizens of the porn world, inexorably ravenous, are also perfectly sexually compatible with one another. Everyone is desired by everyone he or she desires. Serendipitously, as it always turns out, to gratify yourself sexually by imposing your desires on another person is automatically to gratify that person as well.

Here, we see Kant turned on his head. Rather than encouraging us to live as though in a kingdom in which our common capacity for rationality enjoins us to regard all people, ourselves included, as ends-in-themselves, the porn world encourages us to treat ourselves and others as pure means. And what's supposed to license this vision is the idea that desire, not reason, is fundamentally the same from person to person, as though our personal idiosyncrasies were merely generic and reason could have no role to play in a true, and truly moral, sexual utopia.

In the pornutopia, autonomy takes the form of exploring and acting on your sexual desires when and in whatever way you like; to respect your own and other people's humanity, all you have to do is indulge your own sexual spontaneity. No one in the pornutopia has a reason to lose interest in or fear or get bored by sex; no one suffers in a way that can't be cured by it; no one is homeless or dispossessed or morally or spiritually abused or lost. When Daddy fucks Becky, she doesn't experience it as rape. She comes.

Twenty years after the porn wars raged at their height, the triumph of pornography is everywhere evident. Its imagery is just a couple of clicks away for anyone with an internet connection or a cable-TV remote.

According to the old battle lines, the pornographization of everyday life constitutes a victory for the proponents of free speech and a defeat for conservative moralists and radical feminists. But we are past the point, if we ever were there, at which a bipolar politics of pornography, for or against, could be of use to us. It does not help us understand the massive proliferation of porn since the mid-'80s if we insist on analyzing it in terms of free

speech protections or advancements in artistic expression or, on the other side, as incitements to violence against women or a sign of moral lassitude.

We lack the words to articulate the role of pornography in our lives. What we need now is not a new politics of porn but, rather, a candid *phenomenology* of it, an honest reckoning with its powers to produce intense pleasure and to color our ordinary sense of what the world is and ought to be like. Such a reckoning will have to involve a refocusing of our attention, from the male consumers who took center stage in the porn wars to the women for whom the pornutopia provides a new standard both of beauty and of sexual fulfillment. Contemporary pornography is noteworthy for cataloguing the incredibly huge range of things that get our blood flowing. The Meese Commission's interminable list of fetish magazines hardly makes a start on the project. Look on the internet and you will find websites devoted to people who are sexually excited by the sound of balloons popping (and those who find these people disgusting because *they* think that what's sexy about balloons is blowing them up to just *before* the popping point); instructions on how to make love with a dolphin (including an exhortation to go back to the sea the next day to reassure the dolphin that you still respect her, or him); advice on how to tie your leg up so that other people will think it's amputated and stare at you, or how to find a doctor who will actually amputate a limb or digit for you (possibilities which some amputee-obsessed people find sexy and others experience as lifesaving in roughly the way, they say, that transgendered people experience coming out).[1]

Part of the process of becoming civilized—of becoming a genuinely human being—is learning to keep the finer details of your sexual longing to yourself and your consenting intimates. Freud occasionally voiced the view that we are inclined to move too far in that direction: we overestimate the extent to which civilization is incompatible with sexual expression. (I am thinking here of what he says in *Civilization and Its Discontents* about the persecution of homosexuals.) Freud didn't have a T1 connection and so could not possibly have imagined just how polymorphously perverse we human beings are, but I don't think that the vast array of pornography on the web would have fazed him. It might even have pleased him, for pornography allows us to explore and even come to grips with our sexual desire in all its quirks and moral instability. It enables the discovery that the twists and turns of one's erotic longing are not sui generis, that no one is a true sexual freak. Insofar as it substitutes for the psychoanalyst's couch, it can increase our real-world sexual self-awareness.

That ought to be a good thing. But it is not clear what will happen to pornography's power to enlighten us about ourselves, what the cost of it might come to be, as the everyday world gets more and more pornographized and as we accustom ourselves to the mindless enjoyment of all the twinges of arousal that ordinary culture increasingly represents as our birthright.

More than fifty years ago, Simone de Beauvoir observed in *The Second Sex* that, for women, the line between full personhood and complete self-objectification is whisper thin. A genuinely human being, Beauvoir argued, is one who experiences herself as both a subject and an object—and at the same time. A subject, she said, is a being who has the wherewithal to express her sense of what matters in the world, to dare to have a say in it. But part of being a subject, Beauvoir thought, is allowing yourself to be the object of other people's judgment, rational or irrational: to risk being ridiculed or condemned or ignored or, worse, to find yourself convinced that the harsh judgments of others are true—or, maybe worst of all, to be confused about these judgments, to discover that, after all, you don't know who you are.

For Beauvoir herself, the path to humanity took the form of writing about her own experience as that of a representative human being. She was daring to test whether, to invoke Emerson's famous formulation, what she knew in her own heart was true for all people. But the second half of her groundbreaking book is all about how difficult true self-expression is for women. The world sets things up so that we are wildly tempted to expose ourselves to public judgment, yes. But the vehicle of this exposure is not supposed to be self-expression. It's supposed to be self-objectification.

Women are rewarded—we are *still* rewarded—for suppressing our own nascent desires and intuitions and turning ourselves into objects that please the sensibilities of men. It's because it threatens the man-pleasing enterprise that feminism long ago hit a wall as a political movement. The very idea that we are now in some sort of post-feminist era hints at our extraordinary "separate but equal" schizophrenia: we believe that we have achieved full social parity with men, and we take this supposed achievement to license a hyperbolic reinvestment in feminine narcissism. Everywhere we turn we find images daring women of all sexual temperaments to revel in and express their fuckability, as though a woman's transforming herself into the ultimate object of desire should or could satisfy her need for other people to attend to the depth and breadth of her true self, even her true sexual self.

"Look—but don't touch." That's the incoherent rule that used to govern displays of feminine self-objectification. It enjoined women to take their pleasure in arousing desire in men and then withholding the satisfaction of this desire. Some pleasure. Some rule. But the new rule, having emerged from the pornographic subterranean and now ubiquitously shoved in our faces—"Don't just look—touch!"—has proved to be even more bizarre. It makes sense in the pornutopia, where everyone arouses everyone else's desire, and physical contact between and among human beings inevitably leads to orgasm all the way around.

Its oddness in the real world emerges in my female students' explanation for spending their weekend evenings giving unreciprocated blow jobs to drunken frat boys: they tell me they enjoy the sense of power it gives them. You doll yourself up and get some guy helplessly aroused, at which point you *could* just walk away. But you don't. Instead, you take pleasure in arousing the would-be fellatee's desire—and then *not* withholding the satisfaction of it. The source of the first phase of this pleasure is easy to identify, since it is identical to the pleasure afforded women under the old order of female narcissism. It's the pleasure of reveling in someone else's discomfort and frustration—in a word, of sadism. Women who play by the rules—that is, women who wish to survive in a man's world, rather than undertake the daunting work of attempting to transform it—have always been tempted to substitute the pleasures of sadism for the pleasures (and pains) of Beauvoirian subjectivity. But we still have the question of what pleasure there could be, as a young woman affects to walk away from her prey, in turning around and allaying the discomfort and frustration she worked so hard to produce.

I don't want to condescend to my students, and I don't want to speak for them. But I wish I could understand, at least, why they have so little interest in being serviced in return. An astonishingly large number of girls, as they have reverted to calling themselves, have told me that they feel more comfortable confronting a strange man's exposed hard-on than exposing their own, always shaven, vulvas. (We now live in a world where no part of a woman's body is too private to be subject to public standards of beauty.) Here, we are beyond the point of self-objectification. You forgo your own pleasure, be it sadistic or orgasmic, for the sake of another person's; you perhaps experience discomfort and frustration as you carry out this sacrifice; and then you find yourself not just pretending to enjoy, but actually reveling in your own self-effacement.

My students' experience in their sexual interactions with men confirms the logic of the pornutopia: to please someone else sexually is to please yourself, and there's no reason to wonder whether what's making you happy is something that you really desire, or whether you're really fulfilled at all. One wonders: could the pleasure of providing some guy with an unreciprocated blow job be the pleasure of masochism? Of martyrdom, even? Or if it is an internalization of the logic of the pornutopia, what precisely has driven it, and what sustains it in the face of the realities of real-world sexuality? I find that when I ask my students what sense they can make of their experience, they, like all of us, are at a loss for words.

DISCUSSION QUESTIONS

1. How do Bauer's criticisms of pornography differ from more standard feminist criticisms?

2. Explain how the rules for respecting another person are different in the pornutopia than they are in the real world.

3. Bauer thinks the ubiquity of pornography affects people in both positive and negative ways. Describe these effects. Are all of them the same for women as they are for men?

NOTE

1. Carl Elliott, a philosopher at the University of Minnesota who a few years ago in an article in the *Atlantic Monthly* brought wide attention to the phenomenon of voluntary amputation, has raised the question of whether perversions are contagious: whether you can catch one simply from becoming aware of it. It may well be the case that certain sexual preferences are largely a function of learning what's out there. But this does not change the fact that there's a whole lot out there.

Beyond Racism and Misogyny: Black Feminism and 2 Live Crew

BY KIMBERLÉ CRENSHAW

Kimberlé Crenshaw is an American civil rights advocate and a leading scholar of critical race theory. In this essay, Crenshaw discusses the arrests, trial, and obscenity charges against members of the rap group 2 Live Crew. In so doing, she demonstrates the complications of intersectional oppression and argues that collective resistance to racism must not come at the expense of the continued subordination of women.

In June 1990, the members of the rap group 2 Live Crew were arrested and charged under a Florida obscenity statute for their performance in an adults-only club in Hollywood, Florida. The arrests came just two days after a federal court judge had ruled that the sexually explicit lyrics in 2 Live Crew's album, *As Nasty as They Wanna Be*, were obscene. Although the members of 2 Live Crew were eventually acquitted of charges stemming from the live performance, the federal court determination that *As Nasty as They Wanna Be* is obscene still stands. This obscenity judgment, along with the arrests and the subsequent trial, prompted an intense public controversy about rap music, a controversy that merged with a broader debate about the representation of sex and violence in popular music, about cultural diversity, and about the meaning of freedom of expression.

• • •

Two positions dominated the debate about 2 Live Crew. Writing in *Newsweek*, political columnist George Will staked out a case against the Crew, arguing that *Nasty* was misogynistic filth and characterizing their lyrics as a profoundly repugnant "combination of extreme infantilism and menace" that objectified black women and represented them as legitimate targets for sexual violence.

The most prominent defense of 2 Live Crew was advanced by Professor Henry Louis Gates, Jr., an expert on African-American literature. In a *New York Times* op-ed piece, and in testimony at the criminal trial, Gates portrayed 2 Live Crew as brilliant artists who were inventively elaborating distinctively African-American forms of cultural expression. Furthermore, Gates argued, the characteristic exaggeration featured in their lyrics served a political end: to explode popular racist stereotypes about black sexuality precisely by presenting those stereotypes in a comically extreme form. Where Will saw a misogynistic assault on black women by social degenerates, Gates found a form of 'sexual carnivalesque' freighted with the promise to free us from the pathologies of racism.

• • •

As a black feminist, I felt the pull of each of these poles, but not the compelling attractions of either. My immediate response to the criminal charges against 2 Live Crew was ambivalence: I wanted to stand together with the brothers against a racist attack, but I wanted to stand against a frightening explosion of violent imagery directed at women like me. My sharp internal division—my dissatisfaction with the idea that the "real issue" is race or that the "real issue" is gender—is characteristic of my experience as a black woman living at the intersection of racial and sexual subordination. To that experience black feminism offers an intellectual and political response: aiming to bring together the different aspects of an otherwise divided sensibility, it argues that black women are commonly marginalized by a politics of race alone or gender alone, and that a political response to either form of subordination must be a political response to both. When the controversy over 2 Live Crew is approached in light of such black feminist sensibilities, an alternative to the dominant poles of the public debate emerges.

At the legal "bottom line" I agree with the supporters of 2 Live Crew that the obscenity prosecution was wrongheaded. But the reasons for my conclusion are not the same as the reasons generally offered in support of 2 Live Crew. I will come to those reasons shortly, but first I should emphasize that after listening to 2 Live Crew's lyrics, along with those of other rap artists, my defense of 2 Live Crew, (qualified though it is) did not come easy.

The first time I listened to 2 Live Crew, I was stunned. The issue had been distorted by descriptions of "As Nasty as They Wanna Be" as simply "sexually explicit." "Nasty" is much more: it is virulently misogynist, sometimes violently so. Black women are cunts, "'ho's," and all-purpose bitches: raggedy bitches, sorry-ass bitches, lowdown slimy-ass bitches. Good sex is often portrayed as painful and humiliating for women.

This is no mere braggadocio. Those of us who are concerned about the high rates of gender violence in our communities must be troubled by the possible connections between these images and tolerance for violence against women. Children and teenagers are listening to this music, and I am concerned that the range of acceptable behavior is being broadened by the constant propagation of anti-women imagery. I'm concerned, too, about young black women who, like young men, are learning that their value lies between their legs. Unlike men, however, their sexual value is a depletable commodity; by expending it, girls become whores and boys become men.

Nasty is misogynist, and a black feminist response to the case against 2 Live Crew must start from a full acknowledgment of that misogyny. But such a response must also consider whether an exclusive focus on issues of gender risks overlooking aspects of the prosecution of 2 Live Crew that raise

serious questions of racism. And here is where the roots of my opposition to the obscenity prosecution lie.

• • •

An initial problem concerning the prosecution was its apparent selectivity. A comparison between 2 Live Crew and other mass-marketed sexual representations suggests that race played some role in distinguishing 2 Live Crew as the first group ever to be prosecuted for obscenity in connection with a musical recording, and one of only a handful of recording artists to be prosecuted for a live performance. Recent controversies about sexism, racism, and violence in popular culture point to a vast range of expression that might well provide targets for censorship, but that have not been targeted. Madonna has acted out masturbation, portrayed the seduction of a priest, and depicted group sex on stage, yet she has never been prosecuted for obscenity. Moreover, graphic sexual images—many of them violent—were widely available in Broward County where the performance and trial took place. According to the trial testimony of Vice Detective McCloud, "nude dance shows and adult bookstores are scattered throughout the county where 2 Live Crew performed." But again, no obscenity charges were leveled against the performers or producers of these representations.

To clarify this argument, we need to consider the technical use of "obscenity" as a legal term of art. For the purposes of legal argument, the Supreme Court in the 1973 case of Miller v. California held that a work is obscene if and only if it meets each of three conditions: (1) "the average person, applying community standards, would find that the work, taken as a whole, appeals to the prurient interest"; (2) "the work depicts or describes, in a patently offensive way, sexual conduct specifically defined by the applicable state law"; and (3) "the work, taken as a whole, lacks serious literary, artistic, political, or scientific value." The Court held that it is consistent with First Amendment guarantees of freedom of expression for states to subject work that meets all three parts of the Miller test to very restrictive regulations.

An additional concern has as much to do with the obscenity doctrine itself as with the court's application of it to 2 Live Crew. The case illustrates the ways that obscenity doctrine invites racially selective enforcement while at the same time pressing into focus the wrong questions about sexual expression.

As I mentioned earlier, obscenity requires a determination that the material, taken as a whole, appeals to the prurient interest. Although the prurient interest requirement eludes precise definition it seems clear that prurient material must appeal in some immediate way to sexual desire. While it is difficult to say definitively what constitutes such an appeal, one might surmise that the twenty-five-cent peep shows that are standard fare in Broward County rank considerably higher on this scale than the sexual tall tales of 2 Live Crew. But the obscenity doctrine is, as justice Stevens said, "intolerably vague," and the result is that "grossly disparate treatment of similar offenders is a characteristic of the criminal enforcement of obscenity law." More precisely, as the case of 2 Live Crew suggests, the vagueness of the doctrine operating in a world of racial subordination represents an invitation to racially selective enforcement.

While 2 Live Crew should be one of the lesser candidates in the prurient interests sweepstakes mandated by the obscenity doctrine, it is also a lesser contender by another measure that lies entirely outside of obscenity: violence. Compared to such groups as N.W.A., Too Short, Ice Cube, and the Geto Boys, 2 Live Crew's misogynistic hyperbole sounds minor league. Sometimes called "gangsta' rap," the lyrics offered by these other groups celebrate violent assault, rape, rape-murder, and mutilation. Nevertheless, had these other groups been targeted rather than the comparatively less offensive 2 Live Crew, they may have been more successful in defeating the prosecution. The graphic violence in their representations militates against a finding of obscenity by suggesting an appeal not to prurient interests but instead to the fantasy of the social outlaw. Against an historical backdrop that prominently features the image of the black male as social outlaw, gangsta' rap might be read as a subversive form of opposition that aims to challenge social convention precisely by becoming the very social outlaw that society

has proscribed. For this reason, their lyrics might even be read as political, and if they are political they are not obscene. So long, then, as prurience remains an obsession of First Amendment argument, and violent imagery is seen as distinct from sexuality, rap artists may actually be able to strengthen their legal shield by heightening the level of violence in their lyrics.

I do not mean to suggest here that the distinction between sex and violence ought to be maintained in obscenity, nor, more specifically, that the violent rappers ought to be protected. To the contrary, these groups trouble me much more than 2 Live Crew does. My point instead is to emphasize that the obscenity doctrine itself does nothing to protect the interests of those who are most directly implicated in such rap—black women. Because the doctrine is vague, it opens the door to selecting offenders on the basis of race, Because it separates out sexuality and violence, it shields the most violently misogynistic rappers from prosecution. For black women who are hurt by both racism and misogyny, it does no good at all.

Although black women's interests were quite obviously irrelevant in this obscenity judgment, their bodies figured prominently in the public case supporting the targeting of 2 Live Crew. This brings me to my final concern: George Will's *Newsweek* essay provides a striking example of how black women were appropriated and deployed in the broader attack against 2 Live Crew. Commenting on "America's Slide into the Sewers," Will tells us that "America today is capable of terrific intolerance about smoking, or toxic waste that threatens trout. But only a deeply confused society is more concerned about protecting lungs than minds, trout than black women. We legislate against smoking in restaurants; singing 'Me So Horny' is a constitutional right. Secondary smoke is carcinogenic; celebration of torn vaginas is 'mere words.'"

These considerations about selectivity, about the denial of cultural specificity, and about the manipulation of black women's bodies convince me that race played a significant if not determinative role in the shaping of the case against 2 Live Crew. While using anti-sexist rhetoric to suggest a concern for women, the attack simultaneously endorsed traditional readings of black male sexuality. The fact that most perpetrators and victims are of the same race is overshadowed by the mythical image of the black male as the agent of sexual violence and the white community as his victim. The subtext of the 2 Live Crew prosecution thus becomes a re-reading of the sexualized racial politics of the past.

• • •

While concerns about racism fuel my opposition to the obscenity prosecution, I am also troubled by the uncritical support for, and indeed celebration of, 2 Live Crew by other opponents of that prosecution. If the rhetoric of anti-sexism provided an occasion for racism, so, too, the rhetoric of anti-racism provided an occasion for defending the misogyny of black male rappers.

The defense of 2 Live Crew took two forms, one political and one cultural, both of which were advanced most prominently by Henry Louis Gates. The political argument was that 2 Live Crew represents an attack on black sexual stereotypes. The strategy of the attack is, in Gates's words, to "exaggerate [the] stereotypes" and thereby "to show how ridiculous the portrayals are." Thus, Gates concludes, 2 Live Crew and other rap groups are simply pushing white society's buttons to ridicule its dominant sexual images.

I agree with Gates that the reactions by Will and others to 2 Live Crew confirm that the stereotypes still exist and still evoke basic fears. But even if I were to agree that 2 Live Crew intended to explode these mythic fears, I still would argue that their strategy was wholly misguided. These fears are too active, and African-Americans are too closely associated with them, not to be burned when the myths are exploded. More fundamentally, however, I am deeply skeptical about the claim that the Crew was engaged—either in intent or effect—in pursuing a postmodern guerilla war against racist stereotypes.

Gates argues that when one listens to 2 Live Crew the ridiculous stories and the hyperbole make the listener "bust out laughing." Apparently the fact that Gates and many other people react with laughter confirms and satisfies the Crew's objective of ridiculing the stereotypes. But the

fact that the Crew are often successful in prompting laughter neither substantiates Gates's reading nor forecloses serious critique of its subordinating dimensions.

In disagreeing with Gates, I do not mean to suggest that 2 Live Crew's lyrics are to be taken literally. But rather than exploding stereotypes as Gates suggests, I believe that they were simply using readily available sexual images in trying to be funny. Trading in racial stereotypes and sexual hyperbole are well-rehearsed strategies for getting some laughs. 2 Live Crew departs from this tradition only in its attempt to up the ante through more outrageous boasts and more explicit manifestations of misogyny. Neither the intent to be funny, nor Gates's loftier explanations, negate the subordinating qualities of such humor.

Sexual humor in which women are objectified as packages of body parts to serve whatever male-bonding/male competition needs men have subordinates women in much the same way that racist humor subordinates African-Americans. That these are "just jokes" and not meant to be taken literally does little to blunt their demeaning quality—nor for that matter, does the fact that the jokes are told within a tradition of intra-group humor.

Gates advances a second, cultural defense of 2 Live Crew: the idea that Nasty is in line with distinctively African-American traditions of culture and entertainment. It is true that the "dozens" and other forms of verbal boasting have been practiced within the black community for some time. It is true as well that raunchy jokes, insinuations, and boasting of sexual prowess were not meant to be taken literally. Nor were they meant to disrupt conventional myths about black sexuality. They were meant simply to be laughed at, and perhaps to gain respect for the speaker's word wizardry.

Ultimately, however, little turns on whether the "word play" performed by 2 Live Crew is a postmodern challenge to racist sexual mythology or simply an internal group practice that has crossed over into mainstream America. Both versions of the defense are problematic because they each call on black women to accept misogyny and its attendant disrespect in service of some broader group objective. While one version argues that accepting misogyny is necessary to anti-racist politics, the other argues that it is necessary to maintaining the cultural integrity of the community. But neither presents a sufficient reason for black women to tolerate such misogyny. The message that these arguments embrace—that patriarchy can be made to serve anti-racist ends is a familiar one. In Gates's variant, the position of black women is determined by the need to wield gargantuan penises in a struggle to ridicule racist images of black male sexuality. Even though black women may not be the intended targets, they are necessarily attached to these gargantuan penises and are thus made to absorb the impact. The common message of all such strategies is that black women are expected to be vehicles for notions of "liberation" that function to preserve their own subordination.

To be sure, Gates's claims about the cultural aspects of 2 Live Crew's lyrics do address the legal issue about the applicability of the obscenity standard. As I indicated earlier, their music does have artistic value: I believe the Court decided this issue incorrectly and Will was all-too-glib in his dismissal of it. But these criticisms do not settle the issue within the community. "Dozens" and other word plays have long been a black oral tradition, but acknowledging this fact does not eliminate the need to interrogate either the sexism within that tradition or the objectives to which that tradition has been pressed. To say that playing the dozens, for example, is rooted in a black cultural tradition or that themes represented by mythic folk heroes such as Stackalee are "black" does not settle the question of whether such practices are oppressive to women and others within the community. The same point can be made about the relentless homophobia expressed in the work of Eddie Murphy and many other comedians and rappers. Whether or not the black community has a pronounced tradition of homophobia is beside the point; the question instead is how these subordinating aspects of tradition play out in the lives of people in the community, people who otherwise share a common history, culture, and political agenda. While it may be true that the black community is more familiar with the cultural forms that have evolved into rap, that familiarity should not end

the discussion of whether the misogyny within rap is acceptable. Moreover, we need to consider the possible relationships between sexism within our cultural practices and the problem of violence against women.

Violence against women of color is not presented as a critical issue in either the anti-racist or anti-violence discourses. The "different culture" defense may contribute to the disregard for women of color victimized by rape and violence, reinforcing the tendency within the broader community not to take intra-racial violence seriously. Numerous studies have suggested that black victims of crime can count on less protection from the criminal justice system than whites. This is true for rape victims as well—their rapists are less likely to be convicted and on average serve less time when they are convicted.

Although there are times when black feminists should fight for the integrity of the culture, this does not mean that criticism must end when a practice or form of expression is traced to a particular aspect of culture. We must determine whether the practices and forms of expression are consistent with our fundamental interests. The question of obscenity may be settled by finding roots in the culture, but obscenity is not our central issue. Performances and representations that do riot appeal principally to "prurient interests," or that may reflect expressive patterns that are culturally specific, may still encourage self-hatred, disrespect, subordination, and other manifestations of intra-group pathology. These problems require group dialogue. While African-Americans have no plenary authority to grapple with these issues, we do need to find ways of using group formation mechanisms and other social spaces to reflect upon and reformulate our cultural and political practices.

I said earlier that the political goals of black feminism are to construct and empower a political sensibility that opposes misogyny and racism simultaneously. Converging this double vision into an analysis of the 2 Live Crew controversy, it becomes clear that despite the superficial defense of the prosecution as being concerned with the interests of women, nothing about the anti-2 Live Crew movement is about black women's lives. The political process involved in condemning the representations that subordinate black women does not seek to empower black women; indeed, the racism of that movement is injurious to us.

But the implication of this conclusion is not that black feminists should stand in solidarity with the supporters of 2 Live Crew. The spirited defense of 2 Live Crew was no more about defending the black community than the prosecution was about defending women. After all, black women—whose very assault is the object of the representation—are part of that community. Black women can hardly regard the right to be represented as bitches and whores as essential to their interests. Instead the defense of 2 Live Crew primarily functions to protect the cultural and political prerogative of male rappers to be as misogynistic and offensive as they want to be.

The debate over 2 Live Crew illustrates how race and gender politics continue to marginalize black women, rendering us virtually voiceless. Black feminism endeavors to respond to this silencing by constructing a political identity for black women that will facilitate a simultaneous struggle against racism and patriarchy. Fitted with a black feminist sensibility, one uncovers other issues in which the unique situation of black women renders a different formulation of the problem than the version that dominates in current debate. Ready examples include rape, domestic violence, and welfare dependency. A black feminist sensibility might also provide a more direct link between the women's movement and traditional civil rights movements, helping them both to shed conceptual blinders that limit the efficacy of each.

The development of a black feminist sensibility is no guarantee that black women's interests will be taken seriously. In order for that sensibility to develop into empowerment, black women will have to make it clear that patriarchy is a critical issue that negatively impacts the lives not only of African-American women, but men as well. Within the African-American political community, this recognition might reshape traditional practices so that evidence of racism would not constitute justification for uncritical rallying around misogynistic politics and patriarchal values. Although collective opposition to racist practice has been and continues to be crucially important in protecting black interests, an empowered black feminist sensibility would require that the terms of unity no longer reflect priorities premised upon the continued subordination of black women.

DISCUSSION QUESTIONS

1. Explain how Crenshaw argues that the rhetoric of anti-racism can entrench sexism and the rhetoric of anti-sexism can entrench racism.

2. Explain why Crenshaw argues that Black feminists should not stand in solidarity with defenders of 2 Live Crew, but nor should they stand in solidarity with the band's critics.

3. Explain the role of intersectionality in making sense of Crenshaw's "dissatisfaction with the idea that the 'real issue' is race or that the 'real issue' is gender" in the 2 Live Crew controversy.

4. Explain how Crenshaw argues that the vagueness of the obscenity doctrine opens the door for it being applied selectively and thus disproportionately targeting offenders on the basis of race.

Reflections on Race and Sex

BY BELL HOOKS

bell hooks (1952–2021), the pen name for Gloria Jean Watkins, was an American author and social activist best known for her influential writings on race, feminism, and class. In this accessible and disturbing essay, hooks explains how racism and sexism are mutually reinforcing systems of domination, exploring themes such as how rape is condoned as a tool of maintaining both male supremacy and white supremacy, and how the cultural imagery of lustful black male sexuality threatening the purity of white female sexuality is used to perpetuate racist domination.

In order to change the lovelessness in my primary relationships, I had to first learn anew the meaning of love and from there learn how to be loving. Embracing a definition of love that was clear was the first step in the process. Like many who read *The Road Less Traveled* again and again, I am grateful to have been given a definition of love that helped me face the places in my life where love was lacking. I was in my mid-twenties when I first learned to understand love "as the will to extend one's self for the purpose of nurturing one's own or another's spiritual growth." It still took years for me to let go of learned patterns of behavior that negated my capacity to give and receive love. One pattern that made the practice of love especially difficult was my constantly choosing to be with men who were emotionally wounded, who were not that interested in being loving even though they desired to be loved.

I wanted to know love but I was afraid to surrender and trust another person. I was afraid to be intimate. By choosing men who were not interested in being loving, I was able to practice giving love, but always within an unfulfilling context. Naturally, my need to receive love was not met. I got what I was accustomed to getting—care and affection, usually mingled with a degree of unkindness, neglect, and, on some occasions, outright cruelty. At times I was unkind. It took me a long time to recognize that while I wanted to know love, I was afraid to be truly intimate. Many of us choose relationships of affection and care that will never become loving because they feel safer. The demands are not as intense as loving requires. The risk is not as great.

So many of us long for love but lack the courage to take risks. Even though we are obsessed with the idea of love, the truth is that most of us live relatively decent, somewhat satisfying lives even if we often feel that love is lacking. In these relationships we share genuine affection and/or care. For most of us, that feels like enough because it is usually a lot more than we received in our families of origin. Undoubtedly, many of us are more comfortable with the notion that love can mean anything to anybody precisely because when we define it with precision and clarity it brings us face to face with our lacks—with terrible alienation. The truth is, far too many people in our culture do not know what love is. And this not knowing feels like a terrible secret, a lack that we have to cover up.

Had I been given a clear definition of love earlier in my life it would not have taken me so long to become a more loving person. Had I shared with others a common understanding of what it means to love it would have been easier to create love. It is particularly distressing that so many recent books on love continue to insist that definitions of love are unnecessary and meaningless. Or worse, the authors suggest love should mean something different to men than it does to women—that the sexes should respect and adapt to our inability to communicate since we do not share the same language. This type of literature is popular because it does not demand a change in fixed ways of thinking about gender roles, culture, or love. Rather than sharing strategies that would help us become more loving it actually encourages everyone to adapt to circumstances where love is lacking.

Women, more so than men, rush out to purchase this literature. We do so because collectively we are concerned about lovelessness. Since many women believe they will never know fulfilling love, they are willing to settle for strategies that help ease the pain and increase the peace, pleasure, and playfulness in existing relationships, particularly romantic ones. No vehicle in our culture exists for readers to talk back to the writers of this literature. And we do not really know if it has been truly useful, if it promotes constructive change. The fact that women, more than men, buy self-help books, using our consumer dollars to keep specific books on bestseller lists, is no indication that these books actually help us transform our lives. I have bought tons of self-help books. Only a very few have really made a difference in my life. This is true for many readers.

The lack of an ongoing public discussion and public policy about the practice of love in our culture and in our lives means that we still look to books as a primary source of guidance and direction. Large numbers of readers embrace Peck's definition of love and are applying it to their lives in ways that are helpful and transformative. We can spread the word by evoking this definition in day-to-day conversations, not just when we talk to other adults but in our conversations with children and teenagers. When we intervene on mystifying assumptions that love cannot be defined by offering workable, useful definitions, we are already creating a context where love can begin to flourish.

Some folks have difficulty with Peck's definition of love because he uses the word "spiritual." He is referring to that dimension of our core reality where mind, body, and spirit are one. An individual does not need to be a believer in a religion to embrace the idea that there is an animating principle in the self—a life force (some of us call it soul) that when nurtured enhances our capacity to be more fully self-actualized and able to engage in communion with the world around us.

To begin by always thinking of love as an action rather than a feeling is one way in which anyone using the word in this manner automatically assumes accountability and responsibility. We are often taught we have no control over our "feelings." Yet most of us accept that we choose our actions, that intention and will inform what we do. We also accept that our actions have consequences. To think of actions shaping feelings is one way we rid ourselves of conventionally accepted assumptions such as that parents love their children, or that one simply "falls" in love without exercising will or choice, that there are such things as "crimes of passion," i.e., he killed her because he loved her so much. If we were constantly remembering that love is as love does, we would not use the word in a manner that devalues and degrades its meaning. When we are loving we openly and honestly express care, affection, responsibility, respect, commitment, and trust.

Embracing a love ethic means that we utilize all the dimensions of love—"care, commitment, trust, responsibility, respect, and knowledge"—in our everyday lives. We can successfully do this only by cultivating awareness. Being aware enables us to critically examine our actions to see what is needed so that we can give care, be responsible, show respect, and indicate a willingness to learn. Understanding knowledge as an essential element of love is vital because we are daily bombarded with messages that tell us love is about mystery, about that which cannot be known. We see movies in which people are represented as being in love who never talk with one another, who fall into bed without ever discussing their bodies, their sexual needs, their likes and dislikes. Indeed, the message received from the mass media is that knowledge makes love less compelling; that it is ignorance that gives love its erotic and transgressive edge. These messages are often brought to us by profiteering producers who have no clue about the art of loving, who substitute their mystified visions because they do not really know how to genuinely portray loving interaction.

Were we, collectively, to demand that our mass media portray images that reflect love's reality, it would happen. This change would radically alter our culture. The mass media dwells on and perpetuates an ethic of domination and violence because our image makers have more intimate knowledge of these realities than they have with the realities of love. We all know what violence looks like. All scholarship in the field of cultural studies focusing on a critical analysis of the mass media, whether pro or con, indicates that images of violence, particularly those that involve action and gore, capture the attention of viewers more than still, peaceful images. The small groups of people who produce most of the images we see in this culture have heretofore shown no interest in learning how to represent images of love in ways that will capture and stir our cultural imagination and hold our attention.

If the work they did was informed by a love ethic, they would consider it important to think critically about the images they create. And that would mean thinking about the impact of these images, the ways they shape culture and inform how we think and act in everyday life. If unfamiliar with love's terrain, they would hire consultants who would provide the necessary insight. Even though some individual scholars try to tell us there is no direct connection between images of violence and the violence confronting us in our lives, the commonsense truth remains—we are all affected by the images we consume and by the state of mind we are in when watching them. If consumers want to be entertained, and the images shown us as entertaining are images of violent dehumanization, it makes sense that these acts become more acceptable in our daily lives and that we become less likely to respond to them with moral outrage or concern. Were we all seeing more images of loving human interaction, it would undoubtedly have a positive impact on our lives.

Domination cannot exist in any social situation where a love ethic prevails. Jung's insight, that if the will to power is paramount love will be lacking, is important to remember. When love is present the desire to dominate and exercise power cannot rule the day. All the great social movements for freedom and justice in our society have promoted a love ethic. Concern for the collective good of our nation, city, or neighbor rooted in the values of love makes us all seek to nurture and protect that good. If all public policy was created in the spirit of love, we would not have to worry about unemployment, homelessness, schools failing to teach children, or addiction.

Were a love ethic informing all public policy in cities and towns, individuals would come together and map out programs that would affect the good of everyone. Melody Chavis's wonderful book *Altars in the Street: A Neighborhood Fights to Survive* tells a story of real people coming together across differences of race and class to improve their living environment. She speaks from the perspective of a white woman who moves with her family into a predominately black community. As someone who embraces a love ethic, Melody joins her neighbors to create peace and love in their environment. Their work succeeds but is undermined by the failure of support from public policy and city government. Concurrently, she also works to help prisoners on death row. Loving community in all its diversity, Melody states: "Sometimes I think that I've been trying, on death row and in my neighborhood, to gain some control over the violence in my life. As a child I was completely helpless in the face of violence." Her book shows the changes a love ethic can make even in the most troubled community. It also documents the tragic consequences to human life when terror and violence become the accepted norm.

Most of us are raised to believe we will either find love in our first family (our family of origin) or, if not there, in the second family we are expected to form through committed romantic couplings, particularly those that lead to marriage and/or lifelong bondings. Many of us learn as children that friendship should never be seen as just as important as family ties. However, friendship is the place in which a great majority of us have our first glimpse of redemptive love and caring community. Learning to love in friendships empowers us in ways that enable us to bring this love to other interactions with family or with romantic bonds.

Often we take friendships for granted even when they are the interactions where we experience mutual pleasure. We place them in a secondary position, especially in relation to romantic bonds. This devaluation of our friendships creates an emptiness we may not see when we are devoting all our attention to finding someone to love romantically or giving all our attention to a chosen loved one. Committed love relationships are far more likely to become codependent when we cut off all our ties with friends to give these bonds we consider primary our exclusive attention. I have felt especially devastated when close friends who were single fell in love and simultaneously fell away from our friendship. When a best friend chose a mate who did not click with me at all, it caused me heartache. Not only did they begin to do everything together, the friends she stayed closest to were those he liked best.

The strength of our friendship was revealed by our willingness to confront openly the shift in our ties and to make necessary changes. We do not see each other as much as we once did, and we no longer call each other daily, but the positive ties that bind us remain intact. The more genuine our romantic loves the more we do not feel called upon to weaken or sever ties with friends in order to strengthen ties with romantic partners. Trust is

the heartbeat of genuine love. And we trust that the attention our partners give friends, or vice versa, does not take anything away from us—we are not diminished. What we learn through experience is that our capacity to establish deep and profound connections in friendship strengthens all our intimate bonds.

When we see love as the will to nurture one's own or another's spiritual growth, revealed through acts of care, respect, knowing, and assuming responsibility, the foundation of all love in our life is the same. There is no special love exclusively reserved for romantic partners. Genuine love is the foundation of our engagement with ourselves, with family, with friends, with partners, with everyone we choose to love.

DISCUSSION QUESTIONS

1. Why do our culture's psychosexual histories focus almost exclusively on the specter of the black male rapist? Why do progressive attempts to subvert this imagery so often fail?

2. Explain how the use of sexualized metaphors to resist the racist domination of black men, and the related belief that the harms of racist domination are best understood as the loss of black manhood, function to entrench the patriarchal domination of black women.

3. Explain how the equation of black liberation with manhood can give white women reason to be concerned about efforts to resist racism, and can give black women reason to be suspicious of feminism.

Doing Justice to Someone: Sex Reassignment and Allegories of Transsexuality

BY JUDITH BUTLER

Judith Butler is an American philosopher and gender theorist whose work has influenced political philosophy, ethics, and the fields of third-wave feminism, queer theory, and literary theory. In this essay, Butler applies her well-known critique of heteronormativity as hegemonically producing all forms of the body, sex, and gender to the case of David Reimer, a twin whose penis was irreparably damaged during a circumcision accident and who, after spending his childhood being raised as a girl, chose to live as a man and eventually undergo female-to-male sex reassignment surgery.

I want to consider a legal and psychiatric case of a person who was determined without difficulty to be a boy at the time of birth, then was determined again within a few months to be a girl, and then decided to become a man in his teenage years. This is the John/Joan case, brought to public attention by the British Broadcasting Corporation in the early 1990s and recently again in various popular, psychological, and medical journals. I base my analysis on an article cowritten by Milton Diamond, an endocrinologist, and the popular book *As Nature Made Him*, by John Colapinto, a journalist for *Rolling Stone*, as well as on work by John Money, critical commentaries by Anne Fausto-Sterling and Suzanne J. Kessler in their important recent books, and a newspaper account by Natalie Angier. John, a pseudonym for a man who lives in Winnipeg, was born with XY chromosomes. When he was eight months old, his penis was accidentally burned and severed during a surgical operation to rectify phimosis, a condition in which the foreskin thwarts urination. This procedure is relatively risk-free, but the doctor who performed it on John was using a new machine, apparently one that he had not used before, one that his colleagues declared was unnecessary for the job, and he was having trouble

making it work, so he increased the power to the machine to the point that it burned away a major portion of the penis. The parents were, of course, appalled, and they were, according to their own description, unclear how to proceed.

Then one evening, about a year later, they were watching television, and there they encountered Money talking about transsexual and intersexual surgery and offering the view that if a child underwent surgery and started socialization as a gender different from the one originally assigned at birth, he or she could develop normally, adapt perfectly well to the new gender, and live a happy life. The parents wrote to Money, who invited them to Baltimore, and so John was seen at Johns Hopkins University, at which point Money strongly recommended that he be raised as a girl. The parents agreed, and the doctors removed the testicles, made some preliminary preparations for surgery to create a vagina, but decided to wait until Joan, the newly named child, was older to complete the task. So Joan grew up as a girl, was monitored often, and was periodically given over to Money's Gender Identity Institute for the purposes of fostering her adaptation to girlhood. And then, it is reported, between the ages of eight and nine Joan found herself developing the desire to buy a toy machine gun. And then, it is said, between the ages of nine and eleven she started to realize that she was not a girl. This realization seems to have coincided with her desire to buy certain kinds of toys: more guns, apparently, and some trucks. Even without a penis, Joan liked to stand to urinate. And she was caught in this position once, at school, where the other girls threatened to "kill" her if she continued.

At this point the psychiatric teams that intermittently monitored Joan's adaptation offered her estrogen, which she refused. Money tried to talk to her about getting a real vagina, and she refused; in fact, she went screaming from the room. Money had her view sexually graphic pictures of vaginas. He even went so far as to show her pictures of women giving birth, holding out the possibility that Joan could give birth if she acquired a vagina. In a scene that could have inspired the recent film *But I'm a Cheerleader*, he also required that she and her brother perform mock-coital exercises with one another, on command. They both later reported being frightened and disoriented by this demand and did not tell their parents about it at the time. Joan is said to have preferred male activities and not to have liked developing breasts. All of these claims were attributed to Joan by another set of doctors, a team of psychiatrists at her local hospital. These psychiatrists and other local medical professionals intervened, believing that a mistake in sex reassignment had been made. Eventually the case was reviewed by Diamond, a sex researcher who believes in the hormonal basis of gender identity and who has been battling Money for years. This new set of psychiatrists and other doctors offered Joan the choice of changing paths, which she accepted. She started living as a boy, named John, at the age of fourteen. John requested and received male hormone shots; he also had his breasts removed. A phallus, so called by Diamond, was constructed for him between the ages of fifteen and sixteen. John does not ejaculate; he feels some sexual pleasure in the phallus; he urinates from its base. Thus it only approximates some of its expected functions, and, as we shall see, it enters John only ambivalently into the norm.

During the time that John was Joan, Money published papers extolling the success of this sex reassignment. The case was enormously consequential because Joan was an identical twin, and so Money could track the development of both siblings while controlling for genetic makeup. He insisted that both were developing normally and happily into their respective genders. But his own recorded interviews, mainly unpublished, and subsequent research have called his honesty into question. Joan was hardly happy, refused to adapt to many so-called girl behaviors, and was angered by Money's invasive, continual interrogations. Yet the published records from Johns Hopkins claim that Joan's adaptation to girlhood was successful, and certain ideological conclusions immediately followed. Money's Gender Identity Institute, which monitored Joan often, asserted that her successful development as a girl "offers convincing evidence that the gender identity gate is open at birth for a normal child no less than for one born with unfinished sex organs or one who was prenatally over or underexposed to androgen, and that it stays open at least for something over a year at birth." Indeed, the case was used by the public media to prove that what is feminine and what is masculine can be altered, that these cultural terms have no fixed meaning or internal destiny. Even Kate Millett cited the case in arguing that biology is not destiny. Kessler also allied with Money in her essays in favor of the social constructionist thesis. Later Kessler would disavow their alliance and write one of the most important books on the ethical and medical dimensions of sex reassignment, *Lessons from the Intersexed*, which includes a trenchant critique of Money.

Money's approach was to recruit male-to-female transsexuals to talk to Joan about the advantages of being a girl. She was subjected to myriad interviews and was asked again and again whether she felt like a girl, what her desires were, what her image of the future was, whether it included marriage to a man. She was also asked to strip and show her genitals to medical practitioners who were either interested in the case or monitoring it for her adaptational success.

When this case has been discussed in the press recently, and when psychiatrists and other medical practitioners have turned to it, they have done so to criticize the role that Money's institute played and, in particular, its readiness to use Joan's example to substantiate its own theoretical beliefs about the gender neutrality of early childhood, about the malleability of gender, about the primary role of socialization in the production of gender identity. In fact, this is not exactly everything that Money believes, but let us not probe that question here. The individuals who are critical of this case believe that it shows us something very different. When we consider, they argue, that John found himself deeply moved to become a boy and found it unbearable to continue to live as a girl, we have to consider as well that John experienced some deep-seated sense of gender, one linked to his original set of genitals, one seemingly there as an internal truth and necessity that no amount of socialization could reverse. This is the view of Colapinto and of Diamond as well.

So now the case of Joan/John is being used to make a revision and a reversal in developmental gender theory, providing evidence this time that counters Money's thesis, supporting the notion of an essential gender core tied in some irreversible way to anatomy and to a deterministic sense of biology. Indeed, Colapinto clearly links Money's cruelty to Joan to the "cruelty" of social construction as a theory, remarking that Money's refusal to identify a biological or anatomical basis for gender difference in the early 1970s "was not lost on the then-burgeoning women's movement, which had been arguing against a biological basis for sex differences for decades." Colapinto claims that Money's published essays "had already been used as one of the main foundations of modern feminism." He asserts that *Time* engaged in a similarly misguided appropriation of Money's views when it argued that this case, in the magazine's own words, "provides strong support for a major contention of women's liberationists: that conventional patterns of masculine and feminine behavior can be altered." Indeed, Colapinto talks about the failure of surgically reassigned individuals to live as "normal" and "typical" women and men, arguing that normality is never achieved and hence assuming the inarguable value of normalcy itself.

Reporting on the refutation of Money's theory, Natalie Angier claims that the story of John has "the force of allegory." But which force is that? And is this an allegory with closure? Angier reports that Diamond used the case to make an argument about intersexual surgery and, by implication, the relative success of transsexual surgery. Diamond argued, for instance, that intersexed infants, that is, those born with mixed or indeterminate genital attributes, generally have a Y chromosome, and that possession of the Y is an adequate basis for concluding that they ought to be raised as boys. As it is, the vast majority of intersexed infants are subjected to surgery that seeks to assign them to the female sex, since, as Cheryl Chase points out in Angier's article, it is simply considered easier to produce a provisional vaginal tract than to construct a phallus. Diamond argued that these children should be assigned to the male sex, since the presence of the Y is sufficient grounds for the presumption of social masculinity.

In fact, Chase, founder and director of the Intersex Society of North America, voiced skepticism about Diamond's recommendations. Her view, recently defended by Fausto-Sterling as well, is that there is no reason to make a sex assignment at all; society should make room for the intersexed as they are and cease the coercive surgical "correction" of infants. Indeed, recent research has shown that such operations have been performed without the parents knowing about it, without the children themselves ever being truthfully told, and without their having attained the age of consent. Most astonishing, in a way, is the state that their bodies have been left in, with mutilations performed and then paradoxically rationalized in the name of "looking normal." Medical practitioners often say to the parents that the child will not look normal if not operated on; that the child will be ashamed in the locker room, *the locker room*, that site of prepubescent anxiety about impending gender developments; and that it would be better for the child to look normal, even when such surgery may deprive him or her of sexual function and sexual pleasure for life.

So, while some experts, such as Money, claim that the absence of the full phallus makes the social case for rearing the child as a girl, others, such as Diamond, argue that the presence of the Y chromosome is the most compelling fact or, that it is what is indexed in persistent feelings of masculinity, and that it cannot be constructed away. So, on the one hand, how my anatomy looks, how it comes to appear, to others and to myself as I see others looking at me, is the basis of my social identity as woman or man. On the other hand, how the presence of the Y tacitly structures my feeling and self-understanding as a sexed person is decisive. Money argues for the ease with which a female body can be surgically constructed, as if femininity were always little more than a surgical construction, an elimination, a cutting away. Diamond argues for the invisible and necessary persistence of maleness, which does not need to "appear" in order to operate as the key feature of gender identity. When Angier asks Chase whether she agrees with Diamond's recommendations on intersexual surgery, Chase replies, "They can't conceive of leaving someone alone." Indeed, is the surgery performed to create a "normal"-looking body, after all? The mutilations and scars that remain hardly offer compelling evidence that this is accomplished. Or are these bodies subjected to medical machinery that marks them for life precisely because they are "inconceivable"?

Another paradox that emerges here is the place of sharp machines, of the technology of the knife, in debates on intersexuality and transsexuality. If the John/Joan case is an allegory, or has the force of allegory, it seems to be the site where debates on intersexuality (John is not an intersexual) and transsexuality (John is not a transsexual) converge. This body becomes a point of reference for a narrative that is not about this body but that seizes on the body, as it were, to inaugurate a narrative that interrogates the limits of the conceivably human. What is inconceivable is conceived again and again, through narrative means, but something remains outside the narrative, a resistant moment that signals a persisting inconceivability.

Despite Diamond's recommendations, the intersexed movement has been galvanized by the Joan/John case; it is able now to bring to public attention the brutality and coerciveness and lasting harm of the unwanted surgeries performed on intersexed infants. The point is to try to imagine a world in which individuals with mixed or indeterminate genital attributes might be accepted and loved without having to undergo transformation into a more socially coherent or normative version of gender. In this sense, the intersexed movement has sought to ask why society maintains the ideal of gender dimorphism when a significant percentage of children are chromosomally various, and a continuum exists between male and female that suggests the arbitrariness and falsity of gender dimorphism as a prerequisite of human development. There are humans, in other words, who live and breathe in the interstices of this binary relation, showing that it is not exhaustive; it is not necessary. Although the transsexual movement, which is internally various, has called for rights to surgical means by which sex might be transformed, it is clear—and Chase underscores—that there is also a serious and increasingly popular critique of idealized gender dimorphism in the transsexual movement itself. One can see it in the work of Riki Anne Wilchins, whose gender theory makes room for transsexuality as a transformative exercise, but one can see it perhaps most dramatically in the work of Kate Bornstein, who argues that to go from female to male, or from male to female, is not necessarily to stay within the binary frame of gender but to engage transformation itself as the meaning of gender. In some ways, Bornstein now carries the legacy of Simone de Beauvoir: if one is not born a woman, but becomes one, then becoming is the vehicle for gender itself.

But why, we might ask, has John become the occasion for a reflection on transsexuality? Although John comes to claim that he would prefer to be a man, it is not clear whether he himself believes in the primary causal force of the Y chromosome. Diamond finds support for his theory in John, but it is not clear, on the basis of my reading, that John agrees with Diamond. John clearly knows about hormones, has asked for them, and takes them. He has learned about phallic construction from transsexual contexts, wants a phallus, has it made, and so allegorizes a certain transsexual transformation without precisely exemplifying it. He is, in his own view, a man born a man, castrated by the medical establishment, feminized by the psychiatric world, and then enabled to return to who he was to begin with. But to return to who he is, he requires—and wants, and gets—a subjection to hormones and surgery. He allegorizes transsexuality to achieve a sense of naturalness. And this transformation is applauded by the endocrinologists on the case, since they understand his appearance now to be in accord with an inner truth. Whereas Money's institute enlists transsexuals to instruct Joan in the ways of women, and *in the name of normalization*, the endocrinologists prescribe the sex change protocol of transsexuality to John for him to reassume his genetic destiny, *in the name of nature*.

And though Money's institute enlists transsexuals to allegorize Joan's full transformation into a woman, the endocrinologists propose to appropriate transsexual surgery in order to build the phallus that will make John a more legible man. Importantly, it seems, the norms that govern intelligible gender for Money are those that can be forcibly imposed and behaviorally appropriated, so the malleability of gender construction, which is part of his thesis, turns out to require a forceful application. And the "nature" that the endocrinologists defend also needs assistance and augmentation through surgical and hormonal means, at which point a certain nonnatural intervention in anatomy and biology is precisely what is mandated by nature. So in each case the primary premise is in some ways refuted by the means by which it is implemented. Malleability is, as it were, violently imposed, and naturalness is artificially induced. There are ways of arguing social construction that have nothing to do with Money's project, but that is not my aim here. And there are, no doubt, ways of seeking recourse to genetic determinants that do not lead to the same kind of interventionist conclusions arrived at by Diamond and Sigmundson. But that is also not precisely my point. For the record, though, let us consider that the prescriptions arrived at by these purveyors of natural and normative gender in no way follow necessarily from the premises from which they begin, and that the premises with which they begin have no necessity in themselves. (One might well disjoin the

theory of gender construction, for instance, from the hypothesis of gender normativity and have a very different account of social construction from that offered by Money; one might allow for genetic factors without assuming that they are the *only* aspect of nature that one might consult to understand the sexed characteristics of a human: why is the Y chromosome considered the primary determinant of maleness, exercising preemptive rights over any and all other factors?)

But my point in recounting this story and its appropriation for the purposes of gender theory is to suggest that the story as we have it does not supply evidence for either thesis, and to suggest that there may be another way to read this story, one that neither confirms nor denies the theory of social construction, one that neither affirms nor denies gender essentialism. Indeed, what I hope to underscore here is the disciplinary framework in which Joan/John develops a discourse of self-reporting and self-understanding, since it constitutes the grid of intelligibility by which his own humanness is both questioned and asserted.

It seems crucial to remember, as one considers what might count as the evidence of the truth of gender, that Joan/John was intensely monitored by psychological teams through childhood and adolescence, that teams of doctors observed Joan's behavior, that teams of doctors asked her and her brother to disrobe in front of them so that genital development could be gauged, that there was a doctor who asked her to engage in mock-coital exercises with her brother, to view the pictures, to know and want the so-called normalcy of unambiguous genitalia. There was an apparatus of knowledge applied to the person and body of Joan/John that is rarely, if ever, taken into account as part of what John responds to when he reports on his feelings of true gender. The act of self-reporting and the act of self-observation take place in relation to a certain audience, with a certain audience as the imagined recipient, before a certain audience for whom a verbal and visual picture of selfhood is produced. These are speech acts, we might say, that are very often delivered to those who have been scrutinizing, brutally, the truth of Joan's gender for years. Even though Diamond and Sigmundson and indeed Colapinto are in the position of defending John against Money's intrusions, they still ask John how he feels, who he is, trying to ascertain the truth of his sex through the discourse he provides. Of Joan, who was subjected to such scrutiny and, most important, repeatedly subjected to a norm, a normalizing ideal conveyed through a plurality of gazes, a norm applied to the body, a question was continually posed: Is this person feminine enough? Has this person made it to femininity? Is femininity properly embodied here? Is the embodiment working? Is it? Is it? How do we know? What evidence can we marshal in order to know? And surely we must have knowledge here. We must be able to say that we know, and communicate that in the professional journals, and justify our decision, our act. In effect, the question posed through these interrogatory exercises has to do with whether the gender norm that establishes coherent personhood has been successfully accomplished, and the inquiries and inspections can be understood, along these lines, not only as the violent attempt to implement the norm but as the institutionalization of that power of implementation.

The pediatricians and psychiatrists who have revisited the case in recent years cite John's self-description to support their point. John's narrative about his own sense of being male supports the theory that John is really male and that he was, even when he was Joan, always male.

John tells his interviewers the following about himself:

> There were little things from early on. I began to see how different I felt and was, from what I was supposed to be. But I didn't know what it meant. I thought I was a freak or something. . . . I looked at myself and said I don't like this type of clothing, I don't like the types of toys I was always being given, I like hanging around with the guys and climbing trees and stuff like that and girls don't like any of that stuff. I looked in the mirror and [saw] my shoulders [were] so wide, I mean there [was] nothing feminine about me. [I was] skinny, but other than that, nothing. But that [was] how I figured it out.

> [I figured I was a guy] but I didn't want to admit it, I figured I didn't want to wind up opening a can of worms.

So now you hear how John describes himself. And so, if part of my task here is to do justice not only to my topic but to the person I am sketching for you, the person about whom so much has been said, the person whose self-description and whose decisions have become the basis for so much gender theorizing in the last four years, then it seems to me that I must be careful in presenting these words. For these words can give you only something of the person I am trying to understand, some part of that person's verbal instance, and since I cannot truly understand this person, since I do not know this person and have no access to this person, I am left to be a reader of a selected number of words, words that I did not fully select, ones that were selected for me, recorded from interviews and then chosen by those who decided to write their articles on this person for journals such as the *Archives of Pediatrics and Adolescent Medicine*. So we might say that I have been given fragments of the person, linguistic fragments of something called a person, and what might it mean to do justice to someone under these circumstances? Can we?

On the one hand, we have a self-description, and that is to be honored. These are the words by which this individual gives himself to be understood. On the other hand, we have a description of a self that takes place in a language that is already going on, that is already saturated with norms, that predisposes us as we seek to speak of ourselves. And we have words that are delivered in the context of an interview, an interview that is part of the long and intrusive observational process that has accompanied John's formation from the start. To do justice to John is, certainly, to take him at his word, and to call him by his chosen name, but how are we to understand his word and his name? Is this the word that he creates? Is this the word that he receives? Are these the words that circulate prior to his emergence as an "I" that might gain a certain authorization to begin a self-description only within the norms of this language? So when one speaks, one speaks a language that is already speaking, even if one speaks it in a way that is not precisely how it has been spoken before. So what and who is speaking here, when John reports, "There were little things from early on. I began to see how different I felt and was, from what I was supposed to be"? This claim tells us minimally that John understands that there is a norm, a norm of how he was supposed to be, and that he has fallen short of it. The implicit claim is that the norm is femininity, and he has failed to live up to it. And there is the norm, and it is externally imposed, communicated through a set of expectations that others have, and then there is the world of feeling and being, and these realms are, for him, distinct. What he feels is not in any way produced by the norm, and the norm is other, elsewhere, not part of who he is, who he has become, what he feels.

But given what we know about how John has been addressed, we might, in an effort to do justice to John, ask what Joan saw as Joan looked at himself, felt as he felt himself, and please excuse my mixing of pronouns here, but matters are becoming changeable. When Joan looked in the mirror and saw something nameless, freakish, something between the norms, was she not at that moment in question as a human, was she not the specter of the freak against which and through which the norm installed itself? What was the problem with Joan, that people were always asking to see her naked, asking her questions about what she was, how she felt, whether this was or was not the same as what was normatively true? Is that self-seeing distinct from the way s/he is seen? John seems to understand clearly that the norms are external to him, but what if the norms have become the means by which he sees, the frame for his own seeing, his way of seeing himself? What if the action of the norm is to be found not merely in the ideal that it posits but in the sense of aberration and freakishness that it conveys? Consider precisely where the norm operates when John claims, "I looked at myself and said I don't like this type of clothing." To whom is John speaking? And in what world, under what conditions, does not liking that type of clothing provide evidence for being the wrong

gender? For whom would that be true? And under what conditions?

John reports, "I don't like the types of toys I was always being given," and John is speaking here as someone who understands that such a dislike can function as evidence. And it seems reasonable to assume that Joan understood this dislike as evidence of gender dystopia, to use the technical term, because s/he has been addressed time and again by those who have made use of her every utterance about her experience as evidence for or against a true gender. That he happens not to have liked certain toys, certain dolls, certain games, may be significant in relation to the question of how and with what he liked to play. But in what world, precisely, do such dislikes count as clear or unequivocal evidence for or against being a given gender? Do parents regularly rush off to gender identity clinics when their boys play with yarn, or their girls play with trucks? Or must there already be an enormous anxiety at play, an anxiety about the truth of gender that seizes on this or that toy, this or that proclivity of dress, the size of the shoulder, the leanness of the body, to conclude that something like a clear gender identity can or cannot be built from these scattered desires, these variable and invariable features of the body, of bone structure, of proclivity, of attire?

So what does my analysis imply? Does it tell us whether the gender here is true or false? No. And does this have implications for whether John should have been surgically transformed into Joan, or Joan surgically transformed into John? No, it does not. I do not know how to judge that question here, and I am not sure it can be mine to judge. Does justice demand that I decide? Or does justice demand that I wait to decide, that I practice a certain deferral in the face of a situation in which too many have rushed to judgment? And it might be useful, important, even just, to consider a few matters before we decide, before we ascertain whether it is, in fact, ours to decide.

Consider in this spirit, then, that it is for the most part the gender essentialist position that must be voiced for transsexual surgery to take place, and that someone who comes in with a sense of gender as changeable will have a more difficult time convincing psychiatrists and doctors to perform the surgery. In San Francisco female-to-male candidates actually practice the narrative of gender essentialism that they are required to perform before they go in to see the doctors, and there are now coaches to help them, dramaturges of transsexuality who will help you make the case for no fee. Indeed, we might say that Joan/John together went through two transsexual surgeries: the first based on a hypothetical argument about what gender should be, given the ablated nature of the penis; the second based on what the gender should be, based on the behavioral and verbal indications of the person in question. In both cases, certain inferences were made, one that suggested that a body must appear a certain way for a gender to work, another that said that a body must feel a certain way for a gender to work. John clearly came to disrespect and abhor the views of the first set of doctors; he developed, we might say, a lay critique of the phallus to support his resistance:

> Doctor . . . said, it's gonna be tough, you're going to be picked on, you're gonna be very alone, you're not gonna find anybody unless you have vaginal surgery and live as a female. And I thought to myself, you know I wasn't very old at the time but it dawned on me that these people gotta be pretty shallow if that's the only thing they think I've got going for me; that the only reason why people get married and have children and have a productive life is because of what they have between their legs. . . . If that's all they think of me, that they justify my worth by what I have between my legs, then I gotta be a complete loser.

Here John makes a distinction between the "I" that he is, the person that he is, and the value that is conferred on his personhood by virtue of what is or is not between his legs. He was wagering that he would be loved for something other than this or, at least, that his penis would not be the reason he was loved. He was holding out, implicitly, for something called "depth" over and against the "shallowness" of the doctors. And so we might say that, though John asked for and received his new status as male, asked for and received his new phallus, he is also

something other than what he now has, and, though he has undergone this transformation, he refuses to be reduced to the body part that he has acquired. "If that's all they think of me," he says, offering a knowing and critical rejoinder to the work of the norm. There is something here of me that exceeds this part, though I want this part, though it is part of me. He does not want his "worth" "justif[ied]" by what he has between his legs, and what this means is that he has another sense of how the worth of a person might be justified. So we might say that he is living his desire, acquiring the anatomy that he wants in order to live his desire, but that his desire is complex, and his worth is complex.

And this is why, no doubt, in response to many of the questions Money posed—Do you want to have a penis? Do you want to marry a girl?—John often refused to answer, refused the question, refused to stay in the room with Money, refused to visit Baltimore after a while. John did not trade in one gender norm for another, not exactly. It would be as wrong to say that he simply internalized a gendered norm (from a critical position) as it would be to say that he failed to live up to a gendered norm (from a normalizing, medical position), since he has already established that what will justify his worth will be the invocation of an "I" that is not reducible to the compatibility of his anatomy with the norm. He thinks something more of himself than what others think, he does not fully justify his worth through recourse to what he has between his legs, and he does not think of himself as a complete loser. Something exceeds the norm, and he recognizes its unrecognizability; it is, in a sense, his distance from the knowably human that operates as a condition of critical speech, the source of his worth, as the justification for his worth. He says that if what those doctors believe were true, he would be a complete loser, and he implies that he is not a complete loser, that something in him is winning. But he is also saying something more: he is cautioning us against the absolutism of distinction itself, for his phallus does not constitute the entirety of his worth, and so there is an incommensurability between who he is and what he has, between the phallus he has and what it is expected to be (and in this way he is no different from anyone with a phallus), which means that he has not become one with the norm, and yet he is still someone, speaking, insisting, even referring to himself.

And it is from this gap, this incommensurability, between the norm that is supposed to inaugurate his humanness and the spoken insistence on himself that he performs that he derives his worth, that he speaks his worth. We cannot precisely give content to this person at the very moment that he speaks his worth, which means that it is precisely the ways in which he is not fully recognizable, fully disposable, fully categorizable, that his humanness emerges. And this is important, because we might ask that he enter into intelligibility in order to speak and be known, but what he does instead, through his speech, is to offer a critical perspective on the norms that confer intelligibility itself. And he shows, we might say, that there is an understanding to be had that exceeds the norms of intelligibility itself. And he achieves this "outside," we might speculate, by refusing the interrogations that besiege him, by reversing their terms, learning the ways in which he might escape. And if he renders himself unintelligible to those who seek to know and capture his identity, this means that something

about him is intelligible outside the framework of accepted intelligibility. We might be tempted to say that there is some core of a person, and so some presumption of humanism, that emerges here, that supervenes the discourses on sexed and gendered intelligibility that constrain him. But that would mean that he is denounced by one discourse, only to be carried by another discourse, the discourse of humanism. Or we might say that there is some core of the subject who speaks, who speaks beyond what is sayable, and that it is this ineffability that marks John's speech, the ineffability of the other who is not disclosed through speech but leaves a portentous shard of itself in its saying, a self that is beyond discourse itself.

DISCUSSION QUESTIONS

1. Explain why Butler begins with the question of power, and how power works in her argument.
2. How does the case Butler describes change our answers to the question: What can I be? Should those answers be changing? Are there constraints on what we are allowed to be?
3. What does Butler mean by "doing justice to someone"? Explain in detail.

Fear and Loathing in Public Bathrooms, or How I Learned to Hold My Pee

BY IVAN COYOTE

Ivan Coyote is a Canadian spoken word performer, writer, and LGBTQ advocate. In this short and moving essay, Coyote demonstrates how something as simple and ubiquitous as gender-specific bathrooms can affect the quality of life of anyone who does not fit neatly into the gender binary.

I can hold my pee for hours. Nearly all day. It's a skill I developed out of necessity, after years of navigating public washrooms. I hold it for as long as I can, until I can get myself to the theatre or the green room or my hotel room, or home. Using a public washroom is a very last resort for me. I try to use the wheelchair-accessible, gender-neutral facilities whenever possible, always after a thorough search of the area to make sure no one in an actual wheelchair or with mobility issues is en route. I always hold my breath a little on the way out though, hoping there isn't an angry person leaning on crutches waiting there when I exit. This has never happened yet, but I still worry. Sometimes I rehearse a little speech as I pee quickly and wash my hands, just to be prepared. I would say something like, I apologize for inconveniencing you by using the washroom that is accessible to disabled people, but we live in a world that is not able to make room enough for trans people to pee in safety, and after many years of tribulation in women's washrooms, I have taken to using the only place provided for people of all genders.

But I have never had to say any of this. Yet. Once at an airport, I was stopped by a janitor on my way out who reprimanded me for using a bathroom that wasn't meant for me, and I calmly explained to him that I was a transgender person, and that this was the only place I felt safe in, and then I noted that there were no disabled people lined up outside the washroom door, or parents with small children waiting to use the change table.

He narrowed his eyes at me. Then he said, "Okay, but next time you should . . ."

I waited for him to finish. Instead, he shook his head and motioned down the empty hallway with his mop handle that I should be off, that this conversation was now over.

I wondered later in the departure lounge exactly what it was he felt I should do next time? Hold it longer? Not have bodily functions at all? Use the men's room? The ladies'? Be someone else? Look different? Wear a dress? Not wear a tie? Cease and desist with air travel altogether? Do my part to dismantle the gender binary to make more room for people like myself?

I could write an entire book about bathroom incidents I have experienced. It would be a long and boring book where nearly every chapter ends the same, so I won't. But I could. Forty-four years of bathroom troubles. I try to remind myself of that every time a nice lady in her new pantsuit for travelling screams or stares at me, I try to remember that this is maybe her first encounter with someone who doesn't appear to be much of a lady in the ladies' room. That she has no way of knowing this is already the sixth time this week that this has happened to me, and that I have four decades of it already weighing heavy on my back. She doesn't know I have been verbally harassed in women's washrooms for years. She doesn't know I have been hauled out with my pants still undone by security guards and smashed over the head with a giant handbag once. She can't know that I have five cities and seven more airport bathrooms and eleven shows left to get through before I can safely pee in my own toilet. She can't know that my tampon gave up the ghost somewhere between the security line and the food court. I try to remember all that she cannot know about my day, and try to find compassion and patience and smile kind when I explain that I have just as much right to be there as she does, and then make a beeline, eyes down, shoulders relaxed in a non-confrontational slant, into the first stall on the left, closest to the door.

Every time I bring up or write about the hassles trans and genderqueer people receive in public washrooms or change rooms, the first thing out of many women's mouths is that they have a right to feel safe in a public washroom, and that, no offense, but if they saw someone who "looks like me" in there, well, they would feel afraid, too. I hear this from other queer women. Other feminists. This should sting less than it does, but I can't help it. What is always implied here is that I am other, somehow, that I don't also need to feel safe. That somehow their safety trumps mine.

If there is anything I really do understand, it is being afraid in a public washroom. I am afraid in them all the time, with a lifetime of good reason. I wish that I had some evidence that harassing people in public washrooms really did originate from being afraid. I wish I could believe them that it starts with their own fear. What I suspect is more true is that their behaviour begins with and is fed by a phobia. They are afraid of men in a women's washroom, because of what might happen. I am afraid of women in a women's washroom, because of what happens to me all the time.

I don't see cisgendered women who want to feel safe in a public washroom as my adversaries, though; what I see is the potential for many built-in comrades in the fight for gender-neutral, single-stall locking washrooms in all public places. Because the space they seek and the safety I dream of can be accomplished with the very same hammer and nails. Because what I do know for

sure is that every single trans person I have ever spoken to, every single tomboy or woman who wears coveralls for her job or woman with short hair or recovering from chemo, or effeminate boy, or man who likes wearing dresses, or man with long hair that I have ever met is hassled or confronted or challenged nearly every other time they use a public washroom, anywhere. Always. Often. Every day. All the time. Incessantly. Repeatedly. Without mercy or respite. Everything from staring to pointing to screaming to physical violence.

This violence and harassment is justified by people claiming that they were afraid. But very rarely does it feel to me like the person harassing me is actually afraid. Startled, maybe, for a second or two. But when I explain that I was assigned female at birth, just like they were, they usually don't back down. Their fear doesn't disappear, or dissipate. This is right about the time their friend will shake their head at me as if to say, what do you expect? They will pat their friend on the back to comfort them. They both feel entitled to be in a public washroom, entitled enough that they get to decide whether or not I am welcome there. This feels to me like I am being policed, and punished for what I look like. This doesn't smell like fear to me. It reeks of transphobia.

It starts very early. I know a little girl, the daughter of a friend, who is a self-identified tomboy. Cowboy boots and caterpillar yellow toy trucks. One time I asked her what her favourite colour was and she told me camouflage. She came home last October in tears from her half-day at preschool with soggy pants because the other kids were harassing her when she used the girls' room at school and the teacher had instructed her to stay out of the boys' room. She had drunk two glasses of juice at the Halloween party and couldn't hold her pee any longer. She and her peers were four years old, they knew she was a girl, yet already they felt empowered enough in their own bigotries to police her use of the so-called public washrooms. I find it extremely hard to believe that these children were motivated by fear of another little girl. She was four years old and had already learned the brutal lesson that there was no bathroom door with a sign on it that welcomed people who looked like her. She had already been taught that bathrooms were a problem, and that problem started with her, and was hers alone.

My friend asked me to talk to her, and I did. I wanted to tell her that her mom and I were going to talk to the school and that it would all stop, but I knew this wasn't true. I wanted to say that it would be better when she got older, but I couldn't. I asked her to tell me the story of what happened. Asked her how it made her feel. Mad and sad she told me. I told her she wasn't alone. She asked me if I had ever peed in my own pants. I told her yes, I had, but not for a long time. When you get bigger, your bladder grows bigger too, I told her. When you get old like me, you will be able to hold your pee for a lot longer, I promised her. Until you get home? she asked me. I said yes, until you can get home. She seemed to take some comfort in that.

So I get a little tired of having to swallow my lived experience to be force-fed someone else's what-ifs. I get tired of my safety coming second. I get tired of the realities of trans and gender non-conforming people's lives being overshadowed and ignored in favour of a boogey-man that might be lurking in the ladies room. I get really tired of being mistaken for a monster. I get tired of swallowing all these bathroom stories and smiling politely. But the last thing I can do is allow myself to get angry. Because if I get angry, then I am seen as even more of a threat. Then it's all my fault, isn't it? Because then there is a man in the ladies' room, and for some reason, he's angry.

DISCUSSION QUESTIONS

1. Why does Coyote learn to hold pee? Make your answer as detailed as possible, given the information provided in the essay.

2. How do shame and humiliation play into the way we see ourselves as moral agents? Can you give a few examples from your own life?

3. Rates of self-harm and suicide are disproportionately high among LGQBT populations. What did you learn from this essay that might shed light on that sad fact?

Longing for the Male Gaze

BY JENNIFER BARTLETT

Jennifer Bartlett is a poet and disability rights activist. In this short but illuminating discussion of the social construction of disability, Bartlett discusses how her cerebral palsy means she doesn't get sexually harassed by men, and why this invisibility can be in some ways worse than some experiences of harassment.

When I was in my early 30s, I practiced yoga at a studio in my neighborhood in Brooklyn. On most days, I walked there with two friends—one who was in her 20s and one about my age—but occasionally we each got to class on our own. There was a construction site across the street as part of the growing onslaught of gentrification in the neighborhood. My friends would often complain about being harassed and catcalled by the construction workers—even more so when they wore their yoga clothes. I passed the site day after day without incident.

When I was younger, in my 20s, I was a thin, slight woman. I have also always been beautiful and a nice dresser. I also happen to have cerebral palsy, which affects my motor skills, balance and speech, as it does with most people who have it. It is typically caused by damage to or malformation of the brain during birth or infancy. In my case, my mother's umbilical cord was wrapped around my neck in utero. As my mother was unable to have an emergency cesarean section, I was strangled by the cord, and born clinically dead. The temporary lack of oxygen caused damage to a portion of my brain.

Cerebral palsy is not uniform and manifests in a number of ways. It might affect all limbs severely, or just one side of the body; or the effects may be slight, making the disability barely perceptible. It can affect strength, balance and movement; some with the condition may not be able to walk unassisted or care for themselves in typical ways.

To put it bluntly, people with cerebral palsy appear to have strange movements. Since they are not in full control of their muscles, they may have facial expressions or spasticity that most people find surprising, if not unattractive.

People with cerebral palsy are often mistaken for having a mental impairment, although the two are not necessarily linked. I have a speech impediment and awkward gait. My disability is visible, but not necessarily significant. I do have some physical limitations, but am able to do most things that a typical person can do. My primary difficulty has been with people's negative reaction, or what disability-studies scholars call the "social construction" of disability. This primarily means that the main challenges disabled people face come from societal prejudice and inaccessible spaces.

Recently, the popular feminist Jessica Valenti published a memoir titled "Sex Object," which focuses on the toll the "male gaze" has taken on her. Ms. Valenti describes a life of sexual harassment beginning at adolescence. She writes of what seems like countless instances of men exposing themselves to her on the New York City subway. She describes constantly thwarting unwanted advances from men in all areas of her life. Ms. Valenti currently has a 5-year-old daughter, and she wrestles for a way to prepare her child for an onslaught of male harassment. She takes for granted that this will happen.

My experiences have been quite different, nearly the opposite, of Ms. Valenti's and that of most women. I was never hit on or sexually harassed by my professors in college, or later, by my co-workers or superiors. I have not felt as if my male teachers, friends, or colleagues thought less of me because of my gender. I've never been aggressively "hit on" in a bar, despite the fact that I have frequented them alone throughout the years. In fact, I've rarely been approached in a bar at all.

I do remember being sexually harassed by a man on the street. Once. I was 18 years old. I was waiting for a bus, and a man pulled up and offered me a ride in his car. When I declined, he got hostile and asked me if I was wearing panties. I was more startled than anything, and I left the curb to go to the nearby movie theater where my friend worked. I didn't tell my friend what happened, but waited with him for the bus. This was very frightening, but I wouldn't say the incident traumatized me, nor is it something that deeply affected my life. And it happened only once.

Let me rephrase that: It happened only once while I was visibly inhabiting my own body. Virtually, it has been another story.

In 2013, I began experimenting with the dating website OKCupid because I wanted to explore this concept of being desexualized. I created a provocative profile. The photographs were recent, but in photographs, I look "normal." I did not mention that I have cerebral palsy. I wanted to use the opportunity to explore the sexual world as an able-bodied woman, if only online, and see what all the fuss was about.

As a pretend, able-bodied woman, I received all kinds of messages. Men wrote stupid things, aggressive things and provocative things. Often, while I was in a dialogue with a man who didn't know of my impairment, I would disclose it, and almost always, the man vanished, no matter how strong the connection had been beforehand.

After a while, I changed the profile to reflect that I have a disability. Fewer men wrote. Sometimes, no men wrote, depending on the content. But overall, the messages changed. They could be called more respectful. The men who wrote primarily wanted to know how my disability affected me.

This all feels like a political act, and in some ways it is. Strangely, my disability makes me feel as if I have license to play with and deconstruct sexuality in ways I might not have the bravery to do as an able-bodied woman.

I watch men on the street. I will watch a man visually or verbally harass women who pass him. I am invisible enough to do this. Sometimes men look at me, but the reaction is different. There seems to be some level of shame or confusion mixed with the lust in their eyes. Does this mean that I am lucky? Am I blessed to be sexually invisible and given a reprieve from something that has troubled women for centuries?

It certainly does not *feel* that way. On one hand, I know that I am "lucky" not to be sexually harassed as I navigate the New York City streets. But I am harassed in other ways that feel much more damaging. People stare. People insist that I have God's blessing. People feel most comfortable speaking about me in the third person rather than addressing me directly. It is not uncommon that I will be in a situation where a stranger will talk to the nearest able-bodied person, whether it be a friend or a complete stranger, *about me* to avoid speaking *to me*.

I also do understand what it feels like to get attention from the wrong man. It's gross. It's uncomfortable. It's scary and tedious. And in certain cases, traumatic. But I still would much rather have a man make an inappropriate sexual comment than be referred to in the third person or have someone express surprise over the fact that I have a career. The former, unfortunately, feels "normal." The latter makes me feel invisible and is meant for that purpose.

I *like* it when men look at me. It feels empowering. Frankly, it makes me feel like I'm not being excluded.

DISCUSSION QUESTIONS

1. Explain how the social construction of disability affects which people our culture is willing to view as sexual beings.
2. What does Bartlett mean by "sexual invisibility," and how does it complicate existing feminist analyses of the harms of sexual harassment?